A New & Other Exciting News from Frommer's!

In our continuing effort to publish the savviest, most up-to-date, and most appealing travel guides available, we've added some great new features.

Frommer's guides now include a new **star-rating system.** Every hotel, restaurant, and attraction is rated from 0 to 3 stars to help you set priorities and organize your time.

We've also added **seven brand-new features** that point you to the great deals, in-the-know advice, and unique experiences that separate travelers from tourists. Throughout the guide, look for:

Finds	Special finds—those places only insiders know about
Fun Fact	Fun facts—details that make travelers more informed and their trips more fun
Kids	Best bets for kids—advice for the whole family
Moments	Special moments—those experiences that memories are made of
Overrated	Places or experiences not worth your time or money
Tips	Insider tips—some great ways to save time and money
Value	Great values—where to get the best deals

We've also added a **"What's New"** section in every guide—a timely crash course in what's hot and what's not in every destination we cover.

Here's what the critics say about Frommer's:

"Amazingly easy to use. Very portable, very complete."
—*Booklist*

"Detailed, accurate, and easy-to-read information for all price ranges."
—*Glamour Magazine*

"Hotel information is close to encyclopedic."
—*Des Moines Sunday Register*

"Frommer's Guides have a way of giving you a real feel for a place."
—*Knight Ridder Newspapers*

Other Great Guides for Your Trip:

Frommer's New York City 2003
Frommer's New York City with Kids
Frommer's Memorable Walks in New York
New York City For Dummies
Unofficial Guide to New York City
Frommer's Irreverent Guide to Manhattan
Suzy Gershman's Born to Shop New York

New York City
from $90 a Day

2003

by Cheryl Farr Leas

with research assistance from Nathaniel R. Leas

Wiley Publishing, Inc.

About the Author
Cheryl Farr Leas was a senior editor at Frommer's before embarking on a freelance writing career. She also authors the *Frommer's New York City* and *Hawaii For Dummies* travel guides, and has contributed to *Best Places Los Angeles* (Sasquatch Books) and numerous other travel guides. Cheryl also writes about travel, real estate, interior design, and other lifestyle subjects for *Continental, Daily Variety, Bride's,* and other publications. When she's not traveling, she's at home in Park Slope, Brooklyn. Feel free to write her directly at rncleas@yahoo.com.

Published by:

Wiley Publishing, Inc.
909 Third Ave.
New York, NY 10022

Copyright © 2002 Wiley Publishing, Inc., New York, New York. All rights reserved. No part of this publication may be reproduced, stored in a retrieval system or transmitted in any form or by any means, electronic, mechanical, photocopying, recording, scanning or otherwise, except as permitted under Sections 107 or 108 of the 1976 United States Copyright Act, without either the prior written permission of the Publisher, or authorization through payment of the appropriate per-copy fee to the Copyright Clearance Center, 222 Rosewood Drive, Danvers, MA 01923, (978) 750-8400, fax (978) 750-4744. Requests to the Publisher for permission should be addressed to the Legal Department, Wiley Publishing, Inc., 10475 Crosspoint Blvd., Indianapolis, IN 46254, (317) 572-3447, fax (317) 572-4447, E-Mail: permcoordinator@wiley.com.

Wiley and the Wiley Publishing logo are trademarks or registered trademarks of Wiley Publishing, Inc. in the United States and other countries and may not be used without written permission. Frommer's is a trademark or registered trademark of Arthur Frommer. Used under license. All other trademarks are the property of their respective owners. Wiley Publishing, Inc. is not associated with any product or vendor mentioned in this book.

ISBN 0-7645-6628-8
ISSN 8755-5433

Editor: Kathleen Warnock
Production Editor: Suzanna R. Thompson
Cartographer: John Decamillis
Photo Editor: Richard Fox
Production by Wiley Indianapolis Composition Services

Front cover photo: The Statue of Liberty
Back cover photo: A room at the Habitat Hotel

For information on our other products and services or to obtain technical support, please contact our Customer Care Department within the U.S. at 800-762-2974, outside the U.S. at 317-572-3993 or fax 317-572-4002.

Wiley also publishes its books in a variety of electronic formats. Some content that appears in print may not be available in electronic formats.

Manufactured in the United States of America

5 4 3 2 1

Contents

What's New in New York City 1

1 The Best of the Big Apple 4

1 How This Guide Can Save You Money 4
2 Cheap Thrills: Frommer's Favorite Free & Affordable Experiences ...6
3 Best Low-Cost Hotel Bets 9
   Site Seeing: The Big Apple on the Web 12
4 Best Low-Cost Dining Bets 13

2 Planning an Affordable Trip to New York City 16

1 65 Money-Saving Tips 16
   Home Stay Sweet Home Stay ...24
2 Visitor Information 30
3 Money 30
4 When to Go 32
   New York City Calendar of Events 33
5 Health & Insurance 38
6 Tips for Travelers with Special Needs 40
7 Getting There 44
   New Air Travel Security Measures 45
   Money-Saving Package Deals 46
   Newark's New AirTrain: From Jersey to Manhattan in Minutes 48
   Flying into Islip on Southwest 50

3 For International Visitors 54

1 Preparing for Your Trip 54
2 Getting to the United States ...58
   How to Save on International Airfares 59
3 If You're Traveling Beyond New York City 60
   Fast Facts: For the International Traveler 61

4 Getting to Know New York City 66

1 Orientation 66
   Manhattan's Neighborhoods in Brief 69
   Where to Check Your E-mail in the City that Never Sleeps ...76
   Manhattan Address Locator 80
2 Getting Around 83
   Subway Service Interruption Notes 86
   Deals for Visitors with Wheels: Cheap Parking Tips 91
3 Playing It Safe 92
   Fast Facts: New York City 93

5 Accommodations You Can Afford 97

1 TriBeCa 98
2 On the Bowery 98
3 The Lower East Side 99
4 The East Village 100

CONTENTS

- 5 Greenwich Village 102
- 6 Chelsea 103
  - Deal-Making with the Chains ..106
- 7 Union Square, the Flatiron District & Gramercy Park 108
- 8 Times Square & Midtown West 111
- 9 Midtown East & Murray Hill ...120
- 10 The Upper West Side 123
  - Affordable Family-Friendly Hotels 126
- 11 Harlem 129
  - Bed-and-Breakfasting in Brooklyn 130

6 Great Deals on Dining   132

- 1 Restaurants by Cuisine 133
- 2 The Financial District 137
- 3 TriBeCa 138
- 4 Chinatown & Little Italy 141
- 5 The Lower East Side 143
- 6 SoHo & Nolita 146
- 7 The East Village & NoHo 149
  - Dining Zone: Little India 151
- 8 Greenwich Village & the Meat-Packing District 155
- 9 Chelsea 160
- 10 The Flatiron District, Union Square & Gramercy Park 164
- 11 Times Square & Midtown West 168
  - Theme Restaurant Thrills! 174
- 12 Midtown East & Murray Hill ...179
  - Grand Dining at Grand Central 180
- 13 The Upper West Side 181
  - Affordable Family-Friendly Restaurants 188
- 14 The Upper East Side 191
- 15 Harlem 193
- 16 Brooklyn 194

7 Exploring New York City   195

- 1 Sights & Attractions by Neighborhood 195
- 2 Suggested Itineraries 205
- 3 The Top Attractions 206
  - What's Happening in Times Square 216
- 4 More Manhattan Museums ...218
  - Paying Your Respects at Ground Zero 219
  - Where to Find Free Culture ...224
  - Art for Art's Sake: The Gallery Scene 230
- 5 Skyscrapers & Other Architectural Highlights 236
- In Search of Historic Homes ...238
- 6 Places of Worship 240
- 7 Central Park & Other Places to Play 242
- 8 Affordable Sightseeing Tours ...250
  - Absolutely Free Walking Tours 252
- 9 Talk of the Town: Free TV Tapings 253
- 10 Especially for Kids 256
- 11 Highlights of the Outer Boroughs 258
- 12 Spectator Sports 265

8 Shopping for Big Apple Bargains — 267

1. The Top Shopping Streets & Neighborhoods 267
2. The Best Department Stores for Bargain Hunters 271
3. Shopping A to Z 272
   Scouring the Sample Sales 282
   $50 Fabulous: Chinatown's Secret Treasure Trove 294

9 New York City After Dark — 296

1. The Theater Scene 296
   Kids Take the Stage: Family-Friendly Theater 298
   How to Save on Theater Tickets 300
2. Opera, Classical Music & Dance 302
   Bargain Alert: The Classical Learning Curve 303
   Lincoln Center Alert: Last-Minute & Discount Ticket-Buying Tips 304
3. Major Concert Halls & Landmark Venues 307
   Park It! Shakespeare, Music & Other Free Fun 308
4. Live Rock, Jazz, Blues & More 311
   Free Music in the Clubs 316
5. Stand-Up & Sketch Comedy ... 320
6. Cabaret Rooms & Piano Bars 321
7. Bars & Cocktail Lounges 322
8. Dance Clubs & Party Scenes ... 330
9. The Gay & Lesbian Scene 332

Index — 335

List of Maps

Manhattan Neighborhoods   71

Accommodations in the TriBeCa, the Bowery, the Lower East Side, the East Village & Greenwich Village   101

Midtown, Chelsea & Union Square Accommodations   112

Upper West Side Accommodations   125

Harlem-Area Accommodations & Dining   131

Financial District, TriBeCa, Chinatown & Little Italy Dining   139

Lower East Side, SoHo & East Village Dining   145

Greenwich Village Dining   157

Midtown, Chelsea & Union Square Dining   170

Uptown Dining   182

Downtown Attractions   196

Midtown Attractions   198

Uptown Attractions   200

Upper Manhattan Attractions   202

Central Park   243

An Invitation to the Reader

In researching this book, we discovered many wonderful places—hotels, restaurants, shops, and more. We're sure you'll find others. Please tell us about them, so we can share the information with your fellow travelers in upcoming editions. If you were disappointed with a recommendation, we'd love to know that, too. Please write to:

Frommer's New York City from $90 a Day 2003
Wiley Publishing, Inc. • 909 Third Ave. • New York, NY 10022

An Additional Note

Please be advised that travel information is subject to change at any time—and this is especially true of prices. We therefore suggest that you write or call ahead for confirmation when making your travel plans. The authors, editors, and publisher cannot be held responsible for the experiences of readers while traveling. Your safety is important to us, however, so we encourage you to stay alert and be aware of your surroundings. Keep a close eye on cameras, purses, and wallets, all favorite targets of thieves and pickpockets.

New! Frommer's Star Ratings & Icons

Every hotel, restaurant, and attraction listing in this guide has been ranked for quality, value, service, amenities, and special features using a star-rating scale. In country, state, and regional guides, we also rate towns and regions to help you narrow down your choices and budget your time accordingly. Hotels and restaurants are rated on a scale of zero (recommended) to two stars (very highly recommended); exceptional "worth a splurge" options may get three stars. Attractions, towns, and regions are rated according to the following scale: zero stars (recommended), one star (highly recommended), two stars (very highly recommended), and three stars (must-see).

In addition to the rating system, we also use seven icons to highlight insider information, useful tips, special bargains, hidden gems, memorable experiences, kid-friendly venues, places to avoid, and other useful information:

Finds   *Fun Fact*   *Kids*   *Moments*   *Overrated*   *Tips*   *Value*

The following abbreviations are used for credit cards:

AE   American Express   DISC   Discover   V   Visa
DC   Diners Club   MC   MasterCard

FROMMERS.COM

Now that you have the guidebook to a great trip, visit our website at **www.frommers.com** for travel information on nearly 2,500 destinations. With features updated regularly, we give you instant access to the most current trip-planning information available. At Frommers.com, you'll also find the best prices on airfares, accommodations, and car rentals—and you can even book travel online through our travel booking partners. At Frommers.com, you'll also find the following:

- Online updates to our most popular guidebooks
- Vacation sweepstakes and contest giveaways
- Newsletter highlighting the hottest travel trends
- Online travel message boards with featured travel discussions

What's New in New York City

New York will never be the same, of course. The city suffered a devastating blow on September 11, 2001—a blow strong enough to buckle some cities. Now the Twin Towers no longer dominate the skyline with their soaring presence, and thousands of our fellow New Yorkers are gone forever. But despite the violation, the city that awaits you stands strong and sure.

PLANNING YOUR TRIP Travelers looking to make a fast, affordable connection between Newark International Airport and Manhattan can use the new **AirTrain Newark,** which offers a monorail connection from the terminal to the Newark Airport Rail Station, where you can make a one-stop connection into Manhattan's Penn Station. The process takes about a half hour—sometimes less if your timing is right—and costs $11.15 each way (kids under 5 ride free).

ACCOMMODATIONS The edge has come off the Big Apple's legendarily high hotel prices. Rack rates have held steady, even decreased in many cases. Visitors may find they have more bargaining power than they've had in years.

What's more, some new, affordable hotels give budget travelers more options for clean, well-priced lodgings. The top entry is the **Super 8 Hotel Times Square,** 59 W. 46th St. (© **800/567-7720**), with attractive, all-new rooms in the Theater District for as little as $89 double. Trust me—the bargains don't get better than this.

The brand-new **New York City Howard Johnson Express Inn,** 135 E. Houston St. (© **800/406-1411**), is a crowning jewel in the gentrification of the Lower East Side, offering budget-minded travelers quality comforts at a great price—around $119 double—in a trendy location.

Not new, but newly of note, is the **Pioneer of SoHotel,** 341 Broome St. (© **212/226-1482**), a renovated and friendly budget hotel straddling the edge of SoHo and Chinatown, offering double rooms with private baths for less than $80 a night year-round.

Hostellers can head for the **Whitehouse Hotel of New York,** 340 Bowery (© **212/477-5623**), a clean, friendly, well-run hostel in the heart of the hip, wallet-friendly East Village.

Attention nonsmokers: The **Comfort Inn Midtown,** 129 W. 46th St. (© **800/567-7720**), has taken the bold step of becoming New York's first smoke-free hotel. A terrific budget hotel is now better than ever!

RESTAURANTS The emphasis this year is on midpriced meals. Newcomers include the Lower East Side's **AKA Cafe,** 49 Clinton St. (© **212/979-6096**), sister restaurant to chef Wylie Dufresne's pricier 71 Clinton Fresh Food, serving global gourmet at diner prices. **Jeollado,** 116 E. 4th St. (© **212/260-7696**), has brought top-quality sushi at bargain-basement prices to an adoring East Village crowd, while West Villagers line up at **Ony,** 357 Sixth Ave. (© **212/414-8429**), for first-class Japanese noodle bowls in a Zen-stylish setting.

Italian favorite Frank has opened **Lil' Frankie's Pizza,** 19 First Ave. (© 212/420-4900), offering authentic pies in the East Village.

Also new to the East Village is a branch of West Village favorite **A Salt & Battery,** 80 Second Ave. (© 212/254 6610), for authentic fish-and-chips. In Chelsea, the place to go for first-class eats even your old Dublin-born uncle could love is **The Half King,** 505 W. 23rd St. (© 212/462-4300), the literary-minded Irish pub owned by Sebastian Junger, the best-selling author of *The Perfect Storm.*

Budget diners looking for a great date place should head for the Flatiron District's **Via Emilia,** 240 Park Ave. S. (© 212/505-3072).

SIGHTSEEING The biggest news on the museum scene is the temporary move of the **Museum of Modern Art,** to an interim facility across the East River called **MoMA QNS,** 45-20 33rd St., Long Island City, Queens (© 212/708-9400) until 2005. MoMA QNS is an architectural transformation of the old Swingline stapler factory into a 45,000-square-foot exhibition space showcasing the best of MoMA's collection, from Picasso to Warhol.

The grandest of openings has been the glorious new **American Folk Art Museum** (© 212/265-1040), which unveiled its new home at 45 W. 53rd St. This ultramodern museum has been called no less than the city's greatest new museum and best work of architecture since Frank Lloyd Wright built the Guggenheim in 1959.

The **Asia Society,** 725 Park Ave. (© 212/288-6400), has reopened after a $30 million renovation.

Finally open is the **Neue Galerie New York,** 1048 Fifth Ave. (© 212/628-6200), whose collection of 20th-century German and Austrian art and design is housed in a Carrère & Hastings–designed Vanderbilt mansion that's worth a look unto itself.

Back in business in Lower Manhattan is the restaurant at George Washington's old watering hole, the **Fraunces Tavern Museum,** 54 Pearl St. (© 212/425-1778). New on the scene in the city's oldest quarter is the **New York City Police Museum,** 100 Old Slip (© 212/480-3100), an ideal stop for anyone wishing to honor the Big Apple's men and women in blue.

You may encounter some construction. The **Museum of Jewish Heritage,** 18 First Place (© 212/509-6130), is working on a new wing to triple its exhibition-and-events space; it's slated for completion in 2003, but should not affect your visit.

The **Isamu Noguchi Garden Museum,** has relocated to a temporary, indoor space at 36-01 43rd Ave. in Sunnyside, Queens (© 718/204-7088) until 2003. Still, don't pass it up if you're in Queens visiting MoMA QNS, the American Museum of the Moving Image, P.S. 1 Contemporary Art Center, or the Socrates Sculpture Park; the free weekend **Queens Artlink** shuttle will connect you.

Continuing repercussions from the World Trade Center terrorist attacks include, at this writing, the continued closure of the New York Stock Exchange to the public and limited access to the Statue of Liberty; you can take the ferry out to Liberty Island, but the statue itself is closed to visitors.

Be prepared for tighter security everywhere. The most up-to-date information is available from **NYC & Company,** New York City's official tourism office, at © 212/484-1222 or www.nycvisit.com.

THEATER The collapse of the World Trade Center also brought the demise of the Lower Manhattan discount ticket booth TKTS, much to the despair of theatergoers who relied on it for day-before purchases on matinees and shorter lines than at the Times Square booth. But the Theatre Development Fund has opened the **TKTS Downtown Theatre Centre** in the South Street Seaport. The new location offers same-day theater deals, with tickets at 25% to 50% off face value, plus shorter lines and matinee tickets available 1 day in advance.

1

The Best of the Big Apple

Any attempt to define New York City recalls the Zen wisdom that you can't step in the same stream twice. The city is so mutable, so constantly changing, that it's almost impossible to define. Restaurants and nightclubs become trendy overnight, and then die under the weight of their popularity. (Yogi Berra had the perfect comment for that phenomenon: "Nobody goes there anymore; it's too crowded.") Broadway shows, exercise fads, city politics, even neighborhoods are subject to Big Apple fickleness.

But within this ebb and flow lies the answer to why we New Yorkers love our city despite the high rents, the noise, the crowds, the cab drivers who don't know Lincoln Center from the Lower East Side: No other place keeps any of us on our toes like this difficult, magnificent city. Nowhere else is the challenge as tough, the pace as relentless, the stimuli as ever changing—and the payoff as rewarding.

The Big Apple has its own magnetism, unrivaled by any other city. New York remains the nerve center of world finance and trade; the international hub of advertising, publishing, entertainment, and fashion; and the creative core for the arts. Just about every language and any dialect is spoken here, from Mandarin to Brooklynese, and no other dot on the map is quite so ethnically, culturally, socially, and economically diverse.

Despite its almost overwhelming diversity, the city's sense of community is strong. In fact, it's stronger than ever before. Despite the horrendous terrorist attacks of September 11, 2001, New York is still a marvelous place to visit.

After the planes hit, we were devastated. The destruction of the World Trade Center left an empty hole in the Manhattan skyline, and an irrevocable gash in the hearts of New Yorkers. But the city managed to start moving again—believing that we must, as a community, forge ahead, even with tears in our eyes.

Now, at this writing—nearly a year after the attacks—the city is back in full swing, and its spirit is robust. We have not forgotten; we will never forget. But we know we must move onward. So subway lines reopen, new restaurants debut, museums go ahead with exhibits and expansion projects. As talk of memorial parks and redevelopment heats up and the streets begin to bustle with tourism and commerce once again, even Lower Manhattan looks forward to a bright future.

Come witness New York's astonishing resilience for yourself—it's reason enough to visit.

1 How This Guide Can Save You Money

New York City, as everyone knows, is perpetually short on space and overflowing with people. It's a situation that turns the economy of supply and demand in the seller's favor, with vendors charging whatever the market will bear for goods and services. The result has been stratospheric prices, some of the highest in the country. If you're used to getting a simple,

On New York

New York is still here. We've suffered terrible losses and we will grieve for them, but we will be here, tomorrow and forever.

—Rudy Giuliani

comfortable motel room for $60 or so, get set for a shock.

That's the bad news—but there's plenty of good news, too. You *can* stay in New York City comfortably, eat well, and see and do everything you want without blowing your budget. There are plenty of great deals in every category for the intrepid traveler who knows where to look for good value and discounts. And there are more travel and hotel bargains available than there have been in years—if you know where to look.

You've already taken the first step: buying this book. I've done the initial legwork for you, scouring the city from top to bottom and loading the pages that follow with the best money-saving advice, the top values and bargains, and the kind of New York travel know-how that only comes with years of research and experience.

Accommodations will be your biggest hurdle, although visitors have regained their bargaining power in the post-9/11 world. Every other aspect of New York is manageable if you look before you leap, which is how regular New Yorkers manage. The city tends to snag people who, exhausted, sit down at the first restaurant they see and end up with a huge bill—or those who stumble into a chic boutique to buy a souvenir that can be had for a fraction of the price with a little effort. Keep an eye on the goal, and you'll see that New York has more affordable culinary and bargain hunters' delights than you'll have time to enjoy.

With average museum admissions hovering around 10 bucks a pop and guided bus tours starting at $30 for the basic look-see, you could spend a fortune on sightseeing and activities—but you don't have to. Start perusing these pages, and you'll soon find more to see and do for free and on the cheap than you could possibly squeeze into one vacation (or two or three or four). I'm not suggesting that you skip everything that has a price tag; certain New York experiences shouldn't be missed, money be damned. But read the pages that follow and you'll know what's worth your hard-earned dough—and what's not.

THE NEW-YORK-FROM-$90-A-DAY PREMISE

The idea is this: With good planning and a watchful eye, you can keep your basic daily costs—accommodations and three meals a day—down to as little as $90. This budget model works best for two adults traveling together who have at least $180 a day to work with and can share a double room. (Single rooms are much less cost-efficient.) This way, if you aim for accommodations costing around $120 for a double—a reasonable budget these days—you'll be left with about $30 per person per day for food (less drinks and tips). Snare a room for less—doable in this economic climate, especially in a less busy season or if you're willing to share a bathroom—and you'll have more left over from your $180-per-day budget for dining.

In defining this basic premise, we at Frommer's assume that you want to travel comfortably, probably with your own room rather than a hostel bunk (even if it does mean a shared bathroom), and dining on good food. This book will also serve you well even if you don't need to keep your two-person

On New York

The only credential the city asked was the boldness to dream. For those who did, it unlocked its gates and its treasures, not caring who they were and where they came from.

—Moss Hart

budget to a strict $180 a day, but you want to keep the tabs down and get the most for your money. It will, on the other side of the coin, also meet your needs if you want to travel on the ultra-cheap—for less than $90 a day—by camping out in clean hostels and eating as inexpensively as possible.

Sightseeing, transportation, and entertainment are all extra. But don't worry—I've got plenty of suggestions on how to keep those costs down, too. What you choose for entertainment will have a huge effect on your overall budget. If you go to nightclubs every night, you'll come home with a lighter wallet than if you spend time taking in free concerts or browsing galleries. If you seek top-name entertainment on Broadway or the cabaret circuit, you'll pay more than if you take a risk on tomorrow's stars at an Off-Broadway show or a no-cover bar. Only you know how much money you have to spend—but if you follow my advice, you'll be able to make informed decisions on what to see and do so that it's money well spent.

Even if you stick with freebies, the Big Apple guarantees a memorable time. After all, to the late, great Quentin Crisp, every flat surface in New York is a stage—and you're guaranteed a nonstop show.

2 Cheap Thrills: Frommer's Favorite Free & Affordable Experiences

- **Sailing to the Statue of Liberty:** If you have time to do only one thing in New York, this is what it should be. No monument embodies the notion of political freedom and economic potential more than Lady Liberty. The ferry to **Liberty Island** also stops at **Ellis Island,** gateway to America for nearly half of our forefathers and foremothers. The museum's exhibits illustrate what coming to the "promised land" was all about. If you want the view but prefer to skip the tourist crowds—and the fare—consider catching the free **Staten Island Ferry.** The hour-long excursion offers the same brilliant Lower Manhattan skyline views as private harbor cruises with high price tags. See chapter 7.
- **Visiting the Museums:** The number of masterworks in this city is mind-boggling; museum-hopping doesn't get any better. If you've never been before, the place to start is the **Metropolitan Museum of Art,** the best art museum in North America, and one of the best in the world; even if you spend every day here, you couldn't exhaust the possibilities. The new **Rose Center for Earth and Space** at the American Museum of Natural History is an A-1 standout for its breathtaking Harrison Ford–narrated space show. Don't just stick to the biggies; New York boasts a wealth of smaller museums that speak to specific interests—from folk art to photography to financial history—and house some real treasures. For a complete rundown, see chapter 7—and don't miss "Where to Find Free Culture" (p. 224), which will fill you in on which museums

offer free or discounted admission on select days.

- **Walking Across the Brooklyn Bridge:** A marvel of engineering when it first connected Brooklyn to Manhattan in 1883, the Brooklyn Bridge is still able to inspire awe even in jaded New Yorkers. I never tire of admiring its Gothic-inspired stone pylons and steel-cable webs. Get an up-close look and some marvelous—and now devastatingly poignant—views of Manhattan by taking the easy stroll from end to end. Readers often tell me this was the highlight of their trip. Start at the Brooklyn end for best effect, and consider preceding your walk with a stroll through historic Brooklyn Heights for a leafy, lovely afternoon. See chapter 7.

- **Strolling the Neighborhoods:** One of the greatest things about New York is the character of each of its neighborhoods. Rather than trying to quick-scan them all, I recommend picking one and really getting to know it. Wend your way through the historic streets of **Greenwich Village,** saunter the cast-iron canyons of **SoHo,** discover the bustle and exotica of **Chinatown.** All you need is a map and a sense of adventure. If you prefer a little structure, consider one of the excellent guided walking tours available; there's no better way to get to know a neighborhood than with an expert showing it to you. Some of the city's best guided tours are free. See chapters 4 and 7.

- **Stargazing at Grand Central Terminal:** Always a beaux-arts gem, this majestic 1913 railroad station received a remarkable face-lift, unveiled in 1998, that has made it a must-see. Every surface glitters with renewed optimism—but none more than the masterful ceiling, brilliant with 24-karat gold zodiac constellations against a blue-green sky. Walk in, throw your head back, and watch the stars gleam. While you're there, head down to the lower concourse to enjoy a globetrotting bonanza of cheap eats. See chapters 6 and 7.

- **Admiring the City's Magnificent Architecture:** New York boasts such a wealth of architectural treasures that this one could keep you busy for a full day or more. It doesn't cost a penny to admire such works of art and engineering as the neo-Gothic **Woolworth Building; Rockefeller Center,** the nation's most glorious realization of the Art Deco ideal; the chrome-topped **Chrysler Building;** regal uptown apartment buildings such as the legendary **Dakota;** paragons of the International Style such as the **Lever House;** and **Grand Central Terminal,** restored to its original glory. When you visit the **Empire State Building,** don't miss the spectacular mural in the lobby. See chapter 7.

- **Wandering Central Park:** Lots of travelers don't bother with Central Park—and they're making a huge mistake. This beautiful accident of civil planning makes the otherwise uninterrupted urban jungle tolerable for workaday New Yorkers. Be sure to seek out Strawberry Fields, the memorial to John Lennon, which exhorts us all to IMAGINE. If you like things on a smaller scale, head to one of the city's smaller greenbelts, each of which has its own personality, from memorial-rich Battery Park to the pleasing social scene at Union Square. See chapter 7.

- **Watching Your Favorite Talk Show Being Taped—for Free:** If you have the forethought (to send away months in advance) or the patience (to wait in the standby line), you can watch Dave, Conan, Ricki, Regis, Jon Stewart, or the ladies of *The View*. If sketch comedy is more your speed, try your luck at acquiring tickets for the holy grail of live TV tapings, *Saturday Night Live*. To start planning—or for insider tips on how to score last-minute tickets—see "Talk of the Town: Free TV Tapings," in chapter 7.

- **Making a Joyful Noise:** Attending a rousing Sunday gospel service at Abyssinian Baptist or Mother Zion A.M.E. can be a wonderful way to discover the true spirit of Harlem and the famous churches that loom large at the community's heart. Another option is to head to Brooklyn for the afternoon or evening services, where you can witness the Grammy Award–winning Brooklyn Tabernacle Choir belt out their passionate songs of praise. See chapter 7.

- **Dining Out:** New York is the world capital of great eating—and the beauty of New York's restaurant scene is that you don't have to spend a fortune to eat well. You'll find cheap but dazzling Chinese in Chinatown, pastrami to die for at any number of Jewish delis, pasta and cannoli that Carmela Soprano would be proud to call her own . . . the list goes on and on. See chapter 6.

- **Watching the Curtain Rise on a Play:** There's nothing like the immediacy and excitement of live theater. Movie and TV stars know it, which is why more and more are strutting their stuff on New York's stages. Sure, tickets are expensive, but creative minds almost never have to pay top dollar. First, consider the city's wealth of affordable Off-Broadway productions. If your heart's set on a big Broadway show, buy your tickets through the TKTS booth, where you can save 25% to 50%. See chapter 9.

- **Catching Some Classical Music:** Juilliard is one of New York's greatest cultural bargains. The nation's premier music school sponsors excellent performances, ranging from classical concerts to opera to drama to dance, throughout the year—and most are free. The Manhattan School of Music also offers a similar calendar of gratis performances. For further details, see "Bargain Alert: The Classical Learning Curve" on p. 303.

- **Celebrating the Holidays:** Christmas and New Year's can be nightmarish times in New York, with crowds choking the city and every merchant charging top dollar. But the city can be a dream on other, less attention-grabbing holidays—and a veritable bargain to boot. On Chinese New Year, a dragon promises great fortune ahead—and bargain-basement winter getaway rates. With the summer heat keeping both visitors and city dwellers out of town, a peaceful hush comes over the city on July 4th—until the fireworks explode overhead, lighting up the night sky with patriotic flair. The huge balloons of the Macy's Thanksgiving Day Parade bring out the kid in all of us—and some of the best hotel bargains in the city can be had over the holiday weekend away from the parade route. See "When to Go," in chapter 2.

- **Spending Saturday Afternoon Gallery-Hopping:** You don't have to be carting a fat checkbook to peruse New York's world-class art galleries. Ironically enough, this is a very budget-friendly activity since virtually all galleries are free to the public—and most people who come through the door don't buy, so nobody will be expecting you to whip out the gold card.

Consider going Saturday afternoon, a popular time for gallery hopping. See "Art for Art's Sake: The Gallery Scene" on p. 230.

- **Cheering on Your Favorite Teams from the Cheap Seats:** While the top tickets at Big Apple sporting events can cost a fortune, you don't have to blow a bundle to see the game. The Yankees still offer bleacher seats for $8, and the Mets have a low ticket price of $12. But everybody's favorite baseball teams these days are New York's minor league teams, the Brooklyn Cyclones (the mini-Mets) and the Staten Island Yankees. Each boasts its own gorgeous and easily reachable retro-cool stadium, and tickets run just $8 for the Cyclones, $10 for the junior Yanks.

    If basketball is your game, skip the big-ticket Knicks for the WNBA's equally thrilling New York Liberty, who play in Madison Square Garden, and whose upper-tier seats go for $8 and $13. See "Spectator Sports," in chapter 7.

- **Taking Advantage of Free Events:** New York's parks overflow with alfresco freebies in the warm months. Most famous are the renowned **Shakespeare in the Park** annual productions, but Central Park also hosts a slate of concerts at **SummerStage** that can range from Yoko Ono to Verdi operas, as well as performances by the **Metropolitan Opera** and the **New York Philharmonic.** See "Park It! Shakespeare, Music & Other Free Fun" on p. 308 for details on these and other free summer events, including under-the-stars movies at the **Bryant Park Summer Film Festival.** Check out **Club freeTime** (www.clubfreetime.com) for free entertainment anytime of the year. See "Entertainment" under "65 Money-Saving Tips," in chapter 2, for newsstand locations where you can pick up a copy of Club freeTime's monthly magazine while you're in town.

- **Paying Your Respects:** As you rush about the city, pause to take time to reflect and remember those who were lost on September 11, 2001. You can head to lower Manhattan, study the remembrances at **Trinity Church,** and see **Ground Zero**—but you don't have to. You'll find tributes to the city's lost throughout New York, at attractions as diverse as the *Intrepid* **Sea-Air-Space Museum** and the **Cathedral of St. John the Divine.** The bronze sphere that once stood on the plaza between the Twin Towers as a symbol of global peace now stands—damaged but still whole—in **Battery Park** as a temporary memorial to the victims of 9/11. The **New York City Fire Museum** is an ideal place to pay tribute to 343 of New York's Bravest who were lost in one tragic day. You can also check the calendars at museums such as the **New-York Historical Society** and the **Museum of the City of New York** for 9/11-related exhibits. Or just stop to shake hands and say thanks to the NYPD officers you see keeping the city's streets safe—they'll appreciate it. See chapter 7 for details on attractions.

3 Best Low-Cost Hotel Bets

You'll likely spend more than you like on a hotel room; it's a fact of life in the big city. But New York has a wealth of wallet-friendly choices for bargain hunters who know where to look. For the details on these and other affordable hotels, see chapter 5.

- **Best Budget Newcomer:** The **Super 8 Hotel Times Square,** 59 W. 46th St. (© **800/567-7720;** www.applecorehotels.com), made a Theater District splash in 2002 with its large rooms (by New York standards), all-new comforts, luxury amenities like a state-of-the-art exercise room, and a heart-of-it-all location—all for as little as $89 double. Even in the prime tourist seasons, when Super 8 rates can climb into the mid-$100s, you'll still get your money's worth. Free continental breakfast adds the crowning touch to this already-stellar value. See p. 118.

  Also of note is the terrific **New York City Howard Johnson Express Inn,** 135 E. Houston St. (© **800/406-1411** or 212/358-8844; www.hojo.com), which has introduced reliable hotel comforts to the gentrified Lower East Side. This spanking-new hotel boasts newly outfitted rooms and a friendly staff that are both much nicer than they have to be for the money. See p. 99.

- **Best Overall Value—Downtown:** It's hard to beat the **Cosmopolitan Hotel–TriBeCa,** 95 W. Broadway (© **888/895-9400;** www.cosmohotel.com), for value. Each of the small, comfy, modern rooms comes with its own petite but immaculate private bathroom for as little as $119 a night. The high-rent neighborhood is hip as can be and subway-convenient to the rest of the city. See p. 98.

  On the fringe of the East Village is the **Union Square Inn,** 209 E. 14th St. (© **212/614-0500;** www.unionsquareinn.com), another excellent choice thanks to freshly remade rooms with new bathrooms, autumn-hued decor, and pillow-top mattresses (unheard of in the under-$200 price category) that offer a great night's sleep. See p. 110.

- **Best Overall Value—Midtown:** The **Super 8 Hotel Times Square,** 59 W. 46th St. (© **800/567-7720;** www.applecorehotels.com), my favorite budget newcomer, scores in this category with its first-class combination of location, quality, comforts, and space, at rates that are a bargain in any town, much less the Big Apple: as low as $89 double, with breakfast! See p. 118.

  The **Chelsea Savoy,** 204 W. 23rd St. (© **866/929-9353;** www.chelseasavoy.qpg.com), is another great choice, offering reliable comforts for an affordable price—no small thing in a hotel market where "budget" goes hand in hand with "quirky." The hallways are attractive and wide, the elevators swift and silent, and the rooms have big closets and roomy, well-kept bathrooms with lots of counter space. See p. 104.

- **Best Overall Value—Uptown:** The **Hotel Newton,** 2528 Broadway (© **888/HOTEL-58;** www.newyorkhotel.com), doesn't expect you to put up with a tiny room or myriad inconveniences just because you don't have a king's ransom to spend. With rates starting at $85 double, you'll get more than your money's worth here—and you'll save an additional 10% if you're a AAA member. See p. 124.

  The **Comfort Inn—Central Park West,** 31 W. 71st St. (© **800/228-5150;** www.comfortinn.com), can be the best deal in town if you book at the right time. It's loaded with comforts and is in one of the city's best residential neighborhoods. You can sometimes find rates as low as $72 double—with breakfast! See p. 123.

- **Best Value for Bargain Hunters Who Don't Mind Sharing:** If you're willing to share a hall bathroom, you'll be pleased with the **Larchmont Hotel,** in the loveliest part of Greenwich Village at 27 W. 11th St. (© **212/989-9333;** www.larchmonthotel.com). See p. 103.

- **Best Value for Bargain Hunters Who Do Mind Sharing:** Kudos to the **Pioneer of SoHotel,** 341 Broome St. (© **212/226-1482;** www.pioneerhotel.com), which has done something that no one else has managed to do: offer clean, friendly accommodations with private bathrooms for just $77 double year-round. The staff is professional, the decor is more attractive than most hotels in the shoestring category, and the edge-of-Chinatown location is safe and convenient. See p. 98.

- **Best for Bargain Hunters Willing to Compromise: Chelsea Lodge,** 318 W. 20th St. (© **800/ 373-1116;** www.chelsealodge. com), offers the perfect compromise: You'll have an in-room sink and shower, so all you have to share is a toilet in the hall. If you're willing to do that, you'll find yourself in one of the cutest, cleanest, most comfortable hotels in New York—and at one of the cheapest rates in town. One of my all-time budget favorites! See p. 103.

- **Best Service for the Budget-Minded:** The staff at the **Broadway Inn,** 264 W. 46th St. (© **800/ 826-6300;** www.broadwayinn. com), might be the most helpful in the city. They're so committed to making their guests feel welcome that they give you a hot-line number to call when you're out and about if you need directions, advice on where to eat, or any other assistance. And you thought New York wasn't friendly! See p. 111.

- **Best for Creative Spirits:** Reminiscent of Warhol's Factory at the height of its creativity and style, the supercool **Gershwin Hotel,** 7 E. 27th St. (© **212/545-8000;** www.gershwinhotel.com), is the winner in this category. Billy Name is the house photog; what more do I need to say? See p. 109.

- **Best for Families:** Located on the Upper West Side, one of the city's most desirable and kid-friendly residential neighborhoods, is the **Milburn,** 242 W. 76th St. (© **800/ 833-9622;** www.milburnhotel. com), which offers the best value-for-dollar ratio on suite accommodations in town. A queen-size sleeper sofa in the living room makes the junior and one-bedroom suites large enough to accommodate four, and a kitchenette with microwave, minifridge, and coffeemaker means you can save on breakfast bills. Kids under 13 stay free. See p. 127.

- **Best for Style Hounds on a Shoestring:** The **Habitat Hotel,** 130 E. 57th St. (© **800/255- 0482;** www.habitatny.com), is carving out a niche for itself as the "upscale budget" choice among style-conscious consumers. The narrow rooms are fresh and outfitted with flair, and the neighborhood is about as high fashion as it gets. See p. 120.

  Another excellent choice is **The Marcel,** 201 E. 24th St. (© **888/ 66-HOTEL;** www.nychotels.com), whose mod designer-outfitted rooms go for just $125, sometimes less—and the lounge downstairs is one of the hottest in town.

  Fashionistas who don't mind sacrificing space for style might try to score one of the handful of $95 rooms at Ian Schrager's ultra-fashionable **Hudson,** 356 W. 58th St. (© **800/444-4786;** www.ian schragerhotels.com). See p. 110.

- **Best for Gay & Lesbian Travelers:** New York is such a hub of gay

Site Seeing: The Big Apple on the Web

The New York Convention & Visitors Bureau's official site, **www.nycvisit.com**, is an excellent online resource offering information on the city, from trip-planning basics to tips on where to take the kids. But there's much more to be learned about New York in cyberspace.

Citysearch (www.newyork.citysearch.com) is the city's hippest general-information site, with reviews and listings for restaurants, shopping, hotels, attractions, and nightlife. It's not as up-to-the-minute as it used to be, but it's still an excellent source for current happenings. Beware the search engine: If you're looking for a specific restaurant or shop, you're best off heading to the "Restaurants" or "Shopping" page and searching from there—and it still may take a few tries to find what you're looking for.

New York Today (www.nytoday.com) is the online arts, leisure, and entertainment arm of the *New York Times*. The *Times* created this site for those of us who wanted access to their excellent cultural coverage and restaurant reviews without having to wade through the main site (www.nytimes.com), which requires you to register.

Tops these days may be **New York Metro** ★ **(www.nymetro.com)**, the online arm of glossy weekly magazine *New York*. New York Metro is the most up-to-date site covering city happenings. (Although keep in mind that these things can change by the moment.) The site is particularly strong in restaurant and shopping coverage; in fact, the magazine's shopping columnists update the site daily with news of sales and bargains.

All of the city's high-profile weeklies also maintain sites that are very useful for current happenings, including:

- *Time Out New York:* www.timeoutny.com
- The *Village Voice:* www.villagevoice.com
- The *New Yorker:* www.newyorker.com
- *Paper:* www.papermag.com
- The *New York Press:* www.nypress.com

For more on these city-focused magazines, see "Publications" in "Orientation," in chapter 4.

Digital City New York (www.digitalcity.com/newyork) is much like Citysearch, and good for an alternative view. **About.com** also maintains a somewhat useful New York page at **www.gonyc.about.com**.

For the most up-to-date information on Lower Manhattan and Ground Zero, visit the website of the **Alliance for Downtown New York,** the stellar Business Improvement District so productive in Lower Manhattan both before and after 9/11, at **www.downtownny.com**.

In addition, you'll find subject-specific sites listed in the appropriate chapters of this book.

---

life and culture that virtually all of the city's hotels welcome gay and lesbian visitors. But if you're looking for like-minded folks, try the fabulous Hollywood-themed **Chelsea Pines Inn,** 317 W. 14th St. (© **888/546-2700;** www.chelseapinesinn.com; p. 104), or the more low-key but equally welcoming **Colonial House Inn,** 318 W. 22nd St. (© **800/689-3779;** www.colonialhouseinn.com; p. 105).

- **Best Freebies:** The **Travel Inn,** 515 W. 42nd St. (© **800/869-4630;** www.newyorkhotel.com), wins on *two* counts. First is the free garage parking—a $25-a-day value at minimum for visitors driving to the city and free in-and-out privileges to boot. And summer visitors, can take advantage of Travel Inn's rooftop swimming pool and huge sun deck. The **Skyline Hotel** (see directly below) offers similar value-minded perks. See p. 119.
- **Best for Travelers with Disabilities:** The comfortable, budget-minded **Skyline Hotel,** 725 Tenth Ave. (© **800/433-1982;** www.skylinehotelny.com), has seven generously sized wheelchair-accessible rooms, ramps, and fire-safety alarms for deaf and blind visitors, plus free parking. See p. 118.
- **Best Splurge:** The Art Deco–style **Hotel Metro,** 45 W. 35th St. (© **800/356-3870;** www.hotelmetronyc.com), is a midpriced Midtown gem that feels much more expensive than it is, with stylish furnishings, marble bathrooms, an attentive staff, and a rooftop terrace with the best view of the Empire State Building in town. You'll get a surprisingly good value for your dollar here, and free continental breakfast softens the blow. See p. 115.

4 Best Low-Cost Dining Bets

One of the joys of being in New York is that there's fabulous food at nearly every turn—and you don't have to be toting a platinum card to pay for it. Go ethnic—Chinese, Japanese, Jewish, Italian, Mexican, and much more—to indulge in the best cheap eats you'll find anywhere. For the details on these and other terrific affordable city restaurants, see chapter 6.

- **Best for Romance: Bayou,** 308 Lenox Ave. (© **212/426-3800**), serves captivating Creole fare in an intimate, low-lit dining room with casually sophisticated service. This is special-occasion dining for *a lot* less than you'd pay below 96th Street. See p. 193.
- **Best Newcomer:** The Flatiron District's **Via Emilia,** 240 Park Ave. S. (© **212/505-3072**), is my find of the year. This lovely, candlelit trattoria that specializes in homemade stuffed tortellini is an affordable oasis in the heart of a high-rent district, and another first-class date place. See p. 167.
- **Best Chinese:** With all the culinary wonders that Chinatown has to offer, this is a tough choice. But whenever I think about the steamy soup dumplings at **Joe's Shanghai,** 9 Pell St. (© **212/233-8888**), I can't help but swoon. See p. 141.
- **Best Affordable French:** The charming, affordable Chelsea creperie **Rue des Crepes,** 104 Eighth Ave. (© **212/242-9900**), is my favorite in this category, thanks to a winning combination of food, setting, service, and low prices. See p. 163.
- **Best Affordable Italian:** For most-bang-for-your-buck Italian, the award goes to **Frank,** 88 Second Ave. (© **212/420-0202**), for meatballs, pasta, and tomato "gravy" better than Carmela Soprano could make. See p. 152.

The other top choice is Mario Batali's **Lupa,** 170 Thompson St. (② **212/982-5089**), a fantastic Roman-style trattoria and *salumeria* (Italian grocery store). Kudos to Batali for being the one celebrity chef in town who doesn't think you should have to spend a fortune on a first-class meal. See p. 158.

- **Best Affordable Seafood:** You can't do better for your money than at **Pisces,** 95 Ave. A (② **212/260-6660**), where the top-quality fish is always fresh and creatively prepared. The early-bird prix-fixe dinner—two courses for just $15—makes an already terrific value even more wallet-friendly. See p. 153.

- **Best Diner:** It's so nice that it hardly deserves to be called a diner. But **Bubby's,** 120 Hudson St. (② **212/219-0666**), serves up the best comfort food in town. Don't miss the home-style pies. See p. 138. Another top choice with great prices is Ukrainian stalwart **Veselka,** 144 Second Ave. (② **212/228-9682**), which serves their mouth-melting pirogi and other eastern European diner fare around the clock to old-school East Villagers and tattooed clubhoppers alike. See p. 154.

- **Best Burger and Beer:** Ask a hundred New Yorkers and you'll get a hundred opinions. But as far as I'm concerned, there's no argument: The best burger is at **Paul's,** 131 Second Ave. (② **212/529-3033**), an unpretentious East Village diner where the hefty half-pounders (beef or turkey, your choice) are perfect every time—well charred on the outside, juicy on the inside. See p. 153.

- **Best Pizza:** Pizza doesn't get any better than the fresh mozzarella-topped pies at **Lombardi's,** 32 Spring St. (② **212/941-7994**), which has been baking its coal-oven pies since 1905. See p. 147.

If you're feeling adventurous, head across the river to **Grimaldi's Pizzeria,** 19 Old Fulton St., Brooklyn Heights (② **718/858-4300**), where you'll have stellar views in addition to real *Noo Yawk* pizza. See p. 194.

- **Best Fine Dining at a Discount:** Dining values don't get any better than the **Tavern Room at Gramercy Tavern,** 42 E. 20th St. (② **212/477-0777**), which allows you to experience one of the city's finest restaurants for a fraction of what expense-account diners pay in the main dining room. I actually prefer this friendly bistro-style alternative, which offers excellent New American food without the pretension. See p. 166.

- **Best All-U-Can-Eat Meal Deal:** **Salaam Bombay,** 317 Greenwich St. (② **212/226-9400**), has reinvented the buffet with its top-quality pan-Indian lunch spread, offered daily. You simply can't eat better anywhere in the city for just $12.95. See p. 141.

- **Best Early-Bird Dining Bargain:** Authentic French bistro and wine bar **Le Pere Pinard,** 175 Ludlow St. (② **212/777-4917**), offers three courses—starter, entree, and dessert—for just $14 to diners who order between 5 and 7pm daily. It's an excellent deal, especially since you could easily spend that much on just a main course. Pair it with a glass of *vin* from the extensive, affordable list, and you have a meal to remember for 20 bucks. See p. 144.

- **Best Breakfast:** Uptown, head to **Sarabeth's Kitchen,** 423 Amsterdam Ave. (② **212/496-6280**), whose sophisticated home-style cooking and sigh-inducing pastries inspire lines around the block (go early on weekends). See p. 188. Downtown, head to TriBeCa fave **Bubby's,** 120 Hudson St. (© **212/ 219-0666**)—and don't be surprised if Harvey Keitel is chowing down on a monster-size omelet at the next table. See p. 138.

- **Best Late-Night Hangout:** Half authentic-French bistro, half all-American diner, **Florent,** 69 Gansevoort St. (© **212/989-5779**), is the hipster crowd's favorite after-hours hangout. Thanks to its good food, great people-watching, and sense of humor, it's mine, too. See p. 156.

In a neighborhood notoriously underserved in the late-night department, we-never-close **Pigalle,** 790 Eighth Ave. (© **212/ 489-2233**), deserves props for offering affordable French fare to after-hours Theater District crowds. See p. 176.

- **Best Fast Food:** For value, it's hard to beat the terrific, health-minded Tex-Mex fare at **Burritoville,** at 36 Water St. (© **212/ 747-1100**) and throughout the city. See p. 137. It's also hard to beat **Emerald Planet,** at 2 Great Jones St. (© **212/353-9727**), whose wraps and smoothies are made with fresh ingredients and a world of ethnic influences. A Rockefeller Center location makes a delicious, healthful, and easy lunch stop during a day of Midtown sightseeing. See p. 156.

- **Best Old New York Experience: Eisenberg's Coffee Shop,** 174 Fifth Ave. (© **212/675-5096**), has served the same retro fare in the same space since 1929—and prices are retro, too. New Yorkers consider this the best tuna salad in town, but the Reuben is my ticket to culinary happiness. See p. 164.

In the *Noo Yawk* deli wars, **Katz's Delicatessen,** 205 E. Houston St. (© **212/254-2246**), is the choice among those who know their kreplach, knishes, and pastrami. No cutesy sandwiches here—just top-notch classics. The all-beef wieners are the best in a town known for its dogs. What's more, prices are a fraction of what those tourist-targeted Midtown delis charge. See p. 144.

- **Best for Families:** It's hard to beat **Virgil's Real BBQ,** 152 W. 44th St. (© **212/921-9494**), for eat-with-your-hands fun. See p. 177. Kids of all ages love **Serendipity 3,** 225 E. 60th St. (© **212/838-3531**), a classic ice-cream parlor that's just like your memories of Farrell's, but *better*. See p. 192. For more kid-friendly choices, see "Affordable Family-Friendly Restaurants," in chapter 6.

- **Best for Vegetarians:** A perennial favorite among vegetarians is the Asian-inspired fare at **Zen Palate,** 34 Union Square E. (© **212/ 614-9345**). See p. 167. But I prefer **Pongal,** 110 Lexington Ave. (© **212/696-9458**), which recreates the flavorful vegetarian fare of southern India—and thanks to a daily visit from a rabbi, it's kosher, too! See p. 180.

- **Best Baked Goods and Sweets:** There's a lot of competition in this category, but the ultimate kudos go to Franco-Brussels import **Le Pain Quotidien,** 100 Grand St. (© **212/625-9009**), for its fresh-baked breads (baked in small batches five times daily) and scrumptious pastries and sweets, served in a SoHo-loft-goes-farmhouse setting. (You'll find locations in the Flatiron District and on the Upper West and Upper East Sides, too.) See p. 147.

2

Planning an Affordable Trip to New York City

In the pages that follow, you'll find everything you need to know to handle the practical details of planning your trip in advance—airlines and area airports, a calendar of events, resources for those with special needs, and much more—plus time-tested advice on how to save money at every turn.

1 65 Money-Saving Tips

Here are some tips to help you keep your travel costs down:

1. **Buy a package deal.** A package that includes transportation and hotel for one price might be the best bargain. In some cases, you'll get airfare, accommodations, and transportation to and from the airport, plus extras—maybe a sightseeing tour or restaurant and shopping discount coupons—for less than the cost of a hotel room alone had you booked it yourself. For tips on where and how to get the best package, see "Money-Saving Package Deals" on p. 46.
2. **Order the discount-loaded *Entertainment* book.** Each annual edition, which sells for $15 (or $25 in retail stores), is packed with discounts on hotel stays (including top hotels at 50% off the rack rate), dining (including many two-for-one deals), and attractions and entertainment. You can preview available discounts online. The coupons are good for the whole year, so you can use the book on multiple trips, or pass it on to friends visiting later in the year. To order, call **800/933-2605** or go to **www.entertainment.com**. Even if you don't buy it, visit the website; at press time, there were many discounts ranging from restaurants to attractions, free for the printing.
3. **Buy a *New York for Less* guidebook.** The big value in this guide ($19.95) is its discount card, which offers hundreds of discounts from 20% to 50% at restaurants, attractions (including the Empire State Building), shops, theaters, and nightspots. The card is good for up to four people for up to 8 days and comes with a handbook detailing the places that honor *New York for Less*. It even includes a phone card that gives you $8 in free calls. To order, call ✆ **888/463-6753** or 937/846-1411; or visit **www.for-less.com**, where you can also view a list of participating establishments.
4. **Check with NYC & Company for special offers.** The city's Convention & Visitors Bureau has been keeping visitors apprised of special offers since tourism took a dip following September 11, 2001. They offer programs and deals, from savings cards for discounts at shops and attractions to package deals. There's no telling what will be on offer, but check for the latest at **www.nycvisit.com**.

5. **Flash your AAA, AARP, military, senior, or student ID card.** American Automobile Association membership is valuable for hotel and car-rental discounts, often in the neighborhood of 10%, but may also score savings on Gray Line bus tours, harbor cruises, and the like. Seniors and students will usually find a valid ID will snare reduced-rate admission to most attractions. Military and government folks should always ask about discounts; they can get as much as 40% off. Also check your corporate affiliations; a friend of mine who works at Kraft gets free admission to every cultural attraction that Philip Morris underwrites. The rule of thumb is to always ask.

WHEN TO GO

6. **Choose your season carefully.** How much you pay for your hotel room and airfare depends on the season. Prices can vary by hundreds of dollars in some cases, depending on the time of year. January to mid-April is the best season for bargains, with summer from June to mid-August being second best. Spring and fall are the busiest, most expensive seasons, as is the Christmas season, but negotiating a decent rate is possible, especially in spring. Budget-minded travelers should skip Christmas and New Year's. Thanksgiving is a bargain hunter's delight. For more on this, see "Money Matters" in "When to Go," later in this chapter.

GETTING TO NEW YORK CITY
AIR TRAVEL

7. **Plan ahead, be flexible.** You'll likely pay a lot less than full fare if you buy a 7-, 14-, or 21-day advance-purchase ticket. If you stay over Saturday or travel on Tuesday, Wednesday, or Thursday, you'll likely save even more. You can often save by opting for connecting flights rather than nonstop. Sure, it's more time-consuming and can be a hassle, but if saving money is your top priority, this can be a way to do it. Airlines won't generally volunteer this information, so be sure to ask.

8. **Always ask for the lowest fare.** Yes, reservations and travel agents should take for granted that you want the lowest possible fare—but they don't always do so. Be sure to ask specifically for the lowest fare. As with every aspect of your trip, ask about discounts for groups, seniors, children, and students.

9. **Consider all three airports when you're shopping.** Fares can be markedly different depending on which airport you fly into—LaGuardia, JFK, or Newark—and none of them are that far from Manhattan. Continental, for instance, almost always has cheaper flights into Newark because it's one of its hubs; United is another airline that often has cheaper prices into Newark. Even though it's in New Jersey, Newark can be more convenient to your Manhattan destination than the other airports, especially now that the Newark AirTrain links the airport to midtown Manhattan.

10. **Keep an eye out for airfare sales.** Check newspapers for advertised discounts or call the airlines and ask if any special deals are available. You'll almost never see a sale during July and August or during the Thanksgiving or Christmas seasons, but in periods of low-volume travel, you should be able to get a cross-country flight for $400 or less.

   The lowest-priced fares are often nonrefundable, require a Saturday-night stay, and carry penalties for changing dates of travel. So, when you're quoted a fare, know exactly what the restrictions are before you commit.

11. **Try the discount carriers, too.** Don't forget to check with the smaller, no-frills airlines including jetBlue, AirTran, and Southwest (which flies into Long Island's MacArthur Airport, about 50 miles/81km east of Manhattan). See p. 44 for a rundown of discount carriers that fly into area airports.

12. **Check for discounted fares with consolidators.** Also known as "bucket shops," consolidators are a good place to find low fares, often below even the airlines' discounted rates. Basically, these companies buy airfare in bulk and pass some of the savings on to you. Before you pay, ask for a confirmation number and then call the airline to confirm your seat. Be prepared to book with a different consolidator—and there are many—if the airline can't confirm your reservation. Also be aware that consolidator tickets are usually nonrefundable or come with stiff cancellation penalties.

    I've found great deals at **Cheap Tickets** (© **888/922-8849;** www.cheaptickets.com); I almost always do better by calling than I do on their website. **Council Travel** (© **800/226-8624;** www.counciltravel.com) and **STA Travel** (© **800/781-4040;** www.statravel.com) cater to young travelers, but offer discount fares to people of all ages. **The TravelHub** (© **888/AIR-FARE;** www.travelhub.com) represents nearly 1,000 travel agencies, many of whom offer consolidator and discount fares. Other reliable consolidators include **1-800-FLY-CHEAP** (www.1800flycheap.com); **TFI Tours International** (© **800/745-8000** or 212/736-1140;

www.lowestairprice.com), which serves as a clearinghouse for unused seats; and "rebators" like **Travel Avenue** (© **800/333-3335;** www.travelavenue.com), which rebate part of their commissions to you.

13. **Search the Internet for cheap fares.** You can tap into the same databases once accessible only to travel agents through sites like **Travelocity.com, Expedia.com,** and **Orbitz.com.** You might also check out **Qixo** (**www.qixo.com**), another search engine that allows you to search for flights and accommodations from some 20 airline and travel-planning sites (such as Travelocity) at once.

    Going straight to the source can be an excellent strategy, since the major carriers frequently offer "Internet only" sales on their websites. A fare can pop up today that wasn't available yesterday, and won't be around tomorrow. (I was able to snare a $195 round-trip fare between New York and Phoenix on Continental's website in early 2002.)

    Or check megasites that compile comprehensive lists of last-minute specials, notably **Smarter Living** (smarterliving.com) and **WebFlyer** (www.webflyer.com).

    If you don't care who your carrier is, consider **Priceline** (www.priceline.com), which lets you "name your price" for airline tickets (as well as hotel rooms and rental cars). For airline tickets, you have to accept any flight between 6am and 10pm on the dates you've selected. Tickets are nonrefundable, and while they say no frequent-flier miles are awarded, we've been given them more than once.

    A word of warning: Avoid online auctions. Sites that auction airline tickets and frequent-flier

Frommers.com: The Complete Travel Resource

For an excellent travel-planning resource, we highly recommend **Frommers.com** (www.frommers.com). We're a little biased, of course, but we guarantee that you'll find the travel tips, reviews, monthly vacation giveaways, and online-booking capabilities indispensable. Among the special features are our popular **Message Boards,** where Frommer's readers post queries and share advice (sometimes even our authors show up to answer questions); **Frommers.com Newsletter,** for the latest travel bargains and inside travel secrets; and Frommer's **Destinations Section,** where you'll get expert travel tips, hotel and dining recommendations, and advice on the sights to see for more than 2,500 destinations around the globe. When your research is done, the **Online Reservation System** (www.frommers.com/booktravelnow) takes you to Frommer's favorite sites for booking your vacation at affordable prices.

---

miles are the No. 1 perpetrators of Internet fraud, according to the National Consumers League.

14. **Sign up for e-mail notification of last-minute specials.** Each week, airlines send subscribers a list of discounted flights, usually leaving that Friday or Saturday and returning the next Monday or Tuesday. You can sign up at each airline's website; for URLs, see "By Plane" in "Getting There," later in this chapter.

15. **Know when sales start.** You can often score the best online deal if you know when sales start, since last-minute deals may vanish in minutes. So, if you have a favorite booking site or airline, find out when last-minute deals are released to the public. (For example, Southwest's specials are posted every Tues at 12:01am Central.)

16. **Book a seat on a charter flight.** Most charter operators advertise and sell their seats through travel agents, thus making these local professionals your best source of information for available flights. Before deciding to take a charter, check the restrictions: You might be asked to purchase a package tour, pay in advance, be amenable to a change in departure date, fly on an airline you're not familiar with, and/or pay stiff penalties if you cancel—as well as be understanding if the charter doesn't fill and is canceled up to 10 days before departure. Summer charters fill up more quickly and are almost sure to fly, but if you go with one, consider cancellation and baggage insurance.

OTHER TRANSPORTATION OPTIONS

17. **Consider taking a train or bus instead of flying.** Traveling by train or bus may be cheaper than flying. More importantly, even if the cost of your train ticket is the same as an airline ticket, train travel saves you money because you'll come into and out of Midtown without the additional cost of airport transfers. If you're as close to New York as Boston, Philly, or Washington, D.C., a train or bus can save time, now that Amtrak has added the new high-speed Acela trains. Your cheapest transportation method will always be the bus, but keep in mind that unless it's an express, it can take a lot of time.

18. **Have a flexible schedule when booking train travel, and always ask for the lowest fare.** When you're offered a fare, always ask if

you can do better by traveling at different times or days. You can often save money by traveling at off-peak hours and on weekends. Don't forget to ask for discounts for kids, seniors, passengers with disabilities, military personnel, or anything else that you think might qualify you for a lower fare.

19. **Keep an eye out for sales.** Go to www.amtrak.com and click on "Rail Sale," where you'll find discounts of up to 90% on select routes. If you register your e-mail address, you'll be notified of sale fares as they happen. Keep in mind, though, that if you buy a rail sale ticket, it is not refundable and cannot be exchanged. While you're online, also check the "Savings & Promotions" page for a whole range of discounted and/or value-added deals.

    Greyhound advertises sales at www.greyhound.com. They usually have a number of money-saving deals, ranging from "Friendly Fares" that let you travel for as little as $49 to free companion fares.

20. **Make reservations as soon as possible.** As with the airlines, discounts on buses and trains are often based on advanced purchase.

GETTING AROUND NEW YORK CITY

21. **Don't rent a car.** Driving is a nightmare and parking is ridiculously expensive. It's much easier to use public transportation.

22. **Take a bus or the subway from the airport.** You have to allot a bit more time, but public transportation offers great savings over taxis and car services. A shuttle bus connects JFK Airport to the A train, which whisks you into the city for $1.50. The M60 bus comes into Manhattan from LaGuardia for the same price.

(Note that a Metropolitan Transit Authority fare hike was being discussed at press time.) From Newark, convenient, affordable buses can drop you off around the city for around 10 bucks, and the new AirTrain connects the airport with Manhattan for just $11.15.

23. **Use the subway and bus to get around the city.** The transit system is probably the city's best bargain. It's safe, relatively clean, quick, efficient, and cheap. Use taxis only late at night, when trains and buses can be few and far between, or when traveling a short distance in a group of three or four, when the fare might be less than multiple subway or bus fares.

24. **Buy a MetroCard.** If you're going to be in the city for a few days, or you're traveling in a group (up to four people can use a MetroCard at any given time), buy a $15 pay-per-ride MetroCard, which will get you 11 rides for the price of 10, and allow you to transfer within a 2-hour period of each ride you use. If you're going to do a lot of running around, consider a $4 daily **Fun Pass** or a $17 **7-Day MetroCard,** each of which allows unlimited rides for the life of the card. There's one strong caveat, however: Every person has to have his or her own unlimited-use MetroCard; you can't double-up as you can with pay-per-ride MetroCards.

25. **In the daytime, walk.** No other American city is more welcoming or so rewarding to explore on foot. Walking will save you money—and work off all the meals you'll no doubt buy with the savings.

ACCOMMODATIONS

26. **Stay uptown or downtown.** The advantages of a Midtown location are overrated, especially when saving money is your object.

Manhattan is a petite island, and the subway can whisk you anywhere in minutes. You'll get the best value by staying in the neighborhoods where real New Yorkers live, such as Greenwich Village, Chelsea, Murray Hill, or—my favorite neighborhood for space-seekers and bargain hunters—the Upper West Side. These are the neighborhoods where real New Yorkers hang out, too, so you won't want for good eats, nightlife, or Big Apple bustle.

27. **Visit over a weekend.** If your trip includes a weekend, you might save big. Business hotels tend to empty, and rooms that go for $300 or more Monday through Thursday can drop to as low as $150 or less once the execs have gone home. These deals are prevalent in the Financial District, but are often available in Midtown, too. See "Deal-Making with the Chains" on p. 106 for tips on packages.

28. **Watch for advertised discounts.** Scan ads in the travel section of your Sunday paper, which can be an excellent source for up-to-the-minute hotel deals. Also check the back of the travel section of the Sunday *New York Times,* where the best weekend deals and other hotel bargains are usually listed.

29. **Don't be afraid to bargain.** Always ask for a lower price than the first one quoted. Most rack rates include commissions for travel agents, which many hotels will cut if you make your own reservations and haggle a bit. Ask whether a less-expensive room is available than the first one mentioned or if any special rates apply: corporate, student, military, seniors. Mention membership in AAA, AARP, frequent-flier programs, corporate or military organizations, or unions, which might entitle you to deals. The chains, such as Best Western and Comfort Inn, tend to be good about trying to save you money, but reservations agents often won't volunteer the information; you have to pull it out of them.

30. **Dial direct.** When booking a room in a chain hotel, call the hotel's local line, as well as the toll-free number, and see where you get the best deal. The clerk who runs the place is more likely to know about booking patterns and will often grant deep discounts in order to fill up.

31. **Rely on a qualified professional.** Certain hotels give travel agents discounts in exchange for steering business their way, so if you're shy about bargaining, an agent may be better equipped to negotiate discounts for you.

32. **Shop online.** New York hotels often offer "Internet-only" deals that can save you 10% to 20% over what you'd pay if you booked by telephone. Also, hotels often advertise all of their available weekend and other package deals on their websites.

   Also try such booking engines as **Travelocity.com, Expedia.com,** and **Orbitz.com.** I've found that Expedia, in particular, sometimes offers excellent rates that cannot be booked elsewhere. Expedia will require you to pay up front, but you can usually cancel up to 72 hours in advance for a $25 fee. (Check the exact rules for your booking.)

   Some of the discount reservations agencies (see tip 33) have sites that allow you to book online. **American Automobile Association** members may be able to score the best discounts by booking at **www.aaa.com.**

33. **Investigate reservations services.** These work like consolidators, buying up or reserving rooms in

bulk, and then dealing them to customers at a profit. You can get 10% to 50% off; but remember, these discounts apply to rack rates, prices that people rarely end up paying. You may get a decent rate, but call the hotel directly to see if you can do better.

Start with **Quikbook** (ⓒ **800/789-9887** or 212/779-7666; www.quikbook.com), the best of the bunch since they book more than 100 hotels, require no prepayment, and allow you to make changes and cancellations (penalties depend on the hotel). Another good bet is **Hotel ConXions** (ⓒ **800/522-9991** or 212/840-8686; www.hotelconxions.com). Both Quikbook and Hotel ConXions have guaranteed room blocks in select properties, so they can sometimes get you into a hotel that's otherwise sold out. You might also try the **Hotel Reservations Network,** also known as HotelDiscount!com (ⓒ **800/364-0801;** www.180096 HOTEL.com or www.hoteldiscount.com), and **Accommodations Express** (ⓒ **800/950-4685;** www.accommodationsexpress.com).

Important tips: Never just rely on a reservations service. Do a little homework; compare the rack rates to the discount rates to see what kind of deal you're getting. That way you'll know whether you're being offered a substantial savings. Always check the rate a reservations service offers you with the rate you can get directly from the hotel, which can be better. If you're being offered a stay in a hotel I haven't recommended, do more research to learn about it. It's not a deal if you end up at a dump.

34. **Take a chance with Priceline.** I admit it: I'm a little afraid of Priceline (**www.priceline.com**). But I have an aunt who travels constantly, and she won't book a hotel any other way. She's had great luck scoring luxury rooms for as little as $50 through their "name your price" program. If you're a gambler, Priceline can be a great way to win the budget war. You won't know the name of your hotel until it's bought and paid for, but you can choose your neighborhood and the class of hotel (from economy to deluxe), and Priceline guarantees that you'll stay in a nationally recognized, name-brand or independent hotel trusted for their quality, service, and amenities. Please write and let me know how it goes.

35. **If you find a rate that seems like a good value, book it early.** If somebody quotes you an attractive rate, don't assume it'll be waiting for you in a month, a week, or even a day. Occupancy rates have shot through the roof in New York these days, and everyone is on the lookout for a decent rate. As hotels fill up and the number of empty rooms goes down, rates go up.

36. **If you find yourself without a room at the last minute, work it to your advantage.** I never recommend coming to town without reservations; a convention or some other event can hit town and fill up the city's hotels. But if you find yourself without a room, you might be able to strike a bargain. As the hours progress, the hotel becomes more anxious to fill empty rooms and will lower the rate to get your business. I've seen desk clerks sell $179 rooms for $79. But remember—this is a risky way to go, because if the hotel is full, you're out of luck.

37. **Be willing to share a bathroom.** For the best bargains, do as the Europeans do: Share a hall bathroom with your fellow travelers. Usually there are two or three

bathrooms to a floor, often with separate rooms for the toilet and the shower and/or tub so all the facilities aren't tied up at once. If you can wrap your mind around this idea, you can get a lot of bang for your buck. If you're on a tight budget, you'll be able to stay at a nicer hotel than if you insist on a private bathroom. Many rooms have private sinks, so you can brush your teeth or wash your face without leaving your room. A couple of very good bargain-rate places, the Chelsea Lodge and the Chelsea Pines Inn, have private in-room showers, so the only thing you have to share is the toilet.

38. **Consider a suite.** It sounds like the ultimate splurge, but if you're traveling with another couple or your family, a suite can be a bargain. They're always cheaper than two hotel rooms. The living room almost always features a sofa bed, and there's often a kitchenette where you can prepare coffee and light meals for yourself. Some places charge for extra guests beyond two; some don't.

39. **If you're traveling with the kids, stay at a hotel that lets them stay for free.** Most hotels add a surcharge—anywhere from $10 to $30 per night—for each extra person beyond two sharing a room, and that can add up. So if you're traveling with kids, choose a hotel that lets them stay free. Age limits for free kid stays can range from 10 to 18, so you might even be able to have your teens stay for free. Even if the hotel usually charges for kids, it might be willing to drop this extra charge to draw you in, so always ask.

40. **Save on hotel tax by booking an apartment or home stay.** Booking a hosted or unhosted apartment stay can save you dollars on taxes. These agencies are able to charge just 8.25% sales tax, as opposed to 13.25% plus $2 per night for a regular hotel room. Even better: Tax is often included in the rates quoted by booking agencies; thus, a $130 room is just $130, while a regular hotel will charge you $149.23 per night for a $130 room. A tax loophole eliminated entirely the tax on many 7-night or longer stays (which are classified as short-term leases rather than hotel stays). Be sure to get the specific rules for your rental at booking to avoid any surprises at bill time. See "Home Stay Sweet Home Stay," below, for recommended agencies.

41. **Look into group or long-stay discounts.** If you come as part of a group, you may be able to negotiate a bargain because the hotel can guarantee occupancy in a number of rooms. If you're planning a long stay (5–7 days or more), you might qualify for a discount, so be sure to ask.

42. **If you're on a shoestring budget, book a hostel bed.** You'll have no privacy—you'll share a room with fellow travelers and all facilities are common—but there's no arguing with the rate. The largest hostel in the **Hostelling International–American Youth Hostels** system houses travelers in bunk-bedded rooms for $29 to $35 per person per night. You'll save about $3 a night if you become an AYH member. Also consider the dorms at the **Chelsea Star,** the **Chelsea International Hostel, Chelsea Center Hostel,** the **Big Apple Hostel,** the East Village's **Whitehouse Hotel of New York,** Harlem's **Park View Hostel** and **Sugar Hill International House,** and the **Central Park Hostel & Inn.** See chapter 5 for individual listings. For additional hostel possibilities, surf to **The Hostel**

Finds Home Stay Sweet Home Stay

New York apartment or home stays can be a great way to go. They usually fall on the lower end of the price continuum and can range from spartan to splendid, and from a hosted bedroom in a private home to an unhosted, fully equipped apartment. No matter what, you can pretty much guarantee that you'll get more for your money than with a regular hotel room.

The city's best-kept accommodations secret is **Homestay New York** (© and fax **718/434-2071;** www.homestayny.com). Lovely owner Helayne Wagner can book you into a private room with a family (including her own) that welcomes travelers. Homes are in residential neighborhoods in Brooklyn, Queens, or Upper Manhattan, all within a half-hour of Midtown or downtown via subway or bus, and most are beautifully restored 19th- and early-20th-century houses. Not only can this save you money, it can be fun, too: Visitors are matched to hosts by age, interests, and occupation, and the hosts are more than happy to provide advice and assistance. You'll be the only in-house guest, so it's much like staying with a friend who delights in seeing you happy and enjoying the city.

Rates run $100 to $130 single or double, with shared or private bathroom depending on the home. Most rooms have TV, air-conditioning, and a small fridge, and towels are provided. Buffet breakfast is included; the price also often includes a welcome dinner, plus a farewell dinner if your stay lasts 5 or more days. Also included are free MetroCards and phone cards (values depend on the length of your stay), plus Broadway show information and discount coupons for live performances, comedy clubs, and other entertainment. In summer, guests staying 7 nights or more get a 3-hour evening cruise. With these extras, Homestay New York is an excellent value. Tax is included, which saves you an additional 13.25% plus $2 per night over what you'd pay in a hotel. Helayne also has access to theater discounts that you can't get on your own. A 3-night minimum is requested, and no credit cards are accepted. Children 3 and over are welcome.

Handbook (www.hostelhandbook.com) and **Hostels.com** on the Internet.

43. **Try the Y.** The Y isn't as cheap as hostel living, but the facilities are better. The **YMCA of Greater New York** (© **212/630-9600;** www.ymcanyc.org) has eight residences throughout the city's five boroughs. You'll have a private room (some have private bathrooms) and access to the on-site fitness center—many feature state-of-the-art equipment, pools, and exercise classes—free. The Y is popular with families, older travelers, and singles. Contact the **West Side YMCA,** adjacent to Central Park at 5 W. 63rd St. (© **212/875-4100**), and the **Vanderbilt Y,** 224 E. 47th St. (© **212/756-9600**), as far in

A number of agencies can book you into a B&B room (hosted or unhosted) or a private apartment. The place to start is **Manhattan Getaways** ★ (① 212/956-2010; www.manhattangetaways.com). Judith Glynn maintains a beautifully kept and managed network of bed-and-breakfast rooms (from $105 nightly) and unhosted apartments (from $145) around the city. There's a 3-night minimum, and credit cards are accepted. Another decent bet is **A Hospitality Company** (① 800/987-1235 or 212/965-1102; www.hospitalityco.com), with more than 300 apartments they own and manage around Manhattan starting at $115 a night, or $795 weekly for a basic studio. These are rather sparsely furnished apartments and the company offers little in the way of service (it took me 5 days to get my TV fixed when I was displaced from home by renovation), but the apartments are clean and do the trick. There's no minimum stay, and credit cards are accepted. Optional cleaning services are available for longer stays. Additional agencies that can book you into a B&B room or a private apartment, with prices starting at $90 nightly, include **As You Like It** (① 800/277-0413 or 212/695-0191; www.furnapts.com), **Abode Apartment Rentals** (① 800/835-8880 or 212/472-2000; www.abodenyc.com), **CitySonnet** (① 212/614-3034; www.citysonnet.com), **Manhattan Lodgings** (① 212/677-7616; www.manhattanlodgings.com), and **New York Habitat** (① 212/255-8018; www.nyhabitat.com).

Another advantage to booking a B&B or apartment accommodation is that taxes are lower, usually just 8.25% (as opposed to 13.25% plus $2 per night for a regular hotel room).

A few words of warning: If you go this route, keep in mind that you won't have the amenities that a hotel—even a budget hotel—can offer, such as maid service and tour planning. In fact, many accommodations called "B&Bs" don't even offer breakfast, so be sure to ask. You'll have a host on hand to offer personal assistance if you book through Homestay New York. I've received complaints about agencies that offer one thing and deliver another, so get all promises in writing and an exact total up front. Try to pay by credit card if possible, so you can dispute payment if the agency fails to live up to its promises.

advance as possible, as these locations are popular. Manhattan locations are the most expensive, with prices starting around $80; if you can stay up in Harlem or in Brooklyn or Queens, nightly rates start as low as $40. For information, visit the Y's website (www.ymcanyc.org) and click on "Guest Rooms & Group Rates."

44. **Dorm it.** At Columbia University, **International House,** 500 Riverside Dr. on the Upper West Side (① 212/316-8436 or 212/316-8473; www.ihouse-nyc.org), offers dormitory-style accommodations in July and August, priced at $40 or $45 depending on your length of stay (up to 20 nights); you must be 18 or older to stay. International

House has 11 guest rooms with private baths and maid service, ranging from $110 to $150 for up to four people. These are especially reasonable if there are three or four of you, or if you're traveling in the autumn, when everybody else is charging an arm and a leg. Book well ahead.

45. **Make a spiritual connection.** Fully outfitted and maid-serviced guest rooms are offered at Columbia's **Union Theological Seminary** (© **212/280-1313**; www.uts.columbia.edu), for a pricey $130 to $175 per night.

    More affordable accommodations are offered at **The House of the Redeemer,** a former Vanderbilt mansion on the elegant Upper East Side, just steps from Museum Mile, at 7 E. 95th St. (© **212/289-0399**; www.houseoftheredeemer.org). This Episcopal worship center offers short-term accommodations (2–6 nights) to adult travelers of all faiths when groups are not in residence. Accommodations are $60 single, $75 double with hall bath, $100 double with private bath. Rooms are not available from late June to early September.

    The Community of the Holy Spirit, an Episcopal monastic community of nuns, welcomes guests into their simple but neat private rooms (most with shared baths) at **St. Hilda's House,** 621 W. 113th St. (© **212/932-8098**; www.chssisters.org). Rates are $65 single, $110 to $130 double, and $165 triple. Because this is a contemplative environment, it's best suited for visitors looking for the same. You are welcome to share meals with the sisters, but no meals are served and no guests are welcomed on Monday. Reserve well in advance, as these accommodations fill up early.

46. **Do as little business as possible through the hotel.** Any service the hotel offers will cost you dearly. You can find dry cleaners or other services in most areas of Manhattan. Find out before you dial whether your hotel imposes a surcharge on local or long-distance calls; it might be cheaper to use the pay phone in the lobby.

47. **If you're driving into the city and will need to garage your car, check parking rates with the hotel before you book.** Many hotels negotiate discounts at nearby garages. Choose a hotel that has a good rate, or you might end up paying a fortune for parking (negating any savings you've earned by booking a cheap hotel). For more on this, see "Deals for Visitors with Wheels: Cheap Parking Tips" on p. 91.

DINING

48. **Book a room with a kitchenette.** This allows you to eat some meals in. Even if you only prepare breakfast, you're bound to save money this way.

49. **Stay at a hotel, guesthouse, or bed-and-breakfast that includes breakfast.** And be sure to confirm that it's included before you book, because some city guesthouses keep rates down by not offering breakfast. Ask what's included; the offering will most likely be a limited continental breakfast.

50. **Use any coupons you can get your hands on.** The New York Convention & Visitors Bureau offers a free visitor's guide that includes coupons in the back. Even if you order one in advance (see "Visitor Information," below), stop in at the local visitor centers, where the wall racks sometimes have coupons and advertisements for freebies, two-for-ones, and dining discounts.

Also consider buying one or both of the discount/coupon books recommended in tips no. 2, 3, and 4 above. Before you leave home, check the deals offered through the **Playbill Online Theatre Club** (www.playbillclub.com), which often include a few dining discounts. If you use a dining discount coupon, remember to tip your waiter based on the full value of the meal; he's on a budget, too.

51. **Eat ethnic.** New York probably has the best collection of ethnic restaurants in the country, and the best offer first-class eats for low, low prices. Chinatown is always a good bet for top-quality meals for a pittance, as are the restaurants on East 6th Street east of Second Avenue, known as Little India. Jewish delis are first-rate in Manhattan—and the pile of pastrami can keep you fueled for days. New York's excellent selection of pizza parlors serves up bargains by the slice all over town.

52. **During warm weather, picnic.** New York is full of marvelous delis, greenmarkets, and gourmet groceries where you can assemble a delicious, affordable meal. The city is rich with parks that serve as great picnic spots: Battery Park, Bryant Park, and Union Square—and perhaps best of all, Central Park. If you don't feel like going through the hassle of assembling a picnic at a grocery, try takeout, which will save you the cost of the tip you'd leave if you ate in.

53. **Eat street food.** Although dirty-water hot dogs and pretzels still have their appeal, New York's street-food offerings have expanded considerably. You'll find vendors all over the city hawking soups, gyros, falafels, baked potatoes with a variety of toppings, fresh fruit, and more. The best vendors congregate in high-end business districts, such as around Rockefeller Center in Midtown (vendors often line up just off Sixth Ave.; 50th St. is a hot corner) and in the Financial District. Sixth Avenue is lined with plazas where you can enjoy your alfresco lunch, and Lower Manhattan offers a wealth of even more pleasant open spaces.

54. **Order the prix-fixe special.** Fixed-price specials that include appetizers, side dishes, and dessert (as well as beverages in some cases) will almost always get you more bang for your buck. Just one example: Diners willing to eat between 5 and 7pm can have three courses for just $14 at authentic French wine bar **Le Pere Pinard** (p. 144). Also consider buffets like the great lunchtime one at **Salaam Bombay** (p. 141).

55. **Bring your own wine.** This is a great way to save. Some restaurants, even those with their own wine lists, will let you bring your own if you call and ask. At press time, places that are BYOB as policy include **Snack,** the **Zen Palate** in Union Square, **Afghan Kebab House,** the **Pink Tea Cup,** and just about any restaurant in Little India; all of these places are happy to open your bottle and provide glasses. (See chapter 6 for individual reviews.) However, *always* call and ask in advance. (The only exception is Little India, where you can just arrive with a bottle or a six-pack and ask at the door.) If the answer is "no," be gracious and accept it. If the answer is "yes," ask whether a corkage fee is charged. See chapter 8 for tips on shops with good values on wine.

SIGHTSEEING

56. **Buy a CityPass.** CityPass may be New York's best sightseeing deal. Pay one price ($38, or $31 for

kids 12–17) for admission to seven major attractions: The American Museum of Natural History (does not include Space Show); the Solomon R. Guggenheim Museum; the Empire State Building; the *Intrepid* Sea-Air-Space Museum; the Whitney Museum of American Art; MoMA QNS; and a 2-hour Circle Line cruise. If you purchased separate admission to each of these, you'd spend more than twice as much.

CityPass is not a coupon book. It contains actual tickets, so you can bypass ticket lines. This can save you hours, since sights like the Empire State Building often have lines of an hour or more.

CityPass is good for 9 days from the first time you use it. It's sold at all participating attractions and online at www.citypass.net. Your best bet is to buy it at the first attraction you visit, because online orders rack up service and shipping fees. Start sightseeing at an attraction that's likely to have the shortest admission line, like the Guggenheim or the Whitney, or arrive before opening to avoid a wait. A preorder may be the way to go, however, if that's not convenient for you or you're starting your sightseeing on a weekend or during holiday time, when even those museums can have ugly ticket lines.

Get more info by calling CityPass at © **707/256-0490**. (CityPass is not sold over the phone.) The pricing and attraction list is confirmed through March 2003; call or check the website for updated information if your visit falls later in the year.

57. **Take advantage of freebies.** Many of the best things to do and see in Manhattan are free, from walking the Brooklyn Bridge to riding the Staten Island Ferry to exploring Central Park to attending TV show tapings. Additionally, some organizations offer walking tours at no charge. Many museums and attractions that charge admission have free or pay-as-you-wish programs 1 day or evening a week. See "Where to Find Free Culture" (p. 224) and "Absolutely Free Walking Tours" (p. 252).

SHOPPING

58. **Ship major purchases home.** If you're buying high-ticket items, you can often save on the 8.25% New York sales tax by having items shipped home. Depending on the laws of your state, you can pay a lesser tax or skip the duty completely.

Value   Museum & Entertainment Deals for Teens

High 5 Tickets to the Arts (© 212/HI5-TKTS; www.high5tix.org) makes theater and culture more accessible for kids between the ages of 13 and 18. Teens can buy tickets for select theatrical performances and events for $5 each for weekend performances, or $5 for two (for the teen and a guest of any age) for Monday through Thursday performances. High 5 also offers discounted museum passes at the wallet-friendly price of two for $5 (for the teen and a guest of any age). Check the website for details on obtaining theater or museum tickets, which can usually be purchased with proof of age at any New York City Ticketmaster outlet or online. Also check the High 5 website for listings of free and nearly free events going on while you and your teen are in town.

59. **Seek out sample sales.** Garment designers and manufacturers often sell off their newest items (sometimes not even available in stores) for a song to raise quick cash; see "Scouring the Sample Sales" on p. 282.

60. **Do your homework and bargain on electronic equipment.** You'll also notice a wealth of electronics stores throughout the Theater District, many trumpeting GOING OUT OF BUSINESS sales. These guys have been going out of business since the Stone Age. That's the bait and switch; these guys will suck you dry given half a chance. Trust me: The only way you'll do well is if you know your stuff. And play hard to get; I've seen prices tumble the closer I got to the door.

61. **Always ask for a better price on anything used or vintage.** It won't always work, but a lot of vintage, antiques, and collectibles dealers—even those with shops in high-rent districts such as SoHo and the Village—will drop their price if you're just savvy enough to ask. Always be polite, however, and don't push if you're told "no."

ENTERTAINMENT

62. **Buy discounted theater tickets through Playbill Online.** Joining Playbill's Online Theater Club (**www.playbillclub.com**) can yield substantial savings on advance-purchase theater tickets for Broadway and Off-Broadway shows, including some of the top draws (even *Oklahoma!*, at press time). Becoming a member is free; all you have to do is register, and you'll have access to discounts that can range from a few dollars to as much as 50% off regular prices. The club also offers its members deals at some nice hotels as well as a few dining discounts, and you can sign up to receive e-mail updates on new offers. Other sites that offer similar services are **TheaterMania** (**www.theatermania.com**) and **Broadway.com** (**www.broadway.com**), although the Broadway.com site wants a bit too much personal information for my taste. At TheaterMania, be sure to click on "Get the Insider Scoop" for instant discounts.

63. **Buy discounted same-day tickets at the TKTS booth.** If your heart is set on seeing a particular show, order your tickets before you come to the city. But if you're flexible, check out TKTS, which sells day-of-show tickets to plays on and Off-Broadway for 25% to 50% off face value, plus a $2.50 per-ticket service charge. In-the-know theatergoers skip the Theater District location for the far-less-crowded downtown booth, where you can also score matinee tickets a day in advance. For complete details, see "Top Ticket-Buying Tips" in chapter 9.

64. **Take advantage of free events.** Summertime is a great time to be in the city if you're a culture buff. Some of the city's top cultural organizations offer free outdoor events, from Shakespeare in the Park to the Metropolitan Opera. See "Park It! Shakespeare, Music & Other Free Fun" on p. 308.

But you don't have to wait until summer: Comb the listings in *Time Out New York, New York* magazine, the *New Yorker,* and the *New York Times* for free events ranging from dance performances to readings at Barnes & Noble. Or pick up a copy of **Club freeTime,** a monthly paper listing free events around Manhattan—usually 15 to 45 events per day, including movies, theater, dance, concerts, readings, and more. You can subscribe for $25 a year by calling ✆ **212/545-8900,** but there's no need to; there are short-term Internet subscriptions (1 week, $1.95; 1 month, $2.95; 3 months, $7.95) which score you the wealth of free listings, plus discounts to member events, including concerts and discussion groups. If you don't have Web access, you can pick up the current issue at many newsstands. Limited event listings and newsstand locations are online at **www.clubfreetime.com**.

65. **Eschew high-priced, star performances for lesser-known, lower-priced surprises.** Seeing the New York Philharmonic or a Broadway extravaganza is a must if you can afford it. But you'll save money—and maybe enjoy yourself more—by looking beyond the obvious. For instance, the nation's top music education institution, the **Julliard School,** offers a full slate of free and cheap events, from first-rate student concerts to lectures by celebrities of the performing-arts world. Smaller venues such as **Bargemusic,** the **92nd Street Y,** and the **Amato Opera Theatre** offer intimate, only-in-New-York performances, sometimes by nationally known artists, at rock-bottom prices. Off- and Off-Off-Broadway theater is usually significantly less expensive than Broadway, and the quality doesn't have to suffer one bit.

2 Visitor Information

For information before you leave, your best source (besides this book, of course) is NYC & Company, the organization behind the **New York Convention & Visitors Bureau** (NYCVB), 810 Seventh Ave., New York, NY 10019. You can call © **800/ NYC-VISIT** or 212/397-8222 to order the **Official NYC Visitor Kit,** which has the *Official NYC Guide* detailing hotels, restaurants, theaters, attractions, events, and more; a fold-out map; a newsletter on the latest goings-on in the city; and brochures on attractions and services. It costs $5.95 to receive the packet (payable by credit card) in 7 to 10 days, $9.95 for rush delivery (3–4 business days) to U.S. addresses and international orders. (*Note:* I have received complaints that packages don't always strictly adhere to these time frames.)

Money-saving tip: You can order the *Official NYC Guide,* the heart of the kit, for free at **www.nycvisit.com** (click on "Visitors"). The site is also a terrific information source. To speak to a travel counselor call © **212/ 484-1222.**

For visitor-center and information-desk locations once you arrive, see "Visitor Information" in "Orientation," in chapter 4.

Also check out "Site Seeing: The Big Apple on the Web" on p. 12. There, you'll find details on the best online resources for planning your trip.

FOR U.K. VISITORS The **NYCVB Visitor Information Center** is at 33–34 Carnaby St., London W1V 1PA (© **0207/437-8300**). You can order the Official NYC Visitor Kit by sending them an A5-size self-addressed envelope and 72p postage. For New York–bound travelers in the London area, the center also offers free travel-planning assistance.

3 Money

You never have to carry too much cash in New York, and while the city's pretty safe, it's best not to overstuff your wallet (but make sure you have at least $20 in taxi fare on hand).

In most neighborhoods, you can find **ATMs** every couple of blocks. They're scarce in a few neighborhoods, like the East Village or in Harlem. The city's biggest banks are Citibank, Chase, Fleet, and HSBC, which belong to the **Cirrus** (✆ 800/424-7787; www.mastercard.com) and **PLUS** (✆ 800/843-7587; www.visa.com/atms) networks. Expect to pay $1.50 or $2 each time you withdraw money from an ATM, in addition to what your home bank charges. Stay away from commercial machines, like those in hotel lobbies and corner delis, which often charge $3 or more per transaction. Avoid poorly lit or out-of-the-way ATMs, especially at night.

Traveler's checks are something of an anachronism from the days before the ATM. But if you want to avoid ATM withdrawal charges, you might go with traveler's checks—provided you don't mind showing identification every time you cash one. You can get them at almost any bank, usually incurring a service charge ranging from 1% to 4%. **American Express** traveler's checks are available at ✆ 800/221-7282 or www.americanexpress.com. Amex gold or platinum cardholders can avoid paying the fee by ordering over the telephone. **American Automobile Association members** can get checks for no fee at most AAA offices.

Visa offers traveler's checks at Citibanks nationwide, as well as at several other banks; call ✆ 800/732-1322 for information. **MasterCard** also offers traveler's checks; call ✆ 800/223-9920 for a location near you.

As for credit cards, **American Express, MasterCard,** and **Visa** are accepted almost everywhere in New York. **Carte Blanche** and **Diner's Club** have made a comeback in hotel circles, and **Discover** is also popular (though don't count on it being accepted everywhere). Because New York has so many international visitors, cards like **enRoute, Eurocard,** and **JCB** are widely accepted, particularly at hotels. Budget travelers should remember, that many of New York's most affordable restaurants accept cash only. See if they take credit cards *before* you order.

WHAT TO DO IF YOUR WALLET GETS STOLEN

Block charges against your account as soon as you discover a card has been lost or stolen. Then file a police report.

Almost every credit-card company has a toll-free number to call if your card is stolen. They may be able to wire you a cash advance immediately, and in many places, they can deliver an emergency credit card in a day or two. The issuing bank's toll-free number is usually on the back of your credit card—though if your card has been stolen, that won't help you unless you recorded the number elsewhere.

Visa's U.S. emergency number is ✆ 800/336-8472. American Express cardholders and traveler's check holders should call ✆ 800/221-7282. MasterCard holders call ✆ 800/307-7309. Otherwise, call the toll-free directory at ✆ 800/555-1212.

Odds are that if your wallet is gone, the police won't be able to recover it. However, it's still worth informing the authorities. Your credit-card company or insurer may require a police report number or record of the theft.

If you carry traveler's checks, keep a copy of their serial numbers separate from your checks. You'll get a refund faster if you know the numbers.

If you need emergency cash when the banks are closed, you can have money wired to you from **Western Union** (✆ 800/325-6000; www.westernunion.com). You must present valid ID to pick up the cash at the Western Union office. You can pick up a money transfer even if you don't have valid identification, as long as you can answer a test question provided by the sender. Be sure to let the sender know in advance that you don't have ID. If you need to use a test question instead of ID, the sender must take cash to his or her local Western Union office, rather than transferring the money over the phone or online.

4 When to Go

Summer or winter, rain or shine, New York City always has fun things going on, so there's no real "best" time to go.

MONEY MATTERS At press time, it was still unclear as to what kinds of effects 9/11 would have on the city's tourism fortunes. While hotel prices are more flexible than they've been in years, New York hotels are by no means throwing a fire sale. Therefore, if money is a big concern, you might want to follow these rough seasonal guidelines.

The least expensive time to visit is in winter, between the first of the year and early April. Sure, the weather can suck, but hotels are suffering from the post-holiday blues, and rooms often go for a relative song. In the winter of 2002, for instance, rooms at the Comfort Inn–Central Park West were going for as little as $80 to $90, for AAA members. However, the occasional convention or event, such as February's annual Fashion Week, can sometimes throw a wrench in your winter savings plans.

Spring and autumn are traditionally the busiest, most expensive, seasons after holiday time. Don't expect hotels to be handing you deals, but you might be able to negotiate a good rate. Spring is generally easier than fall; many hotels consider their peak season to be the last 4 months of the year.

The city is drawing more families these days, and they usually visit in the summer. Still, the prospect of heat and humidity keeps some people away, making July and the first half of August a significantly cheaper time to visit than later in the year, and good hotel deals are often available.

Christmas is not a good time for budget-minded travelers. The first two weeks of December—the shopping weeks—are the worst when it comes to scoring an affordable room; that's when shoppers converge on the town to catch the holiday spirit and spend, spend, spend. Hotel prices go sky high, and the crowds can be intolerable. If you'd rather have more of the city to yourself, with better chances at discount Broadway-show tickets and easier access to attractions, you'll be happier visiting another time of year.

But Thanksgiving can be a great time to visit: Business travelers have gone home for the holiday, and the holiday shoppers haven't yet arrived. It's a little-known secret that most hotels away from the Thanksgiving Day Parade route have empty rooms sitting, and they're usually willing to make great deals to fill them. Hotels practically give away hotel rooms for the week following Thanksgiving.

WEATHER The worst weather in New York is during that long week or 10 days that arrives each summer between mid-July and mid-August, when temperatures go up to around 100°F with 90% humidity. You feel sticky, the streets smell, everyone's cranky, and the concrete canyons become furnaces. But summer has its compensations, such as wonderful free open-air concerts and other events. And you might luck out, as the last few summers have been downright lovely. But if you are at all temperature sensitive, your odds of getting comfortable weather are better in June or September.

Another period when you might not like to stroll around is during January or

February, when temperatures are commonly in the 20s and those concrete canyons turn into wind tunnels. The city looks gorgeous just after a snowfall, but the streets soon become an ugly, slushy mess. Again, you never know: Temperatures have regularly been in the 30s and mild 40s during the past few winters. If you hit the weather jackpot, you could have a bargain bonanza (see "Money Matters," above).

Fall and spring are the best times in New York (which is why they're the most expensive). From April to June and September to November, temperatures are mild and pleasant, and the light is beautiful. With the leaves changing in Central Park and just the hint of crispness in the air, October is fabulous—but expect to pay for the privilege of being here.

If you want to know how to pack, check the Weather Channel's online 10-day forecast at **www.weather.com**; I like to balance it against CNN's forecast at **www.cnn.com/weather**. You can also get the local weather by calling ✆ **212/976-1212**.

New York's Average Temperature & Rainfall

	Jan	Feb	Mar	Apr	May	June	July	Aug	Sept	Oct	Nov	Dec
Daily Temp. (°F)	38	40	48	61	71	80	85	84	77	67	54	42
Daily Temp. (°C)	3	4	9	16	22	27	29	29	25	19	12	6
Days of Precipitation	11	10	11	11	11	10	11	10	8	8	9	10

NEW YORK CITY CALENDAR OF EVENTS

The following is subject to change. Always confirm before you make plans around a specific event. Call the venue or the **NYCVB** at ✆ **212/484-1222**, go to **www.nycvisit.com**, or pick up a copy of *Time Out New York* for the latest details.

January

Restaurant Week. This twice-yearly event allows you to lunch for $20 at some of New York's finest restaurants. Call ✆ **212/484-1222** or check www.restaurantweek.com for the dates and restaurants. *Reserve immediately.* Late January or early February.

February

Chinese New Year. Every year Chinatown rings in its own new year with 2 weeks of celebrations, including parades with dragon and lion dancers and costumes. The parade winds through Chinatown along Mott, Canal, and Bayard streets, and along East Broadway. The year 2003 is the Year of the Goat, and Chinese New Year falls on February 1. Call the **NYCVB** hot line at ✆ **212/484-1222** or the **Chinese Information and Culture Center** at ✆ **212/373-1800**.

Valentine's Day Weddings atop the Empire State Building. You and your honey can become lifetime members of the **Empire State Building** Wedding Club by getting hitched on the 80th floor observation deck on February 14, 2003. Just 15 lucky couples will be chosen based on "Why We Want to Get Married at the Empire State Building" essays, which are judged on originality, uniqueness, and style. The deadline is November 30; call ✆ **212/736-3100** or visit www.esbnyc.com for details.

Westminster Kennel Club Dog Show. The ultimate purebred-pooch fest. Some 30,000 dog fanciers congregate at **Madison Square Garden** for the 125th "World Series of Dogdom." All 2,500 dogs are American Kennel Club Champions of Record, competing for the Best in Show trophy. Call ✆ **800/455-3647** or visit www.westminsterkennelclub.org for information. Tickets are available through **Ticketmaster** (⌒ **212/307-7171;** www.ticketmaster.com). February 10 and 11.

March

St. Patrick's Day Parade. More than 150,000 marchers join in the world's largest civilian parade, as Fifth Avenue from 44th to 86th streets rings with the sounds of bands and bagpipes, and an inordinate amount of beer is consumed (much of it green). The parade usually starts at 11am, but go extra early if you want a good spot. Call ⌒ **212/484-1222.** March 17.

April

Easter Parade. This isn't a traditional parade, per se: There are no bands, baton twirlers, or protesters. Once, New York's gentry came out to show off their tasteful but discreet toppings. Today, if you were planning to slip on a tasteful little number—you will *not* be the grandest lady along Fifth Avenue from 48th to 57th streets. It's more about flamboyant exhibitionism, with hats and costumes that get more outrageous every year—and anybody can join right in for free. The parade generally runs Easter Sunday from 10am to 3 or 4pm. Call ⌒ **212/484-1222.** April 20.

New York International Auto Show. Hot wheels from all over the world whirl into the **Jacob K. Javits Convention Center** for the largest auto show in the United States. Many concept cars show up. Call ⌒ **800/282-3336** or 212/216-2000, or visit www.autoshowny.com or www.javitscenter.com. One week in early or mid-April.

May

Bike New York: The Great Five Boro Bike Tour. The largest mass-participation cycling event in the United States attracts about 30,000 cyclists from all over the world. After a 42-mile (68km) ride through the five boroughs, finalists are greeted with a New York–style celebration of food and music. Call ⌒ **212/932-BIKE** or visit www.bikenewyork.org to register. First or second Sunday in May.

Ninth Avenue International Food Festival. Spend the day sampling Italian sausages, homemade pirogi, spicy curries, and an assortment of other ethnic dishes. Street musicians, bands, and vendors add to the atmosphere at one of the city's best street fairs, stretching along Ninth Avenue from 37th to 57th streets. Call ⌒ **212/484-1222.** One weekend in mid-May.

Fleet Week. About 10,000 Navy and Coast Guard personnel are "at liberty" in New York at the end of May. Usually from 1 to 4pm daily, you can visit the ships and aircraft carriers as they dock at the piers on the west side of Manhattan, and watch some exhibitions by the U.S. Marines. Even if you don't take in any of the events, you'll know it's Fleet Week because those 10,000 sailors invade Midtown in their white uniforms. It's simply wonderful—like *On the Town* come to life. Call ⌒ **212/245-0072,** or visit www.fleetweek.com (the best source for a full list of events) or www.uss-intrepid.com. Late May.

June

Museum Mile Festival. Fifth Avenue from 82nd to 102nd streets is closed to cars from 6 to 9pm as 20,000-plus strollers enjoy live music from Broadway tunes to string quartets, street entertainers from juggling to giant puppets, and free admission to nine Museum Mile institutions, including the Metropolitan Museum of Art and the Guggenheim. Call ⌒ **212/606-2296** or any participating institutions for details. Usually the second Tuesday in June.

Lesbian and Gay Pride Week and March. A week of cheerful happenings precedes a parade commemorating the Stonewall Riot of June 27, 1969, which for many marks the beginning of the gay liberation movement. Fifth Avenue goes wild as the LGBT community celebrates with bands, marching groups, floats, and plenty of panache. The parade starts on upper Fifth Avenue around 52nd Street and continues into the Village, where a street festival and a dance with fireworks cap the day. Call ⓒ **212/807-7433** or check www.nycpride.org. Late June.

SummerStage. A summer-long festival of outdoor performances in **Central Park,** featuring world music, pop, folk, and jazz artists ranging from Steve Earle to Craig David to the New York Grand Opera (always performing Verdi) to the Chinese Golden Dragon Acrobats. Performances are often free, but certain big-name events require tickets (usually less than $30). Call ⓒ **212/360-2777** or visit www.summerstage.org. June through August.

Shakespeare in the Park. The Delacorte Theater in **Central Park** is the setting for first-rate free performances under the stars—including at least one Shakespeare production each season—often with stars on the stage. For details, see "Park It! Shakespeare, Music & Other Free Fun" on p. 308. Call ⓒ **212/539-8750** or visit www.publictheater.org. June through August.

Restaurant Week. Lunch for only $20 at some of New York's finest restaurants. Participating places vary each year, so watch for the ads in the *New York Times,* call the NYCVB at ⓒ **212/484-1222,** or check www.restaurantweek.com for the schedule and participants, usually available by mid-May. *Reserve immediately.* One week in late June; some restaurants extend their offers to Labor Day.

July

Independence Day Harbor Festival and Fourth of July Fireworks Spectacular. Start the day amid the crowds at the Great July Fourth Festival in Lower Manhattan, and then catch Macy's fireworks over the East River (the best vantage point is from FDR Dr., which closes to traffic several hours before sunset). Call ⓒ **212/484-1222** or Macy's Visitor Center at 212/494-2922. July 4th.

August

Lincoln Center Out of Doors. This series of free music and dance performances is held outdoors on the plazas of **Lincoln Center.** Call ⓒ **212/875-5108** or 212/546-2656, or visit www.lincolncenter.org for this year's schedule (usually available in mid-July). Throughout August.

New York International Fringe Festival. Held in a variety of Lower East Side venues for a mainly hipster crowd, this arts festival presents alternative and traditional theater, musicals, dance, comedy, and all manner of performance art. Hundreds of events are held over about 10 days in August. The quality can vary, and some performances push the envelope, but you'd be surprised at how many shows are *good.* Call ⓒ **888/FRINGE-NYC** or 212/420-8777, or point your browser to www.fringenyc.org. Throughout August.

U.S. Open Tennis Championships. The Grand Slam event is held at the Arthur Ashe Stadium at the USTA National Tennis Center, the largest public tennis center in the world, at **Flushing Meadows**

Park in Queens. Tickets go on sale in May or early June. The event sells out immediately, because many tickets are held by corporate sponsors who give them to customers. (It's worth it to check the list of sponsors to determine if anyone you know has a connection for tickets.) You can usually scalp tickets (an illegal practice, of course), next to Shea Stadium. The last few matches are the most expensive, but you'll see a lot more tennis early on, when your ticket allows you to wander the outside courts and view several matches. Call ⓒ **888/OPEN-TIX** or 718/760-6200 in advance; visit www.usopen.org or www.usta.com for information. Two weeks around Labor Day.

Harlem Week. The world's largest black and Hispanic cultural festival actually spans almost the whole month to include the Black Film Festival, the Harlem Jazz and Music Festival, and the Taste of Harlem Food Festival. Expect a full slate of music, from gospel to hip-hop, and lots of other festivities. Visit www.discoverharlem.com or call ⓒ **212/484-1222** for this year's schedule of events and locations. Throughout August.

September

West Indian–American Day Parade. This Brooklyn event is New York's largest street celebration. Come for the costumes, pulsating rhythms (soca, calypso, reggae), bright colors, folklore, food (jerk chicken, oxtail soup, Caribbean soul food), and two million hip-shaking revelers. The route can change from year to year, but usually runs along Eastern Parkway from Utica Avenue to Grand Army Plaza (at the gateway to Prospect Park). Call ⓒ **212/484-1222** or 718/625-1515. Labor Day.

Broadway on Broadway. This free afternoon show features the songs and casts from virtually every Broadway show on a stage in the middle of Times Square. This event keeps getting bigger—and is usually broadcast on TV—so you can expect the big stars. Call ⓒ **212/768-1560** or visit www.timessquarebid.org and click on "Events." One Sunday in mid-September.

Feast of San Gennaro. This atmospheric Little Italy street fair, honoring the patron saint of Naples, may have seen its final days. (It was cancelled in 2001 following the terrorist attacks.) Let's hope not, because it's a blast, with great food, traditional music, carnival rides, games, and vendors along Mulberry Street north of Canal Street. And who knows? You may even spot a Godfather or two. Call **212/768-9320** or visit www.sangennaro.org to see if this year's event is on. Usually 10 days in mid-September.

New York Film Festival. Legendary hits *Pulp Fiction* and *Mean Streets* had their U.S. premieres at the Film Society of Lincoln Center's festival, a major stop on the film fest circuit. Screenings are held in Lincoln Center venues; advance tickets are advised, and a necessity for certain events (especially evening and weekend screenings). Call ⓒ **212/875-5600** for information, 212/875-5050 for tickets, or check www.filmlinc.com. Two weeks, late September to early October.

October

Feast of St. Francis. Animals from goldfish to elephants are blessed as thousands of Homo sapiens look on at the **Cathedral of St. John the Divine.** A magical experience; pets, of course, are welcome. A festive fair follows. Buy tickets in advance because they can be hard to get.

Call ✆ **212/316-7540** or 212/662-7133 for tickets, or visit www.stjohndivine.org. First Sunday in October.

Ice-Skating. Show off your skating style at the diminutive **Rockefeller Center** rink (✆ **212/332-7654**), from mid-October to mid-March or early April (you'll skate under the Christmas tree for the month of Dec), or at the larger **Wollman Rink** in Central Park, on the east side between 62nd and 63rd streets (✆ **212/439-6900;** www.wollmanskatingrink.com), which usually closes in early April.

Greenwich Village Halloween Parade. This is Halloween at its most outrageous. You may have heard Lou Reed singing about it on his classic album *New York*—he wasn't exaggerating. Drag queens and assorted other flamboyant types parade in wildly creative costumes. The parade route has changed over the years, but it generally starts after sunset at Spring Street and marches up Sixth Avenue to 23rd Street or Union Square. Call the *Village Voice* Parade hot line at ✆ **212/475-3333**, ext. 4044, point your browser to www.halloweennyc.com, or check the papers for the route so you can watch—or participate, if you have the threads and the imagination. October 31.

November

New York City Marathon. Some 30,000 runners from around the world participate in the largest U.S. marathon, and more than a million fans cheer them on as they run through all five New York City boroughs and finish in Central Park. Call ✆ **212/423-2249** or 212/860-4455, or surf to www.nyrrc.org for applications. November 3 in 2002, November 2 in 2003.

Radio City Music Hall Christmas Spectacular. A gaudy extravaganza, but a lot of fun nonetheless. Starring the Rockettes and a cast that includes live camels. After undergoing an extensive restoration for most of 1999, Radio City itself is a sight to see. For information, call ✆ **212/247-4777** or visit www.radiocity.com; buy tickets at the box office or Ticketmaster's **Radio City Hot Line** (✆ **212/307-1000**), or visit www.ticketmaster.com. Throughout November and December.

Macy's Thanksgiving Day Parade. The procession from Central Park West and 77th Street down Broadway to Herald Square continues to be a national tradition. Huge hot-air balloons of Rocky and Bullwinkle, Snoopy, the Pink Panther, Bart Simpson, and other cartoon favorites are the best part of the fun. The night before, you can see the big blow-up on Central Park West at 79th Street; call in advance to find out whether it will be open to the public. Call ✆ **212/484-1222** or Macy's Visitor Center at 212/494-2922. Thanksgiving Day.

Big Apple Circus. New York City's homegrown, not-for-profit circus is a favorite with children and everyone who's young at heart. Big Apple is committed to maintaining the classical circus tradition with sensitivity and only features animals that have a traditional working relationship with humans. A tent is pitched in **Damrosch Park** at **Lincoln Center.** Call ✆ **212/268-2500** or visit www.bigapplecircus.org. November through January.

December

Lighting of the Rockefeller Center Christmas Tree. Ice-skating, singing, entertainment, and a crowd accompany the annual lighting ceremony. The tree stays lit around the clock until after the new year. Call ✆ **212/332-6868** or visit www.rockefellercenter.com for this year's date. Early December.

Holiday Trimmings. Stroll down Fifth Avenue and you'll see doormen dressed as wooden soldiers at **FAO Schwarz,** a 27-foot snowflake over the intersection outside **Tiffany's,** the **Cartier** building beribboned in red, wreaths warming the necks of the **New York Public Library**'s lions, and fanciful figures in the windows of **Saks Fifth Avenue** and **Lord & Taylor.** Madison Avenue between 55th and 60th streets is a good bet; **Sony Plaza** usually boasts some fabulous windows, as does **Barneys New York.** Throughout December.

Christmas Traditions. In addition to the **Radio City Music Hall Christmas Spectacular,** traditional holiday events include *A Christmas Carol* at **The Theater at Madison Square Garden** (C 212/465-6741 or www.thegarden.com; C 212/307-7171 or www.ticketmaster.com), usually featuring a big name to draw in the crowds. Tchaikovsky's holiday favorite, *The Nutcracker* (C 212/870-5570; www.nycballet.com) is performed by the New York City Ballet at **Lincoln Center.** At **Avery Fisher Hall** is the National Chorale's sing-along performances of Handel's *Messiah* (C 212/875-5030; www.lincolncenter.org) for a week before Christmas. Don't worry if the only words you know are "Alleluia, Alleluia!"—a lyrics sheet is given to ticket holders.

Lighting of the Hanukkah Menorah. Everything is done on a grand scale in New York, so it's no surprise that the world's largest menorah (32 ft./9.5m high) is at Manhattan's **Grand Army Plaza,** Fifth Avenue and 59th Street. Hanukkah celebrations begin at sunset on the first night of the holiday, with the lighting of the first of the giant electric candles. Early to mid-December.

New Year's Eve. The biggest party of them all happens in **Times Square,** where thousands of revelers count down the year's final seconds until the ball drops at midnight at 1 Times Sq. I don't understand it, because it's always a crowded, cold, boozy madhouse, but hey! Call C **212/768-1560** or 212/484-1222, or visit www.timessquarebid.org. December 31.

Other year-end events include **fireworks** followed by the New York Road Runner's Club's annual **5K Midnight Run** in **Central Park;** call C **212/860-4455** or visit www.nyrrc.org. Head to Brooklyn for the city's largest New Year's Eve **fireworks** celebration at Prospect Park; call **718/965-8999** or visit www.prospectpark.org.

The Cathedral of St. John the Divine is known for its annual **New Year's Eve Concert for Peace.** Past performers have included the Manhattan School of Music Chamber Sinfonia, Tony award–winning composer Jason Robert Brown (*Parade*), soprano Lauren Flanigan, and the Forces of Nature Dance Company. Call C **212/316-7540** for information or 212/662-2133 for tickets, or go online to www.stjohndivine.org.

5 Health & Insurance

WHAT TO DO IF YOU GET SICK AWAY FROM HOME

If you suffer from a chronic illness, consult your doctor before you leave. For conditions like epilepsy, diabetes, or heart problems, wear a **Medic Alert Identification Tag** (C **800/825-3785;** www.medicalert.org), which will alert doctors to your condition and give them access to your records

HEALTH & INSURANCE

through Medic Alert's 24-hour hot line.

Pack **prescription medications** in your carry-on luggage and in their original containers. Also bring along copies of your prescriptions in case you lose your pills or run out. If you do get sick, ask the concierge at your hotel to recommend a local doctor. This will probably yield a better recommendation than a toll-free number would. There are also several walk-in medical centers, like **DOCS at New York Healthcare,** 55 E. 34th St., between Park and Madison avenues (✆ **212/252-6001**), for nonemergency illnesses. The clinic, affiliated with Beth Israel Medical Center, is open Monday through Thursday from 8am to 8pm, Friday from 8am to 7pm, Saturday from 9am to 3pm, and Sunday from 9am to 2pm. The **NYU Downtown Hospital** also offers physician referrals at ✆ **888/698-3362.**

If you have dental problems, a nationwide referral service known as **1-800-DENTIST** (✆ **800/336-8478**) will provide the name of a nearby dentist or clinic.

If you can't find a doctor right away, try the emergency room at a local hospital. Many emergency rooms have walk-in clinics for emergency cases that are not life threatening. You may not get immediate attention, but you won't pay the high price of an emergency-room visit (usually a minimum of $300 just for signing your name, plus the price of whatever treatment you receive). For a list of local hospitals, see "Fast Facts: New York City," at the end of chapter 4.

Most health insurance policies cover you if you get sick away from home—but check, particularly if an HMO insures you.

TRAVEL INSURANCE

Check your existing insurance policies before you buy travel insurance to cover trip cancellation, lost luggage, medical expenses, or car rentals. You're likely to have partial or complete coverage. But if you need some, ask your travel agent about a package. The cost of travel insurance varies, depending on the cost and length of your trip, your age and health, and the type of trip you're taking. For information, contact one of these popular insurers:

- **Access America** (✆ **800/284-8300;** www.accessamerica.com/)
- **Travel Guard International** (✆ **800/826-1300;** www.travelguard.com)
- **Travel Insured International** (✆ **800/243-3174;** www.travelinsured.com)
- **Travelex Insurance Services** (✆ **800/228-9792;** www.travelex-insurance.com)

There are three major types of **trip-cancellation insurance** (TCI)—one, in the event that you prepay a tour or package that gets cancelled and you can't get your money back; a second when you or someone in your family gets sick or dies and you can't travel (but you may not be covered for a pre-existing condition); and a third, when bad weather makes travel impossible. Some insurers provide coverage for events like jury duty; natural disasters close to home, like floods or fire; even the loss of a job. A few have added provisions for cancellations due to terrorist activities. Always check the fine print, and don't buy trip-cancellation insurance from the tour operator who may be responsible for the cancellation; buy it only from a reputable travel insurance agency. Don't overbuy. You won't be reimbursed for more than the cost of your trip. Your homeowner's or renter's insurance may cover stolen luggage. The airlines are responsible for losses up to $2,500 on domestic flights if they lose your luggage; if you plan to carry anything valuable, keep it in your carry-on bag.

6 Tips for Travelers with Special Needs

FOR FAMILIES
As a result of the decrease in crime and the increase in family-oriented entertainment (exemplified by the "new" Times Square), city sidewalks are full of pint-sized visitors. There are myriad ways to keep them entertained, from kid-oriented museums and theater to theme park–style shopping and restaurants.

For the best places to stay and eat, see "Affordable Family-Friendly Hotels," in chapter 5, and "Affordable Family-Friendly Restaurants," in chapter 6. For sightseeing, check out "Especially for Kids," in chapter 7. For more extensive recommendations, you might want a copy of *Frommer's New York City with Kids,* dedicated to family visits to the Big Apple.

Good bets for the most timely information include the "Weekend" section of Friday's *New York Times,* which has a section dedicated to the best kid-friendly activities; the weekly *New York* magazine, which has a calendar of children's events in its "Cue" section; and *Time Out New York,* which also has a great weekly kids section with a bit of an alternative bent. The *Big Apple Parents' Paper* is usually available for free at children's stores and other locations in Manhattan; you can also find good information from the folks behind the paper at www.parentsknow.com.

The Busy Person's Guide to Travel with Children (http://wz.com/travel/TravelingWithChildren.html) offers a "45-second newsletter" where experts weigh in on the best websites and resources for tips for traveling with children.

The first place to look for **babysitting** is in your hotel (ask about it when you reserve). Many hotels have services or will provide you with lists of sitters. Or you can call The Baby Sitters' Guild (© 212/682-0227; www.babysittersguild.com). The sitters are licensed, insured, and bonded, and can even take your child on outings.

FOR TRAVELERS WITH DISABILITIES
New York is more accessible to disabled travelers than ever. The city's bus system is wheelchair-friendly, and most of the major attractions are easily accessible. Even so, **always call first** to be sure that the places you want to go to are fully accessible.

Most hotels are ADA compliant, with suitable rooms for wheelchair-bound travelers as well as those with other disabilities. But before you book, **ask lots of questions based on your needs.** Many budget hotels are housed in older buildings that have had to be modified to meet requirements; still, elevators and bathrooms can be on the small side. If you have mobility issues, you'll probably do best to book into a newer hotel. You'll find links to New York's accessible accommodations, evaluated by people skilled to make such judgments, at **www.access-able.com** (click on "World Cities"). Some Broadway theaters and other venues provide total wheelchair accessibility; others provide partial accessibility. Many also offer lower-priced tickets for disabled theatergoers, though you'll need to check individual policies and reserve in advance.

GENERAL TRAVEL INFORMATION MossRehab ResourceNet (© 215/456-9900; www.mossresourcenet.org) is a great source for information, tips, and resources relating to accessible travel. You'll find links to a number of travel agents who specialize in planning trips for travelers with disabilities here and through **Access-Able Travel Source** (© 303/232-2979; www.access-able.com), another excellent source. You'll also find relay and voice numbers for hotels, airlines, and car-rental companies on Access-Able's site, as well as links to accessible accommodations, attractions, transportation, tours, local medical resources and equipment repair, and much more.

The **Society for Accessible Travel and Hospitality** (✆ 212/447-7284; www.sath.org) offers a wealth of resources for all types of disabilities and recommendations on destinations, access guides, travel agents, tour operators, vehicle rentals, and companion services. Annual membership costs $45 for adults, $30 for seniors and students.

CITY-SPECIFIC INFORMATION Hospital Audiences, Inc. (✆ 212/575-7676; www.hospitalaudiences. org), arranges attendance and provides details about accessibility at cultural institutions as well as cultural events adapted for people with disabilities. Services include "Describe!," which allows visually impaired theatergoers to enjoy theater events; and the **HAI Hot Line** (✆ 212/575-7676), which offers accessibility information for hotels, restaurants, attractions, and much more. This organization also publishes *Access for All,* a guidebook on accessibility, available by calling ✆ 212/575-7663 or by sending a $5 check to 548 Broadway, 3rd Floor, New York, NY 10012-3950.

Another good source is **Big Apple Greeter** (✆ 212/669-8159; www. bigapplegreeter.org). All of its employees are well versed in accessibility issues. They can provide a list of agencies that serve the city's disabled community, and sometimes have discounts to theater and music performances. Big Apple Greeter even offers one-to-one tours that pair volunteers with visitors with disabilities; they can introduce you to the public transportation system if you like. Reserve at least 1 week ahead.

GETTING AROUND Gray Line Air Shuttle (✆ 800/451-0455 or 212/315-3006; www.graylinenewyork.com) operates minibuses with lifts from JFK, LaGuardia, and Newark airports to Midtown hotels by reservation; arrange pickup 3 or 4 days in advance. **Olympia Trails** (✆ 877/894-9155 or 212/964-6233; www.olympiabus.com) provides service from Newark International Airport, with half-price fares for travelers with disabilities. (Prepurchase your tickets to guarantee the discount fare, as drivers can't sell discounted tickets.) Not all buses are appropriately equipped, so call ahead for the daily schedule of accessible buses (press "0" [zero] to reach a real person).

A licensed ambulette company, **Upward Mobility Limousine Service** (✆ 718/645-7774; www.brainlink. com/~phil) is a wheelchair-accessible car service that can provide door-to-door airport shuttle service as well as taxi service anywhere in the metropolitan area. Arrange airport pickups with as much advance notice as possible.

Taxis are required to carry people who have folding wheelchairs and guide or therapy dogs. However, don't be surprised if they don't run each other down trying to get to you; even though you shouldn't have to, you may have to wait for a friendly (or fare-desperate) driver to come along.

Public buses are an inexpensive, easy way to get around New York. All buses' back doors are supposed to be equipped with wheelchair lifts (though the city has had complaints that not all are in working order). Buses also "kneel," lowering their front steps for people who have difficulty boarding. Passengers with disabilities pay half-price fares (75¢). The **subway** isn't fully wheelchair accessible, but a list of about 30 accessible stations and a guide to wheelchair-accessible subway itineraries is on the MTA website. Call ✆ **718/596-8585** for transit info, or go to www.mta.nyc.ny.us/nyct and click on "Accessibility."

You're better off not trying to rent your own car to get around the city. But if you consider it the best mode of transportation for you, **Wheelchair Getaways** (© **800/379-3750** or 800/344-5005; www.wheelchair-getaways.com) rents specialized vans with wheelchair lifts and features for travelers with disabilities throughout the New York metropolitan area.

FOR SENIOR TRAVELERS

Mention your senior status when you make your travel reservations, because all major airlines and many hotels offer discounts. Major airlines also offer coupons for domestic travel for seniors over age 60. Typically, a book of four coupons costs less than $700, which means you can fly anywhere in the continental United States for under $350 round-trip.

Also mention the fact that you're a senior when you first make your travel reservations. Both **Amtrak** (© **800/USA-RAIL;** www.amtrak.com) and **Greyhound** (© **800/229-2424;** www.greyhound.com) offer discounts to persons over 62, and most of the major domestic airlines offer discount programs for senior travelers.

Many hotels offer senior discounts; **Choice Hotels** (which include Comfort Inns, some of my favorite Midtown hotels; see chapter 5), for example, gives 30% off their published rates to anyone over 50, provided you book your room through their nationwide toll-free reservations number (that is, not directly with the hotels or through a travel agent). For a complete list of Choice Hotels, visit **www.hotelchoice.com**.

New York subway and bus fares are half price (75¢) for people 65 or older. Many museums and sights (and some theaters and performance halls) offer discounted entrance and tickets to seniors; so do ask for it. Always bring an ID card, especially if you've kept your youthful glow.

Members of **AARP** (© **800/424-3410** or 202/434-2277; www.aarp.org), get discounts on hotels, airfares, and car rentals, as well as other wide-ranging benefits. Anyone over 50 can join. The **Alliance for Retired Americans** (© **301/578-8422;** www.retiredamericans.org) also offers members discounts on hotel and auto rentals. *Note:* Members of the former National Council of Senior Citizens receive membership in the Alliance.

FOR GAY & LESBIAN TRAVELERS

Gay and lesbian culture is as much a part of New York's basic identity as yellow cabs, high-rises, and Broadway theater. Indeed, in a city with one of the world's largest, loudest, and most powerful gay and lesbian populations, homosexuality is hardly seen as "alternative"—it's squarely in the mainstream. So city hotels tend to be neutral on the issue, and gay couples shouldn't have a problem; for gay-friendly accommodations, see "Best for Gay & Lesbian Travelers" under "Best Low-Cost Hotel Bets," in chapter 1. You'll want to see "The Gay & Lesbian Scene," in chapter 9, for nightlife suggestions.

The **International Gay & Lesbian Travel Association** (IGLTA; © **800/448-8550** or 954/776-2626; www.iglta.org) links travelers up with gay-friendly hoteliers as well as tour operators and airline representatives. **Now, Voyager** (© **800/255-6951;** www.nowvoyager.com), a San Francisco–based gay-owned travel service, is an excellent source for those who want assistance with trip planning. All over Manhattan, but especially in neighborhoods like the **West Village** (particularly Christopher St., famous as the main drag, so to speak, of New

York gay male life) and **Chelsea** (Eighth Ave. from 16th to 23rd sts. and West 17th to 19th sts. from Fifth to Eighth aves.), shops, services, and restaurants have a lesbian and gay flavor. **The Oscar Wilde Bookshop,** 15 Christopher St. (✆ **212/255-8097;** www.oscarwildebooks.com), is the city's best gay and lesbian bookstore, and a good source for information on the city's gay community.

The **Lesbian, Gay, Bisexual & Transgender Community Center** is at 208 W. 13th St., between Seventh and Eighth avenues (✆ **212/620-7310;** www.gaycenter.org). The center is the meeting place for more than 400 organizations. You can check the online events calendar, which lists hundreds of happenings—lectures, dances, concerts, readings, films—or call. Their site offers links to gay-friendly hotels and guesthouses, plus tons of other information; the staff is also friendly and helpful.

Other good sources for lesbian and gay events are *HX* (www.hx.com), *New York Blade* (www.nyblade.com), *Next* (www.nextnyc.com), *Gay City News* (www.lgny.com); and the *Village Voice* (www.villagevoice.com)—all free weeklies you can pick up in bars, clubs, stores, and sidewalk boxes throughout town.

In addition, there are lesbian and gay musical events, such as performances by the **New York City Gay Men's Chorus** (✆ **212/242-1777;** www.nycgmc.org); health programs sponsored by the **Gay Men's Health Crisis** (GMHC; ✆ **800/AIDS-NYC** or 212/807-6655; www.gmhc.org); the **Gay and Lesbian Switchboard of NY Project** (✆ **212/989-0999;** www.glnh.org), which offers peer counseling and information on upcoming events; and many other organizations.

FOR STUDENTS
Many museums, sights, and theaters offer reduced admission to students, so don't forget to bring your student ID and valid proof of age.

Your best resource is the **Council on International Educational Exchange,** or **CIEE** (www.ciee.org). They can set you up with an International Student ID card, and their travel branch, **Council Travel Service** (✆ **800/226-8624;** www.counciltravel.com), the world's biggest student travel agency, can get you discounts on plane tickets and the like. In New York City, they have offices at 254 Greene St., in Greenwich Village (✆ **212/254-2525**); and in Midtown at 205 E. 42nd St. (✆ **212/822-2700**).

STA Travel (✆ **800/781-4040;** www.statravel.com) is another travel agency catering to young travelers, although their bargain-basement prices are available to people of all ages. STA has offices in the Village at 10 Downing St. (Sixth Ave. at Bleecker St.; ✆ **212/627-3111**); 30 Third Ave. (✆ **212/473-6100**); and locations at Columbia University, in Alfred Learner Hall, 2871 Broadway (✆ **212/854-0150**), and 2871 Broadway (✆ **212/865-2700**).

Hostelling International–American Youth Hostels (✆ **202/783-6161;** www.hiayh.org) has its largest hostel in New York City at 891 Amsterdam Ave., at 103rd Street (✆ **212/932-2300;** www.hinewyork.org); see chapter 5 for a review. Reserve well ahead. You'll also find other, privately run hostels with cheap dorm beds in chapter 5. For additional hostelling choices in the city (and North America), order *The Hostel Handbook* with a check or money order for $5 (payable to Jim Williams) to: The Hostel Handbook, Dept: HHB, 722 St. Nicholas Ave., New York, NY 10031. You can also find ordering information and a selection of listings at **www.hostelhandbook.com**. More info and recommendations can also be found online at **Hostels.com**.

7 Getting There

BY PLANE

Three major airports serve New York City: **John F. Kennedy International Airport** (© 718/244-4444) in Queens, about 15 miles/24km (1 hr.) from Midtown; **LaGuardia Airport** (© 718/533-3400), also in Queens, about 8 miles/13km (30 min.) from Midtown; and **Newark International Airport** (© 973/961-6000) in New Jersey, about 16 miles/26km (45 min.) from Midtown. Information about all three airports is available online at **www.panynj.gov**; click on the "Airports" tab on the left.

Even though LaGuardia is the closest airport to Manhattan, it earned the dubious distinction of being the worst in the nation for flight delays in 2000, according to the Transportation Safety Administration (TSA). (Flight delays rose 20% overall in 2000, so the picture isn't pretty anywhere.) What's more, LaGuardia has a hideous reputation for chaos, in both ticket-desk lines and baggage claim. You may want to arrive and depart at JFK or Newark instead.

Almost every major domestic carrier serves a New York–area airport; most serve two or all three. Among them are **American** (© 800/433-7300; www.aa.com), **America West** (© 800/235-9292; www.americawest.com), **Continental** (© 800/525-0280; www.continental.com), **Delta** (© 800/221-1212; www.delta.com), **Northwest** (© 800/225-2525; www.nwa.com), **United** (© 800/241-6522; www.united.com), and **US Airways** (© 800/428-4322; www.usairways.com).

In recent years there has been rapid growth in the number of no-frills airlines serving New York. You might check out Atlanta-based **AirTran** (© 800/247-8726; www.airtran.com); Chicago-based **ATA** (© 800/435-9282; www.ata.com); Denver-based **Frontier** (© 800/432-1359; www.flyfrontier.com); Raleigh/Durham-based **Midway** (© 800/446-4392; www.midwayair.com); Milwaukee- and Omaha-based **Midwest Express** (© 800/452-2022; www.midwestexpress.com); Las Vegas–based **National** (© 888/757-5387; www.nationalairlines.com); Detroit-based **Spirit** (© 800/772-7117; www.spiritair.com); and Kansas City–based **Vanguard** (© 800/VANGUARD; www.flyvanguard.com). The JFK-based cheap-chic airline **jetBlue** ✶ (© 800/JETBLUE; www.jetblue.com) has taken New York by storm with its low fares and high-class service. The nation's leading discount airline, **Southwest** (© 800/435-9792; www.iflyswa.com), flies into MacArthur (Islip) Airport on Long Island, 50 miles (81km) east of Manhattan.

Most major international carriers serve New York; see "Getting to the United States," in chapter 3, for details.

For advice on getting the best airfare, see "65 Money-Saving Tips" at the beginning of this chapter.

Tips Choosing Your NYC-Area Airport

It's more convenient to fly into Newark than JFK if your destination is Manhattan, and fares to Newark are often cheaper than those to the other airports. Newark is particularly convenient if your hotel is in Midtown West or downtown. Taxi fare into Manhattan is roughly equivalent to the fare from JFK—and now, with the new AirTrain in place (see "Transportation to & from the New York–Area Airports," below), Newark has the quickest and easiest-to-use public transportation link with Manhattan.

Tips: New Air Travel Security Measures

In the wake of the terrorist attacks of September 11, 2001, the airline industry began implementing new security measures in airports. Expect a lengthy check-in process and extensive delays, both at New York's area airports and at your home airport. Although regulations vary from airline to airline, you can expedite the process by taking these steps:

- **Arrive early.** Arrive at the airport *at least* 2 hours before your departure time, because you'll have to negotiate extensive lines at the ticket counter and the security gate. E-tickets seldom speed up the check-in process these days, since interacting with a check-in agent is essential to the new security processes.
- **Try not to drive your car to the airport.** Parking and curbside access to the terminal may be limited. Call ahead and check.
- **Curbside check-in may not be available.** While a few offer it on a limited basis, you can't count on handing off your bag to a skycap anymore. For the latest on this, check with the individual airlines.
- **Carry plenty of documentation.** A government-issued photo ID (federal, state, or local) is now required. With an E-ticket, you may be required to have with you printed confirmation of purchase, and even the credit card with which you bought your ticket. This varies from airline to airline, so call ahead to make sure you have the proper documentation. Be sure that your ID is **up-to-date:** An expired driver's license or passport may keep you from boarding. Be prepared to show it multiple times: at the ticket counter, the security gate, and at boarding.
- **Know what you can carry on—and what you can't.** Travelers in the United States are limited to one carry-on bag, plus one personal bag (such as a purse or a briefcase). The Transportation Safety Administration (TSA) has also issued a list of newly restricted carry-on items that includes knives (yep, including the Swiss Army variety); for the latest restrictions, visit **www.tsa.gov**.
- **Prepare to be searched.** Expect spot-checks, both at the security and boarding gates. Electronic items, such as laptops and cell phones, should be readied for additional screening. Limit the metal items you wear on your person.
- **Remember: No ticket, no gate access.** Only ticketed passengers will be allowed beyond the screener checkpoints, except for those travelers with specific medical or parental needs.

TRANSPORTATION TO & FROM THE NEW YORK–AREA AIRPORTS

For transportation information for all three airports (JFK, LaGuardia, and Newark), call **Air-Ride** (© **800/247-7433**), which offers recorded details on bus and shuttle companies and car services 24 hours a day; live operators staff the line Monday through Friday from 8am to 6pm EST. Similar information is online at **www.panynj.gov/airports**.

The Port Authority also runs staffed Ground Transportation Information counters on the baggage claim level in

> ## Tips Money-Saving Package Deals
>
> Before you start your search for the lowest airfare, you may want to consider booking your flight as part of a travel package that allows you to buy airfare and accommodations (and sometimes extras like sightseeing tours and theater tickets) at a pay-one-price discount.
>
> Here are a few tips to help you tell one package from another, and figure out which one is right for you:
>
> - **Read this guide.** Research New York City. Compare the rack rates we've published to the discounted rates offered by the packagers. If you're being offered a stay in a hotel that we haven't recommended, do more research to learn about it, especially if it isn't a reliable franchise like Holiday Inn or Hyatt. It's not a deal if you end up at a dump.
> - **Read the fine print.** Make sure you know *exactly* what's included in the package. Are hotel taxes and airport transfers included, or are they extra? Conversely, don't pay for a rental car you don't need—and you won't need one in New York. Before you commit, make sure you know how much flexibility you have, say, if your kid gets sick or your boss suddenly asks you to adjust your vacation schedule.
> - **Use your best judgment.** If a deal appears to be too good to be true, it probably is. Go with a reputable firm with a proven track record. This is where your travel agent can come in handy; he or she should be knowledgeable about different packagers.
>
> So how do you find a package deal?
>
> The best place to start is the travel section of your Sunday newspaper. Check the ads in the back of travel magazines like *Travel Holiday*, *National Geographic Traveler*, and *Arthur Frommer's Budget Travel*.
>
> A terrific source for Big Apple packages is **New York City Vacation Packages** (© 888/692-8701 or 570/714-4692; www.nycvp.com),

each terminal at each airport, where you can get information and book transport. Most transportation companies have courtesy phones near the baggage-claim area.

Generally, travel time between the airports and midtown Manhattan by taxi or car is 45 to 60 minutes for JFK, 20 to 35 minutes for LaGuardia, and 35 to 50 minutes for Newark. Always allow extra time, especially during rush hour, peak holiday travel times, and if you're taking a bus.

SUBWAYS & PUBLIC BUSES Taking the MTA to and from the airport can be a hassle, but it's the cheapest way to go—just $1.50 each way. (Note that a fare hike was a possibility at press time.) However, keep in mind that the subways and buses that serve the airports involve multiple transfers and staircases; count on more hauling to your hotel (or a taxi fare) once you arrive in Manhattan. This won't work for travelers with lots of luggage, because you won't have anywhere to store it on the bus or subway. You might not want to take the bus or the subway if you're traveling very early or very late, as you may have to go through some dicey neighborhoods.

which can sell you a complete package including hotel, theater tickets, and more—usually for significantly less than you can do on your own. What's more, NYCVP can often build a package that includes otherwise sold-out tickets to Broadway shows like *The Lion King* and sporting events; they'll even book airport transportation and dining reservations for you if you wish.

One of the biggest packagers in the Northeast, **Liberty Travel** (© 888/271-1584; www.libertytravel.com) offers 2- to 7-night New York packages that usually include freebies like a Circle Line cruise or tickets to the Empire State Building, plus lots of good hotels at every price point.

The major airlines offering good-value packages to New York include **Continental Airlines Vacations** (© 800/634-5555; www.coolvacations.com), **Delta Vacations** (© 800/872-7786; www.deltavacations.com), **US Airways Vacations** (© 800/455-0123; www.usairwaysvacations.com), **United Vacations** (© 800/328-6877; www.unitedvacations.com), **American Airlines Vacations** (© 800/321-2121; www.aavacations.com), and **Northwest WorldVacations** (© 800/800-1504; www.nwa.com/vacpkg). You may want to choose the airline that has frequent service to your hometown or the one on which you accumulate frequent-flier miles.

If you're a late planner, check out the discounted packages offered by **Site59.com.** Their last-minute getaways can save you up to 60% on your entire package, and can be booked anytime between 3 hours and 14 days in advance. Various combinations are available, including flight and hotel, land only (if you've already booked your flight or will be arriving by car), and others that include dining, entertainment, and more.

If you'd prefer to take the train rather than fly, check with **Amtrak Vacations** (© 800/321-8684; www.amtrak.com/services/amtrak-vacations.html) for all-inclusive ride-and-stay packages.

For more subway and bus information, see "Getting Around" in chapter 4.

From/to JFK You can take the **A train** to JFK, which connects to one of two free **shuttle buses** that serve all the JFK terminals. Plan on 2 hours in each direction, maybe more if you're traveling at rush hour: The subway ride from Midtown takes about 75 minutes, and you'll need another 20 to 30 minutes for the shuttle ride to your terminal; also be sure to factor in waiting time at both ends.

Upon exiting the terminal, pick up the shuttle bus (marked LONG TERM PARKING LOT); it takes you to the **Howard Beach station,** where you get the A train to Manhattan. Service is every 10 to 15 minutes during rush hour and every 20 minutes at midday, and the subway fare is $1.50. If you're traveling to JFK from Manhattan, take the A train that says FAR ROCKAWAY or ROCKAWAY PARK—*not* LEFFERTS BOULEVARD. Get off at the Howard Beach/JFK Airport station and connect to the shuttle bus, A or B, which goes to your terminal (they're clearly marked). The subway can actually be more reliable than taking a car or taxi at the height of rush hour.

Newark's New AirTrain: From Jersey to Manhattan in Minutes

In 2001, there was a new way to get to the airport: the **AirTrain Newark,** which now connects Newark International Airport with Manhattan via a speedy monorail/rail link.

Even though you have to make a connection, the system is fast, pleasant, and easy to use. Each arrivals terminal at Newark International Airport has a boarding station, so follow the signs once you collect your bags. All AirTrains head to **Newark International Airport Station,** where you transfer to a **NJ Transit** train. NJ Transit will deliver you to New York Penn Station, where you can pick up a cab to your hotel.

The whole process can have you in Manhattan in 20 minutes if you catch a quick connection. NJ Transit trains run 2 to 3 times an hour during peak travel times (once an hour during early and late hours); you can check the schedules on monitors before you leave the terminal, and again at the train station. Tickets can be purchased from vending machines at both the air terminal and the train station (no ticket is required to board the AirTrain). The one-way fare is $11.15 (children under 5 ride free). Once you arrive at Penn Station, a taxi can take you directly to your hotel.

The AirTrain is an excellent alternative to the taxi system, and so far, it's getting good reviews. Even if you have to wait 15 minutes or so to make a connection, you're likely to find the transfer from the airport to Manhattan is actually quicker than taking a cab, especially during rush hours, when it's easy to get stuck in bumper-to-bumper traffic.

On your return trip, the AirTrain is far more predictable than subjecting yourself to the whims of traffic. What's more, you can check your flight's status at the Newark International Airport Station—and, if you're flying on **Continental,** you can get your boarding pass, which allows you to skip the long lines at the terminal (although those with bags to check must still stand in line at the terminal and follow all security procedures).

Note that travelers heading to points beyond the city can also pick up Amtrak and other NJ Transit trains at Newark International Airport Station to their final destinations.

A word of warning: If you have mobility issues, mountains of luggage, or a bevy of small children to keep track of, you'll find it easier to rely on a taxi, car service, or shuttle that can offer you door-to-door transfers.

For more information on AirTrain Newark, call Ⓒ **888/EWR-INFO** or go online to **www.airtrainnewark.com**. For connection details, click on the links on the AirTrain website or contact **NJ Transit** (Ⓒ **800/626-RIDE;** www.njtransit.com) or **Amtrak** (Ⓒ **800/USA-RAIL;** www.amtrak.com).

From/to LaGuardia The **M60 bus** serves all LaGuardia terminals. When leaving LaGuardia, follow the GROUND TRANSPORTATION signs and look for the **M60** stop sign at the curb. The bus will take you to Broadway and 116th Street on Manhattan's west side, where you can transfer to a downtown bus or the 1 or 9 subway; you can also pick up the N subway into Manhattan by disembarking at the Astoria Boulevard station in Queens. The bus runs daily between 4am and 1am, leaving at half-hour intervals and taking 40 to 50 minutes. Be sure to allow at least 1¼ hours, however; you never know about traffic. *Money-saving tip:* Use a MetroCard to pay your fare and you'll save the extra $1.50 it usually costs for the transfer. For the complete schedule and other pickup and drop-off points, visit **www.mta.nyc.ny.us/nyct**.

PRIVATE BUSES & SHUTTLES
Buses and shuttle services are more expensive than using the MTA for airport transfers, but they're less expensive than taxis if there's only one or two of you (though they're usually more time-consuming).

Gray Line Air Shuttle and **Super Shuttle** serve all three airports; **New York Airport Service** serves JFK and LaGuardia; **Olympia Trails** serves Newark. These services are my favorite option for getting to and from Newark during peak travel times because the drivers usually take lesser-known surface streets that make the ride much quicker than if you go with a taxi or car, which will virtually always stick to the traffic-clogged main route.

Gray Line Express Shuttle USA (© **800/451-0455** or 212/315-3006; www.graylinenewyork.com) vans depart JFK, LaGuardia, and Newark every 20 to 30 minutes between 7am and 11:30pm. They will drop you off at most hotels between 21st and 103rd streets in Manhattan. No reservation is required; go to the ground-transportation desk or dial **24** on the Gray Line courtesy phone in the baggage-claim area. Service from mid-Manhattan to all three airports operates daily from 5am to 9pm; call a day in advance to arrange a hotel pickup.

The regular one-way fare to and from JFK is $19, to and from LaGuardia is $16, and to and from Newark is $19, but you can save a few bucks by pre-paying your round-trip at the airport ($28 for JFK and Newark, $26 for LaGuardia).

The blue vans of **Super Shuttle** (© **800/BLUE-VAN** or 212/258-3826; www.supershuttle.com) serve all three area airports, providing door-to-door service to Manhattan and points on Long Island every 15 to 30 minutes around the clock. As with Gray Line, you don't need to reserve your airport-to-Manhattan ride; go to the ground-transportation desk or use the courtesy phone in the baggage-claim area and ask for Super Shuttle. Hotel pickups for your return trip require 24 to 48 hours' advance booking; you can make your reservations online. Fares run $13 to $22 per person, depending on the airport, with discounts available for additional persons in the same party.

New York Airport Service (© **718/875-8200;** www.nyairportservice.com) buses travel from JFK and LaGuardia to the Port Authority Bus Terminal (42nd St. and Eighth Ave.), Grand Central Terminal (Park Ave. between 41st and 42nd sts.), and to select Midtown hotels between 27th and 59th streets, plus the Jamaica LIRR station in Queens, where you can pick up a train for Long Island. Follow the GROUND TRANSPORTATION signs to the curbside pickup or look for the uniformed agent. Buses depart the airport every 20 to 70 minutes (depending on your departure point and destination) between 6am and midnight. Buses to JFK and LaGuardia depart the Port Authority and Grand Central Terminal on the Park Avenue side every 15 to 30 minutes, depending on the time of day and the day of the week. To request direct shuttle service from your hotel, call at

Tips: Flying into Islip on Southwest

Southwest Airlines, the nation's leading discount carrier, flies into the New York area via Long Island MacArthur Airport, 50 miles (81km) east of Manhattan. If you're on one of these flights, your cheapest option is to pick up the shuttle that **Colonial Transportation** (© 631/589-3500; www.colonialtransportation.com) offers, which traverses the 3 miles (5km) from the airport to the Ronkonkoma Long Island Rail Road Station, and take the LIRR train to Manhattan. The shuttle fare is $5 per person, $1 for each additional family member accompanying a full-fare customer. From Ronkonkoma, it's about a 1½-hour train ride to Manhattan's Penn Station; the one-way fare is $9.50 at peak hours, $6.50 off-peak (half fare for seniors 65 or older and kids 5–11). You can also catch the Suffolk County Transit bus S-57 between the airport and the station Monday through Saturday for $1.50. Trains usually leave Ronkonkoma once or twice every hour, depending on the day and time. For more information, call © 718/217-LIRR or go online to www.mta.nyc.ny.us/lirr.

For more money but less hassle, you can catch the **Hampton Jitney** coach (© 631/383-4600; www.hamptonjitney.com) to drop-off points on Midtown's east side. The cost is $25 per person, plus taxi fare from the terminal to the Hampton Jitney stop. They can explain the details and arrange for taxi transport (usually through Colonial Transportation, above).

Colonial Transportation (© 631/589-3500; www.colonialtransportation.com), **Classic Transportation** (© 631/567-5100; www.classictrans.com), and **Legends** (© 888/LEGENDS or 718/788-1234; www.legendslimo.com) will pick you up at Islip Airport and deliver you to Manhattan via car, but expect to pay $110 to $125 plus tolls and tip. Still, this may not be a bad deal if there are four of you and you have a lot of luggage. Be sure to arrange for it 24 hours in advance.

For additional options and the latest information, call **631/467-3210** or visit **www.macarthurairport.com**.

---

least 24 hours in advance. One-way fare for JFK is $13, $23 round-trip; to and from LaGuardia, it's $10 one way, $17 round-trip.

Olympia Airport Express (© 877/894-9155 or 212/964-6233; www.olympiabus.com) provides service every 5 to 30 minutes (depending on the time of day) from Newark International Airport to Penn Station (the pickup point is the northwest corner of 34th St. and Eighth Ave. and the drop-off point is the southwest corner), the Port Authority Bus Terminal (on 42nd St. between Eighth and Ninth aves.), and Grand Central Terminal (on 41st St. between Park and Lexington aves.). Passengers to and from the Grand Central Terminal location can connect to Olympia's Midtown shuttle vans, which service select Midtown hotels. Call for the exact schedule for your return trip to the airport. The fare runs $11 one way, $21 round-trip; it's $5 more if you connect to the hotel shuttle. Seniors and travelers with disabilities ride for $5.

TAXIS Taxis are a quick and convenient way to travel to and from the airports, but you'll pay for the convenience of door-to-door service. They're available at taxi stands outside the terminals, with dispatchers on hand during peak hours at JFK and LaGuardia, around the clock at Newark. Follow the GROUND TRANSPORTATION or TAXI signs. There may be a line, but it generally moves pretty quickly. Fares, whether fixed or metered, do not include bridge and tunnel tolls ($3.50–$6) or a tip for the cabbie (15%–20% is customary). They include all passengers and luggage—never pay more than the metered or flat rate, except for tolls and a tip (from 8pm–6am a 50¢ surcharge also applies on New York yellow cabs). Taxis have a limit of four passengers, so if there are more in your group, you'll have to take more than one cab. For more on taxis, see "Getting Around" in chapter 4. Cab fares from the airports to the city are as follows:

- **From JFK:** A flat rate of $35 to Manhattan (plus tolls and tip) is charged. The meter will not be turned on and the surcharge will not be added. The flat rate does not apply on trips from Manhattan to the airport.
- **From LaGuardia:** $16 to $26, metered, plus tolls and tip.
- **From Newark:** The dispatcher for New Jersey taxis gives you a slip of paper with a flat rate ranging from $30 to $38 (toll and tip extra), depending on where you're going in Manhattan, so be precise about your destination. New York yellow cabs aren't permitted to pick up passengers at Newark. The yellow-cab fare from Manhattan to Newark is the meter amount plus $10 and tolls (about $40–$50, perhaps a few dollars more with tip). New Jersey taxis aren't permitted to take passengers from Manhattan to Newark.

Note that a taxi fare increase was being discussed at press time, so fares may be higher by the time you arrive.

PRIVATE CAR SERVICES Private car companies provide 24-hour door-to-door airport transfers. The advantage they offer over taking a taxi is that you can arrange your pickup in advance and avoid the hassles of the taxi line. A taxi is virtually always cheaper from JFK thanks to the flat fare; otherwise, as a general rule of thumb, expect to pay a tad less with a car service during rush hour (because there's no ticking meter in bumper-to-bumper traffic), slightly more at other times.

Call at least 24 hours in advance (even earlier on holidays), and a driver will meet you near baggage claim (or at your hotel for a return trip). You'll probably be asked to leave a credit-card number to guarantee your ride. You'll likely be offered the choice of indoor or curbside pickup; indoor pickup is more expensive, but makes it easier to hook up with your driver (who usually waits in baggage claim holding a sign with your name on it). You can save a few dollars if you arrange for an outside pickup; call the

---

Tips **An Airport Warning**

Never accept a car ride from the hustlers who hang out in the terminal halls. They're illegal, don't have proper insurance, and aren't safe. You can tell who they are because they'll approach you with a suspicious conspiratorial air and ask if you need a ride. Not from them, you don't. Sanctioned city cabs and car services wait outside the terminals.

Tips: Getting to the Other Boroughs & the 'Burbs

If you're traveling to a borough other than Manhattan, call **ETS Air Service** (© 718/221-5341) for shared door-to-door service. For Long Island service, call **Classic Transportation** (© 631/567-5100; www.classictrans.com) for car service, or **JFK Flyer** (© 516/766-6722) for bus service. For service to Westchester County or Connecticut, contact **Connecticut Limousine** (© 800/472-5466 or 203/878-2222; www.ctlimo.com) or **Prime Time Shuttle of Connecticut** (© 800/733-8267; www.primetimeshuttle.com).

If you're traveling to points in New Jersey from Newark Airport, call **Olympic Limousine** (© 800/822-9477 or 732/938-4300) for Ocean and Monmouth counties; the **Airporter** (© 800/385-4000 or 609/587-6600; www.goairporter.com) to Middlesex and Mercer counties, plus Bucks County, Penn.; or **State Shuttle** (© 800/427-3207 or 973/729-0030; www.stateshuttle.com) for destinations throughout New Jersey.

Additionally, **New York Airport Service** express buses (© 718/875-8200; www.nyairportservice.com) serve the entire New York metropolitan region from JFK and LaGuardia, offering connections to the Long Island Rail Road; the Metro North Rail Road to Westchester County, upstate New York, and Connecticut; and New York's Port Authority, where you can pick up buses to points throughout New Jersey.

---

dispatcher as soon as you land, then take your luggage to the waiting area, where you'll wait for the driver, which can take anywhere from 10 minutes to a half-hour. Besides the wait, the other disadvantage is that curbside can be chaos during prime deplaning hours.

Vehicles range from sedans to vans to limos and tend to be relatively clean and comfortable. Prices vary slightly by company and the size of car reserved, but expect a rate equivalent to taxi fare (except for the fare from JFK, as noted above) if you request a basic sedan and have only one stop; toll and tip policies are the same. Ask when booking what the fare will be and if you can use your credit card to pay for the ride so there are no surprises at drop-off time. There may be waiting charges tacked on if the driver has to wait an excessive amount of time for your plane to land, but the car companies will usually check on your flight beforehand to get an accurate landing time.

I've had the best luck with **Carmel** (© 800/922-7635 or 212/666-6666) and **Legends** (© 888/LEGENDS or 718/788-1234); **Allstate** (© 800/453-4099 or 212/333-3333) and **Tel-Aviv** (© 800/222-9888 or 212/777-7777) also have reasonable reputations. (Keep in mind, though, that these services are only as good as the individual drivers—and sometimes there's a lemon in the bunch. If you have a problem, report it to the office.)

BY TRAIN

Amtrak (© 800/USA-RAIL; www.amtrak.com) runs frequent service to New York City's **Penn Station,** on Seventh Avenue between 31st and 33rd streets, where you can pick up a taxi, subway, or bus.

If you're traveling to New York from a city along Amtrak's Northeast Corridor, Amtrak may be your best bet now that they've rolled out their new Acela trains, which cut travel time from D.C. down to 2½ hours, and travel time from Boston to 3 hours. Trains can also be less hassle, because they take you into Manhattan (thereby avoiding time-consuming and expensive airport transfers).

To get the best rates, book early (as much as 6 months in advance) and travel on weekends. See "65 Money-Saving Tips," at the beginning of this chapter, for more wallet-friendly advice, and check Amtrak's website for special discounted fares.

BY BUS

Buses arrive at the **Port Authority Terminal,** on Eighth Avenue between 40th and 42nd streets, where you can transfer to your hotel by taxi, subway, or bus. Buses can be slow and uncomfortable, but fares are usually much lower than trains and airlines.

Greyhound Bus Lines (© 800/229-9424; www.greyhound.com) is the nation's biggest bus carrier. You'll find a list of their special fares and discounts on their Web page; ask about special deals if you call.

Peter Pan Lines (© 800/343-9999, 212/564-8484, or 212/967-2900; www.peterpanbus.com) services the entire Northeast Corridor, from New Hampshire to Albany, N.Y., to Washington, D.C.; rates are low, and buses are much more comfortable than Greyhound's. For a complete list of bus carriers that serve Manhattan's Port Authority Bus Terminal, visit **www.panynj.gov/tbt/busline.HTM**.

Although the bus is likely to be the cheapest option, especially for East Coast short hauls, don't just assume. Always compare fares; sometimes, a full-fare bus ticket is no cheaper than the train. If you get lucky, you might even catch an airline fare sale that will make flying the most prudent option.

BY CAR

From the **New Jersey Turnpike** (I-95) and points west, there are three Hudson River crossings into the city's west side: the **Holland Tunnel** (lower Manhattan), the **Lincoln Tunnel** (Midtown), and the **George Washington Bridge** (Upper Manhattan). At press time, cars with only one passenger were prohibited from traveling from New Jersey through the Holland Tunnel during morning rush hour.

From **upstate New York,** take the **New York State Thruway** (I-87), which crosses the Hudson River on the Tappan Zee Bridge and becomes the **Major Deegan Expressway** (I-87) through the Bronx. For the east side, continue to the Triborough Bridge and down the FDR Drive. For the west side, take the Cross Bronx Expressway (I-95) to the Henry Hudson Parkway or the Taconic State Parkway to the Saw Mill River Parkway to the Henry Hudson Parkway south.

From **New England,** the **New England Thruway** (I-95) connects with the **Bruckner Expressway** (I-278), which leads to the Triborough Bridge and the FDR Drive on the east side. For the west side, take the Bruckner to the Cross Bronx Expressway (I-95) to the Henry Hudson Parkway south.

Note that you'll have to pay tolls along some of these roads and at most crossings.

Once you arrive in Manhattan, park your car in a garage (expect to pay $20–$45 per day) and leave it there. Don't use your car for traveling within the city. Public transportation, taxis, and walking will get you where you want to go without the headaches of parking, gridlock, and dodging crazy cabbies. See "Deals for Visitors with Wheels: Cheap Parking Tips" on p. 91.

3

For International Visitors

New York's global media profile might make it appear familiar, but movies and TV, music videos, and news images distort as much as they reflect. The gap between image and reality can make certain situations puzzling for the international—or even the domestic—visitor. This chapter will help prepare you for the more common issues that you might encounter.

1 Preparing for Your Trip

ENTRY REQUIREMENTS

Be sure to check with any U.S. embassy or consulate for the latest information, requirements, and travel advisories, as there may be changes and more restrictions in the wake of the September 11, 2001, terrorist attacks. You can obtain a visa application and other information online at the **U.S. State Department**'s website, **http://travel.state.gov**. Click on "Visas for Foreign Citizens" for entry info, while "Foreign Consular Offices" and "Links to Foreign Embassies" provides information for U.S. embassies and consulates worldwide.

VISAS The U.S. State Department has a **Visa Waiver Program** that allows citizens of certain countries to enter the country without a visa for stays of up to 90 days. At press time, this visa waiver program applied to citizens of Andorra, Australia, Austria, Belgium, Brunei, Denmark, Finland, France, Germany, Iceland, Ireland, Italy, Japan, Liechtenstein, Luxembourg, Monaco, the Netherlands, New Zealand, Norway, Portugal, San Marino, Singapore, Slovenia, Spain, Sweden, Switzerland, the United Kingdom, and Uruguay. Citizens of these countries need only a valid passport and a round-trip ticket in their possession upon arrival. Further information is available from any U.S. embassy or consulate. *Note:* This list can change at any time—Argentina was removed in February 2002—so never assume. Always check visa requirements well in advance. Canadian citizens may enter the United States without visas; they need only proof of residence.

Citizens of other countries must have: (1) a valid passport that expires at least 6 months later than the scheduled end of their visit, and (2) a tourist visa, which may be obtained from any U.S. consulate.

To obtain a visa, submit a completed application (in person or by mail) with two 1½-inch-square photos and $45, and demonstrate binding ties to a residence abroad.

Usually you can obtain a visa at once or within 24 hours, but it may take longer during the summer. If you cannot go in person, contact the nearest U.S. embassy or consulate for directions on applying by mail. Your travel agent or airline may be able to provide you with visa applications and instructions. The U.S. consulate or embassy will determine if you will be issued a multiple- or single-entry visa and any restrictions regarding the length of your stay.

Tips: Immigration Questions

Automated information and live assistance is available from the **Immigration and Naturalization Service's Customer Service Call Center** (© 800/375-5283; www.ins.usdoj.gov). A list of overseas offices is on the INS website. Immigrant visa information is available from the **National Visa Center** (© 603/334-0700).

Note: Make sure you have the Nonimmigrant Visa Application form labeled DF-156, as the old OF-156 form is no longer accepted. All relevant forms can be downloaded from the State Department website.

Inquire about visa cases and the application process at © **202/663-1225**.

MEDICAL REQUIREMENTS

Unless you're arriving from an area known to be suffering from an epidemic (particularly cholera or yellow fever), inoculations or vaccinations are not required for entry into the United States. If you have a disease that requires treatment with narcotics or syringe-administered medications, carry a valid signed prescription from your physician.

Upon entering the United States, foreign nationals are required to declare any dangerous contagious diseases they carry, which includes infection with HIV, the AIDS virus. Anyone who has such a disease is excluded from entry as a tourist. However, you may be able to apply for a waiver if you are attending a conference or have another compelling nontourism reason for your visit (call the **Immigration and Naturalization Service** [INS] at © **800/375-5283** to inquire). Doubtless many HIV-positive visitors come in without declaring their condition, their way of dealing with an archaic law that was originally intended to halt the spread of tuberculosis and the like.

CUSTOMS
WHAT YOU CAN BRING IN

Every visitor over 21 years of age may bring in, duty-free: (1) 1 liter of wine or liquor; (2) 200 cigarettes, 150 cigars (but not from Cuba), or 3 pounds of smoking tobacco; and (3) $100 worth of gifts. These exemptions are offered to travelers who spend at least 72 hours in the United States and who have not claimed them within the preceding 6 months.

International tourists may bring in or take out up to $10,000 in U.S. or foreign currency with no formalities; larger sums must be declared to U.S. Customs upon entering or leaving, which includes filing form CM 4790.

Declare any medicines you are carrying and be prepared to present a letter or prescription from your doctor; you may bring in no more than you would normally use in the duration of your visit.

In the post-9/11 world, restrictions are tighter than ever, and subject to change at any moment. If you have any questions, check before you go. For many more details, check the informative U.S. Customs website at **www.customs.ustreas.gov** and click "Traveler Information," where you can download the latest *Know Before You Go* pamphlet and other customs-related news. If you have questions, call the **U.S. Customs Information Line** at © **202/354-1000**.

WHAT YOU CAN BRING HOME

Rules governing what you can bring back duty-free vary from country to country, but they're generally posted on the Web. **Canadians** should check the booklet *I Declare,* which you can download or order from Revenue

Canada (© 800/461-9999, 204/983-3500, or 506/636-5064; www.ccra-adrc.gc.ca). **British** citizens should contact HM Customs & Excise (© **0845/010-9000,** or 44-208/929-0152 from outside the U.K.; www.hmce.gov.uk). **Australians** can contact the Australian Customs Service (© **1-300/363-263** within Australia, or 61-2/6275-6666 from outside Australia; www.customs.gov.au). **New Zealand** citizens should contact the New Zealand Customs Service (© **0800/428-786,** or 64-09/300-5399; www.customs.govt.nz).

INSURANCE

Although it's not required of travelers, health insurance is recommended. Unlike many European countries, the United States does not usually offer free or low-cost medical care. Doctors and hospitals are expensive, and in most cases will require advance payment or proof of coverage before treatment. Travel insurance policies can cover everything from the loss or theft of baggage and trip cancellation to the guarantee of bail in case you're arrested. Good policies will also cover the costs of an accident, repatriation, or death. See "Health & Insurance" in chapter 2, for more information. Packages such as **Europ Assistance (www.europassistance.com)** in Europe are sold by automobile clubs and travel agencies at attractive rates. **Worldwide Assistance Services, Inc.** (© **800/821-2828** or 703/204-1897; www.worldwideassistance.com) is their agent in the United States.

Though lack of health insurance may prevent you from being admitted to a hospital in nonemergencies, don't worry about being left on a street corner to die: The American way is to fix you now and bill the living daylights out of you later.

FOR BRITISH TRAVELERS Most big travel agents offer their own insurance and will probably try to sell you their package when you book a holiday. Britain's Consumers' Association recommends that you insist on seeing the policy and read the fine print. The **Association of British Insurers** (© **0171/600-3333;** www.abi.org.uk) gives advice by phone and publishes the free *Holiday Insurance Information Sheet,* a guide to policy provisions, as well as *Putting Customers First,* a buyer's awareness brochure, both downloadable from their website. You might also try **Columbus Direct** (© **020/7375-0011;** www.columbusdirect.net).

FOR CANADIAN TRAVELERS Canadians should check with their provincial health plan offices or call **HealthCanada** (© **613/957-2991;** www.hc-sc.gc.ca) to find out the extent of their coverage and what documentation and receipts they must take home in case they are treated in the United States.

MONEY

CURRENCY The most common **bills** (all green) are the $1 (a "buck"), $5, $10, and $20 denominations. There are $2 bills (seldom encountered), $50 bills, and $100 bills (the last two are usually not welcome for small purchases). Redesigned bills were recently introduced, but the old-style bills are still legal tender.

There are six denominations of **coins:** 1¢ (1 cent, or a penny); 5¢ (5 cents, or a nickel); 10¢ (10 cents, or a dime); 25¢ (25 cents, or a quarter); 50¢ (50 cents, or a half dollar); and a gold-toned $1 piece), increasingly common in New York City; you may receive one as change from a subway MetroCard machine.

CURRENCY EXCHANGE The foreign-exchange bureaus so common in Europe are rare even at airports in the United States and nonexistent outside major cities. You'll find them in

New York's tourist areas like Times Square, but expect a lousy exchange rate. **American Express** (© **800/ AXP-TRIP;** www.americanexpress. com) has many offices in the city, including 1185 Sixth Ave., at 47th Street (© 212/398-8585); at the New York Marriott Marquis hotel, 1535 Broadway, in the 8th-floor lobby (© 212/575-6580); on the mezzanine level at Macy's Herald Square, 34th Street and Broadway (© 212/ 695-8075); and at 374 Park Ave., at 53rd Street (© 212/421-8240). Visit **http://travel.americanexpress.com/ travel/personal/resources/tso** to locate additional travel service offices.

Thomas Cook Currency Services (© 800/CURRENCY; www.us. thomascook.com) are at 1590 Broadway at 48th Street (© 212/265-6063); 1271 Broadway, at 32nd Street (© 212/679-4877); 317 Madison Ave. at 42nd Street (© 212/883-0401); 29 Broadway, south of Wall Street (© 212/363-6206); and 511 Madison Ave., at 53rd Street (© 212/ 753-2595).

It's best not to expect to change foreign money (or traveler's checks in a currency other than U.S. dollars) at a small-town bank, or even a bank branch in New York. In fact, it's best to just leave any currency other than U.S. dollars at home—it may prove a greater nuisance to you than it's worth.

TRAVELER'S CHECKS Though traveler's checks are widely accepted, *make sure that they're denominated in U.S. dollars,* as foreign-currency checks are often difficult to exchange. The three traveler's checks most widely recognized—are **Visa, American Express,** and **Thomas Cook/MasterCard.** Be sure to record the numbers of the checks, and keep that information separate from the checks in case they get lost or stolen. Most businesses are good about taking traveler's checks, but you're better off cashing them in at a bank (in small amounts) and paying in cash. *Remember:* You'll need identification, such as a driver's license or passport, to change a traveler's check.

CREDIT CARDS Credit cards are the most widely used form of payment in the United States: **Visa** (Barclay-Card in Britain), **MasterCard** (Eurocard in Europe, Access in Britain, Chargex in Canada), **American Express, Diners Club, Discover,** and **Carte Blanche;** New York vendors may accept cards like **enRoute, Eurocard,** and **JCB,** but not as universally as Amex, MasterCard, or Visa. Some stores and restaurants do not take credit cards, so ask in advance. Some businesses require a minimum purchase, anywhere from $10 or $20, to use a credit card.

I recommend that you bring at least one major credit card. Hotels, car-rental companies, and airlines usually require a credit-card imprint as a deposit, and in an emergency a credit card can be priceless.

ATMs Automated teller machines (ATMs) are on just about every block

---

> **Tips** **Getting the Best Exchange Rate**
>
> You'll actually get the best exchange rate for your national currency if you withdraw money from an ATM. But keep in mind that many banks impose a fee every time a card is used at an ATM (anywhere from $1–$3, depending on the ATM you choose and what your home bank is), so you may want to factor these fees in when you weigh your options.

in Manhattan. Some will allow you to draw U.S. currency against your bank (and even against your credit cards if you have a personal identification number [PIN]—though you should only do this in an emergency since the transaction will be treated as a cash advance, and you'll pay dearly for the privilege). Check with your bank and ask if you'll need to reprogram your PIN in the United States. Expect to be charged up to $3 per transaction if you're not using your own bank's ATM. Rather than taking out small denominations again and again, it makes sense to take out larger amounts every 2 or 3 days.

SAFETY

Tourist areas in Manhattan are generally safe, and the city has experienced a dramatic drop in its crime rate of late. Still, crime is a national problem, and U.S. urban areas tend to be less safe than those in Europe or Japan. Always stay alert, use your head, and trust your instincts. If you feel you're in an unsafe area or situation, you probably are and should leave as quickly as possible.

GENERAL SAFETY SUGGESTIONS Leave your valuables at home if you can. Don't display expensive cameras or flashy jewelry as you walk around. If you are using a map, consult it as discreetly as possible, with one eye on what's going on around you at all times.

Remember that hotels are open to the public, and in a large hotel, security may not be able to screen everyone entering. Always lock your door—don't assume that once inside your hotel you no longer need to keep an eye on your valuables or be aware of your surroundings.

Avoid deserted areas, especially at night, and don't go into parks at night unless there's a concert or similar occasion that will attract a crowd.

For more about personal security, see "Playing It Safe," in chapter 4.

DRIVING An inviolable rule of thumb for New York: Don't even think of driving in the city. Like many cities, New York has its own arcane rules of the road, one-way streets, incomprehensible street-parking signs, and expensive parking garages. Public transportation—buses, subways, or taxis—will get you anywhere you want to go quickly and easily.

If you do drive to New York in a rental car, return it as soon as you arrive and rent another when you're ready to leave. Always keep your car doors locked. Never leave any packages or valuables in sight because thieves will break car windows. If someone attempts to rob you or steal your car, don't resist. Report the incident to the police immediately.

2 Getting to the United States

In addition to the domestic airlines listed in chapter 2, many international carriers serve John F. Kennedy International and Newark airports. **British Airways** (© **0845/77-333-77** or 0870/55-111-55 in the U.K., or 800/ AIRWAYS in the U.S.; www.british-airways.com) has daily service from London as well as direct flights from Manchester and Glasgow. **Virgin Atlantic** (© **01293/747-747** or 01293/511-581 in the U.K., or 800/ 862-8621 in the U.S.; www.virgin-atlantic.com) flies from London's Heathrow to New York.

Canadian readers might book flights on **Air Canada** (© **888/247-2262;** www.aircanada.ca), which offers direct service from Toronto, Montréal, Ottawa, and other cities.

Tips: How to Save on International Airfares

The idea of traveling abroad on a budget is something of an oxymoron, especially when New York is your destination, but you can reduce the price of your airfare by a significant amount if you take the time to shop around.

If you're on a tight budget and you're coming from Europe, consider traveling to New York between January and March. That's when airlines such as British Airways and Virgin Atlantic pull out all the stops to fill their post-holiday flights, and fares plummet. Hotels are also suffering the after-Christmas blues, and rooms often go for a relative song.

If you're coming from anywhere else overseas, you can take advantage of the APEX (Advance Purchase Excursion) reductions offered by all major U.S. and European carriers. These usually require 7 to 21 days advance booking, cannot be canceled, and might come with significant change fees, but they'll save you hundreds of dollars over full-fare rates. For the best rates, compare fares by calling a number of airlines that serve your departure city and be flexible with your dates and times of travel.

Operated by the European Travel Network, **www.discount-tickets.com** is a great online source for regular and discounted airfares. You can use this site to compare rates and book accommodations, cars, and tours. Click on "Special Offers" for the latest package deals. Students should also try **USIT World** (© 0171/730-2101; www.usitworld.com/index.html).

Canadian travelers should check out the deals offered by **Travel CUTS** (© 866/246-9762; www.travelcuts.com).

For more money-saving airline advice, see "65 Money-Saving Tips," at the beginning of chapter 2.

Aer Lingus flies from Ireland to New York (© 0818/365000 in Ireland, 800/IRISH-AIR in the U.S.; www.aerlingus.ie). The following U.S. airlines fly to New York from most major European cities: **Continental** (© 0800/776-464 in the U.K., or 800/231-0856 in the U.S.; www.continental.com); **United** (© 0845/844-4777 in the U.K., or 800/538-2929 in the U.S.; www.ual.com); **American** (© 0208/572-5555 or 0845/778-9789 in the U.K., or 800/433-7300 in the U.S.; www.aa.com); and **Delta** (© 0800/414-767 in the U.K., or 800/241-4141 in the U.S.; www.delta.com).

Qantas (© 13-13-13 in Australia, 800/227-4500 in the U.S.; www.qantas.com.au) and **Air New Zealand** (© 0800/737-000 in New Zealand, 800/262-1234 in the U.S.; www.airnewzealand.co.nz) fly to the West Coast and will book you through to New York City on a partner airline.

IMMIGRATION & CUSTOMS CLEARANCE Visitors arriving by air, no matter what port of entry, should cultivate patience and resignation—now more than ever. Getting through immigration control may take up to 2 hours on some days, maybe longer in the heightened security following the September 11, 2001, terrorist attacks, so be sure to have this guidebook or something else to read. Add the time it takes to clear Customs, and you'll see that you should make a 2- to 3-hour allowance for delays when you plan your connections between flights.

For the traveler arriving by car or rail from Canada, the border-crossing formalities have been streamlined. People traveling by air from Canada, Bermuda, and some places in the Caribbean can sometimes clear Customs and Immigration at the point of departure, which is much quicker.

3 If You're Traveling Beyond New York City

BY PLANE Some major American carriers—including Delta and Continental—offer travelers on their transatlantic or transpacific flights low-price tickets on U.S. flights under the **Discover America** program (sometimes called **Visit USA**). Offering one-way travel between U.S. destinations at significantly reduced prices, this coupon-based airfare program is the best and easiest way to tour the United States at low cost.

These discounted fare coupons are not available in the United States and must be purchased abroad in conjunction with your international ticket. Ask your travel agent or the airline reservations agent about this program in advance of your departure—preferably when you buy your international ticket—since the regulations and conditions can change.

BY TRAIN If you're making a short hop to an East Coast city like Boston or Washington, D.C., rail is the best way to go. **Amtrak** (© **800/USA-RAIL;** www.amtrak.com) trains leave from New York's Penn Station, at Seventh Avenue and 34th Street. For more on Amtrak, see "Getting There" in chapter 2.

If you're visiting more than one city, you might want to consider a **USA Rail Pass,** which can save you money over individual tickets. It's available to international visitors only and good for 15 or 30 days of unlimited travel on Amtrak. The pass is available through many foreign travel agents; with a foreign passport, you can buy passes at some Amtrak offices in the United States. Call Amtrak for details or visit the website.

BY BUS Far from pleasant or speedy, buses nevertheless are your most economical option for traveling around the United States. **Greyhound** (© **800/229-9424** or 402/330-8552; www.greyhound.com) links destinations throughout the U.S., although smaller companies like **Peter Pan Bus Lines** (© **800/237-8747** or 413/781-2900; www.peterpanbus.com) offer better service to destinations between Boston and Washington, D.C., including New York City, at similar prices. Many companies offer discounts to students, travelers linking multiple destinations, or off-season travelers. For a list of long-distance bus carriers serving New York City, visit **www.panynj.gov/tbt/pabframe.HTM.**

Tips Toll-Free Numbers (And Ones That Aren't!)

Calls to area codes **800, 888,** and **877** are toll-free. However, calls to area codes **700** and **900** (chat lines, "dating" services, and so on) can be expensive—they usually charge 95¢ to $3 or more per minute, and sometimes have minimum charges that run as high as $15 or more.

FAST FACTS: For the International Traveler

Also see "Fast Facts: New York City," in chapter 4, for more city-specific information.

Automobile Organizations Auto clubs will supply maps, suggested routes, guidebooks, accident and bail-bond insurance, and emergency road service. The **American Automobile Association** (AAA) is the major auto club in the United States. If you belong to an auto club at home, inquire about AAA reciprocity. You may be able to join AAA even if you're not a member of a reciprocal club; to inquire, call © **800/AAA-HELP** (also the nationwide emergency road service number), or visit **www.aaa.com**. AAA is actually an organization of regional auto clubs, so look under "AAA Automobile Club" in the White Pages of the telephone directory.

Automobile Rentals To rent a car in the United States, you need a valid driver's license, a passport, and a major credit card. The minimum age is usually 25, but some companies will rent to younger people and add a surcharge. It's a good idea to buy maximum insurance coverage unless you're positive your own auto or credit-card insurance is sufficient. All major car-rental agencies have branches in Manhattan; try **Hertz** (© 800/654-3131; www.hertz.com), **National** (© 800/227-7368; www.nationalcar.com), or **Avis** (© 800/230-4898; www.avis.com). Stick to the major companies because what you might save with smaller companies might not be worth the headache if you have mechanical troubles on the road. Rates vary, so it pays to call around.

Business Hours In general, **retail stores** are open Monday through Saturday from 10am to 6pm or 7pm, Thursday from 10am to 8:30 or 9pm, and Sunday from noon to 5pm (see chapter 8). **Banks** tend to be open Monday through Friday from 9am to 3pm, sometimes Saturday mornings.

Currency & Currency Exchange See "Money" under "Preparing for Your Trip," earlier in this chapter. For the latest market conversion rates, go online to **www.oanda.com** or **www.x-rates.com**.

Drinking Laws The legal age for purchase and consumption of alcoholic beverages is 21; proof of age is required and often requested at bars and clubs, so always bring ID with you. Liquor stores, the only retail outlets for wine and hard liquor in New York, are closed on Sundays, holidays, and election days while the polls are open. Beer can be purchased in grocery stores and delis Monday through Saturday and Sunday after noon. Last call at city bars is 4am, although many close earlier.

Do not carry open containers of alcohol in your car or any public area not zoned for alcohol consumption. The police can, and probably will, fine you on the spot. And nothing will ruin your trip faster than getting a citation for DUI ("driving under the influence").

Electricity Like Canada, the United States uses 110 to 120 volts AC (60 cycles), compared to 220 to 240 volts AC (50 cycles) in most of Europe, Australia, and New Zealand. If your small appliances use 220 to 240 volts, you'll need a 110-volt transformer and a plug adapter with two flat parallel pins here. Downward converters that change 220 to 240 volts to 110 to 120 volts are difficult to find in the United States, so bring one with you.

Embassies & Consulates All embassies are in Washington, D.C. Some countries have consulates general in major U.S. cities, and most have a mission to the United Nations in New York City. If your country isn't listed below, call for directory information in Washington, D.C. (© **411** or 202/555-1212), or go online to **www.embassy.org/embassies** for the location and phone number of your national embassy.

Australia: Embassy, 1601 Massachusetts Ave. NW, Washington, DC 20036 (© 202/797-3000; www.austemb.org); Consulate General, 150 E. 42nd St., New York, NY 10117 (© 212/351-6500). **Canada:** Embassy, 501 Pennsylvania Ave. NW, Washington, DC 20001 (© 202/682-1740; www.canadianembassy.org); Consulate General, 1251 Ave. of the Americas, New York, NY 10020 (© 212/596-1628; www.canada-ny.org). **Ireland:** Embassy, 2234 Massachusetts Ave. NW, Washington, DC 20008 (© 202/462-3939; www.irelandemb.org); Consulate General, 1251 Ave. of the Americas, New York, NY 10020-1175 (© 212/596-1628). **Japan:** Embassy, 2520 Massachusetts Ave. NW, Washington, DC 20008 (© 202/238-6700; www.embjapan.org); Consulate General, 299 Park Ave., 18th Floor, New York, NY 10171 (© 212/371-8222; http://ny.cgj.org). **New Zealand:** Embassy, 37 Observatory Circle, Washington, DC 20008 (© 202/328-4800; www.nzemb.org); Consulate General, 780 Third Ave., Suite 1904, New York, NY 10017 (© 212/832-4038). **United Kingdom:** Embassy, 3100 Massachusetts Ave. NW, Washington, DC 20008 (© 202/588-6500; www.britainusa.com); Consulate General, 845 Third Ave., New York, NY 10022 (© 212/745-0200; www.britainusa.com/consular/ny/ny.asp).

Emergencies Call © **911** to report a fire, call the police, or get an ambulance anywhere in the United States. This is a toll-free call (no coins are required at public telephones).

If you have a medical emergency that doesn't require an ambulance, you can walk into a hospital's 24-hour emergency room (usually a separate entrance). For a list of hospitals, see "Fast Facts: New York City," in chapter 4. Because emergency rooms are often crowded, one of the walk-in medical centers listed under "What to Do if You Get Sick Away from Home" under "Health & Insurance," in chapter 2, might be a better option.

Gasoline (Petrol) Petrol is known as gasoline (or simply "gas"), and petrol stations are known as both gas stations and service stations. Gasoline costs about half as much here as it does in Europe (though prices were rising at press time), and taxes are already included in the printed price. One U.S. gallon equals 3.8 liters or .85 imperial gallons.

Holidays Banks, government offices, post offices, and many stores, restaurants, and museums are closed on the following national holidays: January 1 (New Year's Day), the third Monday in January (Martin Luther King Jr. Day), the third Monday in February (Presidents' Day), the last Monday in May (Memorial Day), July 4th (Independence Day), the first Monday in September (Labor Day), the second Monday in October (Columbus Day), November 11 (Veterans' Day/Armistice Day), the fourth Thursday in November (Thanksgiving Day), and December 25 (Christmas). Also, the Tuesday following the first Monday in November is Election Day and is a federal holiday in presidential-election years (next in 2004).

Legal Aid Most foreign tourists will probably never become involved with the American legal system. If you are stopped for a minor infraction (for example, speeding), never attempt to pay the fine directly to a police officer; this could be construed as bribery, a more serious crime. If it's a traffic infraction, do not get out of the car; stay seated with your hands on the wheel until the officer approaches. Pay fines by mail, or to the clerk of the court. If accused of a more serious offense, say and do nothing before consulting a lawyer. Everyone has the right to remain silent. Once arrested, a person can make one telephone call to a party of his or her choice. Call your embassy or consulate.

Mail Generally found at intersections, mailboxes are blue with a white eagle logo and carry the inscription U.S. MAIL. If your mail is addressed to a U.S. destination, don't forget to add the five-digit postal code (or ZIP code), after the two-letter abbreviation of the state to which the mail is addressed.

At press time, domestic postage rates were 22¢ for a postcard and 37¢ for a letter. For international mail, a first-class letter of up to 1 ounce costs 80¢ (60¢ to Canada and Mexico); a first-class postcard costs 70¢ (including Canada and Mexico); and a preprinted postal aerogramme costs 70¢. Point your browser to **www.usps.com** for U.S. postal information, or call © **800/275-8777** for the nearest post office. Most branches are open Monday through Friday from 8am to 5 or 6pm, and Saturday from 9am to noon or 3pm.

Newspapers/Magazines In addition to the *New York Times* and other city papers, many newsstands carry a selection of international newspapers and magazines. For nearly all major newspapers and magazines from around the world, head to **Universal News & Magazines,** at 977 Eighth Ave., between 57th and 58th streets (© **212/459-0932**), and 234 W. 42nd St., between Seventh and Eighth avenues (© **212/221-1809**); or **Hotalings News Agency,** 142 W. 42nd St., between Broadway and Sixth Ave. (© **212/840-1868**). Other good bets include the **Hudson** newsdealers located in Grand Central Terminal, at 42nd Street and Lexington Avenue, and Penn Station, at 34th Street and Seventh Avenue.

Taxes There is no value-added tax (VAT) at the national level, but every state, county, and city has the right to levy its own local tax on all purchases, including hotel and restaurant checks, airline tickets, and so on. Sales tax is usually not included in the price tags on merchandise but is added at the cash register. These taxes aren't refundable. In New York City, the **sales tax** is 8.25% (clothing purchases under $110 are exempt). The **hotel tax** is 13.25% plus $2 per room per night (including sales tax). The **parking garage tax,** added to already high basic fees, is 18.25%.

Telephone & Fax The telephone system in the United States is run by private corporations, so rates, especially for long-distance and operator-assisted calls, can vary. Generally, hotel surcharges on long-distance and local calls are astronomical, so use a **public pay telephone,** which you'll find in most public buildings as well as hotel lobbies and on the street. Many convenience stores and newsstands sell **prepaid calling cards** in denominations up to $50; these can be the least expensive way to call home. Many public phones at airports accept American Express, MasterCard, and Visa credit cards. **Local calls** made from pay phones usually cost 25¢, though some hotel pay phones will charge 50¢.

Most long-distance and international calls can be dialed direct from any phone. **For calls within the United States and to Canada,** dial 1 followed by the area code and the seven-digit number. **For other international calls,** dial 011 followed by the country code, city code, and the telephone number of the person you are calling. Some country and city codes are as follows: **Australia** 61, Melbourne 3, Sydney 2; **Ireland** 353, Dublin 1; **New Zealand** 64, Auckland 9, Wellington 4; **United Kingdom** 44, Belfast 232, Birmingham 21, Glasgow 41, London 71 or 81. If you're calling the **United States** from another country, the country code is 01.

For **reversed-charge, collect, operator-assisted,** and **person-to-person calls,** dial 0 (the number zero) followed by the area code and number you want; an operator will then come on the line, and you should specify that you are calling collect, or person-to-person, or both. If your operator-assisted call is international, ask for the overseas operator.

For local and national directory assistance ("information"), dial © **411.**

Most hotels have **fax machines** for guest use (be sure to ask about the charge to use it), and many hotel rooms have in-room fax machines. Receiving faxes is usually free (always ask first), but a less expensive way to send faxes is at stores such as **Mail Boxes Etc.,** a national chain of packing-service shops (look in the Yellow Pages under "Packing Services"), or **Kinko's,** a chain of copy shops offering business services.

There are two kinds of telephone directories. The **White Pages** list private households and businesses in alphabetical order. The inside front cover lists emergency numbers. The first few pages will tell you how to make long-distance and international calls, and lists country and area codes. Printed on yellow paper, the **Yellow Pages** list all local services, businesses, industries, and houses of worship according to activity with an index at the front or back. The Yellow Pages also include city plans or detailed area maps, postal ZIP codes, and public transportation routes. A useful online "yellow pages" for finding phone numbers and addresses in New York and other U.S. cities is **www.smartpages.com**.

Time The continental United States is divided into four time zones: Eastern Standard Time (EST), the time zone New York is in, which is 5 hours behind Greenwich mean time (GMT); Central Standard Time (CST); Mountain Standard Time (MST); and Pacific Standard Time (PST). Alaska and Hawaii have their own zones. For example, noon in New York City (EST) is 11am in Chicago (CST), 10am in Denver (MST), 9am in Los Angeles (PST), 8am in Anchorage (AST), and 7am in Honolulu (HST).

Daylight saving time is in effect from 1am on the first Sunday in April through 1am on the last Sunday in October, except in Arizona, Hawaii, part of Indiana, and Puerto Rico. Daylight saving time moves the clock 1 hour ahead of standard time. When daylight saving time is in effect, New York is only 4 hours behind Greenwich mean time.

For the correct local time in New York, dial © **212/976-1616.**

Tipping Tips are a very important part of certain workers' salaries, so it's important that you leave appropriate gratuities. Unlike most of Europe, tips aren't automatically added to restaurant and hotel bills. In restaurants, a tip to the waitperson of 15% to 20% of the total check is customary; in New York City, you can double the 8.25% tax to figure the appropriate tip.

Other tipping guidelines: 15% to 20% of the fare to taxi drivers; 10% to 15% of the tab to bartenders; $1 to $2 per bag to bellhops; at least $1 per day to hotel maids; $1 per item to checkroom attendants; $1 to valet parking attendants; and 15% to 20% to hairdressers. Tipping theater ushers, gas-station attendants, and fast-food employees isn't expected.

Toilets In general, you won't find public toilets or "restrooms" on the streets in New York, but they can be found in hotel lobbies, bars, restaurants, museums, department stores, or railway and bus stations. See "Restrooms" under "Fast Facts: New York City" at the end of chapter 4.

Traveler's Assistance **Travelers Aid** helps travelers with problems, including accidents, sickness, and lost or stolen luggage. There is an office on the second floor of the International Arrivals Building at JFK Airport (© **718/656-4870**), and in Newark Airport's Terminal B (© **973/623-5052**).

4

Getting to Know New York City

This chapter gives you an insider's take on Manhattan's most distinctive neighborhoods and streets, tells you how to get around, and serves as a reference to everything from personal safety to libraries and liquor laws.

1 Orientation

VISITOR INFORMATION
INFORMATION OFFICES

- The **Times Square Visitors Center,** 1560 Broadway, between 46th and 47th streets (where Broadway meets Seventh Ave.), across from the TKTS booth (© **212/768-1560;** www.timessquarebid.org), is the city's top info stop. This attractive center features a helpful info desk offering loads of information. There's also a Metropolitan Transportation Authority (MTA) desk that sells MetroCards, offers transit maps, and answers your questions on the transit system; a Broadway Ticket Center providing show information and selling full-price tickets; ATMs and currency-exchange machines; and computers with free Internet access. It's open daily from 8am to 8pm.
- The New York Convention and Visitors Bureau runs the **NYCVB Visitor Information Center** at 810 Seventh Ave., between 52nd and 53rd streets. In addition to information on attractions and a multilingual counselor, the center also has interactive terminals that provide touch-screen access to visitor information via Citysearch and sell advance tickets to major attractions, which can save you from standing in long lines (you can also buy a CityPass using these; see p. 27). There's also an ATM, a gift shop, and phones that connect you directly with American Express card member services. The center is open Monday through Friday from 8:30am to 6pm, Saturday and Sunday from 9am to 5pm. For phone assistance, call © **212/484-1222.**

PUBLICATIONS

For comprehensive listings of films, concerts, performances, sports, museum and gallery exhibits, street fairs, and special events, the following are your best bets:

- The *New York Times* (www.nytimes.com or www.nytoday.com) features great arts and entertainment coverage, particularly in the Friday "Weekend" section and Sunday's "Arts & Leisure" section. Both days have full guides to the latest happenings in theater, music, dance, film, and the art world. Friday is good for cabaret, family fun, and general-interest events.
- *Time Out New York* (www.timeoutny.com) is my favorite weekly magazine. It's attractive, well organized, and easy to use. *TONY* features excellent coverage in categories from music, theater, and clubs (gay and straight) to museums, dance, book and poetry readings, and kids' stuff. The regular

"Check Out" section, unequaled in any other listings magazine, will fill you in on upcoming sample and closeout sales, crafts and antiques shows, and other shopping scoops. A new issue hits newsstands every Thursday.
- The famous free weekly *Village Voice* (www.villagevoice.com), is available late Tuesday downtown and early Wednesday elsewhere. From classical music to clubs, the arts and entertainment coverage couldn't be more extensive, and just about every music venue advertises its shows. But I find the paper a bit unwieldy, and the exposé tone of its features can be tiresome.

Other useful weeklies include the glossy *New York* magazine (www.newyorkmag.com or www.nymetro.com), which offers restaurant reviews and whose "Cue" section is a selective guide to city arts and entertainment; the *New Yorker* (www.newyorker.com), which features "Goings On About Town" at the front of the magazine; and the *New York Press* (www.nypress.com), a free, vaguely libertarian weekly in the *Village Voice* vein. The monthly *Paper* (www.papermag.com) is a glossy alterna-mag that serves as good prep for those of you who want to experience the hipper side of the city.

CITY LAYOUT

Open the sheet map that comes with this book and you'll see the city is comprised of five boroughs: **Manhattan,** where most of the visitor action is; the **Bronx,** the only NYC borough on the mainland United States; **Queens,** where Kennedy and LaGuardia airports are located; **Brooklyn,** south of Queens, which is also on Long Island and is famed for its attitude, accent, and Atlantic-front Coney Island; and **Staten Island,** the least populous borough, bordering Upper New York Bay on one side and the Atlantic Ocean on the other.

It is Manhattan, the finger-shaped island pointing southwest off the mainland—surrounded by the Harlem River to the north, the Hudson River to the west, the East River (really an estuary) to the east, and Upper New York Bay to the south—that most visitors think of when they envision New York City. Despite the fact that it's the city's smallest borough (13½ miles/22km long, 2¼ miles/3.5km wide, 22 sq. miles/35 sq. km), Manhattan contains the city's most famous attractions, buildings, and institutions. For that reason, almost all of the accommodations and restaurants in this book are in Manhattan.

In most of Manhattan, finding your way around is a snap because of the grid system by which the streets are numbered. If you can discern uptown and downtown, and East Side and West Side, you can find your way around pretty easily. In real terms, **uptown** means north of where you happen to be and **downtown** means south, although sometimes these labels have deeper meanings (generally speaking, "uptown" chic vs. "downtown" bohemianism).

Avenues run north and south (uptown and downtown). Most are numbered. **Fifth Avenue** divides the East Side from the West Side of town, and serves as the eastern border of Central Park north of 59th Street. **First Avenue** is all the way east and **Twelfth Avenue** is all the way west. The three most important unnumbered avenues on the East Side you should know are between Third and Fifth avenues: **Madison** (east of Fifth), **Park** (east of Madison), and **Lexington** (east of Park, just west of Third). Important unnumbered avenues on the West Side are **Avenue of the Americas,** which all New Yorkers call Sixth Avenue; **Central Park West,** which Eighth Avenue north of 59th Street as it borders Central Park on the west (hence the name); **Columbus Avenue,** Ninth Avenue north of 59th Street; and **Amsterdam Avenue,** or Tenth Avenue north of 59th.

Broadway is the exception to the rule—it's the only major avenue that doesn't run uptown to downtown. It cuts a diagonal path across the island, from the northwest tip down to the southeast corner. As it crosses most major avenues, it creates **squares** (Times Sq., Herald Sq., and Union Sq., for example).

Streets run east to west (crosstown) and are numbered as they proceed uptown from Houston (*House*-ton) Street. To go uptown, walk north of, or to a higher-numbered street than, where you are. Downtown is south of (or a lower-numbered street than) your current location. If you can see a landmark like the Empire State Building, it's easy to determine uptown and downtown if you know what street you are on; remember the Empire State Building is on 34th Street.

Fifth Avenue is the dividing line between the **East Side** and **West Side** of town (except below Washington Sq., where Broadway serves that function). On the east side of Fifth Avenue, streets are numbered with the distinction "East"; on the west side of Fifth Avenue, they are numbered "West." East 51st Street, for example, begins at Fifth Avenue and runs east to the East River, while West 51st Street begins at Fifth Avenue and runs west to the Hudson River.

If you're looking for a particular address, remember that even-numbered street addresses are on the south side of streets and odd-numbered addresses are on the north. Street addresses increase by about 50 per block starting at Fifth Avenue. For example, nos. 1 to 50 East are just about between Fifth and Madison avenues, while nos. 1 to 50 West are just about between Fifth and Sixth avenues. Traffic generally runs east on even-numbered streets and west on odd-numbered streets, with a few exceptions, like the major east-west thoroughfares—**14th, 23rd, 34th, 42nd, 57th, 72nd, 79th, 86th**—which have two-way traffic. Therefore 28 W. 23rd St. is a short walk west of Fifth Avenue; 325 E. 35th St. would be a few blocks east of Fifth.

Avenue addresses are irregular. For example, 994 Second Ave. is at East 51st Street, but so is 320 Park Ave. Thus, it's important to know a building's cross street to find it. If you don't have the cross street and want to figure out the exact location using just the address, use the **Manhattan Address Locator,** later in this chapter.

Unfortunately, the rules don't apply to neighborhoods in Lower Manhattan, south of 14th Street—like Wall Street, Chinatown, SoHo, TriBeCa, the Village—since they sprang up before engineers devised this brilliant grid scheme. A good map is essential when exploring these areas.

STREET MAPS You'll find a pullout map of Manhattan at the back of this book. There's also a decent one available for free as part of the **Official NYC Visitor Kit** if you write ahead for information (see "Visitor Information," in chapter 2); you can also pick it up for free at the visitor centers listed above.

Even with all these freebies, I suggest investing in a map with more features if you want to zip around the city like a pro. **Hagstrom** maps are my favorites

---

> ### Tips Orientation Tips
>
> I've indicated the cross streets for every destination in this book, but be sure to ask for the cross street (or avenue) if you call for an address.
>
> When you give a taxi driver an address, always specify the cross streets. New Yorkers, even most cab drivers, probably wouldn't know where to find 284 E. 81st St., but they do know where to find 81st and Second. If you're heading to the Afghan Kebab House, for example, tell them that it's on Ninth Avenue between 51st and 52nd.
>
> If you have only the numbered address on an avenue, you can figure out the cross street using the **Manhattan Address Locator** on p. 80.

because they feature block-by-block street numbering—so instead of trying to guess the cross street for 125 Prince St., you can see that it's Greene Street. Hagstrom and other visitor-friendly maps are available at any good bookstore. You might also want to look for *The New York Map Guide: The Essential Guide to Manhattan* (Penguin), by Michael Middleditch, a 64-page book that maps the entire city, including attractions, restaurants, and nightlife spots.

Keep in mind that, due to construction and the World Trade Center disaster, some subway lines will be in flux through 2002 and 2003, especially downtown. Don't rely on a subway map that hasn't been printed by the Metropolitan Transit Authority; more on this in "Getting Around," later in this chapter.

MANHATTAN'S NEIGHBORHOODS IN BRIEF

Since they grew up over the course of hundreds of years, Manhattan's neighborhoods have multiple personalities and fluid boundaries. Still, it's relatively easy to agree upon what they stand for in general—so if you stop a New Yorker and ask him or her to point you to, say, the Upper West Side or the Flatiron District, they'll know where you want to go. From south to north, here is how I've defined Manhattan's neighborhoods throughout this book.

Downtown

Lower Manhattan: South Street Seaport & the Financial District
This is where New York City originated. Established by the Dutch in 1625 (the city's original name was Nieuw Amsterdam), New York's first settlements were here, on the southern tip of Manhattan; everything uptown was farmland and wilderness. While all that's changed, this is still the best place in the city to search for the past.

Lower Manhattan is everything south of Chambers Street. **Battery Park,** the point of departure for the Statue of Liberty, Ellis Island, and Staten Island, is on the south tip of the island. The **South Street Seaport,** now touristy but still a reminder of times of when shipping was the lifeblood of the city, lies a bit north on the east coast; it's just south of the Brooklyn Bridge, which stands proudly as the ultimate engineering achievement of New York's 19th-century Industrial Age.

The rest of the area is the **Financial District,** but may even be more famous now as **Ground Zero.** Until September 11, 2001, the Financial District was anchored by the **World Trade Center,** with the World Financial Center complex and Battery Park City to the west, and **Wall Street** running crosstown south and to the east. Now, a gaping hole sits where the Twin Towers and their five sister buildings stood.

Despite the devastation, the Financial District deserves to be celebrated as an incredible story of recovery. Within 6 months after that horrific day, the neighborhood was running pretty much normally just about everywhere but the World Trade Center site itself. Some nearby hotels and offices remain closed at this writing, but the World Financial Center was up and running by early 2002, and even discount department store Century 21 (p. 271), across the street, had reopened by March 2002.

At press time, the Ground Zero site was still in the clean-up process. Since no redevelopment plan is in place, there's no way to know what's to come. However, one thing's for sure: Ground Zero will still be a massive construction zone throughout 2003. Whether viewing platforms will remain in place is anybody's guess; see chapter 8 for information on how to find the latest on the site.

The surrounding area—including Wall Street, the South Street

Seaport, and Battery Park—is open and ready for your business. **City Hall** remains the northern border of the district, abutting Chambers Street (look for City Hall Park on the map). Most of the streets of this neighborhood are narrow concrete canyons, with Broadway serving as the main uptown-downtown artery.

Most of the major subway lines congregate here before they end or head to Brooklyn (the exceptions: the B, D, F, J, M, Q, V, W, and Z lines cross into Brooklyn from the Lower East Side, over the Manhattan Bridge). At this writing, all but the 1 and 9 lines were running again—even the stop named "World Trade Center" on the E line is reopened (it actually lets you out to the north of the site). The 1 and 9 were scheduled to resume service to the southern tip of Manhattan by autumn 2002. Any event can cause delays, so see "Getting Around" later this chapter for information on where to gather the latest subway information.

TriBeCa Bordered by the Hudson River to the west, the area north of Chambers Street, west of Broadway, and south of Canal Street is the *Tri-angle Below Ca*nal Street, or TriBeCa. Since the 1980s, as SoHo became saturated with chic, the spillover transforming TriBeCa into one of the city's hippest neighborhoods, where celebrities and families coexist in cast-iron warehouses converted into spacious, expensive loft apartments. Artists' lofts and galleries as well as hip antique and design shops pepper the area, as do as some of the city's best restaurants. Standing in the north shadow of the World Trade Center, TriBeCa suffered greatly in the wake of the disaster; however, it has recovered beautifully.

Robert DeNiro gave the neighborhood a boost when he established the TriBeCa Film Center.

Still, historic streets like White (especially the Federal-style building at no. 2) and Harrison (the stretch west from Greenwich St.) evoke a bygone, more human-scaled New York, as do a few hold-out businesses and old-world pubs. I love this neighborhood because it seems to have brought together the old city and the new without bastardizing either. Because retail spaces are usually a few doors apart rather than right on top of one another, it manages to be more peaceful than other neighborhoods. It also happens to be home to one of my favorite budget hotels, the Cosmopolitan (p. 98).

The main uptown-downtown drag is **West Broadway** (2 blocks to the west of Broadway). Consider the Franklin Street subway station on the 1/9 line to be your gateway to the heart of the action. (Note that the nos. 1 and 2 trains will stop there until the 1 and 9 trains are running normally again.) Take your map; the streets are a maze.

Chinatown New York City's most famous ethnic enclave is bursting past its traditional boundaries and encroaching on Little Italy. The former marshlands northeast of City Hall and below Canal Street, from Broadway to the Bowery, are where Chinese immigrants were forced to live in the 1870s. This booming neighborhood is a conglomeration of Asian populations. It offers tasty cheap eats in cuisines from Sichuan to Hunan to Cantonese to Vietnamese to Thai. Exotic shops offer strange foods, herbs, and souvenirs; bargains on clothing and leather. The area is also home to sweatshops and doesn't have quite the character you'd find in San Francisco, although it does feel authentic. Walking down Canal Street, peering into the myriad stores and watching crabs cut loose from their

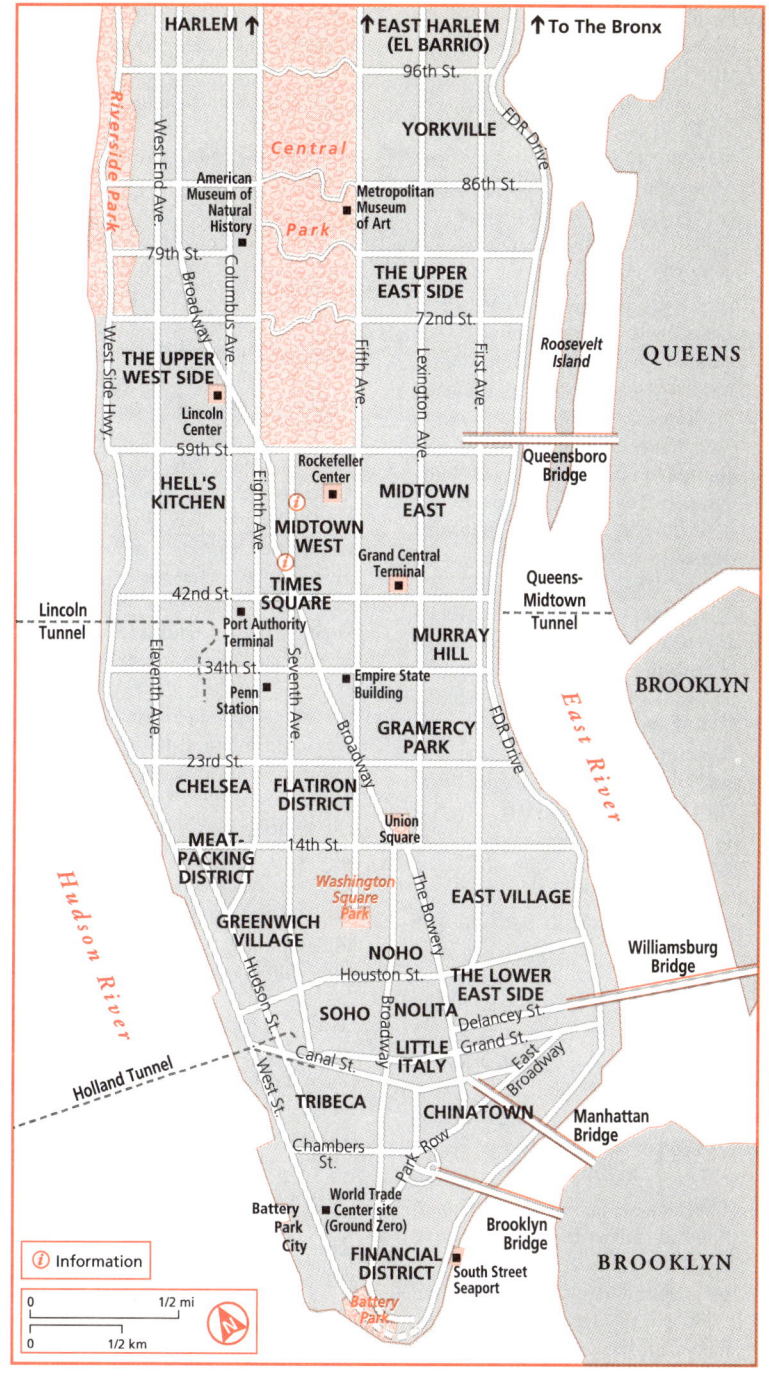

handlers at the exotic fish markets, is some of the city's best free entertainment.

The Canal Street (J, M, Z, N, R, 6, Q, W) station will get you to the heart of the action. The streets are crowded during the day and empty out after around 9pm; they remain quite safe, but the neighborhood is more enjoyable during the bustle.

Little Italy Near Chinatown is Little Italy, just as ethnic if not quite so vibrant, and compelling for its own culinary treats. Traditionally the area east of Broadway between Houston and Canal streets, the community is shrinking, due to the encroachment of Chinatown. It's now limited mainly to **Mulberry Street,** where you'll find most restaurants, and a few offshoots. With rents going up in the trendy Lower East Side, a few chic spots are moving in, further intruding on the old-world landscape. Since the Grand Street subway station is scheduled to be closed until 2005 (except for a shuttle service from the Broadway–Lafayette St. station), the best way to reach Little Italy is to walk east from the Spring Street station, on the no. 6 line, to Mulberry Street; turn south for Little Italy (you can't miss the year-round red, green, and white street decorations). September, when Mulberry Street comes alive during the Feast of San Gennaro, is a great time to visit (the 2001 feast was cancelled due to the terrorist attacks; check with the NYCVB, p. 66, for status of the 2002 festival).

The Lower East Side The Lower East Side boasts the best of old and new New York: Witness the stretch of Houston between Forsyth and Allen streets, where Yoneh Shimmel's Knish Shop sits next to the city's newest art-house cinema—and both are thriving. Some say that the Lower East Side has come full circle: Hipster 20-somethings have been drawn back to the neighborhood their immigrant grandparents worked to escape.

Of all the successive waves of immigrants and refugees who passed through this densely populated tenement neighborhood from the mid–19th century to the 1920s, eastern European Jews left the most lasting impression. Drugs and crime supplanted the Jewish communities, which first popped up between Houston and Canal streets, east of the Bowery, dragging the Lower East Side into the gutter—until recently. The neighborhood has experienced a renaissance over the last few years, and makes a fascinating stop for both nostalgia and nightlife hounds. Still, the blocks south of Houston can be grungy, so walk with confidence and care after dark.

There are some remnants of what was once the largest Jewish population in America along **Orchard Street,** where you'll find great bargain hunting in its many old-world fabric, clothing, and accessories stores still thriving between the club-clothes boutiques and trendy lounges. Keep in mind that many shops close early on Friday and all day on Saturday (the Jewish Sabbath). The expanding trendy set can be found in the blocks between Allen and Clinton streets south of Houston and north of Delancey, with more shops, bars, and restaurants popping up in the blocks to the east every day.

This area is not well served by the subway (one cause for its years of decline), so your best bet is to take the F train to Second Avenue and walk east on Houston; when you see Katz's Deli, you'll know you've arrived. You can also reach the neighborhood from the Delancey

> **Tips Visiting the Lower East Side**
>
> The **Lower East Side Business Improvement District** operates a visitor center at 261 Broome St., between Orchard and Allen streets (© **888/825-8374** or 212/226-9010), open daily from 10am to 4pm. Stop in for an Orchard Street Bargain District shopping guide, plus other information on this historic yet hip 'hood. You can also find shopping, dining, and nightlife directories online at www.lowereastsideny.com.

Street station on the F line, and the Essex Street station on the J, M, and Z lines.

SoHo & Nolita No relation to the London neighborhood of the same name, **SoHo** got its name as an abbreviation of "*So*uth of *Ho*uston Street". This fashionable neighborhood extends down to Canal Street, between Sixth Avenue to the west and Lafayette Street (1 block east of Broadway) to the east. It's accessible by subway: Take the N or R to Prince Street; the C, E, or 6 to Spring Street; or the F or V train to the Broadway-Lafayette stop (the B, D, and Q trains will not be serving Broadway-Lafayette during the life of this book due to Manhattan Bridge construction).

An industrial zone during the 19th century, SoHo retains the cast-iron architecture of the era, and in many places, cobblestone peeks out beneath the asphalt. In the early 1960s, cutting-edge artists began to occupy the drab, deteriorating buildings, turning it into the city's trendiest neighborhood. SoHo is now a prime example of urban gentrification and a major attraction thanks to its impeccably restored buildings, fashionable restaurants, and stylish boutiques. On weekends, the cobbled streets and narrow sidewalks are crowded with shoppers, with the prime action between Broadway and Sullivan Street north of Grand Street.

Some critics claim that SoHo is a victim of its popularity—witness the departure of several imaginative galleries and independent boutiques for TriBeCa and Chelsea as well as the influx of suburban chains like J. Crew and Victoria's Secret. However, SoHo is still one of the best shopping neighborhoods in the city, and few are more fun to browse. High-end street peddlers set up along the boutique-lined sidewalks, hawking jewelry, coffee-table books, and their own art. At night, the neighborhood is a terrific, albeit pricey, dining and barhopping neighborhood (I recommend some affordable options in chapter 6).

In recent years SoHo has been crawling east, taking over Mott and Mulberry streets—and Elizabeth Street in particular—north of Kenmare Street, an area now known as **Nolita** for its *No*rth of *Li*ttle I*ta*ly location. Nolita is becoming increasingly well known for its shopping. Some of the city's most promising clothing designers have set up shop, but don't expect bargains. Good, affordable restaurants abound, making the neighborhood well worth a browse. Taking the 6 to Spring Street will get you closest by subway, but it's a short walk east from SoHo proper.

The East Village & NoHo The **East Village,** which extends between 14th Street and Houston Street, from Broadway east to First Avenue and beyond to Alphabet City—avenues A, B, C, and D—is where the city's bohemia has gone.

Impressions

Nobody's going to come from the boondocks anymore and live in SoHo and be an artist. You can't afford to park there, let alone live there.
—Pete Hamill

Once, flower children tripped along St. Marks Place and listened to music at the Fillmore East; now the East Village is a mix of ethnic and trendy restaurants, upstart clothing designers and kitschy boutiques, punk-rock clubs (yep, still), and folk cafes—plus a half-dozen or so Off-Broadway theaters—all of which give the neighborhood a youthful vibe and a low-budget appeal for visitors and locals alike. In fact, you'll find the city's highest concentration of high-quality budget dining in these precincts.

The city has made a huge impact on the East Village, but there's still a seedy element that some won't find appealing—and some will. I love the East Village more than the West Village for its melting-pot vibe. Now yuppies and other ladder-climbing types make their homes alongside Russian immigrants who have lived in the neighborhood forever, and the cross-dressers and squatters who settled here in between. The neighborhood still embraces ethnic diversity, with elements of its Ukrainian and Irish heritage, while more recent immigrants have taken over 6th Street between First and Second avenues, now called "Little India."

The East Village isn't very subway accessible; unless you're traveling along 14th Street (the L line will drop you off at Third and First aves.), take the 4, 5, 6, N, R, Q, or W to 14th Street/Union Square; the N, R to 8th Street; or the 6 to Astor Place and walk east.

Until 1998 or so, **Alphabet City** resisted gentrification. No more. Bolstered by a major real-estate boom, this way-east area of the East Village has blossomed. Bistros and smart shops are popping up on every corner. Nevertheless, the neighborhood can get deserted late at night, since it's generally the province of locals. It's far off the subway lines, so know where you're going if you venture here.

The southwestern section of the East Village, around Broadway and Lafayette between Bleecker and 4th streets, is called **NoHo** (for *No*rth of *Ho*uston), and has a completely different character. As you might have guessed, this area has developed more like its neighbor to the south, SoHo. Here you'll find trendy lounges, stylish restaurants, cutting-edge designers, and upscale antiques shops. NoHo is wonderful fun to browse; the Bleecker Street stop on the no. 6 line will land you in the heart of it, and the Broadway-Lafayette stop on the F/V line will drop you at its southern edge.

Greenwich Village Tree-lined streets crisscross and wind, following ancient streams and cow paths. Each block reveals yet another row of Greek Revival town houses, a well-preserved Federal-style house, or a peaceful courtyard or square. This is "the Village," from Broadway west to the Hudson River, bordered by Houston Street to the south and 14th Street to the north. It defies Manhattan's orderly grid system with streets that predate it, and unless you live here, it may be impossible to master the lay of the land—so take a map along.

The Seventh Avenue line (1, 2, 3, 9) is the area's main subway artery, while the West 4th Street stop (where the A, C, and E lines meet the F and V lines) serves as its central hub. (Note that, due to rail work, the B, D, and Q subway trains will not be serving W. 4th St. during the life of this book.)

Nineteenth-century artists like Mark Twain, Edgar Allan Poe, Henry James, and Winslow Homer first gave the Village its reputation for embracing the unconventional. Artists like Edward Hopper and Jackson Pollock were drawn in, writers like Eugene O'Neill, e. e. cummings, and Dylan Thomas. Radical thinkers from John Reed to Upton Sinclair basked in the neighborhood's liberal ethos, and beatniks Allen Ginsberg, Jack Kerouac, and William Burroughs dug the free-swinging atmosphere. Now the Village is the roost of choice for the young celebrity set, with the likes of Gwyneth Paltrow, Matthew Broderick and Sarah Jessica Parker drawn by its historic, low-rise charms. Gentrification and escalating real-estate values conspire to push out the artistic element, but culture and counterculture still rub shoulders in cafes, jazz clubs, neighborhood bars, off-Broadway theaters, and an endless variety of tiny shops and restaurants. With a few charming and affordable hotels (see chapter 5), the Village makes a great base for visitors who prefer to avoid more touristy areas in favor of a quirkier, residential view of the city.

The Village is probably the most chameleon-like of Manhattan's neighborhoods. Some of the highest-priced real estate in the city runs along lower Fifth Avenue, which dead-ends at **Washington Square Park.** Serpentine **Bleecker Street** stretches through most of the neighborhood and is emblematic of the area's historical bent. The anything-goes attitude in the Village has fostered a large gay community around **Christopher Street** and Sheridan Square. The streets west of Seventh Avenue, an area known as the **West Village,** boast a more relaxed vibe and some of the city's most charming and historic brownstones. Three colleges—New York University, Parsons School of Design, and the New School for Social Research—keep the area thinking young, which explains the popularity of 8th Street, lined with shops selling cheap, hip clothes.

Streets are often crowded with weekend warriors and teenagers, especially on Bleecker, West 4th, 8th, and surrounding streets, and have been known to become increasingly sketchy west of Seventh Avenue in the late hours, especially on weekends. Keep an eye on your wallet when navigating the throngs. And Washington Square Park was cleaned up a couple of years back, but it's still best to stay out after dark.

Midtown

Chelsea & the Meat-Packing District Chelsea has come on strong in recent years as a hip address, especially for the gay community. A low-rise composite of town houses, tenements, lofts, and factories, the neighborhood comprises roughly the area west of Sixth Avenue from 14th to 30th streets. (Sixth Ave. below 23rd St. is considered part of the Flatiron District; see below.) Chelsea has also evolved into one of the city's best-value accommodations neighborhoods for travelers looking for something special as well as affordable (see chapter 5). Its main arteries are Seventh and Eighth avenues, and it's primarily served by the C, E and 1, 9 subway lines.

Where to Check Your E-mail in the City that Never Sleeps

You don't have to be out of touch while you travel. There are ways to get your e-mail using any computer.

Your **Internet Service Provider** (ISP) may have a Web-based interface that lets you access your e-mail on computers other than your own. Just find out how it works before you leave home.

Or check out **www.mail2web.com**. This free service allows you to type in your regular e-mail address and password and retrieve your e-mail from any Web browser, as long as your home ISP hasn't blocked it with a firewall.

Or open a free mail account with a Web-based e-mail provider, such as **Hotmail (hotmail.com)** or **Yahoo! Mail (mail.yahoo.com)**. Your home ISP may be able to forward your home e-mail to the Web-based account.

All you'll need to check your e-mail away from home is a Web connection, available via your hotel's business center or cash-and-credit-card Internet-access machine (which many hotels now feature in the lobby), as well as Internet cafes and copy shops through the city. After logging on, point the browser to your ISP. Enter your user name and password, and you'll have access to your e-mail, usually for a few dollars an hour.

The **Times Square Visitors Center,** 1560 Broadway, between 46th and 47th streets (© **212/768-1560;** open daily 8am–8pm), has computer terminals that you can use to send e-mails courtesy of Yahoo!. You can even send an electronic postcard with a photo of yourself home to Mom.

The **Chelsea Piers** sports complex to the far west and a host of shops (both unique boutiques and big names like Williams-Sonoma), well-priced bistros, and bars along the main drags have contributed to the area's rebirth. Even the Hotel Chelsea—the neighborhood's most famous architectural and literary landmark, where Thomas Wolfe and Arthur Miller wrote, Bob Dylan composed "Sad-Eyed Lady of the Low Land," Viva and Edie Sedgwick of Andy Warhol fame lived, and Sid Vicious killed girlfriend Nancy Spungeon—has undergone a renovation. Prices put it beyond reach of most budget travelers, but pop into the lobby if you're a pop-culture buff. You'll find a number of very popular flea markets set up in parking lots along Sixth Avenue, between 24th and 27th streets, on the weekends.

One of the most recent trends in Chelsea has been the establishment of **West Chelsea** (from Ninth Ave. west) and the adjacent **Meat-Packing District** (south of West Chelsea in the far west Village, roughly from 17th St. to Little West 12th St.) as the style-setting neighborhoods for the 21st century. What SoHo was in the '60s, this industrial west world (dubbed "the Lower West Side" by *New York* magazine) is today. New restaurants, cutting-edge shopping, and hot nightspots pop up daily in the still-beefy Meat-Packing District, while the area from West 22nd to West 29th streets between Tenth

Open 24/7 in the heart of Times Square, **easyEverything** ⭐, 235 W. 42nd St., between Seventh and Eighth avenues (📞 **212/398-0775**; www.easyeverything.com), is the first stateside branch of a worldwide web of Internet cafes. With 15-inch flat-screen monitors and superfast T-3 connections, this mammoth place makes accessing the Internet cheap through high volume: Access is available for $1, and the length of time that buys you fluctuates depending on the occupancy at the time you log on. This generally works out to the cheapest Web time you can buy in the city.

CyberCafe (www.cyber-cafe.com)—in Times Square at 250 W. 49th St., between Broadway and Eighth Avenue (📞 **212/333-4109**), and in SoHo at 273 Lafayette St., at Prince Street (📞 **212/334-5120**)—is more expensive at $6.40 per half-hour, with a half-hour minimum (it's $3.20 for every subsequent 15 min.). But their T1 lines give you speedy access, and they offer a full range of other cyber, copy, fax, and printing services.

Kinko's (www.kinkos.com) charges 30¢ per minute ($15 per hr.) and is open at 100 Wall St., at Water Street (📞 **212/269-0024**); near City Hall at 105 Duane St., between Broadway and Church Street (📞 **212/406-1220**); 250 E. Houston St., between avenues A and B (📞 **212/253-9020**); 21 Astor Place, between Broadway and Lafayette Street in the Village (📞 **212/228-9511**); 245 Seventh Ave., at 24th Street (📞 **212/929-2679**); 60 W. 40th St., between Fifth and Sixth avenues (📞 **212/921-1060**); 221 W. 72nd St., at Broadway (📞 **212/362-5288**); and about a billion other locations around town.

and Eleventh avenues is home to the cutting edge of today's art scene, with West 26th the unofficial "gallery row." This area is still seriously industrial and in the early stages of transition. With galleries and bars in converted warehouses and former meat lockers, browsing can be frustrating, and the sometimes-desolate streets a tad intimidating. Your best bet is to have a destination in mind, be it a restaurant, gallery, or nightclub, before you come.

The Flatiron District, Union Square & Gramercy Park These adjoining and at places overlapping neighborhoods are some of the city's most appealing. Their streets have been rediscovered by New Yorkers and visitors alike, largely thanks to the boom-to-bust dot-com revolution of the last half-dozen or so years; the Flatiron District served as its heart and earned the nickname "Silicon Alley." These neighborhoods boast great shopping and dining, plus a central location that's hard to beat (and a handful of affordable hotels). The commercial spaces are often large expanses with witty designs and graceful columns.

The **Flatiron District** lies south of 23rd Street to 14th Street, between Broadway and Sixth Avenue, and centers around the historic Flatiron Building on 23rd (so named for its triangular shape) and Park Avenue South, which has become a sophisticated Restaurant Row. Below 23rd Street along Sixth Avenue (once known as the Ladies'

Tips Touring Tip

If you'd like to tour a particular neighborhood with an expert, call **Big Apple Greeter** (© **212/669-8159;** www.bigapplegreeter.org) at least 1 week ahead of your arrival. This nonprofit organization has specially trained volunteers who take visitors around town for a 2- to 4-hour tour of a specific neighborhood. And they say New York isn't friendly!

Mile shopping district), discounters like Filene's Basement, Bed Bath & Beyond, and others have moved in. The shopping gets classier on Fifth Avenue, where you'll find a mix of national names and hip boutiques. Lined with Oriental-carpet dealers and high-end fixture stores, Broadway has become the city's home-furnishings alley; its crowning jewel is the and justifiably famous ABC Carpet & Home.

Union Square is the hub of the area; the N, R, 4, 5, 6, and L trains stop here, as do Q and W trains (until 2004), making it easy to reach. Long in the shadows of the more bustling (Times and Herald) and high-toned (Washington) squares, Union Square has experienced a renaissance in the last decade. Local businesses joined forces with the city to rid the park of drug dealers, and now it's a delightful place to spend an afternoon. Union Square is best known as the setting for New York's premier greenmarket every Monday, Wednesday, Friday, and Saturday. In-line skaters take over the space in the after-work hours. A number of hip and affordable restaurants rim the square, as do superstores like Toys"R"Us, the city's best Barnes & Noble superstore, and a Virgin Megastore.

From about 16th to 23rd streets, east from Park Avenue South to about Second Avenue, is the leafy, largely residential district known as **Gramercy Park.** The pity of the district is that so few can enjoy the park: Built by Samuel Ruggles in the 1830s to attract buyers to the area, it is the only private park in the city and locked to all but those who live on its perimeter (your windows have to look over the park for you to have a key). At the southern end of Lexington Avenue (at 21st St.), it is one of the most peaceful spots in the city. If you know someone who has a key, go there. Or book a room at the midpriced Gramercy Park Hotel (p. 109), whose guests have park privileges.

At the northern edge, fronting the Flatiron Building on 23rd Street and Fifth Avenue, is lovely little **Madison Square.** Across from its northeast corner stood Stanford White's original Madison Square Garden (in whose roof garden White was murdered in 1906 by jealous millionaire Harry K. Thaw). It's now presided over by the New York Life Insurance Building, the New York State Supreme Court, and the Metropolitan Life Insurance Company, whose tower, at 700 feet (210m), was the tallest in the world when it was built in 1909.

Midtown West & Times Square
Midtown West, the area from 34th to 59th streets west of Fifth Avenue to the Hudson River, encompasses several famous names: Madison Square Garden, the Garment District, Rockefeller Center, the Theater District, and Times Square. This is New York's tourism central, where you'll find the bright lights

and bustle that draw people from all over the world. This is the city's biggest hotel neighborhood. While there are a lot of budget and mid-priced choices, rates can fluctuate dramatically, since this is where everybody wants to stay; in periods of high demand, even "budget" hotels can price around the $200 mark. You're likely to find your best bargains elsewhere, especially in fall and the holiday season.

The 1, 2, 3, 9 subway line serves the massive neon station at the heart of Times Square, at 42nd Street between Broadway and Seventh Avenue, while the F, V line runs up Sixth Avenue to Rockefeller Center (B and D lines also serve Rockefeller Center, but travel no farther south than 34th St. until Manhattan Bridge work is complete in 2004). The N/R line cuts diagonally across the neighborhood, following the path of Broadway before heading up Seventh Avenue at 42nd Street (the Q and W trains also use this line until 2004). The A, C, E line serves the west side, running along Eighth Avenue.

If you know New York but haven't been here in a few years, you'll be quite surprised by the "new" **Times Square.** Longtime New Yorkers kvetch about the glory days of the peep-show-and-porn-shop Times Square that this cleaned-up version supplanted, but the truth is that it's a successful regentrification. Old theaters have come back to life as Broadway and children's playhouses, and scores of family-friendly restaurants and shops have opened (including the Virgin Megastore on Broadway). Plenty of businesses have moved in—MTV studios overlook Times Square at 1515 Broadway, and *Good Morning America* has its own studio at Broadway and 44th Street. The lights have never been brighter, and Middle America has never been more welcome. Expect dense crowds; it's often tough just to make your way along the sidewalks.

Most of the Broadway theaters light up the streets just off Times Square, in the West 40s just east and west of Broadway. At the heart of the **Theater District,** where Broadway meets Seventh Avenue, is the TKTS booth, where crowds line up to buy discount tickets.

To the west, in the 40s and 50s between Eighth and Tenth avenues, is **Hell's Kitchen,** which has become much nicer than it sounds. The neighborhood resisted gentrification until the mid-1990s but has grown into a charming, less touristy adjunct to the Theater District. Ninth Avenue has blossomed into one of the city's finest dining avenues; stroll along and you'll have a world of affordable cuisine to choose from, from American diner to hearty German to traditional Thai. Stylish boutiques and bars (including a few gay bars) have also popped up in this area. Realtors tried to rename the area Clinton, but locals hold fast to the Hell's Kitchen moniker, clearly delighting in the increasing juxtaposition.

Unlike Times Square, **Rockefeller Center** has needed no renovation. Between 46th and 50th streets from Sixth Avenue east to Fifth, this Art

---

Impressions

I'm opposed to the redevelopment. I think there should be one neighborhood in New York where tourists are afraid to walk.
                —Fran Lebowitz on the "new" Times Square

Manhattan Address Locator

To locate avenue addresses, cancel the last figure, divide by 2, and add (or subtract) the key number below. The answer is the nearest numbered cross street, approximately.

Avenue A: add 3
Avenue B: add 3
Avenue C: add 3
First Avenue: add 3
Second Avenue: add 3
Third Avenue: add 10
Sixth Avenue: subtract 12
Eighth Avenue: add 9
Ninth Avenue: add 13
Tenth Avenue: add 14

Eleventh Avenue: add 15
Amsterdam Avenue: add 59
Columbus Avenue: add 59 or 60
Lexington Avenue: add 22
Madison Avenue: add 27
Park Avenue: add 34
Park Avenue South: add 8
West End Avenue: add 59
York Avenue: add 4

Note special instructions for finding address locations on the following:

Fifth Avenue
63 to 108: add 11
109 to 200: add 13
201 to 400: add 16
401 to 600: add 18
601 to 775: add 20
776 to 1286: cancel last figure of house number and subtract 18 (do not divide house number by 2)

For 1310 to 1494: cancel last figure of house number. For 1310, subtract 20 and for every additional 20 street numbers, increase deduction by 1.

Seventh Avenue
1 to 1800: add 12

above 1800: add 20

Broadway
Anything from 1 to 754 is south of 8th Street, and hence a named street.

756 to 846: subtract 29
847 to 953: subtract 25

above 953: subtract 31

Central Park West
Cancel last figure and add 60.

Riverside Drive
Cancel last figure and

Up to 567: add 72
568 and up: add 78

Deco complex contains some of the city's great architectural gems, which house offices, a number of NBC studios (including *Saturday Night Live, Late Night with Conan O'Brien,* and the glass-walled *Today* show studio at 48th St.), and some upscale boutiques. Holiday time is a great time to be here, as ice-skaters take over the central plaza, the huge Christmas tree twinkles against the night sky, and merry lines wind past the festive holiday windows of Saks Fifth Avenue, across the street.

Along Seventh Avenue south of 42nd Street is the **Garment District,** of little interest to tourists except for its sample sales, where some great new fashions are sold to serious bargain hunters willing to scour the racks (see chapter 8 for details). Other than that, it's a grim commercial area. Between Seventh and Eighth avenues and 31st and 33rd streets, **Penn Station** sits beneath ugly **Madison Square Garden,** where the Rangers, Knicks, and Liberty play. Taking up 34th Street between Sixth and Seventh avenues is **Macy's,** the world's largest department store; exit Macy's at the southeast corner and you'll find more famous-label shopping around **Herald Square.** The blocks around 32nd Street west of Fifth Avenue have developed into a Koreatown, with midpriced hotels and Asian restaurants that offer some of the best-value stays and eats in Midtown.

Midtown West is also home to some of the city's most revered museums and institutions, including **Carnegie Hall,** the **Museum of Modern Art, Radio City Music Hall,** and the *Intrepid* Sea-Air-Space Museum, to name just a few.

Midtown East & Murray Hill Midtown East, the area including Fifth Avenue and everything east from 34th to 59th streets, is the more upscale side of Midtown. This side of town is short of subway trains, served mostly by the Lexington Avenue 4, 5, 6 line.

Midtown East is where you'll find many of the city's grand hotels along Lexington Avenue and near the park at the top of Fifth. The stretch of **Fifth Avenue** from Saks at 49th Street extending to FAO Schwarz at 59th is home to the city's most high-profile haute shopping, including Tiffany & Co. and Bergdorf Goodman, but midpriced names like Banana Republic and Liz Claiborne have moved in over the last 5 years. The stretch of 57th Street between Fifth and Lexington avenues is also known for high-fashion boutiques (Chanel, Hermès) and galleries, but change is underway since names like Levi's and Niketown have arrived. You'll find more spillover along **Madison Avenue,** a great strip for shoe shopping in particular.

Architectural highlights include the recently repolished **Chrysler Building,** with its stylized gargoyles glaring down on passersby; the beaux-arts tour de force that is **Grand Central Terminal; St. Patrick's Cathedral;** and the glorious **Empire State Building.**

Far east, swank Sutton and Beekman places are enclaves of beautiful town houses and tiny pocket parks that look out over the East River. Along the river is the **United Nations,** which isn't officially in New York City, or even the United States, but on a parcel of land belonging to member nations.

Claiming territory east from Madison Avenue, **Murray Hill** begins somewhere north of 23rd Street (the line between it and Gramercy Park is fuzzy), and is most clearly recognizable north of 30th Street to 42nd Street. This brownstone-lined quarter is largely residential, notable for its handful of budget and midpriced hotels. The stretch of Lexington Avenue in the high 20s is **Curry Hill,** and has usurped the East Village's Little India as a destination for inexpensive, good Indian food.

Uptown

The Upper West Side North of 59th Street and encompassing everything west of Central Park, the Upper West Side contains **Lincoln Center,** one of the world's premier performing-arts venues; the **American Museum of Natural History,** whose renovated Dinosaur Halls and Rose Center for Earth and Space garner rave reviews; and a growing number of affordable hotels whose larger-than-Midtown rooms and nice residential location make them some of the best values—and some of my favorite places to stay—in the entire city.

Unlike the more stratified Upper East Side, the Upper West Side is home to an egalitarian mix of middle-class yuppiedom, laid-back wealth (lots of celebs and moneyed media types call Central Park West home), and ethnic families who were here before the gentrification.

The neighborhood runs all the way up to Harlem, around 125th Street, and includes **Morningside Heights,** where you'll find **Columbia University** and the perennial construction project known as the **Cathedral of St. John the Divine.** North of 59th Street is where Eighth Avenue becomes Central Park West, the eastern border of the neighborhood (and the western border of Central Park); Ninth Avenue becomes Columbus Avenue, lined with boutiques and cafes; and Tenth Avenue becomes Amsterdam Avenue, less charming than Columbus to the east and less trafficked than Broadway (whose highlights are the gourmet megamarts Zabar's and Fairway) to the west. Amsterdam in the 70s and 80s has blossomed into a restaurant-and-bar strip the last few years, but becomes sketchy to the north, while Broadway stays safe and pleasant from Lincoln Center in the mid-60s, where Broadway crosscuts Amsterdam, to 125th Street.

Two subway lines serve the area: The 1, 2, 3, 9 line runs up Broadway, while the B and C trains go up Central Park West, stopping outside the Dakota (where John Lennon was shot and Yoko lives) at 72nd Street, and at the Museum of Natural History at 81st Street.

Upper East Side North of 59th Street and east of Central Park is some of the city's most expensive residential real estate. This is New York at its most gentrified: Walk along Fifth and Park avenues, especially between 60th and 80th streets, and you're sure to encounter some of the wizened WASPs and Chanel-suited socialites that make up the most rarefied of the city's population. Madison Avenue from 60th Street well into the 80s is the moneyed crowd's main shopping strip, in recent years vaunting ahead of Hong Kong's Causeway Bay to become the most expensive retail real estate *in the world*. The main attraction of this neighborhood is **Museum Mile,** the stretch of Fifth Avenue fronting Central Park that's home to no fewer than 10 cultural institutions, including Frank Lloyd Wright's **Guggenheim,** and anchored by the **Metropolitan Museum of Art.** But the elegant rows of landmark town houses are worth a look: East 70th Street, from Madison east to Lexington, is one of the world's most charming residential streets. If you want to see where real people live, move east to Third Avenue and beyond; that's where affordable restaurants and active street life start popping up.

A second subway line is in the works, but that's far in the future. For now, the Upper East Side is served by the crowded Lexington Avenue line (4, 5, 6 trains) and rather slow buses, so wear your walking shoes (or bring taxi fare) if you head here to explore.

Harlem Now that Bill Clinton has moved his post-presidential office—and more than a few Secret Service agents—into this uptown neighborhood, the world has heard the news about Harlem, which has benefited from a dramatic image makeover in the last few years.

Harlem is really two areas. Harlem proper stretches from river

> **Finds Discovering Harlem**
> You'll find sightseeing, restaurants, arts, and nightlife information about Harlem in this book. But if you want to learn more, a great source is the **Harlem Association for Travel & Tourism** website at www.hatt.org.

to river, beginning at 125th Street on the West Side and 96th Street on the East Side. East of Fifth Avenue, **Spanish Harlem** (El Barrio) runs between East 100th and East 125th streets. Harlem proper is benefiting from the revitalization that has swept much of the city, with national retailers moving in, restaurants and nightspots opening, and visitors touring historic sites related to the Golden Age of African-American culture, when bands like the Count Basie and Duke Ellington orchestras played the Cotton Club and Sugar Cane Club, and literary giants like Langston Hughes and James Baldwin soaked up the scene. Some houses date back to when the area was a country retreat and represent some of the best brownstone mansions in the city. On Sugar Hill (from 143rd to 155th sts., between St. Nicholas and Edgecombe aves.) and Striver's Row (W. 139th St. between Adam Clayton Powell Jr. and Frederick Douglass blvds.) are a significant number of fine town houses. For cultural visits, there's the Morris-Jumel Mansion, the Schomburg Center, the Studio Museum, and the Apollo Theatre.

Do come to Harlem—it's one of the city's most vital, historic neighborhoods, and no other feels quite so energized. Your best bet is to take a guided tour (see "Affordable Sightseeing Tours," in chapter 7); if you come on your own, do it during the day. Don't wander without a plan, especially at night. If you head up after dark to a restaurant or club, be clear about where you're going and stay alert.

Washington Heights & Inwood
At the northern tip of Manhattan, Washington Heights (the area from 155th St. to Dyckman St., with adjacent Inwood running to the tip) is home to a large segment of Manhattan's Latino community, plus an increasing number of yuppies who don't mind trading a half-hour subway commute to Midtown for lower rents. **Fort Tryon Park** and **the Cloisters** are the two big reasons visitors come up this way. The Cloisters houses the Metropolitan Museum of Art's medieval collection, with excellent views across the Hudson to the Palisades.

2 Getting Around

Frankly, Manhattan's transportation systems are a marvel. It's miraculous that so many people can gather on this little island and move around on it. For the most part, you can get where you're going pretty easily using some combination of subways, buses, and cabs; this section will tell you how to do just that.

But between traffic gridlock and subway delays, sometimes you just can't get there from here—unless you walk. Walking can be the fastest way to navigate the island. During rush hours, you'll beat car traffic on foot, as taxis and buses stop and groan at gridlocked corners (don't even *try* going crosstown in a cab or bus in Midtown at midday). You'll also see a lot more by walking than by riding beneath the street or flying by in a cab. So pack comfortable shoes and hit

> **Tips On the Sidewalks**
>
> New Yorkers stride across wide, crowded pavements without any regard for the traffic light, weaving through crowds, dodging taxis and buses whose drivers. **Never take your walking cues from the locals.** Wait for walk signals and always use crosswalks—don't jaywalk. Do otherwise and you could quickly end up as a flattened statistic.
>
> **Always pay attention to the traffic flow.** Walk as if you're driving, staying to the right. At intersections, keep an eye out for drivers who don't yield, turn without looking, or think a yellow traffic light means "Hurry up!" Unfortunately, most bicyclists seem to think that the traffic laws don't apply to them; they'll often blithely fly through red lights and dash the wrong way on one-way streets, so be on your guard.
>
> For more safety tips, see "Playing It Safe," later in this chapter.

the pavement—it's the best, cheapest, and most appealing way to experience the city.

BY SUBWAY

Run by the **Metropolitan Transit Authority** (MTA), the much-maligned subway system is actually the best way to travel around New York, especially during rush hours. Some three-and-a-half million people a day agree, as it's their primary mode of transportation. The subway is quick, inexpensive, relatively safe, and pretty efficient, as well as being a genuine New York experience.

The subway runs 24 hours a day, 7 days a week. The rush-hour crushes are roughly from 8 to 9:30am and from 5 to 6:30pm on weekdays; the rest of the time the trains are relatively uncrowded.

PAYING YOUR WAY

The subway fare is $1.50 (half price for seniors and those with disabilities), and children under 44 inches tall ride free (up to three per adult). *Note:* As of this writing, a fare increase was being discussed, so it's entirely possible that the fare might be higher by the time you visit.

While **tokens** still exist (they'll soon be phased out eventually), most people pay fares with the **MetroCard,** a magnetically encoded card that debits the fare when swiped through the turnstile (or the fare box on a bus). Once you're in the system, you can transfer to any subway line that you can reach without exiting your station. MetroCards—*not* tokens—also allow you **free transfers** between the bus and subway within a 2-hour period.

MetroCards can be purchased from each station's staffed booth, where you must pay cash; at the ATM-style vending machines located in just about every subway station in the city accept cash, credit cards, and debit cards; and from a MetroCard merchant, such as most Rite Aid drugstores or Hudson News at Penn Station and Grand Central Terminal; or at the MTA information desk at the Times Square Visitor Center, 1560 Broadway, between 46th and 47th streets.

MetroCards come in a few different configurations:

Pay-Per-Ride MetroCards, which can be used for up to four people by swiping up to four times (bring the whole family). You can put any amount from $3 (two rides) to $80 on your card. Every time you put $15 on your Pay-Per-Ride MetroCard, it's automatically credited 10%—that's one free ride for every $15. You can buy Pay-Per-Ride MetroCards in any denomination at any subway station; many stations have MetroCard vending machines, which allow you to buy MetroCards using your credit or debit card. MetroCards are also available from shops and newsstands in $15 and $30 values. You can refill your card until the expiration date, usually about a year from the date of purchase.

Unlimited-Ride MetroCards, which can't be used for more than one person at a time or more frequently than 18-minute intervals, are available in four values: the **daily Fun Pass,** which allows you a day's worth of unlimited subway and bus rides for $4; the **7-Day MetroCard,** for $17; and the **30-Day MetroCard,** for $63. Seven- and 30-day Unlimited-Ride MetroCards can be purchased at any subway station or MetroCard merchant. Fun Passes cannot be purchased at token booths—you can only buy them from a MetroCard vending machine; from a MetroCard merchant; or at the MTA information desk at the Times Square Visitor Center. Unlimited-Ride MetroCards go into effect not at the time you buy them but the first time you use them—so if you buy a card on Monday and don't begin to use it until Wednesday, Wednesday is when the clock starts ticking. A Fun Pass is good from the first time you use it until 3am the next day, while 7- and 30-day MetroCards run out at midnight on the last day. These MetroCards cannot be refilled; throw them out once they've been used up and buy a new one.

Tips for using your MetroCard: The MetroCard swiping mechanisms at turnstiles are the source of much grousing among subway riders. If you swipe too fast or too slow, the turnstile will ask you to swipe again. If this happens, ***do not move to a different turnstile,*** or you may end up paying twice. If you've tried repeatedly and really can't make it work, tell the token-booth clerk; chances are good, though, that you'll get the movement down after a couple of uses.

If you're not sure how much money you have left, or when the card expires, use the station's MetroCard Reader, usually near the station entrance or the token booth (on buses, the fare box will also provide you with this information).

To locate the nearest MetroCard merchant, or for any other MetroCard questions, call © **800/METROCARD** or 212/METROCARD (212/638-7622) Monday through Friday between 7am and 11pm, Saturday and Sunday from 9am to 5pm. Or go online to **www.mta.nyc.ny.us/metrocard**, which can give you a full rundown of MetroCard merchants in the tri-state (N.Y., N.J., and Conn.) area.

USING THE SYSTEM

As you can see from the full-color subway map on the inside back cover, the subway system basically mimics the lay of the land above ground, with most lines in Manhattan running north and south, and a few lines east and west.

To go up and down the east side of Manhattan (and to the Bronx and Brooklyn), take the 4, 5, or 6 train.

To travel up and down the west side (and also to the Bronx and Brooklyn), take the 1, 2, 3, or 9 line; the A, C, E, or F line; or the B or D line.

The N, R, Q, and W lines first cut diagonally across town from east to west and then snake under Seventh Avenue before shooting out to Queens.

The crosstown S line, the Shuttle, runs back and forth between Times Square and Grand Central Terminal. Farther downtown, across 14th Street, the L line works its own crosstown magic.

Note: For service changes, see "Subway Service Interruption Notes," below.

Lines have assigned colors on subway maps and trains—red for the 1, 2, 3, 9 line; green for the 4, 5, and 6 trains; and so on—but nobody refers to them by color. Always use the number or letter when asking questions. Within Manhattan,

Subway Service Interruption Notes

Due to ongoing work by the Metropolitan Transit Authority (MTA) on the Manhattan Bridge, and the World Trade Center disaster—subway service will experience numerous interruptions during the life of this book.

Changes resulting from **Manhattan Bridge work** are clear. So far, the rerouting of the B, D, and Q lines serving Sixth Avenue, Chinatown, Brooklyn, and Queens seems to be working out well. Here's a summary of the changes affecting visitors to Manhattan:

- Chinatown's Grand Street subway station is served only by a shuttle train that runs between SoHo's Broadway-Lafayette Street station and Grand Street. To reach Chinatown, take the F train to Broadway–Lafayette Street (no longer served by the B, D, or Q trains) and change to the gray S train to Grand Street; or take the N or R train to Canal Street instead.
- The 34th Street/Herald Square station is now the southern terminus of the B and D trains. For Sixth Avenue service below 34th Street, use the F train, or the new V train, which makes all local stops in Manhattan along the Sixth Avenue line from Second Avenue at the south end to 47th–50th streets/Rockefeller Center before veering east to Queens.
- Q trains now run express along the N and R track (which runs along Broadway) instead of along their normal Sixth Avenue path in Manhattan, as does the new temporary (until 2004) W train. Both the Q and W trains stop at express stops only from 34th Street south.

Kudos to the MTA, because train interruptions resulting from the **World Trade Center disaster** had largely been rectified. Service interruptions are mostly limited to the 1 and 9 lines, which run local along the west side of Manhattan to the southern tip of the island. At press time, the nos. 1 and 2 trains were running local to Chambers Street, where they veered to Brooklyn; no. 3 trains run express from 14th Street north; and no. 9 service was suspended altogether.

However, 1, 2, 3, and 9 service was scheduled to return to normal—with 2/3 trains running express and 1/9 trains running local to South Ferry—by autumn 2002. All stations on the 1/9 line should reopen with the exception of Cortlandt Street (which was the World Trade Center stop on this line).

The subway map inside the back cover of this book was as accurate as possible at press time. However, since reopening of the 1/9 line could be delayed and service is always subject to change, your best bet is to contact the **MTA** for the latest details; call ✆ **718/330-1234**, or visit **www.mta.nyc.ny.us**, where you'll find system updates that are timely and clear. Once in town, you can stop at the MTA desk at the **Times Square Visitors Center,** 1560 Broadway, between 46th and 47th streets (where Broadway meets Seventh Ave.) to pick up the latest subway map. (You can also ask for one at any token booth, but they might not always be stocked.)

the distinction between numbered trains that share the same line is usually that some are express and others are local. **Express trains** often skip about three stops for each one that they make; express stops are indicated on subway maps with a white (rather than solid) circle. Local stops usually come about 9 blocks apart.

Directions are almost always indicated using "Uptown" (northbound) and "Downtown" (southbound), so be sure to know what direction you want to head in. The outsides of some subway entrances are marked UPTOWN ONLY or DOWNTOWN ONLY; read carefully, as it's easy to head in the wrong direction. Once you're on the platform, check the signs overhead to make sure that the train you're waiting for will be traveling in the right direction. If you do make a mistake, it's a good idea to wait for an express station, like 14th Street or 42nd Street, so you can get off and change for the other direction without paying again.

The days of graffiti-covered cars are gone, but the stations—and an increasing number of trains—are not nearly as clean as they could be. Trains are air-conditioned (move to the next car if yours isn't), though during the dog days of summer the platforms can be sweltering. In theory, all subway cars have PA systems to allow you to hear the conductor's announcements, but they don't always work well. It's a good idea to move to a car with a working PA system in case sudden service changes are announced that you'll want to know about.

For **subway safety tips,** see "Playing It Safe," later in this chapter.

BY BUS

Less expensive than taxis and more pleasant than subways (they provide a mobile sightseeing window on Manhattan), MTA buses are a good transportation option. Their big drawback: They can get stuck in traffic, sometimes making it quicker to walk. They also stop every couple of blocks, rather than the eight or nine blocks that local subways traverse between stops. So for long distances, the subway is your best bet; but for short distances or traveling crosstown, try the bus.

> *Tips* **For More Bus & Subway Information**
>
> For transit information, call the Metropolitan Transit Authority's **MTA/New York City Transit's Travel Information Center** at ✆ **718/330-1234.** Automated information is available at this number 24 hours a day, and agents are on hand to answer your questions and provide directions daily from 6am to 9pm. For online information, visit **www.mta.nyc.ny.us**; kudos to the MTA, because the information on the site is always current.
>
> To request maps, call the Customer Assistance Line at ✆ **718/330-3322** (although recent service changes may not be reflected on printed maps). Riders with disabilities should direct inquiries to ✆ **718/596-8585;** hearing-impaired riders can call ✆ **718/596-8273.** For MetroCard information, call ✆ **212/638-7622** weekdays from 7 to 11am, weekends from 9am to 5pm, or go online to **www.mta.nyc.ny.us/metrocard**.
>
> You can get bus and subway maps and additional information at most information centers (see "Visitor Information," earlier in this chapter). A helpful MTA transit information desk is located at the Times Square Visitor Center, 1560 Broadway, between 46th and 47th streets, where you can also buy MetroCards. Maps are sometimes available in subway stations (ask at the token booth), but rarely on buses.

> **Value Money-Saving Transit Tips: Free Transfers**
>
> If you pay your subway or bus fare with a **MetroCard,** you can transfer to another bus or to the subway (or from the subway to a bus) for up to 2 hours. You don't need to do anything special: Just swipe your card at the token box or turnstile, and the automated system keeps track.
>
> If you use a token or coins to board a bus and need to transfer to another line, request a free **transfer slip** that allows you to change to an intersecting bus route only (transfer points are listed on the transfer itself) within 1 hour of issue. Transfer slips cannot be used to enter the subway.

PAYING YOUR WAY

Like the subway fare, **bus fare** is $1.50, half price for seniors and riders with disabilities, free for children under 44 inches (up to three per adult). As of this writing, a fare increase was being discussed, so it's possible that the fare might be higher by the time you visit. The fare is payable with a **MetroCard,** a **token** (for now, anyway), or **exact change.** Bus drivers don't make change, and fare boxes don't accept dollar bills or pennies. You can't purchase MetroCards or tokens on the bus, so get them before you board; for details on where to get them, see "Paying Your Way" under "By Subway," above.

USING THE SYSTEM

You can't flag a city bus down—you have to wait at a bus stop. **Bus stops** are located every 2 or 3 blocks on the right-side corner of the street (facing the direction of traffic flow). They're marked by a curb painted yellow and a blue-and-white sign with a bus emblem and the route number or numbers. Guide-A-Ride boxes at most stops show a route map and a somewhat optimistic schedule.

Almost every major avenue has its own **bus route.** They run either north or south: downtown on Fifth, uptown on Madison, downtown on Lexington, uptown on Third, and so on. There are **crosstown buses** at strategic locations all around town: 8th Street (eastbound); 9th (westbound); 14th, 23rd, 34th, and 42nd (east- and westbound); 49th (eastbound); 50th (westbound); 57th (east- and westbound); 65th (eastbound across the West Side, through the park, and then north on Madison, continuing east on 68th to York Ave.); 67th (westbound on the East Side to Fifth Ave. and then south on Fifth, continuing west on 66th St. through the park and across the West Side to West End Ave.); and 79th, 86th, 96th, 116th, and 125th (east- and westbound). Some bus routes, however, are erratic: The M104, for example, starts at the East River, then turns at Eighth Avenue and goes up Broadway. The buses of the Fifth Avenue line go up Madison or Sixth and follow various routes around the city.

Most routes operate 24 hours a day, but service is infrequent at night. Some say that New York buses have a herding instinct: They come only in groups. During rush hour, main routes have "limited-stop" buses, identifiable by the orange card in the front window; they stop only at major cross streets.

To make sure the bus you're boarding goes where you're going, check the maps on the sign that's at every bus stop, get your hands on a route map (see "For More Bus & Subway Information," above), or **just ask.** The drivers are helpful, as long as you don't hold up the line too long.

While traveling, look out the window not only to take in the sights but also to keep track of cross streets. Signal for a stop by pressing the tape strip above and beside the windows and along the metal straps, about 1 block before you want to stop. Exit through the back doors (not the front door) by pushing on the yellow tape strip; the doors open automatically (pushing on the handles is useless). Most city buses are equipped with wheelchair lifts, making buses the preferable mode of public transportation for wheelchair-bound travelers; for more on this topic, see "Tips for Travelers with Special Needs," in chapter 2. Buses also "kneel," lowering down to the curb to make boarding easier.

BY TAXI

If you don't want to deal with public transportation, finding an address that might be a few blocks from the subway station, or sharing your ride with three-and-a-half million other people, then take a taxi. The biggest advantages are that cabs can be hailed on any street (provided you find an empty one—often simple, yet at other times nearly impossible) and will take you right to your destination.

Official New York City taxis, licensed by the Taxi and Limousine Commission, are yellow, with the rates printed on the door and a light with a medallion number on the roof. You can hail a taxi on any street. *Never* accept a ride from any other car except an official city yellow cab (private livery cars are not allowed to pick up fares on the street).

If you're planning to take taxis, be prepared to pay. The base fare on entering the cab is $2. The cost is 30¢ for every one-fifth mile or 20¢ per minute in stopped or very slow-moving traffic (or for waiting time). There's no extra charge for each passenger or for luggage. However, you must pay bridge or tunnel tolls (sometimes the driver will front the toll and add it to your bill at the end; most times, however, you pay the driver before the toll). You'll also pay a 50¢ night surcharge after 8pm and before 6am. A 15% to 20% tip is customary.

Note: Taxi drivers were lobbying for a fare increase at press time, and the mayor supports it, so don't be surprised if you find higher fares when you arrive.

Because it's going to cost you at least $2 just to get in the car, taxis are far more expensive than other forms of transportation. Visitors on a limited budget are generally better off relying on subways and buses, using taxis only late at night (after 11pm or midnight, when buses and subway trains start getting fewer and farther between) or to reach an out-of-the-way destination (maybe a bar or restaurant on the Lower East Side or the far East Village, neighborhoods not well served by the subway). You'll also get your money's worth out of a taxi at night, when there's little traffic to keep them from speeding you to your destination.

Although taxis are generally far more expensive than the subway or a bus, consider taking cabs for short hauls if there's three or four in your group. A taxi might not actually save you money, but you'll get door-to-door service for about the same price: It costs four people $6 to take the subway, which is no less than you'd pay for a short taxi ride from Times Square to the West Village, say, or

---

Tips Taxi-Hailing Tips

When you're waiting on the street for a taxi, look at the **medallion light** on the top of the coming cabs. If the light is out, the taxi is in use. When the center part (the number) is lit, the taxi is available—then raise your hand to flag the cab. If all the lights are on, the driver is off-duty.

Note: A taxi can't take more than four people.

from Carnegie Hall to your Murray Hill hotel. Skip taxis entirely at rush hour, when it's more convenient and cheaper to take the subway, because you don't want to end up stuck in traffic, delayed, and paying for unnecessary wait time.

Forget about hopping into the back seat and having some double-chinned, cigar-chomping driver slowly turn and ask, "Where to, Mac?" Nowadays most taxi drivers speak only an approximation of English and drive in engagingly exotic ways. Always wear your seat belt—taxis are required to provide them.

The TLC has posted a **Taxi Rider's Bill of Rights** in every cab. Drivers are required to take you anywhere in the five boroughs, to Nassau or Westchester counties, or to Newark Airport. They are supposed to know how to get you to any address in Manhattan and major points in the outer boroughs. They are required to provide air-conditioning and turn off the radio on demand, and they cannot smoke while you're in the cab. They are required to be polite.

You are allowed to dictate the route that is taken. It's a good idea to look at a map before you get in a taxi. Taxi drivers have been known to jack up the fare on visitors who don't know better by taking very circuitous routes. Know enough about where you're going to know that something's wrong if you hop in a cab at Sixth Avenue and 57th Street to go to the Empire State Building (Fifth Ave. and 34th St.), say, and you suddenly find yourself on Ninth Avenue.

On the other hand, listen to drivers who propose an alternate route. These guys spend 8 or 10 hours a day on these streets, and they know them well—where the worst traffic is, where Con Ed has dug up an intersection. A knowledgeable driver will know how to get you to your destination quickly and efficiently.

Another important tip: **Always make sure the meter is turned on at the start of the ride.** You'll see the red readout register the initial $2 and start calculating the fare as you go. I've witnessed unscrupulous drivers hauling unsuspecting visitors around with the meter off, and then overcharging them at drop-off time.

Always ask for the receipt—it comes in handy if you need to make a complaint or leave something behind. It's a good idea to make a mental note of the driver's four-digit medallion number (usually posted on the divider between the front and back seats) just in case. You probably won't, but it's a good idea.

For driver complaints and lost property, call the 24-hour Consumer Hot Line at ⓒ **212/NYC-TAXI.** For details on getting to and from the local airports by taxi, see "By Plane" under "Getting There," in chapter 2. For further taxi information—including a complete rundown of your rights as a taxi rider—point your Web browser to **www.ci.nyc.ny.us/taxi**.

BY CAR

Forget driving yourself around the city. It's not worth it. Traffic is horrible, the streets have all the civility of the Wild West, street parking is nearly impossible (not to mention the security risks), and garage parking *will* cost you a fortune.

If you arrive in New York City by car, park it in a garage and leave it there. If you drive a rental car in, return it as soon as you arrive and rent another on the day you leave. Just about all of the major car-rental companies, including

Impressions

Traffic signals in New York are just rough guidelines.
—David Letterman

Tips — Deals for Visitors with Wheels: Cheap Parking Tips

If you're driving and have to find somewhere to put your car, don't despair. Even under the best of circumstances, you'll probably pay more for parking in New York than in other cities, but it doesn't have to break the bank.

When planning your trip, try to pick a hotel that has a parking agreement with a nearby garage. This is common practice, and the rate that management has negotiated will be better than the rate you would pay on your own. Many hotels are able to negotiate daily rates between $15 and $25 in neighborhoods where the rate is anywhere from $25 to $50. In chapter 5, "Accommodations You Can Afford," you'll see estimated parking rates in listing,. There are even two hotels, **Travel Inn** and the **Skyline Hotel**, that provide garage parking to guests for free.

If you have to find your own parking, your best bet is to choose a lot on the far west or far east fringes of Midtown, near the West Side Highway to the west or the FDR Drive to the east. You won't have easy access to your wheels, but you'll pay a much lower daily rate than you would in prime Midtown—probably between $15 and $20 as opposed to $25 to $50.

If you'd rather have your car closer at hand, Midtown west of Seventh Avenue is cheaper than more eastern Midtown areas (around $25 instead of $50, which is what you'll pay near Fifth or Sixth aves.). Residential Murray Hill is also cheaper than more commercial Midtown East, although garages near the East River can be supercheap, and a steal on weekends. At press time, a garage on 53rd Street between First and Second avenues offered a daily rate of $8 on weekends; look for similar weekend specials in deserted Lower Manhattan. If you're staying on the Upper West Side, you'll save a few dollars by garaging your car north of 96th Street.

If you drive into the city, garage your car and use it again only when you're ready to leave. Most city garages do not provide in-and-out privileges, so expect to pay a much higher rate if you use your car and return it later the same day.

Also remember that a steep **parking garage tax** of 18.25% is added to every parking bill, so factor that in to your calculations. See why I recommend that you just leave your car at home?

One last note: Despite the fact that some New Yorkers do it, don't try street parking. You don't know the arcane alternate-side-of-the-street regulations. You don't want to find out the price of parking violations or the Kafkaesque tragedy of liberating a car from the tow pound. And your car is sure to come home with a new dent or two if you leave it on the street. As expensive as garaging it may be, trust me—it's cheaper in the long run.

National (© 800/227-7368; www.nationalcar.com), **Hertz** (© 800/654-3131; www.hertz.com), and **Avis** (© 800/230-4898; www.avis.com), have multiple Manhattan locations.

TRAVELING FROM THE CITY TO THE SUBURBS

The **PATH** (© 800/234-7284; www.panynj.gov/path) system connects urban communities in New Jersey, including Hoboken and Newark, to Manhattan by subway-style trains. Stops in Manhattan are at Christopher and 9th streets, and along Sixth Avenue at 14th, 23rd, and 33rd streets. A new lower Manhattan station, to replace the one destroyed underneath the World Trade Center, is not expected to be up and running until 2004. The fare is $1.50.

New Jersey Transit (© 800/626-RIDE; www.njtransit.com) operates commuter trains from Penn Station, and buses from the Port Authority at Eighth Avenue and 42nd Street, to points throughout New Jersey.

The **Long Island Rail Road** (© 718/217-LIRR; www.mta.nyc.ny.us/lirr) runs from Penn Station, at Seventh Avenue between 31st and 33rd streets, to Queens and points beyond on Long Island.

Metro-North (© 800/METRO-INFO or 212/532-4900; www.mta.nyc.ny.us/mnr) departs from Grand Central Terminal, at 42nd Street and Lexington Avenue, for areas north of the city, including Westchester County, the lovely Hudson Valley, and Connecticut.

If you'd prefer to rely on substantially cheaper buses to reach your suburban destination, visit **www.panynj.gov/tbt/pabframe.HTM**, where you'll find a complete list of bus companies (in addition to NJ Transit, above) that service Manhattan's Port Authority bus terminal at Eighth Avenue and 42nd Street.

3 Playing It Safe

Sure, there's crime in New York City, but millions of people spend their lives here without being robbed and assaulted. In fact, New York is safer than any other big American city, and is listed by the FBI as somewhere around 150th in the nation for total crimes. While that's quite encouraging, it's still important to take precautions. Criminals are expert at spotting newcomers who appear disoriented or vulnerable.

Men should carry their wallets in their front pockets and women should keep hold of their purse straps. Cross camera and purse straps over one shoulder, across your front, and under the other arm. Never hang a purse on the back of a chair or on a hook in a bathroom stall; keep it in your lap or between your feet with one foot through a strap. Avoid carrying large amounts of cash. You might carry your money in several pockets so that if one is picked, the others might escape. Skip the flashy jewelry and keep valuables out of sight on the street.

Panhandlers are seldom dangerous and can usually be ignored (more aggressive pleas can be answered, "Not today"). If a stranger walks up to you on the street with a sob story ("I live in the suburbs and was attacked and don't have the money to get home...."), it's likely a scam. You have every right to walk away. Be wary of an individual who "accidentally" falls in front of you or causes some other commotion, because he or she may be working with someone else who will take your wallet when you try to help. And remember: You *will* lose if you place a bet on a sidewalk card game or shell game.

Impressions

I like it here in New York. I like the idea of having to keep eyes in the back of your head all the time.

—John Cale

FAST FACTS: NEW YORK CITY 93

> **Tips The Top Safety Tips**
>
> Trust your instincts, because they're usually right. You'll rarely be hassled, but it's always best to walk with a sense of purpose, and don't stop in the middle of the sidewalk to look at your map. If you find yourself on a deserted street that feels unsafe, it probably is; leave as quickly as possible. If you do find yourself accosted by someone with or without a weapon, remember to keep your anger in check and that the most reasonable response (maddening though it may be) is not to resist.

Certain areas should be avoided late at night. I don't recommend going to the Lower East Side, Alphabet City in the far East Village, Harlem, or the Meat-Packing District unless you know where you're going. Don't be afraid to go, but head straight for your destination and don't wander onto deserted side streets. Times Square has been cleaned up, and there'll be crowds around until midnight, when theater- and moviegoers leave the area. Still, stick to the main streets, such as Broadway or Ninth Avenue, Midtown West's newest restaurant row. The areas south of Times Square are best avoided after dark, as they're largely abandoned once the business day ends. Take a cab or bus when visiting the Jacob Javits Center on 34th Street and the Hudson River. Don't wander the parks after dark, unless you're going to a performance; if that's the case, stick with the crowd.

If you plan on visiting the outer boroughs, go during the daylight hours. If the subway doesn't go directly to your destination, your best bet is to take a taxi. Don't wander the side streets; many areas in the outer boroughs are absolutely safe, but neighborhoods change quickly, and it's easy to get lost.

All this said, don't panic. New York has experienced a dramatic drop in crime and is safer than many other major U.S. cities these days, especially in the neighborhoods that visitors are prone to frequent. There's a good police presence on the street, so don't be afraid to stop an officer, or even a friendly-looking New Yorker (trust me—you can tell) if you need help getting your bearings.

SUBWAY SAFETY TIPS In general, the subways are safe, especially in Manhattan. Still, stay alert and trust your instincts. Always keep a hand on your personal belongings.

When using the subway, **do not wait for trains near the edge of the platform** or on extreme ends of a station. During nonrush hours, wait for the train in view of the token-booth clerk or under the yellow DURING OFF HOURS TRAINS STOP HERE signs, and ride in the train operator's or conductor's car (usually in the center of the train; you'll see his or her head stick out of the window when the doors open). Choose crowded cars over empty ones—there's safety in numbers.

Avoid subways late at night, and take a cab after about 10 or 11pm—it's money well spent to avoid a long wait on a deserted platform. Or take the bus.

 FAST FACTS: New York City

American Express Travel service offices are at many Manhattan locations, including 1185 Sixth Ave., at 47th Street (© 212/398-8585); at the New York Marriott Marquis, 1535 Broadway, in the 8th-floor lobby (© 212/575-6580); on the mezzanine level at Macy's Herald Square, 34th Street and Broadway (📞 212/695-8075); and at 374 Park Ave., at 53rd St. (📞 212/421-8240). Call 📞 **800/AXP-TRIP** or go online to www.americanexpress.com for other city locations or general information.

Area Codes There are four area codes in the city: two in Manhattan, the original **212** and the new **646,** and two in the outer boroughs, the original **718** and the new **347.** Also common is the **917** area code, which is assigned to cell phones, pagers, and a few land lines. All calls between these area codes are local calls, but you'll have to dial 1 + the area code + the seven digits if the number you're calling is not within your area code.

Dentists See "Health & Insurance," in chapter 2.

Doctors For emergencies requiring immediate attention, head to the nearest emergency room (see "Hospitals," below). New York also has several walk-in centers, like **DOCS at New York Healthcare,** 55 E. 34th St., between Park and Madison avenues (📞 **212/252-6001**), for nonemergency illnesses. The clinic, affiliated with Beth Israel Medical Center, is open Monday through Thursday from 8am to 8pm, Friday from 8am to 7pm, Saturday from 9am to 3pm, and Sunday from 9am to 2pm. The **NYU Downtown Hospital** offers referrals at 📞 **888/698-3362.**

Embassies/Consulates See "Fast Facts: For the International Traveler," in chapter 3.

Emergencies Dial 📞 **911** for fire, police, and ambulance. The **Poison Control Center** is at 📞 **800/222-1222** toll-free from any phone.

Hospitals The following hospitals have 24-hour emergency rooms. Don't forget your insurance card.

Downtown: New York Downtown Hospital, 170 William St., between Beekman and Spruce streets (📞 212/312-5063 or 212/312-5000); **St. Vincents Hospital and Medical Center,** 153 W. 11th St., at Seventh Avenue (📞 212/604-7000); and **Beth Israel Medical Center,** First Avenue and 16th Street (📞 212/420-2000).

Midtown: Bellevue Hospital Center, 462 First Ave., at 27th Street (📞 212/562-4141); **New York University Medical Center,** 560 First Ave., at 33rd Street (📞 212/263-7300); and **Roosevelt Hospital,** 425 W. 59th St., between Ninth and Tenth avenues (📞 212/523-6800).

Upper West Side: St. Luke's Hospital Center, Amsterdam Avenue and 113th Street (📞 212/523-3335); and **Columbia Presbyterian Medical Center,** 622 W. 168th St., between Broadway and Fort Washington Avenue (📞 212/305-2500).

Upper East Side: New York Presbyterian Hospital, 525 E. 68th St., at York Avenue (📞 212/746-5050); **Lenox Hill Hospital,** 100 E. 77th St., between Park and Lexington avenues (📞 212/434-2000); and **Mount Sinai Medical Center,** Fifth Avenue at 100th Street (📞 212/241-6500).

Hot Lines The 24-hour **Rape and Sexual Abuse Hot Line** is 📞 212/267-7273. The **Bias Crimes Hot Line** is 📞 212/662-2427. The **LIFENET hot line** for suicide prevention, substance abuse, and other crises is 📞 800/543-3638. For **Mental Health and Alcoholism Services Crisis Intervention,** call 📞 212/219-5599. You can reach **Alcoholics Anonymous** at 📞 212/870-3400 (general office) or 212/647-1680 (for alcoholics who need immediate counseling from a sober, recovering alcoholic). The **Domestic Violence Hot**

Line is ✆ 800/621-4673. Other useful numbers are the **Crisis Help Line** ✆ 212/532-2400; **Samaritans' Suicide Prevention Line** ✆ 212/673-3000; to locate local **police** precincts ✆ 646/610-5000 or 718/610-5000; **Department of Consumer Affairs** ✆ 212/487-4444; and **taxi complaints** ✆ 212/NYC-TAXI or 212/676-1000. If you suspect your car was towed, call the **Department of Transportation TOWAWAY Help Line** at ✆ 212/869-2929.

Libraries The **New York Public Library** is on Fifth Avenue at 42nd Street (✆ **212/930-0830**). This beaux-arts beauty houses more than 38 million volumes, and the reading rooms have been restored to their former glory. More efficient and modern, if less charming, is the mid-Manhattan branch at 455 Fifth Ave., at 40th Street, across from the main library (✆ **212/340-0833**). For other branches, see the list online at www.nypl.org.

Liquor Laws The legal age to purchase and consume alcoholic beverages in New York is 21. Liquor and wine are sold only in licensed stores, which are closed on Sundays, holidays, and election days while the polls are open. Beer can be purchased in grocery stores and delis 24 hours a day, except Sundays before noon. Last call in bars is at 4am.

Newspapers/Magazines There are three major daily newspapers: the *New York Times,* the *Daily News,* and the *New York Post.* For details on where to find arts and entertainment listings, see "Publications," under "Visitor Information," earlier in this chapter.

If you want to find your hometown paper, visit **Universal News & Magazines,** at 234 W. 42nd St., between Seventh and Eighth avenues (✆ **212/221-1809**); and 977 Eighth Ave., between 57th and 58th streets (✆ **212/459-0932**); or **Hotalings News Agency,** 624 W. 52nd St., between Eleventh and Twelfth avenues (✆ **212/974-9419**).

Pharmacies **Duane Reade** (www.duanereade.com) has 24-hour pharmacies in Midtown at 224 W. 57th St., at Broadway (✆ **212/541-9708**); on the Upper West Side at 2465 Broadway, at 91st Street (✆ **212/799-3172**); and on the Upper East Side at 1279 Third Ave., at 74th Street (✆ **212/744-2668**).

Police Dial ✆ **911** in an emergency; otherwise, call ✆ **646/610-5000** or 718/610-5000 (NYPD headquarters) for the number of the nearest precinct.

Restrooms There are public restrooms at the visitor centers in Midtown (1560 Broadway, between 46th and 47th sts.; and 810 Seventh Ave., between 52nd and 53rd sts.). Grand Central Terminal, at 42nd Street between Park and Lexington avenues, also has clean restrooms. On the street, try Starbucks or another java chain—there's practically one on every block. The big bookstores are good for restrooms, too. You can also head to hotel lobbies (especially the big Midtown ones) and department stores like Macy's and Bloomingdale's. On the Lower East Side, stop into the Lower East Side BID Visitor Center, 261 Broome St., between Orchard and Allen streets (open Sun–Fri 10am–4pm, sometimes later).

Smoking Smoking is prohibited on public transportation, in the lobbies of hotels and office buildings, in taxis, and most shops. It also may be restricted or not permitted in restaurants; for more, see p. 132.

Taxes **Sales tax** is 8.25% on meals, most goods, and some services, but not charged on clothing and footwear under $110. **Hotel tax** is 13.25% plus $2 per room per night (including sales tax). **Parking-garage tax** is 18.25%.

Time For the correct time, dial © **212/976-1616**.

Transit Information For information on getting to and from the airport, see "Getting There" on p. 44 or call **Air-Ride** at © **800/247-7433**. For information on subways and buses, call the **MTA** at © **718/330-1234**, or see "Getting Around," earlier in this chapter.

Traveler's Assistance **Travelers Aid International (www.travelersaid.org)** helps distressed travelers with all kinds of problems, including accidents, sickness, and lost or stolen luggage. There is an office on the second floor of the International Arrivals Building at John F. Kennedy International Airport (© **718/656-4870**), and one in Newark International Airport's Terminal B (© **973/623-5052**).

Weather For the current temperature and next day's forecast, look in the upper-right corner of the front page of the *New York Times* or call © **212/976-1212**. If you want to know how to pack before you arrive, point your browser to **www.cnn.com/weather** or **www.weather.com**.

Accommodations You Can Afford

In 2001, the average hotel room rate in New York reached a whopping $227. That's the bad news. The good news? There are more hotel bargains these days than there have been in a decade, largely in response to a building boom; visitors who were less willing to part with their hard-earned dollars prior to September 11, 2001; and the effects of the World Trade Center disaster on the city's tourism fortunes.

So visitors have more bargaining power than they've had in years. Still, don't expect cheap. While the city does have a handful of good inexpensive hotels, it can be difficult to score a room with a private bathroom, nice furniture, closet space, and elevator—for $100 or less. Still, there are some bargains if you know where to look, and in the next pages, I'll tell you about some wonderful places.

To stay in New York on a tight budget, you must weigh what you're willing to spend versus what you're willing to put up with. If you only want to spend 100 or so bucks a night—a very budget-basic rate in this city—you're going to have to live with some inconveniences.

First, be aware that many of New York's budget hotels have **shared bathrooms.** There are a few exceptions to the rule—but in general, don't count on a double room with its own bathroom for less than $100.

Even if you're willing to spend a bit more, don't expect much in the way of **space,** New York's most coveted commodity. Don't be surprised if your hotel room isn't much bigger than the bed in it, the closet is a rack screwed to the wall, and the bathroom is the smallest you've ever seen. Pack light.

It's almost always more expensive to stay in the Theater District than in a residential **neighborhood** like Chelsea, Murray Hill, the Upper West Side, or Harlem; in fact, uptown has become a haven of affordable sleeps for travelers looking for the highest value-for-dollar ratio. Staying in a residential area is almost always quieter, and will give you better access to affordable restaurants where locals eat. Most travelers who choose residential areas end up thrilled with their advantages.

Remember: Hotel rooms are subject to **13.25% tax plus $2 per night,** unless otherwise noted.

HOW TO SAVE ON YOUR HOTEL ROOM

The **rates** quoted in the listings below are the rack rates (the maximum rates that a hotel charges). But rack rates are only guidelines, and there are ways around them. Before you start calling, review the "65 Money-Saving Tips" in chapter 2, including the box on p. 24 "Home Stay Sweet Home Stay," where you'll find time-tested advice on how to get the most for your accommodations dollar.

The hotels below have provided us with their best rate estimates for 2002, and all quoted rates were correct at press time. Be aware that **rates can change at**

any time, subject to availability, seasonal fluctuations, and plain old increases. All bets are off at Christmas; expect everyone to charge over their rack rates.

1 TriBeCa

Cosmopolitan Hotel–Tribeca *Value* Hiding behind a plain-vanilla TriBeCa awning is one of the best hotel deals in Manhattan for travelers who insist on a private bathroom. Everything is budget but nice: The IKEA-ish furniture includes a work desk and an armoire (a few rooms have a dresser and hanging rack instead); for a few extra bucks, you can have a love seat. Beds are comfy, and sheets and towels are of good quality. Rooms are small but make the most of the limited space, and the whole place is pristine. The two-level minilofts have lots of character, but expect to duck on the second level: Downstairs is the bathroom, TV, closet, desk, and club chair, while upstairs is a low-ceilinged bedroom. Management does a great job keeping everything fresh. The TriBeCa location is safe, hip, and subway-convenient; Ground Zero is a walk away (for better or worse). There's no room service, but a range of restaurants will deliver. In fact, all services are kept at a bare minimum to keep costs down, so you must be a low-maintenance guest to be happy here. If you are, this place is a great deal.

95 W. Broadway (at Chambers St.), New York, NY 10007. © **888/895-9400** or 212/566-1900. Fax 212/566-6909. www.cosmohotel.com. 113 units. $119–$159 double. Inquire about discounts. AE, DC, MC, V. Parking $20, 1 block away. Subway: 1, 2, 3, 9 to Chambers St. *In room:* A/C, TV, dataport, ceiling fan.

2 On the Bowery

Off SoHo Suites Hotel *Value* Once you had to put up with an industrial, edge-of-Chinatown neighborhood to enjoy Off SoHo Suites—a hotel with clean, welcoming rooms with full kitchen facilities at surprisingly low prices. But the neighborhood is getting nicer by the minute, and it's a stone's throw from the city's coolest dining, shopping, and nightlife: Nolita's Elizabeth Street is 2 blocks west, and the Lower East Side's Orchard and Ludlow streets are a half-dozen blocks east, not to mention Chinatown's nearby cheap eats. You'll get a lot for your dough: Each deluxe suite has a living and dining area with a pullout sofa, kitchen, private bathroom with hair dryer, and separate bedroom. In the economy suites, kitchens and bathrooms (with hair dryers) are shared with another room; if four of you are traveling, you can combine two economy suites into a sizable apartment. Everything is basic and the beds are a bit harder than I like, but the whole place is nicely kept. Telephones have voice mail and dataports. *Note:* If you don't like a youth-oriented, gentrifying scene, stay elsewhere.

11 Rivington St. (btwn Chrystie St. and the Bowery), New York, NY 10002. © **800/OFF-SOHO** (633-7646) or 212/979-9808. Fax 212/979-9801. www.offsoho.com. 38 units (10 with shared bathroom). $66–$89.50 economy suite (2 people maximum), $99–$199 deluxe suite (4 people maximum). AE, MC, V. Parking $20 nearby. Subway: F to Second Ave., 6 to Spring St. Pets allowed (in deluxe suites only). **Amenities:** Cafe for breakfast and lunch; exercise room; access to nearby health club; activities desk; limited room service; dry cleaning/laundry; coin-op laundry. *In room:* A/C, TV w/free movies, dataport, kitchen with fridge and coffeemaker, hair dryer, iron.

Pioneer of SoHotel *Finds* One of my favorite finds is this little Euro-style hotel, which has done something no other Manhattan hotel has managed: It offers clean, quiet, friendly accommodations with private bathrooms for as little as $77 double (plus tax, or $89 nightly) on a year-round basis.

This older hotel has steadily improved and come into its own, and the friendly manager continues to make improvements. The same can be said for the neighborhood: The hotel is in a four-story walkup off a stretch of the Bowery lined with restaurant suppliers that was crusty and desolate a few years ago. But these days it's clean, safe, and convenient.

It's one level up to the lobby, which is older but bright and agreeable. Here you'll find a professional staff and morning coffee (the pot's usually on all day). Decorative painting adds an attractive flair to rooms, and hanging plants add color in the halls. Rooms have black linoleum floors, mix-and-match lamps and chairs, ceiling fans, and fresh and firm platform beds (which may be a tad too firm for some). Some have armoires, while others have a rack on the wall in lieu of a closet. Most rooms have a tiny but spotless bathroom with a shower stall (a handful have tubs). Shared-bathroom units (which have small sinks) are petite, but many spacious configurations are available, and the standard doubles are a good size. Room no. 11D is a family-friendly triple with two doubles and a twin and a sizable bathroom with a tub, while a room with three twins is a great configuration for friends. A few rooms have no windows, but they're blissfully silent and will even save you a few dollars. Ask for a renovated room (most are). Service is delightfully old-fashioned; a wake-up call consists of a clerk who'll knock on your door (BYO alarm and hair dryer if you'll want them).

341 Broome St. (btwn Elizabeth St. and the Bowery), New York, NY 10013. © **212/226-1482.** Fax 212/226-3525. www.pioneerhotel.com. 125 units (about 35 with shared bathroom). $69–$89 single or double with shared bathroom, $99 quad with shared bathroom; $89–$99 double with private bathroom, $116–$158 triple, quad, or family room with private bathroom. Rates include tax. AE, DC, DISC, MC, V. Parking $10–$15 nearby. Subway: F to Second Ave., 6 to Spring St. **Amenities:** Morning coffee in lobby. *In room:* A/C, TV, ceiling fan, no phone.

3 The Lower East Side

New York City Howard Johnson Express Inn *Value* This brand-new hotel is a boon to travelers looking for quality at a great price, a trendy location, or both. It's the kind of hotel where recent college grads could put up their parents—*and* where they'd like to stay themselves.

The hotel sits on a wide thoroughfare next to a renovated Yiddish vaudeville house that houses a state-of-the-art movie complex. Bars, live-music clubs, restaurants, and offbeat shops abound on the surrounding blocks; East Village action is across Houston Street, and SoHo is to the west. The neighborhood may be on the cutting edge, but this HoJo is wonderfully predictable. In the second-floor lobby, I was greeted by a welcome bowl of Tootsie Rolls and a staff that's more attentive than most working in this price range. The building was completed in December 2001, so everything is new. Rooms are small, but furnishings and textiles are attractive and of good quality: Mattresses are firm, work desks boast desk-level inputs and an ergonomic chair, and the granite bathrooms are nicer than those in some luxury hotels (some even have Jacuzzis).

Most rooms have queen beds, while some have two doubles; don't expect much elbowroom in either configuration. Those with room numbers ending in 01, 02, or 03 are the largest. Not much noise comes off of Houston, but request a back-facing or high-floor room for total quiet. Coffee's on all day in the lobby, and a basic continental breakfast (Danishes, donuts) is laid out in the morning.

135 E. Houston St. (at Forsyth St.), New York, NY 10002. © **800/406-1411** or 212/358-8844. Fax 212/473-3500. www.hojo.com. 54 units. $119–$149 double. Rates include continental breakfast. Inquire about AAA, AARP, and corporate discounts. AE, DC, DISC, MC, V. Parking $29, 4 blocks away. Subway: F to Second Ave. **Amenities:** Dry cleaning/laundry. *In room:* A/C, TV, dataport, hair dryer, iron.

4 The East Village

East Village Bed & Coffee *Finds* *Fair warning:* This little guesthouse isn't for everyone. If you're turned off by the idea of staying behind a graffiti-covered facade in a space that's a work in progress, in an up-and-coming neighborhood, skip this one. But if you're an adventurous traveler who likes a communal vibe, willing to put up with a few eccentricities for a super deal, read on.

Friendly innkeeper Carlos Delfin has created a series of private guest rooms on two floors. All are small and basic, with little more than a high-quality bed and a work desk. Best is the sunlit French room, with queen bed and a chest of drawers. Also on the second floor are some very petite rooms, including the Mexican room plus a common kitchen, living room with TV, and bathroom. Downstairs is a loftlike space with Carlos's workroom, office, and the main kitchen; a second bathroom; and two more Japanese-style bedrooms (with low ceilings and low platform beds) built as enclosed lofts over the main space (best for heavy sleepers). Furnishings are hodgepodge; everything is well worn but clean and comfortable—Carlos makes constant improvements—and a wonderful art collection brightens the mix. He lives in the space (with his shepherd Fang, whose name belies her sweet disposition). The back garden is open in warm weather. The Alphabet City neighborhood is gentrifying, but it's still the hinterlands as far as most visitors are concerned. Subways are a significant walk away, so use the money you save on your room to take cabs back late at night.

110 Ave. C (btwn 7th and 8th sts.), New York, NY 10009. © and fax **212/533-4175.** www.eastvillagebed.citysearch.com or www.bedandcoffee.com. 6 units (all with shared bathroom). $65–$75 single; $75–$80 double. Rates include tax. AE, MC, V. Subway: L to First Ave., 6 to Astor Place. **Amenities:** Common kitchen with coffee and tea, living room with TV/VCR; Internet connection for guest use; fax; free local calls from common phone. *In room:* A/C, no phone.

Second Home on Second Avenue ⭐ *Finds* Here's another guesthouse run by gregarious innkeeper Carlos Delfin, this one a big step up in quality, location, and price from his East Village Bed & Coffee (see above). It's a guesthouse for young, independent-minded travelers who prefer the restaurant- and club-heavy East Village. The rooms are large and decently, if eclectically, furnished. Each is outfitted with two full beds, good closet space, a large TV with VCR, a CD player (unheard of in this price category), an alarm, and a phone (free local calls!) with answering machine in every room. If there are more than two of you, the suite, which has a separate living room with a leather sofa that pulls out into a queen bed and a big private bathroom, is a good bet. Bathrooms are older but clean. A nice, new common kitchen is fully outfitted and offers free coffee and tea.

A few words of caution: Don't expect lots in the way of service, as Carlos lives off-site. Rooms are on the third and fourth floors of a walk-up. The guesthouse is popular with European travelers, who tend to smoke; you may still want to stay elsewhere if the possibility bothers you.

221 Second Ave. (btwn E. 13th and 14th sts.), New York, NY 10003. © and fax **212/677-3161.** www.secondhome.citysearch.com. 6 units (2 with private bathroom). $75–$145 single; $85–$165 double. Rates include tax. Extra person $20. 2-night minimum stay required. AE, MC, V. Parking about $20 nearby. Subway: L to Third Ave.; N, R, 4, 5, 6 to Union Sq. **Amenities:** Common kitchen. *In room:* A/C, TV/VCR, CD player.

St. Mark's Hotel ⭐ This renovated hotel from the folks behind the Chelsea Savoy (p. 104) and Park Savoy (p. 107) is a welcome addition to the budget hotel scene. It's in a four-story walkup on St. Marks Place, the hot spot for the East Village's youth, lined with used-record stores, restaurants and bars, and a

Accommodations in the TriBeCa, the Bowery, the Lower East Side, the East Village & Greenwich Village

Abingdon Guest House **1**
Cosmopolitan Hotel—Tribeca **11**
East Village Bed & Coffee **6**
Larchmont Hotel **3**
New York City
   Howard Johnson Express Inn **8**
Off SoHo Suites **9**
Pioneer of SoHotel **10**
Second Home on Second Avenue **4**
St. Mark's Hotel **5**
Washington Square Hotel **2**
Whitehouse Hotel of New York **7**

parade of tattooed hipsters. Folks in search of peace and quiet will abhor the location, but anybody interested in being at the heart of the action will love it.

In a city where dingy paint and 20-year-old carpet is the norm in budget hotels, St. Mark's pretty Parisian mural (in the stairwell leading up to the second-floor front desk), lighting, finished oak, and marble floors are a welcome sight. Rooms are basic and furnishings are simple, but even the smallest—one double bed—is a decent size and boasts new carpet, a firm bed, a TV, a phone with voice mail, and a tiled bathroom with a tiny sink, shower, and nice towels; butter-yellow walls and framed prints brighten most rooms. Services are minimal, but the staff is professional. There's no dedicated public space, but a pub sits on the ground level. Some of New York's best affordable restaurants are within shouting distance.

2 St. Marks Place (at Third Ave.), New York, NY 10003. © **212/674-0100** or 212/674-2192. Fax 212/420-0854. www.stmarkshotel.qpg.com. 70 units. $80–$150 single or double. No credit cards. Subway: 6 to Astor Place. *In room:* A/C, TV.

Whitehouse Hotel of New York ★ *Value*
This newly renovated, youth-oriented hotel is a wonderful addition, because it offers private rooms at hostel prices, and the location is smashing. Rooms are tiny and plain, each with either a full bed or twins, so expect no perks; but everything is clean, well maintained, and relatively new. Good quality linens and towels are provided. All rooms share simple shower-stall bathrooms off the hall. There's a lobby lounge with a TV, tables and chairs for lounging, a cafe area selling continental-style breakfast items, and friendly, grandfatherly service around the clock. A coin-op laundry and an Internet-access machine in the lobby add to the convenience. The city's best budget dining lines the East Village blocks; the heart of Greenwich Village is to the west, and SoHo and the Lower East Side are both just a 5-minute walk away. No smoking allowed, and no travelers under 18.

340 Bowery (btwn 2nd and Great Jones/3rd sts.), New York, NY 10012. © **212/477-5623**. Fax 212/473-3150. www.whitehousehotelofny.com. 468 beds (all with shared bathroom). $30–$32 single; $58–$63 double; $75–$91 triple. Rates include tax. AE, DC, MC, V. Subway: 6 to Bleecker St. No children under 18 accepted. *Amenities:* Common kitchen w/microwave; Internet access machine and dataport in lobby; coin-op laundry; continental breakfast for a charge (daily 6–10am). *In room:* A/C.

5 Greenwich Village

Abingdon Guest House ★★ *Finds*
Steve Austin and his partner, Zachary Stass, run this lovely guesthouse (and its downstairs coffee bar, **Brewbar**) in a retail-and-residential West Village neighborhood. Both men have an eye for style—the Abingdon is beautifully outfitted and professionally run. Accommodations with in-room bathrooms are pricey for most wallet-watching travelers (but worth the price if you feel like a splurge), but those with hall bathrooms are well priced—as low as $115, no more than $177—and still come with private bathrooms, just outside your room off the hall. All of the rooms are done in bold colors and outfitted with well-chosen art and furnishings. No matter which you choose, you'll get a quality mattress and linens, soft bathrobes, an alarm clock, a telephone with free local calls and your own answering machine (a splitter can be provided for your laptop), and maid service.

The neighborhood is terrific, with good restaurants and shops. The Abingdon is best for mature, independent travelers, because there's no regular staff on-site, and the area is geared to locals rather than tourists. The thoughtful style and privacy make it ideal for a romantic escape, but friends traveling won't feel out of place (in fact, two rooms feature two twin beds). It's a nonsmoking property.

13 Eighth Ave. (btwn W. 12th and Jane sts.), New York, NY 10014. © **212/243-5384.** Fax 212/807-7473. www.abingdonguesthouse.com. 9 units. $115–$222 double. 4-night minimum on weekends, 2-night minimum on weekdays. Rates $10 less for single travelers. Extra person $25. AE, DC, DISC, MC, V. Parking $20 nearby. Subway: A, C, E, L, 1, 2, 3, 9 to 14th St. **Amenities:** Coffee bar. *In room:* A/C, TV, dataport, hair dryer, iron, safe.

Larchmont Hotel *Value* Located on a tree-lined block in a quiet part of the Village, this European-style hotel is a gem. If you're willing to share a bathroom, it's hard to do better for the money. The entire place has an air of warmth and sophistication. Each bright guest room is done in rattan and outfitted with a writing desk, a minilibrary, an alarm clock, a washbasin, and a few extras you normally have to pay a lot more for, such as bathrobes, slippers, and ceiling fans. Every floor has two shared bathrooms (with hair dryers) and a small kitchen. The management is constantly renovating, so everything feels clean and fresh. Those looking for a hip downtown base couldn't be better situated, because some of the city's best shopping, dining, and sightseeing—plus your choice of subway lines—is all close. A free continental breakfast that includes fresh-baked goods every morning is the crowning touch that makes the Larchmont a terrific deal. Book *well* in advance (the management suggests 6–7 weeks' lead time).

27 W. 11th St. (btwn Fifth and Sixth aves.), New York, NY 10011. © **212/989-9333.** Fax 212/989-9496. www.larchmonthotel.com. 58 units (all with shared bathroom). $70–$95 single; $90–$125 double. Rates include continental breakfast. Children under 13 stay free in parents' room. AE, DC, DISC, MC, V. Parking $18 nearby. Subway: A, C, E, F, V to W. 4th St. (use 8th St. exit); F to 14th St. **Amenities:** Common kitchenette; tour desk; fax service; room service (10am–6pm). *In room:* A/C, TV, hair dryer, safe, washbasin, ceiling fan.

Washington Square Hotel Popular with a young international crowd, this hotel sits behind a facade facing Washington Square Park (historically Henry James territory, now the heart of New York University). A marble-and-brass lobby leads to tiny rooms that benefited from a freshening in 2000. Each comes with a firm bed, private bathroom, and a small closet with a pint-size safe. It's worth paying extra for a south-facing room on a high floor, because others can be dark. Both the Union Square Inn and Murray Hill's Thirty Thirty offer a bit more space and brand-new everything for a similar price; but the heart-of-campus location is ideal for travelers who want to be near Village restaurants, bars, and clubs. On site is a very good restaurant and lounge, **C3,** which draws locals with its stylish design, well-priced cocktails and bistro fare, and Sunday jazz brunch. The staff has been known to be terse, but service seems to be on an upswing.

103 Waverly Place (btwn Fifth and Sixth aves.), New York, NY 10011. © **800/222-0418** or 212/777-9515. Fax 212/979-8373. www.wshotel.com. 170 units. $101–$131 single; $118–$151 double; $145–$188 quad. Rates include continental breakfast. Inquire about special rates and jazz packages. Rollaway $20 extra. AE, MC, V. Parking $20 nearby. Subway: A, C, E, F, V to W. 4th St. (use 3rd St. exit). **Amenities:** Restaurant; lounge; exercise room; dry cleaning/laundry. *In room:* A/C, TV, dataport, hair dryer, iron, safe.

6 Chelsea

Chelsea Lodge *Finds* Housed in a brownstone on a landmarked block, this small hotel is charming and a terrific value—arguably the best in the city for budget-minded travelers. The husband-and-wife owners, Paul and GG Weisenfeld, have put in an incredible effort: renovations have restored original woodwork and created a country-in-the-city vibe with beautiful wallpapers and wainscoting, refinished vintage furniture, and lovely touches like Hershey's Kisses on the pillows. The beds are the finest and best outfitted I've seen in this price category. Ongoing renovations, which include redecorated common areas and bathrooms at this writing, show how much Paul and GG continue to care.

The only place with a similar grown-up sensibility for the same money is Greenwich Village's Larchmont (p. 103), but there, bathroom facilities are shared; at Chelsea Lodge, each room has its own sink and in-room shower stall, so you only have to share a toilet. I won't kid you—rooms are petite, the closets are small, and beds are full-size (queens wouldn't cut it). But considering the stylishness, the amenities—which include TV, a ceiling fan, a desk, and an alarm clock—and the neighborhood, you'd be hard-pressed to do better. Best for couples rather than shares. *Tip:* Try to book 2A, which is bigger than most, or one of the first-floor rooms, whose high ceilings make them feel more spacious.

318 W. 20th St. (btwn Eighth and Ninth aves.), New York, NY 10011. © 800/373-1116 or 212/243-4499. Fax 212/243-7852. www.chelsealodge.com. 24 units (all with semiprivate bathroom). $90 single; $105 double. AE, DC, DISC, MC, V. Parking about $20 nearby. Subway: 1, 9 to 18th St.; C, E to 23rd St. *In room:* A/C, TV, ceiling fan.

Chelsea Pines Inn ★★ *Value* This inn caters largely to gay travelers, but all adult travelers are welcome as long as they'll be comfortable in a gay-oriented atmosphere. The inn straddles the border of the West Village, the heart of New York's gay community, and Chelsea, the latest hip address for the GLBT scene.

The rooms have comfortable furnishings, floral-print textiles, and a terrific collection of movie posters. Each room is dedicated to a Golden-Age-of-Hollywood star; the Paul Newman room boasts posters from movies such as *Hud* and *The Drowning Pool.* Rooms aren't big, but are well outfitted and arranged. Each has a minifridge, free HBO, a clock radio, and an answering machine; most have queen beds and daybeds for extra seating, and a half-dozen have breakfast areas with cafe tables and microwaves. Private bathrooms are bright and new; the cheapest (semiprivate) rooms have showers and sinks, so you just have to share a hall toilet. There's a payoff if you're willing to stay at the top of the five-story walkup: The Rock Hudson room sleeps four and has a terrific green-and-white bathroom with a skylight. The friendly staff mans the front desk around the clock, and continental breakfast is served in a cute breakfast room. There's also a greenhouselike enclosed patio and a backyard garden with blooming flowers.

317 W. 14th St. (btwn Eighth and Ninth aves.), New York, NY 10014. © 888/546-2700 or 212/929-1023. Fax 212/620-5646. www.chelseapinesinn.com. 24 units (15 with private bathroom). $89–$139 double with semiprivate bathroom, $119–$189 double with private bathroom; $159–$199 triple or quad with continental breakfast. Rates include expanded continental breakfast. Check website for special deals. Extra person $20. 3-night minimum stay on weekends. AE, DC, DISC, MC, V. Parking $25 nearby. Subway: A, C, E to 14th St. Inappropriate for children. *In room:* A/C, TV, dataport, fridge, hair dryer, iron.

Chelsea Savoy Hotel ★★ *Kids* This newish hotel has been a welcome addition to Chelsea, a neighborhood abloom with galleries, restaurants, nightclubs, and flea markets. The six-story Savoy was built from the ground up in 1995, so it isn't subject to the eccentricities of older hotels. The hallways are attractive and wide, the elevators swift and silent, and the cheery rooms of good size with big closets and roomy, immaculate bathrooms with tons of counter space. The reasonably priced quad rooms are suitable for a family of four (children stay free). Creature comforts abound: The rooms boast mattresses, furniture, and linens of high quality, plus the kinds of amenities you usually have to pay more for, like minifridges, in-room safes, and toiletries. Free continental breakfast makes a good value even better. Most rooms are street facing and sunny; corner rooms tend to be brightest but noisiest. Ask for a back-facing room if you crave total silence. The staff is young and helpful, and the increasingly hip neighborhood makes a good base for exploring both Midtown and downtown. A plain but pleasant sitting room off the lobby makes an excellent place to enjoy your morning coffee over a selection of newspapers and magazines.

204 W. 23rd St. (at Seventh Ave.), New York, NY 10011. © 866/929-9353 or 212/929-9353. Fax 212/741-6309. www.chelseasavoy.qpg.com or www.chelseasavoynyc.com. 90 units. $99–$115 single; $125–$175 double; $145–$195 quad. Rates include continental breakfast. Children stay free in parents' room. AE, MC, V. Parking $25 nearby. Subway: 1, 9 to 23rd St. *In room:* A/C, TV, dataport, fridge, hair dryer, iron, safe.

Chelsea Star Hotel/Chelsea Suites Industrial-chic hallways lead to private rooms that are minuscule and bare-bones basic at this Generation Y–targeted hotel—more hostel than hotel-like, with nothing more than a firm bed and an open closet. But they're spotless, the mattresses and linens are of good quality, and designer Rob Graf has infused them with enough style so they don't feel as dour as most supercheap sleeps. They're individually dressed in cheeky themes ranging from the Disco Room (graced by a *Fever*-era poster of Travolta in all his white-suited glory) to the Asian mod Madame Butterfly Room (tiny but lovely) to the glow-in-the-dark cosmos of the Orbit Room (complete with black light). Try to grab the Madonna Room, a relatively spacious quad where Mrs. Ritchie lived for a year in leaner days. The shared hallway bathrooms have showers only, but they're smart and clean. Shoestring travelers who don't mind snoozing with strangers can opt for a single bunk in one of the serviceable dorms.

For a bit more, you can have your own pad: a stylish, fully loaded apartment with an equipped kitchen, private bathroom, and TV in the furnished living room. These are the best values in the house—and some of the best in Midtown—so book way ahead. *Tip:* The courtyard-facing apartments are quietest.

The Chelsea Star is a great addition to the budget hotel scene, but a word of warning: It is decidedly youth-oriented; mature travelers looking for standard amenities may be disappointed. The location—at the back door of Penn Station, more Midtown than Chelsea—may not be New York's finest, but it's cleaner and safer than ever, and cheap eateries and Irish pubs abound.

300 W. 30th St. (at Eighth Ave.), New York, NY 10011. © 877/827-6969 or 212/244-7827. Fax 212/279-9018. www.chelseastar.com or www.chelseasuites.com. 25 rooms (all with shared bathroom); 5 apts; 24 dorm beds. $59–$69 single; $79–$89 double; $89–$99 triple or quad. $25.50 per person in dorm. $159–$179 apt (sleeps up to 4); $900 weekly; $3,000 monthly (tax included in monthly rate). AE, DISC, MC, V. Parking about $25 nearby. Subway: A, C, E to 34th St./Penn Station. No children under 18 accepted. **Amenities:** Pay Internet PC; fax service; dry cleaning/laundry; shared pay phones. *In room:* A/C, no phone (TV, phone, and dataport in apts).

Colonial House Inn This charming 1850 brownstone, on a pretty residential block in the heart of gay-friendly Chelsea, was the first permanent home of the Gay Men's Health Crisis. The four-story walk-up caters to a largely gay and lesbian clientele, but the friendly staff welcomes everyone. The place is beautifully maintained and professionally run. Rooms are small and basic but clean; all have radios and those that share a hall bathroom (at a ratio of about three rooms per bathroom) have in-room sinks. Deluxe rooms—those with private bathrooms—have minifridges, and a few have working fireplaces. Both private and shared bathrooms are basic but nice. A terrific art collection brightens the public spaces. Book at least a month in advance for weekend stays. At parlor level is a breakfast room where a continental spread is put out from 8am to noon daily; coffee and tea are available all day. Rooms don't have hair dryers and irons, but the front desk will lend them. There's a nice roof deck split by a privacy fence (the area behind the fence is clothing optional). The neighborhood is chock-full of great restaurants and shopping, and offers easy access to the rest of the city.

106 CHAPTER 5 · ACCOMMODATIONS YOU CAN AFFORD

> **Tips Deal-Making with the Chains**
>
> Most hotels—particularly chains like Comfort Inn, Holiday Inn, and Best Western—are market-sensitive. Because they hate to see rooms sit empty, they'll often negotiate good rates at the last minute and in slow seasons.
>
> The chains are also where you're able to pull out all the stops for discounts, from auto-club membership to senior status. And you might be able to take advantage of corporate rates or discounted weekend stays. Most chain hotels let the kids stay with parents for free. Ask for every possible kind of discount; if you find that you get an unhelpful reservation agent, call back and try again. And it's worth calling the hotel direct, where the front-desk staff will deal to keep their occupancy rate high.
>
> Of course, there's no guarantee. Your chances of getting a deal aren't great if you're visiting in a busy season. But if you're willing to make a few extra calls, or spend some time surfing online—which might net you a 10% discount for booking online—you might get a deal at hotels that would otherwise be out of your price range.
>
> **Best Western's** (© **800/528-1234;** www.bestwestern.com) rack rates for their New York hotels are higher than you'd expect. At the **Best Western President Hotel,** in the Theater District at 234 W. 48th St. (© **800/826-4667** or 212/246-8800), doubles go for $129 to $229 but can drop to $99—a great deal on a centrally located hotel. Ditto for **Hampshire Hotels & Suites (www.bestnyhotels.com)** the company that manages this and chain hotels such as the **Quality Hotel on Broadway** (p. 128) and the **Comfort Inn–Central Park West** (p. 123), where rooms can go as low as $72 (with breakfast), as well as two Midtown Best Westerns and Howard Johnsons on Park Avenue; check their website for all the details.
>
> At these and other franchised hotels—such as the ones run by **Apple Core Hotels** (© **800/567-7720;** www.applecorehotels.com), a small

318 W. 22nd St. (btwn Eighth and Ninth aves.), New York, NY 10011. © **800/689-3779** or 212/243-9669. Fax 212/633-1612. www.colonialhouseinn.com. 20 units (12 with shared bathroom). $80–$99 single or double with shared bathroom; $125–$140 double with private bathroom. Rates include expanded continental breakfast. 2-night minimum on weekends. Extra person $15. Weekly rates available. MC, V. Parking $20 nearby. Subway: C, E to 23rd St. **Amenities:** Internet-access PC in lounge; fax service. *In room:* A/C, TV, dataport.

SUPERCHEAP SLEEPS
Also consider the dorm beds ($25.50) at the **Chelsea Star Hotel** (see above).

Chelsea Center Hostel   Going strong since 1981, this small, pleasant hostel is ideal for travelers who prefer a laidback ambience and a good night's sleep over the standard hostel bustle. It's on two floors of a Chelsea brownstone. Rooms are bunk-bedded and hostel-simple, but everything is bright and clean, and rates include decent-quality sheets and blankets; each bed also has its own night light for late-night reading and writing. Plenty of top-flight dining and nightlife is nearby; there's no curfew, and the owners will be happy to point you in the right direction. One of the nicest perks is the light continental breakfast included in the

management company that handles the **Comfort Inn Midtown** (p. 114), the **Ramada Inn Eastside** (p. 122), Manhattan's first **Red Roof Inn** (p. 117), and the **Super 8 Hotel Times Square** (p. 118), and the **Best Western Manhattan,** 17 W. 32nd St. (© **212/736-1600**), doubles can go for as little as $89. Check with the franchiser if you're not quoted a good advance-booking rate directly or through the management company's online reservations system; their global 800 and online reservations systems will often garner you a better rate, which might include a promotion—or, at minimum, an "Internet User's Rate" that's 10% lower than the standard.

A good source for deals is **Choice Hotels** (© **800/4-CHOICE;** www.hotelchoice.com), which oversees Comfort Inn, Quality Hotel, and Clarion Hotel chains, all of which have terrific Manhattan branches.

Also try **Holiday Inn** (© **800/HOLIDAY;** www.holiday-inn.com), which has a handful of terrific hotels in Manhattan, all of which carry rack rates that are too high for most budget travelers. However, discounted weekend and slow-season rates can drop as low as $109 double—at the **Holiday Inn Wall Street,** 15 Gold St. (© **212/232-7800;** www.holidayinnwsd.com), New York's most high-tech hotel. Shoppers might like the **Holiday Inn Downtown/SoHo,** 138 Lafayette St. (© **212/966-8898;** www.holidayinn-nyc.com), straddling the border between Chinatown and SoHo.

Another hotel to try is the **Days Hotel Midtown,** 790 Eighth Ave., at 48th Street (© **800/544-8313** or 212/581-7000; www.daysinn.com). The bistro **Pigalle** (p. 176) gives it a better-than-budget flair, and the motel-like rooms are worth the $105-to-$130 rate you might be able to snare in slower seasons. Be sure to ask about senior, AAA, corporate, and promotional rates at all three hotels, and check for online-booking discounts.

rate; guests sit around their morning table to chat. There's also a common room, plus a garden for warm-weather relaxation. You can request a dorm bed at their eastside location, in the East Village (exact location provided upon booking).

313 W. 29th St. (just west of Eighth Ave.), New York, NY 10031. © 212/643-0214. www.chelseacenterhostel.com. 20 dorm beds in each location (all with shared bathroom). $30 dorm bed. Rate includes continental breakfast and tax. No credit cards. Subway: C, E to 23rd St. **Amenities:** Common kitchen and lounge rooms. *In room:* No phone.

Chelsea International Hostel As hostels go, this is a good one. The only other private hostel in this league, both in terms of cleanliness and location, is the Big Apple Hostel (p. 120). The well-managed, well-maintained Chelsea International consists of a warren of low-rise buildings around a central courtyard, like a cottage complex. It's hugely popular with international travelers.

Accommodations and shared bathrooms are older and plain but fine; the shared rooms come with nice extras such as wall hooks, sinks, and in-room lockers big enough for most backpacks (BYO combination lock and towels).

108 CHAPTER 5 · ACCOMMODATIONS YOU CAN AFFORD

The miniscule private rooms have little more than a double bed and some shelf units, but you can call one your own for just 60 bucks. Some rooms have air-conditioning, so request one if it matters to you.

The two fully equipped common kitchens (with microwaves) are the best I've seen in a hostel, and free coffee, tea, sugar, and cream is on hand. The private courtyard has picnic tables and barbecues. There are also dining and lounge areas with TV, Internet-access machines, self-service laundry, and soda machines; free luggage storage is another plus. The neighborhood is great, the desk is attended 24 hours, and maintenance is on hand around the clock. At press time, free pizza was part of the package for Wednesday-night guests.

251 W. 20th St. (btwn Seventh and Eighth aves.), New York, NY 10011. © **212/647-0010.** Fax 212/727-7289. www.chelseahostel.com. 223 dorm beds; 57 private units (all with shared bathroom). $25 dorm bed; $60–$65 double. Rates include tax. AE, MC, V. Subway: 1, 9 to 18th St. **Amenities:** 2 kitchens; dining areas; Internet access; fax; coin-op laundry. *In room:* No phone.

7 Union Square, the Flatiron District & Gramercy Park

Carlton Arms The motto here is THIS AIN'T NO HOLIDAY INN! The spirit of bohemianism and artistic freedom reigns in this backpacker's delight, where every room is a work of art by an artist given license to go hog wild. Think of this as the legendary Hotel Chelsea as it used to be. Some spaces are sublime, such as Robin Banks's Cartoon Room (#5B), Thias Charbonet's Underwater Room (#1A), Olivia Hamlin's super-realist 12A, the ocean-blue lobby (complete with fish in the TV), and the first-floor mosaic bathroom; others are simply bizarre. Whether you end up with a mermaid mural or a wall of teddy bears, you'll see why this is one of the most extraordinary hotels in the city.

But if you're looking for creature comforts, this is *not* the place for you. The cramped rooms are *very* basic. The beds are lumpy, and there's no air-conditioning. Each room has a sink, but you'll most likely end up sharing a bathroom with your fellow travelers (mainly students, international travelers, and existentialists). The place is clean, but there's no maid service. Still, the staff is friendly, and they'll be happy to take messages (rooms don't have phones; there's a pay phone in the lobby). The neighborhood is unhip, but it's safe, quiet, residential, and overflowing with affordable restaurants. Reserve 1 to 2 months in advance, because despite the inconveniences, this place is almost always full.

160 E. 25th St. (btwn Lexington and Third aves.), New York, NY 10010. © **212/679-0680** or 212/684-8337. www.carltonarms.com. 54 units (20 with private bathroom). $60–$90 single or double with shared bathroom; $99–$130 triple or quad with shared bathroom; $75–$100 single or double with private bathroom; $111–$140 triple or quad with private bathroom. 10% discount on 7-night stays paid upon arrival. MC, V. Subway: 6 to 23rd St. *In room:* No phone.

Chelsea Inn The name may say Chelsea, but the east-of-Sixth-Avenue address is really Flatiron. It's still a great location, what with Union Square just a stone's throw in one direction and Chelsea in the other.

The inn is in two 19th-century brownstones, but don't expect too much. Staying here is like living in your own New York City tenement for a few days: The rooms feature a mix of thrift-store furniture, the beds in the twin rooms are little more than rollaways, and the quality of the mattresses is a crapshoot. Everything's faded, but the place is clean and well kept. More on the upside: Closets are big, bathrooms are fine, and all rooms feature a hot plate, minifridge, coffeemaker, cups and utensils, a safe, voicemail, and free coffee; those without a bathroom have their own sinks. Shared bathrooms are livened with murals, and you'll only have to split yours with one other room. If there's more than two of you, pair up two doubles that share a bathroom, and you can usually negotiate a discount. Groups of three or four will like no. 102, a spacious suite with a private bathroom, a dining table and kitchenette. The staff is accommodating, and deals are often available. It's a reasonable, well-priced budget choice.

46 W. 17th St. (btwn Fifth and Sixth aves.), New York, NY 10011. © 800/640-6469 or 212/645-8989. Fax 212/645-1903. www.chelseainn.com. 26 units (18 with private bathroom). $109–$129 double with shared bathroom, $139–$159 double with private bathroom; $179–$259 suite (for up to 4). Check website for available specials (as low as $89 at press time). AE, DISC, MC, V. Parking about $20 nearby. Subway: 4, 5, 6, N, R, Q, W to 14th St./Union Sq. *In room:* A/C, TV, fridge, coffeemaker, safe.

Gershwin Hotel ★ *Kids*   If you see glowing horns protruding from a lipstick-red facade, you're in the right place. This Warholesque hotel caters to up-and-coming artistic types—and names with an eye for good value—with its art collection and wild style. The lobby is a postmodern cartoon of kitschy furniture and pop art. The standard rooms are clean and bright, with Picasso-style wall murals, Philippe Starck–ish takes on motel furnishings, and more modern art. Superior rooms are best, worth the extra $10; all have either a queen bed, two twins, or two doubles, plus a newish private bathroom with colorful tile. Families and groups of friends will love the family room, a two-room suite that nicely accommodates four with a queen bed in one room, two twins in the other.

One of the best things about the Gershwin is its great Factory-esque vibe: There's always something going on, whether it's live jazz, alt-rock, or stand-up comedy in the **Living Room,** nightly happy hour (7–9pm) in the **Red Room** beer bar, summer film screenings in the rooftop garden, or a show at the hotel's own art gallery (usually twice monthly). The hotel is more service-oriented than you usually see at this price level, and the staff is very professional.

7 E. 27th St. (btwn Fifth and Madison aves.), New York, NY 10016. © 212/545-8000. Fax 212/684-5546. www.gershwinhotel.com. 121 units. $99–$189 double (usually less than $150); $189–$219 family unit. Check website for discounts, 3rd-night-free specials, or other value-added packages. Extra person $10. AE, MC, V. Parking $25, 3 blocks away. Subway: N, R, 6 to 28th St. **Amenities:** Cafe (breakfast only); beer bar; tour desk; Internet-access PC; dry cleaning/laundry. *In room:* A/C, TV, dataport, hair dryer, iron.

Gramercy Park Hotel   Opened in 1924, this old-world hotel has one of the best settings in the city. It's in one of New York's loveliest neighborhoods, on the edge of the private park—restricted to area residents and to hotel guests, who can also get a key—that gives Gramercy Park the air of a quiet London square.

Management has this dowager looking good. You'll still have to overlook the finer details, including ancient TVs and mix-and-match bathrooms that have been updated haphazardly. But rooms are huge by city standards, and comfortable, and the hotel has an old–New York feel, due to an incredibly loyal staff, many of whom have worked here since the Nixon administration. Each standard double has a king bed or two doubles, and some suites have pullout sofas that make them large enough to sleep six; all have big closets and fluffy towels in the roomy bathrooms. Request a park-facing room, which costs no more but features a great view and a small kitchenette (most suites have kitchenettes, too). Off the bustling lobby is a continental restaurant (renovated in 2001) and a divey piano lounge with nightly entertainment that draws a young, retro-obsessed crowd.

2 Lexington Ave. (at 21st St.), New York, NY 10010. © 800/221-4083 or 212/475-4320. Fax 212/505-0535. www.gramercyparkhotel.com. 509 units. $150–$160 single; $160–$170 double; $200–$220 suite. Extra person $10. Children under 12 stay free in parents' room. AE, DC, DISC, MC, V. Parking $28 nearby. Subway: 6 to 23rd St. Pets accepted. **Amenities:** Restaurant; lounge; salon; limited room service; in-room massage; dry cleaning/laundry. *In room:* A/C, TV, fridge, hair dryer.

Hotel 17 Hotel 17 has managed to garner a hip reputation; Madonna, David Bowie, and Maxwell have all been photographed in the eclectic, eccentric rooms. The neighborhood is great, the block is peaceful, and the individually decorated rooms are attractive (all have been freshened in the last year). Look beyond the stylish veneer and you'll find rooms that are cramped, dark, and basic—not for travelers looking for creature comforts. Each has its own sink, hair dryer, and alarm clock; the shared bathrooms are older but clean. The lobby has a funky modern feel, but the security glass separating you from the staff detracts from the ambience. It's a decent deal, especially if you're the sort who requires some individuality in your lodgings. Expect lots of younger and international travelers, who don't mind the inconveniences and the lingering smell of smoke.

225 E. 17th St. (btwn Second and Third aves.), New York, NY 10003. **212/475-2845.** Fax 212/677-8178. www.hotel17.citysearch.com. 120 units (all with shared bathroom). $60–$70 single; $65–$95 double; $85–$115 triple. No credit cards. Parking about $20 nearby. Subway: 4, 5, 6 to 14th St.; L to Third Ave. No children under 18 accepted. **Amenities:** Coin-op laundry. *In room:* A/C, TV, hair dryer (no A/C or TV in singles).

The Marcel ★★ *Value* Being budget-challenged doesn't mean you have to settle for boring. This Gramercy Park hotel offers style and a superhip scene at low, low prices. Thanks to designers Goodman Charlton, who love to infuse retro styles with futuristic freshness, the Marcel sits on the cutting edge style-wise. Fab faux *Mod Squad*-era Scandinavian stylings in the lobby lead to guest rooms boasting blond-wood built-ins that make clever use of limited space, and a bold geometric cushioned headboard adds a downright luxurious flair. The designer furnishings and textiles look and feel expensive, even if the lumpy-ish beds don't; still, budget travelers will be thrilled. And trust me—you're going to have to look long and hard for another hotel in town that supplies marble bathrooms, dual-line phones, and CD players at this price. Even if the service isn't fabulous or the little details aren't perfect, you should feel like you're getting a great deal here.

One of the strongest appeals of the Marcel is **Spread** (www.spreadnyc.com), a restaurant/lounge hybrid offering a small-plates menu, a sushi bar, cocktails, and a blast of an after-dark scene. The subterranean lounge **Coal** is an even more seductive space—just ask Natasha Richardson, who celebrated a birthday here.

201 E. 24th St. (at Third Ave.), New York, NY 10011. **888/66-HOTEL** (664-6835) or 212/696-3800. Fax 212/696-0077. www.nychotels.com. 97 units. $125–$175 double. AE, DISC, MC, V. Parking $24. Subway: 6 to 28th St. **Amenities:** Restaurant; lounge; coffee/cappuccino bar; limited room service; dry cleaning/laundry. *In room:* A/C, TV w/pay movies, CD player, dataport, hair dryer, iron.

Union Square Inn ★★ *Value* A stone's throw east of Union Square on the fringe of the East Village, this unassuming hotel is a welcome addition. Rooms aren't as cheap as at sister hotel the Murray Hill Inn, but comforts are better-quality, every unit has a private bathroom, and everything feels fresh and new.

Four standard rooms are tiny twins with trundle beds; a handful in the deluxe category are spacious double/doubles that can accommodate more than two. Most fall in the moderate category, with one double bed and little room to spare—but you're not in the Big Apple to hang out in your room! All rooms boast terrific brand-new pillow-top mattresses and good-quality sheets (probably the best bedding you'll find in this price category), cheery autumn-hued textiles and art, cute contemporary redwood furnishings, nice bedside lamps, and pretty all-new Italian-tile bathrooms. On the downside, all rooms lack views, open wall racks substitute for closets, most bathrooms have shower only, halls are narrow, and there's no elevator—but those are minimal sacrifices considering the low prices.

Services are virtually nonexistent in order to keep costs down, but everything you'll need, from restaurants to dry cleaners to a slate of subway lines, is right at hand in the hip, central-to-everything location.

209 E. 14th St. (btwn Second and Third aves.), New York, NY 10003. © **212/614-0500.** Fax 212/614-0512. www.unionsquareinn.com. 40 units. $99–$169 double. Rates include continental breakfast. Extra person $20. AE, MC, V. Parking $25 nearby. Subway: L to Third Ave.; or 4, 5, 6, N, R to 14th St./Union Sq. **Amenities:** Coffee bar w/light meals. *In room:* A/C, TV, dataport.

8 Times Square & Midtown West

Americana Inn ★ *Value* The cheapest hotel from the Empire Hotel Group—the people behind the Upper West Side's Newton and pricier properties—is a star in the budget category. Linoleum floors give the rooms a somewhat unfortunate institutional quality, but the hotel is well run and immaculately kept. Rooms are spacious, with good-size closets and private sinks, and an alarm built into the TV; the beds are the most comfortable I've found at this price. Most come with a double bed or two twins; a few can accommodate three guests in two twin beds and a pullout sofa or three twins. One hall bathroom accommodates every three rooms or so; all are spacious and spotless, and the front desk lends hair dryers. Every floor has a kitchenette with microwave, stove, and fridge (BYO cooking utensils, or go plastic). The five-story building has an elevator (uncommon at this price), and four rooms are accessible for travelers with disabilities. Ask for a back-facing room away from the street noise.

69 W. 38th St. (at Sixth Ave.), New York, NY 10018. © **888/HOTEL-58** (468-3558) or 212/840-6700. Fax 212/840-1830. www.newyorkhotel.com. 50 units (all with shared bathroom). $65–$75 single; $75–$115 double. Check website for specials (winter rates as low as $60 double). Extra person $10. AE, MC, V. Parking $25–$35 nearby. Subway: B, D, F, V to 34th St. **Amenities:** Common kitchen. *In room:* A/C, TV.

Broadway Inn ★★ *Finds* More like a San Francisco B&B than a Theater District hotel, this lovely, welcoming inn is a charmer. The second-floor lobby sets the homey, easygoing tone with bookcases, cushy seating, and cafe tables where free continental breakfast is served. The rooms are basic but comfy, outfitted in an appealing neo-Deco style with firm beds, good-quality linens and textiles, and nice bathrooms (about half have showers only). The place is impeccably kept. The standard doubles are fine for couples; if there's more than two of you or you're looking to stay a while, the suites—with pullout sofa, microwave, minifridge, and lots of closet space—are a great deal. Double-paned windows keep the rooms surprisingly peaceful; still, ask for a back-facing one if you're extrasensitive.

The inn's biggest asset is its staff, who go above and beyond the call to make guests happy; they'll even give you a hot-line number so you can call while you're on the town for directions, advice, and other assistance. Service just doesn't get any better in this price range. This nicely gentrified corner of the Theater District makes a great base, especially for theatergoers. The inn has a loyal following, so reserve early. However, there's no elevator in the four-story building, so overpackers and travelers with limited mobility should book elsewhere.

264 W. 46th St. (at Eighth Ave.), New York, NY 10036. © **800/826-6300** or 212/997-9200. Fax 212/768-2807. www.broadwayinn.com. 41 units (about half with shower only). $99–$139 single; $135–$225 double; $199–$299 suite. Rates include continental breakfast. Check the website for special deals (as low as $79 single, $99 double at press time). Extra person $10. Children under 12 stay free in parents' room. AE, DC, DISC, MC, V. Parking $20, 3 blocks away. Subway: A, C, E to 42nd St. **Amenities:** 2 nearby restaurants offer guest discounts; concierge; fax and copy service. *In room:* A/C, TV, dataport, fridge, hair dryer, iron.

Midtown, Chelsea & Union Square Accommodations

- Americana Inn **16**
- Big Apple Hostel **7**
- Broadway Inn **14**
- Carlton Arms **28**
- Chelsea Center Hostel **38**
- Chelsea Inn **32**
- Chelsea International Hostel **34**
- Chelsea Lodge **36**
- Chelsea Pines Inn **35**
- Chelsea Savoy Hotel **33**
- Chelsea Star Hotel/Chelsea Suites **39**
- Colonial House Inn **37**
- Comfort Inn Manhattan **17**
- Comfort Inn Midtown **9**
- Gershwin Hotel **26**
- Gramercy Park Hotel **29**
- Habitat Hotel **4**
- Helmsley Middletowne **6**
- Herald Square Hotel **20**
- Hotel 17 **30**
- Hotel Edison **10**
- Hotel Grand Union **22**
- Hotel Metro **18**
- Hotel Wolcott **21**
- Hudson **1**
- Mayfair Hotel **11**
- Murray Hill Inn **25**
- New York Inn **13**
- Park Savoy Hotel **2**
- Pickwick Arms Hotel **5**
- Portland Square Hotel **8**
- Ramada Inn Eastside **24**
- Red Roof Inn **19**
- Skyline Hotel **12**
- Super 8 Hotel Times Square **40**
- The Marcel **27**
- The Wyndham **3**
- Thirty Thirty **23**
- Travel Inn **15**
- Union Square Inn **31**

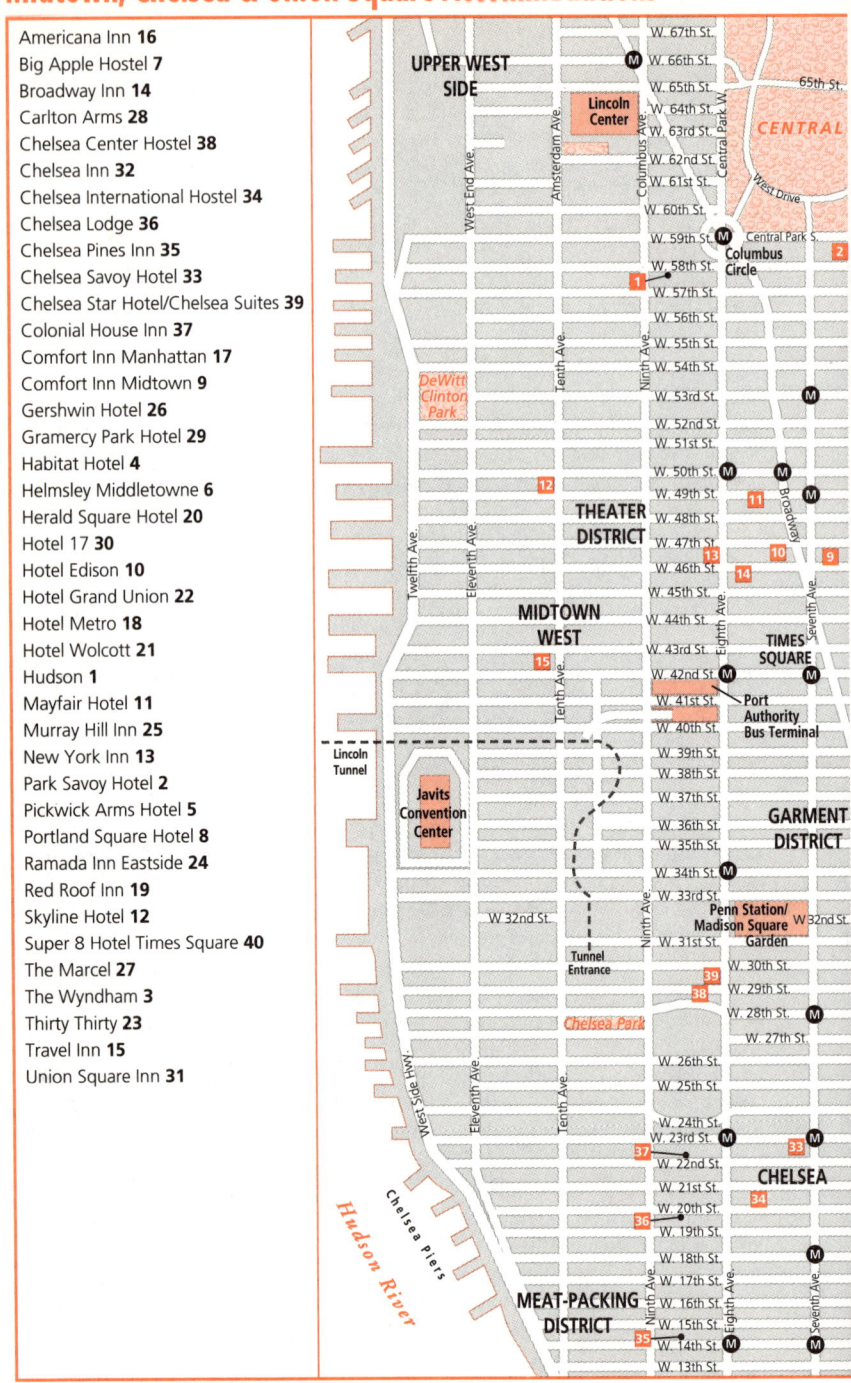

112

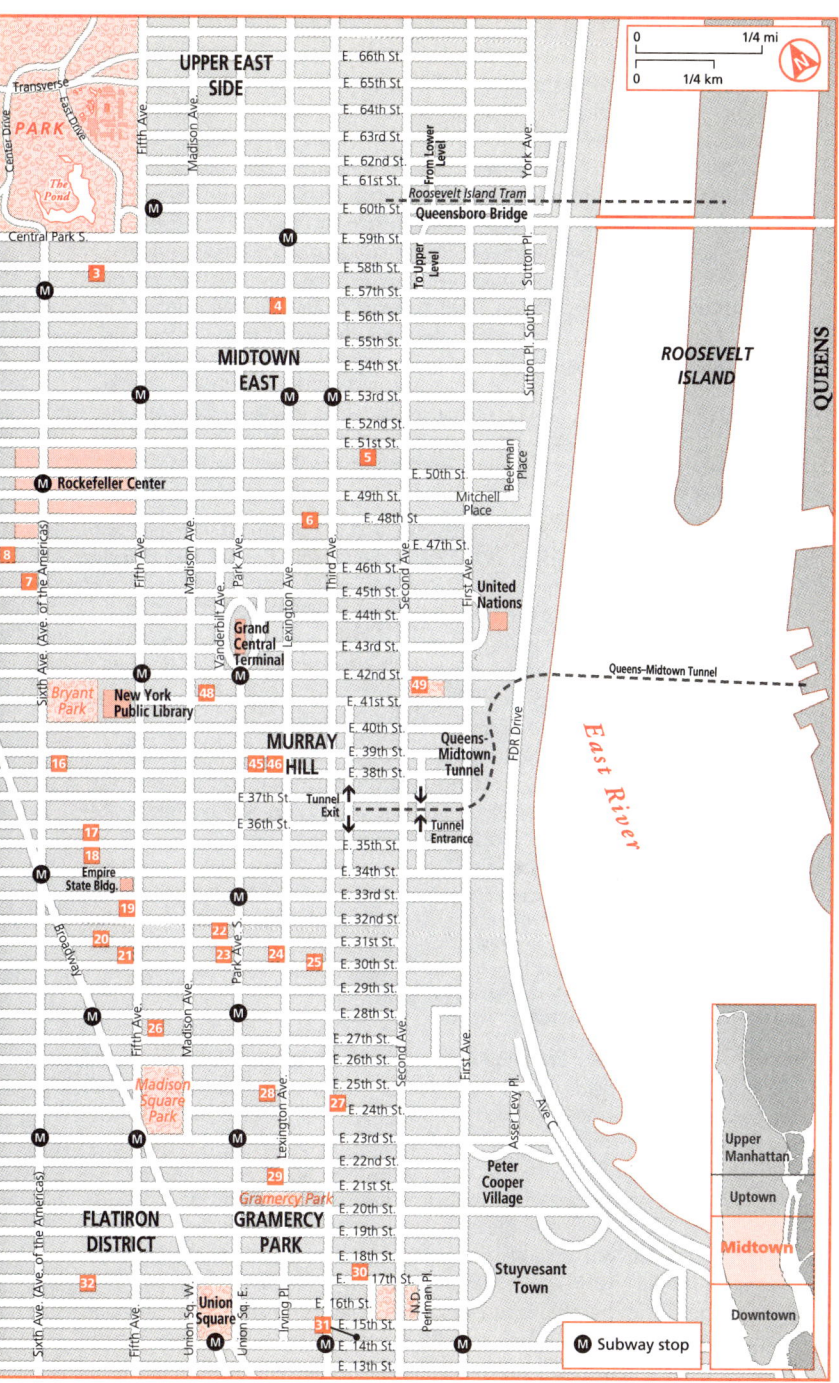

Comfort Inn Manhattan This centrally located hotel is a good choice for those who prefer to go with a national chain with a proven reputation. It's on a block just a stone's throw from some of Midtown's biggest attractions, including the Empire State Building and Macy's. This is a standard chain hotel, but the rooms are clean, well maintained, and large by Manhattan standards. In fact, Hotel Choice (Comfort Inn's parent company) presented this location its gold award for the quality of its professionalism, housekeeping, and hospitality. Nice extras include big closets, hair dryers, in-room safes, on-command movies, and voice mail on the phones. A number of rooms have microwaves and minifridges, and about 30 king-bedded rooms come with sleeper sofas. The lobby is attractive enough to invite lounging, and the front desk staff is friendly and helpful. The substantial continental breakfast spread that's included in the rates is a big plus.

42 W. 35th St. (btwn Fifth and Sixth aves.), New York, NY 10001. © 800/228-5150 or 212/947-0200. Fax 212/594-3047. www.comfortinnmanhattan.com or www.comfortinn.com. 131 units. $139–$219 double. Rates include continental breakfast. Ask about senior, AAA, corporate, and other discounts (as low as $116 at press time). Extra person $15. Children under 19 stay free in parents' room. AE, DC, DISC, MC, V. Parking $18 nearby. Subway: B, D, F, N, Q, R, V, W to 34th St. **Amenities:** Restaurant; dry cleaning/laundry. *In room:* A/C, TV, dataport, hair dryer, iron.

Comfort Inn Midtown As of August 1, 2001, this simple but pleasant member of the Comfort Inn chain has taken a bold step forward by officially declaring itself a nonsmoking hotel.

A major renovation turned the Hotel Remington into a value-oriented Comfort Inn in 1998. Rates can climb in autumn or at Christmas, but low-season rates can make the rooms one of Midtown's best bargains. A mahogany-and-marble lobby leads to the petite but comfortable and nicely outfitted guest rooms, which boast neo-Shaker furnishings, coffeemakers, blackout drapes, and marble-and-tile bathrooms; all rooms have tub/shower combinations. Every room previously in the "smoking allowed" category has been disinfected. Don't expect much in the way of service, but the location is excellent—steps from Times Square, Rockefeller Center, Broadway theaters, and a wealth of dining options.

129 W. 46th St. (btwn Sixth Ave. and Broadway), New York, NY 10036. © 800/567-7720 or 212/221-2600. Fax 212/790-2760. www.applecorehotels.com or www.comfortinn.com. 79 units. $89–$329 double. Rates include continental breakfast. Ask about senior, AAA, corporate, and other discounts; check www.comfortinn.com for online discounts. Extra person $10. Children under 14 stay free in parents' room. AE, DC, DISC, MC, V. Parking $20 nearby. Subway: 1, 2, 3, 9 to 42nd St./Times Sq.; N, R to 49th St.; B, D, F, V to 47–50th sts./Rockefeller Center. **Amenities:** Small fitness room; self-serve business center; dry cleaning/laundry. *In room:* A/C, TV, dataport, coffeemaker, hair dryer, iron.

Herald Square Hotel Presiding regally over the entrance, Philip Martiny's gilded sculpture *Winged Life* is emblematic of the new life in this older Manhattan hotel. The owners took the Carrère & Hastings beaux-arts building that was once home to *Life* magazine and reinvented it as a budget hotel with a sense of history. *Life* covers decorate the lobby, and some of the rooms. The rooms are small and basic, with laminated furniture, florescent lighting, and good-size but older bathrooms; plus voicemail and in-room safes. Still, if you're looking for a great location, this is a good bet (although I'd try the Portland Square, the Herald Square's sister hotel, which I like better, first; see below). The hotel is popular with Europeans and other visitors who love the nearby shopping (Macy's, Lord & Taylor, the Manhattan Mall) and sightseeing (the Empire State Building). The friendly staff can arrange bus tours and airport transportation.

19 W. 31st St. (btwn Fifth Ave. and Broadway), New York, NY 10001. © 800/727-1888 or 212/279-4017. Fax 212/643-9208. www.heraldsquarehotel.com. 120 units (109 with private bathroom). $60–$95 single;

TIMES SQUARE & MIDTOWN WEST 115

$95–$120 double; $109–$140 triple or quad. Extra person $10. Children under 12 stay free in parents' room. AE, DISC, MC, V. Parking from $21 nearby. Subway: N, R to 28th St.; B, D, F, N, Q, R, V, W to 34th St. *In room:* A/C, TV, dataport, hair dryer, iron, safe.

Hotel Edison *Kids*   A big jump in prices means that the Edison is no longer one of the Theater District's best bargains, but it's still a reasonably good deal. A grand, block-long Art Deco–style lobby leads to rooms that have been nicely renovated. Don't expect much more than the basics, but you will find a firm bed, decor that's more attractive than most in this category, and a clean tile bathroom. Most double rooms feature two twins or a full bed, but there are some queens; request one at booking and show up early for your best chance at one. The larger quad rooms, with two doubles, are the best reason to consider the Edison, especially if you're traveling with the kids. Off the lobby is the **Cafe Edison,** an old-style Polish deli that's a favorite among theater types and downmarket ladies who lunch; **Sofia's,** a just-fine Italian restaurant; and the **Rum House tavern,** which has a Caribbean flair and live entertainment most nights.

228 W. 47th St. (btwn Broadway and Eighth Ave.), New York, NY 10036. © **800/637-7070** or 212/840-5000. Fax 212/596-6850. www.edisonhotelnyc.com. 850 units. $150–$170 single; $170–$200 double; $185–$230 triple or quad; $225–$275 suite. Extra person $15. AE, DC, DISC, MC, V. Parking $35. Subway: N, R to 49th St.; 1, 9 to 50th St. **Amenities:** 2 restaurants; cocktail lounge; exercise room; tour desk; dry cleaning/laundry. *In room:* A/C, TV, dataport.

Hotel Metro ★★★ *Kids*   One of my all-time favorites, the Metro is the handsdown best choice in Midtown for those who don't want to sacrifice style or comfort for affordability. This glamorous Art Deco–style jewel has larger rooms than you'd expect. They're outfitted with retro furnishings, playful fabrics, fluffy pillows, alarm clocks, and small but beautiful marble bathrooms. Only about half the bathrooms have tubs, but the others have huge shower stalls (junior suites have whirlpool tubs). The family room—a two-room suite with a second bedroom in lieu of a sitting area—is an ingenious invention, while families on tighter budgets can opt for a roomy double/double. There's a comfy, fire-lit library/lounge area off the lobby, where complimentary buffet breakfast is laid out and the coffeepot's on all day. The well-furnished rooftop terrace boasts a breathtaking view of the Empire State Building, and makes a great place to order up room service from the stylish and very good **Metro Grill.**

Prices skyrocket in fall, but it's relatively easy to score a rate between $150 and $180 through August, as long as you book well ahead; also check with airlines and other package operators for great-value package deals.

45 W. 35th St. (btwn Fifth and Sixth aves.), New York, NY 10001. © **800/356-3870** or 212/947-2500. Fax 212/279-1310. www.hotelmetronyc.com. 179 units. $150–$250 double; $165–$300 triple or quad; $200–$350 family room; $225–$400 suite. Rates include continental breakfast. Check with airlines and other package operators for great-value package deals. Extra person $25. 1 child under 14 stays free in parents' room. AE, DC, MC, V. Parking $17 nearby. Subway: B, D, F, V, N, R to 34th St. **Amenities:** Restaurant; rooftop bar in summer; fitness room; salon; limited room service; dry cleaning/laundry. *In room:* A/C, TV, dataport, fridge, hair dryer, iron.

Hotel Wolcott   This was once one of the grande dames of Manhattan hotels. Now, the Wolcott has been reinvented as a good-value option for bargain hunters. Only the lobby hints at its former grandeur; these days, the rooms are motel-standard, but they're rather large, well kept, and quite serviceable. Plusses include spacious bathrooms and phones with voice mail, plus minifridges in most rooms. On the downside, the decor is less than stylish and the closets tend to be small—but these are small sacrifices for prices this low. Some of the triples are poorly configured—but they're big enough for three, and come with two (as do the suites). What's more, the services—fitness room, business center, coin-op laundry, Nintendo and TV Internet access in every room—far exceed most competitors in the budget category. All in all, you get your money's worth here.

4 W. 31st St. (at Fifth Ave.), New York, NY 10001. © **212/268-2900.** Fax 212/563-0096. www.wolcott.com. 250 units. $99–$160 single or double; $115–$180 triple; $120–$220 junior suite for 2 or 3. Discounted AAA, AARP, and promo rates may be available. AE, MC, V. Parking $17 next door. Subway: B, D, F, V, N, R to 34th St. **Amenities:** Exercise room; tour desk; business center; coin-op laundry. *In room:* A/C, TV w/pay movies, dataport, fridge, hair dryer, video games, Internet access.

Hudson ✦ If you're a style hound on a budget, it's never too early to book one of the handful of the cheapest rooms at Hudson. Unveiled in October 2000, by celebrity hotelier Ian Schrager, it has become the white-hot center of the style universe, attracting an adoring crowd and star-studded events to its Philippe Starck–designed digs. The eye-popping hotel boasts an Ivy-League-on-Acid design that radiates energy. The ivy-draped lobby and the second-level "Private Park" deck—the best outdoor space in any Big Apple hotel—serve as the quad from which everything radiates, including the hot **Hudson Bar,** the classic-goes-Warhol **Library,** and the surprisingly affordable cafeteria-style restaurant.

It's a good thing about the public spaces, because the handful of budget-friendly guest rooms are miniscule—think budget cabin on a Carnival cruise and you'll get the picture. There's no arguing with their beauty or luxury comforts, though: They were designed on the retro-romantic ocean liner model, with rich African Makore paneling, hardwood floors, beautifully made white-on-white beds, clever bedside lamps featuring translucent art by Francesco Clemente, a petite steel desk, and studded white-leather steamer trunk upholstery. Ultra-efficient appointments make even the smallest feel like a treat, but anybody who values spreading-out room over style should *definitely* book elsewhere.

356 W. 58th St. (btwn Eighth and Ninth aves.), New York, NY 10019. © **800/444-4786** or 212/554-6000. Fax 212/554-6001. www.ianschragerhotels.com. 1,000 units. $95–$295 double; $350–$450 studio. AE, DC, DISC, MC, V. Parking $46. Subway: 1, 9, A, B, C, D to 59th St./Columbus Circle. **Amenities:** Restaurant; 2 bars; 24-hr. fitness center; 24-hr. concierge; business center; room service (6:30am–midnight); dry cleaning/laundry; CD library. *In room:* A/C, TV w/pay movies, CD player, dataport and high-speed connectivity, minibar, hair dryer, safe.

Mayfair Hotel Be prepared—the rooms here are *tiny.* The elevator is, too. That's it for the bad news. Now the good: The Mayfair is one of the Theater District's friendliest and best-kept budget hotels, and the location couldn't be better. Each room boasts a small but nice black-and-white tile bathroom (all but a few singles have tub/shower combos) and unstylish but perfectly nice decor. The wood-paneled lobby is more elegant than most in this price range; just off it is the cute French bistro **Le Garrick,** an attraction in its own right. A super-nice staff is merely the icing on the cake. Don't be frightened off by the rack-rate range; while prices can soar in peak seasons, rates usually stay below $200, and it's easy to score a room for around $150 or less before the end of June. The ridiculous end of the price spectrum is only charged in autumn, when you *should* stay elsewhere.

242 W. 49th St. (btwn Broadway and Eighth Ave.), New York, NY 10019. © **800/55-MAYFAIR** or 212/586-0300. Fax 212/307-5226. www.mayfairnewyork.com. 78 units. $90–$250 single or double ($100–$150 in most seasons). Corporate rates $10–$20 less; also check for low-season specials. AE, DC, DISC, MC, V. Parking $18 nearby. Subway: 1, 9, C, E to 50th St. **Amenities:** Restaurant; concierge. *In room:* A/C, TV, dataport, hair dryer, iron, safe.

New York Inn Don't expect much from this dingy little hotel on a still-ratty block of Eighth Avenue. But if you're committed to finding a room with private bathroom, TV, and phone in the Theater District for a low rate, this is probably your best choice—especially in the second half of the year, when prices skyrocket at most neighboring budget hotels. A half-staircase leads up to the lobby, where you'll check in and proceed up a narrow staircase to three floors of rooms. Guest rooms are small and dark but have firm beds with relatively new spreads, new desktop TVs with cable, telephones with voice mail, and cramped bathrooms with stall showers that could use some serious retiling. Maintenance is less than perfect, but everything is clean—frankly, as good as can be expected considering the location and rate. I'd choose the St. Mark's Hotel (p. 100) first—but it's not in the heart of the Theater District. While this specific block is less than pretty, this area is gentrifying well, and great affordable eats abound.

765 Eighth Ave. (btwn 46th and 47th sts.), New York, NY 10036. © **888/450-5555** or 212/247-5400. Fax 212/586-6201. www.newyorkinn.com. 40 units. $89–$130 single or double. Rates include continental breakfast and tax. AE, DISC, MC, V. Subway: C, E to 50th St. *In room:* A/C, TV, hair dryer.

Park Savoy Hotel The Park Savoy isn't as nice as its sibling, the Chelsea Savoy (p. 104), but the lower prices reflect the quality difference, making it a good deal. Rooms are basic, and a few I saw were in need of a fresh coat of paint. All have voice mail and alarm clocks, most have walk-in closets, and a few have minifridges. All rooms have newish tiled private bathrooms that are petite (with showers only, no tubs) but attractive and clean. If your budget is tight, two of you can make do in the smallest rooms; the biggest ones can accommodate three or four in two double beds. Services are kept to a minimum to keep rates low, but there's a decent restaurant next door. Best of all is the convenient location—a block from Central Park and a stone's throw from Carnegie Hall, Lincoln Center, and the Columbus Circle subways, which give easy access to the rest of the city.

158 W. 58th St. (btwn Sixth and Seventh aves.), New York, NY 10019. © **212/245-5755.** Fax 212/765-0668. 70 units. $95–$145 single or double. AE, MC, V. Parking $20 next door. Subway: A, B, C, D, 1, 9 to 59th St./Columbus Circle; N, R to 57th St. *In room:* A/C, TV.

Portland Square Hotel Another Puchall family project (see the Herald Square Hotel, above), the Portland Square is a good Theater District bet for budget travelers. I like this hotel better than the Herald Square: The public spaces have been renovated, and everything seems to be in good shape. The rooms are small, simple, and cheaply furnished (laminated furniture, fluorescent lighting), but clean. Ask for one with an extra-large bathroom; some are almost as big as the bedroom. Avoid the shared-bathroom singles if you can: The ratio is a high four rooms to a bathroom, the hall bathrooms I saw were on the crusty side, and most of the shared bathrooms had a smoky odor. But the private bathrooms are a decent deal if money's tight. The staff is friendly and cooperative, but don't expect much in the way of service (that's one way they keep rates low).

132 W. 47th St. (btwn Sixth and Seventh aves.), New York, NY 10036. © **800/388-8988** or 212/382-0600. Fax 212/382-0684. www.portlandsquarehotel.com. 145 units (115 with private bathroom). $65–$75 single or double with shared bathroom; $99–$120 single with private bathroom; $125–$135 double with private bathroom; $135–$170 triple or quad with private bathroom. Extra person $10. AE, MC, V. Parking $24 across the street. Subway: B, D, F, V to 47th–50th sts./Rockefeller Center. **Amenities:** Luggage lockers. *In room:* A/C, TV, dataport.

Red Roof Inn ★★ Manhattan's first Red Roof Inn opened in mid-2000, and it offers relief from Midtown's high-priced hotel scene. The hotel occupies a former office building that was gutted and laid out fresh, allowing for more spacious rooms and bathrooms than you'll usually find in this price category. The lobby feels smart, and elevators are quiet and efficient. In-room amenities—including coffeemakers and TVs with on-screen Web access—are better than most competitors', and furnishings are new and comfortable. The location—on a bustling block lined with nice hotels and affordable Korean restaurants, just a stone's throw from the Empire State Building and Herald Square—is excellent.

The rack-rate range is ridiculous, but it's usually easy to score a room for less than $150 if you book well in advance. Be sure to compare the rates offered by Apple Core Hotel's reservation line (the management company) and those quoted on Red Roof's national reservation line and website, as they can vary significantly. Complimentary continental breakfast adds to the good value.

6 W. 32nd St. (btwn Broadway and Fifth Ave.), New York, NY 10001. © **800/567-7720**, 800/RED-ROOF, or 212/643-7100. Fax 212/643-7101. www.applecorehotels.com or www.redroof.com. 171 units. $89–$329 double (usually less than $159). Rates include continental breakfast. Children under 14 stay free in parents' room. AE, DC, DISC, MC, V. Parking $22. Subway: B, D, F, V, N, R to 34th St. **Amenities:** Breakfast room; wine-and-beer lounge; exercise room; concierge; business center; dry cleaning/laundry. *In room:* A/C, TV w/pay movies, dataport, fridge, coffeemaker, hair dryer, iron; video games, Internet access.

Skyline Hotel *Kids*   This newly renovated motor hotel offers predictable comforts and some uncommon extras—free storage parking (easily worth $25 or more a day) and an indoor pool—that make it an excellent value. A pleasant lobby leads to motel-standard rooms that are a far cry from stylish, but bigger than most in this price range. They boast decent-size closets, small work desks (in most), and double-paned windows that open to let fresh air in, and shut out a surprising amount of street noise. Some rooms have brand-new bathrooms, but the older ones are fine. Each junior suite is basically one large room with a pullout sofa bed, while each full suite has a sitting room with a pullout sofa and a separate room with two double beds and an extra TV, making them great for families. Everything is very well kept. On the downside, some closets are open to the room, there are no bedside alarm clocks, and hair dryers and irons must be requested from housekeeping. The pool has a nicely tiled deck and plush deck chairs, but it's only open limited hours, so call ahead if it matters.

725 Tenth Ave. (at 49th St.), New York, NY 10019. © **800/433-1982** or 212/586-3400. Fax 212/582-4604. www.skylinehotelny.com. 230 units. $109–$209 double or suite. Check website or inquire about special rates (as low as $89 at press time). Extra person $15. Children 14 and under stay free in parents' room. AE, DC, DISC, MC, V. Free storage parking (charge for in/out privileges). Subway: A, C, E to 50th St. Pets accepted with $200 deposit. **Amenities:** Restaurant; bar with live entertainment; indoor pool; Gray Line tour desk; Internet-access machine in lobby. *In room:* A/C, TV w/pay movies, hair dryer, iron, safe; video games, Internet access.

Super 8 Hotel Times Square ★★ *Value*   This brand-new lodging is my favorite new budget hotel of the year. The Super 8 folks, in alliance with Apple Core Hotels (the franchisee behind such hotels as the Comfort Inn Midtown and Red Roof Inn, reviewed earlier), have done a terrific job reinventing the former Hotel Wentworth (more recently, the former Quality Hotel & Suites) into a bright, attractive hotel offering better-than-budget accommodations in a heart-of-Midtown location. The Wentworth was built in 1902 as a hotel for women, so it boasts extra-large rooms (by New York standards), outfitted with a king or two doubles, and all-new bathrooms. Decor isn't what you'd call stylish, but it's attractive, with woods, pastel wallpaper, green carpeting, and floral spreads. Everything is new, and all rooms are well outfitted with fridges, coffeemakers, small work desks, hair dryers, irons, and alarm clocks, plus Nintendo and on-screen e-mail access. Mom and Dad will love the family suite, which features a king in one room and two twins (in lieu of a sitting area) in the other; be flexible in your travel and you may be able to snare this suite for as little as $129.

FREE TRIAL ISSUE

AWARD-WINNING MAGAZINE

☑ **YES!** Please send my **FREE** trial issue of *Arthur Frommer's Budget Travel* magazine. If I wish to continue, I'll pay my bill for just $12.00 for a one-year subscription (10 issues in all)—**a savings of 69% off the newsstand price.** If I choose not to subscribe, I'll simply return my invoice marked "Cancel" and owe nothing.

_____
Name   (please print)

_____
Address   Apt.#

_____
City   State   Zip

_____
E-mail (optional)

Please allow 4-6 weeks for delivery. Canadian orders add $12 per year for postage. Foreign orders add $18 per year. U.S. funds must accompany foreign orders. Residents of GA please add applicable sales tax.

C202A1

BUSINESS REPLY MAIL

FIRST-CLASS MAIL PERMIT NO. 183 FLAGLER BEACH FL

POSTAGE WILL BE PAID BY ADDRESSEE

ARTHUR FROMMER'S

vacations for real people

PO BOX 420772
PALM COAST FL 32142-8518

NO POSTAGE
NECESSARY
IF MAILED
IN THE
UNITED STATES

The lobby is bright and elegant, and service is professional. Perks include a state-of-the-art exercise room and a breakfast room serving a continental meal that's included in the rate—for as little as $89 double! Even in high seasons, when Super 8 rates can climb into the mid-$100s, you'll still get your money's worth. In fact, Apple Core always keeps their hotels priced ahead of the curve.

59 W. 46th St. (btwn Fifth and Sixth aves.), New York, NY 10036. © **800/567-7720** or 212/719-2300. Fax 212/790-2760. www.applecorehotels.com or www.super8.com. 160 units. $89–$329 double (usually less than $179); family suite from $129. Rates include continental breakfast. Check for AAA, AARP, and other discounts. Children under 14 stay free in parents' room. AE, DC, DISC, MC, V. Parking $20 next door. Subway: B, D, F, V to 42nd St. **Amenities:** Breakfast room; exercise room; business center with computer, fax, copier; dry cleaning/laundry. *In room:* A/C, TV w/pay movies, dataport, fridge, coffeemaker, hair dryer, iron, video games, Internet access.

Travel Inn *Kids* Extras like a huge outdoor pool and sun deck, a sunny, up-to-date fitness room, and free parking (with in-and-out privileges!) make the Travel Inn another terrific deal. Like the Skyline (see above), the Travel Inn may not be loaded with personality, but it offers the clean, bright regularity of a good chain hotel—an attractive trait in a city where "quirky" is the catchword at most affordable hotels. Rooms are oversize and comfortable, furnished with extra-firm beds and desks; even the smallest double is sizable and has a roomy bathroom, and double/doubles make affordable shares for families. A renovation over the last couple of years has made everything feel like new, even the tiled bathrooms. The neighborhood has gentrified and isn't as far off as you might think: Off-Broadway theaters and good restaurants are nearby, and it's a 10-minute walk to the Theater District. It's a good bet even if you don't have a car.

515 W. 42nd St. (just west of Tenth Ave.), New York, NY 10036. © **888/HOTEL58** (468-3558), 800/869-4630, or 212/695-7171. Fax 212/967-5025. www.newyorkhotel.com. 160 units. $125–$200 double. AAA discounts available. Check website for Internet deals (as low as $105 at press time). Extra person $10. Children under 16 stay free in parents' room. AE, DC, DISC, MC, V. Free self-parking. Subway: A, C, E to 42nd St./Port Authority. **Amenities:** Coffee shop; outdoor pool; fitness center; tour desk; 24-hr. room service. *In room:* A/C, TV, dataport, hair dryer, iron.

The Wyndham ★ *Finds* This hotel isn't part of the upscale chain of the same name; rather, it's a family-owned charmer that's one of Midtown's best hotel deals: perfectly located, on a great block steps away from Fifth Avenue and Central Park. The Wyndham is stuck in the '70s on all fronts, but its guest rooms are enormous, comfortable, and loaded with character. The hotel features a wild collection of wallpaper, from candy stripes to crushed velvets, so some rooms cross the ticky-tacky line. But others are lovely, with such details as rich Oriental carpets and well-worn libraries, and the eclectic art collection that lines the walls boasts some real gems. If you're put in a room that's not to your taste, just ask politely to see another one; the staff is usually willing to accommodate.

Most important, it's a great deal: The rooms are quite large and feature huge walk-in closets (the biggest I've seen). The surprisingly affordable suites also have full living rooms, dressing areas, and cold kitchenettes (fridge only). You'll need a two-bedroom suite if you bring the kids (only two guests are allowed in standard rooms or one-bedroom suites), but the rate is a steal considering the space. Don't expect an alarm clock, hair dryer, luxury toiletries, or other modern amenities. But at these prices, you can afford to invest in travel sizes.

42 W. 58th St. (btwn Fifth and Sixth aves.), New York, NY 10019. © **800/257-1111** or 212/753-3500. Fax 212/754-5638. 212 units. $130–$150 single or double; $160–$195 1-bedroom suite; $290–$330 2-bedroom suite (up to 4 guests included in rate). AE, DC, MC, V. Parking $40 nearby. Subway: N, R to Fifth Ave.; B, Q to 57th St. **Amenities:** New upscale Mediterranean restaurant with excellent cocktail lounge; salon; dry cleaning/laundry. *In room:* A/C, TV, dataport.

SUPERCHEAP SLEEPS

Big Apple Hostel ⭐ This is the nicest hostel in Midtown, if not in all of Manhattan. It's not fancy, but it's well run, spotlessly clean, and in the heart of the Theater District; many luxury hotels wish they had it so good. All dorm rooms are four-bedded; they're well spaced and well kept, with metal bunks and good mattresses with blankets and linens. Only guests in private rooms get towels, so dormers should bring their own. Private rooms are basic but better than most in hostels; all have phones (free local calls!), radio, and alarm, and some have a table and chairs. The shared bathrooms are better than average. There's a stocked kitchen with microwave, a small backyard patio with barbecue, and a luggage storage room. It's popular with Japanese and other international travelers who like the location. It doesn't get much better at bargain-basement prices—much better than the more well-known Aladdin Hostel farther west on 45th Street.

119 W. 45th St. (btwn Sixth and Seventh aves.), New York, NY 10036. © **212/302-2603.** Fax 212/302-2605. www.bigapplehostel.com. 112 dorm beds; 11 private doubles. $28–$38.50 dorm bed; $78–$109 double. MC, V. Subway: N, R, S, 1, 2, 3, 7, 9 to Times Sq./42nd St. **Amenities:** Common kitchen. *In room:* Fans, no phone in dorm units.

9 Midtown East & Murray Hill

Habitat Hotel ⭐ This new-in-1999 hotel is marketed as "upscale budget," to appeal to travelers who are short on funds but big on style. Rooms are well designed in a palette accented with black-and-white photos. Everything is of better quality and more attractive than in most hotels in this price range, from the mattresses to the plush towels to the pedestal sinks in every room. The bathrooms are new; choose between shared (one for every three to four rooms), private, or a semiprivate "minisuite" (two rooms sharing an adjacent bathroom).

The only downside—and it may be a big one for some—are the sleeping accommodations. A few queens are available (at the high end of the price spectrum), but most of the double rooms have a twin bed with a pullout trundle, which takes up most of the width of the room when it's open. Despite that drawback, rates are attractive, especially for the rooms with shared bathroom, considering the *Metropolitan Home* mind-set and the A-1 location. I prefer the private-bathroom units at sister hotel Thirty Thirty (see below), because they don't have the space limitations, but this hotel has a more thrilling location and a more exciting vibe thanks to the popular restaurant and bar, **Opus.**

The second-floor lobby is designer-stylish and professionally staffed, the bar scene hops, and the neighborhood is safe, chic, and convenient—especially for shoppers, since Bloomingdale's is just 2 blocks away. You won't even have to put on your shoes to visit Kenneth Cole, whose new boutique is just downstairs.

130 E. 57th St. (at Lexington Ave.), New York, NY 10022. © **800/255-0482** or 212/753-8841. Fax 212/829-9605. www.habitatny.com. 300 units (about 40 with private bathroom). $85–$115 single or double with shared bathroom, $125–$195 single or double with private bathroom; $240–$270 minisuite (2 rooms with shared bathroom). Rates include continental breakfast. Inquire or check website for student rates and promotions (from $79 at press time). AE, DC, DISC, MC, V. Parking $25. Subway: 4, 5, 6 to 59th St.; E, F to Lexington Ave. **Amenities:** Restaurant/bar; tour desk. *In room:* A/C, TV, dataport.

Helmsley Middletowne ⭐ This value-laden member of the Helmsley chain (yes, as in Leona Helmsley) boasts little in the way of style, services, or amenities, but rooms and suites are large, comfortable, and well priced, and the location is fantastic—you usually have to spend more to stay in this 'hood. The hotel started life as an apartment building and still has the vibe and the large rooms. The lobby is virtually nonexistent, but the front-desk staff—most of whom have worked here for *years*—is brisk and friendly. Room decor is generic and furnishings are older, but beds are firm and everything is well kept. Each room has a refrigerator (usually with a wet bar), multiple-line phones, a dated but fine bathroom, and a wealth of closet space. The one- and two-bedroom suites are well priced and big enough to accommodate families. They also boast walk-in kitchenettes (some lack dishware, though, so request it or bring plastic); some have fireplaces and/or balconies as well. Business travelers can request an in-room fax machine. Not sexy but, all in all, a nice choice in the midprice range.

148 E. 48th St. (btwn Third and Lexington aves.), New York, NY 10017. © 800/221-4982 or 212/755-3000. Fax 212/832-0261. www.helmsleyhotels.com. 192 units. $195–$205 double; from $235 1- or 2-bedroom suite. Rates include continental breakfast. Ask about packages. Children under 12 stay free in parents' room. AE, DC, MC, V. Parking $30. Subway: 6 to 51st St. **Amenities:** Restaurant; dry cleaning/laundry. *In room:* A/C, TV, fridge, hair dryer, iron, kitchenettes in suites.

Hotel Grand Union This centrally located hotel is big with budget-minded international travelers. A pleasant white-on-white lobby leads to clean, spacious rooms with nice extras that are uncommon in this price category, like hair dryers and free HBO. Bad florescent lighting, unattractive furniture, and a lack of natural light dampen the mood—but considering the roominess, rates, and central-to-everything location, the Grand Union is a deal. A nicely configured quad with two twins and a queen in a separate alcove, no. 309 is a great bet for families. Most bathrooms have been outfitted in granite or tile; ask for a newly renovated one. The staff is helpful, there's a pleasant sitting room off the lobby, and an adjacent coffee shop is convenient for morning coffee or a quickie burger.

34 E. 32nd St. (btwn Madison and Park aves.), New York, NY 10016. © 212/683-5890. Fax 212/689-7397. www.hotelgrandunion.com. 95 units. $116–$138 single or double; $132–$158 twin or triple; $158–$190 quad. Call or check website for special rates (as low as $90 at press time). AE, DC, DISC, MC, V. Parking $22 nearby. Subway: 6 to 33rd St. **Amenities:** Coffee shop; tour desk; fax service. *In room:* A/C, TV, dataport, fridge, hair dryer.

Murray Hill Inn ★ *Value* Housed in a five-story walk-up in a pleasant neighborhood, the Murray Hill Inn is shoestring-basic—but there's no arguing with its cleanliness, key in judging accommodations in this price range. Rooms are tiny and outfitted with one or two beds with motel-standard bedspread and furnishings, a wall rack, a phone, and small TV; most rooms with shared bathroom also have private sinks (request one when booking). These Euro-style rooms share the in-hall bathrooms that are new and spotless. Some of the doubles have an alcove that can accommodate a third traveler on a cot if you're on an extra-tight budget. Rooms with private bathrooms are the nicest; they're spacious, with new bathrooms and dataports on the telephones. Most have pullout sofas that can accommodate an extra traveler. Don't expect much in terms of facilities beyond a pleasant (if tiny) lobby, plus a sitting area with a vending machine, an ATM, and a luggage-storage area. The rooms with private bathrooms go fast, so book early; you can often deal on shared-bathroom units, though.

143 E. 30th St. (btwn Lexington and Third aves.), New York, NY 10016. © 888/996-6376 or 212/683-6900. Fax 212/545-0103. www.murrayhillinn.com. 50 units (10 with shared bathroom). $60–$65 single with shared bathroom; $75–$80 double with shared bathroom, $125 double with private bathroom. Ask about discounts and special rates (as low as $95 with private bathroom at press time). Extra person $20. Children under 12 stay free in parents' room. AE, MC, V. Parking about $25 nearby. Subway: 6 to 28th St. *In room:* A/C, TV.

Pickwick Arms Hotel What keeps the Pickwick booked up is its prices. For a Midtown hotel on the East Side, this is like entering an economic time warp. The location couldn't be better. The older, sometimes astoundingly small rooms are spare (think monk's cell), but they're well kept, and the place is safe and well run. There are a few doubles and twins with private bathrooms (the larger deluxe twins can accommodate a rollaway), but the majority of rooms are singles with private, semiprivate, or shared hall bathrooms. Two friends traveling together can take advantage of the semiprivate situation: Two singles (each with sink, TV, desk, closet, and telephone) that share a bathroom can be had for the same price as a twin room. All of the bathrooms are worn-looking and have showers only, but they're clean. A renovation has spiffed up the halls and rooms. If you want a great location for a low price, this is the place. On site is a rooftop patio with skyline views, and an affordable restaurant serving three squares a day.

230 E. 51st St. (btwn Second and Third aves.), New York, NY 10022. © **800/742-5945** in the U.S., 800/874-0074 in Canada, or 212/355-0300. Fax 212/755-5029. www.pickwickarms.com. 320 units (200 with private bathroom). $79–$125 single; $129–$150 double or twin; $155–$165 triple. AE, DC, MC, V. Parking $30–$35 nearby. Subway: 6 to 51st St. **Amenities:** Restaurant. *In room:* A/C, TV, dataport.

Ramada Inn Eastside   The most affordable of the Apple Core Hotels (which also include the Red Roof Inn, the Comfort Inn Midtown, and the Super 8 Hotel; see "Times Square & Midtown West," earlier in this chapter), this former Quality Hotel fell under the Ramada banner in 2002. It's nothing special—small, basic rooms with older bathrooms—but a complete renovation has given them a fresh look in greens and beige. Its other features are the location, in quiet Murray Hill, which abounds with affordable restaurants; the value-added amenities, which include free continental breakfast, free local phone calls, business center, and fitness room; and the usually low rates. Don't expect anything in the way of service, but considering how expensive an average room has become, this hotel is a value. It's quite easy to score a room for $139 or less most of the year.

161 Lexington Ave. (at 30th St.), New York, NY 10016. © **800/567-7720** or 212/545-1800. Fax 212/790-2760. www.applecorehotels.com. 96 units. $89–$209 double. Rates include continental breakfast. Inquire about seasonal/weekend discounts (as low as $79 at press time). Children under 13 stay free in parents' room. AE, DC, DISC, MC, V. Parking $20 nearby. Subway: 6 to 33rd St. **Amenities:** Coffee shop; business center, exercise room (both under renovation at press time). *In room:* A/C, TV w/pay movies, dataport, coffeemaker, hair dryer, iron, video games, Internet access.

Thirty Thirty ★★ *Value*   This new-in-2001 hotel is just right for bargain-hunting travelers looking for a splash of style for an affordable price. The building (which formerly housed the Martha Washington women's hotel and the nightclub Danceteria) has been gutted, renovated, and redone with brand-new everything. The design-conscious tone is set in the loftlike industrial-modern lobby. Pretty hallways lead to rooms that are mostly on the smallish side but do the trick for those who intend to spend their days out on the town rather than holed up here. They're done in a natural palette with a creative edge—purplish carpet, khaki bedspread, woven wallpaper—that comes together more attractively than you might expect. Configurations are split between twin/twins (great for friends), queens, and queen/queens (great for triples, budget-minded quads, or shares that want more spreading-out room). Features include cushioned headboards, firm mattresses, stylish bedside lamps, two-line phones, built-in wardrobes, and spacious tiled bathrooms. No. 1135 is a large L-shaped queen with a nice granite bathroom. A few larger units have kitchenettes—try to book one if you're staying for awhile, as you'll appreciate the extra room and the fridge. There's no room service, but delivery is available from nearby restaurants, and we're told the hotel will be adding a restaurant soon.

30 E. 30th St. (btwn Madison and Park aves.), New York, NY 10016. © **800/497-6028** or 212/689-1900. Fax 212/689-0023. www.thirtythirty-nyc.com. 240 units. $125–$175 double, $145–$195 double with kitchenette; $185–$245 quad. Call for last-minute deals, or check website for special promotions (as low as $99 at press time). AE, DC, DISC, MC, V. Parking $35, 1 block away. Subway: 6 to 28th St. Pets accepted with advance approval. **Amenities:** Concierge; dry cleaning/laundry. *In room:* A/C, TV, dataport, hair dryer.

10 The Upper West Side

Amsterdam Inn *Value* This renovated five-story walk-up offers basic accommodations that add up to a great value in a terrific neighborhood. The private bathrooms are bigger and better at the Murray Hill Inn (p. 121), but you might be able to do better on the rates here, and I prefer this property if you're going to share a bathroom. The inn's biggest assets are its prime Upper West Side location—where one-bedroom apartments rent for $2,000 or more per month—its newness, its consistent cleanliness, and its professional management.

The rooms are small and narrow, with a bed, a rack to hang your clothes on, a set of drawers with a TV on top, a side table with a lamp and a phone that requires a deposit to activate, and a sink if there's no private bathroom. The Euro-style rooms share the in-hall bathrooms at a ratio of about 2½ to 1. The bathrooms are new but have showers only. If you book a double, make sure it's a *real* double, with a double bed. The singles with trundles can (theoretically) accommodate two, but don't expect to have any space left over. Management seems willing to negotiate, so always ask for a lower rate.

340 Amsterdam Ave. (at 76th St.), New York, NY 10023. © 212/579-7500. Fax 212/579-6127. www.amsterdaminn.com. 25 units (12 with private bathroom). $60–$75 single with shared bathroom; $75–$95 bunk-bed twin or double with shared bathroom, $95–$115 double with private bathroom. Extra person $20. Children under 12 stay free in parents' room. AE, MC, V. Parking $20–$25 nearby. Subway: 1, 9 to 79th St. *In room:* A/C, TV.

Comfort Inn–Central Park West *Value* This chain hotel is a great place to stay if you can snag a good rate—which you usually can. It's fabulously located, tucked in the Upper West Side's best residential territory, just steps from Central Park—in fact, the hotel is so understated and attractive that most locals don't even realize it's there. Everything is fresh, new, and professionally done. Rooms aren't huge or stylish, but there's no arguing with the quality. Layout is smart; bedding, fabrics, and window treatments are good; and blackout drapes let you sleep till noon. Closets are on the small side, but you'll have a new bathroom, some with hair dryers (which can otherwise be provided upon request). Most rooms have desks, too. Executive rooms are outfitted in a more modern, less chain-standard style, with mahogany built-ins and individual climate controls.

An extended continental breakfast is served in the breakfast room (with free newspapers), which ups the ante on the value. Rates are seasonal, but low $80 deals are common in the slowest seasons and for AAA cardholders and seniors.

31 W. 71st St. (btwn Columbus Ave. and Central Park W.), New York, NY 10023. © **800/228-5150** (worldwide reservations), 877/727-5236 (direct), or 212/721-4770. Fax 212/579-8544. www.comfortinn.com or www.bestnyhotels.com. 96 units. $119–$209 standard double, $179–$299 executive double. Rates include continental breakfast. Ask about senior, AAA, corporate, and promotional discounts; check www.hotelchoice.com for excellent rates (often as low as $80–$90). Extra person $15. Children under 13 stay free in parents' room. AE, DC, DISC, MC, V. Parking $25 nearby. Subway: B, C to 72nd St. **Amenities:** Small exercise room; concierge; business center; dry cleaning/laundry; executive-level units. *In room:* A/C, TV, dataport, iron.

Holmes Bed & Breakfast *Finds* This terrific, well-priced B&B is an excellent choice for independent-minded travelers who like a residential feel and a little personality in their lodgings. Four guest rooms are available on two floors of a nicely maintained brownstone on a tree-lined block in the heart of the Upper West Side. Owner Marguerite Holmes is an accomplished artist; not only do her terrific multigenre paintings (which run the gamut from pastoral scenes to impressive abstracts) fill the hallways and guest rooms, but her creative eye has turned what could be very basic accommodations into something really special.

Each well-maintained guest room has cable TV (a couple have a VCR), a well-chosen mix of vintage furnishings and original art, good-quality bedding, and a direct-dial phone. The two rooms with private bathrooms each have a fridge, coffeemaker, microwave, and toaster oven, while the two shared-bathroom units share a similarly outfitted pantry kitchenette. The Cranberry Room is the nicest; it boasts a marble bathroom with shower, generous closet space, and a terrace, while the Blueberry Room has a private bathroom with a tub and a sleeper sofa that can sleep a third person. The two shared-bathroom units share an older but nice bathroom.

There's no formal breakfast serving, but a cupboard is stocked with help-yourself breakfast items. A friendly resident innkeeper is on hand and glad to help if you need advice or assistance. No smoking allowed.

W. 91st St. (off Amsterdam Ave.), New York, NY 10024. © 917/838-4808. Fax 518/854-7148. www.holmesnyc.com. 4 units (2 with shared bathroom). $90–$120 double. Rates include morning breakfast items. Discounts on weekly and monthly stays Jan–Mar. AE, DC, MC, V. Subway: 1, 2, 3, 9 to 96th St. *In room:* A/C, TV, kitchenette w/fridge, toaster oven, microwave.

Hotel Belleclaire This beaux-arts hotel boasts a great Upper West Side location and renovated, stylish guest rooms that are larger than most but could use a little more attention to detail. Still, the accommodations do the job, and the management seems intent on pleasing. The rooms have small, freshly tiled bathrooms with tub/shower combos (six have roll-in showers to accommodate travelers with disabilities). Cushioned headboards, nice fabric-covered cubes for modular seating, small TVs, minifridges, and alarm clocks are the main amenities. Closets are small. The shared-bathroom units are the same but have in-room sinks and share hall bathrooms at a ratio of 3 to 1. The family suite features two attached, semiprivate bedrooms with a bathroom, a minifridge, and a big walk-in closet. You'll get more for your money at the Milburn around the corner. Still, it's a perfectly decent choice in a first-class residential neighborhood.

250 W. 77th St. (at Broadway), New York, NY 10024. © 877/HOTEL-BC (468-3522) or 212/362-7700. Fax 212/362-1004. www.hotelbelleclaire.com. 189 units (39 with shared bathroom). $109 double with shared bathroom, $169–$189 double with private bathroom; $229 family suite. Ask about AAA, corporate, group, and other discounts. AE, DC, DISC, MC, V. Parking $25 nearby. Subway: 1, 9 to 79th St. **Amenities:** Access to nearby health club; tour desk; fax; dry cleaning/laundry. *In room:* A/C, TV w/pay movies and games, dataport, fridge, hair dryer, iron.

Hotel Newton *Value* Finally—an inexpensive hotel that's *nice*. Unlike many of its peers, the Newton doesn't scream "budget!" at every turn, or require you to have the attitude of a college student to put up with it. As you enter the pretty lobby, a uniformed staff that's attentive and professional greets you.

The rooms are large, with good, firm beds, work desks, and new bathrooms, plus roomy closets in most (a few have wall racks only). Some are big enough to accommodate families with two doubles or two queen beds. Each suite features two queen beds in the bedroom, a sofa in the sitting room, plus niceties like a microwave, minifridge, and iron, making them worth the few extra dollars. The bigger rooms and suites have been upgraded with cherrywood furnishings, but even the older laminated furniture is much nicer than I usually see in this price

Upper West Side Accommodations

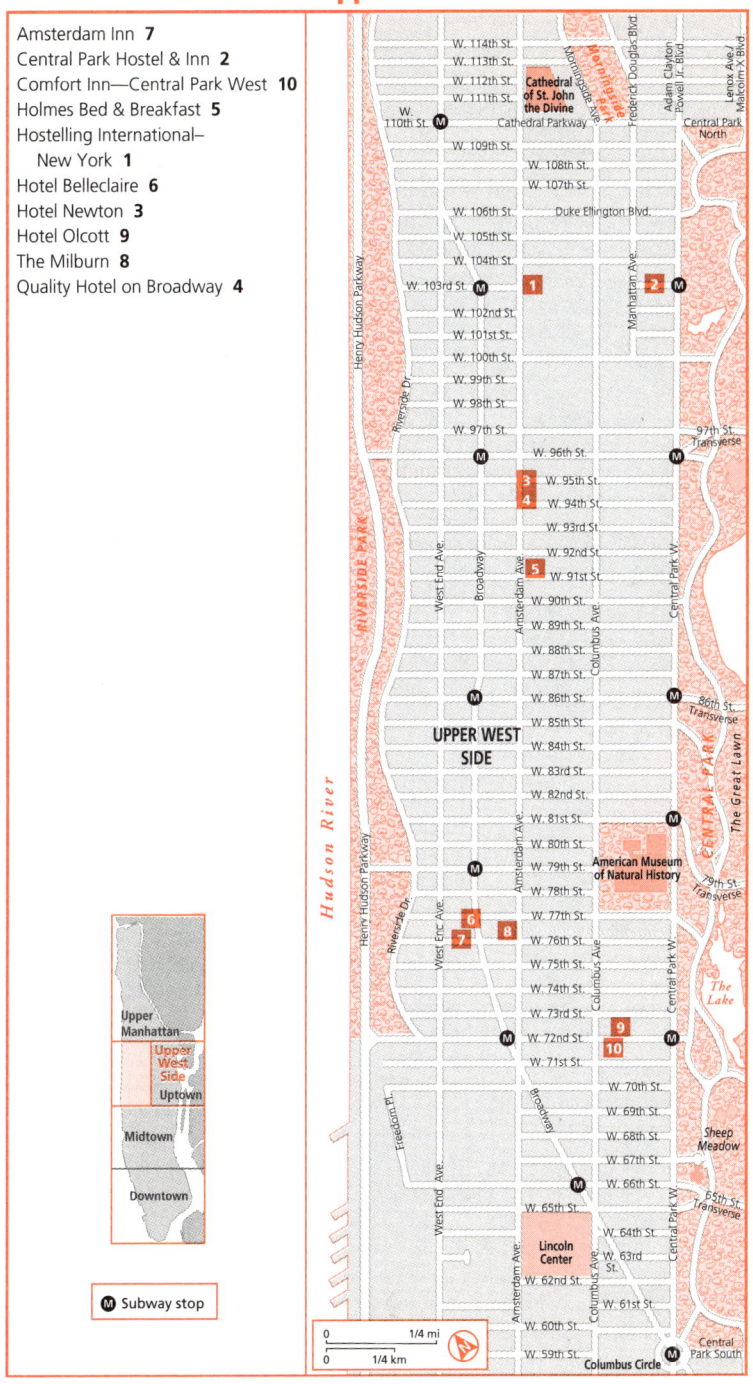

Amsterdam Inn **7**
Central Park Hostel & Inn **2**
Comfort Inn—Central Park West **10**
Holmes Bed & Breakfast **5**
Hostelling International–
  New York **1**
Hotel Belleclaire **6**
Hotel Newton **3**
Hotel Olcott **9**
The Milburn **8**
Quality Hotel on Broadway **4**

125

Kids Affordable Family-Friendly Hotels

The best way for families on a budget to save is to bunk together in a larger room with two double or queen beds. Some hotels have wallet-friendly suite deals that allow the kids to sleep on a pullout sofa in the living room, thus giving everybody a little well-deserved privacy.

Chelsea Savoy Hotel (p. 104) These attractive, affordable rooms are large and comfy enough to accommodate four. Big closets and roomy, immaculate bathrooms with tons of counter space make sharing even easier. Children stay free, and continental breakfast is included.

Gershwin Hotel (p. 109) This funky Flatiron District hotel looks like the domain of the artsy crowd, but it suits families extremely well. Parents in search of a high space-to-dollar ratio will love the family room, a two-room suite that accommodates Mom and Dad in a queen bed in one bedroom, two kids in two twins in the adjacent one.

Hotel Edison (p. 115) Quads can accommodate four in two double beds, and value-priced suites with pullout sofas offer even more space. The nearly 1,000-room hotel bustles around the clock with families and tour groups from around the world, so you can feel comfortable allowing the kids to act like kids here. A coffee shop/deli serves wallet-friendly meals.

Hotel Metro (p. 115) This Art Deco–inspired hotel is an excellent choice for families who want more in the way of room, service, and

---

range. The AAA-approved hotel is impeccably kept, and there was lots of sprucing up going on—new drapes here, fresh paint there—during my last visit.

The 96th Street express subway stop is just a block away. It's a nice bet all the way around. The neighborhood boasts lots of affordable restaurants, and a cute diner in the same block provides room service.

2528 Broadway (btwn 94th and 95th sts.), New York, NY 10025. ℂ **888/HOTEL-58** (468-3558) or 212/678-6500. Fax 212/678-6758. www.newyorkhotel.com. 110 units. $85–$160 double or junior suite. AAA, corporate, senior, and group rates available; check website for Internet deals (from $75 double at press time). Extra person $10. Children under 15 stay free in parents' room. AE, DC, DISC, MC, V. Parking $20 nearby. Subway: 1, 2, 3, 9 to 96th St. **Amenities:** 24-hr. room service. *In room:* A/C, TV, hair dryer.

Hotel Olcott Value Kids   Before I moved to New York, I stayed at the Olcott—and all these years later, this old dowager remains one of New York's best budget bargains. About half of this residential hotel houses permanent and long-term residents, but the rest is open to out-of-towners. The studios and suites are a steal. The apartments are about as stylish as Aunt Edna's house—built around 1970—but they're maintained with care, and even the studios are bigger than most NYC apartments (the suites are enormous). If only I had this much closet space! The discount furnishings are not pretty, but they're perfectly comfortable. Every apartment has a big bathroom and a kitchenette with minifridge, hot plate with kettle, toaster, and basic dishes and utensils; studios generally have dining tables for two and suites have four-tops. Phones have voice mail. Suites have TV only in the living room and sofas don't pull out, but the friendly management will lend you a cot (or even an additional bed) if you're bringing the family or sharing with friends. Ask for a renovated room when you book; most of the

comforts thanks to the hotel's "family room": a two-room suite with a second bedroom in lieu of a sitting area. This configuration gives mom and dad privacy, and kids their own real beds.

Hotel Olcott (see above) Every one-bedroom apartment has a stocked kitchenette, dining table, and space to spread out. Sofas don't pull out, but the bedroom usually has two queens, and the management will lend you a cot or extra bed for the living room if you prefer. Central Park is steps away, and a barbecue joint in the building serves affordable family meals.

The Milburn (see below) This Upper West Sider is a real suite deal for any visitor, but their kids-under-12-stay-free policy makes it a stellar choice for families. Every room has a fully outfitted kitchenette (with microwave) and a dining area. The one-bedroom suites are a bargain, and a pullout queen sofa in the living room makes them comfortable for families. The neighborhood is kid-friendly, and Central Park is an easy walk away.

Skyline Hotel (p. 118) and **Travel Inn** (p. 119) If you're driving, take advantage of the free parking—which saves you at least $25 a day—at these two motor hotels. And you'll like the family-size rooms, and the kids will love the pools (a rarity in affordable hotels). *And* children stay free (under 14 at the Skyline, under 16 at the Travel Inn).

suites and about half of the studios have brand-new, bright-white kitchenettes and freshly laid tile in the bathroom.

The Olcott is steps from Central Park on one of Manhattan's most high-class blocks (the Dakota apartment building is just doors way). Nearby Columbus Avenue bustles with boutiques and restaurants, and just off the surprisingly sophisticated lobby is **Dallas BBQ** for cheap eats and bathtub-size cocktails.

27 W. 72nd St. (btwn Columbus Ave. and Central Park W.), New York, NY 10023. © **212/877-4200.** Fax 212/580-0511. www.hotelolcott.com. 200 units. $130 studio double ($840 weekly); $150 suite ($980 weekly), $1,600 weekly 2-bedroom suite (sleeps up to 4). Extra person $15. MC, V (check or money order deposit required to guarantee room). Parking $35, 4 blocks away. Subway: B, C to 72nd St. **Amenities:** Restaurant; bar. *In room:* A/C, TV, dataport, kitchenette with fridge.

The Milburn *Kids* On a quiet street a block from the Beacon, the Milburn offers reasonably priced rooms and suites with kitchenettes in the same neighborhood—at about half the price. These suites might not be as nice as the Beacon's, but they're a better value. Every suite is rife with amenities, including a dining area; a newish bathroom and kitchenette (with free coffee); two-line phones; and more. Junior and one-bedroom suites boast a pullout queen sofa, an extra TV, a CD player, and a desk. Don't expect much from the decor (the laminated furniture is a cheaper grade than at the Beacon), but everything is attractive and in good shape. The conscientious management keeps the whole place spotless and in good order. In fact, what makes the Milburn a find is that it's more service-oriented than most hotels in this price range: The friendly staff will do everything from providing free copy, fax, and e-mail services to picking up your laundry at the dry cleaner next door. All in all, this is a great choice for bargain hunters—especially families, for whom rollaways and cribs are on hand.

242 W. 76th St. (btwn Broadway and West End Ave.), New York, NY 10023. © **800/833-9622** or 212/362-1006. Fax 212/721-5476. www.milburnhotel.com. 114 units. $129–$179 studio double; $149–$185 junior suite, $169–$205 1-bedroom suite. Extra person $10. Children under 13 stay free in parents' room. AE, DC, MC, V. Parking $20–$29. Subway: 1, 9 to 79th St. **Amenities:** Fitness room; access to nearby health club; business services; coin-op laundry; free video library. *In room:* A/C, TV/VCR (Sony PlayStation on request), dataport, kitchenette with fridge and coffeemaker, hair dryer, iron, safe, CD player in suites.

Quality Hotel on Broadway *Value* The Comfort Inn–Central Park West (see above) is a bit smarter, but stay at this reliable, freshly renovated hotel if you like lots of space; some rooms are large enough for two doubles or a king bed. Rooms feature dark-wood, hotel-standard furnishings that include a work desk with a good ergonomic chair; an armoire holds the TV and good drawer space. Each room has an alarm clock, two phones with voice mail and free local calls, and a makeup mirror in the bathroom. Some also have a minifridge or a kitchenette; request one when you book. Most bathrooms have spacious granite countertops. A library-style sitting room is off the lobby. The location is terrific—cheaper than staying on the Upper West Side in the 70s and 80s, but just as nice neighborhood-wise, surrounded by affordable restaurants and 2 blocks from an express subway station that will whisk you to Times Square in two stops. Best of all, the online discount deals can be stellar (as low as $70 at press time).

215 W. 94th St. (at Broadway), New York, NY 10025. © **800/228-5151** or 212/866-6400. Fax 212/866-1357. www.bestnyhotels.com. 350 units. $119–$149 single or double; $179–$219 junior suite (sleeps 2 or 3). Ask about senior, AAA, corporate, and promotional discounts; check www.hotelchoice.com for online-booking discounts (as low as $70 at press time). Extra person $15. Children under 18 stay free in parents' room. AE, DC, DISC, MC, V. Parking $20. Subway: 1, 2, 3, 9 to 96th St. **Amenities:** Restaurant; fax service; coin-op laundry; dry cleaning/laundry. *In room:* A/C, TV, dataport, coffeemaker, hair dryer, iron.

SUPERCHEAP SLEEPS

Central Park Hostel & Inn There's really no inn here—just a hostel. Run by the folks behind the Amsterdam, Murray Hill, and Union Square inns, this cheap choice offers newness and cleanliness. Everything is fresh and of decent quality; mattresses, pillows, and linens are better than in most hostels (BYO towels). The shared bathrooms are brand-new (shared at a ratio of about 10 beds to a bathroom). Each floor has a locker area and the building is generally bright and sunny; the front desk is staffed around the clock, morning coffee and munchies are available at the corner deli, and a basement rec room and TV lounge with Internet access machine was in the works at press time.

Now the downside: Most dorm rooms have one too many bunk beds; there's barely any floor space for luggage. Columbia University is helping by building student housing throughout the area, but the location is still sketchy. It's separated from virtually all commercial activity (along Broadway and Amsterdam Ave.) by a major housing project. Luckily, the B and C trains' stops are at the end of the block. I'd try another city hostel first—the Big Apple (p. 120), Chelsea Center (p. 106), and Chelsea International (p. 107) are as clean and much better located.

19 W. 103rd St. (btwn Central Park W. and Manhattan Ave.), New York, NY 10025. © **877/PARK-BED** (727-5233) or 212/678-0491. Fax 212/678-0453. www.centralparkhostel.com. 150 dorm beds. $26–$36 dorm bed; $75–$85 private twin. Rates include tax. Inquire about discounted rates. No credit cards. Subway: B, C to 103rd St. *In room:* A/C, no phone.

Hostelling International–New York Staying here is like going back to college—a very international college, with clocks set for six different time zones behind the front desk and a backpack-toting clientele from around the globe. Beds are cheap, but expect to bunk it (upper or lower?) with people you don't know in rooms of 4, 6, 8, or 12. Everything is extremely basic, but the mattresses are firm and the shared bathrooms are nicely kept. There are four rooms with one double and two bunk beds that have private bathrooms. The well-managed hostel feels like a student union, with bulletin boards and listings of events posted; a coffee bar with an ample menu and pleasant seating; two TV rooms; a game room; and a library with bill- and credit-card-operated Internet access computers. There's also a common kitchen, vending machines, a coin-op laundry, a terrace, and a yard with picnic tables and barbecues in summer. The neighborhood has improved over the years, but it's still a little sketchy; 1 block over is much nicer Broadway, lined with affordable restaurants and shops.

891 Amsterdam Ave. (at 103rd St.), New York, NY 10025. © 800/909-4776 or 212/932-2300. Fax 212/932-2574. www.hinewyork.org. 624 beds; 4 units with private bathroom. $29–$38 dorm bed; $120–$135 for family room (sleeps up to 4) or private quad. Travelers must be 18 or older. AE, DC, MC, V. Subway: 1, 9 to 103rd St. **Amenities:** Coffee bar; access to nearby health club; game room; activities desk; coin-op laundry. *In room:* A/C, locker (BYO lock), no phone.

11 Harlem

Urban Jem Guest House ★   This B&B is the best place to stay in once-again-hip Harlem. Jane Alex Mendelson, a refugee from the corporate world, has successfully reinvented herself as an innkeeper. In the Mount Morris Historic District, her renovated 1878 brownstone is graced with fine woodwork and beautiful original (nonworking) fireplaces. The house is a work in progress, so don't expect perfection; there's still plenty to be done, and the furnishings are largely an odds-and-ends mix. But the accommodations offer good value. The second floor has two guest rooms with firm queen beds, new private bathrooms, and spacious kitchenettes with stove, minifridge, microwave, and the basic tools for preparing and serving a meal. On the third floor are two nice rooms that share a hall bathroom and fully equipped kitchen: one a pretty bedroom with a queen bed, the other a spacious room with two foldout futon sofa beds. They can also be combined into a two-bedroom suite, which gives you a whole floor to yourself. Every room has a phone, and local calls are free.

You can pay an extra $7.50 for daily maid service (the trash is taken out daily); otherwise, sheets and towels are changed weekly. Jane is friendly and helpful and can provide lots of neighborhood information. The bustling urban neighborhood has welcomed the inn, and it makes a good starting point for exploring jazz-, gospel-, and history-rich Harlem. Midtown is about a half-hour subway ride away, but Jane recommends taking a cab back after 11pm or so.

2005 Fifth Ave. (btwn 124th and 125th sts.). © 212/831-6029. Fax 212/831-6940. www.urbanjem.com. 4 units (2 with shared bathroom that can be combined into a suite). $90–$215 single or double. Rates include continental breakfast upon request. Extra person $15. 2-night minimum on weekends or holidays. AE, DISC, MC, V. Subway: 2, 3 or 4, 5, 6 to 125th St. **Amenities:** Self-serve laundry (small fee). *In room:* A/C, TV, CD player, dataport, kitchenette with fridge and microwave, hair dryer, iron.

SUPERCHEAP SLEEPS

Sugar Hill International House   This intimate hostel is a good choice for looking for a quiet, nonsmoking, hostel. It's in two brownstones in the Sugar Hill Historic District, a residential, predominantly African-American section of Harlem. Owner Jim Williams has been here since 1984, and he and his partners have literally written the book on hostelling—or one of them, anyway:

Bed-and-Breakfasting in Brooklyn

Leafy, lovely brownstone Brooklyn is the best-kept secret for B&B-loving budget travelers. The neighborhoods are jewels; these are some of the most desirable areas in the city for folks who don't want to hassle with the bustle of Manhattan. What's more, they're safe and subway-convenient, with Manhattan just 15 to 30 minutes away via subway. Each boasts a good selection of affordable restaurants catering to a local crowd.

The historic neighborhood of Park Slope is the heart of brownstone Brooklyn, and home to **Bed & Breakfast on the Park,** 113 Prospect Park W. (© 718/847-4444; www.bbnyc.com). Housed in an 1895 Victorian town house across the street from Prospect Park, this inn has two beautifully outfitted shared-bathroom units ($125 or $150 double). A sumptuous breakfast is served in the formal dining room. Six more rooms with private bathrooms are available for guests who are looking to splurge. However, be aware that there is a 10% service charge added to all bills.

Another excellent choice is **Akwaaba Mansion,** 347 MacDonough St. (© 718/455-5958; www.akwaaba.com), a meticulously restored 1860s Italianate villa in Bedford-Stuyvesant, outfitted with Afrocentric elegance. Four suites are available in the 18-room home, each with private bathroom with either a claw-foot or a Jacuzzi tub, for $120 to $150 double—including a hearty, Southern-style breakfast. The innkeepers are a lovely and helpful couple who love welcoming guests into their home; they also operate an affordably elegant restaurant with live jazz on Friday and Saturday nights, plus an all-you-can-eat Sunday brunch for just $11.95, just down the street.

In Carroll Gardens is the **Baisley House Bed-and-Breakfast,** 294 Hoyt St. (© 718/935-1959; www.virtualcities.com/ons/ny/n/nyn1901.htm), a Victorian mansion that offers three guest rooms: one single and two doubles, each with shared bathroom, all including cable TV with VCR and a full breakfast. There's an opulent drawing room for lounging, plus an English-style garden out back. Rates are $95 to $150 double.

Also consider **Garden Green Bed-and-Breakfast,** 641 Carlton Ave. (© 718/783-5717; www.virtualcities.com/ons/ny/n/nyn7601.htm), in the Prospect Heights section of brownstone Brooklyn, near Park Slope, the Brooklyn Museum of Art, and Prospect Park. Two double rooms (one with a full-size bed, one with two twins) share a hall bathroom, while a full-floor garden apartment—the best value of the three—boasts a queen bed, a sleeper sofa, a kitchen, and access to the lovely garden out back. Rates run an affordable $95 to $135 single or double; breakfast is not served.

Be prepared for a 2-night minimum at any bed-and-breakfast.

The Hostel Handbook, a guide to hostels across North America with an accompanying website (www.hostelhandbook.com).

Hand-hewn bunk beds fill spacious, high-ceilinged rooms accommodating six to eight; a few highly coveted double rooms are available on a first-come,

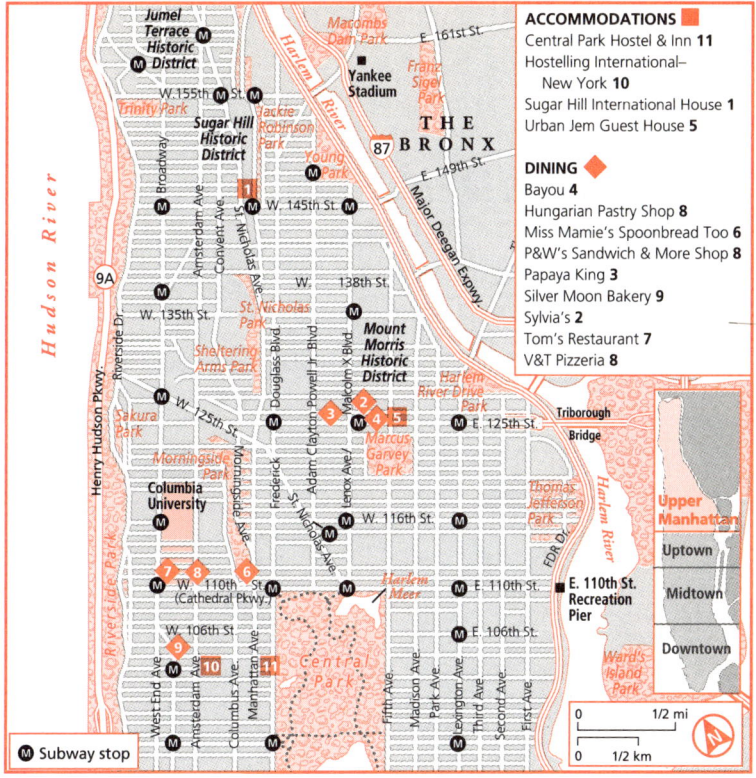

Harlem-Area Accommodations & Dining

ACCOMMODATIONS
Central Park Hostel & Inn **11**
Hostelling International–
  New York **10**
Sugar Hill International House **1**
Urban Jem Guest House **5**

DINING
Bayou **4**
Hungarian Pastry Shop **8**
Miss Mamie's Spoonbread Too **6**
P&W's Sandwich & More Shop **8**
Papaya King **3**
Silver Moon Bakery **9**
Sylvia's **2**
Tom's Restaurant **7**
V&T Pizzeria **8**

first-served basis. Accommodations are hostel basic: you'll get a mattress, pillow, and linens (BYO towels), plus plenty of floor space for your stuff; you can store valuables in a safe in the main office. Bathrooms are older but well kept, and divided into toilet, shower, and sink sections for easy sharing. The buildings are works in progress, but the place is well kept and well run. The owners are very friendly and helpful, long term staff lives on site, and security is tight: A passport ID is required for check-in (required at most private hostels these days), you will be assigned a code for the front door and provided with a key for your specific dorm, and no guests are allowed. One dorm is for women only. There's a common kitchen with a fridge, a cooktop, and basic tools; takeout is available, and St. Nick's Pub is across the street for genuine Harlem jazz.

722 St. Nicholas Ave. (btwn 146th and 147th sts.), New York, NY 10031. ⓒ **212/926-7030.** www.sugarhillhostel.com. 25 dorm beds. $25 single dorm bed; $60 bunk-bed twin. No credit cards. Subway: A, B, C, D to 145th St. **Amenities:** Free Internet access; kitchen. *In room:* No phone.

6

Great Deals on Dining

Without a doubt, New York is the best restaurant town in the country. Other cities might have particular specialties—Paris has better bistros, Hong Kong better Chinese, Los Angeles better Mexican—but no culinary capital spans the globe as successfully as NYC.

The sheer variety is astounding. That's due in part to New York's vibrant immigrant mix. Let a newcomer arrive and see that his or her native foods aren't being served and *zap!*—there's a restaurant, cafe, or grocery to fill the void. Yet we New Yorkers can be fickle: One moment a restaurant is hot, the next it's passé. Do call ahead to see if it's still there!

But eating in New York ain't cheap. The primary cause? The high rents, which are reflected in your tab. Wherever you're from, New York's restaurants will seem *expensive*. Yet as you peruse this chapter, you'll see that values abound—especially if you eat ethnic and venture beyond tourist zones into the neighborhoods where real New Yorkers eat, such as Chinatown, the Upper West Side, and the East Village. But even if you're not venturing beyond Times Square, I've included inexpensive restaurants in every neighborhood.

For a quick summary, check out "Best Low-Cost Dining Bets," in chapter 1. Also revisit the dining section in "65 Money-Saving Tips," in chapter 2, for ideas on how to save.

RESERVATIONS Reservations are always a good idea, and a virtual necessity if your party consists of more than two people. Do yourself a favor and make them, so you won't be disappointed. If you're booking dinner on a weekend night, call a few days to a week in advance; even farther in advance never hurts, especially if you're set on a certain dining hour.

But lots of city restaurants, especially at the affordable end of the spectrum, don't take reservations. One of the ways they're able to keep prices down is by packing people in as quickly as possible. This means that the best cheap and midpriced restaurants often have a wait. Your best bet is to go early or late. Often, you can get in more quickly on a weeknight. Or go knowing that you'll have to wait; there are worse things than sipping a glass of wine or a margarita at the bar.

THE LOWDOWN ON SMOKING

New York City enacted strict no-smoking laws a few years back that made the majority of the city's dining rooms smoke-free. However, that doesn't mean that smokers are completely prohibited from lighting up. Restaurants with more than 35 seats cannot allow smoking in their dining rooms. They can allow smoking in their bars, lounges, and alfresco areas; most do.

Whether you're a smoker or nonsmoker, call ahead if it matters to you. If you're hell-bent on enjoying an after-dinner cigarette indoors, make sure that the restaurant has a bar or lounge that allows smoking. Some restaurants, such as Bar Pitti, Le Pere Pinard, and Mexican Radio, offer dinner tables in designated areas where you can puff away during the meal. Smoking is usually allowed in outdoor dining areas, but always ask. If you're a nonsmoker who doesn't want to be bothered by secondhand smoke, make sure your seat is away from the bar.

TIPPING Tipping is easy in New York. Double the 8.25% sales tax and voilà! Happy waitperson. If you check your coat, leave a dollar per item for the checkroom attendant.

1 Restaurants by Cuisine

AMERICAN
All State Cafe (Upper West Side, p. 184)
Bendix Diner (East Village, p. 150)
Big Nick's Burger Joint/Pizza Joint (Upper West Side, p. 184)
Blondie's ✶ (Upper West Side, p. 185)
Bubby's ✶✶ (TriBeCa, p. 138)
Bulgin' Waffles (East Village, p. 150)
Chat 'n' Chew (Union Square, p. 164)
Comfort Diner (Midtown East, Upper East Side, p. 179)
Corner Bistro (Greenwich Village, p. 156)
EJ's Luncheonette (Greenwich Village, Upper East and Upper West Sides, p. 156)
Empire Diner (Chelsea, p. 161)
ESPN Zone ✶ (Times Square, p. 174)
Fanelli's Cafe (SoHo, p. 146)
Gray's Papaya (Greenwich Village, p. 160; Upper West Side, p. 190; Upper East Side, p. 192)
Hard Rock Cafe ✶ (Midtown West, p. 174)
Jackson Hole (Midtown East, Murray Hill, Upper East and Upper West Sides, p. 191)
Jekyll & Hyde Club (Midtown West, p. 175)
Joe Allen ✶✶ (Midtown West/Times Square, p. 172)
Johny's Grill & Luncheonette (Chelsea, p. 162)
Kitchenette (TriBeCa, p. 140)
Lyric Diner (Midtown East, p. 165)
Manhattan Chili Co. (Midtown West/Times Square, p. 175)
Mars 2112 (Midtown West, p. 175)
Old Town Bar & Restaurant ✶ (Flatiron District p. 165)
Paul's ✶✶ (East Village, p. 153)
Papaya King (Times Square, p. 178; Upper East Side, p. 192; Harlem, p. 194)
Planet Hollywood (Midtown West, p. 175)
Popover Cafe (Upper West Side, p. 187)
Prime Burger (Midtown East, p. 181)
Route 66 Cafe (Midtown West, p. 176)
Serendipity 3 (Upper East Side, p. 192)
Tom's Restaurant (Upper West Side, p. 190)
Vynl ✶ (Midtown West, p. 177)
Walker's ✶ (TriBeCa, p. 141)
WWE New York ✶✶ (Times Square, p. 174)

ASIAN FUSION/PAN-ASIAN
Republic (Union Square, p. 166)
Rice ✶ (Nolita, p. 148)
Zen Palate ✶ (Union Square, Midtown West, Upper West Side, p. 167)

BELGIAN
B. Frites (Midtown West, p. 178)
Le Pain Quotidien ✶✶ (SoHo, Flatiron District, Midtown East, Upper East and Upper West Sides, p. 147)
Petite Abeille (Chelsea, p. 163; TriBeCa, p. 138; Greenwich Village, p. 155)

BRAZILIAN
Brazil Grill ★ (Midtown West, p. 168)
Rice 'n' Beans (Midtown West, p. 176)

BRITISH
A Salt & Battery (Greenwich Village, p. 155)
Christer's (Midtown East, p. 180)
Puck Fair (Nolita/SoHo, p. 148)
Tea & Sympathy (Greenwich Village, p. 160)

CHINESE
Flor de Mayo (Upper West Side, p. 185)
Funky Broome ★ (Chinatown, p. 141)
Grand Sichuan International ★ (Chelsea, Midtown West, p. 161)
Hunan Park (Upper West Side, p. 186)
Joe's Shanghai ★★ (Chinatown, Midtown West, p. 141)
La Caridad 78 (Upper West Side, p. 186)
New York Noodletown ★★ (Chinatown, p. 142)
Sammy's Noodle Shop & Grill (Greenwich Village, p. 160)
Sweet-n-Tart Cafe (Chinatown, p. 142)

CONTEMPORARY AMERICAN
AKA Cafe (Lower East Side, p. 143)
Eatery ★ (Midtown West, p. 169)
Josie's Restaurant & Juice Bar (Upper West Side, Midtown East, p. 186)
Sarabeth's Kitchen ★★ (Upper West Side, Upper East Side, p. 188)
Tavern Room at Gramercy Tavern ★★ (Union Square, Flatiron District & Gramercy Park, p. 166)
Time Cafe ★ (Upper West Side, original location in NoHo, p. 189)

CREOLE
Bayou ★ (Harlem, p. 193)

FRENCH
Florent (Meat-Packing District, p. 156)
Franklin Station Cafe (TriBeCa, p. 140)
La Bonne Soupe ★ (Midtown West, p. 173)
L'Express (Flatiron District/Union Square, p. 164)
Le Pain Quotidien ★★ (SoHo, Flatiron District, Midtown East, Upper East and Upper West Sides, p. 147)
Le Pere Pinard ★ (Lower East Side, p. 144)
Le Zinc ★★★ (TriBeCa, p. 140)
Pigalle (Midtown West, p. 176)
Rue des Crepes ★★ (Chelsea, p. 163)

GERMAN
Hallo! Berlin ★ (Midtown West, p. 169)
Knödel (Midtown East, p. 180)

GOURMET SANDWICHES/ CAFE/TAKEOUT
Amy's Bread (Midtown West, p. 178; Chelsea, p. 163; Upper East Side, p. 192)
Antique Cafe ★ (Chelsea, p. 160)
Bagel & Bean (Midtown West, p. 178)
Canova Market (Times Square, p. 178)
Dean & Deluca (Greenwich Village, p. 160; SoHo, p. 149; Midtown West, p. 179)
Eisenberg's Coffee Shop (Flatiron District, p. 164)
Emerald Planet ★ (Greenwich Village, Midtown West, p. 156)
Ess-A-Bagel ★ (Midtown East, p. 179)
F&B ★ (Chelsea, p. 161)
Ferrara ★ (Little Italy, p. 143)
H&H Bagel (Upper West Side, p. 190; Midtown West, p. 179; Upper East Side, p. 192)

RESTAURANTS BY CUISINE

Housing Works Used Books Cafe ✪ (SoHo, p. 149)
Hungarian Pastry Shop (Upper West Side, p. 190)
Island Burgers & Shakes (Midtown West, p. 172)
Le Pain Quotidien ✪✪ (SoHo, Flatiron District, Midtown East, Upper East and Upper West Sides, p. 147)
Little Pie Company (Chelsea, p. 163; Midtown East, p. 180)
Mangia (Financial District, Midtown East, Midtown West, p. 137)
Mike's Take-Away (Midtown East, p. 180)
P&W's Sandwich & More Shop (Upper West Side, p. 190)
Silver Moon Bakery (Upper West Side, p. 191)
Xando/Cosí (locations all over the city, p. 190)
Yura & Company (Upper East Side, p. 192)

GREEK

Johny's Grill & Luncheonette (Chelsea, p. 162)
Niko's Mediterranean Grill & Bistro (Upper West Side, p. 187)
Snack (SoHo, p. 148)

INDIAN

Bombay Dining (East Village, p. 151)
Cafe Spice Express (Midtown East, p. 180)
Gandhi (East Village, p. 151)
Mavalli Palace (Murray Hill, p. 181)
Mitali East (East Village, p. 151)
Pongal ✪✪ (Murray Hill, p. 180)
Rose of India (East Village, p. 151)
Salaam Bombay ✪ (TriBeCa, p. 141)

INTERNATIONAL

Emerald Planet ✪ (Greenwich Village, Midtown West, p. 156)
F&B ✪ (Chelsea, p. 161)

IRISH

The Half King ✪ (Chelsea, p. 162)
Molly's Pub & Restaurant Sheeben (Gramercy Park, p. 165)

ITALIAN

Bardolino (Upper East Side, p. 191)
Bar Pitti ✪ (Greenwich Village, p. 155)
Cucina di Pesce (East Village, p. 151)
Ferrara ✪ (Little Italy, p. 143)
44 Southwest ✪ (Midtown West, p. 169)
Frank ✪✪ (East Village, p. 152)
Frutti di Mare (East Village, p. 151)
Lupa ✪✪ (Greenwich Village, p. 158)
Umberto's Clam House (Little Italy, p. 143)
Via Emilia ✪ (Flatiron District, p. 167)

JAPANESE

Go Sushi (Midtown East, Greenwich Village, Midtown West, p. 179)
Jeollado (East Village, p. 152)
Katsu-Hama (Midtown East, p. 180)
Ony (Greenwich Village, p. 159)
Otafuku (East Village; p. 155)
Sandobe Sushi (East Village, p. 152)
Sapporo ✪ (Midtown West/Times Square, East Village, p. 176)
Soba-Ya ✪✪ (East Village, p. 153)
Village Yokocho (East Village, p. 154)
Won Jo ✪✪ (Midtown West, p. 178)

JEWISH

Artie's Delicatessen (Upper West Side, p. 184)
Barney Greengrass, the Sturgeon King (Upper West Side, p. 184)
Carnegie Deli (Midtown West, p. 173)
Junior's (Midtown East, p. 180)

Katz's Delicatessen ★★ (Lower East Side, p. 144)
Stage Deli (Midtown West, p. 173)

KOREAN
Mandoo Bar (Midtown West, p. 174)
Village Yokocho (East Village, p. 154)
Won Jo ★★ (Midtown West, p. 178)

LATIN AMERICAN/ CARIBBEAN
AKA Cafe (Lower East Side, p. 143)
Cafe con Leche (Upper West Side, p. 185)
Cafe Habana ★ (Nolita, p. 146)
Flor de Mayo (Upper West Side, p. 185)
La Caridad 78 (Upper West Side, p. 186)
La Taza de Oro (Chelsea, p. 162)
Rice ★ (Nolita, p. 148)

MALAYSIAN
Franklin Station Cafe (TriBeCa, p. 140)

MEXICAN/TEX-MEX
Burritoville ★★ (locations all over the city, p. 137)
Gabriela's ★★ (Upper West Side, p. 186)
Los Dos Rancheros Mexicanos (Midtown West, p. 174)
Manhattan Chili Co. (Midtown West/Times Square, p. 175)
Mexican Radio (SoHo, p. 147)
Nacho Mama (Upper West Side, p. 187)
Taco & Tortilla King (Gramercy Park, p. 166)
Tajin Restaurant (Financial District, p. 138)

MIDDLE EASTERN
Afghan Kebab House (Midtown West, p. 168)
Bereket ★ (Lower East Side, p. 144)
Lemon Tree Cafe (Midtown West, p. 173)
Moustache (Greenwich Village, East Village, p. 159)

PIZZA
Big Nick's Burger Joint/Pizza Joint (Upper West Side, p. 184)
California Pizza Oven (Union Square, p. 166)
Grimaldi's Pizzeria ★★ (Brooklyn, p. 194)
John's Pizzeria ★ (Times Square, original in Greenwich Village and locations on the Upper West and Upper East Sides, p. 172)
Lil' Frankie's Pizza (East Village, p. 152)
Lombardi's ★★ (SoHo/Little Italy, p. 147)
Pintaile's Pizza (Union Square, p. 166; Upper East Side, p. 192)
Totonno's Pizzeria Napolitano (Upper East Side, p. 192)
Two Boots (East Village and Greenwich Village, p. 158; Midtown East, p. 180)
V&T Pizzeria ★ (Upper West Side, p. 189)

SEAFOOD
New York Noodletown ★★ (Chinatown, p. 142)
Pisces ★ (East Village, p. 153)
Umberto's Clam House (Little Italy, p. 143)

SOUTHERN/SOUL FOOD/BARBECUE
Acme Bar & Grill (NoHo, p. 150)
Miss Mamie's Spoonbread Too ★ (Harlem, p. 193)
The Pink Tea Cup (Greenwich Village, p. 159)
Sylvia's ★★ (Harlem, p. 193)
Virgil's Real BBQ ★★ (Times Square, p. 177)

THAI
Chanpen (Midtown West, p. 169)
Siam Inn ★ (Midtown West, p. 177)

TIBETAN
Tsampa (East Village, p. 154)

UKRAINIAN
Veselka ★ (East Village, p. 154)

VEGETARIAN/HEALTH-CONSCIOUS
Angelica Kitchen (East Village, p. 150)
Josie's Restaurant & Juice Bar (Upper West Side, Midtown East, p. 186)
Mavalli Palace (Murray Hill, p. 181)
Pongal ★★ (Murray Hill, p. 180)
The Pump (Murray Hill, Midtown West, p. 181)
Spring Street Natural Restaurant (SoHo, p. 149)
Tiengarden (Lower East Side, p. 146)
Time Cafe ★ (Upper West Side, original location in NoHo, p. 189)
Tsampa (East Village, p. 154)
Zen Palate ★ (Union Square, Midtown West, Upper West Side, p. 167)

VIETNAMESE
Nha Trang ★ (Chinatown, p. 142)

2 The Financial District

If you'd like to chow down where George Washington once did (it's a splurge), consider the beautifully restored, Revolutionary-era **Fraunces Tavern** (p. 222).

Burritoville ★★ *Value* TEX-MEX   This bright, cheerful minichain serves up the best "fast food" in the city. In fact, Burritoville fare doesn't deserve to be called fast food. This is forward-thinking Mexican, prepared with healthy ingredients—fresh produce, brown rice, and black beans—using no lard, preservatives, or canned goods. Even the tortillas are pressed every day. Options range from well-stuffed tacos and quesadillas to only-at-Burritoville creations such as a spicy white chicken chili with cumin, salad burritos, and a number of wraps. The extensive menu offers a wealth of options for vegetarians, as well as anyone looking for a quick, healthy bite. Another nice thing is their flexibility—you can make substitutions and special requests easily, and usually without an extra charge. *Tip:* The green salsa is hot, the red salsa (made with open-flame-roasted tomatoes) is not.

In addition to this location (a short walk from Battery Park and the Statue of Liberty and Staten Island ferry landings), a second lower Manhattan location is in the Financial District at 20 John St., between Broadway and Nassau (✆ **212/766-2020**). There are 11 more Burritovilles throughout the city, most with attractive decor and good table seating that makes Burritoville more attractive and comfortable than your average fast-food joint.

36 Water St. (just north of Broad St.). ✆ **212/747-1100**. www.burritoville.com. Reservations not accepted. Main courses $4.50–$9. AE, DISC, MC, V. Daily 11am–10pm. Subway: 2, 3 to Wall St.; 1, 9 to South Ferry.

Mangia MEDITERRANEAN CAFE   This gourmet cafeteria is an ideal place to take a break while sightseeing. Between the giant salad and soup bars, the sandwich and hot-entree counters, and expansive cappuccino-and-pastry counter, even the most finicky eater will have a hard time deciding what to eat. Everything is freshly prepared and beautifully presented. The soups and stews are particularly good (there are a number of daily choices), and a cup goes well with a fresh-baked pizzette (a minipizza). Pay-by-the-pound salad bars don't get any better than this, hot-meal choices (such as grilled mahimahi or cumin-marinated lamb kebab) are cooked to order, and sandwiches made as you watch. It's packed with Wall Streeters between noon and 2pm, but things move quickly and there's enough seating that usually no one has to wait. Come in for a late breakfast or an afternoon snack and you'll virtually have the place to yourself. At press time, Mangia was in the process of adding a sit-down section with waiter service in addition to the cafeteria. In addition to Wall Street, Mangia has two cafeteria-style cafes in Midtown that offer similar, if not quite such expansive, menus.

40 Wall St. (btwn Nassau and William sts.). © 212/425-4040. www.mangianet.com. Reservations not accepted. Soups and salads $3.50–$5; sandwiches and main courses $6–$14 (most less than $10). AE, DC, DISC, MC, V. Mon–Fri 7am–5pm (waiter service available 11:30am–4pm). Subway: 2, 3, 4, 5 to Wall St.; J, M, Z to Broad St. Also at 50 W. 57th St. (btwn Fifth and Sixth aves.); © 212/582-5554; Mon–Fri 7am–8pm; Sat 8:30am–6pm; subway: B, Q to 57th St.); 16 E. 48th St. (btwn Fifth and Madison aves.; © 212/754-0637; Mon–Fri 7am–6pm; subway: B, D, F, Q to 47th–50th sts./Rockefeller Center.).

Tajin Restaurant *Value* MEXICAN This Mexican luncheonette is a favorite among Wall Streeters, who love the bullish portions of authentic south-of-the-border cooking at low prices. Tostadas might be the best deal: Crisp tortillas come piled with traditional fillings, including your choice of chicken and beef, for $2.95. The enchiladas are fresh-made and saucy; I love the spinach-and-mushroom version, topped with cheese and salsa verde. There's always something interesting on the "specials" board. Come early, before you begin your sightseeing, to launch your day with huevos rancheros, *huevos con chorizo* (eggs with sausage), or a breakfast burrito stuffed with scrambled eggs, potatoes, green pepper, onions, and a touch of jalapeño. The small dining room is spare but not unpleasant. Food comes on real plates but with plastic forks. Service can be a tad gruff on occasion, but it's generally fine. There may be a short line for a table at the height of the lunch hour (noon–1:30pm), but it moves very quickly.

85 Greenwich St. (south of Rector St.). © 212/509-5017. Reservations not accepted. Main courses 65¢–$6 at breakfast, $5–$10 at lunch and dinner. AE, MC, V. Mon–Fri 7am–9pm; Sat 9am–5pm. Subway: 1, 9 to Rector St.

3 TriBeCa

In addition to the choices below, **Burritoville** (p. 137) is at 144 Chambers St., at Hudson Street (© **212/964-5048**). There's a branch of the Belgian cafe **Petite Abeille** (p. 163) at 134 W. Broadway, between Duane and Thomas streets (© **212/791-1360**).

Bubby's ★★ AMERICAN How do I love Bubby's? Let me count the ways. I love it for the sublime macaroni and cheese, for divine garlic burger and fries (accompanied by Bubby's own "wup-ass" ketchup), for the homemade meat loaf with cider gravy and garlic mashies. I love it for the roasted rosemary chicken and chipotle-crusted Black Angus steak, and the classic cocktail the bartender will make when I'm in the mood. I love Bubby's generous portions and fresh-from-the-field greens. I love the big home-style breakfasts so much that I don't even mind lining up with the crowds for weekend brunch. The high-ceilinged, brick-walled, loftlike space is very homey—very TriBeCa—and I love the candlelight that adds a touch of romance to the evening. I love the wait staff that doesn't neglect me, even when Harvey Keitel is sitting two tables over. Best of all, I love Bubby's pies: baked fresh daily, a half dozen from which to choose (along with another half dozen homemade cakes), and topped with fresh-made whipped cream (pumpkin's my favorite). Yum, yum, Bubby!

120 Hudson St. (at N. Moore St.). © **212/219-0666**. www.bubbys.com. Reservations recommended for dinner (not accepted for brunch). Main courses $2–$16 at breakfast, brunch, and lunch; $10–$22 at dinner. AE, DC, DISC, MC, V. Mon–Thurs 8am–11pm; Fri 8am–midnight; Sat 9am–4:30pm and 6pm–midnight; Sun 9am–10pm. Subway: 1, 9 to Franklin St.

Financial District, TriBeCa, Chinatown & Little Italy Dining

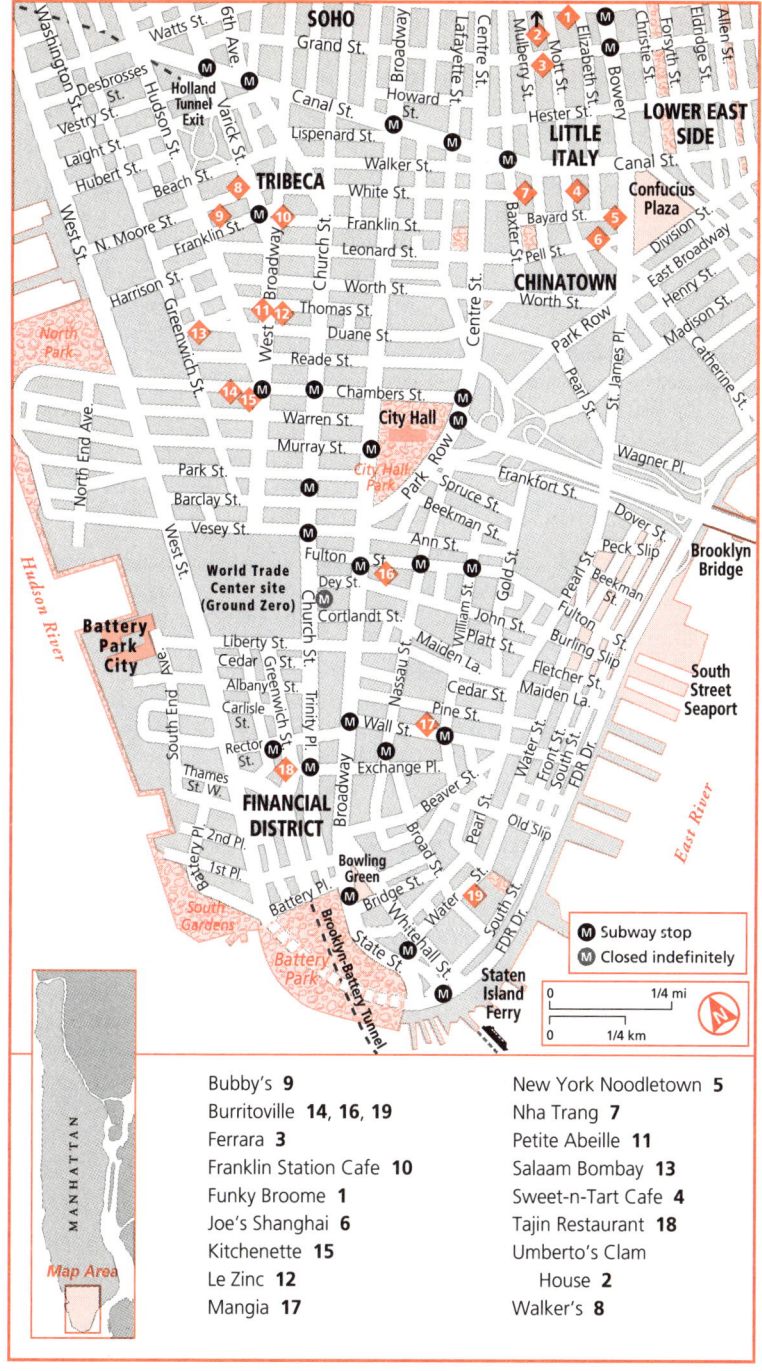

Bubby's **9**
Burritoville **14, 16, 19**
Ferrara **3**
Franklin Station Cafe **10**
Funky Broome **1**
Joe's Shanghai **6**
Kitchenette **15**
Le Zinc **12**
Mangia **17**

New York Noodletown **5**
Nha Trang **7**
Petite Abeille **11**
Salaam Bombay **13**
Sweet-n-Tart Cafe **4**
Tajin Restaurant **18**
Umberto's Clam House **2**
Walker's **8**

139

Franklin Station Cafe FRENCH-MALAYSIAN This charming brick-walled cafe is a winner for affordable Malaysian noodle and curry bowls and French-inspired sandwiches. The dishes on the handwritten-and-illustrated menu are prepared by the kitchen with all-natural ingredients. Sandwiches are simple but satisfying creations such as home-baked ham with honey mustard, lettuce, and tomato; mozzarella with basil, vine-ripened tomato, and extra-virgin olive oil; smoked salmon with mascarpone and chives; and tuna salad with jalapeño. For warm and cozy, you can't do better than one of the noodle bowls, such as tom yum shrimp, with sprouts, pineapple, and cucumber in a hot-and-sour broth; or seafood udon, with helpings of squid, shrimp, and salmon in a milder vegetable broth. For a more substantial meal, check the blackboard for such specials as Chilean sea bass in cardamom sauce. Service is friendly and efficient, wine and beer is available, and the desserts (a scrumptious fresh-baked tart and banana or carrot-raisin cake are usually among the choices) are well priced and pleasing. Omelets dominate the morning menu. It's a great choice for a casual meal.

222 W. Broadway (at Franklin St.). © 212/274-8525. Reservations not accepted. Breakfast $4.50–$7.50; sandwiches $6.50–$7; Malaysian specialties and noodle bowls $7–$13.50; house specials $10.50–$16.50. AE, DC, MC, V. Daily 8am–11pm. Subway: 1, 9 to Franklin St.; 2, 3 to Chambers St.

Kitchenette AMERICAN HOME COOKING This TriBeCa luncheonette has become a prime contender on the comfort-food circuit, thanks to Hungry Man–size breakfasts and just-like-home cooking. The little room has the feel of a New England diner, with folk art on the walls and country-rustic chairs at the tables. Expect high-cholesterol breakfasts and hearty salads and sandwiches. Weekly lunchtime blue-plate specials include shepherd's pie with mashed potato crust on Tuesday and gooey and four-cheese mac and cheese on Friday (specials are subject to change). Everything is well prepared and filling. Service is sit-down at breakfast, but lunch is more cafeteria-style, with orders taken at the counter.

80 W. Broadway (at Warren St.). © 212/267-6740. www.kitchenettenyc.com. Main courses $4.50–$7 at breakfast, $5.25–$9.25 at lunch and brunch, $9.50–$17 at dinner. AE ($20 minimum). Mon–Fri 7:30am–4:30pm; Sat–Sun 9am–4:30pm. Subway: 1, 2, 3, 9 to Chambers St.

Le Zinc ★★★ *Value* FRENCH BISTRO The new restaurant from David and Karen Waltuck (the team behind glorious, big-ticket Chanterelle) is this affordable and authentic French bistro. Despite its TriBeCa address, Le Zinc is unfussy and unpretentious, boasting genuine warmth and creative bistro cuisine. The space is open and comfortable, with big, well-spaced tables, banquette seating, unframed art posters glazed into the walls, and soft, sexy lighting.

The menu features bistro favorites with gentle accents, some of which reach beyond France to Eastern Europe, Asia, and even New Orleans. Winning choices include a skate wing browned in butter and capers; Grandma Gaby's Hungarian stuffed cabbage; mussels in snail butter; an excellent duck, foie gras, and pistachio terrine from the charcuterie; rib steak and frites; and a thick, juicy bacon cheeseburger. Reservations aren't taken, but any wait is worth it—put yourself in the competent hands of the bartenders at the mahogany bar. The crowd is grown-up and easygoing. This is a real winner—and reason enough to visit TriBeCa.

139 Duane St. (btwn W. Broadway and Church St.). © 212/513-0001. www.lezincnyc.com. Reservations not accepted. Main courses $2–$7 at breakfast, $7–$16 at lunch, $10–$21 at dinner. AE, DISC, MC, V. Sun–Thurs 8am–1am; Fri–Sat 8am–3am. Subway: 1, 2, 3, 9 to Chambers St.

Salaam Bombay ✦ *Value* PAN-INDIAN   Salaam Bombay is much more attractive than most curry houses, and the Pan-Indian cuisine is a cut above the standard fare. Dinner is more expensive than Indian should be, but the daily $12.95 all-you-can-eat lunch is a bargain for travelers willing to make lunch their main mealtime. I know the notion can be a turnoff (Buffet? Yuck!), but this is a freshly prepared, top-quality spread—you'll watch the tandoori chef pulling fresh-baked *naan* (flatbread) from the clay oven. There are a dozen or so fresh-made meat and vegetarian dishes, as well as all the traditional accompaniments. The location is convenient for a sightseeing break.

The room is romantically low-lit and formally outfitted in the evening, and service is attentive, so dinner is worth the expense if you care to splurge.

317 Greenwich St. (btwn Duane and Reade sts.). © 212/226-9400. www.salaambombay.com. Main courses $9–$18; daily all-you-can-eat buffet lunch $12.95. AE, DC, DISC, MC, V. Sun–Fri 11:30am–3pm; Sun–Thurs 5–10:30pm; Fri–Sat 5–11pm. Subway: 1, 2, 3, 9 to Chambers St.

Walker's ✦ AMERICAN   Down-to-earth as ever, Walker's is an old holdout from pre-fabulous TriBeCa. I love this pub and restaurant; prices are low, and the space is charming, with a tin ceiling, a long wooden bar, oldies on the sound system, friendly bartenders, and cozy tables. The affordable—and surprisingly good—meat-and-potatoes fare includes an 8-ounce sirloin burger, a yummy grilled rib-eye, and well-roasted organic chicken with mashies among an extensive list of entrees and specials, plus crisp, fresh salads. The fried oysters with Cajun aioli make a great starter. Low lighting sets a nice dinnertime mood, and service is friendly and attentive enough, as long as you're not in a hurry.

16 N. Moore St. (at Varick St.). © 212/941-0142. Reservations accepted for dinner. Main courses $8–$15 at dinner. AE, DC, DISC, MC, V. Daily noon–1am (bar usually open to 4am). Subway: 1, 9 to Franklin St.; 2, 3 to Chambers St.

4 Chinatown & Little Italy

Funky Broome ✦ CANTONESE   This neon-bright Chinese joint straddles the Nolita/Chinatown border geographically and in attitude—and the crowd, a mix of hipsters and Chinese nationals, loves the fusion. The mind-set is evident in the playful decor and the mainly Cantonese menu. The kitchen keeps preparations authentic, but presentations are a joy: Rice is served in a section of bamboo, and miniwoks are presented over an open flame to keep the contents sizzling (the pork with enoki mushrooms is my favorite). There's a wealth of seafood, poultry, stir-fry, sizzling, and vegetarian dishes, ranging from favorites like General Tso's chicken to wild offerings like marinated goose intestines and stir-fried conch with sweet peas and jellyfish for the more adventuresome. It's a great place to try Chinatown eats without having to surmount a language barrier.

176 Mott St. (at Broome St.). © 212/941-8628. Reservations accepted. Main courses $3.50–$16 (most less than $12). AE, MC, V. Sun–Thurs 11:30am–11pm; Fri–Sat 11:30am–midnight. Subway: 6 to Spring St.

Joe's Shanghai ✦✦ SHANGHAI CHINESE   Tucked away on a little side street off the Bowery is this Chinatown institution, which serves up authentic cuisine. The stars of the extensive menu are the soup dumplings, quivering steamed pockets filled with broth and your choice of pork or crab, accompanied by a side of seasoned soy. Listed as "steamed buns" (item nos. 1 and 2), these culinary marvels never disappoint. Neither does the rest of the Shanghai-inspired menu, which boasts such main courses as whole yellowfish bathed in spicy sauce; excellent "mock duck," a saucy bean-curd dish similar to Japanese *yuba* that's a hit with vegetarians and carnivores alike. The room is set mostly with round tables of 10 or so, and you'll be asked if you're willing to share. It's a great way to watch and learn from your neighbors (many of whom are Chinese), who are usually happy to tell you what they're eating. If you want a private table, expect a wait. *Note:* The Midtown location is geared more to Western diners, and is more expensive across the board, but it takes major credit cards.

9 Pell St. (btwn Bowery and Mott sts.). ☎ **212/233-8888**. Reservations recommended for 10 or more. Main courses $4.25–$17. No credit cards. Daily 11am–11pm. Subway: N, R, Q, W, 6 to Canal St.; F to Delancey St. Also at 24 W. 56th St. (btwn Fifth and Sixth aves.; ☎ **212/333-3868**; subway: B, Q to 57th St.).

New York Noodletown ★★ CHINESE/SEAFOOD

This just may be the best Chinese food in New York City. Among its fans are Ruth Reichl, editor-in-chief of *Gourmet* magazine, who consistently puts it at the top of the heap. So what if the florescent-lit room has all the ambience of a school cafeteria? The food is fabulous. The mushroom soup is a lunch in itself, thick with earthy chunks of shiitakes, vegetables, and noodles. Another appetizer that can serve as a meal is the hacked roast duck in noodle soup. The kitchen excels at seafood preparations, so be sure to try at least one: Looking like a snow-dusted plate of meaty fish, the salt-baked squid is sublime. The quick-woked Chinese broccoli or the crisp sautéed baby *bok choy* are great accompaniments. Other special dishes are various sandy pot casseroles, hearty, flavorful affairs slow-simmered in clay vessels. Unlike most of its neighbors, New York Noodletown keeps very long hours, which makes it the best late-night bet in the neighborhood, too.

28½ Bowery (at Bayard St.). ☎ **212/349-0923**. Reservations accepted. Main courses $4–$13. No credit cards. Daily 9am–3:30am. Subway: N, R, 6 to Canal St.

Nha Trang *Finds* VIETNAMESE

The decor may be standard-issue, Chinatown (glass-topped tables, linoleum floors, mirrored walls), but this friendly, bustling place serves up the best Vietnamese fare in Chinatown. A plate of six crispy, finger-size spring rolls is a nice way to start; the slightly spicy pork-and-shrimp filling is offset by the wrapping of lettuce, cucumber, and mint. The *pho* noodle soup comes in a quart-size bowl brimming with bright vegetables and meats and seafood. But my favorite dish is the simple barbecued pork chops—sliced paper-thin, soaked in a soy/sugarcane marinade, and grilled to utter perfection. Everything is well prepared, though, and your waiter will be glad to help you design a meal to suit your tastes.

If there's a line, and you don't want to wait, head a couple of blocks over to the nice second location, **Nha Trang Centre,** which accepts credit cards.

87 Baxter St. (btwn Canal and Bayard sts.). ☎ **212/233-5948**. Reservations accepted. Main courses $4–$12.50. No credit cards. Daily 11am–9:30pm. Subway: N, R, 6 to Canal St. Also at 148 Centre St. (at Walker St.; ☎ **212/941-9292**; MC, V; subway: N, R, 6 to Canal St.).

Sweet-n-Tart Cafe *Value* CHINESE

Here's Chinatown's best supercheap cuisine. There's almost nothing over $6—and, considering the prices, the quality is stellar. Rarely is Chinese food described as airy and light, but this is, especially the noodle soups. The scallion pancake is beautifully seasoned, and the Taiwan-style salt-baked chicken, served on broth-soaked rice, is a don't-miss. There are plenty of familiar dishes—fried rice, lo mein, pan-fried dumplings, and the like—but this is also a good bet for adventurous diners who'd like to try something new, be it shredded jellyfish, chicken with sea cucumber, or broiled frog. Sweet-n-Tart's specialty is *tong shui,* a broth or gelatin made with herbal, nut, or fruit essences. Served cold or hot, they're taken as invigorating medicinal tonics. You can have yours at any time during the meal, but I've found they offer a clean, fresh finish; consider the quail eggs with lotus seed in a light, peppery broth.

There's zero ambience, but it's pleasant enough, and the service is some of the best I've experienced in Chinatown. No alcohol is served, but the servers keep your glass filled with tea, and a juicer blends papaya and other fresh-fruit shakes.

76 Mott St. (just south of Canal St.). © 212/334-8088. Reservations not accepted. Main courses $2–$10. No credit cards. Sun–Thurs 9am–11pm; Fri–Sat 9am–midnight. Subway: N, R, 6 to Canal St.

Umberto's Clam House ITALIAN/SEAFOOD   Umberto's has true-crime cachet. It was at the Mulberry Street location in 1973 where "reputed" Mafioso Joey Gallo was assassinated while savoring a plate of scungilli. Umberto's moved here a few years back, leaving those famed bullet holes behind, but it still brims with classic Little Italy ambience.

The traditional, seafood-heavy menu is pleasing. I found the *scungilli* (conch) to be a bit chewy, but the baked clams were divine. You can also expect first-rate cherrystones on the half-shell; perfectly al dente linguine with a generous helping of fresh shelled clams in red sauce or extra-virgin olive oil; and lobster ravioli stuffed with chunks of lobster (a steal at $15). Plenty of meat and pasta dishes are on hand for nonseafood eaters. The wine list is decent and affordable. The atmosphere is unpretentious, old-world nautical, with comfortably spaced tables and a small outdoor patio. Autographed pictures on the walls run the gamut from Sinatra to never-beens with big dreams. The restaurant is staffed with career waiters who are friendly and attentive. It's a bit pricey, but a very good bet.

386 Broome St. (btwn Mulberry and Mott sts.). © 212/431-7545. www.umbertosclamhouse.com. Reservations required for Fri–Sat dinner, and for parties of 5 or more. Pastas $10–$19.50; main courses $7–$30 (most $10–$20). AE, DISC, MC, V. Daily 11am–4am. Subway: N, R to Prince St.; 6 to Spring St.

QUICK BITES

America's first espresso bar was **Ferrara**, 195 Grand St., between Mott and Mulberry streets (© **212/226-6150**), founded in 1892. This big, pleasant Little Italy *pasticceria* is still the place for Italian treats such as cannoli (fresh-squeezed in the pastry shell as you watch), zeppoles, *pastiacotti* (Italian cream puffs), *sfogliatelle* (a flaky shell stuffed with baked ricotta, and a *Sopranos* favorite), napoleons, pignolis, macaroons, and more. Cafe seating is available. Open Sunday to Friday from 8am to midnight, Saturday from 8am to 1am.

5 The Lower East Side

AKA Cafe NEW AMERICAN/LATIN AMERICAN   This bare-bones sibling to the much-pricier 71 Clinton Fresh Food down the block, serves similarly creative and well-prepared cuisine with a Latin flair—and for less than half the price. The menu is small, but budget diners with adventurous palates will love the rich and flavorful oyster soup, seasoned with white wine, aromatic veggies, smoked bacon and quinoa; inventive empanadas, cornbread pastries stuffed with fillings like roast turkey and smoked pumpkin; the pressed Cuban sandwich, made with Smithfield ham, Swiss, and pickled peppers; and my favorite, super-tender braised pork with celery root purée in a carrot-cumin broth. Portions are small, so order one more dish than you think you'll need. I'm less enamored with the fruity martinis than many, but there's an affordable and nicely chosen by-the-glass wine list, plus a full bar. "Super bueno" *dulce de leche* makes the perfect finish. The room is decor-free, but service is friendly.

49 Clinton St. (btwn Stanton and Rivington sts.). © **212/979-6096**. Reservations recommended. Main courses $5–$12. AE, MC, V. Mon–Fri noon–4:30pm; Mon–Sat 6pm–midnight. Subway: F, J, M, Z to Delancey/Essex sts.

Bereket ★ *Value* TURKISH   This popular kebab house has undergone an expansion that has more than doubled the number of tables and upgraded its hole-in-the-wall ambience to shiny diner-style decor—and the quality of their grilled meats is as excellent as ever. Order at the counter, where you'll see the kebabs displayed behind glass, waiting to hit the grill, and then snare a table as your plate is being prepared. The *kofte,* ground lamb with spices, is a favorite, but you won't go wrong with any of the choices. Complete dinners—two skewers of your choice, rice, and salad—are a steal for a 10 spot, especially the mixed grill, which features chicken, *shish* (beef), and *doner* (lamb) kebabs. Vegetarians have a lot to choose from, including excellently herbed hummus, falafel, great *piyaz* (white-bean salad with chopped onions and parsley), and babaganoush. Everything is freshly prepared in-house, and the counter staff is friendly and accommodating. No alcohol is served, but Turkish coffee should provide the necessary jolt.

187 Houston St. (at Orchard St.). © **212/475-7700.** Reservations not accepted. Main courses $3.50–$13.50. No credit cards. Open daily 24 hr. Subway: F to Second Ave.

Katz's Delicatessen ★★ *Value* JEWISH DELI   The motto here is, "There's Nothing More New York than Katz's," and it's spot-on. Founded in 1888, this brightly lit place is suitably Noo Yawk, with dill pickles, Dr. Brown's cream soda, and old-world attitude to spare. The Lower East Side institution draws everybody from housewives in for a day of shopping to tattooed club-goers looking for after-hours nutrition. Half of the space is dedicated to cafeteria-style counter service—perfect for budget-minded travelers who'd rather save on tip money—the other half offers waiter service (though it's considered appropriate to tip the carver who slices the meat for your sandwich if you get it at the counter).

All of Katz's traditional eats are first-rate: matzo ball and chicken noodle soups, potato knishes, cheese blintzes, egg creams (made with Katz's very own seltzer), and the beloved all-beef hot dogs. There's no faulting the pastrami—smoked to perfection and piled high on rye—or the dry-cured roast beef, either. All of the well-stuffed sandwiches are substantially cheaper than you'll find at any other deli in town. What's more, Katz's is the only deli cool enough to let you split one with your travel partner without adding a bogus $2 to $3 "sharing" charge.

205 E. Houston St. (at Ludlow St.). © **212/254-2246.** Reservations not accepted. Sandwiches $2.15–$10; other main courses $5–$17.50. AE, MC, V ($20 minimum). Sun–Tues 8am–10pm; Wed–Thurs 8am–11pm; Fri–Sat 8am–2:30am. Subway: F to Second Ave.

Le Pere Pinard ★ *Finds* FRENCH BISTRO/WINE BAR   This authentic French wine bar and bistro is a charming slice of Le Marais, with high ceilings, burnished brick walls, well-spaced tables with mix-and-match chairs, and an authentic come-as-you-are air. Everything is well worn in a comfortable way. The kitchen specializes in the Gallic version of comfort food: steak frites, shell steak with Roquefort sauce, shepherd's pie with a delightfully cheesy crust, a terrific *brandade* (a dish of salt fish puréed with olive oil, milk and garlic) and a charcuterie and cheese plate—the perfect match for the sublime crusty-on-the-outside, soft-in-the-middle bread that accompanies every meal. Greens are fresh and well prepared; even a simple mesclun salad wears a just-right vinaigrette.

There's a wonderful and affordable wine selection by the bottle, carafe, and glass; I like the restaurant's protocol, which allows you to taste first even if you're ordering by the glass. Service is attentive in an easygoing way. I've eaten here

Lower East Side, SoHo & East Village Dining

A Salt & Battery **13**	Frutti de Mare **22**	Rice **42**
Acme Bar & Grill **23**	Gandhi **8**	Rose of India **11**
AKA Café **40**	Housing Works	Sandobe Sushi **3**
Angelica Kitchen **2**	Used Books Café **28**	Sapporo East **5**
Bendix Diner **4**	Jeollado **35**	Snack **31**
Bereket **33**	Katz's Delicatessen **38**	Soba-Ya **17**
Bombay Dining **10**	Le Pain Quotidien **44**	Spring Street
Bulgin' Waffles **36**	Le Pere Pinard **39**	Natural Restaurant **43**
Burritoville **16**	Lil' Frankie's Pizza **34**	Tiengarden **41**
Cafe Habana **32**	Mitali East **9**	Time Café **24**
Cucina di Pesce **21**	Moustache **6**	Tsampa **19**
Dean & Deluca **29**	Otafuku **18**	Two Boots **37**
Dean & Deluca Cafe **1**	Paul's **14**	Two Boots to GoGo **26**
Emerald Planet **25**	Pisces **7**	Veselka **15**
Fanelli's Café **30**	Puck Fair **27**	Village Yokocho **20**
Frank **12**		

145

plenty, and both food and service are consistently good. Smoking is allowed in the front (bar) room, while the back room is dedicated to nonsmokers. There's also a pleasant garden in warm weather. Attention diners happy to eat on the early side (before 7pm): The pre-theater meal—three courses for $14—is a stellar deal.

175 Ludlow St. (south of Houston St.). ✆ 212/777-4917. Reservations recommended. Main courses $11.50–$19.50; pre-theater menu daily 5–7pm, $14 for 3 courses. AE. Mon–Thurs 5pm–midnight; Fri 5pm–1am; Sat 11am–1am; Sat–Sun 11am–midnight. Subway: F to Second Ave.

Tiengarden VEGAN   This petite restaurant serves up first-rate vegan fare. As with much vegetarian fare, the emphasis is on Asian flavors and spices. The kitchen uses all-natural ingredients, with no preservatives, MSG, or egg or dairy. Veggies are always fresh and never overcooked. Among my favorites are the spicy organic tofu, with shiitakes, bell peppers and soy in a zippy Sichuan sauce; the steaming noodle soups, made with a clear mushroom stock and your choice of wheat, rice, or udon noodles; and the herbed home fries. I'm not a fan of faux meats, but these are some of the best in town. No beer or wine—but lest it all sound too austere, the vegan cakes and cookies are downright devilish.

170 Allen St. (1½ blocks south of Houston St.). ✆ 212/388-1364. Main courses $5–$10.50; lunch specials $5–$6 (until 4pm). No credit cards. Mon–Sat noon–4pm and 5pm–10pm. Subway: F to Second Ave.

6 SoHo & Nolita

Cafe Habana ★   LATIN AMERICAN   I love this update on a typical Hispanic luncheonette. It's hip without being pretentious, and what the food may lack in authenticity it more than makes up for in quality and flavor: Shrimps are big and hearty; pork is moist and flavorful; cilantro and other spices fresh and aromatic. Starters include *pozole,* hominy corn stew with shredded chicken or pork in a clear broth that you season to taste with oregano, chili, and lime; and Mexican corn on the cob, which is skewered, coated with lime juice and grated cheese, sprinkled with chili powder, and grilled into a messy but sweet popcorny treat. Main courses include the moist roast pork (perfect with a squeeze of lime) and *camarones al ajillo,* shrimp in spicy garlic sauce. Most everything comes with your choice of red or black beans and rice; go with the yellow rice. Wine and Mexican beers are served, but I enjoyed the not-too-sweet red hibiscus tea.

The room is narrow and tables are petite (especially those for two), but a middle aisle keeps the place from feeling too crowded, and service is easygoing and friendly. Don't be surprised if there's a wait for a table.

If you're strolling Nolita and need a bite, stop into the adjacent storefront sandwich shop around the corner on Elizabeth Street for a pressed sandwich, burrito, or other takeout treat (open daily noon–10pm).

17 Prince St. (at Elizabeth St.). ✆ 212/625-2001. Reservations not accepted. Main courses $5–$15. AE, MC, V. Daily 9am–midnight. Subway: F, S to Broadway/Lafayette St.; 6 to Spring St.

Fanelli's Cafe   AMERICAN   Once upon a time, SoHo consisted of a few galleries, a gaggle of artists living in loft space no one wanted, a few Italian bakeries, and Fanelli's. It couldn't be more different now: The galleries have given way to Banana Republic, the bakeries have moved over for Balthazar, and people pay millions for the lofts. Thankfully, Fanelli's remains the same. This is a classic New York pub, with a long bar propped up by regulars, and a corner door and pressed-tin ceiling that have locked in the 1847 atmosphere. If smoke bothers you, ask to be seated in the back. The giant burgers are great, the pastas fresh, the beer served in pint glasses. The daring will give the mussels a shot.

Wine? House red. The Bloody Marys are a godsend for a hangover (white wine is the secret ingredient). If you're coming for dinner, especially on a weekend, your best bet is to arrive before 7pm, which is when the noise level really starts to escalate.

94 Prince St. (at Mercer St.). © **212/226-9412**. Reservations not accepted. Main courses $6–$15 (most less than $12). AE, MC, V. Sun–Thurs 10am–12:30am; Fri–Sat 10am–1am. Subway: N, R to Prince St.

Le Pain Quotidien ★★ FRENCH-BELGIAN/BAKERY CAFE   This airy neoclassical-goes-farmhouse cafe is one of my favorites for a sophisticated casual meal at a bargain-basement price. Take a seat at a table for two or cozy up to one of the generous and comfy common tables (the one in the sunlit front room is best). The light menu is comprised mostly of beautiful sandwiches and salads. Excellent choices include the open-faced beef carpaccio sandwich dressed with basil, Parmesan, and virgin olive oil on dark country bread; Paris ham with three mustards on crusty French; and a board of fine French cheeses—brie, chavignol, Gruyère—and your choice of walnut bread, rye, wheat, or a baguette. All are garnished with seasonal greens and fresh herbs. Salads are a good value because they come piled high and accompanied by a plate of French bread. Soups are homemade, hearty, and warming. Breads are baked five times daily in small batches. Save room for a divine dessert—fruit tarts, pies, brownies, cookies, brioches—or stop just for a sweet and a cappuccino; the warm Belgian waffle sprinkled with powdered sugar and fresh blueberries makes a light-as-air choice. Tables are waiter-serviced, but an up-front counter serves walk-ins and takeout.

100 Grand St. (between Mercer and Greene sts.). © **212/625-9009**. www.painquotidien.com. Reservations not accepted. Breakfast $3–$7.50; sandwiches and salads $7.50–$18 (most less than $12). No credit cards. Daily 8am–7pm. Subway: N, R to Canal St. Also at ABC Carpet & Home, 38 E. 19th St. (btwn Broadway and Park Ave. S.; © **212/625-9009**; subway: 4, 5, 6, N, R, L to 14th St./Union Sq.); 50 W. 72nd St. (btwn Columbus Ave. and Central Park W.; © **212/712-9700**; subway: B, C to 72 St.); 833 Lexington Ave. (btwn 63rd and 64th sts.; © **212/755-5810**; subway: 4, 5, 6 to 59th St.; N, R to Lexington Ave.); 1336 First Ave. (btwn 71st and 72nd sts.; © **212/717-4800**; subway: 6 to 68th St.); 1131 Madison Ave. (btwn 84th and 85th sts.; © **212/327-4900**; subway: 4, 5, 6 to 86th St.).

Lombardi's ★★ *Kids* PIZZA   Lombardi's makes the best pizza in Manhattan. First opened in 1905, "America's first licensed pizzeria" cooks its delectable pies in its original coal brick oven. The smoky crust (a generations-old family recipe that Gennaro Lombardi carried from Naples) is topped with fresh mozzarella, basil, pecorino Romano, and San Marzano tomato sauce. From there, the choice is yours. Topping options are suitably old-world (Citterio pancetta, kalamata olives, Esposito sweet Italian sausage, meatballs, beefsteak tomatoes, and the like), but Lombardi's specialty is the fresh clam pie, with hand-shucked clams, oregano, fresh garlic, Romano, extra-virgin olive oil, and fresh-ground pepper (no sauce). The dining room is narrow but pleasant, with checkered tablecloths and exposed brick walls. A big draw is the back garden; walk past the kitchen and up a flight of stairs to reach the second-floor deck, where tables sport Cinzano umbrellas. Another plus: In a city where rudeness is a badge of honor, Lombardi's wait staff is extremely affable.

32 Spring St. (btwn Mott and Mulberry sts.). © **212/941-7994**. Reservations accepted for parties of 6 or more. Pies $11.50–$21; extra charge for additional toppings. No credit cards. Mon–Thurs 11:30am–11pm; Fri–Sat 11:30am–midnight; Sun 11:30am–10pm. Subway: 6 to Spring St.; N, R to Prince St.

Mexican Radio MEXICAN   The hip SoHo-goes-south-of-the-border decor—mango walls, candles, folk art, rough-hewn furniture—creates an artsy-rustic atmosphere in which to dig into surprisingly good Old Mexico fare. The multicolored corn chips (not free; $2.50) come with a fresh and tangy salsa.

Main choices range from well-stuffed burritos to heaping fajita platters. Fans shouldn't pass on the chocolatey mole (one of the best in the city). Another winner is the *carnitas,* tender shredded pork soaked in a marinade of oranges, lemons, limes, and garlic, then grilled with a pepper salsa and served with fresh-made white corn tortillas. The spice meter is turned up high, so ask your young, friendly waiter to point you to the cooler dishes if you shy away from fiery spices. The margaritas are terrific. Beware: The room can get *loud* as weekend evenings wear on.

19 Cleveland Place (just south of intersection of Spring and Lafayette sts.). © 212/343-0140. Reservations accepted for parties of 6 or more. Main courses $8–$16. AE, MC, V. Sun–Thurs noon–11:30; Fri–Sat noon–midnight. Subway: 6 to Spring St.

Puck Fair *Finds* BRITISH   This pub looks as if it could have been lifted wholesale from a stylish corner of London and plunked down on this side of the pond. It's genuine through and through, but a young crowd and a hip soundtrack make it feel fresh (unlike Fanelli's, which is an old-time institution). Twenty beers are on tap (including Guinness), and the kitchen serves up good pub grub: chicken pot pie, bangers and mash, beef-stuffed cottage pie topped with the fluffy mashies, Guinness-battered fish and chips, and "toasties" (hot sandwiches) filled with your choices of cheese, ham, mushrooms, and Irish sausage. A nice yellowfin tuna niçoise adds a nouveau edge to the menu. The best tables are on the mezzanine; come post-lunch or for early dinner to try to snare one.

298 Lafayette St. (just south of Houston St.). © 212/431-1200. www.puckfair.citysearch.com. Main courses $6–$10 at brunch, $8–$17 at dinner (most $8–$13). AE, MC, V. Daily noon–4am. Subway: F, S to Broadway/Lafayette St.; N, R to Prince St.

Rice ★ *Value* PAN-ASIAN/INDO-CARIBBEAN   This sleek restaurant has a Japanese vibe and a superaffordable seasonal menu built around—you guessed it—rice. Pick your grain from the seven choices, which range from brown to Bhutanese red or Thai black, and pair it with any of 10 toppings. Vietnamese-grilled lemongrass chicken goes well with short-grain Japanese or sticky rice, while Jamaican jerk chicken wings are an ideal match for yellow rice and peas. Basmati is a must for the warm lentil salad or Indian curry. If you're just not sure, go with the pairing suggestions on the short but appealing menu. Thick Portuguese soup, flavored with potatoes and distinctive caraway-flavored rice, is a vegan's delight; it pairs up well with grilled eggplant maki or rice balls topped with tomato cumin sauce for a complete vegetarian meal for about $10. Rice bowls come small or large to suit your appetite, but all portions tend to be on the daintier side, so big appetites should order accordingly.

A word of warning: Like so many affordable downtown restaurants, the dining room is tiny, so come early to snare a table along the comfortable banquette; otherwise, you may end up perched at postage-stamp-size high tables on the opposite wall. Rice is best for twosomes at busy dinnertime, as only two tables can accommodate larger parties. A takeout outlet is in the adjacent storefront.

227 Mott St. (btwn Prince and Spring sts.). © 212/226-5775. Reservations not accepted. Main courses $6–$13. No credit cards. Daily noon–midnight. Subway: 6 to Spring St.

Snack GREEK   This SoHo newcomer draws a chic crowd with its beautifully prepared Hellenic eats. Tables are tiny and seating is tight, but a tin ceiling, Art Nouveau light fixtures, and shelves lined with Greek grocery goods transform the storefront dining room into a charmer. Even with paper plates and plastic utensils, this place is atmospheric enough to enjoy a wallet-friendly date (you're welcome to BYO wine or beer). The menu is traditional Greek cooking, and the kitchen usually strikes gold. The *taramosalata* (carp roe dip) is the best I've had, and the *spanikopitakia* (spinach squares) come close. Dressed with fresh tomatoes, roasted red onions, and a roasted tomato aioli and served on fresh, crusty *ciabatta*, the braised lamb sandwich was terrific. If the wait is too long at lunch and the weather's nice, order to go and head down the block to the park, where chess tables and benches come in handy for alfresco dining. Come after 6pm for yummy entrees like *saganaki* (fried cheese), vegetarian moussaka, grilled octopus, and chicken slow-roasted with lemon, rosemary, and garlic.

105 Thompson St. (btwn Prince and Spring sts.). © 212/925-1040. Reservations not accepted. Main courses $6–$14. No credit cards. Sun–Mon 11am–8:30pm; Tues–Sat 11am–10:30pm. Subway: C, E to Spring St.

Spring Street Natural Restaurant HEALTH-CONSCIOUS This 3-decade-old spot is as comfortable and easygoing as your old college hangout—and about as affordable. The brick-walled room is filled with leafy greenery and anchored by an oak bar. This is the kind of place where you can set up camp for a while, poring over a book while you nosh on a farm-fresh entree-size salad or a terrific tempeh burger; the staff will refill your coffee mug as you relax. But although the food is fresh, all-natural, unprocessed, and prepared with good health in mind, it's not strictly vegetarian: There's lots of fresh seafood from which to choose, plus free-range chicken and turkey. And the menu isn't restricted to soups, sandwiches, and salads, as at many other health-minded restaurants. You can come for a full meal, dining on such entrees as broiled New England bluefish with shiitake mushrooms, roasted chicken with pommery mustard glaze, or any number of pastas and stir-fry dishes. Everything is well prepared and satisfying. The kitchen can also satisfy sugar, dairy, and other dietary restrictions. There's pleasant outdoor seating along Lafayette Street in good weather.

62 Spring St. (at Lafayette St.). © 212/966-0290. Reservations accepted for parties of 8 or more. Main courses $7–$16.25. AE, DC, MC, V. Sun–Thurs 11:30am–11:30pm; Fri–Sat 11:30am–12:30am. Subway: 6 to Spring St.

QUICK BITES

If you need a coffee break, skip Starbucks and head to **Housing Works Used Books Cafe**, 126 Crosby St. (1 block east of Broadway), south of Houston Street (© 212/334-3324; www.housingworksubc.com). This attractive and airy used-book shop (whose proceeds support AIDS charities) has an appealing cafe that serves coffee and tea, salads, sandwiches, sweets, and other light bites. There are tables where you can pull up a chair, and you're welcome to read while you nosh. Beer and wine are served, and such events as literary readings and wine tastings are common in the evenings

Dean & Deluca also has a walk-up cafe for coffee, sandwiches, and sweets at the front of their store at 560 Broadway, at Prince Street (© **212/431-1691**).

7 The East Village & NoHo

In addition to the choices below, a great choice for wallet-friendly Middle Eastern fare is **Moustache** (p. 159), at 265 E. 10th St., between First Avenue and Avenue A (© **212/228-2022**). There's also an East Village branch of Sapporo (p. 176) called **Sapporo East,** on the corner of First Avenue and 10th Street (© **212/260-1330**), with a good sushi bar in addition to the cheap-eats Japanese menu offered here and at the sushi-less Theater District location.

The original **Time Cafe** is located at 380 Lafayette St., at Great Jones Street (© **212/533-7000**); this location serves breakfast, and I've spotted Michael

Stipe here more than once. **Burritoville** (p. 137) is at 141 Second Ave., between St. Marks Place and 9th Street (✆ **212/260-3300**). Additionally, a second location of British chippery **A Salt & Battery** (p. 155) will be open by the time you arrive, at 80 Second Ave., between 4th and 5th streets (✆ **212/254 6610**).

Acme Bar & Grill Kids SOUTHERN/BARBECUE   Acme's motto is AN OKAY PLACE TO EAT. This NoHo joint is divey in a pleasing way, with a good-natured staff, a Louisiana roadhouse theme, and the ambience of a well-worn neighborhood favorite. Acme serves up platters of Southern cooking and barbecue, including po' boys, crawfish, jambalaya, seafood gumbo, thick-cut pork chops, chicken-fried steak, baby back ribs—good, cheap, filling eats. Kids are welcome, and there are plenty of choices for them on the menu. The restaurant is a hot-sauce lover's delight, with dozens of bottles lining the walls so you can douse your dish with the perfect measure of heat. Fresh-baked cornbread starts the meal, and a range of beers is available.

9 Great Jones St. (at Lafayette St.). ✆ **212/420-1934.** Reservations accepted for parties of 8 or more. Main courses $6–$14 at lunch, $7–$16 at dinner; fixed-price weekend brunch $10 (includes coffee and tea, plus juice, Bloody Mary, beer, or mimosa). AE, DC, DISC, MC, V. Mon–Thurs 11:30am–midnight; Fri–Sat 11am–1am; Sun 11am–11pm. Subway: 6 to Bleecker St.

Angelica Kitchen ORGANIC VEGETARIAN   This cheerful restaurant is serious about vegan cuisine. The kitchen prepares everything fresh daily; they guarantee at least 95% of all ingredients are organically grown. But good-for-you (and good-for-the-environment) doesn't have to mean boring—this is flavorful, beautifully prepared cuisine served in a country-kitchen–style setting. Salads spill over with sprouts and crisp veggies and are crowned with homemade dressings. The Dragon Bowls, a specialty, are heaping portions of rice, beans, tofu, and steamed vegetables. The daily specials feature the best of what's fresh and in season in such dishes as fiery three-bean chili, slow-simmered with sun-dried tomatoes and a blend of chili peppers; baked tempeh in a sourdough baguette dressed in mushroom gravy; and lemon-herb baked tofu layered with roasted vegetables and fresh pesto on mixed-grain bread. Breads and desserts are fresh-baked and similarly wholesome (and made without eggs, of course). If you like the eats, you can take home *The Angelica Home Kitchen* cookbook.

300 E. 12th St. (just east of Second Ave.). ✆ **212/228-2909.** www.angelicakitchen.com. Reservations accepted for parties of 6 or more. Main courses $6–$14.50. No credit cards. Daily 11:30am–10:30pm. Subway: L, N, R, 4, 5, 6 to 14th St./Union Sq.

Bendix Diner AMERICAN DINER   For the same reason that it's just plain wrong to order healthy at Big Boy, it's nutty to go for the gentler side of the menu at this funky diner. Ignore the bizarro Thai dishes and indulge in the all-American grub. The burgers are served deluxe with a heap of fries, the chili con carne (over rice with onions, peppers, and cheese) is heavy with beef and beans, and the meat loaf and mashed potatoes are better than Ma used to make. I love the chicken noodle soup, with its richer-than-usual broth (no bouillon cubes here). Breakfast is available any time, and it's as hearty and wholesome as you'd expect. Sunday brunch gets alarmingly crowded, so bring a chunk of the *Times* to tide you over.

167 First Ave. (btwn 10th and 11th sts.). ✆ **212/260-4220.** Main courses $4.50–$15 (most under $10). AE, MC, V. Sun–Tues 8am–11pm; Wed–Sat 8am–1am. Subway: L to First Ave.

Bulgin' Waffles Finds WAFFLES   This unpretentious joint does one thing—waffles—and does them very well. The waffles come in two sizes—normal, or

Dining Zone: Little India

East 6th Street between First and Second avenues in the East Village is called "Little India," thanks to the dozen or more Indian restaurants that line the block (Subway: F to Second Ave.). Dining here isn't exactly high style, its restaurants offer decent food at discount prices, sometimes accompanied by live sitar music. It's fun to grab a bottle of wine or a six-pack (many of Little India's restaurants don't serve alcohol, but even those that do will often let you bring in your own) and cruise the strip. In warm weather, each usually stations a hawker out front to convince you that theirs is *so* much better than the competition's.

Some people speculate that there's one big kitchen behind East 6th, but a few of Little India's restaurants deserve special attention. **Bombay Dining,** at 320 E. 6th St. (© **212/260-8229**), is a standout, serving excellent *samosa* (vegetable-and-meat patties), *pakora* (banana fritters), and *papadum* (crispy bean wafers with coarse peppercorns). Also try **Gandhi,** 345 E. 6th St. (© **212/614-9718**), for a touch of low-light romance; **Mitali East,** 334 E. 6th St. (© **212/533-2508**), the king of curry; and **Rose of India,** 308 E. 6th St. (© **212/533-5011**), most notable for the pure spectacle of its every-day-is-Christmas decor.

"wafflette," and extra-thick, or "bulgin'." You have a number of varieties, from plain to hazelnut to pumpkin, and a full slate of toppings—so if you have a problem making choices, skip this place. Everybody else will love the fabulous food, superlow prices, and ambience. It's great for breakfast, brunch, dinner, or dessert! The "Dream Machine" is the ultimate ice-cream sandwich—made with waffles. The room is comprised of a bustling order counter and a collection of rough-hewn tables where you'll stake a post-order claim; your food is delivered to your table on paper plates. There's also an ice cream and Italian ice counter.

49½ First Ave. (at 3rd St.). © 212/477-6555. Main courses $2–$8. MC, V ($10 minimum). Sun 10am–10pm; Mon–Thurs 8am–10pm; Fri 8am–2am; Sat 10am–2am. Subway: F to Second Ave.

Cucina di Pesce *Value* ITALIAN   This crowded East Village stalwart—left over from the neighborhood's pre-trendy days—is legendary for its value. It's charming, too, if a little loud. The focus is on old-world basics like lasagna, marinara-topped pasta, shrimp scampi, and veal Marsala. Every once in a while somebody in the kitchen goes too far with a shellfish-and-mollusk combo, but by and large the offerings satisfy. The wide selection of pastas (fettuccine primavera, linguine with clam sauce) is always fresh-made and properly sauced, the veal tender, and the calamari well seasoned and crisp. The great-meal/low-price combo means that the place can be a mob scene, but free mussels marinara at the bar makes the wait easier to take. Try to snare a seat in the garden if the weather suits. As for wine: Stick with the house red, or opt for beer instead.

Note: If the wait is too long, head across the street to **Frutti di Mare,** 84 E. 4th St., at Second Avenue (© **212/979-2034**), which offers up basically the same schtick, minus the mussels at the bar.

87 E. 4th St. (btwn Second and Third aves.). © 212/260-6800. www.cucinadipesce.com. Main courses $8–$13 (specials may be slightly higher); 3-course pre-theater dinner with glass of wine $10 (daily 3–6:30pm). No credit cards. Daily 2:30pm–midnight. Subway: F to Second Ave.

Frank ★★ (Value) ITALIAN   The first thought that pops into my mind when I try an Italian restaurant is, "What would Tony Soprano think?" T would definitely give Frank the thumbs up. This home-style restaurant serves straight-from-the-boot cuisine. The menu is small but satisfying, focusing on what the kitchen does well: Rigatoni al ragu wears a meat-and-tomato "gravy" slow-cooked to perfection. It appears again on the house specialty, the *polpettone*—literally "the big meatball"—a beautifully seasoned mound of beef with a potato-and-pancetta gratin that's better than dessert in my book. The spaghetti with garlic and extra-virgin olive oil is simple, but the pasta is al dente and tossed to perfection with just the right bit of finely grated cheese; anchovy lovers should go with the fishy version. There's homemade gnocchi and ravioli, plus spiced meat loaf. The wine list is well priced, with a good selection by the glass.

The young wait staff is easygoing and earnest, and the brick-walled room is dimly lit and attractive in a cozy way. On the downside, the tables are so close together that you can't help but overhear your neighbors' conversation; the open kitchen can make the dining room rather smoky at times; and there's often a wait (Vera, Frank's bar, offers a place to unwind with a glass of wine). But these minor inconveniences are well worth it for the marvelous payoff that is Frank fare.

88 Second Ave. (btwn 5th and 6th sts.). © 212/420-0202. Reservations accepted only for parties of 8 or more. Main courses $9–$14. No credit cards. Mon–Thurs 10:30am–4pm and 5pm–12:45am; Fri–Sat 10:30am–4pm and 5pm–1:45am; Sun 10:30am–11:45pm. Subway: 6 to Astor Place.

Jeollado (Value) SUSHI   Sushi chef Kirjin Kim expanded to this cavernous space, which he named after his South Korean hometown. Just like its plain-Jane sister joint, Sandobe Sushi, Jeollado offers probably the best price-to-quality ratio in the city for bargain-hunting sushi lovers. Take it from this sushi hound: You'll pay significantly more—and wait just as long—for sushi of this high quality anywhere else. The fresh fish is generously and expertly cut. The sushi combos are a good-value starting point; supplement with some sea-salty *edamame* (soybean pods) and one or two of the creative house rolls, such as the Hawaiian (ruby-red tuna and real crabmeat). The Korean side of the menu features Korean pancakes, teriyaki and noodle dishes, and (spiced vegetables served over rice). Service can be slow, the room can get loud, and it's almost always packed, but the efficient servers turn the tables over quickly, and the payoff is worth it.

Note: If you're in the neighborhood, Kim's original no-decor **Sandobe Sushi,** 330 E. 11th St., between First and Second avenues (© **212/780-0328**), still offers excellent sushi-meal deals at similarly low prices.

116 E. 4th St. (between First and Second aves.). © **212/260-7696.** Reservations not accepted. Sushi rolls $3.40–$11.75; sushi combos $9.75–$17.75; nonsushi entrees $8–$15. No credit cards. Daily 5pm–1am. Subway: F to Second Ave.

Lil' Frankie's Pizza PIZZA   If Frank (see above) sounds appealing but you're in the mood for pizza, head to this new place. Lil' Frankie's feels like grandma's Italian kitchen, complete with wood tables, family photos, and lace curtains; frankly, this must be the most adorable pizza joint in town. The wood-burning brick oven at the heart of the open kitchen was handcrafted by a third-generation Neapolitan oven builder and features real lava from Vesuvio. Thin, crisp crusts are topped with zesty sauce and some of the best ingredients in town, including tiny meatballs (on the pizza Polpettine), gorgeous fresh mushrooms (on the pizza funghi), and Sicilian salted anchovies (on the Napoletana and the Romana). A few other dishes come from the oven if you're not in the mood for pie, such as Thursday's excellent lasagna alla Bolognese, and I defy you to find another pizza joint that serves such gorgeous green salads. Service is friendly, and the wine list is inexpensive. A back garden for warm-weather dining and late hours—until 2am weekdays, 4am weekends—add the perfect crowning touches.

19 First Ave. (btwn 1st and 2nd sts.). © 212/420-4900. Reservations not accepted. Main courses $9–$14. No credit cards. Sun–Thurs 9:30am–2am; Fri–Sat 9:30am–4am. Subway: F to Second Ave.

Paul's ★★ *Value* BURGERS/DINER   This neighborhood diner serves the best burgers in town—period. It's a bold claim, but I'll stand by it. Every burger is a half-pounder, made from 100% pure beef or turkey. Both versions are thick, juicy, and delicious. Variations run the gamut from a slate of cheeseburgers (American, Swiss, mozzarella, cheddar, Monterey Jack, blue) to concoctions like the Texas (topped with a fried egg) and the Eastsider (a bacon cheeseburger with ham, mushrooms, tomatoes, and onions). If you're in the mood for something else, consider a Philly cheese steak, a tuna melt, or any one of a dozen omelets. Fries are crisp and yummy. A better-than-average selection of beers is on hand, while egg creams, milk shakes, and root-beer floats offer old-fashioned comfort.

131 Second Ave. (btwn 7th St. and St. Marks Place). © 212/529-3033 or 212/529-3097. Reservations not accepted. Burgers and main courses $2.30–$10.60. No credit cards. Sun–Thurs 11am–midnight; Fri–Sat 11am–1am. Subway: 6 to Astor Place.

Pisces ★ *Value* SEAFOOD   This pleasing fish house serves up the best inexpensive seafood in the city. All the fish is top quality and fresh daily, and all smoked items are prepared in the restaurant's own smoker. The mesquite-smoked whole trout in sherry oyster sauce is better than trout I've had for twice the price; start with the phyllo-fried shrimp or the tuna ceviche with curried potato chips and roasted pepper coulis, and the world is yours. Other winning dishes include flaky pan-fried skate in a burgundy reduction with garlicky mashed potatoes and roasted pearl onions. Last time we dined here, I feasted on an excellent grilled mako shark with chard in a cockle stew. The creative kitchen shows surprising skill with vegetables as well as fish.

The wine list is appealing and well priced, the decor nautical without being kitschy, and the service friendly and attentive. For wallet-watchers, the early-bird fixed-price makes an already terrific value even better. The Alphabet City locale gives Pisces serious hip, but it's laid-back, ensuring that anyone will be comfortable here. Tables spill out onto the sidewalk on warm evenings, giving you a ringside seat for the funky East Village show.

95 Ave. A (at 6th St.). © 212/260-6660. Reservations recommended. Main courses $8–$20; 2-course fixed-price dinner (Mon–Thurs 5:30–7pm; Fri–Sun 5:30–6:30pm) $15. AE, DC, MC, V. Mon–Thurs 5:30–11:30pm; Fri 5:30pm–1am; Sat 11:30am–3:30pm and 5:30pm–1am; Sun 11:30am–3:30pm and 5:30–11:30pm. Subway: 6 to Astor Place; F to Second Ave.

Soba-Ya ★★ *Finds* JAPANESE NOODLES   *Shhh*—don't tell anybody about Soba-Ya. It has a loyal following, but the masses haven't discovered it yet. That makes it easy to walk in and enjoy an affordable, healthful Japanese meal without a wait. Go with one of the special starters, which might be grilled shiitakes or luscious *toro* (tuna belly) sashimi, and then move on to one of the house specialties: generous, steaming noodle bowls. They come with *soba* (thin buckwheat) or *udon* (a very thick noodle much like pasta) and in a number of combinations. A menu with descriptions and pictures makes it easy for noodle novices to order. I love the *nabeyaki*, an udon bowl with shrimp tempura, and the excellent-quality *una-don*, broiled eel over rice. Cold soba dishes topped with your choice of ingredients are also available. Everything is beautifully presented on Japanese dishware, and there's a lengthy list of sakes. The lovely blond-wood dining room is blessed with a soothing, Zen-like vibe and attentive service.

229 E. 9th St. (btwn Second and Third aves.). © **212/533-6966**. Reservations not accepted. Main courses $6.50–$14. AE, DC, DISC, MC, V. Daily noon–4pm and 5:30–10:30pm. Subway: 6 to Astor Place.

Tsampa *Finds* TIBETAN/VEGETARIAN   Here's something you're unlikely to stumble across in your hometown: Tibetan food. It's light, wholesome, and vegetarian-friendly, prepared with mostly organic produce, but not strictly vegetarian. Some of the dishes are a bit bland (skip the curry), but most are flavorfully spiced. Start with an order of momo, Tibet's signature dish. *Momo* are steamed or fried dumplings stuffed with your choice of ingredients—from chicken and veggies to tofu and chives—served with a pair of spicy red and green hot sauces. A baked udon noodle dish makes a pleasing follow-up, as does the whole grilled fish and the *sherpa khala,* baby potatoes sautéed with chicken, greens, garlic, and ginger served with Tibetan bread. A candlelit ambience and mature service makes Tsampa a good bet for budget-friendly romance.

212 E. 9th St. (btwn Second and Third aves.). © **212/614-3226**. Reservations accepted. Main courses $9–$16 (most less than $13). AE, MC, V. Daily 5pm–11:30pm. Subway: 6 to Astor Place.

Veselka ★ UKRAINIAN DINER   Whenever the craving hits for eastern European fare at old-world prices, Veselka fits the bill with *pirogi* (dumplings filled with potatoes, cheese, or sauerkraut), *kasha varnishkes* (cracked buckwheat and noodles with mushroom sauce), stuffed cabbage, Polish kielbasa, potato pancakes, and classic soups like a borscht, voted best in the city by the *New York Times* and *New York* magazine. Try the buckwheat pancakes or cheese blintzes; the Christmas borscht, which hits the menu in early December and stays through January, is a simple but divine rendering of the eastern European classic. But if all you want is a burger, don't worry—it's a classic, too.

Despite the authentic fare, the diner is comfortable, modern, and appealing, with an artsy slant and house-made desserts. Regional beers from the Ukraine and Poland and a nice selection of wines from California and South America add a sophisticated touch. No wonder Veselka surpasses its status as a popular after-hours hangout with club kids and other night owls to be a favorite at any hour.

144 Second Ave. (at 9th St.). © **212/228-9682**. Reservations not accepted. Main courses $5–$13. AE, DC, DISC, MC, V. Daily 24 hr. Subway: 6 to Astor Place.

Village Yokocho *Value* JAPANESE/KOREAN BARBECUE   Village Yokocho is about as authentic as Japanese restaurants get. Entering this second-floor spot feels like stepping into a Tokyo yakitori bar, complete with a hip clientele that's a mix of Japanese and in-the-know Americans. Between the regular menu and the handwritten specials on the wall, the choices are vast. Dishes run the gamut from dumplings and yakisoba noodles to exotica such as deep-fried squid eggs. The broiled-eel bowl is finer quality than you'll get at many restaurants and a deal at $8. The yakitori skewers, both meat and veggie choices grilled over an open flame, are excellent. Korean dishes include oxtail soup and *bibinbop,* a rice bowl topped with veggies, ground beef, and a fried egg. The specials change depending on the season, but you might find soft-shell crab in ponzu sauce, broiled yellowtail with teriyaki sauce, and any number of sashimi appetizers. There's a big, affordable sake menu as well as a several beers.

8 Stuyvesant St. (at Third Ave. and E. 9th St.), 2nd floor. © **212/598-3041**. Reservations not accepted. Main courses $4–$12. AE, MC, V. Sun–Wed 5pm–3am; Thurs–Sat 5pm–4am. Subway: 6 to Astor Place.

QUICK BITES
Adventuresome diners should seek out **Otafuku**, 236 E. 9th St., between Second and Third avenues (✆ **212/353-8503**). Run by two Japanese women, this tiny takeout specializes in *okonomiyaki*, a Japanese pancake made with egg and flour, blended with shredded cabbage and either meat or seafood, then grilled on a hot plate, and topped with a traditional sauce and curly dried bonito flakes. *Okonomiyaki* means, "cook what you like," and you can choose your ingredients: beef, pork, shrimp, or squid. It's a delicious, filling, and healthy one-dish meal that's also dirt cheap—I defy you to spend $10 here. There are no tables, but you can take your food to the Starbucks across Third Avenue, which has plenty of outdoor seating, or head to a bench in Union Square Park a few blocks north.

8 Greenwich Village & the Meat-Packing District

In addition to the choices below, there's an outpost of the coffeehouse/sandwich bar **Xando/Cosí** (p. 190) at 504 Sixth Ave., at 13th Street (✆ **212/462-4188**). There's also a **Burritoville** (p. 137) at 298 Bleecker St., near Seventh Avenue (✆ **212/633-9249**). The ultrafresh, supercheap **Go Sushi** (p. 179) is at 3 Greenwich Ave. (Sixth Ave. at 8th St.; ✆ **212/366-9272**). There's also a branch of the Belgian **Petite Abeille** (p. 163) in the West Village at 466 Hudson St., at Barrow Street (✆ **212/741-6479**), and another at 200 W. 14th St., between Ninth and Tenth avenues (✆ **212/727-1505**).

A Salt & Battery BRITISH   Adjacent to tearoom Tea & Sympathy (see below) and a shop selling Cadbury Flake bars, Hob Nob biscuits, and other English groceries and trinkets, this is this newest addition to Nicky Perry's burgeoning Pax Brittania. This shop is so genuine that they serve the goods wrapped in newspaper. Stick with the traditional varieties (halibut, cod) and you'll enjoy the real thing (crisp-battered outside, flaky and greaseless inside). The room is tiny, with no more than six or eight seats, so come at an off hour or be prepared for a wait—but it's worth it. Word is that the deep-fried Mars Bar makes a divine dessert; if you dare, write and let me know—I've been too chicken to try it myself. English beers are available, of course.

112 Greenwich Ave. (btwn 12th and 13th sts.). ✆ 212/691-2713. www.asaltandbattery.com. Reservations not accepted. Main courses $5–$13. AE, MC, V. Daily noon–10pm. Subway: A, C, E, 1, 2, 3, 9 to 14th St. Also at 80 Second Ave. (btwn 4th and 5th sts.; ✆ 212/254-6610; subway: F to Second Ave.).

Bar Pitti ★ *Value* TUSCAN ITALIAN   This indoor/outdoor trattoria is a hip sidewalk scene, and one of downtown's best dining bargains. Waiting for a table can be a chore, but all is forgiven once you take a seat, thanks to authentic, affordably priced cuisine and some of the friendliest waiters in town. Despite the packed seating, Bar Pitti wins you over with Italian charm—it's the kind of place where the waiter brings over the list of daily specials on a well-worn blackboard, and if you want more cheese, a block of Parmesan and a grater suddenly appear. Peruse the laminated menu, but don't get your heart set on anything until you see the board, which boasts the best of what the kitchen has to offer; on my last visit, they wowed me with fabulous veal meatballs. Winners off the regular menu, which focuses heavily on pastas and panini, include excellent beef carpaccio; grilled country bread with prosciutto, garlic, and olive oil; and spinach-and-ricotta ravioli in a creamy sage and Parmesan sauce. The all-Italian wine list is high-priced compared to the menu, but you'll find a few good-value choices.

268 Sixth Ave. (btwn Bleecker and Houston sts.). © 212/982-3300. Reservations accepted for parties of 4 or more. Main courses $7.50–$13 (some specials may be higher). No credit cards. Daily noon–midnight. Subway: A, C, E, F, V to W. 4th St. (use 3rd St. exit).

Corner Bistro BURGERS This old-time neighborhood bar serves up what some people (including *The Daily Show*'s Jon Stewart) consider to be the best burger in the city. Its well-charred, beefy burgers are deservedly famous—and you'd be hard-pressed to dine so well for so little anywhere else. The top of the line is the bistro burger, with bacon, cheese, lettuce, and tomato, for 5 bucks. The thin, crispy fries, served up on a paper plate, are an appropriate accompaniment. Head elsewhere if you want something besides a burger, because the other offerings are limited and half-hearted, except for the chili. Service can be slow, but why bother being in a rush at an atmospheric neighborhood local like this?

331 W. 4th St. (at Jane St., near Eighth Ave.). © 212/242-9502. Reservations not accepted. Burgers and sandwiches $2.50–$6. No credit cards. Mon–Sat 11am–3:30am; Sun noon–3:30am. Subway: A, C, E to 14th St.

EJ's Luncheonette *Kids* AMERICAN DINER This retro diner is popular with all Village types, including yuppies and their kids, who come for hearty American fare in a 1950s setting—vinyl booths, Formica tabletops, a soda fountain, and a lunch counter with stools that spin. The menu features a large selection of breakfasts so good you won't be ashamed of indulging in a stack of banana-pecan pancakes for dinner. There's also a terrific selection of burgers (including a great veggie version), sandwiches, salads, and main dishes such as meat loaf with mashed potatoes. Everything is better than you'd expect, and service is friendly. Don't miss the amazing sweet-potato fries. Weekend brunch is a big deal at all three locations, but expect a wait.

432 Sixth Ave. (btwn 9th and 10th sts.). © 212/473-5555. Reservations not accepted. Main courses $4–$12. AE. Sun–Thurs 8:30am–10:30pm; Fri–Sat 8:30am–11pm. Subway: Subway: A, C, E, F, V to W. 4th St. (use 8th St. exit). Also at 447 Amsterdam Ave. (btwn 81st and 82nd sts.; © 212/873-3444; subway: 1, 9 to 79th St.); 1271 Third Ave. (at 73rd St.; © 212/472-0600; subway: 6 to 77th St.).

Emerald Planet *✪* INTERNATIONAL WRAPS This San Francisco import has buried the sandwich and replaced it with the wrap. The Emerald Planet ideology is simple: You can eat wraps at every meal, from bacon and eggs (the Omaha) in the morning to grilled veggies with goat cheese (the Sonoma) at noon to jerk chicken, mango salsa, and jasmine rice (the Kingston) at dinner. The tortilla-like wrapping changes depending on the ingredients, from flour to whole wheat to tomato to spinach. All ingredients are fresh, and the emphasis is on healthy. Supplement your wrap with one of the smoothies, or opt for a margarita, fresh-brewed iced tea, a latte, fresh sangria, or one of the international bottled beers on offer. The decor is downtown stylish—wee dangling halogen lights, clean woody surfaces, rainforest-green walls. This is one of downtown's best stops for quick, quality chow—just ask Madonna, an Emerald Planet regular.

2 Great Jones St. (at Broadway). © 212/353-9727. www.emeraldplanet.citysearch.com. Wraps $1.50–$3.50 at breakfast, $6–$8 at lunch; smoothies $4–$5. AE, MC, V. Mon–Fri 9am–10pm; Sat noon–10pm; Sun noon–8pm. Subway: 6 to Bleecker St.; N, R to 8th St. Also at 30 Rockefeller Plaza, lower concourse level (down the hall from the skating rink; © 212/218-1133; subway: B, D, F, Q to 47th–50th sts./Rockefeller Center).

Florent *Kids* DINER/FRENCH BISTRO So you get a craving at 3am for *rillettes, boudin noir,* or steak frites and can't decide whether you'd like to eat with club kids, celebrities, transvestites, truckers, or the odd stockbroker? Then get thee down to Florent, the nearly 24-hour French bistro dressed up as a '50s-style

Greenwich Village Dining

A Salt & Battery **4**	Lupa **19**
Bar Pitti **18**	Moustache **15**
Burritoville **13**	Ony **12**
Corner Bistro **3**	Petite Abeille **16**
EJ's Luncheonette **10**	Sammy's Noodle Shop & Grill **7**
Florent **2**	Tea & Sympathy **5**
Go Sushi **9**	The Pink Tea Cup **14**
Gray's Papaya **11**	Two Boots to Go West **6**
John's Pizzeria **17**	Xando/Cosi **8**
Little Pie Company **1**	

157

diner, where you can have it all. Located in the Meat-Packing District, Florent is a hot spot no matter what time of day; a children's menu makes this the perfect place to bring the kids for lunch or early dinner. But it's after the clubs close when the joint really jumps. Tables are packed, almost uncomfortably so, but it's all part of the late-night festivities. This place has a sense of humor (check out the menu boards) and a CD catalog full of the latest indie sounds. The food's good, too: The grilled chicken with herbs and mustard sauce is a winner, as is the French onion soup with Gruyère. There are always faves like burgers and chili in addition to Gallic standards like *moules frites* (fried mussels), and comfort-food specialties such as chicken potpie make regular appearances. The fries are light, crispy, and addictive. The fixed-price lunches and dinners are excellent deals.

69 Gansevoort St. (2 blocks south of 14th St. and 1 block west of Ninth Ave., btwn Greenwich and Washington sts.). © **212/989-5779**. www.restaurantflorent.com. Reservations recommended for dinner. Main courses $4.50–$14.50 at brunch and lunch, $8–$20.50 at dinner (most less than $15); 2-course fixed-price lunches $8.25–$11.95; 3-course fixed-price dinner $18.95 before 7:30pm, $20.95 7:30pm–midnight. No credit cards. Mon–Wed 9am–5am; Thurs–Sun 24 hr. Subway: A, C, E, L to 14th St. L to 8th Ave.

Lupa ★★ *Value* CENTRAL ITALIAN   God bless Mario Batali, New York's big-name chef who thinks you shouldn't have to spend a fortune to eat like a king. The man behind the acclaimed and more expensive Babbo, the Food Network's "Molto Mario" operates this Roman-style trattoria. Reservations are taken for the back room only, and I strongly advise you to get them, as it's quieter and more civilized. The front room is for walk-ins; it's loud and cramped and you'll probably have to wait unless you come early, but the food is worth it.

Don't be scared off by the all-Italian menu; the butcher-coated waiter will steer you through the language and preparations. It's a short list, but one that boasts lots of treats. As always with Mario, the pastas stand out: The *bucatini all'amatriciana*, a classic Italian tube pasta in a smoky tomato sauce made from hog jowl

---

Tips Pizza! Pizza!

In the mood for a slice or two . . . or three? The original location of **John's Pizzeria** (p. 172), 278 Bleecker St. between Sixth and Seventh avenues (© **212/243-1680**), is a New York original and still one of the city's best. The pies are thin-crusted, properly sauced, and fresh and served up piping hot in an authentic old-world setting. Sorry, no slices.

For something more funky, head to **Two Boots to Go West,** 201 W. 11th St., at Seventh Avenue (© **212/633-9096**), or **Two Boots to Go-Go,** 74 Bleecker St., at Broadway (© **212/777-1033**), where variations on the traditional pie are the point: Consider the Larry Tate, a "bewitching" blend of spinach, garlic, and tomatoes on a white pie; or the Bayou Beast, with BBQ shrimp, andouille sausage, crawfish, and jalapeños. (The "two boots" refer to Louisiana and Italy—hence the crawfish.) Both are predominately takeout and delivery locations, but there are a few tables. For full service or a quick slice, head to the original **Two Boots,** 37-45 Ave. A, between 2nd and 3rd streets (© **212/505-2276** or 212/254-1919; www.twoboots.com). The East Village location also boasts two entertainment spaces: The **Pioneer Theater** (© **212/254-3300**), hosting independent films; and the **Den of Cin** at Two Boots Video (© **212/254-1441**), a lounge hosting cult films, music, comedy, and other entertainment. Call or check the website for a schedule.

(bacon), is divine, as is the ricotta gnocchi with Italian sausage and fennel. Don't miss an opportunity to start with the *prosciutto di carpegna* with roasted figs, an ideal marriage of salt and sweet; it's easy to build a value-packed meal from the list of antipasti. Among the main courses, the classic saltimbocca was a disappointment, but the oven-roasted littleneck clams with sweet *soppressata* (salami) was a joy. The wine list is massive and superaffordable.

170 Thompson St. (btwn Houston and Bleecker sts.). © 212/982-5089. www.luparestaurant.com. Reservations highly recommended. Antipasti $5–$12; main courses $9–$17; 4-course prix fixe $30 at lunch, $45 at dinner (only for parties of 7 or more). AE, DC, MC, V. Daily noon–2:45pm and 5:30–11:30pm. Subway: 1, 9 to Houston St.

Moustache *Value* MIDDLE EASTERN Moustache (pronounced moo-*stahsh*) is the sort of exotic neighborhood spot that's just right. On a side street in the West Village, this charming hole-in-the-wall boasts a Middle Eastern vibe and fare that's both palate-pleasing and wallet-friendly. Delicately seasoned dishes bear little resemblance to the food at your average falafel joint. Expect subtly flavored hummus, tabbouleh, and spinach-chickpea-tomato salad (or a large plate of all three); oven-roasted "pitzas," thin, matzolike pita crusts topped with spicy minced lamb and other ingredients; and—best of all—homemade pita bread, which puts any of those store-bought Frisbees to shame. Moustache is hugely and popular, so don't be surprised if there's a line—but it's worth the wait.

90 Bedford St. (btwn Barrow and Grove sts.). © 212/229-2220. Reservations not accepted. Main courses $5–$12. No credit cards. Daily noon–midnight (last order at 11pm). Subway: 1, 9 to Christopher St. Also at 265 E. 10th St. (btwn First Ave. and Ave. A; © 212/228-2022; L to First Ave.).

Ony JAPANESE NOODLES This smart, stylish noodle shop is a welcome addition to a less-than-attractive stretch of Sixth Avenue. The specialty is *menchanko*, a ramen-noodle soup served in a soy, miso, or tomato broth with your choice of fresh ingredients, from chicken and shrimp to tofu to kimchee and fresh vegetables—or all of the above. Menchanko arrives piping hot at your table in a large metal bowl, with both chopsticks and a ladle for easy sipping and slurping. A handful of other noodle dishes are also on hand, including udon bowls and cold soba (buckwheat) noodle dishes, plus a short sushi-roll menu—but this place is all about the noodles. The room is attractive, and service professional. Pony up to the sleek noodle bar if you're in a hurry.

357 Sixth Ave. (btwn W. 4th St. and Washington Place). © 212/414-8429. Reservations not accepted. Noodle bowls $7.75–$9.75; sushi $4.50–$11. AE, MC, V. Daily 11am–1am. Subway: A, C, E, F, V to W. 4th St. (use 3rd St. exit).

The Pink Tea Cup *Value* SOUL FOOD This simple soul fooder has been serving smothered pork chops, fried chicken, barbecue, and other hearty, fare to New Yorkers since 1954. Portions are huge, and every dinner comes with your choice of two vegetables (I love the black-eyed peas), soup *and* salad, bread, and jello or a bread pudding for dessert. Tops among the main courses are the divine chicken and dumplings, in a thick, flavorful broth. If you're in the mood for something simpler, opt for a fried-catfish or roast-beef sandwich, or a satisfying burger (served with pie and coffee for just $5.50). Spend a couple extra dollars on a side of macaroni and cheese—trust me, you won't be disappointed. Another worthy extra: the coconut cake. Service is efficient and attentive, and the old-fashioned jukebox boasts selections from songsters like Aretha, Isaac Hayes, and Kirk Franklin. Feel free to bring your own beer or wine. One word of warning: The restroom sits at the bottom of a tiny, vertigo-inducing spiral staircase.

42 Grove St. (btwn Bleecker and Bedford sts.). © 212/807-6755. www.thepinkteacup.com. Reservations not accepted. Breakfast $4–$9.25; sandwiches and burger combos $3–$9.25; complete dinners (including soup, salad, and dessert) $9.25–$15.25. No credit cards. Mon–Thurs 8am–midnight; Fri–Sun 8am–1am. Subway: 1, 9 to Christopher St.

Sammy's Noodle Shop & Grill CHINESE   This colorful, brightly lit restaurant is perpetually packed with neighborhood regulars and NYU students, but it's large enough that there's rarely a wait for a table. The cuisine isn't Chinatown authentic, but it is delicious. Cantonese wonton and Mandarin noodle soups, barbecue roasted meats (pork, ribs, duck, and chicken), and dim sum are all well done—especially the roasted meats, which hang in the window, dripping with succulent juices—and the choice of Chinese mains is encyclopedic. Noodle soups are made with delicious udon noodles and come stuffed with fresh veggies and sliced meats. Dumplings, egg rolls, and steamed buns are monstrous—one is enough for two to share. In fact, all portions are huge; you can pretty much expect leftovers. Service is friendly and efficient at this reliable choice.

453–461 Sixth Ave. (at 11th St.). © 212/924-6688. Main courses $3.50–$17 (most less than $10). AE, DC, DISC, MC, V. Daily 11:30am–midnight. Subway: A, C, E, F, V to W. 4th St. (use 8th St. exit); F to 14th St.

Tea & Sympathy BRITISH   When Londoner Nicky Perry moved to New York, she was disappointed to find no proper British tearoom, so she opened her own. Tea & Sympathy seems transplanted wholesale from Greenwich or Highgate, complete with an oddball collection of creamers and teapots, snappy British wait staff, and plenty of charm. Elbow room is at a minimum and the place is usually packed, but it's worth the squeeze for the full afternoon tea, which comes on a tiered tray with crust-off finger sandwiches like chicken salad and egg and 'cress, scones with jam and Devonshire cream, and cakes and cookies for a sugary finish. The menu also features such traditional British comforts as shepherd's pie, bangers and mash, and a chicken-and-leek pie. Anglophiles line up for the Sunday dinner—roast beef and Yorkshire pudding, of course. For dessert, try the treacle pudding, ginger cake, or yummy sherry trifle.

108 Greenwich Ave. (btwn 12th and 13th sts.). © 212/807-8329 or 212/989-9735. www.teaandsympathynewyork.com. Reservations not accepted. Main courses $5.50–$12 at lunch and brunch, $10.50–$17 at dinner; full afternoon tea $19 ($35 for 2). MC, V. Daily 11:30am–10pm. Subway: 1, 2, 3, 9, A, C, E to 14th St.

QUICK BITES

Ask any New Yorker—one of the cheapest, most satisfying meals in the city is the $2.45 two-dogs-and-drink deal from **Gray's Papaya**, 402 Sixth Ave., at 8th Street (© **212/260-3532**). This legendary hot-dog stand hawks nothing but all-beef dogs, fries, and your choice of tropical-flavored fruit drinks ranging from piña colada to Orange Julius–style OJ. Best of all, you can indulge in a Gray's frank and juice at any hour, because they never close.

Gourmet grocer **Dean & Deluca** has a cafe at 11th Street and University Place (© **212/473-1908**), a great stop for a sandwich or cafe au lait and pastry.

9 Chelsea

In addition to the choices below, **Burritoville** (p. 137) is at 264 W. 23rd St., between Seventh and Eighth avenues (© **212/367-9844**).

Antique Cafe CAFE   I love the atmosphere and the beautifully prepared food at this brick-walled cafe, named for the flea markets that fill the nearby Sixth Avenue parking lots on weekends (see chapter 8) always fragrant with the aroma of fresh-baked goods. There's no printed menu; instead, the day's bill of fare features whatever's fresh, including homemade soups, bounteous salads, gourmet sandwiches that run the gamut from roast beef to peanut butter and jelly, quiche, and pastries and cappuccino. Making regular appearances are a terrific bruschetta with melted Swiss, mushroom, and onion ($3.50); a dynamite haddock chowder ($3.75); a London broil salad boasting a beautiful cut, tomatoes, red onions, and cilantro over mixed greens ($6.25); and a simple, healthy chicken paella with salad ($6). Order at the friendly counter and take a seat at one of the small cafe tables indoors or out, or take your food over to Madison Square Park.

101 W. 25th St. (just west of Sixth Ave.). © 212/675-1663. All items less than $8. No credit cards. Daily 7:30am–6:30pm. Subway: F to 23rd St.

Empire Diner AMERICAN DINER This throwback to the all-American diner looks like an Airstream camper plunked down on the corner. This classic joint boasts an Art Deco vibe, honest coffee, and great mashed potatoes. The food is diner fare: eggs, omelets, burgers, sandwiches, and a nice turkey platter. Frankly, I think the Empire Diner is overrated—you'll find better breakfast fare elsewhere—but there's no denying its status as a fixture on the late-night scene. If you want quiet, go early. If you want an eyeful, wait for the after-hours crowd; 1 to 3am offers the best people-watching. There's live music courtesy of a regular pianist. When the weather's warm, a pleasing sidewalk cafe appears, and the limited traffic this far over—mostly aiming for the Lincoln Tunnel—keeps the soot-and-fumes factor down.

210 Tenth Ave. (at 22nd St.). © 212/243-2736. Reservations not accepted. Main courses $9–$18. AE, DC, DISC, MC, V. Daily 24 hr. Subway: C, E to 23rd St.

F&B *Finds* INTERNATIONAL Budget-minded New Yorkers have rejoiced at the arrival of F&B, which serves a global menu of European street food (Danish and German hot dogs, Swedish meatballs, Belgian frites, New Orleans beignets) in a stylish powder-blue space. The signature dog comes in a variety of styles, from the Great Dane, a Danish dog dressed with rémoulade, roast onions, marinated cucumber slices, Danish mustard and ketchup on a toasted bun, to Pups in a Blanket, adorable minidogs in puff pastry served with honey mustard. A veggie dog is also available. The warm beignets come brushed with powdered sugar and your choice of dips, including chocolate, maple syrup, and crème anglaise. The crispy twice-cooked frites come accompanied with your choice of a range of flavored butters, oils, and dips, including a yummy garlic aioli. You can wash it down with Belgian-style beers, ciders, wine, and even champagne. Delivery is available if you're staying in the area.

269 W. 23rd St. (btwn Seventh and Eighth Aves.). © 646/486-4441. Reservations not accepted. Main courses $1.50–$10. AE, MC, V. Daily 11am–11pm. Subway: C, E to 23rd St.

Grand Sichuan International *Value* SICHUAN CHINESE Grand Sichuan serves up real Chinese here in Chelsea. This comfortable spot has garnered raves for its authentic Sichuan cuisine. Spicy-food lovers will be thrilled, as the kitchen excels at dishes that are intensely spiced without being numbing—a balance that few Chinatown kitchens can achieve. The flavors are complex and strong, especially in such top choices as Sichuan wontons in red oil, Chairman Mao's pork with chestnuts, and my favorite, boneless whole fish with pine nuts in a modified sweet-and-sour sauce. The house bean curd in spicy sauce is another winner, but only for those with a high tolerance for hot. The staff will be more than happy to recommend milder dishes.

229 Ninth Ave. (at 24th St.). © 212/620-5200. Reservations accepted for parties of 3 or more. Main courses $3.25–$14. AE, DC, MC, V. Daily 11:30am–11pm. Subway: C, E to 23rd St. Also at 745 Ninth Ave. (btwn 50th and 51st sts.; © 212/582-2288; subway: C, E to 50th St.).

Johny's Grill & Luncheonette *Value* GREEK-AMERICAN DINER This neighborhood greasy spoon offers up cheap eats and a dose of local color. Johny has been running the grill for over 25 years; his dad makes the soups and specials from the kitchen in the back. I like the split pea soup because it doesn't have the typical stand-your-spoon-up-thickness and comes topped with lots of croutons. The personal-size pita pizzas are incredible, with the grilled chicken the best among the terrific choices. To order like an insider, sidle up to the long counter and use the burger code (not on the menu—it's secret code among Johny and his regulars): a "full house" is a burger with the works (lettuce, tomato, onion, and pickle), while a "deluxe" is a full house plus fries. Other specialties include the grilled sandwiches like the Big Mo (roast beef, coleslaw, and cheese) or the Florentine (grilled chicken, spinach, and feta cheese). Both the TV and radio are usually on, and Johny usually knows the score.

124 W. 25th St. (btwn Sixth and Seventh aves.). © 212/243-6230. Breakfast $1.25–$4.50; sandwiches, burgers, and salads $2.50–$6. No credit cards. Mon–Sat 8am–3:45pm. Subway: 1, 9, F to 23rd St.

The Half King ★ IRISH Author Sebastian Junger took his earnings from *The Perfect Storm*, teamed up with some other writer/filmmaker friends, and opened the perfect pub in west Chelsea. It's the spitting image of an upscale Dublin watering hole, complete with long wooden bar and an adjacent dining room with a mix of standard dining tables and larger-party booths with low-slung tables and well-stuffed leather sofas; there's also a garden out back for warm-weather dining. The crowd is easygoing, with service having a similar demeanor.

Come at any hour for a beautifully prepared meal. Each menu—breakfast, brunch, lunch, dinner, late-night—features versions of Irish classics and more nouveau fare. Morning starts with a traditional Irish breakfast (bacon, eggs, sausage, black and white pudding, mushrooms, tomatoes, baked beans, and home fries), a smoked-salmon scramble if you're in the mood for something lighter, or a bowl of Weetabix and fruit. Daytime and evening bring crisp, bounteous salads; a rich and creamy seafood chowder; gorgeous realizations of pub standards, including fish and chips made with fresh Chatham cod, pork roast with parsnip hash and capers, and a beef-and-Guinness pie with a flaky crust; and well-prepared pastas, chicken, and burgers. The food isn't cheap, but it's well priced considering the quality, large portions, and pleasing atmosphere.

Look for readings every Monday night, plus art events on select Tuesdays.

505 W. 23rd St. (just west of Tenth Ave.). © 212/462-4300. www.thehalfking.com. Breakfast and brunch $3–$12; lunch $6–$12; dinner $9–$18 (most less than $15); late night $6–$16. AE, DC, DISC, MC, V. Sun–Thurs 9am–2am; Fri–Sat 9am–4am. Subway: C, E to 23rd St.

La Taza de Oro PUERTO RICAN This brightly lit luncheonette serves up some of the most authentic Latin-American food in the city. Tuned-in locals know you won't find better, or better-priced, *chuletas fritas* (fried pork chops—and say yes to the garlic). *Mondongo* is a delicious rendering of traditional tripe soup. If that's just too adventurous, try the beef stew (*carne guisada*), which is slow-cooked until meltingly tender, or steak and onions. The squid and shrimp dishes are always supple, and the chicken is perfectly roasted. Portions are huge, and most come with lots of beans (red, black, or black-eyed) and rice (white or yellow). Service is exuberant and efficient. Both the flan and the coconut pudding are yummy. There's no beer, just soda; the *café con leche* is great. *¡Que bien!*

96 Eighth Ave. (btwn 14th and 15th sts.). ✆ 212/243-9946. Main courses $5–$11 (most under $8). No credit cards. Daily 7am–11pm. Subway: A, C, E to 14th St.

Petite Abeille BELGIAN   This delightful cafe serves Belgian fare to a local crowd that returns regularly for morning pastries, quiches, salads, sandwiches, and sweets. Start with a fresh-from-the-oven *pain au chocolat* or cream-cheese croissant, and return at lunch for a fresh-baked quiche; panini bread dressed with black forest ham, Swiss cheese, and pineapple; a beautiful niçoise salad; or a traditional Belgian dish like *les carbonnades à la Flamande*, a classic Belgian stew. In addition to a first-rate espresso bar, a full selection of Samantha and Looza Nectar juices are on hand. It's usually not tough to score a butcher-block table, even at the height of the lunch hour, as the crowd moves in and out quickly.

107 W. 18th St. (at Sixth Ave.). ✆ 212/604-9350 or 212/367-9062. Main courses $5.25–$11.25 (most under $8). AE, MC, V. Mon–Fri 7am–7pm; Sat–Sun 9am–5pm. Subway: F to 14th St. Also at 400 W. 14th St. (btwn Ninth and Tenth aves.; ✆ 212/727-1505; subway: A, C, E to 14th St.); 466 Hudson St. (at Barrow St.; ✆ 212/741-6479; subway: 1, 9 to Christopher St.); 134 W. Broadway (btwn Duane and Thomas sts.; ✆ 212/791-1360; subway: 1, 2, 3, 9 to Chambers St.).

Rue des Crepes ★★ *Finds* FRENCH   This *creperie* is a real find. Seldom do decor, quality, and service come together so well in such an affordable restaurant. Evoking a Parisian cafe with muraled walls, tiled floors, Art Nouveau lamps, and petite tables, the dining room is comfortable and romantic. Chef Michael Kalajian, a Culinary Institute of America graduate and former student of four-star chef Charlie Palmer, whips up light-as-air buckwheat (and cholesterol-free) crepes and folds them around a host of savory fillings, from classics like turkey and brie to spicy Moroccan *merguez* sausage accompanied by white beans and roasted garlic. Vegetarian options are available, including yummy homemade hummus and roasted veggies. Soups and salads are also served; sandwiches are prepared on fresh baguettes from Amy's Bread, and pre-prepared ones are ready to go in the takeout case. Dessert crepes come with your choice of fillings; my favorite is the "Sidewalk," a classic preparation with butter, sugar, lemon, and chocolate, but fresh-fruit and fat-free vanilla cream options are on hand for waist-watchers. You'll order at the counter, but a server takes over from there. Beer and wine are available. *Money-saving tip:* Check the website for a 10% off coupon.

104 Eighth Ave. (btwn 15th and 16th sts.). ✆ 212/242-9900. www.ruedescrepes.com. Reservations not accepted. Main courses $6–$9. AE, MC, V. Sun–Thurs 11am–11pm; Fri–Sat 11am–1am. Subway: A, C, E to 14th St.

QUICK BITES

At Chelsea Market, 75 Ninth Ave., between 15th and 16th streets, a second branch of **Amy's Bread** (✆ 212/462-4338; p. 178) has cafe tables where you can enjoy a light bite for breakfast or lunch.

There's also the wonderful **Little Pie Company** at 407 W. 14th Street, west of Ninth Avenue (✆ 212/414-2324; www.littlepiecompany.com), where you can sit at a table or pull up a stool at the counter and dig in to one of the classic pies and cakes, which many consider New York's best; the sour-cream apple is divine.

10 The Flatiron District, Union Square & Gramercy Park

In addition to the choices below, you can find **Xando/Cosí** (p. 190: at 841 Broadway, at 13th Street (✆ **212/614-8544**); and 257 Park Ave. S., between 20th and 21st streets (✆ **212/598-9300**). For lovely baked goods and sandwiches and salads, try **Le Pain Quotidien** ★★ (p. 147) at ABC Carpet & Home, 38 E. 19th St., between Broadway and Park Avenue South (✆ **212/625-9009**).

Chat 'n' Chew AMERICAN   Looking for a place to get a square meal that won't break the bank or leave you hungry? Then head to this cute hole-in-the-wall that excels at down-home American cooking. In fact, the space is so down-homey that it's on the brink of becoming a theme restaurant, but the chow's the real thing. Look for honey-dipped fried chicken, roast turkey with all the fixin's, BBQ pork chops with skin-on mashed potatoes, and mac 'n' cheese as crispy on the outside and gooey on the inside. There are a few unnecessary nods to contemporary tastes—if you're looking for grilled tuna, you don't belong here!—but the only real misstep is the meat loaf, which is a disappointment. Weekend brunch sees such standards as oatmeal with brown sugar and omelets with honey-baked ham on the side. Portions are all Hungry Man–size, service is snappy, and beer's available. Desserts are of the Duncan Hines layer-cake variety, and the soda fountain serves up everything from egg creams to Häagen-Dazs shakes. The crowd mainly consists of the young and hip (who can afford to throw caution to the wind when it comes to calories), but everyone will feel perfectly welcome.

10 E. 16th St. (btwn Fifth Ave. and Union Sq. W.). ✆ **212/243-1616.** www.chatnchew.citysearch.com. Reservations not accepted. Sandwiches and salads $6–$11; main courses $7–$14. AE, MC, V. Mon–Fri 11:30am–midnight; Sat 10:30am–midnight; Sun 10:30am–11pm. Subway: L, N, R, Q, W, 4, 5, 6 to 14th St./Union Sq.

Eisenberg's Coffee Shop *Finds* SANDWICHES   Eisenberg's has always been, and remains the real deal. This old-world luncheonette has been dishing up the same eggs/bacon/burgers/sandwiches since 1929, at pretty much the same prices—adjusted for inflation, of course, but still welcomingly wallet-friendly.

One of the best things about Eisenberg's is the folks who work there, some of whom have seemingly been there since the Eisenhower era. More likely than not, you'll be greeted with a growled "Hiya, sweetheart," or a gravelly "What'll it be, love?" Pony up to the long counter or nab one of the four or five tables and place your order. Lots of folks consider this the best tuna salad in town, but I prefer the terrific matzo-ball soup, the dynamite Reuben, and the first-class BLT. AM diners can choose from a number of egg dishes, including a Western omelet or pastrami and eggs. The egg cream—that frothy mix of milk, chocolate syrup, and real from-the-bottle seltzer—is the real deal. Service is fast and efficient.

174 Fifth Ave. (at 22nd St.). ✆ **212/675-5096.** Reservations not accepted. Main courses $2.25–$7.25. No credit cards. Mon–Fri 6am–5pm; Sat 7:30am–4pm. Subway: N, R to 23rd St.

L'Express FRENCH   This round-the-clock French bistro is a favorite of New Yorkers for affordable anytime fare. The service is friendly and attentive, and the mood-lit room comfortable and romantic in the evening; the food is respectable, if not fabulous. I like the appetizers best, especially the escargots in butter and herbs, the onion tart, *boudin noir* (blood sausage) with caramelized apples and mashed potato, and the good house paté. Among the mains are a roasted half-chicken, a juicy lamb burger, and roasted rabbit in Dijon mustard sauce; skip the boeuf bourguignon, which is hiding a poor cut. Wines are somewhat pricey, averaging $7 a glass, but a large selection of imported beers is on hand, including Trappist ales. The dense, gooey French bread that comes with every meal is alone worth the price of a meal. Daytime diners will feel perfectly welcome to camp out for a couple of hours, nursing a cup of tea and delving into a good book.

249 Park Ave. S. (at 20th St.). © 212/254-5858. Reservations accepted for parties of 5 or more only. Main courses $2–$7.50 at breakfast, $5–$15 at lunch, $9–$18 at dinner (most less than $15). AE, MC, V. Open daily 24 hr. Subway: 6 to 23rd St.

Lyric Diner AMERICAN   Want to know where the good diners are? Follow the cops. On the east side, you'll find 'em at the Lyric, which dishes out good, straightforward diner fare in a clean, bright, well-lit space. Expect all the diner standards: hot open sandwiches, Monte Cristos and Reubens, burgers, stuffed baked potatoes. Breakfast is served 'round the clock, of course.

283 Third Ave. (at 22nd St.). © 212/213-2222. Reservations not accepted. Breakfast (served all day) $2.75–$11 (most less than $7); sandwiches and salads $2.25–$11; dinner $10–$18 (including soup or salad). AE, MC, V. Open daily 24 hr. Subway: 6 to 23rd St.

Molly's Pub & Restaurant Sheeben IRISH   If The Half King (p. 162), is the new real-deal Irish pub, Molly's is the *real* real-deal Irish pub, complete with Tudor detailing, a fireplace creating a warm and toasty ambience, and a back room with checked cloths on the tables, photos covering every inch of wall space, and waitresses bringing you three types of mustard with your corned beef and cabbage. The menu also features lamb stew, beer-battered fish and chips, and a perfect shepherd's pie, as well as a good burger and entree-size salads. Sandwiches come with fries, dinners come with salad and Irish soda bread. The jukebox features Dylan and familiar tunes, and is set at a pleasant volume. Tuck into a genuine Irish breakfast on weekends, complete with white and black puddings (baked beans $1.25 extra).

287 Third Ave. (btwn 22nd and 23rd sts.). © 212/254-5858. www.mollys.citysearch.com. Reservations not accepted. Main courses $9–$13 at brunch, $6.50 to $16 at lunch (most less than $12), $8–$19 at dinner (most less than $14). AE, DC, DISC, MC, V. Mon–Wed 11:30am–midnight; Thurs–Sun 11:30am–2am (bar until 4am). Subway: 6 to 23rd St.

Old Town Bar & Restaurant ⭐ AMERICAN   If you've watched TV at all over the last couple of decades, this place should look familiar: It was featured nightly in the old *Late Night with David Letterman* intro, starred as Riff's Bar in *Mad About You,* as well as in such movies as *The Devil's Own, Bullets Over Broadway,* and *The Last Days of Disco.* But this is no stage set—it's a genuine tin-ceilinged 19th-century bar serving up good pub grub, lots of beers on tap, and a sense of New York history. Sure, there are salads on the menu, but everybody comes for the burgers. Whether you go low-fat turkey or bacon-chili-cheddar, they're perfect every time. You have your choice of sides, but go with the shoestring fries. Other good choices include spicy Buffalo wings, fiery bowls of chili with cheddar cheese and dolloped with sour cream, and a Herculean Caesar salad slathered with mayo and topped with anchovies. Food comes up from the basement kitchen courtesy of ancient dumbwaiters behind the bar, where equally crusty bartenders would rather *not* make you a Cosmopolitan, thank you very much. If you want to escape the cigarettes and the predatory singles scene that pulls in on weekends, head upstairs to the blissfully smoke-free dining room.

Tips   Pizza! Pizza!

Pintaile's Pizza, 124 Fourth Ave., between 12th and 13th streets (☎ **212/475-4977;** www.pintailespizza.com), dresses their crisp organic crusts with layers of plum tomatoes, extra-virgin olive oil, and other fresh ingredients. This new branch of the Upper East Side favorite even has lots of seating for in-house eating. Also in the Union Square area is **California Pizza Oven,** at 122 University Place, between 13th and 14th streets (☎ **212/989-4225**), which cooks their thin-crust brick-oven pizzas over hickory and cherrywood, imbuing them with a rich, smoky flavor and topping them with everything from pepperoni and Italian sausage to goat cheese and baby eggplant. A table near the hearth makes a cozy spot to enjoy a quick slice. Both shops are open daily from 11am to 10pm.

---

45 E. 18th St. (btwn Broadway and Park Ave. S.). ☎ 212/529-6732. Reservations not accepted. Main courses $6–$12. AE, MC, V. Mon–Fri 11:30am–midnight; Sat–Sun 12:30pm–midnight. Subway: L, N, R, Q, W, 4, 5, 6 to 14th St./Union Sq.

Republic PAN-ASIAN NOODLES   Proving once and for all that you don't have to sacrifice style for wallet-friendly prices, this chic noodle joint serves up affordable food in a neighborhood where it's getting harder to find an affordable meal. Cushionless, backless benches pulled up to pine-and-steel tables don't encourage lingering, but that's the point: This is the kind of place that knows how to make you feel happy and get you out the door quickly. The Chinese, Vietnamese-, and Thai-inspired noodle menu attracts a stream of on-the-go customers. For a one-bowl meal, try the spicy coconut chicken (chicken slices in coconut milk, lime juice, lemongrass, and galangal) or spicy beef (rare beef with wheat noodles spiced with chilies, garlic, and lemongrass). Service is friendly. The long, curving bar is perfect for solitary diners in the daytime and during the early-dinner hour; later, it livens up with a crowd who come to enjoy such libations as the Sake Dragon (sake and Chambord) and Fuji apple Cosmopolitan.

37 Union Sq. W. (btwn 16th and 17th sts.). ☎ 212/627-7172 or 212/627-7168. Reservations accepted for parties of 10 or more. Main courses $7–$9. AE, DISC, MC, V. Sun–Wed 11:30am–11pm; Thurs–Sat 11:30am–11:30pm. Subway: L, N, R, Q, W, 4, 5, 6 to 14th St./Union Sq.

Taco & Tortilla King *Value* TEX-MEXICAN   This low-profile sleeper is little more than a lunch counter, but the authentic food can't be beat. Sit down to a couple of tacos and you'll think you've been transported to one of those gourmet Mexican joints your friends in Southern California keep raving about. The kitchen won me over with the basics: fresh-made guacamole infused with lime and flour tortillas made from scratch and baked on the premises. All the staples, from well-stuffed burritos to sizzling fajitas, are authentically prepared, hearty, and satisfying; a good portion of the offerings can be prepared meatless for vegetarians. It's an all-around winner for a fast meal at an unbeatable price.

285 Third Ave. (btwn 22nd and 23rd sts.). ☎ 212/679-8882 or 212/481-3930. A la carte items 99¢–$5.60; sandwiches $2.30–$6.80; combo plates $4.90; by-the-lb. fajitas $13–$18. AE, MC, V ($15 minimum). Mon–Fri 11am–11:30pm; Sat–Sun 11:30am–11pm. Subway: 6 to 23rd St.

Tavern Room at Gramercy Tavern ★★ *Value* CONTEMPORARY AMERICAN   Gramercy Tavern's main dining room is one of New York's finest. However, dining there requires reservations weeks in advance and deep,

deep pockets. Not so in the front Tavern Room, a friendly, informal bistro-style alternative where you can decide to eat at the last minute and still dine on some of the best food in town—without breaking the bank in the process.

The compact but appealing menu offers a more casual take on Chef Tom Colicchio's American fare. I love the roasted baby chicken with butternut squash succotash; nobody in town does chicken better. And where else are you going to get a filet mignon this good for an Andrew Jackson? There's a good selection of salads, a terrific tomato garlic-bread soup, and a handful of fish dishes and sandwiches, plus the restaurant's signature selection of cheeses and desserts. The room is comfortable, with well-spaced tables and a pleasant energy that allows for conversation; owner Danny Meyer's no-smoking policy prevents any secondhand smoke from interfering with your meal. Service is top-notch.

42 E. 20th St. (btwn Broadway and Park Ave. S.). © 212/477-0777. Reservations not accepted. Main courses $14–$20. AE, DC, DISC, MC, V. Sun–Thurs noon–11pm; Fri–Sat noon–midnight. Subway: N, R, 6 to 23rd St.

Via Emilia *Value* EMILIA-ROMAGNA ITALIAN   This candlelit, brick-walled trattoria is a haven for budget diners in the high-priced Park Avenue South area. The menu is simple but satisfying, with an emphasis on house-made pastas—as you might expect from a restaurant that emphasizes the cuisine of Emilia-Romagna. The specialty is tortellini; the *tortellini in brodo,* meat-stuffed tortellini in a chicken broth, is a great way to start your meal. Other starters include fresh-grilled squid or thin-sliced tenderloin carpaccio, served with shaved Parmesan and leafy arugula. There's not a dud among the pastas, all of which are oversize, none exceeding $12; I love the tortellini filled with chicken and wild mushrooms in truffle oil. There's also a handful of nonpasta entrees, including veal scallopine in an aromatic sauce with diced asparagus, and the *cosciotto d'agnello,* a thinly sliced leg of lamb with mushrooms, cannelloni beans, and tomatoes, like a lighter, Italian cassoulet. Wines are well priced, too, and service better than you'd expect at a restaurant this affordable. It's a great date place!

240 Park Ave. S. (btwn 19th and 20th sts.). © 212/505-3072. Reservations not accepted. Main courses $7.50–$15. No credit cards. Mon–Sat 5–11pm. Subway: N, R, 6 to 23rd St.

Zen Palate PAN-ASIAN VEGETARIAN   Zen Palate has adopted the healthy, less-is-more approach to Asian cuisine. Each location shares the same Japanese-influenced postmodern decor, with teak and patinated copper; the Union Square flagship is a standout, with a counter downstairs for on-the-run eaters and a warren of spare but attractive dining rooms upstairs, including some with Japanese-style seating.

Tofu is king here, but you're not limited to it. Stars on the wide-ranging menu include taro spring rolls and basil moo-shu rolls for something creative, as well as veggie dumplings and buns for a more traditional Asian choice. Despite the good-for-you approach, main courses such as Rose Petals (homemade soy pasta in a sweet rice ginger sauce with garden vegetables) and Curry Supreme (with tofu, potatoes, and carrots) are very flavorful, and some will particularly appeal to spicy-food lovers. Even more affordable casual grazing dishes are served in the all-day gourmet shop downstairs. All in all, a good bet for health-minded diners.

And as an added attraction, you're welcome to BYOB with no corkage fee in the upstairs dining room at this location.

34 Union Sq. E. (at 16th St.). © 212/614-9395. www.zenpalate.com. Reservations accepted. Main courses $7–$17.50 ($3–$8 in gourmet shop). AE, MC, V. Mon–Sat 11am–10:45pm; Sun noon–10:45pm. Subway: L, N, R, Q, W, 4, 5, 6 to 14th St./Union Sq. Also at 663 Ninth Ave. (at 46th St.; © 212/582-1669); subway: A, C, E to 42nd St.); 2170 Broadway (btwn 76th and 77th sts.; © 212/501-7788; subway: 1, 9 to 79th St.).

11 Times Square & Midtown West

Check out the Asian-nouvelle vegetarian cuisine at **Zen Palate** (p. 167), at 663 Ninth Ave., at 46th Street (✆ **212/582-1669**). **Joe's Shanghai** (p. 141) has a Midtown branch at 24 W. 56th St., west of Fifth Avenue (✆ **212/333-3868**), offering soup dumplings and other dishes—but expect to pay a bit more here than in Chinatown. An outpost of **Grand Sichuan International** (p. 161) dishes up killer Sichuan fare at 745 Ninth Ave., between 50th and 51st streets (✆ **212/582-2288**). A new branch of the ultrafresh, supercheap eat-in/takeout sushi joint, **Go Sushi** (p. 179), is at 756 Ninth Ave., at 51st Street (✆ **212/459-2288**).

There's a cafeteria-style **Mangia** (p. 137) at 50 W. 57th St., between Fifth and Sixth avenues (✆ **212/582-5882**). Two nice branches of **Burritoville** (p. 137) are at 352 W. 39th St., at Ninth Avenue (✆ **212/563-9088**), and 625 Ninth Ave., at 44th Street (✆ **212/333-5352**).

Also consider **Emerald Planet** (p. 156), on the lower concourse at 30 Rockefeller Plaza, near the skating rink (✆ **212/218-1133**), for wraps and yummy smoothies. Healthy eaters will enjoy the all-natural eats at **The Pump** (p. 181), 40 W. 55th St., between Fifth and Sixth avenues (✆ **212/246-6844**), too.

Afghan Kebab House MIDDLE EASTERN *Value*

Bring your own wine or six-pack (there's a liquor store across the street) and dig in to heaping plates of first-rate Middle Eastern fare at this Afghan restaurant. Kebabs are the first order of business: All are pleasing, but my favorite is the *sultani*, chunks of ground lamb marinated in aromatic spices and broiled over wood charcoal with green peppers and tomatoes. The *tikka kebabs*—lamb and beef—are impressive, as is the chicken korma, slow-cooked with fresh onions, tomatoes, peppers, and fresh herbs. All plates come with brown Indian basmati rice and flat Afghan bread. The room is simple and well worn but evocative, with Oriental carpets serving as table runners, and service is attentive. Another plus: No MSG is used.

764 Ninth Ave. (btwn 51st and 52nd sts.). ✆ **212/307-1612** or 212/307-1629. Reservations accepted. Main courses $10–$16 (most less than $12). AE, DC, DISC, MC, V. Daily 11:30am–10:30pm. Subway: C, E to 50th St.

Brazil Grill BRAZILIAN

The Theater District is loaded with overpriced tourist traps, and many affordable restaurants feel dowdy or downscale. So where can you go for a pre- (or post-) theater dinner that won't break the bank? Make a beeline for Brazil Grill, where the tables are spacious, the staff is charming, cobalt-blue accents add a touch of elegance, and the menu showcases the sunny flavors of Brazil. The prix-fixe is an incredible deal: Three filling courses for $19.95 will have you mamboing all the way to the theater. The broader menu offers lots of country cooking to satisfy the meat-and-potatoes crowd (sizzling beef skewers with peppers and onions), while diners with more adventurous palates might try the spicy *camarao baiana* (shrimp sautéed with palm oil and served in a sauce of coconut milk, tomatoes, and garlic). Portions are generous, and main courses come with ample sides of rice and beans. The wine list offers affordable choices, including an array of wines by the glass for only $5 to $6. Don't miss the incredible *doce de leite* for dessert—if you've never tasted this rich and creamy caramel confection of the gods, you'll thank me.

787 Eighth Ave. (at 48th St.). ✆ **212/307-9449.** www.brazilgrill.citysearch.com. Reservations recommended, especially pre-theater. Main courses $10.95–$21.95; 3-course prix-fixe dinner $19.95. AE, DC, MC, V. Daily noon–midnight. Subway: 1, 2 to 50th St.; C, E to 50th St.

Chanpen THAI   This charming restaurant serves Thai food at Chinatown prices. It's a tad cheaper than nearby Siam Inn (p. 177), especially at lunch, when Siam Inn caters to a middle-management crowd; Chanpen's lunch specials are values that draw savvy worker bees from throughout the neighborhood. In addition to the prices, you'll be pleased by the bright dining room, the pleasant and attentive service, and the classic preparations of familiar Thai favorites.

761 Ninth Ave. (at 51st St.). © 212/586-6808. AE, MC, V. Reservations accepted for dinner Sun–Thurs only. Main courses $8–$15; lunch special (Mon–Fri 11:30am–3pm) $7–$8. AE, MC, V. Sun–Thurs 11:30am–11pm; Fri–Sat 11:30am–midnight. Subway: C, E to 50th St.

Eatery *Finds* NEW AMERICAN   Wearing all the mod trappings—celadon hues, black banquette seating, George Nelson light fixtures—this cool nouveau diner is an excellent choice for high-quality food. Eatery is a little pricier than Route 66 Cafe and Vynl (see below), but the fare is a step up, which makes this a good choice for a special pre- or post-theater meal. Come for entree-size salads, such as the grilled Asian chicken salad with jicama and toasted peanuts in a sweet chili vinaigrette; or baby spinach dressed with blue cheese, roasted shallots, Portobello mushrooms, and oven-dried tomatoes. Main courses run the gamut from a terrific burger (beef or veggie) with crisp fries to macaroni and cheese to more elegant choices like miso-glazed salmon with Chinese broccoli and glass noodles. Service is terrific, and a full bar is on hand if you're in a cocktail mood.

798 Ninth Ave. (at 53rd St.). © 212/765-7080. www.eaterynyc.com. Pre-theater reservations highly recommended. Main courses $6–$16 at brunch and lunch (most under $9), $8–$20 at dinner (most under $16). AE, DC, MC, V. Mon–Thurs 11:30am–3:30pm and 5pm–midnight; Fri 11:30am–3:30pm and 5pm–1am; Sat 10:30am–3:30pm and 5pm–1am; Sun 10:30am–3:30pm and 5pm–11pm. Subway: A, C, E to 50th St.

44 Southwest *Finds* ITALIAN   This mom-and-pop restaurant serves up the best Italian food in Midtown for the money. It's simple but charming, with an original tin ceiling, red-checkered tablecloths, and soft lighting; the result is a romantic first-date ambience (very *Lady and the Tramp* sharing spaghetti). The dishes are generously portioned and very satisfying. Pastas are perfectly al dente; I especially love the thick and hearty meat sauce on the linguine Bolognese. The chicken Parmesan is classically yummy, and personal pizzas arrive with wonderfully chewy crusts. The wine list is affordable and the service attentive, making 44 Southwest a winner on all fronts for wallet-watching visitors.

621 Ninth Ave. (at 44th St.). © 212/315-4582 or 212/315-4681. Reservations accepted (recommended for pre-theater dining). Main courses $8–$14. AE, DC, DISC, MC, V. Sun–Thurs noon–11pm; Fri–Sat noon–midnight. Subway: A, C, E to 42nd St.

Hallo! Berlin *Finds* GERMAN   Hallo! Berlin bills itself as "New York's Wurst Restaurant"—and indeed it is. If wurst is best in your book, don't miss it. Hallo! Berlin is straight outta Deutschland, serving up eight varieties of sausage, from boiled beef-and-pork knockwurst to pan-fried veal bavarianwurst and beef currywurst. Sandwiches come with all the fixings, including red cabbage, sauerkraut, onions, and mustard, but I prefer the combo, which lets me choose two kinds of sausage (substitute spaetzle for German fries for maximum satisfaction). There's also a terrific Wiener schnitzel. The potato pancakes make a great starter; one generous order is enough for a few friends to share. A big bowl of lentil, split pea, or potato soup with cut-up wurst and bread and butter makes a satisfying lunch for just $5. The main location is petite and pleasant, with efficient table service and a couple of taps pouring German brews, while the Tenth Avenue location is a full-scale beer hall well equipped for larger parties.

Midtown, Chelsea & Union Square Dining

Afghan Kebab House **10**
Amy's Bread **22**, **42**
Antique Café **61**
B. Frites **14**
Bagel & Bean **5**
Brazil Grill **18**
Burritoville **31**, **33**, **38**, **80**
California Pizza Oven **47**
Canova Market **73**
Carnegie Deli **4**
Chanpen **9**
Chat 'n' Chew **50**
Comfort Diner **71**
Dean & Deluca **74**
Eatery **3**
Eisenberg's Coffee Shop **46**
Emerald Planet **75**
Empire Diner **36**
ESPN Zone **27**
Ess-A-Bagel **58**, **79**
F&B **37**
Florent **38**
44 Southwest **32**
Go Sushi **11**, **68**, **81**
Grand Central Terminal **69**
    Café Spice Express
    Christer's
    Junior's
    Knödel
    Little Pie Company
    Two Boots
Grand Sichuan International **12**, **32**
H&H Bagel **19**
Hallo! Berlin **8**, **20**
Half King **35**
Hard Rock Café **2**
Island Burgers & Shakes **10**
Jackson Hole **68**
Jekyll & Hyde Club **86**
Joe Allen **23**
Joe's Shanghai **82**
John's Pizzeria **1**, **29**, **88**
Johny's Grill & Luncheonette **60**

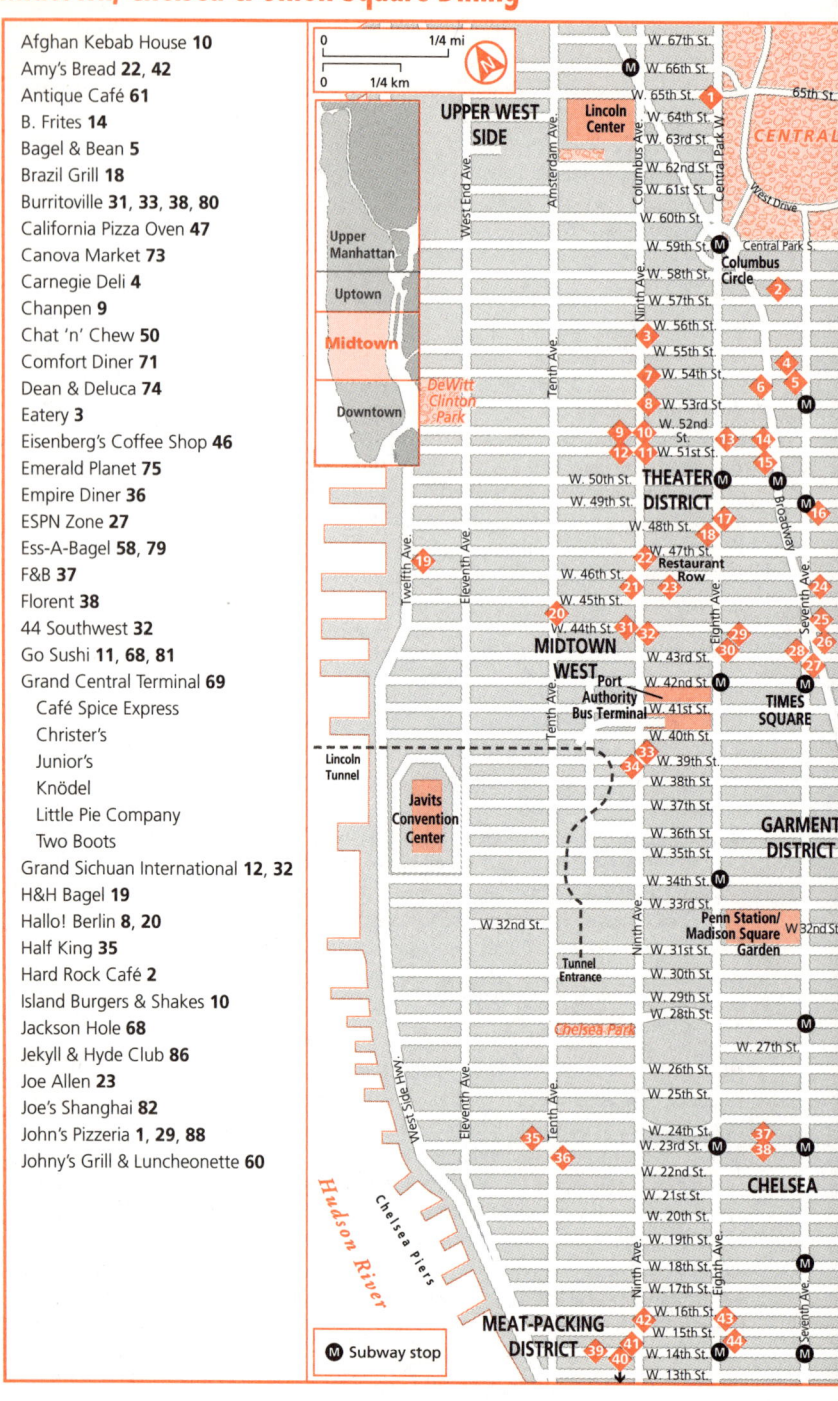

170

Josie's **70**
Katsu-Hama **72**
La Bonne Soupe **84**
La Taza de Oro **44**
Le Pain Quotidien **53**
Lemon Tree Café **9**
L'Express **57**
Little Pie Company **39**
Los Dos Rancheros Mexicanos **34**
Lyric Diner **59**
Mandoo Bar **66**
Mangia **73**, **85**
Manhattan Chili Co. **6**, **26**
Mars 2112 **15**
Mavalli Palace **62**
Molly's Pub
 & Restaurant Sheeben **59**
Old Town Bar & Restaurant **52**
Papaya King **30**
Petite Abeille **41**, **45**
Pigalle **17**
Pintaile's **48**
Planet Hollywood **24**
Pongal **63**
Prime Burger **77**
Republic **51**
Rice 'n' Beans **12**
Route 66 Café **3**
Rue des Crepes **43**
Sapporo **16**
Serendipity 3 **87**
Siam Inn **13**
Stage Deli **5**
Taco & Tortilla King **59**
Tavern Room
 at Gramercy Tavern **54**
The Half King **35**
The Pump **65**, **83**
Via Emilia **56**
Virgil's Real BBQ **25**
Vynl **7**
Won Jo **67**
WWF New York **28**
Xando/Cosí **48**, **55**, **64**, **78**
Zen Palate **21**, **49**

171

402 W. 51st St. (just west of Ninth Ave.). © **212/541-6248.** Reservations not accepted. Sandwiches $3–$3.75; main courses (with soup) $6.50–$15; lunch specials (until 5pm) $5.25–$6.50. MC, V. Mon–Sat 11am–11pm; Sun 4–11pm. Subway: C, E to 50th St. Also at 626 Tenth Ave. (at 44th St.; © **212/977-1944;** subway: A, C, E to 42nd St./Port Authority).

Island Burgers & Shakes *Value* GOURMET BURGERS/SANDWICHES This aisle-size diner glows with the colors of a California surf shop. As the name implies, folks come for the Goliath-size burgers—either beef hamburgers or, the specialty of the house, *churrascos* (flattened grilled chicken breasts). Innovation strikes with the more than 40 toppings: Choose anything from the horseradish, sour cream, and black-pepper burger to the Hobie's (with black-pepper sauce, blue cheese, onion, and bacon). Choose your own bread from a wide selection ranging from soft sourdough to crusty ciabatta. Island Burgers doesn't serve fries; you're meant to eat these fellows with their tasty dirty potato chips. You can also opt for a baked potato slathered in butter and sour cream. Terrifically thick shakes and cookies are available to satisfy your sweet tooth, while health-minded diners have a selection of hearty entree-size salads from which to choose; the Caesar is a delightful rendering of the classic.

766 Ninth Ave. (btwn 51st and 52nd sts.). © **212/307-7934.** www.island.citysearch.com. Reservations not accepted. Sandwiches and main-course salads $5.25–$9.50. No credit cards. Sun–Thurs noon–10:30pm; Fri–Sat noon–11pm. Subway: C, E to 50th St.

Joe Allen ★★ AMERICAN PUB This Restaurant Row pub is a glorious throwback to yesteryear, when theater types went to places like Sardi's and Lüchow's—and yep, Joe Allen. Joe Allen is still going strong; don't be surprised if you spot a stage star or two. The straightforward pub food is reliable and well priced, and served at big, comfortable tables (the kind that restaurant managers don't order anymore because they take up too much room) covered with red-checked cloths. The meatloaf is terrific, but you can't go wrong with the chili, the decent Greek salad, the great burgers, or anything that comes with mashed potatoes. More than 30 beers are available, and some good wines by the glass. The staff is a congenial and neighborhood-appropriate mix of career waiters and aspiring thespians. You'll enjoy perusing the walls covered with posters and other memorabilia from legendary Broadway flops.

326 W. 46th St. (btwn Eighth and Ninth aves.). © **212/581-6464.** Reservations recommended (a must for pre-theater dining). Main courses $9–$22 (most less than $17). MC, V. Mon–Tues and Thurs–Fri noon–11:45pm; Wed and Sat–Sun 11:30am–11:45pm. Subway: A, C, E to 42nd St./Port Authority.

John's Pizzeria ★ *Kids* PIZZA Thin-crusted, properly sauced, and fresh, the pizza at John's has long been one of New York's best—some even consider these *the* best pies in New York. Housed in the century-old Gospel Tabernacle Church, the split-level dining room is vast and pretty, featuring a stained-glass ceiling and chefs working at classic brick ovens. More important, it's big enough to hold pre-theater crowds, so the wait's never too long despite its popularity. At John's you order a whole made-to-order pie rather than ordering by the slice as at most New York pizzerias, so come with friends or family. There's also a good selection of traditional pastas, such as baked ziti and well-stuffed calzones.

This Theater District location is my favorite, but the original Bleecker Street location is loaded with old-world atmosphere, and the Lincoln Center outpost makes for a good and affordable pre-theater meal.

260 W. 44th St. (btwn Broadway and Eighth Ave.). © **212/391-7560.** Reservations accepted for 10 or more. Pizzas $11–$16 (plus toppings); pastas $7–$13. AE, DISC, MC, V. Daily 11:30am–11:30pm. Subway: A, C, E to 42nd St.; N, R, S, 1, 2, 3, 7, 9 to 42nd St./Times Sq. Also at 278 Bleecker St. (btwn Sixth and Seventh aves.;

> **Tips** **The Midtown Deli News**
>
> If you're in Midtown and looking for one of the Big Apple's quintessential Jewish delis, head to the **Stage Deli,** 834 Seventh Ave., between 53rd and 54th streets (✆ **212/245-7850;** www.stagedeli.com), known for its celebrity sandwiches, from the Joe DiMaggio (corned beef, pastrami, chopped liver, and Bermuda onion) to the Julia Roberts (chicken salad, hard-boiled egg, lettuce, and tomato); or the **Carnegie Deli,** 854 Seventh Ave., at 55th Street (✆ **212/757-2245;** www.carnegiedeli.com), for pastrami, corned beef, and cheesecake. But these landmarks specialize in tourist-target pricing, with sandwiches coming in between $12 to $20. You get your money's worth—they're more than most mortals can consume in one sitting—but you'll be charged $2 to $3 to split one with your travel partner. Head down to **Katz's** (p. 144) or up to **Barney Greengrass** (p. 184) for less touristy, less expensive deli experiences.

✆ **212/243-1680;** subway: 1, 9 to Houston St.); 48 W. 65th St. (btwn Broadway and Central Park W.; ✆ **212/721-7001;** subway: 1, 9 to 66th St.); 408 E. 64th St. (btwn First and York aves.; ✆ **212/935-2895;** subway: 6 to 68th St.).

La Bonne Soupe ★ Kids FRENCH BISTRO   This slice of Paris has been around forever; I remember discovering the magic of fondue here on a high school field trip that took place more years ago than I care to think about. For gourmet at good prices, it's still hard to beat it. You'll even see French natives elbow-to-elbow in the newly renovated dining room. "Les bonnes soupes" are satisfying noontime meals of salad, bread, a big bowl of soup (mushroom and barley with lamb is a favorite), dessert (chocolate mousse, crème caramel, or ice cream), and wine or coffee—a great bargain at just $13.95. The menu also features entree-size salads (including a good niçoise), steak burgers, and bistro fare like omelets, quiche Lorraine, croque monsieur, and fancier fare like steak frites and filet mignon au poivre. Rounding out the menu are French fondues: Emmethal cheese, beef, and creamy chocolate to finish off the meal; the silky smooth chocolate mousse is yummy. A kids' menu is available, offering a burger or chicken and fries, plus dessert, for $10.25. Bon appétit!

48 W. 55th St. (btwn Fifth and Sixth aves.). ✆ **212/586-7650.** www.labonnesoupe.com. Reservations recommended for parties of 3 or more. Main courses $9–$19.25 (most less than $15); "les bonnes soupes" fixed price $13.95; 3-course fixed price $20 at lunch and dinner. AE, DC, MC, V. Mon–Sat 11:30am–midnight; Sun 11:30am–11pm. Subway: E, F to Fifth Ave.; B, Q to 57th St.

Lemon Tree Cafe MIDDLE EASTERN   Lemon Tree is bare-bones decor-wise, with institutional furnishings and a few posters of Egypt or Syria distracting you from the fake wood paneling and linoleum floor. But the food is fresh, tasty, and plentiful. Skip those Midtown falafel carts—readers of the *New York Press* voted Lemon Tree's crispy, savory falafel sandwich best in the city. All pita sandwiches come overstuffed with lettuce, tomato, cabbage, onion, and tahini sauce. Veggie platters are light and delicious, particularly the lemony hummus, babaganoush, and tabbouleh. The grilled meat platters (served with salad and rice) could feed an army. Service can be slow and quirky (one day I was served by a 10-year-old girl), but it's worth putting up with for the great meal deal.

769 Ninth Ave. (btwn 51st and 52nd sts.). ✆ **212/245-0818.** Reservations not accepted. Sandwiches $2.50–$4; platters $5–$9. AE, DISC, MC, V ($20 minimum). Daily 11am–11pm. Subway: C, E to 50th St.

Theme Restaurant Thrills!

I may not know the difference between Stone Cold Steve Austin and the Rock, but I know that **WWE New York**, housed in the restored Paramount Building, 1501 Broadway, at 43rd Street (© **212/398-2563**; http://newyork.wwe.com), is cool. It's more than a theme restaurant; rather, the World Wrestling Entertainment's 47,000-square-foot, 2,000-capacity complex is designed to appeal to wrestling fans and nonfans alike. A 30-foot video screen and 110 36-inch video monitors make this the best place to watch a Wrestlemania or Royal Rumble pay-per-view event. Live broadcasts from WWE New York during WWE shows like "RAW" and "Smackdown!" along with appearances by WWE stars, energize things a couple nights a week; call ahead for the schedule and to book a table if you don't want to miss out. Non-head-butting attractions include The World dance club every Saturday night; the occasional headlining concert; plus magic from illusionist Criss Angel (2001 Magician of the Year) 6 nights a week through January 2003. Stop by at anytime for above-average eats. WWE action is broadcast nonstop.

Then there's **ESPN Zone**, 1472 Broadway, at 42nd Street (© **212/921-3776**; www.espnzone.com). This 42,000-square-foot space houses the Studio Grill, with nonstop ESPN programming; the Screening Room, with two giant screens and a dozen 36-inchers, audio and video touch screens, and reclining leather chairs with built-in speakers; the Sports Arena, a full floor of sports-related arcade games; set replicas from ESPN's shows (including *Sportscenter* and *NBA 2night*); and much more.

A perennial favorite, New York's **Hard Rock Cafe**, 221 W. 57th St., between Broadway and Seventh Avenue (© **212/489-6565**; www.hardrockcafe.com), is one of the originals, and a wonderful realization

---

Los Dos Rancheros Mexicanos *Finds* MEXICAN   This is probably the most authentic Mexican restaurant in New York. The decor is no-frills—tables with paper menus beneath the glass, plastic cups, and cheap dishes—but murals and a Wurlitzer jukebox pumping out Latin pop add charm. The Pueblo-style food isn't for the faint of heart: The famous moles are extra-rich; the house-made salsas are hot, hot, hot; and barbecued goat, tripe soup, and tongue tacos are among the specialties. But even the less adventurous will dig in to the enchiladas (don't pass up the beef), burritos, and other choices with gusto. Everything is affordable and excellently prepared, and soft, freshly made corn tortillas are served with just about every dish. Service is attentive, and Mexican beers are available. Check the wall behind the open kitchen for the specials. The south-of–Port Authority neighborhood can be desolate at night, so go earlier rather than later.

507 Ninth Ave. (at 38th St.). © **212/868-7780**. Reservations not accepted. Tacos $2–$3; burritos and sandwiches $4–$7; platters $7–$12. No credit cards. Daily 11am–10:30pm. Subway: A, C, E to 42nd St./Port Authority.

Mandoo Bar *Finds* KOREAN   This bustling block of 32nd Street has grown into a bright, neon-lit haven for lovers of zesty, cheap Korean food. My favorite is this dumpling house, which specializes in all manner of fresh dumplings.

of the concept. The memorabilia collection is terrific, with lots of John Lennon items. The menu boasts the Hard Rock standards, including a good burger and fajitas, and the comfortable bar mixes up great cocktails.

The subterranean red planet–themed **Mars 2112**, 1633 Broadway, at 51st Street (© **212/582-2112**; www.mars2112.com), is a hoot, from the simulated red-rock rooms to the Martian-costumed wait staff to the silly "Man Eats on Mars!" newspaper-style menu. The food is better than you might expect, but skip the Star Tours–style simulated spacecraft ride at the entrance if you don't want to lose your appetite before you get to your table. The kids won't mind—they'll love it, along with the video arcade.

Something to scare you with, my dear? You'll enter the **Jekyll & Hyde Club**, 1409 Sixth Ave., between 57th and 58th streets (© **212/541-9505**; www.eerie.com), through a small, dark room with a sinking ceiling, where a corpse warns you of the oddities to come. There are five floors—grand salon, library, laboratory, mausoleum, observatory—of bizarre artifacts, wall hangings that come to life, and other interactive bone chillers. Kids love it.

Planet Hollywood got a jolt of much-needed energy in 2000, thanks to a new circle of celebrity investors and a move to the heart of Times Square at 1540 Broadway, at 45th Street (© **212/333-7827**). JC and Justin do not stop in for Cap'n Crunch fried chicken, and the movie memorabilia doesn't hold the same excitement as the rock-and-roll goods at the Hard Rock (didn't I see the R2D2 and C3PO robots at three *other* PHs?).

I love the *mool mandoo,* broiled dumplings stuffed with vegetables and meat, and the baby mandoo, bite-size dumplings of beef, pork, and leek. The menu also offers fried-noodle dishes, including great pad Thai and Korean-style noodle soups; fried rice and bibimbob with veggies and beef; and *pajeon,* a Korean pancake with seafood. Plenty of meatless options are on hand. The room is plain but pleasant, with a long blond-wood tables and benches that speak to Mandoo Bar as a quick-bite kind of place. Service is brisk and efficient, in a friendly way. Beer and wine are available. Don't be surprised if there's a lunchtime wait, when ravenous shoppers descend from Macy's, but the line moves quickly.

2 W. 32nd St. (just west of Fifth Ave.). © **212/279-3075**. Reservations not accepted. Main courses $6–$14. AE, DC, MC, V. Daily 11:30am–11pm. Subway: B, D, F, N, Q, R, V, W to 34th St./Herald Sq.

Manhattan Chili Co. *Kids* SOUTHWESTERN/AMERICAN This big, festive Theater District restaurant adjacent to Dave Letterman's Ed Sullivan Theater is a great choice for a casual, affordable meal, especially if you have kids. The hearty chili bowls are geared to young palates, which tend to be suspicious of anything unfamiliar. The extensive list of chili choices is clearly marked by spice level, from traditional Abilene with ground beef, tomatoes, basil, and red wine (mild enough for tenderfeet) to the Texas Chain Gang, which adds jalapeños to the mix for those who prefer hot. In addition, expect favorites like nachos, chicken wings, big salads, and generous burritos and burgers. It's really hard to go wrong here—even vegetarians have lots to choose from. A fun place to eat!

1697 Broadway (53rd and 54th sts.). © 212/246-6555. www.manhattanchilico.com. Reservations accepted. Chili bowls $10; main courses $11–$16; Sat–Sun brunch $10.95. AE, DISC, MC, V. Sun–Mon 11:30am–11pm; Tues–Sat 11:30am–midnight. Subway: B, D, E to Seventh Ave.; 1, 9 to 50th St. Also at 1500 Broadway (entrance on 43rd St.; © 212/730-8666; subway: N, R, S, 1, 2, 3, 7, 9 to 42nd St./Times Sq.).

Pigalle FRENCH BRASSERIE   This French brasserie has been struggling to find an audience, but it deserves one. It's a wonderful addition to the Theater District, with high-quality fare, low prices, and convenient-to-Broadway location—not to mention a we-never-close policy. The beautifully designed room by Nancy Mah boasts the trimmings of a traditional brasserie—zinc bar, rattan, soft ochre lighting—with a designer edge. The room is airy and comfortable, great for couples and larger parties alike. The menu offers classic brasserie fare, including an onion soup gratinée, a *classique* cassoulet, duck confit, and steak au poivre. The food isn't groundbreaking, but it's satisfying.

I love the cocktail menu, reason enough to come in. The Violet Martini is perfectly shaken with Grey Goose and a hint of violet essence, then dressed with a single purple petal. The New Yorker is my husband's new favorite: gin, dry vermouth, dill pickle, and garlic, straight up. The only downside was the service on our last visit; if you're going pre-theater, make it clear the moment you arrive.

790 Eighth Ave. (at 48th St.), adjacent to the Days Hotel. © 212/489-2233. Reservations recommended. Main courses $6.50–$14 at breakfast and lunch, $8–$18 at dinner. AE, DC, DISC, MC, V. Daily 24 hr. Subway: A, C, E to 50th St.

Rice 'n' Beans BRAZILIAN   This cool, dark, hallway-size restaurant dishes up bold-flavored, stick-to-your-ribs fare that'll make you want to stand up and samba. Among the highlights are *feijoada,* the national dish of Brazil, a hearty stew of black beans, pork ribs, and linguiça (Portuguese sausage); and a roasted chicken seasoned with tomato and cilantro. Frankly, I think prices have climbed a bit in recent years, but big eaters will still get a bang for their buck. By far the best bargain is the eponymous dish: For less than $10 you get a large plate mounded with rice, beans, mixed vegetables, collard greens, and plantains—a vegetarian's delight. Portions are monstrous. The weekday lunch specials—full meals with rice, beans, plantains, and your choice of roasted or sautéed chicken, beef stew, thin-cut sautéed pork chops, or the day's fried fish—are a steal. Be forewarned: Service can be slow at times and ambience is almost nonexistent.

744 Ninth Ave. (btwn 50th and 51st sts.). © 212/265-4444. Reservations not accepted. Full plates $5–$8.25 at lunch, $6–$17 at dinner. AE, DISC, MC, V. Sun–Thurs 11am–10pm; Fri–Sat 11am–10:30pm. Subway: C, E to 50th St.

Route 66 Cafe AMERICAN DINER   Here's a good bet for straightforward American eats. The brick-walled room is light, bright, and spacious, making it a nice place to enjoy a casual, affordable meal. Expect an extensive menu with diner standards, from waffles, eggs, and bagels to burgers, salads, triple-decker sandwiches, meat loaf, and pastas. The food satisfies, and isn't as overpriced as most Theater District fare. Service is friendly and a juice bar adds a healthy twist.

858 Ninth Ave. (btwn 55th and 56th sts.). © 212/977-7600. Reservations not accepted. Breakfast $3.75–$7.75; sandwiches and salads $4.70–$10; dinner entrees $10–$22 (most less than $15). AE, DC, DISC, MC, V. Daily 7:30am–midnight. Subway: A, B, C, D, 1, 9 to 59th St./Columbus Circle.

Sapporo JAPANESE   In my world, comfort food doesn't get any better than a big ramen or fried-rice bowl from Sapporo. This no-frills restaurant serves up good, cheap Japanese eats, and the mostly Japanese crowd is testimony to its authenticity. Sapporo is famous for their *gyoza,* pork-filled dumplings that are pan-fried and served with a soy, rice-vinegar, and chili-oil dipping sauce. Other winning choices include *chahan,* lightly fried Japanese rice with veggies, egg, fish cake, and your choice of pork or chicken; sweet beef and tofu sukiyaki; fried pork cutlets; and any of the gargantuan noodle bowls. You can't really go wrong with anything; I've eaten here more times than I can count and have never been disappointed. Some of the servers speak little English, so just point to your choice, and don't hesitate to ask for silverware if you prefer it to chopsticks. Beer and sake are served, and there's a sushi bar at the East Village location.

152 W. 49th St. (btwn Sixth and Seventh aves.). © 212/869-8972. Reservations not accepted. Main courses $6–$9. No credit cards. Mon–Sat 11am–11pm; Sun 11am–10pm. Subway: N, R to 49th St. Sapporo East at 245 E. 10th St. (at First Ave.; © 212/260-1330; subway: L to First Ave.).

Siam Inn THAI Situated on an unremarkable stretch of Eighth Avenue, Siam Inn is an attractive outpost of good Thai food. All your favorites are here, well prepared and served by a brightly attired and courteous staff. *Tom kah gai soup* (with chicken, mushrooms, and coconut milk), chicken satay with peanut sauce, and light, flaky curry puffs all make good starters. Among noteworthy entrees are the *masaman* and red curries (the former rich and peanutty, the latter quite spicy), spicy sautéed squid with fresh basil and chilies, and perfect pad Thai. Unlike many of the drab restaurants in this neighborhood, the decor is pretty and pleasing—black tables and chairs, cushy rugs, and soft lighting.

854 Eighth Ave. (btwn 51st and 52nd sts.). © 212/757-4005. www.siaminn.com. Reservations suggested. Main courses $8–$12 at lunch, $8–$16 at dinner. AE, DC, MC, V. Mon–Fri noon–11:30pm; Sat–Sun 4–11:30pm. Subway: C, E to 50th St.

Virgil's Real BBQ BARBECUE/SOUTHERN Virgil's may look like a theme-park version of a barbecue joint, but they take their barbecue seriously. The meat is house-smoked with a blend of hickory, oak, and fruitwood chips, and most every regional school is represented, from Carolina pulled pork to Texas beef brisket to Memphis ribs. You may not consider this contest-winning chow if you're from barbecue country, but we Yankees are thrilled to have it. I love to start with the barbecued shrimp, with mustard slaw, and a plate of buttermilk onion rings with blue cheese for dipping. The ribs are good and the chicken is moist and tender—go for a combo if you can't choose. Burgers, sandwiches, and other entrees (chicken-fried steak, anyone?) are also available if you can't face up to all that meat 'n' sauce. And cast that cornbread aside for an order of buttermilk biscuits, which come with maple butter so good it's like dessert. So hunker down and don't worry about making a mess; when you're through, you get a hot towel for washing up. Kids will enjoy the atmosphere and friendly staff. The bar offers a huge selection of on-tap and bottled brews.

152 W. 44th St. (btwn Sixth and Seventh aves.). © 212/921-9494. www.virgilsbbq.com. Reservations recommended. Sandwiches $6–$11; main courses and barbecue platters $13–$26 (most less than $19). AE, DC, DISC, MC, V. Sun–Mon 11:30am–11pm; Tues–Sat 11:30am–midnight. Subway: 1, 2, 3, 7, 9, N, R to 42nd St./Times Sq.

Vynl AMERICAN DINER Vynl adds a hip quotient to the traditional diner formula with Lucite and Bakelite decor, a collection of action figures through the ages (from Captain and Tenille to Tyson Beckford), a 1970s-to-now soundtrack, and an affordable menu in a gatefold album cover (ours were from Lionel Richie and Three Dog Night). But Vynl isn't all veneer—the food is terrific. The brioche French toast with sautéed apples and caramel sauce is a great way to launch a weekend. For daytime and evening, the fare runs the gamut from diner fare to Asian-accented dishes including Thai curries, a veggie stir-fry, and Chinese chicken salad. Service is friendly and attentive. Pay with a credit card so you can sign the bill with the coolest pen in town (yours to purchase, if you wish).

824 Ninth Ave. (at 54th St.). © 212/974-2003. Reservations not accepted. Main courses $4.50–$11. AE, MC, V. Mon–Tues 11:30am–11pm; Wed–Fri 11:30am–midnight; Sat 9:30am–midnight; Sun 9:30am–11pm. Subway: C, E to 50th St.

Won Jo ★★ KOREAN BARBECUE/JAPANESE This round-the-clock Korean barbecue is a good bet for first-timers and purists alike. The menu at this brightly lit restaurant is massive, but barbecue is the way to go. All the cuts of meat are high quality (shrimp is available, too), and the table barbecues come with six side dishes (including kimchee), plus rice, dipping sauce, and lettuce leaves for wrapping barbecued meats. This is an interactive meal; you'll cook everything at your table's built-in grill. Unlike some neighboring joints, the food isn't blazingly spiced, but still piquant. The staff may not speak the best English, but they're happy to walk novices through the steps. It's a feast that's particularly fun with a crowd—Asian pop blares through the speakers, and groups keep the place hopping, especially on weekends—but couples will be well contented, too. The sushi, teriyaki, and *bibimbop* (Korean hot-pot dishes) are well prepared, too, if you'd rather forego the cook-your-own option.

23 W. 32nd St. (btwn Broadway and Fifth Ave.). © 212/695-5815. Reservations not accepted. Full barbecue dinners $17–$20; main courses $8–$27 (most less than $12). AE, MC, V. Daily 24 hr. Subway: B, D, F, N, R, Q, W to 34th St.

QUICK BITES

Canova Market, 134 W. 51st St., between Sixth and Seventh avenues (© **212/969-9200**), is a 24-hour gourmet deli where your choices are only limited by your imagination. There's a salad bar, a deli counter, a soup bar, a sushi bar, and the lunchtime-only pay-per-pound Mongolian grill, where you assemble your own concoction of veggies, meats, seafood, rice, noodles, and seasonings and then watch the chefs do their stuff ($5.30 per lb.). There's a large dining area in the back where you can eat. This place really bustles at lunch, but lines move fast.

Amy's Bread, 672 Ninth Ave., between 46th and 47th streets (© **212/ 977-2670;** www.amysbread.com), makes a great daytime stop. The brick-walled bakery/cafe serves up fresh-baked pastries, quiches, sandwiches made on some of the city's best bread, homemade soups, and excellent sweets (including divine old-fashioned layer cake), as well as cappuccino. Pastries are $1 to $4, sandwiches $3 to $6. A few tables are on hand in addition to the takeout counter.

Friendly **Bagel & Bean,** 828 Seventh Ave., at 53rd Street (© **212/ 262-6340**), is a great stop for lunchtime bagel sandwiches. The fresh-baked bagels are first-rate, and fillings range from cream cheese to whitefish salad to an excellent veggie burger. There's no table seating, but it's easy to park yourself on a corporate plaza in this area, and Central Park is a half dozen blocks to the north.

Little more than a jazzy, neon-lit storefront, **B. Frites,** 1657 Broadway, between 51st and 52nd streets (© **212/767-0858**), is a purveyor of authentic Belgian fries. You can choose from at least a dozen sauces, ranging from traditional mayo to herb-seasoned tomato purée. The $7.55 soup-and-fries combo (tax included) is a great deal at lunch.

Papaya King (p. 192) is at 255 W. 43rd St., just off Eighth Ave. (© **212/ 944-4590**). The two-all-beef-franks-and-an-all-natural-fruit-drink combo is a bargain at $4.30.

Gourmet grocer **Dean & Deluca** runs a bustling, airy cafe at 9 Rockefeller Center, at 49th Street, across from the *Today* show studio (© **212/664-1363**).

If you're over by the *Intrepid,* stop into **H&H Bagel**, 639 W. 46th St., at Twelfth Avenue (© **212/595-8000**), to sample incredible fresh-baked bagels.

12 Midtown East & Murray Hill

In addition to the listings below, there's a cafeteria-style branch of **Mangia** (p. 137) at 16 E. 48th St., east of Fifth Avenue (© **212/754-0637**); and a **Burritoville** (p. 137) at 866 Third Ave. (really on 52nd St. between Lexington and Third aves.; © **212/980-4111**). **Jackson Hole** (p. 191) is at 521 Third Ave., at 36th Street (© **212/679-3264**), for burgers and other affordable diner fare. Additionally, there are two area outposts of the coffeehouse/sandwich bar **Xando/Cosí** (p. 190): at 461 Park Ave. S., at 31st Street (© **212/634-3467**); and 320 Park Ave., at 51st Street (© **212/754-6144**).

Also consider the Midtown East outpost of Upper West Side favorite **Josie's** (p. 186), 565 Third Ave., at 37th St. (© **212/490-1558**), serving the same health-conscious New American cooking, and that of **Le Pain Quotidien,** at 833 Lexington Ave. (between 63rd and 64th sts.; © **212/755-5810**).

Comfort Diner *Kids* AMERICAN DINER   This retro-minded diner makes a good choice for a square meal: breakfast, lunch, dinner, or a between-meal snack. Outfitted like a roadside joint, with booths and Formica-topped tables, the diner is comfortable and easygoing. All of your favorite diner standards are well prepared and generously portioned, from the omelets to the Cobb salad to mom's meatloaf. Some of my favorites are the chicken potpie, with creamy filling and flaky crust, and Thanksgiving Every Day, outfitted with all the turkey-day trimmings, but you really can't go wrong with anything here. It's a reliable budget bet.

214 E. 45th St. (btwn Second and Third aves.). © **212/867-4555**. Reservations not accepted. Main courses $5–$15 (most less than $10). AE, DC, DISC, MC, V. Mon–Fri 7:30am–11pm; Sat–Sun 9am–11pm. Subway: 4, 5, 6 to 59th St. Also at 142 E. 86th St. (at Lexington Ave.; © **212/369-8628**; subway: 4, 5, 6 to 86th St.).

Ess-A-Bagel ⭐ BAGEL SANDWICHES   Ess-A-Bagel turns out the city's best bagel, edging out rival H&H, which won't make you a sandwich. Baked daily on-site, the hand-rolled delicacies come in 12 flavors—plain, sesame, poppy, onion, garlic, salt, whole wheat, pumpernickel, pumpernickel raisin, cinnamon raisin, oat bran, and everything. They're so plump, chewy, and satisfying it's hard to believe they contain no fat, cholesterol, or preservatives. Head to the back counter for a baker's dozen or line up for a sandwich stuffed with salads and spreads. Fillings can range from a schmear of cream cheese to Nova salmon or chopped herring salad to sun-dried tomato tofu spread. There also are lots of deli-style meats, plus a range of cheeses, salads (egg, chicken, light tuna, and so on), and vegetarian items. Homemade soups and salads round out the menu. The cheerful dining room has plenty of bistro-style tables.

831 Third Ave. (at 51st St.). © **212/980-1010**. Reservations not accepted. Sandwiches $1.50–$8.50. AE, DC, DISC, MC, V. Mon–Fri 6am–10pm; Sat–Sun 7am–5pm. Subway: E, F to Lexington Ave.; 6 to 51st St. Also at 359 First Ave. (at 21st St.); © **212/260-2252**; subway: L to First Ave.; 6 to 23rd St.).

Go Sushi *Value* SUSHI   This bright, attractive chain of eat-in/takeout joints serves up excellent sushi for wallet-watching fans. It's boxed in bento-style containers, but everything is prepared fresh by a bevy of chefs behind the counter, so you never have to worry about quality; you can also place orders if what you desire is not ready-made. In addition to sashimi, nigiri, and cut-roll choices, you can choose from a selection of fresh-made noodle bowls as well as bentos with teriyaki or tempura. I know locals who eat at Go Sushi three times a week. All in all, it's a wallet-friendly choice for a quick, healthy meal. No alcohol is served.

982 Second Ave. (at 52nd St.). © 212/593-3883. Reservations not accepted. A la carte sushi $1.50–$2; rolls $3.80–$9 (most less than $6); sushi combos and bentos $5–$17 (most less than $10); noodle soups $5.50–$6.50. AE, MC, V. Daily 11:30am–11:10pm. Subway: 6 to 51st St. Also at 511 Third Ave. (btwn 34th and 35th sts.; © 212/679-1999; subway: 6 to 33rd St.); 756 Ninth Ave. (at 51st St.; © 212/459-2288; subway: C, E to 50th St.); 3 Greenwich Ave. (Sixth Ave. at 8th St.; © 212/366-9272; subway: A, C, E, F, V, S to W. 4th St.).

Katsu-Hama *Finds* JAPANESE Even if you've never dined on Japanese cuisine, give this restaurant a try. It specializes in *katsu*, breaded and cleanly fried cutlets, usually pork, friendly to American palates. Katsu-Hama also katsus chicken, prawns, and potatoes ("cream croquettes") in addition to moist pork tenderloin. Dinners start at $8.95 and come with as much rice, miso, and cabbage salad as you can eat. Japanese curries and skewers (yakitori) are also on hand, and there's a kids' menu. The butter-yellow room features modern art and comfy seating. Service is welcoming, knowledgeable, and generous with seconds. Beer and a short but good sake selection are on hand. It's an excellent value offering a more pleasing all-around dining experience than most in this price range.

11 E. 47th St. (btwn Fifth and Madison aves.). © 212/758-5909. www.katsuhama.com. Reservations accepted. Main courses and complete meals $7–$16. AE, DC, DISC, MC, V. Mon–Thurs 11:30am–3pm and 5–10:30pm; Fri 11:30am–10:30pm; Sat–Sun 11:30am–9:30pm. Subway: B, D, F, V to 47th–50th sts./Rockefeller Center.

Pongal VEGETARIAN INDIAN My favorite Indian food is served at this standout on Curry Hill, the stretch of Lexington that's home to a number of Indian restaurants. Pongal specializes in the vegetarian cuisine of southern India, and also happens to be kosher. Trust me—you don't have to be a vegetarian to love it. The dishes are prepared to order (no vats of *saag paneer* sitting

---

Grand Dining at Grand Central

The lower concourse of **Grand Central Terminal** ★★, 42nd Street at Park Avenue, is a haven of cheap eats—and the setting is an architecture-lover's delight. Head downstairs and choose among the outlets offering everything from bratwurst to sushi. Standouts include **Junior's**, a branch of the Brooklyn stalwart, serving deli sandwiches, steak burgers, and their world-famous cheesecake in their own waiter-serviced dining area. (With a few exceptions, most of the outlets are takeout counters; there's abundant, seating at the center of the concourse.) **Mike's Take-Away** serves up soups, salads, and sandwiches, including a warming mushroom stew in winter. **Little Pie Company** serves up the Big Apple's best pies, plus fresh-baked muffins and the concourse's best coffee. **Cafe Spice Express**, serves terrific Indian fare, while **Christer's** and **Knödel** specialize, respectively, in fish 'n' chips and German-style brats, wieners, and sausages. There's also an outpost of pizzeria **Two Boots**. If you want beer or wine, visit one of the two **bar cars**, which sit near tracks 105 and 112. For a complete list of vendors, check out www.grandcentralterminal.com.

around getting stale). Ingredients are top-quality, vegetables and legume dishes never overcooked, and the well-spiced sauces are divine. The specialty is *dosai,* a large golden crepe filled with onions, potatoes, and other goodies, accompanied by coconut chutney and flavorful sauce. The food is very cheap, with almost nothing over $10, but you don't have to put up with a crusty cafeteria to get such a bargain: The restaurant is low-lit and attractive, with professional service and a pleasing ambience, making it a nice choice for a special night on the town.

Note: If Pongal is too crowded, go down the block to their annex at 81 Lexington Ave., at 26th Street. Or head to **Mavalli Palace,** 46 E. 29th St., between Park and Madison avenues (© **212/679-5535** or 212/679-2606), which serves excellent vegetarian Indian cuisine, and is often substantially quieter.

110 Lexington Ave. (btwn 27th and 28th sts.). © **212/696-9458.** www.pongal.org. Reservations not accepted. Main courses $6–$11 (most less than $9). DC, DISC, MC, V. Mon–Fri noon–3pm and 5–10pm; Sat–Sun noon–10pm. Subway: 6 to 28th St.

Prime Burger AMERICAN/HAMBURGERS Across the street from St. Patrick's Cathedral, this no-frills coffee shop is a heavenly find in a high-priced 'hood. The juicy burgers and well-stuffed sandwiches are tasty, the fries crispy and generous. The front seats, which might remind you of old wooden grammar-school desks, are great fun—especially when business-suited New Yorkers take their places at these oddities. A great stop during a day of Fifth Avenue shopping.

5 E. 51st St. (btwn Fifth and Madison aves.). © **212/759-4729.** Reservations not accepted. Main courses $3.25–$9. No credit cards. Mon–Fri 6am–6:30pm; Sat 6am–5pm. Subway: 6 to 51st St.

The Pump HEALTH-CONSCIOUS Here's a terrific stop for diners watching their figures as well as their wallets. An appealing mix of retro-cute and future-chic, with a counter in back and a few tables, The Pump espouses a philosophy that eating right doesn't have to mean boring. Everything is low-fat and high in protein but doesn't sacrifice flavor for healthfulness. This is casual food with natural ingredients: salads, sandwiches, "supercharged" combo platters, fresh juices, and high-protein and health shakes. Although they serve up a great nature burger (a blend of brown rice, sunflower seeds, herbs, and veggies), The Pump isn't a vegetarian restaurant; lean beef, turkey, and chicken are served. Because they cater to a workout crowd that needs energy, portions are substantial. Salad dressings are fat-free, using tahini and honey mustard, and pizzas are prepared with nonfat mozzarella, low-sodium tomato sauce, and whole-wheat crust. At breakfast, eggs, pancakes, and potatoes are baked, never fried—so you can indulge in a steak-and-egg sandwich (served on a whole-wheat pita).

113 E. 31st St. (btwn Park and Lexington aves.). © **212/213-5733.** www.thepumpenergyfood.com. Reservations not accepted. Breakfast $3.75–$8.50; sandwiches and salads $4.75–$7; full plates $8–$14. AE, MC, V. Mon–Thurs 9:30am–9:30pm; Fri 9:30am–8pm; Sat 11am–6:30pm. Subway: 6 to 33rd St. Also at 40 W. 55th St. (btwn Fifth and Sixth aves.; © **212/246-6844;** subway: F to 57th St.).

13 The Upper West Side

For good burgers and diner fare, visit **EJ's Luncheonette** (p. 156), 447 Amsterdam Ave., between 81st and 82nd streets (© **212/873-3444**) or **Jackson Hole** (p. 191), 517 Columbus Ave., at 85th St. (© **212/362-5177**). Vegetarians and health-minded diners might also consider **Zen Palate** (p. 167), 2170 Broadway, between 76th and 77th streets (© **212/501-7768**).

For French baked goods, sandwiches, and salads of a divine order, also consider **Le Pain Quotidien** ★★ (p. 147), at 50 W. 72nd St., between Columbus Avenue and Central Park West (© **212/712-9700**).

Uptown Dining

All State Café **26**
Amy's Bread **36**
Artie's Delicatessen **12**
Bardolino **41**
Barney Greengrass,
 the Sturgeon King **7**
Big Nick's Burger Joint/
 Pizza Joint **20**
Blondie's **18**
Burritoville **13**, **28**, **40**, **48**
Cafe con Leche **5**, **16**
Comfort Diner **46**
EJ's Luncheonette **14**, **38**
Flor de Mayo **4**
Gabriela's **7**, **21**
Gray's Papaya **27**
H&H Bagel **14**, **43**
Hunan Park **6**, **30**
Hungarian Pastry Shop **3**
Jackson Hole **11**, **35**, **44**, **51**
John's Pizzeria **31**, **34**
Josie's Restaurant & Juice Bar **25**
La Caridad 78 **19**
Le Pain Quotidien **29**, **33**, **37**, **45**
Nacho Mama **1**
Niko's Mediterranean
 Grill & Bistro **21**
P&W's Sandwich & More Shop **3**
Papaya King **47**
Pintaile's Pizza **52**
Popover Café **8**
Sarabeth's Kitchen **15**, **39**, **50**
Serendipity 3 **32**
Silver Moon Bakery **2**
Time Café **10**
Tom's Restaurant **1**
Totonno's Pizzeria Napolitano **42**
V&T Pizzeria **3**
Xando/Cosí **23**
Yura & Company **49**
Zen Palate **22**

Ⓜ Subway stop

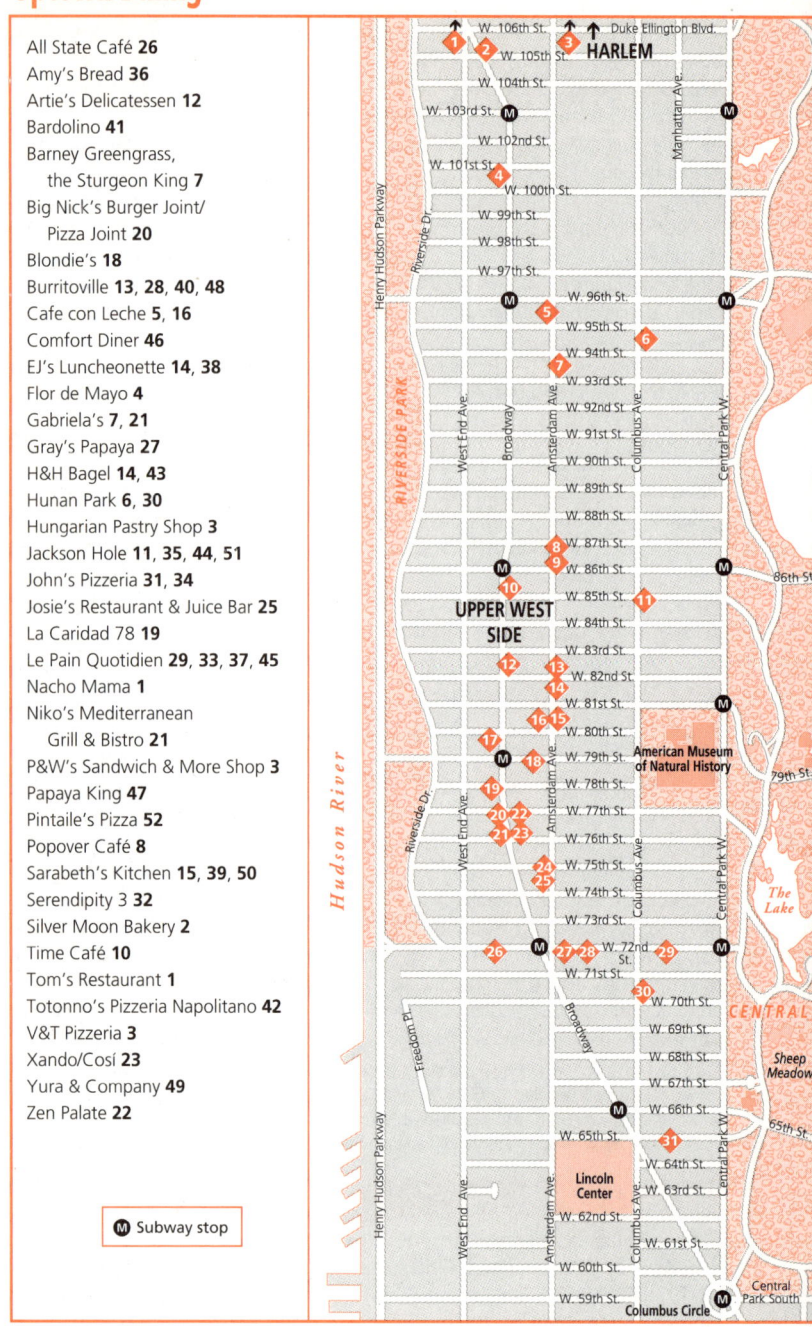

182

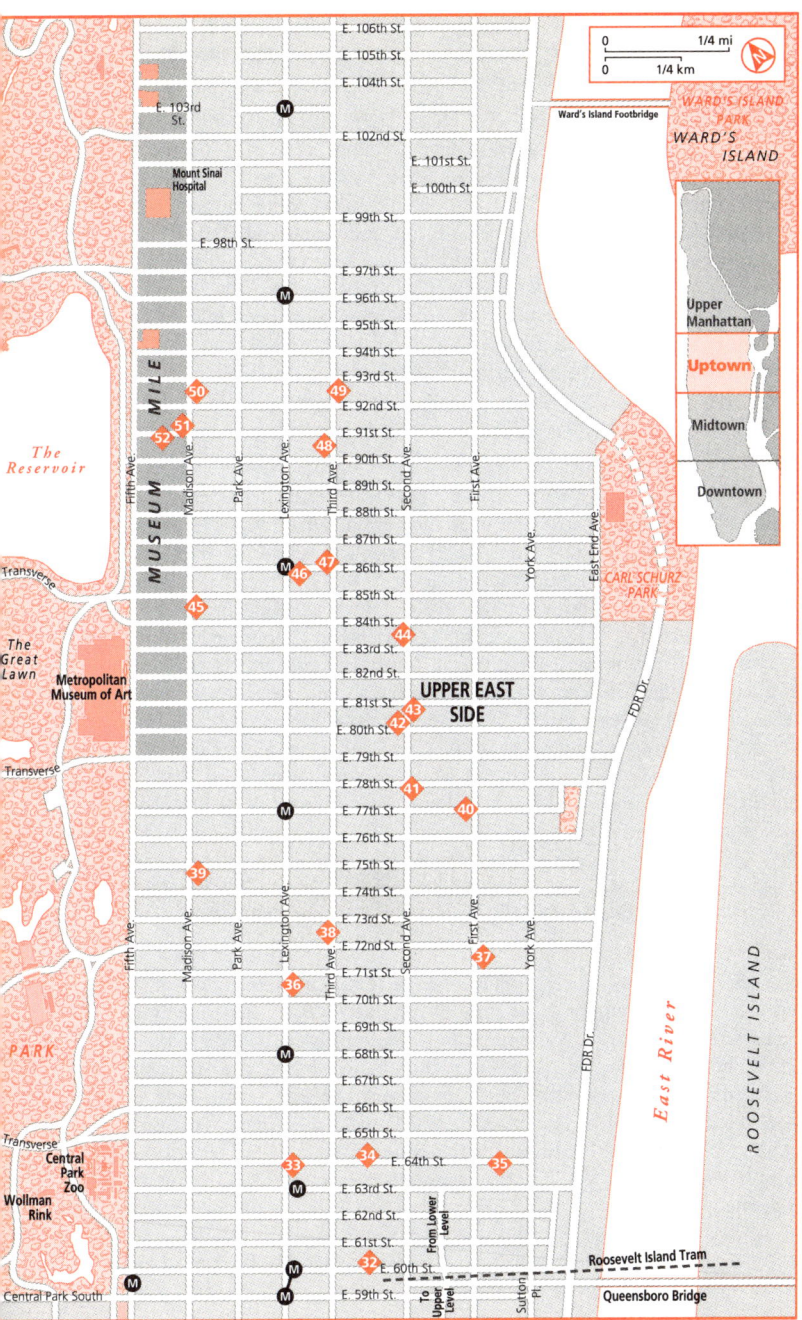

What would the Upper West Side be without its own **Burritoville** (p. 137)—or two? There's one at 166 W. 72nd St., near Broadway (✆ **212/580-7700**), and at 451 Amsterdam Ave., between 81st and 82nd streets (✆ **212/787-8181**).

All State Cafe *Finds* AMERICAN   This subterranean pub is one of Manhattan's undiscovered treasures—a classic neighborhood "snugger." It's easy to miss, and the regulars like it that way. The All State attracts a crowd drawn in by the casual ambience, the outstanding jukebox, and the superior burgers. If you're not in the burger mood, dig in to a variety of fresh salads and sandwiches, plus main courses like homemade fusilli with sautéed shrimp and scallops in a shiitake mushroom sauce. The dining room behind the bar has casual, rough-hewn tables and chairs and an easygoing ambience; a fireplace makes it inviting in cold weather. Draft beers, a wine list focusing on affordable labels from the United States and Australia, and a full bar round out the comfortable picture.

250 W. 72nd St. (btwn Broadway and West End Ave.). ✆ **212/874-1883**. Reservations not accepted. Main courses $10–$14. No credit cards. Daily 11:30am–4am (sometimes earlier; food nightly until 12:45am). Subway: 1, 2, 3, 9 to 72nd St.

Artie's Delicatessen JEWISH DELI   Yay for Artie's, which opened in 1999 but already has the wonderful vibe of an institution. What's more, it's as good as many of the best delis in Manhattan (I prefer it over tourist traps like the Carnegie and the Stage), and far more cheery. In other words, Artie's is tourist-friendly, but in a good way; even New Yorkers appreciate the vibe.

All of your favorites are here—from corned beef to chopped liver to tongue on rye—and arrive at your table in top form. The pastrami is everything it should be, and the chicken soup with kreplach is a sore throat's worst nightmare. Artie's chili dogs deserve special note—they may be the best in town. Burgers, omelets, and salads are also on hand. Nostalgia-inducing desserts include jello, baked apple, New York black-and-white cookies, very good homemade ruggelach, and sliced birthday cake every day ("No birthday necessary—song not included").

2290 Broadway (btwn 82nd and 83rd sts.). ✆ **212/579-5959**. www.arties.com. Reservations not accepted. Main courses $6–$12 at breakfast, $6–$17 at lunch and dinner. AE, DISC, MC, V. Sun–Thurs 9am–11pm; Fri–Sat 9am–11:30pm. Subway: 1, 9 to 86th St.

Barney Greengrass, the Sturgeon King JEWISH DELI   This daytime-only deli, going strong since 1908, is different from other Jewish delis; it's small and quiet, with an emphasis on smoked fish and service that's friendly rather than attitude-laden. It's a legend for its high-quality salmon (sable, gravlax, Nova Scotia, kippered, lox, pastrami—you choose), whitefish, and sturgeon (of course). But meat-lovers won't be disappointed: The triple-deckers are terrific (and much cheaper than at Midtown's delis), and the chicken liver inspired a raging, months-long debate among restaurant critics a few years back. Great for morning eggs and omelets, too; the bagels are fresh from H&H. Purists will be in heaven.

541 Amsterdam Ave. (btwn 86th and 87th sts.). ✆ **212/724-4707**. Reservations not accepted. Breakfast $3.50–$14; sandwiches $2.50–$16 (most less than $10); smoked fish platters $16–$36 (most less than $22). No credit cards. Tues–Fri 8:30am–4pm (takeout 8am–6pm); Sat–Sun 8:30am–5pm (takeout 6am–6pm). Subway: 1, 9 to 86th St.

Big Nick's Burger Joint/Pizza Joint *Kids* AMERICAN/PIZZA   A neighborhood landmark since 1962, this greasy spoon is one of the city's best spots for a midnight snack. Big Nick offers a full menu 24 hours a day, which includes everything from French toast and pancakes to beef burgers. The classic charbroiled burgers come in many varieties, from your all-American cheeseburger to the Mediterranean, stuffed with herbs, spices, and onions and topped with anchovies, feta, and tomato. There's also a good selection of Big Nick–style pizzas, like the Gyromania, topped with well-seasoned gyro meat and onions. Nick's is a real joint, specializing in homegrown Noo Yawk fare; the kitchen gets kudos, though, for a diet-watchers menu, with such specialties as pizzas prepared with skim-milk cheese or whole-wheat crust and lean-ground veal and turkey burgers. There really is something for everyone here on the huge menu. The atmosphere is often chaotic, with brusque waiters and staff scrambling about, cooks calling out orders, and crowded tables full of diners happily chowing down. It's a great place to take the kids for an affordable meal.

2175 Broadway (at 77th St.). © 212/362-9238. www.bignicksnyc.com. Reservations not accepted. Main courses $3.50–$19 (most less than $10). MC, V. Daily 24 hr. Subway: 1, 9 to 79th St.

Blondie's ★ AMERICAN   This bustling sports bar is the place for the best Buffalo wings in town. They're big and meaty; even my husband, who can eat 20 anywhere else, can only manage an order of 10 ($6.50) here. Choose your heat level, from plain to ouch!—the kitchen will get it right. Additional flavors include honey mustard, barbecue, or honey barbecue, but I recommend sticking with the real thing. All the standard fixings are on hand: celery, carrots, and blue cheese. Standard sports-bar fare rounds out the menu: burgers, fries, mozzarella sticks, with most food served in baskets. There's a huge selection of on-tap and bottled beers, but beware—this is where they make their money.

212 W. 79th St. (btwn Amsterdam Ave. and Broadway). © 212/362-3311. Reservations not accepted. Main courses $5.50–$13. AE, DC, DISC, MC, V. Sun–Mon 11:30am–midnight; Tues 11:30am–12:30am; Wed 11:30am–1am; Thurs 11:30am–2am; Fri–Sat 11:30am–3am. Subway: 1, 9 to 79th St.

Cafe con Leche Value CUBAN/DOMINICAN   This longtime favorite serves up terrific Cuban-style fare in a bright and comfortable upscale luncheonette setting. If Cafe Habana (p. 146) is the hip take on a Hispanic luncheonette, and La Taza de Oro (p. 162) is a little *too* authentic for those who cringe at the idea of tripe stew, Cafe con Leche is the just-right choice—authentic, but not off-puttingly so. All of the staples of Latin-Caribbean cuisine are here, including pressed sandwiches; well-stuffed empanadas (the meat-filled are best); terrific *ropa vieja* (Cuban-style slow-cooked and shredded beef); oxtail stew; and a wonderful paella, bursting with seafood and famous as the house specialty. Dishes come with your choice of red or black beans and yellow or white rice. Everything is zesty, but not too much so. Cafe con leche is the drink of choice, of course, but I prefer the fruity shakes.

424 Amsterdam Ave. (btwn 80th and 81st sts.). © 212/595-7000. Reservations not accepted. Main courses $5–$15 (most less than $10). AE, MC, V. Daily 8am–11pm. Also at 726 Amsterdam Ave. (btwn 95th and 96th sts.; © 212/595-7000; subway: 1, 2, 3, 9 to 96th St.).

Flor de Mayo Finds SPANISH/CHINESE   This hybrid Latin/Chinese restaurant far surpasses the more famous La Caridad 78 (see below) for quality. The kitchen excels at both sides of the menu. The best dish on the massive menu is the half *la brasa* chicken lunch special, beautifully spiced and slow-roasted until it's fork tender and falling off the bone, served with a giant pile of fried rice, bounteous with roast pork, shrimp, and veggies. Offered Monday through Saturday until 4:30pm, the whole meal is just $6.95, and it's enough to fortify you for the day. Expect nothing in the way of decor and you won't be disappointed. Service is reminiscent of Chinatown: efficient and lightning-quick.

2651 Broadway (btwn 100th and 101st sts.). © 212/663-5520 or 212/595-2525. Reservations not accepted. Main courses $4.50–$19 (most under $10); lunch specials $5–$7 (Mon–Sat to 4:30pm). AE, MC, V ($15 minimum). Daily noon–midnight. Subway: 1, 9 to 103rd St.

Gabriela's ★★ *Value* MEXICAN   If you love roast chicken, trust me: Gabriela's is the best. A blend of Yucatán spices and a slow-roasting rotisserie results in some of the most tender, juicy chicken in town—and at $7 for a half chicken with two sides and $13 for a whole, it's one of the city's best bargains. All of the authentic Mexican specialties are well prepared, generously portioned, and satisfying, from the monster tacos to the well-sauced enchiladas. The fresh, chunky, perfectly limed guacamole should please even Southwest natives. The dining room is bright and pretty, with a south-of-the-border flair, and the service is quick and attentive. Try one of Gabriela's fruit shakes (both mango and papaya are good bets) or tall *aguas frescas* (fresh-fruit drinks), which come in a variety of tropical flavors; beer, wine, and margaritas are served, too. A real winner!

315 Amsterdam Ave. (at 75th St.). © 212/875-8532. www.gabrielas.com. Reservations accepted for parties of 6 or more. Main courses $5–$9 at lunch, $7–$20 at brunch and dinner (most less than $15); early dinner specials $9.95, includes glass of wine or frozen margarita (Mon–Fri 4–7pm, Sat–Sun 3:30–6:30pm). AE, DC, MC, V. Mon–Thurs 11:30am–11pm; Fri–Sat 11:30am–midnight; Sun 11:30am–10pm. Subway: 1, 2, 3, 9 to 96th St. Also at 685 Amsterdam Ave. (at 93rd St.) © 212/961-0574; subway: 1, 2, 3, 9 to 96th St.).

Hunan Park HUNAN CHINESE   This casual place has been earning kudos for years from *Zagat's* to *New York* magazine to Alan Alda for its well-prepared, inexpensive Chinese standards. Everything about it—quality, service, decor—is a cut above standard. Expect all the familiar favorites, plus satisfying specialties such as ginger chicken, spicy four-flavor beef, Lake Tung-Ting shrimp, and crispy sea bass in a rich Hunan sauce. Service is friendly and efficient.

235 Columbus Ave. (btwn 70th and 71st sts.). © 212/724-4411. Reservations accepted for 5 or more. Main courses $6–$14. AE, MC, V (minimum $20). Sun–Thurs 11am–midnight; Fri–Sat 11am–1am. Subway: B, C, 1, 2, 3, 9 to 72nd St. Also at 721 Columbus Ave. (at 95th St.) © 212/222-6511; subway: B, C to 96th St.).

Josie's Restaurant & Juice Bar HEALTH-CONSCIOUS NEW AMERICAN   You have to admire the sincerity of an organic restaurant that uses chemical-free milk paint on its walls. Chef/owner Louis Lanza doesn't stop there: His menu shuns dairy, preservatives, and concentrated fats. Free-range and farm-raised meats and poultry augment vegetarian choices like baked sweet potato with tofu, tamari brown rice, broccoli, roasted beets, and lemon-tahini sauce; and a sautéed three-grain vegetable burger made from quinoa, bulghur wheat, and couscous with homemade ketchup and barbecued onions. The yellowfin tuna wasabi burger with pickled ginger is another signature. Latin and Asian accents are copious, as in citrus-marinated skirt-steak fajita, accompanied by chipotle corn salsa, guacamole, and whole-wheat tortillas. Everything is made with organic grains, beans, and flour and produce when possible. You don't have to be a health nut to enjoy Josie's; Lanza's eclectic cuisine satisfies. And nobody's gonna make you do without: If beet or arugula juice isn't your thing, a full wine and beer list is served in this pleasing modern space, which boasts enough colorful Jetsons-style touches to give the room a playful, relaxed feel.

300 Amsterdam Ave. (at 74th St.). © 212/769-1212. www.josiesnyc.com. Reservations recommended. Main courses $7.50–$13.50 at brunch, $8–$13.75 at lunch, $8.75–$18.50 at dinner (most less than $15). AE, DC, MC, V. Mon–Wed noon–11pm; Thurs–Fri noon–midnight; Sat 11:30am–midnight; Sun 11am–11pm. Subway: 1, 2, 3, 9 to 72nd St. Also at 565 Third Ave. (at 37th St.) © 212/490-1558; subway: 6 to 33rd St.).

La Caridad 78 LATIN AMERICAN/CHINESE   This neighborhood stalwart is the most famous of a string of New York institutions: the Chino-Latino hybrid restaurant. (Come for the Latino; you can find better Chino in this neighborhood.) The cuisine isn't fusion; rather, the menu features separate Latino and Chinese sections, so you could conceivably start with an egg roll, move on to Cuban-style fried pork with black beans and yellow rice, and follow up with moo goo gai pan if you're still hungry. Atmosphere is not the point, so ignore the bare-bones interior and fluorescent lighting. Instead, line up with the rest of the crowd for the huge portions of good, cheap eats. The lemon pork chops, shrimp with yellow rice, and stir-fried chicken are all recommendable. No beer or wine is served.

2199 Broadway (at 78th St.). © 212/874-2780. Reservations not accepted. Main courses $4–$11.25. No credit cards. Mon–Sat 11:30am–midnight; Sun 11:30am–10:30pm. Subway: 1, 9 to 78th St.

Nacho Mama TEX-MEX   I really like this attractive restaurant and bar, which caters to a Columbia U. crowd with value-minded fare that's more Tex than Mex but won me over with its fresh preparations and creative twists. The space is airy and attractive, with the brick, wood, and terra-cotta look of a Southwestern cantina. Everything is simply and generously prepared. I love the enchiladas with sweetly spiced, slow-braised pork. You can order it in a giant burrito if you prefer or opt for one of the many other fillings: wild mushrooms (crimini, white, and portobello, lightly sautéed in tomato and chilies); white-hominy pozole with red pepper, onion, and a touch of cilantro; steak, chicken, or grilled shrimp. The salsa is fresh and on the mild side, not too heavy on the cilantro, and the guacamole is chunky. Tex-Mex-style salads, sandwiches, and chicken wings are also available, plus a few more-sophisticated entrees at dinner. A terrific bar serves up monster real-lime margaritas and martinis for just $5 to $6, plus good drafts and an extensive bottled-beer list that roams the globe.

2893 Broadway (btwn 112th and 113th sts.). © 212/665-2800. Reservations accepted. Main courses $5–$14 (most less than $10). AE, MC, V. Sun 11:30am–10pm; Mon–Thurs 11:30am–11pm; Fri–Sat 11:30am–midnight (bar open later nightly). Subway: 1, 9 to 110th St./Cathedral Pkwy.

Niko's Mediterranean Grill & Bistro GREEK   If you're in a feta-and-phyllo mood, head to Niko's, where the cuisine of the Greek Isles gets the Big Nick treatment (see above, but expect a more upscale setting). The menu is huge, prices are low, and all the standards are up to snuff. Don't pass on the flaming saganaki, even if you're only stopping in for lunch. They have great falafel, too.

2161 Broadway (at 76th St.). © 212/873-7000. www.nikosgrillnyc.com. Reservations only taken for parties of 6 or more. Main courses $5.50–$8.50 at lunch, $5–$19 at dinner; daily brunch special (11am–4pm) $9; continental breakfast $6. AE, DC, DISC, MC, V. Sun–Thurs 9am–midnight; Fri–Sat 9am–1am. Subway: 1, 9 to 79th St.

Popover Cafe *Kids* HOME-STYLE AMERICAN   The first thing people usually call Popover's is kid-friendly, a nod to its child-size burger, PBJ sandwiches, and decor that's chockablock with teddy bears. But grownups will like it just as much. Everybody gets addicted to the fluffy popovers with strawberry butter or preserves. The full dinner entrees are a bit pricey, but Popover's forte is comfort food that makes hearty and affordable breakfasts and lunches: omelets and scrambles, chili and soups, and salads and sandwiches. A bowl of one of the day's homemade soups (vegetarian three-bean and split pea are two of my favorites) accompanied by a popover makes a more-than-satisfying lunch for a few dollars. Service is warm and welcoming; in fact, eating here feels like stepping into somebody's big old, hospitable New England home. Well worth a stop. Beware the crowds at brunch, however, which can ruin the mood.

Kids Affordable Family-Friendly Restaurants

It's always a smart move to call ahead to make sure a restaurant can accommodate kids with such amenities as children's menus and high chairs, but you can always count on the following places:

EJ's Luncheonette (p. 156) These retro-1950s diners serve up great burgers, fries, and specials. There's a kids' menu featuring peanut-butter-and-jelly sandwiches as well as downsized versions of the classics.

John's Pizzeria (p. 172) The Times Square location is particularly well located and kid-friendly, with family-size tables, chefs cooking up pies in brick ovens in the cavernous room, and an atmosphere where kids are welcome to be kids.

Manhattan Chili Co. (p. 175) This fun restaurant is geared for all-American tastes and palates. Expect kid-friendly nachos, chicken wings, not-too-hot bowls chili, and other faves such as burritos and burgers.

Popover Cafe (p. 187) This country-cozy cafe is especially welcoming for breakfast and lunch, when the home cooking is at its best. Little ones will warm to the teddies that line the banquettes—and everybody loves the baskets of fluffy popovers, which come with delectable strawberry butter.

Serendipity 3 (p. 192) This irony-free charmer even makes grown-ups feel like kids again. The whimsical restaurant and ice-cream shop serves up an extensive menu of American favorites, with colossal ice-cream treats.

Virgil's Real BBQ (p. 177) This pleasing Times Square barbecue joint welcomes kids with open arms—and Junior will be more than happy, I'm sure, to be *allowed* to eat with his hands.

You and the kids might also consider **Acme Bar & Grill** (p. 150); **Comfort Diner** (p. 179); **Artie's Delicatessen** (p. 184); **Lombardi's** (p. 147) for pizza; **Florent** (p. 156) and **La Bonne Soupe** (p. 173) for family dining with a French flair; **Big Nick's Burger Joint/Pizza Joint** (p. 184); **Two Boots** for pizza in a family-friendly atmosphere (p. 158); and **Jackson Hole** (p. 191) for terrific burgers. Don't forget about the city's perennially kid-friendly, and affordable (if you can get past the souvenir counter), theme restaurants; see the "Theme Restaurant Thrills!" box on p. 174.

---

551 Amsterdam Ave. (btwn 86th and 87th sts.). © 212/595-8555. Reservations not accepted. Main courses $6–$11 at breakfast and brunch, $9–$15 at lunch, $8.50–$21 (most less than $15) at dinner. AE, MC, V. Mon–Fri 8am–10pm; Sat–Sun 9am–10pm. Subway: 1, 9 to 86th St.

Sarabeth's Kitchen ★★ CONTEMPORARY AMERICAN Sarabeth's fresh-baked goods, award-winning preserves, and creative American cooking with a European touch keep a loyal following. This country restaurant with a Hamptons feel is best known for its breakfast and weekend brunch, when the menu features porridge with wheatberries, fresh cream, butter, and brown sugar;

pumpkin waffles topped with sour cream, raisins, pumpkin seeds, and honey (a sweet tooth's delight); and a host of farm-fresh omelets. Expect a *long* wait for weekend brunch; weekday breakfast and lunch are just as good, and a lot less crowded. Lunch might be a Caesar salad with Parmesan, brioche croutons, and anchovy dressing, accompanied by cream of tomato soup; a country-style sandwich; or a old-fashioned chicken potpie. Dinner is more sophisticated and splurge-priced, with such specialties as hazelnut-crusted halibut in an aromatic seven-vegetable broth and oven-roasted lamb crusted in black mushrooms, with grilled leeks and Vidalia onion rings. Leave room for the luscious desserts no matter what time you come—or stop by just for dessert!

423 Amsterdam Ave. (btwn 80th and 81st sts.). © **212/496-6280.** Reservations accepted for dinner only. Main courses $4.50–$13 at breakfast and brunch, $10.50–$17.50 at lunch, $10.50–$15.50 afternoon tea (Mon–Fri 3:30–5:30pm), $13–$26 at dinner. AE, DC, DISC, MC, V. Mon–Sat 8am–10:30pm; Sun 8am–9:30pm. Subway: 1, 9 to 79th St. Also at 1295 Madison Ave. (at 92nd St.; © **212/410-7335;** subway: 4, 5, 6 to 96th St.); Cafe inside the Whitney Museum, 945 Madison Ave. (at 75th St.; © **212/570-3670;** subway: 6 to 77th St.); Bakery location at Chelsea Market, 75 Ninth Ave. (btwn 15th and 16th sts.; © **212/989-2424;** subway: A, C, E, L to 14th St.).

Time Cafe ★ HEALTHY NEW AMERICAN   This easygoing, attractive spot can provide a night's entertainment, the perfect brunch, or anything in between. The menu features a selection of contemporary fare with a healthy bent, such as a good arugula salad with red Bartlett pears, blue cheese, walnuts, and a tart raspberry vinaigrette. The appetizer menu ranges from homemade hummus to smoked Scottish salmon rolls, while main courses include seared yellowfin tuna with wild mushrooms and barley risotto; herb-roasted free-range chicken with potato gratin and steamed veggies; a host of creative thin-crust pizzas and entree-size salads. The food is satisfying—I enjoyed a mixed-green salad with a blue corn–crusted chicken breast and buttermilk dressing on my last visit—and I like the health-minded preparations, the friendly service, and the laid-back vibe. The lunch special, which includes a bowl of soup (chicken noodle or the daily variety) and the day's special sandwich or entree-size salad, is a steal at $10. (Note that the lunch special is only offered at the Upper West Side location.) The well-stacked magazine rack offers a good selection of diversions for solo diners.

Both branches have a wonderful Moroccan lounge called **Fez** (see chapter 9), with the downtown location showcasing cutting-edge performances, too.

2330 Broadway (at 85th St.). © **212/579-5100.** www.timecafenyc.com. Reservations recommended on weekends. Main courses $7–$16 at lunch (most less than $13), $9.50–$22 at dinner (most less than $16); 2-course lunch special (soup and main-course salad or sandwich) $10. AE, MC, V. Mon–Thurs 11:30am–midnight; Fri 11:30am–1am; Sat 10am–1am; Sun 10am–midnight. Subway: 1, 9 to 86th St. Also at 380 Lafayette St. (at Great Jones St.; © **212/533-7000;** subway: 6 to Bleecker St.).

Tips **Pizza! Pizza!**

The Upper West Side does not lack for good pizza. Near Lincoln Center, **John's Pizzeria** (p. 172), 48 W. 65th St., between Broadway and Central Park West (© **212/721-7001**), serves up one of the city's best pies.

Farther uptown, the place to go is **V&T Pizzeria** ★, 1024 Amsterdam Ave., between 110th and 111th streets (© **212/666-8051** or 212/663-1708). This is a sit-down (or carry-out) restaurant with red-checked tablecloths, and traditional pies with red sauce and a chewy crust. V&T caters to a Columbia University crowd, so prices stay low—how can you *not* splurge on one of the mascarpone-filled cannolis for dessert, right?

Tom's Restaurant AMERICAN DINER   Tom's would be just any other diner if it weren't for its famous connections: This is the restaurant that served as the exterior for Monk's on *Seinfeld* and inspired Suzanne Vega to write "Tom's Diner." It's worth a pilgrimage if you're a Jerry fan or if you're in the neighborhood. It's popular with Columbia University students, thanks to its long hours and cheap coffee-shop fare. Expect the standards, from three-egg omelets to tuna salad. The '70s-era wait staff emits the requisite attitude and won't think twice of rushing you when it's crowded.

2880 Broadway (at 112th St.). ✆ 212/864-6137. Reservations not accepted. Main courses $3–$10. No credit cards. Sun–Wed 6am–1:30am; Thurs–Sat 24 hr. Subway: 1, 9 to 110th St.

Xando/Cosí   COFFEEHOUSE/SANDWICHES   City coffeehouse chain Xando met sandwich maker Cosí, and it's been a match made in heaven. The stars of the menu are Cosí's sandwiches, superb baked-on-the-premises pocket breads filled with your choice of mix-and-match fillings and spreads, plus combos for those who can't decide. Smoked Nova salmon with goat cheese and cucumber is one of my favorites, but I also love the tandoori chicken with roasted red peppers, and the tomato, basil, and mozzarella. The kitchen bakes personal pizzas on yummy Cosí bread as well, with such toppings as goat cheese and roasted red peppers. The Xando side of the equation serves up coffee drinks; wine, beer, and coffee cocktails like the Mocha Kiss (Irish cream, Kahlúa, Grand Marnier, mocha coffee). In a coffeehouse version of s'mores, all of the necessary ingredients—chocolate, graham crackers, giant marshmallows—are served in a pupu platter tray, and you fire your own over the open flame. The setting is *Friends*-reminiscent coffeehouse style, with bright colors and comfy IKEA-ish furniture. If you see a crowd, don't despair; there's additional seating downstairs.

2160 Broadway (at 76th St.). ✆ 212/595-5616. www.xandocosi.com. Reservations not accepted. Soups and salads $2.50–$8; sandwiches and pizzas $6–$9. AE, MC, V. Sun–Thurs 7am–midnight; Fri–Sat 7am–2am. Subway: 1, 2, 3, 9 to 72nd St. Also at 841 Broadway (at 13th St.; ✆ 212/614-8541; subway: 4, 5, 6, L, N, R to 14th St./Union Sq.); 504 Sixth Ave. (at 13th St.; ✆ 212/462-4188; subway: F to 14th St.); 257 Park Ave. S. (at 21st St.; ✆ 212/505-7978; subway: 6 to 23rd St.); 461 Park Ave. S. (at 31st St.; ✆ 212/634-3479; subway: 6 to 33rd St.); 320 Park Ave. (at 51st St.; ✆ 212/754-6144; subway: 6 to 51st St.). Call ✆ 212/653-1600 or visit website for additional sandwich-bar-only locations.

QUICK BITES

For one of the most satisfying meal deals in the city, head for **Gray's Papaya** (p. 160), 2090 Broadway, at 72nd Street (✆ **212/799-0243**), where all-beef dogs are available around the clock. Add some crispy fries and a tropical juice drink.

H&H Bagel, 2239 Broadway, at 80th Street (✆ **212/595-8003**), is the king of New York bagel makers. Stop in to this we-never-close takeout shop for a piping-hot bagel, which is so good it needs no accompaniment. Traditional toppings—cream cheese, lox, and the like—are sold in the refrigerator cases. In my opinion, this is the best of the three locations.

If you're farther uptown, the lovely, worn **Hungarian Pastry Shop,** 1030 Amsterdam Ave., between 110th and 111th streets (✆ **212/866-4230**)—a landmark for 40 years—makes an ideal stop for coffee and pastry or a late-night plateful of crumbly, buttery cookies. For something more substantial, head next door to **P&W's Sandwich & More Shop** (✆ **212/222-2245**), specializing in homemade soups, bagels, made-to-order sandwiches, by-the-pound salads, and the like. There are no tables, but you're welcome to pick up your food and take it over to the pastry shop to enjoy. If you're staying in the area and your room has kitchen facilities, P&W also makes a good spot at which to stock up on supplies like milk, cereal, peanut butter, coffee, paper plates, plastic utensils, and the like.

Silver Moon Bakery, 2740 Broadway at 105th Street (© **212/866-4717**), is bright, airy, and alive with fresh-baked pastry smells. Come by for a first-rate java fix and a fresh-from-the-oven brioche, a muffin, or other baked goods.

14 The Upper East Side

There's also a branch of **EJ's Luncheonette** (p. 156), the retro all-American diner, at 1271 Third Ave., at 73rd Street (© **212/472-0600**). Like the name says, the **Comfort Diner** (p. 179), at 142 E. 86th St., at Lexington Avenue (© **212/369-8628**), serves similarly satisfying comfort fare.

Sarabeth's Kitchen (p. 188) has two Upper East Side locations for breakfasts or sweet treats: a full-service outpost at 1295 Madison Ave., at 92nd Street (© **212/410-7335**), and a cafe inside the Whitney Museum, 945 Madison Ave., at 75th Street (© **212/606-0218**). **Burritoville** (p. 137) is at 1489 First Ave., between 77th and 78th streets (© **212/472-8800**), and 1606 Third Ave., between 90th and 91st (© **212/410-2255**).

For baked goods and sandwiches and salads, consider **Le Pain Quotidien** ★★ (p. 147), which has three Upper East Side locations: 833 Lexington Ave., between 63rd and 64th streets (© **212/755-5810**); 1336 First Ave., between 71st and 72nd streets (© **212/717-4800**); an easy walk from Museum Mile at 1131 Madison Ave., between 84th and 85th streets (© **212/327-4900**).

Bardolino *Value* ITALIAN *Shhh*—don't tell Bardolino, but they should be charging more. This trattoria prepares terrific pastas in a romantic atmosphere. On my last visit, I enjoyed a traditional Caesar, followed by a fantastic penne alla vodka with peas and prosciutto in a lightly creamy pink sauce so good I dream about it when I'm hungry. Other choices include fusilli *norcia,* in a tomato sauce with hot and sweet Italian sausage; and a first-rate puttanesca. The wine list is well priced and pleasing. This is the kind of solicitous service you usually have to pay twice as much to enjoy. The fixed-price meal deals at weekend brunch, lunch, and early dinner make an already excellent value even better.

1496 Second Ave. (at 78th St.). © **212/734-9050** or 212/734-9395. Reservations accepted. Pastas $7–$11; main courses $11–$13 (specials may be slightly higher); 2-course fixed-price lunch $5.95 (daily to 3:45pm); weekend brunch $7.95 (with mimosa or juice); 2-course fixed-price dinner $9.95 (daily 4–7pm). AE, DC, MC, V. Mon–Fri noon–11:30pm; Sat–Sun 11am–11:30pm. Subway: 6 to 77th St.

Jackson Hole *Kids* AMERICAN The "home of the 7 oz. burger" has been satisfying the hunger pangs of New Yorkers with all-American diner food at low prices since 1972. There's no faulting the juicy burger, which comes in more than 30 topping combos, all piled high on a hefty beef or turkey patty, or a marinated and grilled chicken breast. The Eastsider—a bacon-cheese version topped with ham, mushrooms, tomatoes, and fried onions—is actually trademarked. Hearty salads, blue-plate specials, and stuffed baked potatoes are also on hand, and eggs, omelets, and fluffy pancakes are served all day. This location has garden dining.

232 E. 64th St. (btwn Second and Third aves.). © **212/371-7587.** www.jacksonholeburgers.com. Reservations not accepted. Sandwiches and main courses $5–$14 (most less than $10). AE, MC, V. Mon–Thurs 10:30am–1am; Fri–Sat 10:30am–1:30am; Sun 10:30am–midnight. Subway: 6 to 68th St. Also at 521 Third Ave. (at 35th St.; © **212/679-3264;** subway: 6 to 33rd St.); 1611 Second Ave. (btwn 83rd and 84th sts.;

> **Tips** **Pizza! Pizza!**
> **Pintaile's Pizza,** at 26 E. 91st St., between Fifth and Madison avenues (© **212/722-1967;** www.pintailespizza.com; open daily 11am–9:30pm), dresses their organic crusts with tomatoes, extra-virgin olive oil, and fresh ingredients. Pintaile's is also at 1237 Second Ave., between 64th and 65th streets (© **212/752-6222;** open daily 11am–10:30pm).
> For a more traditional pie, head to **Totonno's Pizzeria Napolitano,** 1544 Second Ave., between 80th and 81st streets (© **212/327-2800**), for coal-oven pies. **John's Pizzeria** (p. 172) has an outpost at 408 E. 64th St. between First and York avenues (© **212/935-2895**).

© 212/737-8788; subway: 4, 5, 6 to 86th St.); 1270 Madison Ave. (at 91st St.; © 212/427-2820; subway: 6 to 96th St.); 517 Columbus Ave. (at 85th St.; © 212/362-5177; subway: B, C to 86th St.).

Serendipity 3 *Kids* AMERICAN   You'd never guess that this whimsical place was once a top stop on Andy Warhol's agenda. Wonders never cease—and neither does the confection at this delightful restaurant and sweet shop. Serendipity's small front-room curiosity shop overflows with odd objects, from jigsaw puzzles to silly jewelry. But the real action is behind the shop, where the quintessential American soda fountain reigns supreme. Happy people gather at marble-topped ice-cream parlor tables for burgers and foot-long hot dogs, meat loaf with mashed potatoes and gravy, and salads and sandwiches with cute names like "The Catcher in the Rye" (their own twist on the BLT, with chicken and Russian dressing—on rye, of course). What they're really there for are the desserts. The restaurant's signature is Frozen Hot Chocolate, a slushie version of everybody's cold-weather favorite; other crowd pleasers include dark double devil mousse, celestial carrot cake, lemon icebox pie, and anything with hot fudge. Serendipity is a charmer to be appreciated by adults and kids alike.

225 E. 60th St. (btwn Second and Third aves.). © 212/838-3531. www.serendipity3.com. Reservations accepted for lunch and dinner (not just dessert). Main courses $7–$18; sweets and sundaes $5–$17 (most under $10). AE, DC, DISC, MC, V. Sun–Thurs 11:30am–midnight; Fri 11:30am–1am; Sat 11:30am–2am. Subway: N, R to Lexington Ave.; 4, 5, 6 to 59th St.

QUICK BITES

In business since 1932, **Papaya King,** 179 E. 86th St., at Third Avenue (© **212/369-0648;** www.papayaking.com), is the originator of the two-franks-and-a-fruit-drink combo that Gray's Papaya (p. 160) has popularized. Papaya King isn't as inexpensive as Gray's—the combo is $4.30 here—but the quality is high.

For more refined tastes, there's **Yura & Company,** 6045 Third Ave., at 92nd Street (© **212/860-8060**), one of the Upper East Side's best-kept secrets. This gourmet bakery/cafe serves good coffee, scones and muffins, and a selection of foods that are perfect for a Central Park picnic (the 90th St. entrance is a few blocks away). Or you can opt for table service in the country-style dining room, a cute spot for breakfast or a well-made sandwich. Good angel-food cake, too.

New on the Upper East Side scene for coffee and pastry is **Amy's Bread** (p. 178), 972 Lexington Ave., between 70th and 71st streets (© **212/537-0270**).

H&H Bagel (p. 190), has an outlet at 1551 Second Ave., between 80th and 81st streets (© **212/734-7441**), where you can stop in around the clock.

15 Harlem

Bayou ★ CREOLE   This casually sophisticated Creole restaurant is a symbol of Harlem's renaissance. The room is stylish in a trend-defying way, with yellow walls, oak tables, a mahogany bar, and dim lighting. The food is pure New Orleans: shrimp and okra gumbo, cornmeal-fried oysters, sautéed chicken livers, and shrimp rémoulade with deviled eggs. Shrimp Creole or crawfish étouffée are served in their own piquant sauces over rice. Farm-raised catfish is marinated and sliced thin, then deep-fried in cornmeal until the outside is perfectly crisp, while the inside stays moist and flaky. Salads are crisp and bounteous. The only disappointment is the shiitake-and-collard-green enchiladas, an attempt at a vegetarian option. Service is attentive and professional. An affordable wine list and well-priced desserts and starters make Bayou a good value, to boot. The fine glass of pinot noir I had would've been $8 anywhere below 96th Street; here, it was just $6. Desserts are divine; don't pass up the bread pudding, made with fresh peaches and a scrumptious bourbon sauce.

308 Lenox Ave. (btwn 125th and 126th sts.). © **212/426-3800.** Reservations recommended for dinner. Main courses $7–$13 at lunch, $13–$22 at dinner (most less than $18); Sun brunch $14–$21 (includes starter and mimosa or Bloody Mary). AE, MC, V. Mon–Thurs 11:30am–4pm and 6–10pm; Fri 11:30am–4pm and 6–11pm; Sat 6–11pm; Sun noon–8pm. Subway: 2, 3 to 125th St.

Miss Mamie's Spoonbread Too ★ *Finds* SOUTHERN   Entering this bright, strawberry-curtained charmer is like stepping straight into South Carolina. Take a seat at one of the retro Formica-topped tables and nibble from the plate of cornbread as you peruse the menu of Southern classics: fried chicken, barbecue shrimp (great sauce!), short ribs falling off the bone and topped with a perfect gravy (zesty but not too peppery). If you can't choose, try the sampler plate, a "smorgasbord of Southern delights." Every entree comes with your choice of two sides, including macaroni and cheese, collard greens, candied yams, and better-than-mom-makes potato salad. Save room for dessert, which follows the traditional line with sweet-potato pie, banana pudding, and home-baked cobblers and cakes. Service is charming and attentive, beer and wine are available.

366 W. 110th St. (btwn Columbus and Manhattan aves.). © **212/865-6744.** Reservations not accepted. Main courses $7–$15. MC, V. Mon–Sat noon–10:30pm; Sun 11am–10:30pm. Subway: 2, 3 to 125th St. Also at 547 Lenox Ave. (btwn 137th and 138th sts.; © **212/690-3100;** subway: 2, 3 to 135th St.).

Sylvia's ★★ SOUL FOOD   South Carolina–born Sylvia Woods is the last word in New York soul food. Despite the lack of decor, this bustling place is so popular that the dining room has spilled into the building next door. Don't be surprised if you have a wait for a table, but the food is worth it. Since 1962, this Harlem institution has dished up finger-lickin' Southern fried goods: turkey with down-home stuffing, smothered chicken and pork chops, fried chicken and baked ham, collard greens and candied yams, and sweet tea. And then there's "Sylvia's World Famous, Talked About, Bar-B-Que Ribs Special"—the sauce is sweet, with a potent afterburn. This Harlem landmark is still presided over by 73-year-old Sylvia, who's likely to greet you at the door. Eating here is still a one-of-a-kind New York experience. Sunday gospel brunch is a joyous time to go.

328 Lenox Ave. (btwn 126th and 127th sts.). © **212/996-0660.** www.sylviassoulfood.com. Reservations only accepted for parties of 10 or more. Main courses $2.50–$8.25 at breakfast, $8–$19 at lunch and dinner; lunch special Mon–Fri 11am–3pm $3.75–$9.25; Sun gospel brunch $17 (includes a cocktail). AE, DISC, MC, V. Mon–Thurs 8am–10:30pm; Fri–Sat 7:30am–10:30pm; Sun 11am–8pm. Subway: 2, 3 to 125th St.

QUICK BITES

Papaya King (p. 192) has another location at 121 W. 125th St., between Lenox Avenue and Adam Clayton Powell Boulevard (✆ **212/665-5732**). The two-all-beef-franks-and-an-all-natural-fruit-drink combo is a bargain at $4.30.

16 Brooklyn

Grimaldi's Pizzeria ★★ PIZZA   Here's New York's best pizza; only Lombardi's (see p. 147) can claim to be Grimaldi's rival in taste and quality. *Zagat's* gives this Brooklyn classic a 26 (out of 30) for food, a rating usually reserved for the likes of Le Cirque. Thin coal-oven crust, crisp and smoky, is topped with perfectly seasoned red sauce, basil, and fresh mozzarella. Crown this pie with your choice of toppings, including pepperoni and house-roasted red peppers. Grimaldi's is a pleasant place, with red-checked tablecloths, photos of Sinatra, and the Chairman of the Board himself crooning from the jukebox. Patsy Grimaldi is likely to greet you himself, warmly, with stogie in hand (despite the no-smoking signs). Otherwise, the service can be gruff, but that's how you'll know you've arrived—in Brooklyn, that is. The best time to come is in summer, when sidewalk tables offer the kind of views of the Brooklyn Bridge and lower Manhattan that usually only big money buys.

19 Old Fulton St. (btwn Front and Water sts.), Brooklyn Heights. ✆ **718/858-4300.** Reservations not accepted. Pies $14 and up, depending on toppings. No credit cards. Sun–Thurs 11:30am–11pm; Fri–Sat 11:30am–midnight. Subway: A, C to High St.; 2, 3 to Clark St. (use Henry St. exit). Walk downslope, toward the water; it will be on your right in the last block, across from the Eagle Warehouse.

Exploring New York City

If this is your first trip to New York, face facts: It will be impossible to take in the entire city. Because New York is almost unfathomably big and constantly changing, you could live your whole life here and still make fascinating daily discoveries. This chapter is designed to give you an overview so you can narrow your choices to an itinerary that's doable in a day, or a week, or in between.

So don't try to tame New York—you can't. Decide on a few must-see attractions, and then let the city take you on its own ride. Inevitably, you'll be blown off course by unplanned diversions that are as much fun as what you meant to see.

1 Sights & Attractions by Neighborhood

MANHATTAN
CHELSEA
Dia Center for the Arts (p. 221)

EAST VILLAGE & NOHO
Merchant's House Museum ★ (p. 238)

THE FLATIRON DISTRICT/UNION SQUARE
Center for Jewish History (p. 220)
Flatiron Building (p. 237)
Theodore Roosevelt Birthplace (p. 236)
Union Square Park (p. 249)

GREENWICH VILLAGE
Forbes Magazine Galleries (p. 222)
Washington Square Park (p. 249)

HARLEM
Abyssinian Baptist Church ★ (p. 240)
Astor Row Houses (p. 237)
Jumel Terrace Historic District (p. 237)
Morris-Jumel Mansion ★ (p. 238)
Mother A.M.E. Zion Church (p. 241)
Schomburg Center for Research in Black Culture (p. 234)
Strivers' Row (p. 237)
Studio Museum in Harlem (p. 235)
Sugar Hill (p. 237)
Sylvan Terrace (p. 237)

LOWER EAST SIDE
Lower East Side Tenement Museum ★ (p. 227)

LOWER MANHATTAN/FINANCIAL DISTRICT/NEW YORK HARBOR
Battery Park ★★ (p. 248)
Bowling Green Park (p. 248)
Brooklyn Bridge ★★ (p. 208)
Castle Clinton National Monument (p. 248)
Ellis Island ★★ (p. 208)
Federal Hall National Memorial (p. 222)
Fraunces Tavern Museum (p. 222)
Museum of American Financial History (p. 228)
Museum of Jewish Heritage—A Living Memorial to the Holocaust ★ (p. 229)
National Museum of the American Indian (p. 232)
New York City Police Museum (p. 233)

Downtown Attractions

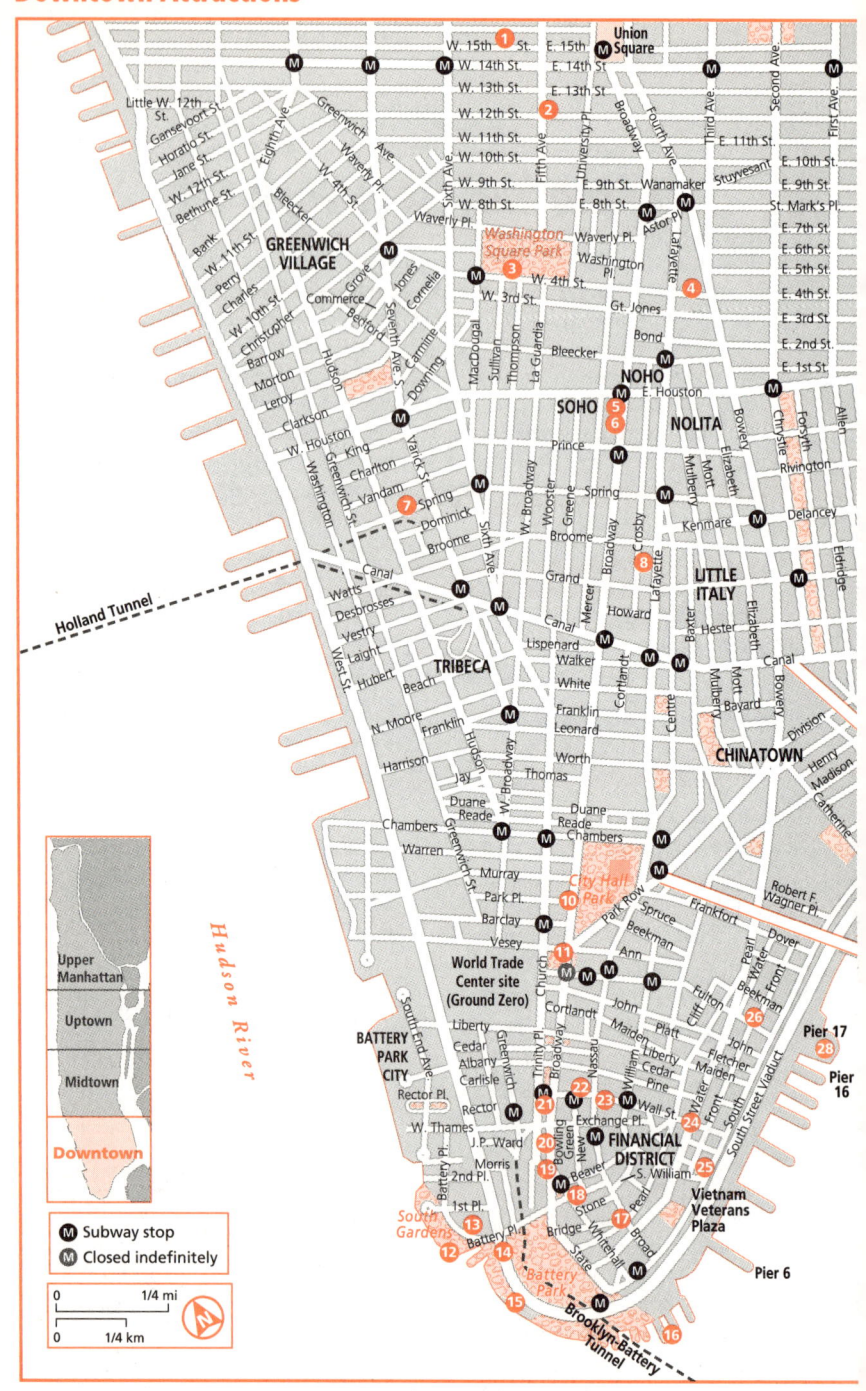

196

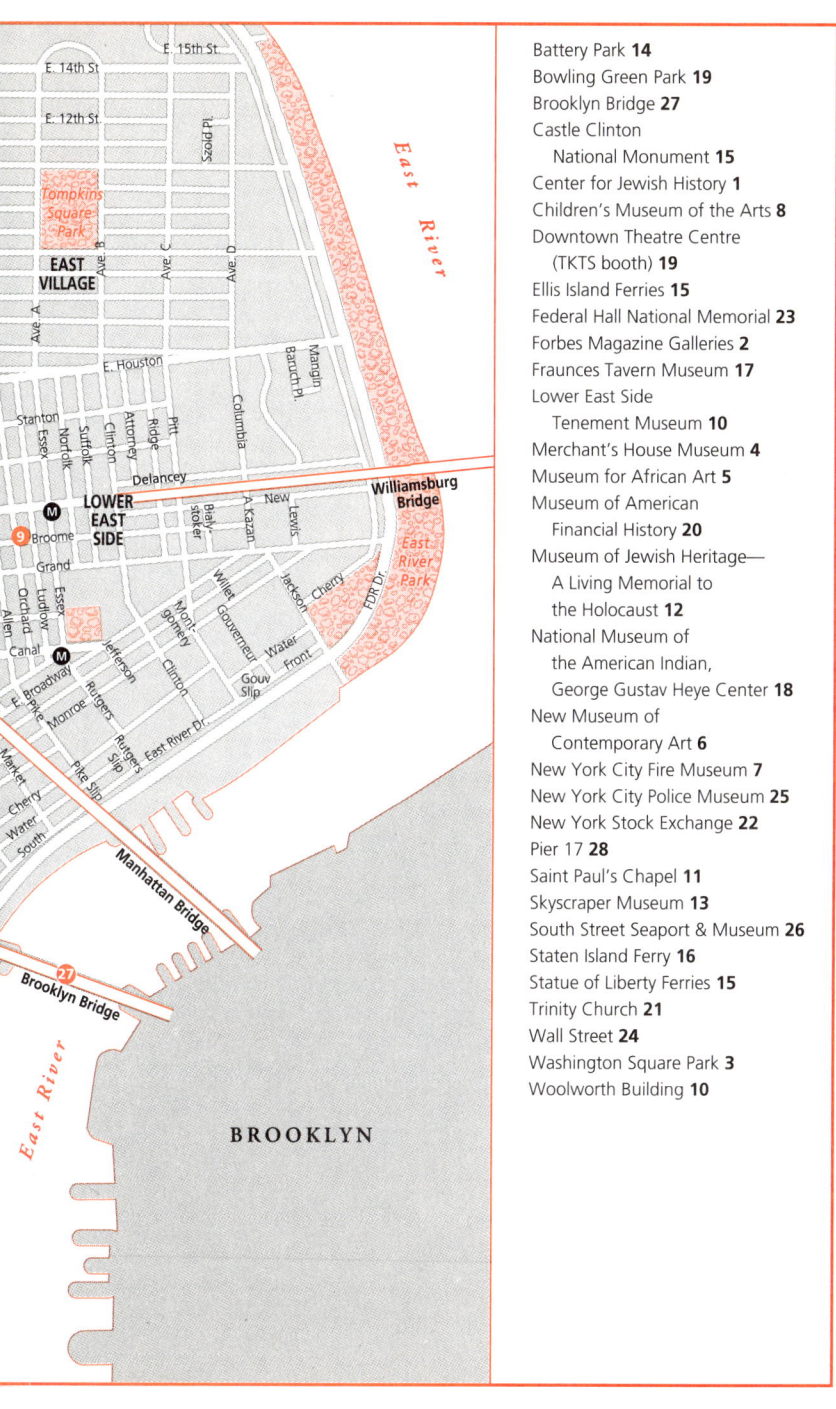

Battery Park **14**
Bowling Green Park **19**
Brooklyn Bridge **27**
Castle Clinton
  National Monument **15**
Center for Jewish History **1**
Children's Museum of the Arts **8**
Downtown Theatre Centre
  (TKTS booth) **19**
Ellis Island Ferries **15**
Federal Hall National Memorial **23**
Forbes Magazine Galleries **2**
Fraunces Tavern Museum **17**
Lower East Side
  Tenement Museum **10**
Merchant's House Museum **4**
Museum for African Art **5**
Museum of American
  Financial History **20**
Museum of Jewish Heritage—
  A Living Memorial to
  the Holocaust **12**
National Museum of
  the American Indian,
  George Gustav Heye Center **18**
New Museum of
  Contemporary Art **6**
New York City Fire Museum **7**
New York City Police Museum **25**
New York Stock Exchange **22**
Pier 17 **28**
Saint Paul's Chapel **11**
Skyscraper Museum **13**
South Street Seaport & Museum **26**
Staten Island Ferry **16**
Statue of Liberty Ferries **15**
Trinity Church **21**
Wall Street **24**
Washington Square Park **3**
Woolworth Building **10**

197

Midtown Attractions

American Craft Museum **30**
American Folk Art Museum **31**
Broadway City **4**
Bryant Park **24**
Carnegie Hall **2**
Center for Jewish History **11**
Central Park Zoo **37**
Chelsea Piers Sports
 & Entertainment Complex **8**
Chrystler Building **20**
Circle Line Cruises **7**
Dahesh Museum of Art **26**
Dia Center for the Arts **9**
Empire State Building **15**
Flatiron Building **14**
Grand Central Terminal **21**
International Center
 of Photography **25**
Intrepid Sea-Air-Space Museum **6**
Japan Society **19**
Lazer Park **3**
Lever House **35**
Lincoln Center **1**
Madame Tussaud's New York **5**
Madison Square Garden **10**
Morgan Library **16**
Mount Vernon Hotel
 Museum and Garden **39**
Museum of Modern Art
 (closed until 2005) **32**
Museum of Television & Radio **33**
New York Public Library **23**
New York Transit Museum,
 Gallery Annex **21**
Radio City Music Hall **27**
Rockefeller Center **28**
Scandinavia House:
 The Nordic Center in America **17**
Seagram Building **36**
Sony Building **34**
Sony Wonder Technology Lab **34**
St. Patrick's Cathedral **29**
Temple Emanu-El **38**
Theodore Roosevelt Birthplace **13**
Tisch Children's Zoo **37**
Union Square Park **12**
United Nations **18**
Whitney Museum of American Art
 at Philip Morris **22**

198

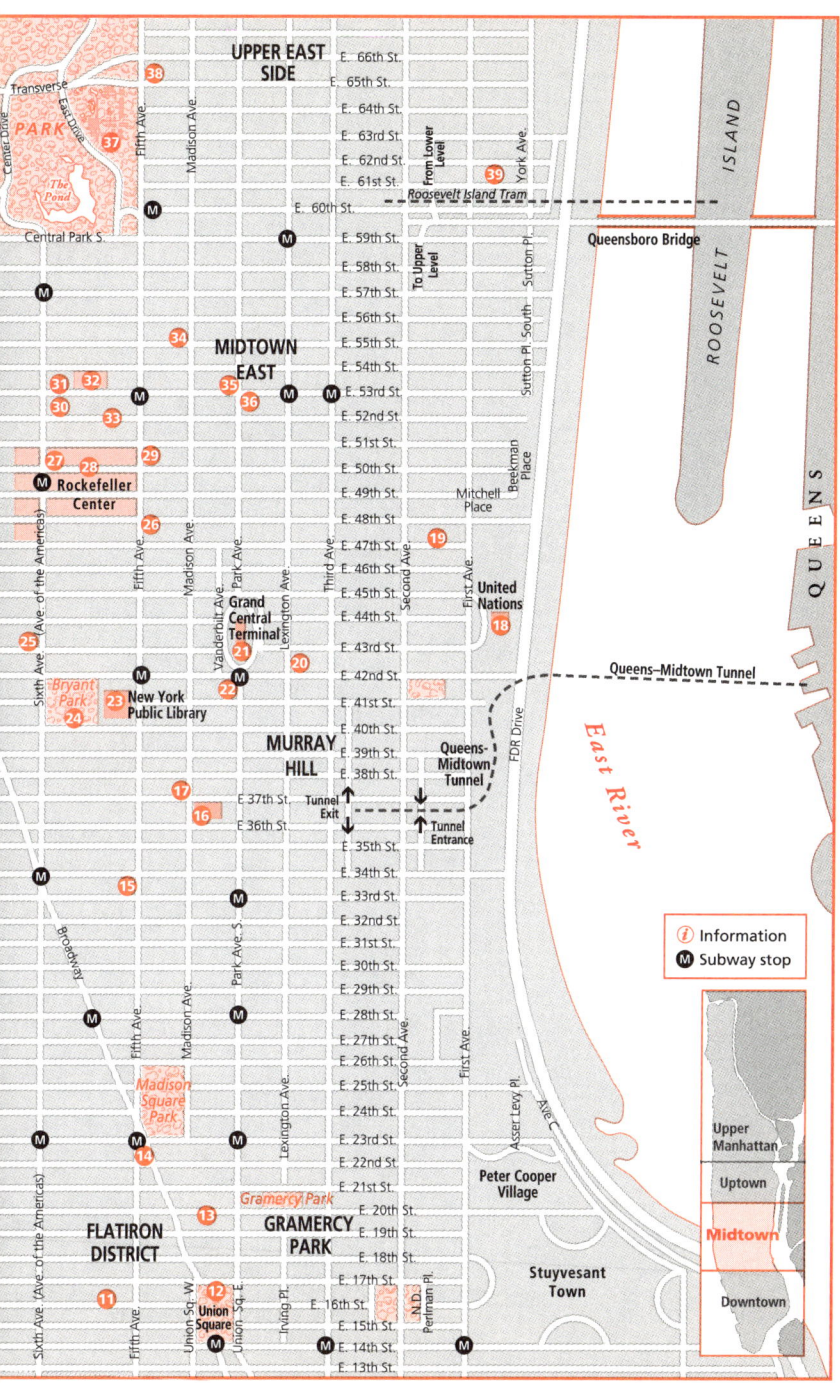

Uptown Attractions

American Folk Art Museum;
 Eva & Morris Feld Gallery **19**
American Museum of
 Natural History **24**
The Ansonia **22**
Asia Society **14**
Cathedral of St. John the Divine **1**
Central Park Zoo **17**
Children's Museum
 of Manhattan **25**
Cooper–Hewitt
 National Design Museum **6**
The Dakota **21**
El Museo del Barrio **2**
The Frick Collection **13**
Gracie Mansion **10**
Guggenheim Museum **8**
Jewish Museum **5**
Lincoln Center **20**
Metropolitan Museum of Art **11**
Mount Vernon Hotel
 Museum & Garden **15**
Museum of the
 City of New York **3**
National Academy of Design **7**
Neue Galerie **4**
New-York Historical Society **23**
92nd Street Y **9**
Rose Center for
 Earth and Space **24**
Temple Emanu-El **16**
Tisch Children's Zoo **17**
Whitney Museum of
 American Art **12**
Wollman Rink **18**

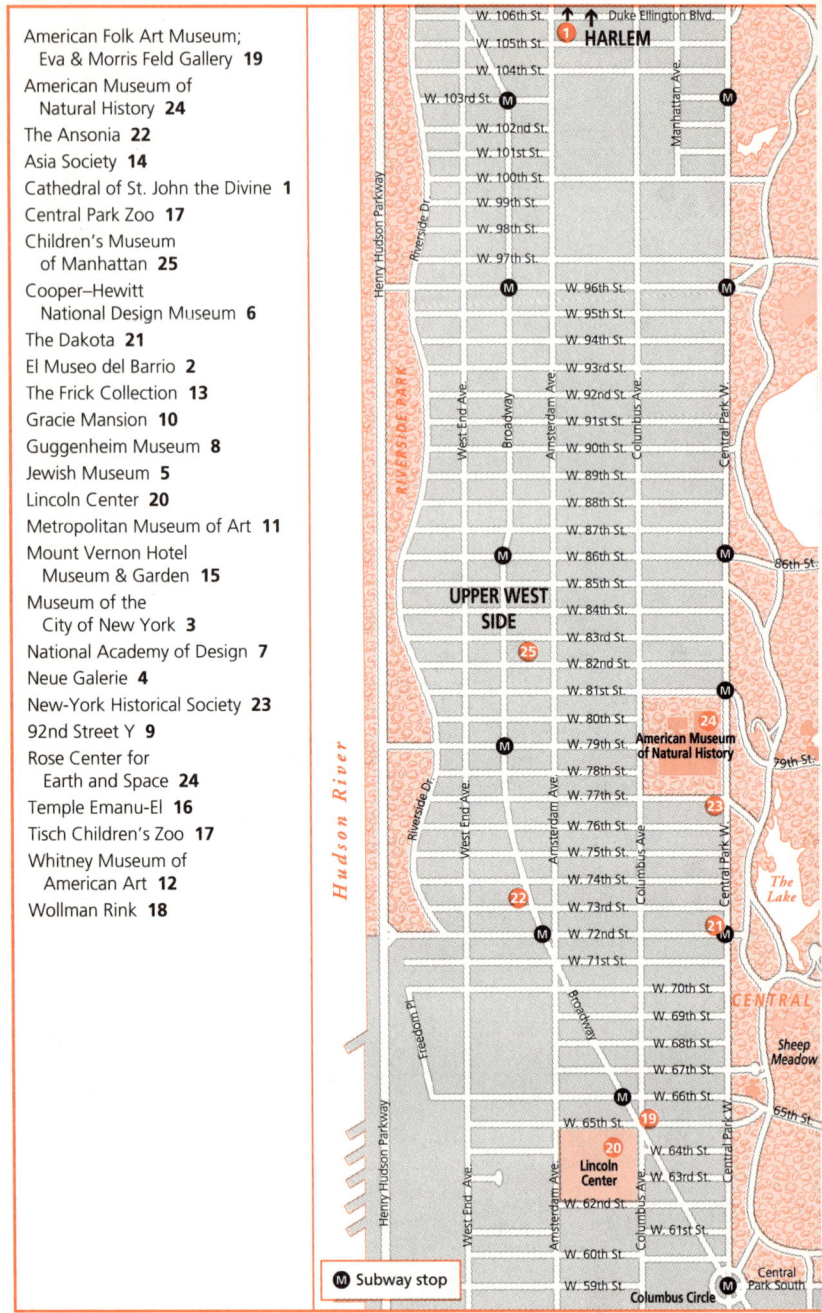

200

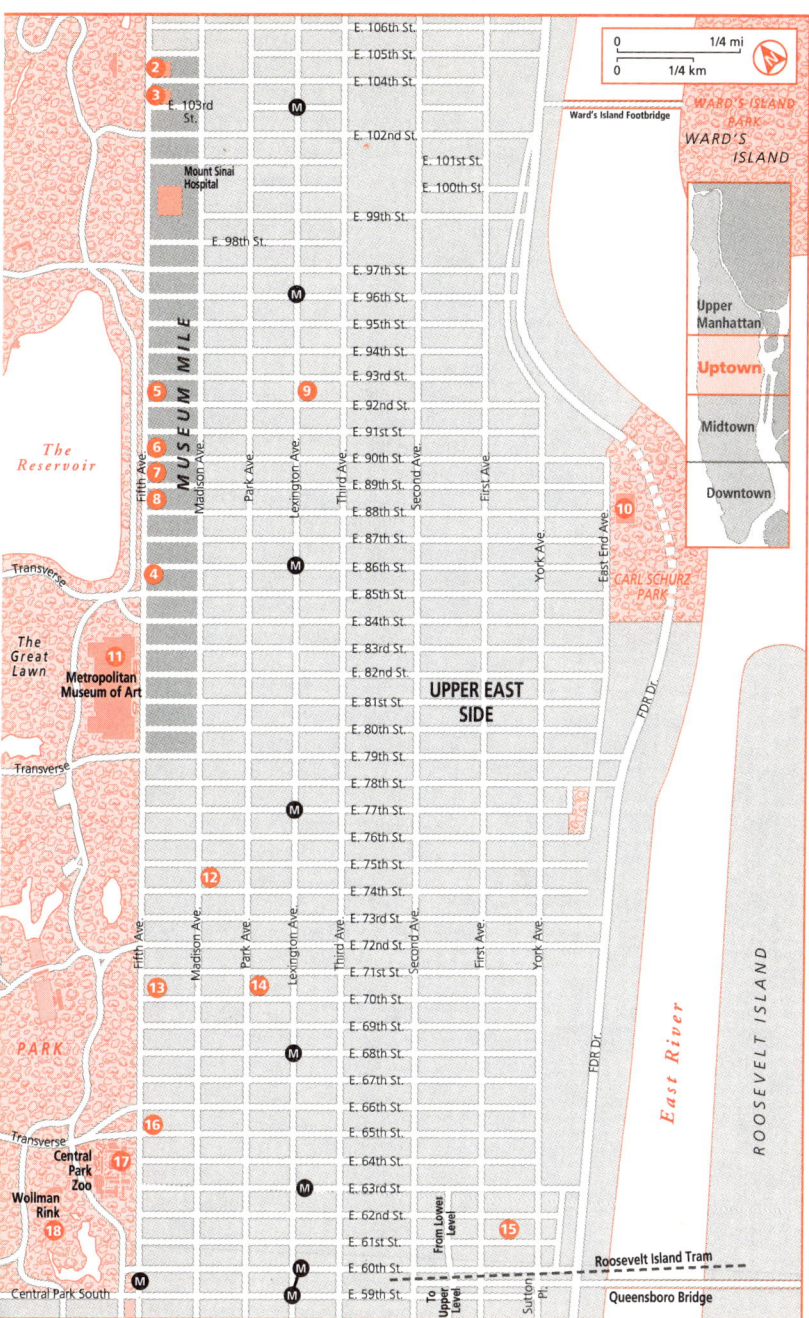

201

Upper Manhattan Attractions

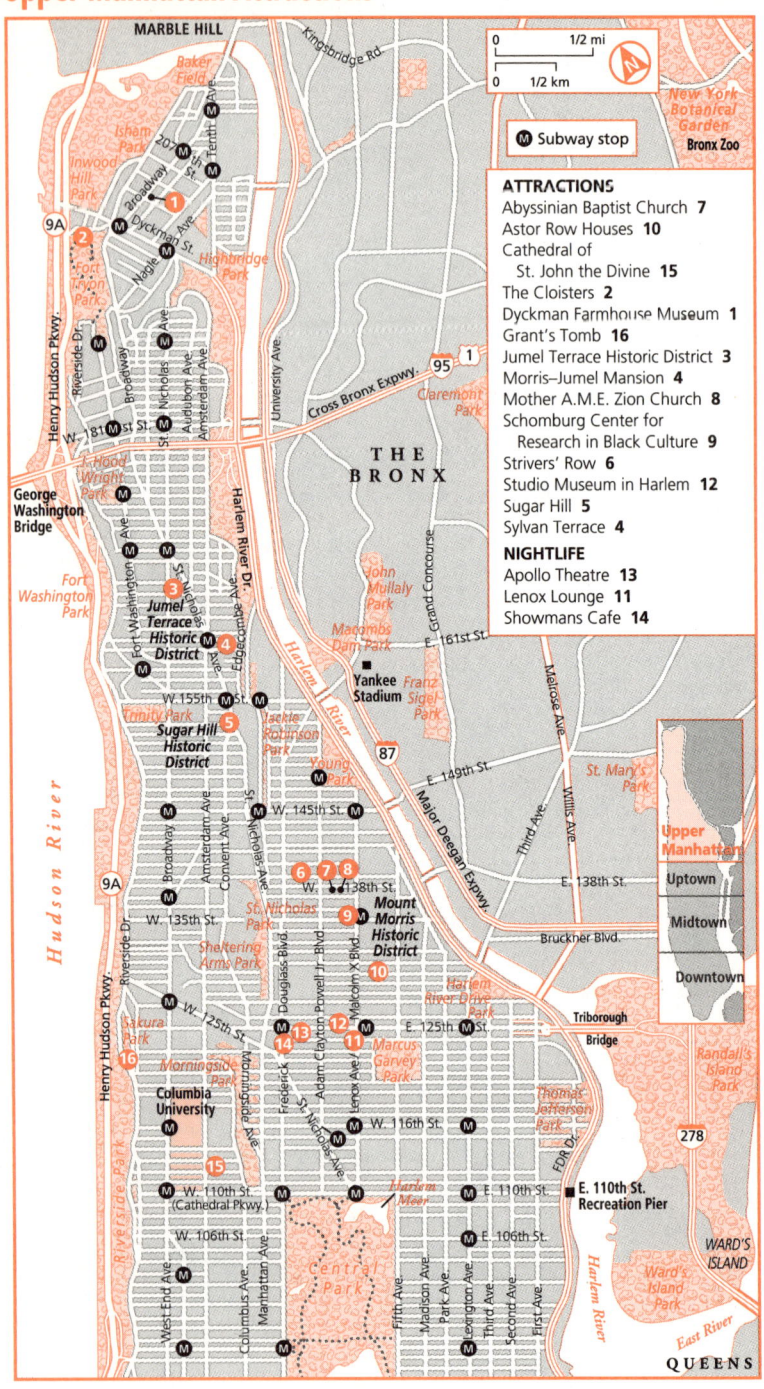

SIGHTS & ATTRACTIONS BY NEIGHBORHOOD

New York Stock Exchange ★★ (p. 217)
St. Paul's Chapel (p. 242)
Skyscraper Museum (p. 234)
South Street Seaport & Museum (p. 235)
Staten Island Ferry ★★ (p. 214)
Statue of Liberty ★★★ (p. 215)
Trinity Church (p. 241)
U.S. Customs House (p. 232)
Wall Street ★★ (p. 217)
Woolworth Building ★ (p. 239)
World Trade Center site (Ground Zero) (p. 219)

MIDTOWN EAST

Chrysler Building ★★ (p. 236)
Dahesh Museum of Art (p. 221)
Empire State Building ★★★ (p. 209)
Grand Central Terminal ★ (p. 210)
Japan Society (p. 226)
Lever House (p. 236)
Morgan Library ★★ (p. 228)
New York Public Library ★★ (p. 238)
New York Transit Museum, Gallery Annex (p. 261)
St. Patrick's Cathedral (p. 241)
Scandinavia House: The Nordic Center in America (p. 234)
Seagram Building (p. 236)
Sony Building (p. 236)
Sony Wonder Technology Lab (p. 257)
United Nations (p. 239)

Whitney Museum of American Art at Philip Morris (p. 236)

SOHO

Children's Museum of the Arts (p. 256)
Museum for African Art (p. 264)
New Museum of Contemporary Art ★ (p. 232)
New York City Fire Museum ★ (p. 233)

TIMES SQUARE & MIDTOWN WEST

American Craft Museum ★ (p. 218)
American Folk Art Museum ★★ (new location; p. 218)
Broadway City ★ (p. 257)
Bryant Park ★ (p. 248)
Circle Line Sightseeing Cruises ★★ (p. 250)
International Center of Photography ★ (p. 223)
Intrepid Sea-Air-Space Museum (p. 224)
Lazer Park (p. 257)
Madame Tussaud's New York (p. 227)
Madison Square Garden (p. 266)
Museum of Modern Art ★ (p. 263)
Museum of Television & Radio (p. 229)
Radio City Music Hall (p. 213)
Rockefeller Center ★★ (p. 212)

Tips Advance Planning Tip

If you're planning your sightseeing itinerary around specific attractions, make sure they'll be open while you're in town. While the majority of city attractions have devised post-9/11 security plans and settled back into regular hours, public access, open hours, or programming schedules can change at any time. This is also a good way to check current programming, such as museum schedules, and prioritize your time—there will always be more to see and do than you'll have time for.

Also, if you're planning on hitting many major attractions while you're in town, consider buying the **CityPass**, which can save you fully half on regular admission to such attractions as the Museum of Natural History, the Empire State Building, and others; see p. 27 for details.

Tips Alert: Lower Manhattan Subway Access Update

At this writing, Lower Manhattan subway service had largely been restored, with the **1/9 line** south of Chambers Street to South Ferry being the chief exception. (No. 1 trains were following the 2/3 express line to Brooklyn south of Chambers St., and 9 service was suspended.)

We have maintained all traditional references to 1/9 local service to South Ferry, however, because 1/9 service is scheduled to be restored (with the exception of the Cortlandt St. station) in autumn 2002. But anything can happen in the interim, so I strongly recommend you check with the **Metropolitan Transit Authority** at ⓒ **718/330-1234** or **www.mta.nyc.ny.us** before you plan your travel routes; your hotel concierge or any token-booth clerk should also be able to assist you.

UPPER EAST SIDE
Asia Society (p. 220)
Central Park ★★★ (p. 242)
Central Park Zoo ★ (p. 246)
Cooper-Hewitt National Design Museum ★ (p. 221)
El Museo del Barrio (p. 222)
The Frick Collection ★★ (p. 223)
Guggenheim Museum ★ (p. 213)
The Jewish Museum (p. 226)
Metropolitan Museum of Art ★★★ (p. 211)
Mount Vernon Hotel Museum & Garden (p. 228)
Museum of the City of New York (p. 229)
National Academy of Design (p. 232)
Neue Galerie New York (p. 232)
92nd Street Y ★ (p. 250 and p. 313)
Temple Emanu-El (p. 241)
Tisch Children's Zoo (p. 246)
Whitney Museum of American Art ★★ (p. 217)

UPPER MANHATTAN
The Cloisters ★ (p. 220)

UPPER WEST SIDE
American Folk Art Museum, Eva and Morris Feld Gallery (p. 219)
American Museum of Natural History ★★★ (p. 206)
The Ansonia (p. 236)
Cathedral of St. John the Divine ★ (p. 240)
Central Park ★★★ (p. 242)
Children's Museum of Manhattan ★ (p. 256)
The Dakota (p. 236)
New-York Historical Society ★ (p. 233)
Rose Center for Earth and Space ★ (p. 206)
Wollman Rink ★ (p. 247)

OUTER BOROUGHS
THE BRONX
Bronx Zoo Wildlife Conservation Park ★★★ (p. 258)
Edgar Allan Poe Cottage (p. 238)
New York Botanical Garden ★ (p. 258)
Wave Hill ★ (p. 259)
Yankee Stadium (p. 266)

BROOKLYN
Brooklyn Botanic Garden ★ (p. 260)
Brooklyn Bridge ★★ (p. 208)
Brooklyn Heights Historic District ★ (p. 262)
Brooklyn Museum of Art ★★ (p. 260)
Brooklyn Tabernacle ★ (p. 260)
Coney Island (p. 266)
Grand Army Plaza (p. 260)
New York Aquarium (p. 261)

New York Transit Museum
  (p. 261)
Prospect Park ⭐⭐ (p. 262)

QUEENS
American Museum of the Moving
  Image ⭐ (p. 263)
Flushing Meadows–Corona Park
  (p. 257)
Isamu Noguchi Garden Museum
  ⭐ (p. 264)

MoMA QNS ⭐ (p. 211)
New York Hall of Science ⭐
  (p. 257)
P.S. 1 Contemporary Art Center
  (p. 264)
Queens Museum of Art (p. 265)
Shea Stadium (p. 265)
Socrates Sculpture Park (p. 265)

2 Suggested Itineraries

If you're a first-time visitor and you'd like a blueprint with which to begin planning your time, consider the following game plan.

Day 1 Start your day off just like the city itself did: At Manhattan's southern tip, New York's oldest precinct. Leave early to catch the first ferry to the **Statue of Liberty** ⭐⭐⭐ and **Ellis Island** ⭐⭐. This will occupy your morning.

Once back on the mainland, pop over to the downtown **TKTS booth** at South Street Seaport (the line is usually shorter than at Times Sq.) to pick up some half-price tickets for a **Broadway** or **Off-Broadway show** (something's always available for the evening, or tomorrow afternoon if you prefer a matinee).

After lunch, you might want to see **Ground Zero.** (Whether the temporary viewing platform at Broadway and Fulton St. will be up while you're in town was not clear at press time; call the NYCVB at © **212/484-1222** or visit www.nycvisit.com for the latest.) You can also pay your respects to the victims of the WTC attack in waterfront **Battery Park** ⭐⭐, where the bronze sphere that stood on the World Trade Center plaza between the Twin Towers now stands, bearing its war wounds, as a temporary memorial to the victims of 9/11.

Or, hop the subway to Brooklyn (the A/C line will whisk you from Manhattan to High St. in minutes) and stroll back to the 212 area code over the **Brooklyn Bridge** ⭐⭐, which offers my favorite view of the Manhattan skyline.

Or use the time to enjoy one of Lower Manhattan's many historic or cultural attractions, such as the moving **Museum of Jewish Heritage—a Living Memorial to the Holocaust** ⭐; surprisingly diminutive **Wall Street** ⭐⭐; or the **National Museum of the American Indian,** housed in the stunning 1907 beaux-arts **U.S. Customs House,** worth a visit for the architecture alone.

Head back to your hotel to freshen up so you can enjoy a leisurely pre-theater dinner. If you've chosen a Broadway show, make time before or afterwards to feel the pulse of nighttime in **Times Square.**

Day 2 Spend most of the day at one of the big museums like the **Metropolitan Museum of Art** ⭐⭐⭐ or the **American Museum of Natural History** ⭐⭐⭐. You could spend a week at either, so you might want to take a Highlights Tour. Don't miss the new Harrison Ford–narrated Space Show at the Natural History Museum's **Rose Center for Earth and Space** ⭐.

After you've had enough museumgoing (you'll give out before you exhaust these collections), head into **Central Park** ⭐⭐⭐; both museums sit right on its fringe. If you still have some energy left, you might stroll out of the south end to do a bit of window-shopping on **Fifth Avenue.** Plan on dinner at one of the city's ethnic enclaves (see chapter 6 for recommendations).

Day 3 Start with the 3-hour **Circle Line Sightseeing Cruise**, which circumnavigates Manhattan and offers a fascinating perspective on the island. In the afternoon, explore one or two of the downtown neighborhoods—perhaps the cast-iron canyons of **SoHo,** the 19th-century streets of **Greenwich Village,** or exotic **Chinatown.** Walk the thoroughfares, poke your head into shops, or sit at a cafe and watch the world go by. If you prefer to have a guide, schedule a **guided walking tour** (see "Affordable Sightseeing Tours," later in this chapter).

Stay downtown for the evening, catching dinner in a stylish (or authentically old-world) restaurant and following up with some out-on-the-town time, perhaps in a live-music or comedy venue, a dance club, a hipper-than-thou cocktail lounge, or a neighborhood tavern (see chapter 9 for recommendations). Or, if you've had enough of downtown, head up to Harlem to catch a soul-food dinner at legendary **Sylvia's** and some smooth jazz at the **Lenox Lounge.**

Day 4 Head to **Rockefeller Center** to start your day with Matt and Katie outside the *Today* show studio, or to score standby tickets for Conan O'Brien. Make your way to the **Empire State Building** to see the view from the 86th-floor of New York's ultimate landmark skyscraper.

Once you're done, head to **Grand Central Terminal** (a pleasant walk on a nice day) to admire the marvelous beaux-arts monument to modern transportation and have lunch. Head for the subterranean **food concourse,** which boasts a wealth of wallet-friendly full-service and casual options (see chapter 6).

Spend the afternoon browsing one or two of the smaller museums—maybe the **Morgan Library**, the *Intrepid* **Sea-Air-Space Museum,** the **Frick Collection**, or the **Whitney.** Afterwards, enjoy another evening at the theater, or, if it's summer, catch one of the city's free alfresco entertainment events (see chapter 9). Or catch a **baseball game;** the Yankees or the Mets are likely to be in residence (sometimes both), and cheap seats aren't usually hard to score.

Day 5 Use the morning to explore one of the major attractions you've missed thus far. If you spent day 2 at the Met, spend today at the **American Museum of Natural History**. Or go see Frank Lloyd Wright's iconic **Guggenheim Museum**. Tour that nerve center of international relations, the **United Nations.** Or, if you haven't seen **Central Park** yet, go now.

After lunch, take stock: What haven't you done yet that you don't want to miss? What do you want to do more of? Perhaps a bit of shopping (see chapter 8), or a visit to a museum that focuses on your interests, such as the **International Center of Photography**, the **American Craft Museum**, or the **Museum of Television & Radio.** You're becoming a pro at exploring the city by now, so take the bull by the horns and make the most of your afternoon.

In the evening, celebrate the end of a great vacation with some live music. Splurge on a night of jazz at one of the Big Apple's legendary clubs, or take in a night of laughs at one of the city's comedy clubs, such as the **Comedy Cellar.** If you're the party type, don your glad rags and dance the night away at one of the city's outrageous clubs. No matter what you choose, make it a night to remember!

3 The Top Attractions

In addition to the choices below, don't forget **Central Park**, the great green swath that is, by virtue of its existence, New York City's greatest marvel. Central Park is so big and multifaceted that it earns its own section (p. 242).

American Museum of Natural History This is one of the hottest museum tickets in town, thanks to the $210 million **Rose Center for Earth and**

Space ⭐, whose planetarium sphere hosts the show "Are We Alone?"—the most technologically advanced sky show on the planet. Prepare to be blown away. The show is short—less than a half-hour—but phenomenal. **Buy your tickets in advance** in order to guarantee admission (they're available online); you can also buy tickets in advance for a specific IMAX film or exhibition, such as the Butterfly Conservatory (see below), which I recommend, especially during peak seasons and for weekend visits; otherwise, you might miss out.

Start your tour of the museum at the Rose Center. Afterwards, follow the Cosmic Pathway, which spirals around the sphere and down to the main level, chronicling the 15-billion-year evolution of the universe. (The sphere itself is used to create a point-of-reference scale that puts the universe into better perspective.) Other must-sees include the Big Bang Theater, which re-creates the birth of the universe; the Hall of the Universe, with its very own 15½-ton meteorite; and the Hall of Planet Earth, which focuses on the geologic processes of our home planet (great volcano display!). All in all, you'll need at least 2 hours to fully explore the Rose Center. *Tip:* Friday night is a great time to plan your visit, as the center isn't overcrowded, live jazz and food fills the Hall of the Universe, and, bathed in blue light, the sphere looks magical.

The rest of the 4-square-block museum is nothing to sneeze at. Founded in 1869, it houses the world's greatest natural-science collection in a group of buildings made of towers and turrets, pink granite, and red brick overflowing with neo-Gothic charm. The diversity is astounding: some 36 million specimens ranging from microscopic organisms to the world's largest cut gem, the Brazilian Princess Topaz (21,005 carats). If you don't have a lot of time, you can see the best of the best on free **Highlights Tours** offered daily every hour at 15 minutes after the hour from 10:15am to 3:15pm. Free daily **Spotlight Tours,** thematic tours that change monthly, are also offered; stop by an information desk for the schedule. **Audio Expeditions,** high-tech audio tours that allow you to access narration in the order you choose, are available to help you make sense of it all.

If you only see one exhibit, see the **dinosaurs** ⭐, on the fourth floor. Start in the **Orientation Room,** where a video gives an overview of the 500 million years of evolutionary history that led to you. Continue to the **Vertebrate Origins Room,** where models of ancient fish and turtles hang overhead, with plenty of interactive exhibits and kid-level displays to keep young minds fascinated. Next come the great **dinosaur halls,** with mammoth, spectacularly reconstructed skeletons and more interactive displays. **Mammals and Their Extinct Relatives** brings what you've learned in the previous halls home, showing how yesterday's prehistoric monsters have evolved into today's modern animals.

The **Hall of Biodiversity** is an impressive multimedia exhibit, but its doom-and-gloom story about the future of rain forests and other natural habitats might be too much for the little ones. Kids 5 and older should head to the **Discovery Room,** with lots of hands-on exhibits and experiments. (Be prepared, Mom and Dad; there seems to be a gift shop filled with fuzzy stuffed animals at every turn.)

I'm thrilled to report that the outmoded **Hall of Ocean Life** is getting a much-needed face-lift, and should reopen in 2003. In the meantime, the **animal habitat dioramas** and **halls of peoples** seem dated but still have something to teach (that's especially true of the Native American halls); these may also be in the process of piecemeal renovation while you're in town. The **IMAX Theater** was also getting an overhaul at press time, but will reopen well before you arrive; it shows films on a four-story screen that puts you right in the heart of the action.

The museum excels at **special exhibitions,** so check to see what's on while you're in town. The **Butterfly Conservatory**, a walk-in enclosure housing nearly 500 free-flying tropical butterflies, has developed into a can't-miss fixture from October through May; check to see if it's in the house while you're in town.

Central Park W. (btwn 77th and 81st sts.). **212/769-5100** for information, or 212/769-5200 for tickets (tickets can also be ordered online). www.amnh.org. Suggested admission $10 adults, $7.50 seniors and students, $6 children 2–12. Space Show and museum admission $19 adults, $14 seniors and students, $11.50 children under 12. Additional charges for IMAX movies and some special exhibitions. Daily 10am–5:45pm; Rose Center open Fri to 8:45pm. Subway: B, C to 81st St.; 1, 9 to 79th St.

Brooklyn Bridge ★★ *Moments* Its Gothic-inspired stone pylons and steel-cable webs have moved poets like Walt Whitman and Hart Crane to sing the praises of this great span, the first to connect Manhattan to Brooklyn. Begun in 1867 and completed in 1883, the beautiful Brooklyn Bridge is the city's best-known symbol of the age of growth that seized the city during the late 19th century. Walk across the bridge and imagine the awe that New Yorkers felt at seeing two boroughs joined by this monumental span. It's still astounding.

Designed by John Roebling, this massive engineering feat was plagued by death and disaster. Roebling was fatally injured in 1869 when a ferry rammed a waterfront piling. His son, Washington, who was subsequently put in charge, contracted the bends in 1872 working underwater, and oversaw the rest of the construction with a telescope from his bed at the edge of the East River (his wife relayed his instructions to the workers). Washington refused to attend the 1883 opening ceremonies, having had a bitter disagreement with the company that financed the construction. Though it was declared the "eighth wonder of the world" upon its completion, the bridge's troubles were not over: Twelve pedestrians were killed in a stampede when a rumor of its imminent collapse spread like wildfire on the day it opened. Things are usually calmer now.

Walking the Bridge: This is one of my all-time favorite New York activities, although there's no doubt that the Lower Manhattan views from the bridge now have a painful resonance. A wide wood-plank pedestrian walkway is elevated above the traffic, making it a relatively peaceful, and popular, walk. It's a great vantage point from which to contemplate the New York skyline.

There's a sidewalk entrance on Park Row, just across from City Hall Park (take the 4, 5, or 6 train to Brooklyn Bridge/City Hall). But why do this walk *away* from Manhattan? For Manhattan skyline views, take an A or C train to High Street, one stop into Brooklyn. From there, you'll be on the bridge in no time: Come above ground, then walk through the little park to Cadman Plaza East and head downslope (left) to the stairwell that will take you up to the foot-path. (Following Prospect Place under the bridge, turning right onto Cadman Plaza E., will also take you directly to the stairwell.) It's about a 20- to 40-minute stroll over the bridge to Manhattan (there are benches along the way). The foot-path will deposit you right at City Hall Park.

If you'd like to extend this walk a bit, I highly recommend pairing it with a quick tour of Brooklyn Heights and its wonderful promenade; see "Highlights of the Outer Boroughs" (p. 258) for exact directions.

Subway: A, C to High St.; 4, 5, 6 to Brooklyn Bridge–City Hall.

Ellis Island ★★ The restored Ellis Island opened in 1990, north of Liberty Island. Roughly 40% of Americans (myself included) can trace their heritage back to an ancestor who came through here. For the 62 years when it was America's main entry point for immigrants (1892–1954), Ellis Island processed some 12 million people. The greeting was often brusque—especially in the early years when as many as 12,000 came through in a single day. The **Immigration Museum** skillfully relates the story of Ellis Island and immigration in America by placing the emphasis on personal experience.

It's difficult to leave the museum unmoved. Today you enter the Main Building's baggage room, just as the immigrants did, and then climb the stairs to the **Registry Room,** with its vaulted tiled ceiling, where millions waited anxiously for medical and legal processing. A step-by-step account of the immigrants' voyage is detailed in the exhibit, with haunting photos and oral histories. What might be the most poignant exhibit is **"Treasures from Home,"** 1,000 objects and photos donated by descendants of immigrants, including family heirlooms, religious articles, and clothing and jewelry. Outside, the **American Immigrant Wall of Honor** commemorates the names of more than 500,000 immigrants and their families, from Myles Standish to Jay Leno. You can research your own family's history at the **American Family Immigration History Center;** start your research at home at www.ellisislandrecords.org. You might also make time to see the award-winning short film *Island of Hope, Island of Tears,* which plays on a continuous loop in two theaters. Short live performances are also often part of the day's events.

Touring Tips: Ferries run daily to Ellis Island and Liberty Island from Battery Park and Liberty State Park (in New Jersey) at frequent intervals; see the Statue of Liberty listing (p. 215) for details.

In New York Harbor. © 212/363-3200 (general info), or 212/269-5755 (ticket/ferry info). www.nps.gov/elis or www.ellisisland.org. Free admission (ferry ticket charge). Daily 9:30am–5pm (last ferry departs around 3:30pm). For subway and ferry details, see the Statue of Liberty listing on p. 215 (ferry trip includes stops at both sights).

Empire State Building ★★★   It took 60,000 tons of steel, 10 million bricks, 2½ million feet of electrical wire, 120 miles of pipe, and 7 million man-hours to build. King Kong climbed it in 1933. A plane slammed into it in 1945. The World Trade Center superseded it in 1970 as the island's tallest building. On September 11, 2001, it regained its status as New York City's tallest building after 31 years of taking second place. And through it all, the Empire State Building has remained one of the city's favorite landmarks, and its signature high-rise. Completed in 1931, the limestone-and-stainless-steel streamline deco dazzler climbs 102 stories (1,454 ft./436m) and now harbors the offices of fashion firms, and, in its upper reaches, a jumble of broadcast equipment.

Always a conversation piece, the Empire State Building glows every night, bathed in colored floodlights to commemorate events of significance—red, white, and blue for Independence Day; green for St. Patrick's Day; red, black, and green for Martin Luther King Day; blue and white for Hanukkah; even lavender and white for Gay Pride Day (you can find a lighting schedule online). The silver spire can be seen from all over the city. My favorite view is from 23rd Street, where Fifth Avenue and Broadway converge. On a lovely day, stand at the base of the Flatiron Building (p. 237) and gaze up Fifth; the crisp, gleaming deco tower jumps out, soaring above the sooty office buildings that surround it.

But the views that keep nearly three million visitors coming every year are the ones from the 86th- and 102nd-floor **observatories.** The lower one is best—you can walk out on a windy deck and look through coin-operated viewers (bring quarters!) over what, on a clear day, can be as much as an 80-mile (129km) radius. The panorama is magnificent. The higher observation deck is glass-enclosed and cramped.

Light fog can create an admirably moody effect, but it goes without saying that a clear day is best. Dusk brings the most remarkable views and the biggest crowds. Consider going in the morning, when the light is still low on the horizon, keeping glare to a minimum. Starry nights are pure magic.

In your haste to go up, don't rush through the beautiful marble **lobby** without pausing to admire its features, which include a wonderful streamline mural.

Time-saving tip: If you don't mind spending about $1 more per ticket—you can avoid ticket lines by purchasing advance tickets online. It's money well spent in the busy seasons. Place your order well before you leave home.

350 Fifth Ave. (at 34th St.). © 212/736-3100. www.esbnyc.com. Observatory admission $10 adults, $9 seniors and children 12–17, $4 children 5–11, free for children under 5. Mon–Fri 10am–midnight; Sat–Sun 9:30am–midnight; tickets sold until 11:25pm. Subway: B, D, F, N, R, V, Q, W to 34th St.; 6 to 33rd St.

Grand Central Terminal ✯   Rededicated with appropriate pomp and circumstance in 1998, the 1913 landmark (designed by Warren & Wetmore with Reed & Stem) has been reborn as one of the most magnificent public spaces in the country. The restoration, by Beyer Blinder Belle, is an utter triumph. Their work has reanimated the genius of the station's original intent: to inspire those who pass through with feelings of civic pride and appreciation for Western architectural traditions. In short, they've put the "grand" back into Grand Central.

Come and visit, even if you're not catching the subway or Metro North trains. Even if you arrive and leave by subway, be sure to exit the station, walking a couple of blocks south, to about 40th Street, before you turn to admire Jules-Alexis Coutan's neoclassical sculpture *Transportation* over the south entrance, with a majestic Mercury, the Roman god of commerce and travel, as its central figure.

The greatest visual impact comes when you enter the vast **main concourse.** Cleaned of decades of grime and cheesy advertisements, it boasts renewed majesty. The high windows again allow sunlight to penetrate the space, glinting off the half-acre Tennessee marble floor. The brass clock over the central kiosk gleams, as do the gold- and nickel-plated chandeliers piercing the side archways. The **sky ceiling,** again a brilliant greenish blue, depicts the constellations of the winter sky above New York. They're lit with 59 stars, surrounded by 24-carat gold and emitting light fed through fiber-optic cables, their intensities replicating the magnitude of the stars as seen from Earth. Look its previous neglect. On the east end of the main concourse is a grand **marble staircase** where there had never been one before, but as the original plans had always intended.

This beaux-arts splendor serves as a hub of activity as well. New retail shops and restaurants have taken over the mezzanine and lower levels. Off the main concourse at street level, there's a mix of specialty shops and national retailers, as well as the truly grand **Grand Central Market** for gourmet foods (see chapter 8). The **New York Transit Museum Gallery Annex & Store,** in the shuttle passage, houses city transit-related exhibitions and a gift shop that's worth a look (see chapter 8). The **lower concourse** houses a food court that's a budget diner's delight, offering everything from bratwurst to New York–style cheesecake, as well as the famous **Oyster Bar & Restaurant** (© 212/490-6650).

The **Municipal Art Society** (© 212/935-3960; www.mas.org) offers a free walking tour of Grand Central Terminal on Wednesday at 12:30pm, which meets at the information booth on the Grand Concourse. The **Grand Central Partnership** (© 212/697-1245) runs its own free tour every Friday at 12:30pm, which meets in front of the Whitney Museum at Philip Morris gallery, at 42nd Street and Park Avenue. Call to confirm before you set out to meet either tour.

42nd St. at Park Ave. © 212/340-2210 (events hot line). www.grandcentralterminal.com. Subway: S, 4, 5, 6, 7 to 42nd St./Grand Central.

Metropolitan Museum of Art ★★★   The Metropolitan Museum of Art draws some five million people a year, more than any other attraction in the city. No wonder: this place is magnificent. At 1.6 million square feet (480,000 sq. m), this is the largest museum in the Western Hemisphere. Nearly all the world's cultures through the ages are on display—from Egyptian mummies to ancient Greek statuary to Islamic carvings to Renaissance paintings to Native American masks to 20th-century decorative arts—and masterpieces are the rule. You could go once a week for a lifetime and find something new on each visit.

So unless you plan on spending your entire vacation here (some people do), you cannot see the entire collection. My recommendation is to give it one good, long day. One way to get an overview is to take the **Museum Highlights Tour,** offered every day (usually 10:15am–3:15pm). Even some New Yorkers who've spent many hours in the museum could profit from this once-over. Visit the museum's website for a schedule of this and subject-specific walking tours (Old Master Paintings, American Period Rooms, Arts of China, Islamic Art, and so on); you can also get a schedule of the day's tours at the Visitor Services desk when you arrive. A daily schedule of free **Gallery Talks** is available as well.

The least overwhelming way to see the Met on your own is to pick up a map at the round desk in the entry hall and concentrate on what you like, whether it's 17th-century paintings, American furniture, or the art of the South Pacific. Highlights include the American Wing's **Garden Court,** with its 19th-century sculpture; the ground-level **Costume Hall;** and the **Frank Lloyd Wright room.** The beautifully renovated **Roman and Greek galleries** are overwhelming, but in a marvelous way, as is the collection of later **Chinese art.** The highlight of the **Egyptian collection** is the **Temple of Dendur,** in a dramatic, specially built glass-walled gallery with Central Park views. The **Greek Galleries,** which at last fully realize McKim, Mead & White's grand neoclassical plans of 1917, and the **Ancient Near East Galleries** are particularly of note. But it all depends on what your interests are. Don't forget the marvelous **special exhibitions,** which can range from "Jade in Ancient Costa Rica" to "Cubism and Fashion."

To purchase tickets for concerts and lectures, call © **212/570-3949** (Mon–Sat 9:30am–5pm). The roof garden is worth visiting from spring to autumn, offering peaceful views over Central Park and the city.

Money-saving tip: The Met's medieval collections are housed in Upper Manhattan at the **Cloisters** ★ (p. 220); admission is included with your Met ticket purchase, but seeing both satisfactorily in a single day is more than only the most die-hard budget travelers should try to accomplish. If you're committed to seeing both on one ticket, start at the Cloisters at opening time on a Friday or Saturday (the Met's extended-hour days, so you can maximize your time), then move downtown to the main museum in the afternoon.

Fifth Ave. at 82nd St. © 212/535-7710. www.metmuseum.org. Admission (includes same-day entrance to the Cloisters) $10 adults, $5 seniors and students, free for children under 12 when accompanied by an adult. Sun and Tues–Thurs 9:30am–5:30pm; Fri–Sat 9:30am–9pm. No strollers allowed Sun (back carriers available at 81st St. entrance coat-check area). Subway: 4, 5, 6 to 86th St.

Museum of Modern Art/MoMA QNS ★   The Museum of Modern Art (or MoMA, as it's called) boasts the world's greatest collection of painting and sculpture from the late 19th century to the present, everything from Monet's *Water Lilies* and Klimt's *The Kiss* to masterworks by Frida Kahlo, Edward Hopper,

Andy Warhol, Robert Rauschenberg, and others. Top that off with an extensive collection of drawings, photography, architectural models and modern furniture, iconic design objects ranging from tableware to sports cars, and film and video (including the world's largest collection of D. W. Griffith films), and you have quite a museum. If you're into modernism, this is the place to be.

Here's the Bad News: MoMA will be closed while you're in town. The museum is undergoing a $650 million renovation of its West 53rd Street building under the guidance of Japanese architect Yoshio Taniguchi that will double the exhibit space when the project is complete, which won't be until 2005.

Here's the Good News: The museum has opened temporary exhibit space called **MoMA QNS** in the old Swingline stapler factory in Long Island City. The spectacularly renovated 45,000-square-foot gallery will exhibit highlights of the collection, among them van Gogh's *Starry Night,* Picasso's *Les Demoiselles d'Avignon,* and Warhol's *Gold Marilyn Monroe.* Workshops, a limited program schedule, and special exhibitions will also be part of the fun: Spring 2003 will showcase masterworks by Matisse and Picasso, while summer visitors can expect an exhibit of Ansel Adams photographs.

Yes—it's definitely worth a short subway ride to Queens. Getting there is quick and easy; in fact, from Midtown, you can be here quicker than you can get to the Village. Also consider visiting the MoMA affiliate **P.S. 1 Contemporary Art Center** (p. 264), also in Long Island City, while you're here. You might consider making a day of it: The **Queens Artlink** (www.moma.org/qal) is a free weekend arts shuttle, running Saturday and Sunday from 11:30am to 5:30pm and linking five top-flight art institutions in the area, including MoMA QNS, P.S. 1, the **Isamu Noguchi Garden Museum** (p. 264), the **American Museum of the Moving Image** (p. 263), and the **Socrates Sculpture Park** (p. 265).

45-20 33rd St., Long Island City, Queens. 212/708-9400. www.moma.org. Admission $12 adults, $8.50 seniors and students, free for children under 16 accompanied by an adult; pay what you wish Fri 4:30–8:15pm. Sat–Tues and Thurs 10:30am–5:45pm; Fri 10:30am–8:15pm. Subway: 7 to 33rd St. (MoMA QNS is across the st.).

Rockefeller Center *Moments* A streamline masterpiece, Rockefeller Center is one of New York's central gathering spots. A prime example of the city's skyscraper spirit, it was erected in the 1930s, when the city was deep in the Depression as well as its most passionate Art Deco phase. Designated a National Historic Landmark in 1988, it's the world's largest privately owned business-and-entertainment center, with 18 buildings on 21 acres.

For a dramatic approach to the entire complex, start at Fifth Avenue between 49th and 50th streets. The builders purposely created the gentle slope of the Promenade, known here as the **Channel Gardens** because it's flanked to the south by La Maison Française and to the north by the British Building. You'll also find a number of shops along here, including a branch of the **Metropolitan Museum of Art Store,** a good stop for elegant gifts (some quite affordable). The

---

Moments Evening Events at the Met

On **Friday and Saturday evenings,** the Met remains open for art viewing and cocktails in the Great Hall Balcony Bar (5–8pm) and live classical music. A slate of after-hours programs (gallery talks, tours) changes by the week; call for schedule. The restaurant stays open until 10pm (last reservation at 8:30pm); dinner is usually accompanied by piano music.

THE TOP ATTRACTIONS 213

> **Tips Avoiding the Crowds at Big Apple Museums**
>
> Many of the city's top museums—including the Natural History Museum, the Met, the Guggenheim, and the Whitney—have late hours on Friday and/or Saturday nights. Take advantage of them. You'll largely have the place to yourself by 5 or 6pm—which, in most cases, leaves you hours left to explore, unfettered by crowds or screaming kids.

Promenade leads to the **Lower Plaza,** home to the famous ice-skating rink and alfresco dining in summer in the shadow of Paul Manship's gilded bronze statue *Prometheus.* All around the flags of the United Nations' member countries flap in the breeze. Just behind *Prometheus,* in December and early January, towers the city's majestic official Christmas tree.

The **Rink at Rockefeller Plaza** (© 212/332-7654; www.rockefeller center.com) is tiny but romantic, especially during the holidays, when the Christmas tree's lights twinkle. It's open mid-October to mid-March, and you'll skate under the tree from early December through the holiday season.

The focal point of this "city within a city" is the **GE Building**, at 30 Rockefeller Plaza, a 70-story showpiece. It's still one of the city's most impressive buildings; walk through for a look at the granite-and-marble lobby, lined with sepia-toned murals by José Maria Sert. You can pick up a walking tour brochure highlighting the center's art and architecture at the main information desk. **NBC** maintains studios throughout the complex. Shows like *Saturday Night Live, Dateline NBC,* and *Late Night with Conan O'Brien* originate in the GE Building (see "Talk of the Town: Free TV Tapings," on p. 253, for tips on getting tickets). NBC's ***Today*** **show** is broadcast live on weekdays from 7 to 10am from the glass-enclosed studio on the corner of 49th Street and Rockefeller Plaza; come early if you want a visible spot, and bring your HI MOM! sign.

The 70-minute **NBC Studio Tour** (© 212/664-3700; www.nbcsuper store.com) will take you behind the scenes, but it's not worth the expenditure for wallet-watching budget travelers ($17.50 adults, $15 for seniors and kids 6–16). If you're committed to the notion, you can reserve your tickets for either tour in advance or buy them right up to tour time at the **NBC Experience** store, on Rockefeller Plaza at 49th Street.

Other notable buildings include the **International Building,** on Fifth Avenue between 50th and 51st streets, worth a look for its Atlas statue; and the **McGraw-Hill Building,** on Sixth Avenue between 48th and 49th streets, with its 50-foot (15m) sun triangle on the plaza. Designed by Donald Deskey, the restored **Radio City Music Hall**, 1260 Sixth Ave., at 50th Street (© 212/247-4777; www.radiocity.com), is one of the city's largest indoor theaters, with 6,200 seats, but its true grandeur derives from its Art Deco appointments. From the distant seats, the stage's proscenium arch evokes a faraway sun setting on the horizon. The men's and women's lounges are also splendid. The theater hosts the annual **Christmas Spectacular,** starring the Rockettes. The 1-hour **Stage Door Tour,** offered Monday through Saturday, is $16 for adults, $10 for children under 12.

Btwn 48th and 50th sts., from Fifth to Sixth aves. © 212/332-6868. www.rockefellercenter.com. Subway: B, D, F, V to 47th–50th sts./Rockefeller Center.

Solomon R. Guggenheim Museum
It's been called a bun, a snail, a concrete tornado, and even a giant wedding cake. Whatever descriptive you choose,

Frank Lloyd Wright's only New York building, completed in 1959, is best summed up as a brilliant work of architecture—so brilliant that it competes with the art for your attention. If you're looking for the city's best modern art, head to MoMA or the Whitney first; come to the Guggenheim to see the house.

It's easy to see the bulk of what's on display in 2 to 4 hours. Inside, a spiraling rotunda circles over a slowly inclined ramp that leads you past changing exhibits. Usually the progression is counterintuitive: from the first floor up, rather than from the sixth floor down. Permanent exhibits of 19th- and 20th-century art, including Kandinsky, Klee, Picasso, and French Impressionists, occupy a stark annex called the **Tower Galleries,** an addition accessible at every level that some critics claimed made the original look like a toilet bowl backed by a water tank (judge for yourself—I think there may be something to that).

The Guggenheim runs some special programs, including free daily docent-led **tours,** lectures, family films, avant-garde screenings for grown-ups, curator-led gallery tours on select Friday afternoons, and the **World Beat Jazz Series,** which resounds through the rotunda on Friday and Saturday from 5 to 8pm.

1071 Fifth Ave. (at 88th St.). 212/423-3500. www.guggenheim.org. Admission $12 adults, $8 seniors and students, free for children under 12; pay as you wish Fri 6–8pm. Sun–Wed 9am–6pm; Fri–Sat 9am–8pm. Subway: 4, 5, 6 to 86th St.

Staten Island Ferry ★★ *Value* Here's New York's best freebie—especially if you just want to glimpse the Statue of Liberty and not climb her steps. You get an hour-long excursion (round-trip) into the world's biggest harbor. This is not strictly a sightseeing ride but commuter transportation to and from Staten Island (remember Melanie Griffith in *Working Girl?*). During business hours you'll share the boat with working stiffs reading papers and drinking coffee, blissfully unaware of the sights outside.

You, however, should go on deck and enjoy the busy harbor traffic. The old orange-and-green boats usually have open decks along the sides or at the bow and stern; try to catch one of these boats if you can, because the newer white boats don't have decks. Grab a seat on the right side of the boat for the best view. On the way out of Manhattan, you'll pass the Statue of Liberty, Ellis Island, and from the left side of the boat, Governor's Island; you'll see the Verrazano Narrows Bridge spanning the distance from Brooklyn to Staten Island in the distance.

Tips **Lady Liberty Touring Updates**

At press time, **only the grounds of Liberty Island were open to the public.** Whether and when the pedestal, museum, and/or the body of the statue itself will reopen was unknown at this writing, but the close-up view from the grounds is breathtaking enough to make the journey worthwhile.

If the statue does reopen, be sure to arrive by noon if your heart's set on experiencing everything. And keep in mind that, for the last few years, the National Park Service has instituted a "crown" policy during the peak **summer** season: Visitors who want to walk up to the crown must be on one of the **first two ferries of the day.** At other times, you must be on line to climb to the crown by 2pm; otherwise, you will not be allowed up.

These and all policies regarding access to the Statue of Liberty and Ellis Island are subject to change at any time. *Please* call or check the website **(www.nps.gov/stli)** for the latest access information.

When the boat arrives at St. George, Staten Island, everyone must disembark. Follow the boat-loading sign on your right as you get off; you'll circle around to the next loading dock. It's all well worth the time spent.

Departs from the Whitehall Ferry Terminal at the southern tip of Manhattan. © 718/815-BOAT. www.ci.nyc.ny.us/html/dot. Free admission ($3 for car transport on select ferries). 24 hr.; every 20–30 min. weekdays, less frequently off-peak and weekend hours. Subway: N, R to Whitehall St.; 4, 5 to Bowling Green; 1, 9 to South Ferry (ride in 1 of the 1st 5 cars).

Statue of Liberty ★★★ *Kids*   For the millions who came by ship to America in the last century—as tourists or immigrants—Lady Liberty, standing in the Upper Bay, was their first glimpse of America. No monument so embodies the nation's, and the world's, notion of freedom and economic potential. Even if you don't make it to Liberty Island, you can get a glimpse from Battery Park, from the New Jersey side of the bay, or from the Staten Island Ferry (see above).

Proposed by French statesman Edouard de Laboulaye as a gift from France to the United States commemorating the two nations' friendship, the statue was designed by sculptor Frédéric-Auguste Bartholdi with the help of Alexandre-Gustave Eiffel (of the famed Paris tower), and unveiled on October 28, 1886. Despite the fact that Joseph Pulitzer had to make a mighty effort to attract donations on this side of the Atlantic for her pedestal (designed by American Richard Morris Hunt), more than a million people watched as the French tricolor veil was pulled away. After nearly 100 years of wind, rain, and exposure to the harsh sea air, Lady Liberty received a successful $150 million face-lift in time for its centennial celebration on July 4, 1986. Feted in fireworks, Miss Liberty became more of a city icon than ever before.

Touring Tips: Ferries leave daily every half hour to 45 minutes from 9am to about 3:30pm (their clock), with more frequent ferries in the morning and extended hours in summer. Try to go early on a weekday to avoid the crowds that swarm in the afternoon, on weekends, and on holidays.

A stop at **Ellis Island** ★★ (p. 208) is included in the fare, but if you catch the last ferry, you can only visit the statue or Ellis Island, not both.

You can **buy ferry tickets in advance** via www.statueoflibertyferry.com, which will allow you to board the boat without standing in the ticket line; however, there is a service charge. Even if you've purchased tickets, arrive as much as 30 minutes before your desired ferry time to allow for increased security procedures. The ferry ride takes about 20 minutes.

Once on Liberty Island, you'll start to get an idea of the statue's immensity: She weighs 225 tons and measures 152 feet (46m) from foot to flame. Her nose alone is 4½ feet (1.5m) long, and her index finger is 8 feet (2.5m) long.

Note that access to the statue itself was severely restricted at this writing; see "Lady Liberty Touring Updates" (below) for details.

If the statue does reopen to the public, you may have to wait as long as 3 hours to walk up into the crown. If it's summer, or you're not in shape, you may want to skip it: It's a grueling 354 steps (the equivalent of 22 stories) to the crown, or you can take the elevator the first 10 stories up (a shortcut I endorse). But even if you take the elevator, the interior is stifling once the temperature starts to climb. You don't have to go all the way up to the crown; there are **observation decks** at different levels, including one at the top of the pedestal that's reachable by elevator. Even if you don't go inside, a stroll around the base is an extraordinary experience, and the views of the Manhattan skyline are stellar.

On Liberty Island in New York Harbor. © **212/363-3200** (general info), or 212/269-5755 (ticket/ferry info). www.nps.gov/stli or www.statueoflibertyferry.com. Free admission; ferry ticket to Statue of Liberty and Ellis

What's Happening in Times Square

The writer O. Henry once observed "New York City will be a great place if they ever finish it." Indeed, no other city is so good at reinventing itself: Witness the "new" Times Square. The dust is settling on the epic renewal where Broadway meets 42nd Street; what was once the city's gritty heart is now the hub of its tourist-friendly rebirth.

The neon lights of Broadway are more dazzling than ever, now that ABC's *Good Morning America* has set up a street-facing studio at Broadway and 44th Street (across from **MTV**'s own); **NASDAQ**'s eight-story billboard—the world's largest video screen, at Broadway and 43rd—has joined the landscape, and World Wrestling Entertainment spent a mint restoring the landmark Paramount Building and installing a 47,500-square-foot entertainment complex, **WWE New York.** (Take note of the WWE's marquee: Between the restored historic scrollwork is a full-color sign that incorporates the latest in LED and fiber-optic technology.) A handful of upper-end new hotels in the heart of the action means that thousands more visitors can stay right on (or just off) the Great White Way—as long as they're willing to shell out big-time to do it.

Along with WWE New York, **ESPN Zone,** the freshly *NSync-funded **Planet Hollywood,** and **B.B. King Blues Club & Grill** all joined the Times Square pack in the 21st century, reinvigorating the notion of themed dining and nightlife (see "Theme Restaurant Thrills!" in chapter 6; chapter 9 for B.B. King's). The rockin' **Virgin Megastore** has a major presence (see chapter 8), as does **MTV,** which draws busloads of *Total Request Live* fans to Broadway and 45th Street every weekday afternoon, giving the entire square a welcome shot of youth appeal.

Forty-Second Street between Seventh and Eighth avenues, the former porn paradise, has been rebuilt from scratch as a family-oriented entertainment mecca. In addition to a spate of renovated theaters—including the **New Victory** (see "Kids Take the Stage: Family-Friendly Theater," in chapter 9), the **New Amsterdam** (home to *The Lion King*), and the former Selwyn, reinvented as the **American Airlines Theatre** and now home of the Roundabout Theater—the neon-bright block is chock-full with retail and amusements, including **Madame Tussaud's New York** (p. 227); the multilevel, state-of-the-art **Broadway City** video arcade; two 20-plus-screen movie complexes; and plenty of mall-familiar shopping and dining, including the **Museum Company,** a Yankees Clubhouse Shop (where you can purchase tickets), and **Chevy's Fresh Mex** and **Applebee's** restaurants. (Don't leave home without it, right?)

To quote the great Bart Simpson: *Ay carumba!*

Island $8 adults, $6 seniors, $3 children 3–17. Daily 9am–5pm (last ferry departs around 3:30pm); extended hours in summer. Subway: 4, 5 to Bowling Green; 1, 9 to South Ferry (note that 1, 9 had not resumed service to Lower Manhattan at press time). Walk south through Battery Park to Castle Clinton, the fort housing the ferry ticket booth.

Wall Street & the New York Stock Exchange ★★ *Value* Wall Street—it's an iconic name, and the world's prime hub for bulls and bears everywhere. This 18th-century lane (you'll be surprised at how little it is) is appropriately monumental, lined with neoclassical towers that reach as far skyward as the dreams of investors who built it into the world's most famous financial market.

At the heart of the action is the **New York Stock Exchange** (NYSE), the world's largest securities trader, where you can watch the billions change hands and get an idea of how the money merchants work. NYSE came into being in 1792, when merchants met daily under a buttonwood tree to pass off to each other the U.S. bonds that had been sold to fund the Revolutionary War. By 1903, they were trading stocks of publicly held companies in this Corinthian-columned beaux-arts "temple" designed by George Post. About 3,000 companies are listed on the exchange, trading nearly 314 billion shares valued at about $16 trillion. Until September 11, 2001, visitors could acquire free tickets to tour a small interactive museum and watch the action on the trading floor from the glass-lined, mezzanine-level observation gallery. However, the facility has been closed to the public since the terrorist attack. It was scheduled to reopen to the public sometime in 2002, but no date could be confirmed at this writing. Your best bet is to call to check the status—as well as the updated ticket procedure—before you arrive.

20 Broad St. (between Wall St. and Exchange Place). © 212/656-5165. www.nyse.com. Free admission. Mon–Fri 9am–4:30pm (ticket booth opens 8:45am). *Note that information may change when the facility reopens in 2002.* Subway: J, M, Z to Broad St.; 2, 3, 4, 5 to Wall St.

Whitney Museum of American Art ★★ Arguably the finest collection of 20th-century American art belongs to the Whitney thanks to the efforts of Gertrude Vanderbilt Whitney. A sculptor herself, she organized exhibitions by American artists shunned by traditional academies, assembled a sizable personal collection, and founded the museum in 1930 in Greenwich Village.

Today's museum is an imposing presence on Madison Avenue—an inverted three-tiered pyramid of concrete and gray granite with seven seemingly random windows designed by Marcel Breuer, a leader of the Bauhaus movement. The rotating permanent collection consists of a selection of major works by Edward Hopper, George Bellows, Georgia O'Keeffe, Roy Lichtenstein, Jasper Johns, and other significant artists. The second floor is devoted to works from its permanent collection from 1900 to 1950, while the rest is dedicated to rotating exhibits.

Shows are usually all well curated and more edgy than what you'd see at MoMA or the Guggenheim, though not as left-of-mainstream as what you'll find at the New Museum. Topics range from topical surveys, such as "American Art in the Age of Technology" and "The Warhol Look: Glamour Style Fashion," to in-depth retrospectives of famous or lesser-known movements (such as Fluxus, the movement that spawned Yoko Ono, among others) and artists (Mark Rothko, Keith Haring, Duane Hanson, Bob Thompson). The next **Whitney Biennial** is scheduled for spring 2004. Biennials serve as the premier launching pad for new American artists working on the vanguard in every media.

Free **gallery tours** are offered daily, and music, screenings, and lectures fill the calendar. The Whitney is also notable for having the best museum restaurant in town: **Sarabeth's at the Whitney,** worth a visit in its own right (see chapter 6).

For details on the **Whitney Museum of American Art at Philip Morris,** the petite Midtown annex, which you can visit for free, see p. 236.

945 Madison Ave. (at 75th St.). © 877/WHITNEY or 212/570-3676. www.whitney.org. Admission $10 adults, $8 seniors and students, free for children under 12; pay as you wish Fri 6–9pm. Tues–Thurs and Sat–Sun 11am–6pm; Fri 1–9pm. Subway: 6 to 77th St.

4 More Manhattan Museums

In 1978, New York's finest cultural institutions on Fifth Avenue from 82nd to 104th streets formed a consortium called **Museum Mile,** the name New York City gave to the stretch several years later. The "mile" begins at the **Metropolitan Museum of Art** ★★★ (see "The Top Attractions," above) and moves north to **El Museo del Barrio.** However, even the smallest museums require some time, so don't plan on just popping into a few as you stroll along. Your best bet is to head directly to the museum that's tops on your list, then proceed to your second choice if you have time. If you're heading to the Metropolitan, you'll only see a portion of the collection there in a full day.

For the **Brooklyn Museum of Art** ★★, the **New York Transit Museum,** the **American Museum of the Moving Image** ★, the **Queens Museum of Art,** the **Isamu Noguchi Garden Museum** ★, and the **P.S. 1 Contemporary Art Center,** see "Highlights of the Outer Boroughs" (p. 258).

If you're traveling with the kids, consider the museums listed under "Especially for Kids" (p. 256), which include the **Children's Museum of Manhattan** ★, the **Sony Wonder Technology Lab,** and the **New York Hall of Science** ★.

If you're interested in historic-house museums, see "In Search of Historic Homes" (p. 238).

Also, don't forget to see what's on at the monumental **New York Public Library** ★★, which regularly holds excellent free exhibitions; see p. 238.

American Craft Museum ★ *Finds* This small but pleasing museum is the nation's top showcase for contemporary crafts. The collection focuses on objects that are prime examples of form and function, ranging from jewelry to baskets to vessels to furniture. You'll see an emphasis on material as well as craft, whether it be fiber, ceramics, or metal. Exhibitions can range from expressionist clay sculpture to bookbinding, and celebrate movements (such as "Memories of Murano: American Glass Artists in Venice") or single artisans ("Elegant Fantasy: The Jewelry of Arline Fisch," Sept 2002–Jan 5, 2003).

40 W. 53rd St. (btwn Fifth and Sixth aves.). © 212/956-3535. www.americancraftmuseum.org. Admission $7.50 adults, $4 students and seniors, free for children under 12; pay as you wish Thurs 6–8pm. Tues–Wed and Fri–Sun 10am–6pm; Thurs 10am–8pm. Subway: E, V to Fifth Ave.

American Folk Art Museum ★★ New Yorkers can't stop raving about the brand-new home of the American Folk Art Museum. Designed by Tod Williams Billie Tsien Architects this ultramodern boutique museum has been called no less than the city's greatest new museum and best work of architecture since the Guggenheim by *House & Garden,* while *New York* magazine called it "brilliant" and "a tour de force." Not only is it a stunning structure, but it also heralds American folk art into the top echelon of museum-worthy art.

The new building quadruples the museum's exhibit space to 30,000 square feet. The modified open-plan interior features an extraordinary collection of traditional works from the 18th century to those of self-taught artists and craftspeople of the present. A splendid variety of quilts, in particular, makes the textiles collection the museum's most popular. Look for "American Anthem Part II: Masterworks from the Permanent Collection," the largest installation of its kind that the museum has ever mounted, through December 2002. The gift-and-book shop is outstanding, filled with one-of-a-kind objects.

Moments: Paying Your Respects at Ground Zero

The World Trade Center dominated Lower Manhattan. The complex occupied 16 acres, and its 12 million square feet (3.6 million sq. m) of office space housed hundreds of firms. About 50,000 people worked there, and some 70,000 others (tourists and businesspeople) visited each day. The complex included, in addition to two 110-story towers—one of which rewarded visitors with breathtaking views from the Top of the World observation deck, more than 1,350 feet (405m) in the air—five additional buildings (including a hotel), a plaza rich with outdoor sculpture, a shopping mall, and a full slate of restaurants, including the spectacular Windows on the World, the city's ultimate special-occasion restaurant.

Then the first plane hit Tower 1, at 8:45am on Tuesday, September 11, 2001. By 10:30am, it was all gone, along with nearly 3,000 people.

We've all seen the photos. The former Trade Center is now a vast crater; at this writing, it is still being cleared of debris, combed for remains, and shored up. Cleanup was scheduled to be complete by the end of 2002, but no decisions had yet been finalized as to what will come next.

At press time, a **temporary viewing platform** was in place at Broadway and Fulton Street, open daily from 9am to 8pm; it is scheduled to remain in place through summer 2002, but its fate thereafter is unknown. Free tickets are available at the South Street Museum's ticket booth at Fulton and South streets, open daily from 11am to 6pm (morning viewing tickets are distributed the previous afternoon). *Please check the sources listed below for the latest viewing and access information.*

As of March 11, 2002, a temporary victims' memorial was in place at **Battery Park** (p. 248): The bronze sphere that once stood on the World Trade Center plaza between the Twin Towers now stands witness, bearing its war wounds, until a permanent one can be erected. Additionally, I expect that the gates of **Trinity Church** (p. 241) will continue to serve as an impromptu memorial, brimming with tokens of remembrance.

Ground Zero is bounded by Church, Barclay, Liberty, and West streets. Call © **212/484-1222** or visit www.nycvisit.com or www.southstseaport.org for viewing information; www.downtownny.com for area information and updates. Subway: C, E to World Trade Center; N, R to Cortlandt St.

The original Lincoln Center location is now the **Eva and Morris Feld Gallery,** which displays art from the permanent collection, including new acquisitions. There's also a second gift gallery here.

45 W. 53rd St. (btwn Fifth and Sixth aves.). © **212/265-1040.** www.folkartmuseum.org. Admission $9 adults, $5 seniors and students, free for children under 12, free to all Fri 6–8pm. Tues–Sun 11:30am–7:30pm. Subway: E or V to 5th Ave. **Eva and Morris Feld Gallery:** 2 Lincoln Sq. (Columbus Ave. between 65th and 66th sts.,). © **212/595-9533.** Free admission. Tues–Sun 11am–7:30pm; Mon 11am–6pm. Subway: 1, 9 to 66th St.

Asia Society The Asia Society was founded in 1956 by John D. Rockefeller III with the goal of increasing understanding between Americans and Asians through art exhibits, lectures, films, performances, and conferences. The society is a leader in presenting contemporary Asian and Asian-American art. Now, after a $30 million renovation that doubled the exhibition space was completed in 2001, the society's headquarters is bigger, smarter, and better than ever. Never has so much of the core collection, comprised of Rockefeller's Pan-Asian acquisitions dating from 2000 B.C. to the 19th century, been on display before. Well-curated temporary exhibits run the gamut from "The New Way of Tea," exploring Japan's elaborate tea ceremony, to "Through Afghan Eyes: A Culture in Conflict, 1987–1995," a study in photographs and video. The mammoth calendar of events runs the gamut from films to lectures to discussions featuring experts in Pan-Asian and global politics, business, and more.

725 Park Ave. (at 70th St.). © 212/288-6400. www.asiasociety.org. Gallery admission $7 adults, $5 seniors and students, free for children under 16, free to all Fri 6–9pm. Tues–Thurs and Sat–Sun 11am–6pm; Fri 11am–9pm. Subway: 6 to 68th St./Hunter College.

Center for Jewish History *Finds* New in late 2000, this 125,000-square-foot complex is the largest repository of Jewish history, art, and literature in the Diaspora. It unites five of America's leading institutions of Jewish scholarship: the **American Jewish Historical Society** (www.ajhs.org), the national archives of the Jewish people in the Americas; the **Leo Baeck Institute** (www.lbi.org), documenting the history of German-speaking Jewry from the 17th century until the Nazis; the **Yeshiva University Museum** (www.yu.edu/museum), which includes general-interest exhibits, plus a collection of Judaica objects confiscated by the Nazis; the **YIVO Institute for Jewish Research** (www.yivoinstitute.org), focusing on exhibits exploring the diversity of the Jewish experience; and the **American Sephardi Federation** (www.amsephfed.org), representing the spiritual, cultural, and social traditions of the American Sephardic communities (Jews from Southern Europe, North Africa, and the Middle East). This union represents about 100 million archival documents, 500,000 books, and thousands of objects of art and ephemera, ranging from Thomas Jefferson's letter denouncing anti-Semitism to memorabilia of famous Jewish athletes.

The main gallery space is the Yeshiva Museum, which comprises four galleries, an outdoor sculpture garden, and a children's workshop; a range of exhibits also showcase holdings belonging to the other institutions. A central feature is the **Reading Room,** home to stacks accessible by serious researchers and lay historians alike, as well as the **Center Genealogy Institute,** which offers assistance in family-history research. Another huge component of the center is its 250-seat home to a packed schedule of events. There's also a kosher cafe.

15 W. 16th St. (btwn Fifth and Sixth aves.). © 212/294-8301. www.cjh.org. Admission to Yeshiva University Museum $6 adults, $4 seniors and students, free admission to all other facilities. Yeshiva University Museum Sun and Tues–Wed 11am–5pm; Thurs 11am–8pm. Reading Room and Genealogy Institute Mon–Thurs 9:30am–4:30pm; Fri by appt. All other exhibition galleries Mon–Thurs 9am–5pm; Fri 9am–4pm. Subway: 4, 5, 6, N, R, L, Q, W to 14th St./Union Sq.; F, V to 14th St.

The Cloisters ★ If it weren't for this branch of the Metropolitan Museum of Art, many New Yorkers would never get to the northernmost point in Manhattan. This remote yet lovely spot is devoted to the art and architecture of medieval Europe. Atop a cliff overlooking the Hudson River, you'll find a 12th-century chapter house, parts of five cloisters from medieval monasteries, a Romanesque chapel, and a 12th-century Spanish apse brought intact from Europe. Surrounded by peaceful gardens, this is the one place on the island that can even approximate the kind of solitude suitable to such a collection. Inside you'll find extraordinary works that include the famed Unicorn tapestries, sculpture, illuminated manuscripts, stained glass, ivory, and precious metal work.

Despite its remoteness, the Cloisters are extremely popular, especially in fine weather, so try to schedule your visit on a weekday. A free guided **Highlights Tour** is offered Tuesday through Friday at 3pm and Sunday at noon; gallery talks are also a regular feature. **Garden Tours** are offered Tuesday through Sunday at 1pm in May, June, September, and October; lectures and other programming are on Sunday from noon to 2pm; medieval-music concerts are held in the 12th-century Spanish chapel.

At the north end of Fort Tryon Park. ✆ 212/923-3700. www.metmuseum.org. Suggested admission (includes same-day entrance to the Metropolitan Museum of Art) $10 adults, $5 seniors and students, free for children under 12. Nov–Feb Tues–Sun 9:30am–4:45pm; Mar–Oct Tues–Sun 9:30am–5:15pm. Subway: A to 190th St., then a 10-min. walk north along Margaret Corbin Dr., or pick up the M4 bus at the station (1 stop to Cloisters). Bus: M4 Madison Ave. (Fort Tryon Park–The Cloisters).

Cooper-Hewitt National Design Museum 🖈 Part of the Smithsonian Institution, the Cooper-Hewitt is in the Carnegie Mansion, built by Andrew Carnegie in 1901 and renovated in 1996. Some 11,000 square feet of space is devoted to changing exhibits that are well conceived, engaging, and educational. Shows are both historic and contemporary in nature, and topics range from "The Work of Charles and Ray Eames: A Legacy of Invention" to "The Architecture of Reassurance: Designing the Disney Theme Parks." Exhibitions scheduled for 2002 to 2003 include "New Hotels for Global Nomads."

Note the Art Nouveau–style copper-and-glass canopy above the entrance. And visit the garden, ringed with Central Park benches from various eras.

2 E. 91st St. (at Fifth Ave.). ✆ 212/849-8400. www.si.edu/ndm. Admission $8 adults, $5 seniors and students, free for children under 12, free to all Tues 5–9pm. Tues 10am–9pm; Wed–Sat 10am–5pm; Sun noon–5pm. Subway: 4, 5, 6 to 86th St.

Dahesh Museum of Art *Value* If you consider yourself a classicist, this small museum is for you. It's dedicated to 19th- and early-20th-century European academic art, a continuation of Renaissance, baroque, and rococo traditions that were overshadowed by the arrival of Impressionism. (If you're not familiar with this academic school, expect lots of painstaking renditions of historical subjects and pastoral life.) Artists represented include Jean-Léon Gérôme, Lord Leighton, and Edwin Long, whose *Love's Labour Lost* is a cornerstone of the collection.

601 Fifth Ave. (btwn 48th and 49th sts.), 2nd floor. ✆ 212/759-0606. www.daheshmuseum.org. Free admission. Tues–Sat 11am–6pm. Subway: B, D, F, V to 47–50th sts./Rockefeller Center.

Dia Center for the Arts Housed in a series of renovated warehouse buildings on the fringe of Chelsea, this contemporary art institution focuses on interdisciplinary art and criticism through a rotating calendar of large-scale, single-artist exhibitions by modern artists with big ideas. Basically, if you think the mainstream museums are too conventional, predictable, and well, *small,* this is the place for you. The main space is the four-story warehouse at 548 W. 22nd,. The exhibition schedule for late 2002 to 2003 had not been announced at press time, but expect the unexpected, such as these recent shows: *Knots + Surfaces,* a multiprojection video installation by L.A. artist Diana Thater that had something intriguing to do with the intersection of mathematics and the dance of the honeybee; or Bruce Neumann's *Mapping the Studio I (Fat Chance John Cage),* an exhibit chronicling the nocturnal activities of the artist's cat with various mice.

Call or check the website for the current exhibition schedule, as well as commissioned-artist Web projects, lectures, poetry readings, screenings, and other events of an avant-garde nature. If you like what you see, inquire about additional exhibition spaces in SoHo and TriBeCa that may be open.

545–548 W. 22nd St. (btwn Tenth and Eleventh aves.). © 212/989-5566. www.diacenter.org. Admission $6 adults, $3 students and seniors. Wed–Sat noon–6pm (hours may vary, so call ahead). Subway: C, E to 23rd St.

El Museo del Barrio   What started in 1969 with a display in a school classroom is today the only museum in America dedicated to Puerto Rican, Caribbean, and Latin American art. The northernmost Museum Mile institution has a permanent exhibit ranging from pre-Columbian artifacts to photographic art and video. The display of *santos de palo,* wood-carved religious figurines, is worth noting, as is "Taíno, Ancient Voyagers of the Caribbean," dedicated to the cultures that Columbus encountered when he landed in the "New World." The changing exhibitions focus on 20th-century artists and contemporary subjects.

1230 Fifth Ave. (at 104th St.). © 212/831-7272. www.elmuseo.org. Suggested admission $5 adults, $3 seniors and students, free for children under 12. Wed–Sun 11am–5pm. Subway: 6 to 103rd St.

Federal Hall National Memorial *Value*   Fronted by 32-foot fluted marble Doric columns, this 1842 neoclassical temple is most famous for what happened here while the site was occupied by the 18th-century City Hall. Peter Zenger, publisher of the outspoken *Weekly Journal,* stood trial in 1735 for "seditious libel" against Royal Governor William Cosby. Defended brilliantly by Alexander Hamilton, Zenger's eventual acquittal (based on the grounds that anything you printed that was true, even if it wasn't very nice, couldn't be construed as libel) set the precedent for freedom of the press, later guaranteed in the Bill of Rights, which was drafted and signed inside this building. New York's first major rebellion against British authority also occurred here, when the Stamp Act Congress met in 1765 to protest King George III's policy of "taxation without representation." J. Q. A. Ward's 1883 statue of George Washington on the steps commemorates the spot of the first presidential inauguration, in 1789. Congress met here after the revolution, when New York was briefly the nation's capital.

Call ahead if you'd like to hook up with one of the 20- to 30-minute guided tours (I recommend it), which usually take place between 12:30 and 3:30pm.

26 Wall St. (at Nassau St.). © 212/825-6888. www.nps.gov/feha. Free admission. Mon–Fri 9am–5pm. Subway: 4, 5 to Wall St.

Forbes Magazine Galleries *Kids*   The late publishing magnate Malcolm Forbes may have been a self-described "capitalist tool," but he had esoteric, almost childish, tastes. With its model boats, toy soldiers, old Monopoly games, trophies, miniature rooms, presidential memorabilia, and Fabergé eggs, this is a great little museum for you and the kids. Personal anecdotes explain why certain objects attracted Forbes's attention and turn the collection into an interesting biographical portrait. The Picture and Autograph Galleries, where you can find Abraham Lincoln's Emancipation Proclamation, are also intriguing.

62 Fifth Ave. (at 12th St.). © 212/206-5548. www.forbes.com/forbescollection. Free admission. Tues–Wed and Fri–Sat 10am–4pm (hours vary, call ahead). Subway: L, N, R, 4, 5, 6 to 14th St./Union Sq.

Fraunces Tavern Museum   This petite museum of early American history and culture is most famous for the Long Room, in which George Washington made his farewell to his soldiers at the end of the American Revolution, but it also houses exhibits such as "Colonists, Revolutionaries, Builders: Freemasons in

America." Built in 1907, this replica of the original 1717 tavern is nevertheless a wonderful example of New York's pre-Revolutionary architectural style.

One of the best ways to experience Fraunces Tavern is to dine there. After a million-dollar renovation, the restaurant reopened in 2001, and serves lunch and dinner Monday through Saturday. The tavern has been painstakingly re-created and the fare significantly upscaled since the Revolutionary War days—as have entree prices, which are in the low $20s. The fare is mainly American, but the menu includes some West Indian dishes in honor of 18th-century restaurateur Samuel Fraunces. For a more cost-efficient but equally atmospheric experience, stop by for a drink in the bar.

54 Pearl St. (near Broad St.). © 212/425-1778, or 212/968-1776 for restaurant reservations. www.fraunces tavernmuseum.org. Admission $3 adults, $2 students and seniors, free for children under 6. Mon–Fri 10am–4:45pm. Restaurant Mon–Fri 6:30am–9:30pm (last seating); Sat noon–5pm (tavern/bar area only) and 5–9:30pm (dining room). Subway: N, R to Whitehall St.; 2, 3 to Wall St.; 4, 5 to Bowling Green.

The Frick Collection ★★   Henry Clay Frick could afford to be an avid collector of European art after amassing a fortune in the coke and steel industries at the turn of the 20th century. To house his treasures and himself, he hired Carrère & Hastings to build this 18th-century French-style mansion (1914).

Most appealing about the Frick is its intimate size and setting. This is a living testament to New York's Gilded Age—the interior still feels like a private home (albeit a really rich guy's home) with beautiful paintings. Come here to see the classics by Titian, Bellini, Rembrandt, Turner, Vermeer, El Greco, and Goya, to name only a few. A highlight is the **Fragonard Room,** graced with the rococo series *The Progress of Love.* The portrait of Montesquieu by Whistler is stunning. Sculpture, furniture, Chinese vases, and French enamels complement the paintings. Included in the price of admission, the AcousticGuide audio tour is useful because it allows you to follow your own path rather than a proscribed route. A free 22-minute **video** presentation is screened in the Music Room every half-hour from 10am to 4:30pm (from 1:30 on Sun).

In addition to the permanent collection, the Frick mounts small, well-focused temporary exhibitions. Fall 2002 visitors can enjoy "Poussin, Claude, and Their World: 17th-Century French Drawings from the Ecole Nationale des Beaux-Arts, Paris" through November 2002. Additionally, Andrea Mantegna's magnificent *Descent into Limbo* (1468), a magnificent example of Italian Renaissance painting, will be on display in the Enamel Room through August 1, 2003.

Free chamber-music concerts are held twice a month, generally every other Sunday at 5pm, select Thursdays at 5:45pm in warm weather, as well as once-a-month **lectures,** select Wednesdays at 5:30pm; call or visit the website for the current schedule and ticket information.

1 E. 70th St. (at Fifth Ave.). © 212/288-0700. www.frick.org. Admission $10 adults, $5 seniors and students. Children under 10 not admitted; children 10–16 must be accompanied by an adult. Tues–Sat 10am–6pm; Sun 1–6pm. Closed all major holidays. Subway: 6 to 68th St./Hunter College.

International Center of Photography ★ *Finds*   In late 2000, the ICP—one of the world's premier educators, collectors, and exhibitors of photographic art—relocated from its Museum Mile location to this expanded Midtown facility. The state-of-the-art gallery space is ideal for viewing exhibitions of the museum's 50,000-plus prints as well as visiting shows. The emphasis is on contemporary photographic works, but historically important photographers aren't ignored.

1133 Sixth Ave. (at 43rd St.). © 212/857-0000. www.icp.org. Admission $9 adults, $6 seniors and students. Tues–Thurs 10am–5pm; Fri 10am–8pm; Sat–Sun 10am–6pm. Subway: B, D, F, V to 42nd St.

Value Where to Find Free Culture

New York's gargantuan stash of museums, galleries, and attractions makes this city one of the cultural capitals of the world. But the cost of this culture can be high, especially because many museums now charge $10 or more. But don't get discouraged; there are ways around these steep fees.

Some city attractions are free all the time. Some set aside an afternoon, evening, or a day during the week when you can explore at no charge. Others offer "pay what you wish" times, be it $1 or the full admission price.

Most museums keep pretty solid schedules, but it's always a good idea to call ahead and confirm free and "pay what you wish" times—because these, like everything else, are always subject to change.

Always Free
- **Abyssinian Baptist Church** (p. 240)
- **American Folk Art Museum's Eva and Morris Feld Gallery** (p. 219)
- **Brooklyn Tabernacle** (p. 260)
- **Center for Jewish History** (all galleries except Yeshiva University Museum; p. 220)
- **Dahesh Museum of Art** (p. 221)
- **Federal Hall National Memorial** (p. 222)
- **Forbes Magazine Galleries** (p. 222)
- **Mother A.M.E. Zion Church** (p. 241)
- **National Museum of the American Indian** (p. 232)
- **New York City Police Museum** (p. 233)
- **New York Public Library** (p. 238)
- **New York Stock Exchange** (p. 217)
- **New York Transit Museum's Gallery Annex** (p. 261)
- **St. Patrick's Cathedral** (p. 241)
- **Schomburg Center for Research in Black Culture** (p. 234)
- **Socrates Sculpture Park** (p. 265)
- **Sony Wonder Technology Lab** (p. 257)
- **South Street Seaport** (charge for museum admission; p. 235)
- **Staten Island Ferry** (p. 214)
- **Temple Emanu-El** (p. 241)
- **Trinity Church** ($2 donation requested for noonday concerts; p. 241)
- **Whitney Museum of American Art at Philip Morris** (p. 236)
- **Zenith Media Lounge** at the New Museum of Contemporary Art (p. 233)

Sometimes Free (or Pay What You Wish)
- **American Craft Museum:** Thursday from 6 to 8pm; regular admission $7.50 (p. 218)
- **American Folk Art Museum:** Friday 6 to 8pm; regular admission $9 (p. 218)

***Intrepid* Sea-Air-Space Museum** *Kids* The most astonishing thing about the aircraft carrier USS *Intrepid* is how it can be simultaneously so big and so

- **Asia Society:** Friday 6 to 9pm; regular admission $7 (p. 220)
- **Bronx Zoo Wildlife Conservation Park:** All day Wednesday; regular admission $9 (p. 258)
- **Brooklyn Botanic Garden:** All day Tuesday and Saturday from 10am to noon year-round, plus all day Wednesday, Thursday, and Friday from mid-November through mid-March; regular admission $3 (p. 260)
- **Brooklyn Museum of Art:** First Saturday of the month from 5 to 11pm; regular admission $6 (p. 260)
- **Children's Museum of the Arts:** Thursday from 4 to 6pm; regular admission $5 (p. 256)
- **Cooper-Hewitt National Design Museum:** Tuesday from 5 to 9pm; regular admission $8 (p. 221)
- **The Jewish Museum:** Tuesday from 5 to 8pm; regular admission $8 (p. 226)
- **MoMA QNS:** Friday from 4:30 to 8:15pm; regular admission $12 (p. 211)
- **New York Hall of Science:** Thursday and Friday from 2 to 5pm; regular admission $7.50 (p. 257)
- **New York Transit Museum:** Seniors enter free Tuesday from noon to 4pm; regular senior admission $1.50 (p. 261).
- **Solomon R. Guggenheim Museum:** Friday from 6 to 8pm; regular admission $12 (p. 213)
- **Studio Museum in Harlem:** First Saturday of the month; regular admission $5 (p. 235)
- **Wave Hill:** All day Tuesday and Saturday mornings in summer, every day in winter; regular admission $4 (p. 259).
- **Whitney Museum of American Art:** Friday from 6 to 9pm; regular admission $10 (p. 217)

Almost Free (admission of $3 or less)
- **Brooklyn Botanic Garden:** $3 (p. 260)
- **Cathedral of St. John the Divine:** $2 ($3 for guided tour; p. 240)
- **Edgar Allan Poe Cottage:** $2 (p. 238)
- **Fraunces Tavern Museum:** $3 (p. 222)
- **Morris-Jumel Mansion:** $3 (p. 238)
- **Museum of American Financial History:** $2 (p. 228)
- **New Museum of Contemporary Art:** Thursday from 6 to 8pm, $3; regular admission $6 (p. 232)
- **New York Botanical Garden:** $3 (p. 258)
- **New York Transit Museum:** $3 (p. 261)
- **Prospect Park Wildlife Conservation Center:** $2.50 (p. 262)
- **Scandinavia House:** $3 (p. 234)
- **Theodore Roosevelt Birthplace:** $3 (p. 236)

small. It's a few football fields long, weighs 40,000 tons, holds 40 aircraft. But stand there and think about landing an A-12 jet on the deck and suddenly it's minuscule. In the passageways below, you'll find it isn't quite the roomiest of vessels. Now a National Historic Landmark, the exhibit also includes the destroyer USS *Edson,* and the submarine USS *Growler,* the only intact strategic missile submarine open to the public anywhere, as well as a collection of vintage and modern aircraft, including the A-12 Blackbird, the world's fastest spy plane.

Kids just love this place. They—and you—can climb inside a replica of a Revolutionary War submarine, sit in an A-6 Intruder cockpit, and follow the progress of America's astronauts as they work in space. There are even navy flight simulators in the Technologies Hall. Look for family-oriented activities and events at least one Saturday a month.

New in 2002 is "All Hands on Deck," which teaches kids and adults how things work on ships, plus a new AH-1 Cobra attack helicopter. The action-packed *Intrepid Wings* shows aircraft carrier take-offs and recoveries in the new Allison and Howard Lutnick Theater; the film runs throughout the day. "Remembering 9-11" recalls those lost, both civilians and rescuers. The $5.5 million visitor center, opened in 2000, makes for an impressive entrance, and the museum store is well stocked; goods include NYPD and FDNY logo gear. But dress warmly for a winter visit—it's almost impossible to heat an aircraft carrier.

Pier 86 (W. 46th St. at Twelfth Ave.). ✆ 212/245-0072. www.intrepidmuseum.org. Admission $13 adults; $9 veterans, seniors, and students; $6 children 6–11; $2 children 2–5. $5 extra for flight simulator rides. Apr–Sept Mon–Fri 10am–5pm, Sat–Sun 10am–7pm; Oct–Mar Tues–Sun 10am–5pm. Last admission 1 hr. before closing. Subway: A, C, E to 42nd St./Port Authority. Bus: M42 crosstown.

Japan Society The Japan Society was founded in 1907 to foster cultural understanding and enlightened relations between East and West, and does so admirably. The society's U.S. headquarters, housed in a striking modern building by Junzo Yoshimuro (1971), mounts exhibits of Japanese art in a serene gallery. Changing displays have included "Japanese Theater in the World" and "Frank Lloyd Wright and the Art of Japan: The Architect's Other Passion"; upcoming in spring 2003 is "Early Buddhist Art from Korea and Japan, 6th–9th Centuries." The tranquil, elegant building also features a bamboo pond garden as well as a 278-seat auditorium that hosts a wide variety of performances, from contemporary Japanese dance and music to *butoh* and kabuki. The extensive program schedule also features lectures, gallery talks, films, and classes.

333 E. 47th St. (btwn First and Second aves.). ✆ 212/832-1155. www.japansociety.org. Admission $5 adults, $3 seniors and students. Gallery Tues–Fri 11am–6pm; Sat–Sun 11am–5pm. Subway: E, V to Lexington Ave.; 6 to 51st St.

The Jewish Museum Housed in a Gothic-style mansion renovated in 1993 by AIA Gold Medal winner Kevin Roche, this museum now has the world-class space it deserves to showcase its collections, which chronicle 4,000 years of Jewish history. The permanent exhibit, "Culture and Continuity: The Jewish Journey," tells the story of the Jewish experience from ancient times through today. Artifacts include daily objects that might have served the authors of the books of Genesis, Psalms, and Job, and an assemblage of Torahs. A collection of classic TV and radio programs is available for viewing through the Goodkind Resource Center (as any fan of television's golden age knows, its finest comic moments were Jewish comedy). The scope of the exhibit is phenomenal, and its story an enlightening—and intense—one. A random-access audio guide is geared to families (free with admission). In addition to the in-house shop, don't miss the Jewish Museum Design Shop in the adjacent brownstone. *Money-saving tip:* Check the website for online admission discounts (50% off at press time).

1109 Fifth Ave. (at 92nd St.). © 212/423-3200. www.thejewishmuseum.org. Admission $8 adults, $5.50 seniors and students, free for children under 12, pay what you wish Thurs 5–8pm. Sun 10am–5:45pm; Mon–Wed 11am–5:45pm; Thurs 11am–8pm; Fri 11am–3pm. Subway: 4, 5 to 86th St.; 6 to 96th St.

Lower East Side Tenement Museum ★ This museum is the first-ever National Trust for Historic Preservation site that was not the home of someone rich or famous. It's a five-story tenement that 10,000 people from 25 countries called home between 1863 and 1935—people who had come to the United States looking for the American dream. The museum tells the story of the immigration boom of the late 19th and early 20th centuries, when the Lower East Side was considered the "Gateway to America." A visit here is a good follow-up to an Ellis Island trip—what happened to the people who passed through that way station?

The only way to see the museum is by guided tour. Two tenement tours, held on all open days and lasting an hour, offer an exploration of the museum: **Piecing It Together: Immigrants in the Garment Industry,** which focuses on the apartment and the lives of its turn-of-the-century tenants, an immigrant Jewish family named Levine from Poland; and **Getting By: Weathering the Great Depressions of 1873 and 1929,** featuring the homes of the German-Jewish Gumpertz family and the Sicilian-Catholic Baldizzi family, respectively. A guide leads you into each dingy urban time capsule, where several apartments have been restored to their lived-in condition, and recounts the stories of the families who occupied them. You can pair them for an in-depth look at the museum.

These tours are not really for kids, who won't enjoy the serious tone and "don't touch" policy. Much better for them is the 45-minute, weekends-only **Confino Family Apartment** tour, a living history program geared to families, which allows kids to converse with an interpreter playing teenage immigrant Victoria Confino (ca. 1916); kids can handle whatever they like and try on period clothes.

The hour-long **Streets Where We Lived** neighborhood heritage walking tour is offered on weekends from April through December. Small permanent and rotating exhibits, including photos, videos, and a model tenement, are housed in the Visitors' Center and exhibition space in the tenement building at 97 Orchard St. Special tours and programs are sometimes on the schedule.

Tours are limited in number and sell out quickly, so it pays to buy tickets in advance, which you can do online, or over the phone by calling **Ticketweb** at © **800/965-4827.** Note that the potential acquisition of a neighboring tenement at 99 Orchard St. may change programming, so confirm schedules.

Visitor Center at 90 Orchard St. (at Broome St.). © 212/431-0233. www.tenement.org. Tenement and walking tours $9 adults, $7 seniors and students; Confino Apartment $8 adults, $6 seniors and students. Tenement tours depart every 40 min. Tues–Fri 1–4pm; Sat–Sun every half hr. 11am–4:45pm. Confino Apartment tour Sat–Sun hourly noon–3pm. Walking tour Apr–Dec Sat–Sun 1 and 2:30pm. Subway: F to Delancey St.; J, M, Z to Essex St.

Madame Tussaud's New York *Overrated* A branch of the garish London institution, this wax museum is just plain *overpriced.* Admission should be $6 or $7, not $20. Because there are far better things a family of four could do with 70 or 80 bucks, budget travelers should save their money and skip this place.

If you do go, bring your camera, because half the fun is having yourself photographed alongside replicas of famous figures ranging from Joan Rivers to Gandhi. Best is the "Opening Night Party," in which a range of contemporary stars are arranged in such candid poses that it's sometimes hard to distinguish the real folks from the fakes; in fact, it's almost creepy. While most of the figures are excellent likenesses, a few are off target (the Beatles win the "What Were They Thinking?" award). Despite the wealth of John Travoltas and Woody Allens and

Michael Jordans, my favorite figure is a surprisingly handsome Napoleon; the rest of the "Madame Tussaud's Story" exhibit is gruesome (she was a French Revolution–era death-mask sculptor), so skip it if you have little ones.

An extra $2 buys you admission to a ridiculous 10-minute virtual-reality movie that's not even entertaining—the best thing about it is a fake "snowfall" at the end (actually some shaving cream–like substance). If you insist on wasting your money here, at least pass on paying the additional bucks for this shoddy extra.

234 W. 42nd St. (btwn Seventh and Eighth aves.). © 212/512-9600. www.madame-tussauds.com. Admission $19.95 adults, $17.95 seniors, $15.95 children 4–12. $2 extra for "New York, New York" screening. Daily 10am–6pm (last ticket sales). Subway: 1, 2, 3, 7, 9, N, R, S, Q, W to 42nd St./Times Sq.

Morgan Library ★★ *Finds*   Here's an undiscovered New York treasure, boasting one of the world's most important collections of manuscripts, rare books and bindings, drawings, and personal writings. Among the artifacts on display under glass are stunning illuminated manuscripts (including Gutenberg bibles), a draft of the U.S. Constitution with copious handwritten notes, and handwritten scores by Beethoven, Mozart, and Puccini. The collection of mostly 19th-century drawings—featuring works by Seurat, Degas, Rubens, and other great masters—have an excitement of immediacy about them.

This rich repository originated as the private collection of turn-of-the-20th-century financier J. Pierpont Morgan and is housed in a landmark Renaissance-style palazzo building (1906) he commissioned from McKim, Mead & White. Morgan's library and study are preserved virtually intact and are worth a look themselves for their architecture (particularly the rotunda) and detailed fittings.

The special exhibitions are well chosen and curated; subjects can range from medieval bookbinding techniques to the literary genesis of the mystery novel and pulp fiction to a display of treasures from the royal tombs of Ur. A reading room is available by appointment, and an exceptional calendar of concerts, lectures, film screenings, gallery talks, and family tours can be found online.

29 E. 36th St. (at Madison Ave.). © 212/685-0610. www.morganlibrary.org. Admission $8 adults, $6 students and seniors, free for children 12 and under. Tues–Thurs 10:30am–5pm; Fri 10:30am–8pm; Sat 10:30am–6pm; Sun noon–6pm. Subway: 6 to 33rd St.

Mount Vernon Hotel Museum & Garden *Finds*   It's a pleasant shock to find such a little-known jewel on this thoroughly modern block. This survivor from the early American republic was built as a carriage house for Abigail Adams Smith, daughter of President John Adams, and her husband, William Stephens Smith, in 1799. It's been restored by the Colonial Dames of America to its early-19th-century condition, when the house served as the Mount Vernon Hotel—a country hotel for overnights away from the city. On a guided tour you can explore nine period rooms, outfitted in Federal style, as well as the grounds, planted as a late-18th-century garden would be. An orientation center offers a scale model of the building as it looked in 1799 and screens a video on New York City in the early 19th century. Special events take place throughout the year.

421 E. 61st St. (btwn First and York aves.). © 212/838-6878. Admission $4 adults, $3 seniors, free for children under 12. Tues–Sun 11am–4pm (last tour 3:15pm). Closed Aug. Subway: N, R to Lexington Ave.; 4, 5, 6 to 59th St.

Museum of American Financial History   Real money buffs (and who among us isn't?) may want to make a stop here. The exhibits housed in this Smithsonian-affiliate museum include numismatic and vintage ticker-tape displays; murals and photos depicting historic Wall Street scenes; and interactive financial news terminals, so little bulls and bears can learn how to keep up with the market. Temporary installations have run the gamut from "Morgan," a chronicle of the lasting influence of J. Pierpont Morgan, to "High Notes," an oddly compelling exhibit of high-denomination currency.

The **World of Finance Walking Tour** of the Financial District is Fridays at 10am; tickets cost $15 for adults, $10 for students and seniors. Reservations are required for parties of six or more, but call and confirm to avoid disappointment. (The tour was suspended at press time but is scheduled to resume in mid-2002.)

28 Broadway (just north of Bowling Green Park). © **877/98-FINANCE**, 212/908-4110, or 212/908-4519. www.financialhistory.org. Admission $2. Tues–Sat 10am–4pm. Subway: 4, 5 to Bowling Green; J, M to Broad St.; 2, 3 to Wall St.

Museum of Jewish Heritage—A Living Memorial to the Holocaust ⭐

In the south end of Battery Park City, the Museum of Jewish Heritage occupies a six-sided building designed by award-winning architect Kevin Roche, with a six-tier roof alluding to the Star of David and the six million murdered in the Holocaust. The permanent exhibits ("Jewish Life a Century Ago," "The War Against the Jews," and "Jewish Renewal") recount the daily prewar lives, the horror that destroyed them, and the renewal experienced by European and immigrant Jews in the years from the late 19th century to the present. The museum's power derives from the way it tells that story: through the objects, photographs, documents, and, most poignantly, the videotaped testimonies of Holocaust victims, survivors, and their families, all chronicled by Steven Spielberg's Survivors of the Shoah Visual History Foundation. Thursday evenings are dedicated to panel discussions, performances, and music, while Sundays are for family programs and workshops; a film series is also a regular part of the calendar. A new East Wing that will triple the exhibition and events space and add a Family History Center is slated for completion in fall 2003.

While advance tickets are not usually necessary, you may want to purchase them to guarantee admission; call © **212/945-0039.** Audio tours narrated by Meryl Streep and Itzhak Perlman are available for an additional $5.

Money-saving tip: Check the website for $2-off admission coupon (available at press time), which you'll need to print out and bring with you.

18 First Place (at Battery Place), Battery Park City. © **212/509-6130.** www.mjhnyc.org. Admission $7 adults, $5 seniors and students, free for children under 5. Sun–Wed 10am–5:45pm; Thurs 9am–8pm; Fri and eves of Jewish holidays 10am–3pm. Subway: 4, 5 to Bowling Green.

Museum of Television & Radio

If you can resist the allure of this museum, I'd wager you've spent the last 70 years in a bubble. You can watch and hear the great personalities of TV and radio—from Uncle Miltie to Johnny Carson to Jerry Seinfeld—at a private console. You can conduct computer searches to pick out the great moments of history, viewing almost anything that made its way onto the airwaves, from the Beatles' appearance on *The Ed Sullivan Show* to the crumbling of the Berlin Wall. The collection consists of 75,000 programs and commercials, only a fraction of which are available for instant viewing (call at least a week in advance to arrange for a specific reel); you're allowed to watch up to four shows in one sitting. Selected programs are also presented in two theaters and two screening rooms.

25 W. 52nd St. (btwn Fifth and Sixth aves.). © **212/621-6800** or 212/621-6600. www.mtr.org. Admission $6 adults, $4 seniors and students, $3 children under 13. Tues–Sun noon–6pm (Thurs until 8pm, Fri theater programs until 9pm). Subway: B, D, F, V to 47–50th sts./Rockefeller Center; E, V to 53rd St.

Museum of the City of New York

A wide variety of objects—costumes, photographs, prints, maps, dioramas, and memorabilia—trace the history of

Art for Art's Sake: The Gallery Scene

Manhattan has more than 500 private art galleries, selling everything from old masters to tomorrow's news. Galleries are free to the public, generally Tuesday through Saturday from 10am to 6pm. Nobody will expect you to buy, so don't worry—it's all about looking.

The best way to choose where to browse is by perusing the "Art Guide" in the Friday "Weekend" section of the *New York Times,* or the Sunday "Arts & Leisure" section; the "Cue" section of *New York* magazine; the Art section in *Time Out New York;* or the *New Yorker*'s "Goings on About Town." You can find the latest listings at **www.nymetro.com**, whose Arts page gives you access to *New York* magazine's listings; **www.newyork.citysearch.com** (click on "Arts"); **www.artnet.com**; and **www.galleryguide.org**. An excellent source—more for practicals on the galleries and the artists and genres—is **www.artincontext.org**. The *Gallery Guide* is available at most galleries.

I suggest picking a gallery or a show in a neighborhood that suits your taste, and start browsing. I've listed a few starting points in the neighborhoods below—uptown in Midtown East and on the Upper East Side; Chelsea, Manhattan's *avant* gallery row; and downtown, mainly in SoHo, hub for the modern art establishment. This list doesn't begin to scratch the surface; there are many more galleries as well as concentrations of galleries in areas like the East Village, TriBeCa, and Brooklyn (the Art in Context site is a good way to locate them).

When choosing a browsing territory, keep in mind that uptown galleries tend to be more traditional, downtown galleries more contemporary, and far west Chelsea galleries the most cutting-edge. Museum-quality works dominate uptown, while raw talent and emerging artists are most common in west Chelsea. But you'll find constant surprises in all neighborhoods.

UPTOWN Uptown galleries are clustered in and around the crossroads of Fifth Avenue and 57th Street and on and off Madison Avenue in the 60s, 70s, and 80s. These blue-chip galleries maintain their white-glove demeanor. They include **Hirschl & Adler Galleries,** 21 E. 70th St. (© 212/535-8810; www.hirschlandadler.com), for 18th- to 20th-century European and American painting and decorative arts; powerhouses **Gagosian Gallery,** 980 Madison Ave. (© 212/744-2313; www.gagosian.com), and **Pace Wildenstein,** 32 E. 57th St. (© 212/421-3292), whose focus is on classic modernism, representing such artists as Barbara Hepworth, and Claes Oldenburg; **Margo Feiden Galleries,** 699 Madison Ave. (© 212/677-5330; www.alhirschfeld.com), the authorized representative of the works of Al Hirschfeld; **James Cohan Gallery,** 41 W. 57th St.

New York City from its beginnings as a Dutch colony in the 16th century to its present-day prominence. Two outstanding exhibits are the re-creation of John D. Rockefeller's master bedroom and dressing room, and the space devoted to "Broadway!" a history of New York theater. Kids will love "New York Toy

(📞 212/755-7171; www.jamescohan.com), strong in modern photography; **Mary Boone Gallery,** 745 Fifth Ave. (📞 212/752-2929), known for such artists as Ross Bleckner and Nancy Ellison; and **Richard L. Feigen & Co.,** 34 E. 69th St. (📞 212/628-0700; www.rlfeigen.com), and **Wildenstein,** the classical big brother of Pace Wildenstein, 19 E. 64th St. (📞 212/879-0500; www.wildenstein.com), specializing in big-ticket works: old masters, Impressionism, and Renaissance paintings and drawings.

CHELSEA The West 20s between Tenth and Eleventh avenues are home to the avant-garde, with West 26th serving as the unofficial "gallery row." Most galleries are not in storefronts but in the large spaces of multistory former garages and warehouses. Galleries worth seeking out include **Paula Cooper,** 534 W. 21st St. (📞 212/255-1105), specializing in conceptual and minimal art; **George Billis Gallery,** 526 W. 26th St., 9F (📞 212/645-2621; www.georgebillis.com), who shows works by emerging artists like still-life modernist Tom Gregg and avant-photographer Matt Ernst; **Gagosian Gallery,** 555 W. 24th St. (📞 212/741-1111; www.gagosian.com), shows such major modern artists as Richard Serra and Julian Schnabel; **Cheim & Read,** 547 W. 25th St. (📞 212/242-7727), which often shows works by such high-profile pop artists as Diane Arbus, Larry Clark, Robert Mapplethorpe, and Nan Goldin; **DCA Gallery,** 525 W. 22nd St. (📞 212/255-5511; www.dcagallery.com), specializing in contemporary Danish artists; and **Alexander and Bonin,** 132 Tenth Ave. (📞 **212/367-7474;** www.alexanderandbonin.com), which mounts excellent solo exhibitions by artists from the Americas and Europe.

SOHO SoHo remains colorful, if less edgy than it used to be, with the action centered around West Broadway. Start with **Bronwyn Keenan,** 3 Crosby St. (📞 212/431-5083), who's known for a keen eye for emerging talent; **Peter Blum Gallery,** 99 Wooster St. (📞 212/343-0441), who showcased Kim Sooja, a Korean artist who uses traditional Korean bedcovers to comment on the promise of wedded bliss, in early 2002; **Lehmann Maupin,** 39 Greene St. (📞 212/965-0753), whose exhibitions run the gamut from unknowns to contemporary masters like Ross Bleckner; **O. K. Harris,** 383 W. Broadway (📞 212/431-3600; www.okharris.com), which shows a wide and fascinating variety of contemporary painting, sculpture, and photography; and **Louis K. Meisel,** 141 Prince St. (📞 212/677-1340; www.meiselgallery.com), specializing in photo realism and American pinup art (yep, Petty and Vargas girls).

Stories," a permanent exhibit of toys and dolls owned and adored by centuries of New York children. The "Painting the Town: Cityscapes of New York" explores the changing cityscape from 1809 to 1997, and carries new profundity in the wake of September 11, 2001. Check for a schedule of other exhibits relating to the terrorist attack, curated as part of the museum's Project September 11.

1220 Fifth Ave. (at 103rd St.). © 212/534-1672. www.mcny.org. Suggested admission $7 adults; $4 seniors, students, and children; $12 families. Wed–Sat 10am–5pm; Sun noon–5pm. Subway: 6 to 103rd St.

National Academy of Design Founded in 1825 and housed in a landmarked beaux-arts town house, the National Academy is one of the oldest art institutions in the country and is dedicated to preserving the academic tradition. It has three components: a fine-arts school; an honorary professional association of artists; and a museum, which mounts exhibits from its large collection on such themes as "Art in the Age of Queen Victoria" and "The Watercolors of Charles Hawthorne." The Annual Exhibition is the nation's oldest juried show.

1083 Fifth Ave. (btwn 89th and 90th sts.). © 212/369-4880. www.nationalacademy.org. Admission $8 adults, $4.50 seniors, $5 students. Wed–Thurs noon–5pm; Fri 10am–6pm; Sat–Sun 10am–5pm. Subway: 4, 5, 6, to 86th St.

National Museum of the American Indian, George Gustav Heye Center
Value This collection represents the Smithsonian Institution's Native People holdings. It's housed in New York until its new home on the Mall in Washington, D.C., is completed in 2004. Until then, enjoy items spanning more than 10,000 years of native heritage, collected a century ago mainly by New York banking millionaire George Gustav Heye. About 70% of the collection is dedicated to the natives of North America and Hawaii; the rest represents the cultures of Mexico and Central and South America. There's a wealth of material, but it's not as well organized as it could be. The museum also hosts temporary themed exhibitions and interpretive programs plus free storytelling, music, and dance presentations.

The museum is housed in the 1907 beaux-arts **U.S. Customs House**, designed by Cass Gilbert and a National Historic Landmark. The statues lining the front of this granite structure personify *Asia* (pondering philosophically), *America* (bright-eyed and bushy-tailed), *Europe* (decadent, whose time has passed), and *Africa* (sleeping) by Daniel Chester French (of Lincoln Memorial fame). The most interesting, if unintentional, sculptural statement—keeping in mind the building's current purpose—is the giant seated woman to the left of the entrance representing America and surrounded by references to Native America: Mayan pictographs adorning her throne, Quetzalcoatl under her foot, the plains Indian scouting out from over her shoulder. Inside, the oval rotunda designed by Raphael Guastavino was frescoed by Reginald Marsh to glorify the shipping industry (and, by extension, the Customs office once housed here).

1 Bowling Green (btwn State and Whitehall sts.). © 212/514-3700. www.nmai.si.edu. Free admission. Daily 10am–5pm. Subway: 4, 5 to Bowling Green; N, R to Whitehall.

Neue Galerie New York *Finds* This new museum is dedicated to German and Austrian art and design, with a focus on the early 20th century. The collection features painting, works on paper, decorative arts, and other media from such artists as Klimt, Kokoschka, Kandinsky, Klee, and leaders of the Wiener Werkstätte decorative arts and Bauhaus movements such as Adolf Loos and Mies van der Rohe. Once occupied by Mrs. Cornelius Vanderbilt III, the landmark-designated 1914 Carrère & Hastings building (they built the New York Public Library as well) is worth a look. Cafe Sabarsky is modeled on a Viennese cafe, so museumgoers in need of a snack break can expect a fine linzer torte.

1048 Fifth Ave. (at 86th St.). © 212/628-6200. www.neuegalerie.org. Admission $10. Fri–Mon 11am–7pm. Subway: 4, 5, 6 to 86th St.

New Museum of Contemporary Art With 33,000 square feet of space and the former curator of contemporary art at the Whitney as its director, the

New Museum is now a prime contender on the museum scene. Expect adventurous and well-curated exhibitions. The 2003 exhibition calendar had not been announced at press time, but previous schedules have included "Portrait of the Lost Boys," New Zealander Jacqueline Fraser's narrative made of sumptuous fabric and wire sculptures that examines the high incidence of suicide among teenage boys; the experimental film and slide projections of Brazilian artist Hélio Oiticica; Belgian artist Wim Devoye's *Cloaca,* a fascinating sculptural installation using an array of laboratory glassware, electric pumps, computer monitors, and plastic tubing to both scientifically and artistically replicate the organic function of the human digestive system. The **Zenith Media Lounge,** a digital and media-arts technology space housing rotating installations, is free to the public.

583 Broadway (btwn Houston and Prince sts.). ☏ **212/219-1222.** www.newmuseum.org. Admission $6 adults, $3 on Thurs 6–8pm. Free for children 18 and under. Tues–Wed and Fri–Sun noon–6pm (Zenith Media Lounge to 6:30pm); Thurs noon–8pm. Subway: N, R to Prince St.; F, S to Broadway/Lafayette St.

New York City Fire Museum ★ *Kids* Housed in a 1904 firehouse, the former quarters of FDNY Engine Co. 30, this museum houses one of the country's most extensive collections of fire-service memorabilia from the 18th century to the present. It's also the best place to pay tribute to the 343 heroic firefighters who lost their lives in the World Trade Center disaster. Expect changing exhibits relating to the 9/11 disaster. Other displays range from vintage fire marks to fire trucks to the gear and tools of modern firefighters. Also look for leather hoses, fireboats, and Currier & Ives prints, plus a new exhibit on fire safety and burn prevention geared to families. Real firefighters are almost always on hand to share stories and fire-safety information. The retail store sells FDNY logo wear and souvenirs. Call ahead for details on scheduling a guided tour.

278 Spring St. (btwn Varick and Hudson sts.). ☏ **212/691-1303.** www.nycfiremuseum.org. Admission $4 adults, $2 seniors and students, $1 children under 12. Tues–Sat 10am–5pm; Sun 10am–4pm. Subway: C, E to Spring St.

New York City Police Museum *Kids* Newly opened in this Lower Manhattan location in early 2002, this small museum tells the story of the NYPD and offers a look at the present-day world of law enforcement through the eyes of NYPD officers. Exhibits include arrest records of famous criminals, fingerprinting and forensic art stations, and crime-fighting weapons galore.

100 Old Slip (at South St., 2 blocks south of Wall St.). ☏ **212/480-3100.** www.nycpolicemuseum.org. Free admission (donation suggested). Mon–Fri 10am–5pm. Subway: N, R to Whitehall St.; 2, 3 to Wall St.

New-York Historical Society ★ Launched in 1804, the New-York Historical Society is a major repository of American history, culture, and art, with a focus on New York. The neoclassical edifice near the Museum of Natural History has emerged from the renovation tent. Now open on the fourth floor is the Henry Luce III Center for the Study of American Culture, a state-of-the-art facility and gallery of fine and decorative arts, which displays more than 40,000 objects amassed over 200 years—including paintings, sculpture, Tiffany lamps, textiles, furniture, even carriages—that had been in storage for decades. Also look for paintings from Hudson River School artists Thomas Cole, Asher Durand, and Frederic Church, including Cole's five-part masterpiece, *The Course of Empire.* Of particular interest to scholars and ephemera buffs are the extensive Library Collections, which include books, manuscripts, maps, newspapers, photographs, and more documents chronicling the American experience. (An appointment may be necessary to view some or all of the Library Collections, so call ahead.)

Also of note are the society's temporary exhibits; a 2002 series called "History Responds" was one of the best in the city dealing with the 9/11 terrorist attack and its aftermath. World Trade Center–related exhibits are likely to continue, so interested visitors should be sure to check the exhibition schedule.

An extensive calendar of public programs runs the gamut from family story hours to Irving Berlin music nights to lectures by such luminaries as Ric Burns and Susan Sontag to expert-led walks through Manhattan neighborhoods.

2 W. 77th St. (at Central Park W.). ✆ 212/873-3400. www.nyhistory.org. Admission $5 adults, $3 seniors and students, free for children 12 and under. Tues–Sun 10am–5pm. Subway: B, C to 81st St.; 1, 9 to 79th St.

Scandinavia House: The Nordic Center in America *Finds*
Opened in October 2000, this center is dedicated to the shared and unique cultures of Denmark, Finland, Iceland, Norway, and Sweden. Two floors of galleries and an outdoor sculpture terrace display rotating art and design exhibits that can range from "Scandia: Important Early Maps of the Northern Regions" to "Strictly Swedish: An Exhibition of Contemporary Design." The rest of the space, including the 168-seat Victor Borge Hall, is dedicated to a calendar of lectures, films, music and drama, and scholarly presentations, all of a Nordic ilk. The exquisite modern building—designed to showcase Scandinavian materials and aesthetics—is worth a look itself. Guided tours are offered Tuesday and Thursday at 2pm, and last a half-hour; they're free, but reservations are recommended.

The shop is a riot of fine Scandinavian design, and the excellent **AQ Cafe**—an affordable offshoot of the elegant Midtown restaurant Aquavit—serves up Swedish meatballs and other Scandinavian delicacies.

58 Park Ave. (btwn 37th and 38th sts.). ✆ 212/879-9779. www.scandinaviahouse.org. Suggested admission to 3rd- and 4th-floor galleries $3 adults, $2 seniors and students; free admission to other spaces. Exhibitions Tues–Sun noon–6pm. Cafe Mon–Sat 10am–5pm. Store Mon–Sat 10am–6pm. Subway: 6 to 33rd St.; 4, 5, 6, 7, S to 42nd St./Grand Central.

Schomburg Center for Research in Black Culture *Value*
Arturo Alfonso Schomburg, a black Puerto Rican, set himself to accumulating materials about blacks in America, and his massive collection is now housed and preserved at this research branch of the New York Public Library. The Exhibition Hall, the Latimer/Edison Gallery, and the Reading Room host exhibits related to black culture, such as "Lest We Forget: The Triumph over Slavery" and "Masterpieces of African Motherhood." A rich calendar of talks and performing-arts events is part of the continuing program. Make an appointment for a guided tour so you can see the 1930s murals by Harlem Renaissance artist Aaron Douglas; it'll be worth your while. Academics and others interested in a more complete look at the center's holdings can preview what's available online. Call to inquire about current exhibitions and information on tours and public programs.

515 Malcolm X Blvd. (Lenox Ave., btwn 135th and 136th sts.). ✆ 212/491-2200. www.nypl.org. Free admission. Gallery Mon–Sat 10am–6pm; Sun 1–5pm. Subway: 2, 3 to 135th St.

Skyscraper Museum
Awed by the architectural marvel that is the high-rise? You're not alone. If you'd like to learn more about the technology, culture, and muscle behind it all, seek out this formerly itinerant museum, moving into its permanent home sometime in 2002 in a new 38-story Skidmore, Owings & Merrill tower that houses the Ritz-Carlton New York, Battery Park hotel. The space is comprised of two galleries, one housing a permanent exhibition dedicated to the evolution of Manhattan's skyline, the other for changing shows. Committed to telling the multifaceted story of the multistory high-rise, the museum has always done a bang-up job, so you can expect them to shine once

they settle in. Not all details were in place at this writing—including admission fees or an exact opening date—so call or check the website before you go.

2 West St., Battery Park City. © 212/968-1961. www.skyscraper.org. Subway: 4, 5 to Bowling Green.

South Street Seaport & Museum *Kids*   This landmark district encompasses 11 blocks of historic buildings, a museum, several piers, shops, and restaurants.

You can explore most of the Seaport on your own. It's an odd place. The 18th- and 19th-century buildings lining the cobbled streets and alleyways are beautifully restored but have a theme-park air about them, no doubt due to the mall-familiar shops housed within. The height of the Seaport's cheesiness is Pier 17, a barge converted into a mall, complete with food court and jewelry kiosks.

Despite its rampant commercialism, the Seaport is worth a look. There's a good amount of history to be discovered here, most of it around the **South Street Seaport Museum,** a fitting tribute to the sea commerce that once thrived here.

In addition to the galleries—which house paintings and prints, ship models, scrimshaw, and nautical designs, as well as exhibitions—there are a number of historic ships berthed at the pier, including the 1911 *Peking* and the 1893 Gloucester fishing schooner *Lettie G. Howard.* The museum also offers a number of guided **walking tours;** call or check www.southstseaport.org for details.

Even **Pier 17** has its merits. Head up to the third-level deck overlooking the East River, where the wooden chairs will have you thinking about what it was like to cross the Atlantic on the *Normandie.* From here, you can see south to the Statue of Liberty, north to the Brooklyn Bridge, and across to Brooklyn Heights.

At the gateway to the Seaport, at Fulton and Water streets, is the **Titanic Memorial Lighthouse,** a monument to those who lost their lives when the ocean liner sank on April 15, 1912. It was erected overlooking the East River in 1913 and moved to this spot in 1968, just after the historic district was so designated.

A variety of events take place year-round, ranging from street performers to concerts to fireworks; check the website or dial © **212/SEA-PORT.**

At press time, the ticket booth at the Seaport corner of Fulton and South streets was the place to pick up free tickets to climb the **Ground Zero viewing platform,** at Broadway and Fulton streets. For more on this process, see p. 219. You can also pick up discounted Broadway and other theater tickets at the downtown **TKTS booth.**

At Water and South sts.; museum Visitor Center is at 12 Fulton St. © **212/748-8600** or 212/SEA-PORT. www.southstseaport.org or www.southstreetseaport.com. Museum admission $6 adults, $5 seniors, $4 students, $3 children. Museum Apr–Sept Fri–Wed 10am–6pm, Thurs 10am–8pm; Oct–Mar Wed–Mon 10am–5pm. Subway: 2, 3, 4, 5 to Fulton St. (walk east, or downslope, on Fulton St. to Water St.).

Studio Museum in Harlem   The small but lovely museum is devoted to 19th- and 20th-century African-American art as well as 20th-century African and Caribbean art and traditional African art and artifacts. Rotating exhibitions are a big part of the museum's focus, such as "Smithsonian African-American Photography: The First 100 Years, 1842–1942"; the silk-screens and lithographs of Jacob Lawrence; and an annual exhibition of works by emerging artists as part of its Artists-in-Residence program. There's also a small sculpture garden, a good gift shop, and a full calendar of special events. A just-completed renovation and expansion has added 2,500 feet of gallery space, a cafe, and an auditorium, and also gave a much-needed face-lift to the formerly dour facade.

144 W. 125th St. (btwn Lenox Ave. and Adam Clayton Powell Blvd.). © **212/864-4500.** www.studiomuseum inharlem.org. Admission $5 adults, $3 seniors, $1 children under 12, free for all on first Sat of the month. Sun and Wed–Fri noon–6pm; Sat 10am–6pm. Subway: 2, 3 to 125th St.

Theodore Roosevelt Birthplace This National Historic Site is a reconstruction on the same site of the brownstone where Theodore Roosevelt was born on October 27, 1858 and lived his first 14 years. Period rooms appear as they did in Teddy's youth. The powder-blue parlor is in the rococo-revival style popular at the time, the dining room boasts horsehair-covered chairs, and the nursery has a window that leads to a small gymnasium built to help the frail Teddy get stronger. There's also a collection of Roosevelt memorabilia.

28 E. 20th St. (btwn Broadway and Park Ave. S.). © 212/260-1616. www.nps.gov/thrb. Admission $3 adults, free for children under 18 and National Park Passport holders. Mon–Fri 9am–5pm (tours hourly from 10am–4pm). Subway: N, R to Broadway/23rd St.; 6 to 23rd St.

Whitney Museum of American Art at Philip Morris *Value* This Midtown branch of the Whitney Museum of American Art (p. 217) features an airy sculpture court and a petite gallery that hosts changing exhibits, usually the works of living contemporary artists. Well worth peeking into if you happen to be in the neighborhood; I popped in recently and found a wonderful exhibition that juxtaposed the organic-inspired sculptures and drawings of Isamu Noguchi and Ellsworth Kelly. Free gallery talks are offered Wednesday and Friday at 1pm.

120 Park Ave. (at 42nd St., opposite Grand Central Terminal). © 917/663-2453. www.whitney.org. Free admission. Gallery Mon–Wed and Fri 11am–6pm; Thurs 11am–7:30pm. Sculpture Court Mon–Sat 7:30am–9:30pm; Sun 11am–7pm. Subway: S, 4, 5, 6, 7 to 42nd St./Grand Central.

5 Skyscrapers & Other Architectural Highlights

For details on the **Empire State Building**, see p. 209; **Grand Central Terminal**, see p. 210; **Rockefeller Center**, see p. 212; the **U.S. Customs House**, p. 232; and the **Brooklyn Bridge**, p. 208. "Places of Worship," below, covers **St. Patrick's Cathedral, Temple Emanu-El,** and the **Cathedral of St. John the Divine**.

In addition to the landmarks below, architecture buffs may want to seek out the **Lever House,** at 390 Park Ave., between 53rd and 54th streets, and the **Seagram Building** (1958), at 375 Park Ave., which are the city's best examples of the glass-and-steel International style, with the latter designed by master architect Mies van der Rohe himself. Also in Midtown East is the **Sony Building,** at 550 Madison Ave., designed in 1984 by Philip Johnson with a rose-granite facade and a playful Chippendale-style top that puts it a cut above the rest on the block.

The Upper West Side is home to two of the city's prime examples of residential architecture. On Broadway, between 73rd and 74th streets, is the **Ansonia,** looking like a flamboyant architectural wedding cake. This splendid beaux-arts building has been home to the likes of Stravinsky, Toscanini, and Caruso, thanks to its virtually soundproof apartments. (It was also the spot where members of the Chicago White Sox plotted to throw the 1919 World Series.) Even more notable is the **Dakota,** at 72nd Street and Central Park West. Legend has it that the angular 1884 apartment house—accented with gables, dormers, and oriel windows that give it a brooding appeal—earned its name when its developer, Edward S. Clark, was teased by friends that he was building so far north of the city that he might as well be building in the Dakotas. The building's most famous resident, John Lennon, was gunned down outside the 72nd Street entrance on December 8, 1980; Yoko Ono still lives inside.

Chrysler Building Built as Chrysler Corporation headquarters in 1930, this is perhaps the 20th century's most romantic architectural achievement, especially at night, when the lights in its triangular openings play off its steely

> **Fun Fact Harlem's Architectural Treasures**
> Originally conceived as a suburb for 19th-century Manhattan's moneyed set, Harlem has always had more than its share of historic treasures. Pay a call on the **Astor Row Houses,** 130th Street between Fifth and Lenox avenues, a series of 28 town houses built in the early 1880s by the Astors, graced with wooden porches, yards, and ornamental ironwork.
>
> Equally impressive is **Strivers' Row,** West 139th Street between Adam Clayton Powell Jr. and Frederick Douglass boulevards, where hardly a brick has changed among the McKim, Mead & White neo-Italian Renaissance town houses since 1890. Once the original white owners had moved out, these houses attracted the cream of Harlem, "strivers" like Eubie Blake and W. C. Handy.
>
> Handsome brownstones, town houses, and row houses are atop **Sugar Hill,** 145th to 155th streets, between St. Nicholas and Edgecombe avenues, named for the "sweet life" enjoyed by its residents. In the early 20th century, such prominent blacks as W.E.B. DuBois, Thurgood Marshall, and Roy Wilkins lived in the building at 409 Edgecombe Ave.
>
> While you're uptown, don't miss the **Jumel Terrace Historic District,** west of St. Nicholas Avenue between 160th and 162nd streets. Of particular note is **Sylvan Terrace,** which feels more like a Hudson River town than a part of Harlem. A walk along it will lead you to the **Morris-Jumel Mansion** ★ (see "In Search of Historic Homes," below).

crown. As you admire its facade, be sure to note the gargoyles reaching out from the upper floors, looking for all the world like streamline-Gothic hood ornaments.

There's a fascinating tale behind this building. While it was under construction, architect William Van Alen hid his final plans for the spire that now tops it. Working at a furious pace in the last days of construction, the workers assembled the elegant pointy top in secrecy—and then they raised it right through what people had assumed was going to be the roof, and for a brief moment it was the world's tallest building (a distinction taken by the Empire State Building a few months later). The observation deck closed long ago, but you can visit its lavish ground-floor interior, which is Art Deco to the max. The ceiling mural depicting airplanes and other marvels of the first decades of the 20th century evince the bright promise of technology. The elevators are works of art, covered in exotic woods (especially note the lotus-shaped marquetry on the doors).
405 Lexington Ave. (at 42nd St.). Subway: S, 4, 5, 6, 7 to 42nd St./Grand Central.

Flatiron Building   This triangular masterpiece was one of the first skyscrapers. Its knife-blade wedge shape is the only way the building could fill the triangular property at the intersection of Fifth Avenue and Broadway, and that coincidence created one of the city's most distinctive buildings. Built in 1902 and fronted with limestone and terra cotta, the Flatiron measures only 6 feet (2m) across at its narrow end. It was originally named the Fuller Building, then later "Burnham's Folly," because folks were certain that architect Daniel Burnham's 21-story structure would fall down. It didn't. There's no observation deck, and the building mainly houses publishing offices, but there are a few shops on the ground floor. The building's existence has served to name the neighborhood around it— the Flatiron District, home to a bevy of smart restaurants and shops.
175 Fifth Ave. (at 23rd St.). Subway: N, R to 23rd St.

Finds In Search of Historic Homes

New York's appetite for change often means that older architecture is torn down so that money-earning high-rises can go up. Surprisingly, the city maintains a fine collection of often-overlooked historic houses that are more than a tale of architecture—they're the stories of the people who passed their lives in buildings that range from humble to magnificent.

The **Historic House Trust of New York City** preserves 19 houses in all five boroughs. Those worth seeking out include the **Morris-Jumel Mansion**, in Harlem at 65 Jumel Terrace (at 160th St. east of St. Nicholas Ave.; © 212/923-8008; open Wed–Sun 10am–4pm; admission $3, $2 seniors and students), a grand colonial mansion built in the Palladian style around 1765 and now Manhattan's oldest surviving house.

The **Edgar Allan Poe Cottage**, 2460 Grand Concourse, at East Kingsbridge Road, the Bronx (© 718/881-8900; www.bronxhistoricalsociety.org; open Sat 10am–4pm, Sun 1–5pm; admission $2), was the final home of the poet and author, who moved his wife here because he thought the "country air" would be good for her tuberculosis. Among the works he penned in residence (1846–49) are "The Bells" and "Annabel Lee." The house is outfitted with period furnishings and exhibits on Poe's life and times.

The **Merchant's House Museum**, 29 E. 4th St. between Lafayette Street and Bowery in NoHo (© 212/777-1089; www.merchantshouse.com; open Thurs–Mon 1–5pm; admission $5, $3 for seniors and students), is a rare jewel: a perfectly preserved 19th-century home, complete with intact interiors, whose last resident is said to have been the inspiration for Catherine Sloper in Henry James's *Washington Square*. The house is a prime example of Greek Revival architecture. Seven rooms are outfitted with the belongings of the original inhabitants, offering a prime look at domesticity in the 19th century.

Each of the 16 others also has its own fascinating story to tell, and admission is generally no more than $2 or $3. A brochure listing the locations and touring details of all 19 of the historic homes is available by calling © 212/360-8282; recorded information is available at © 212/360-3448. You'll also find information online at www.preserve.org/hht or http://nycparks.completeinet.net (click on "Things to Do," then "Attractions").

New York Public Library ★★ *Value*   The New York Public Library, adjacent to Bryant Park (p. 248) and designed by Carrère & Hastings (1911), is one of the country's finest examples of beaux-arts architecture, a majestic structure of white Vermont marble with Corinthian columns and allegorical statues. Before climbing the broad flight of steps to the Fifth Avenue entrance, take note of the famous lion sculptures—*Fortitude* on the right, and *Patience* on the left. At Christmastime they don natty wreaths to keep warm.

This library is actually the **Humanities and Social Sciences Library,** only one of the research libraries in the New York Public Library system. The interior is one of the finest in the city and features **Astor Hall,** with arched marble ceilings and grand staircases. The **Main Reading Rooms** have now reopened after a massive restoration and modernization that brought them back to their stately glory and moved them into the computer age (goodbye, card catalogs!).

Even if you don't stop in to peruse the periodicals, you may want to check out one of the **exhibitions;** look for "Drawings by Charles Addams: The Unnatural," "Urban Neighbors: Images of New York City Wildlife," and "New York Eats Out," tracing the history of the Big Apple as the world's ultimate restaurant city, among other exhibitions in late 2002 to 2003. There's also a full calendar of **lecture programs,** with speakers ranging from Tom Stoppard to Cokie Roberts; popular speakers often sell out, so it's a good idea to purchase tickets in advance.

Fifth Ave. and 42nd St. © **212/869-8089** (exhibits and events), or 212/661-7220 (library hours). www.nypl.org. Free admission to exhibitions. Mon and Thurs–Sat 10am–6pm; Tues–Wed 11am–7:30pm. Subway: B, D, F, V to 42nd St.; S, 4, 5, 6, 7 to Grand Central/42nd St.

United Nations The U.N. headquarters occupies 18 acres of international territory—neither New York City nor the United States has jurisdiction here—along the East River from 42nd to 48th streets. Designed by an international team of architects (led by American Wallace K. Harrison and including Le Corbusier), the complex along the East River weds the 39-story glass slab Secretariat with the free-form General Assembly on grounds donated by John D. Rockefeller Jr. One hundred eighty nations use the facilities to arbitrate worldwide disputes.

Guided tours last 45 minutes to an hour and take you to the General Assembly Hall and the Security Council Chamber and introduce the history and activities of the United Nations and its related organizations. Along the tour you'll see donated objects and artwork, including charred artifacts that survived the atomic bombs at Hiroshima and Nagasaki, stained-glass windows by Chagall, a replica of the first *Sputnik,* and a colorful mosaic called *The Golden Rule,* based on a Norman Rockwell drawing, which was a gift from the United States in 1985.

If you take the time to wander the landscaped **grounds,** you'll be rewarded with lovely views and some surprises. The monument *Good Defeats Evil,* donated by the Soviet Union in 1990, fashioned a contemporary St. George slaying a dragon from parts of Russian and American missiles. At press time, the **Delegates' Dining Room** was closed to the public for lunch; feel free to call © **212/963-7625** to see if it has reopened to visitors.

At First Ave. and 46th St. © **212/963-8687.** www.un.org/tours. Guided tours $8.50 adults, $7 seniors, $6 high school and college students, $5 children 5–14. Children under 5 not permitted. Daily tours every half hr. 9:30am–4:45pm; closed weekends Jan–Feb; limited schedule may be in effect during the general debate (late Sept to mid-Oct). Subway: S, 4, 5, 6, 7 to 42nd St./Grand Central.

Woolworth Building ★ This soaring "Cathedral of Commerce" cost Frank W. Woolworth $13.5 million worth of nickels and dimes in 1913. Designed by Cass Gilbert, it was the world's tallest edifice until 1930, when the Chrysler Building surpassed it. At its opening, Pres. Woodrow Wilson pressed a button from the White House that illuminated the building's 80,000 electric light bulbs. The neo-Gothic architecture is rife with spires, gargoyles, flying buttresses, vaulted ceilings, 16th-century–style stone-as-lace traceries, turrets, and a churchlike interior.

Step into the marble entrance arcade to view the mosaic Byzantine-style ceiling and gold-leafed neo-Gothic cornices. The corbels (carved figures under the crossbeams) in the lobby include portraits of the building's engineer Gunwald Aus measuring a girder (above the staircase to the left of the main door), Gilbert holding a model of the building, and Woolworth counting coins (both above the left-hand corridor of elevators). Stand near the security guard's podium and crane your neck for a glimpse of Paul Jennewein's murals of *Commerce* and *Labor,* half hidden on the mezzanine. Cross Broadway for the best view of the exterior.

233 Broadway (at Park Place, near City Hall Park). Subway: 2, 3 to Park Place; N, R to City Hall.

6 Places of Worship

New York has an incredible range of religious institutions, notable for their history, architecture, and/or inspirational music. I've listed two of Harlem's premier gospel institutions below; if you would rather go to one of these gospel services in the company of a guide, see "Affordable Sightseeing Tours," on p. 250. Those who would like to hear the rousing gospel of the multiple Grammy Award–winning **Brooklyn Tabernacle Choir** should see p. 261.

If you do plan to attend a gospel service, be prepared to stay for the entire 1½- to 2-hour service. It is impolite to exit early. (Services are extremely popular, so you'll find it just plain difficult to leave before the end, anyway.)

Abyssinian Baptist Church ★ The most famous of Harlem's more than 400 houses of worship is this Baptist church, founded downtown in 1808 by African-American and Ethiopian merchants. It was moved uptown to Harlem back in the 1920s by Adam Clayton Powell Sr., who built it into the largest Protestant congregation in America. His son, Adam Clayton Powell Jr. (for whom the adjoining boulevard was named), carried on his tradition, and also became a U.S. congressman. Abyssinian is now the domain of the activist-minded Rev. Calvin O. Butts, whom the Chamber of Commerce has declared a "Living Treasure." The Sunday-morning services—at 9 and 11am—offer a wonderful opportunity to experience the Harlem gospel tradition.

132 Odell Clark Place (W. 138th St., btwn Adam Clayton Powell Blvd. and Lenox Ave.). ✆ 212/862-7474. www.abyssinian.org. Subway: 2, 3, B, C to 135th St.

Cathedral of St. John the Divine ★ The world's largest Gothic cathedral, has been a work in progress since 1892. Its sheer size is amazing enough—a nave that stretches two football fields and a seating capacity of 5,000—but keep in mind that there is no steel structural support. The church is being built using Gothic engineering; blocks of granite and limestone are carved by master masons and their apprentices—which may explain why construction is still ongoing, more than 100 years after it began, with no end in sight. That's precisely what makes this place so wonderful: Finishing isn't necessarily the point. A December 2001 fire destroyed the north transept, which housed the gift shop. But this phoenix rose from the ashes; the cathedral was reopened to visitors within a month, even though the scent of charred wood was still in the air.

Though the seat of the Episcopal Diocese of New York, St. John's embraces an interfaith tradition. Each chapel is dedicated to a different national, ethnic, or social group. The genocide memorial in the Missionary chapel—dedicated to the victims of the Ottoman Empire in Armenia (1915–23), of the Holocaust (1939–45), and in Bosnia-Herzegovina since 1992—moved me to tears, as did the FDNY memorial in the Labor chapel. Although it was originally conceived to honor 12 firefighters killed in 1966, hundreds of personal notecards and trinkets of remembrance have evolved it into a moving tribute to the 343 firefighting heroes murdered on September 11, 2001.

You can explore the cathedral on your own, or on the **Public Tour,** offered 6 days a week; also inquire about periodic (usually twice-monthly) **Vertical Tours,** which take you on a hike up the 11-flight circular staircase to the top, for spectacular views. St. John the Divine is also known for presenting outstanding workshops, musical events, and important speakers. The free **New Year's Eve concert** draws thousands of New Yorkers; so, too, does its annual **Blessing of the Animals,** held in early October (see "Calendar of Events," in chapter 2). To hear the pipe organ in action, attend the weekly **Choral Evensong and Organ Meditation** service Sunday at 6pm.

1047 Amsterdam Ave. (at 112th St.). ⓒ **212/316-7540**, 212/932-7347 (tour information and reservations), or 212/662-2133 (event information and tickets). www.stjohndivine.org. Suggested admission $2; tour $3; vertical tour $10. Mon–Sat 7am–6pm; Sun 7am–8pm. Tours offered Tues–Sat 11am; Sun 1pm. Worship services Mon–Sat 8 and 8:30am (morning prayer and holy Eucharist), 12:15pm, and 5:30pm (1st Thurs service 7:15am); Sun 8, 9, and 11am and 6pm; AIDS memorial service 4th Sat of the month at 1pm. Subway: B, C, 1, 9 to Cathedral Pkwy.

Mother A.M.E. Zion Church Another of Harlem's great gospel churches is this African Methodist Episcopal house of worship, the first black church to be founded in New York State. Established on John Street in Lower Manhattan in 1796, Mother A.M.E. was known as the "Freedom Church" for the central role it played in the Underground Railroad. Among the escaped slaves the church hid was Frederick Douglass; other famous congregants have included Sojourner Truth and Paul Robeson. Rousing Sunday services are at 11am.

140–7 W. 137th St. (btwn Adam Clayton Powell Blvd. and Lenox Ave.). ⓒ **212/234-1544**. www.motherafricanmethodistezchurch.com. Subway: 2, 3 or B, C to 135th St.

St. Patrick's Cathedral This Gothic white marble–and-stone structure is the largest Catholic cathedral in the United States, as well as the seat of the Archdiocese of New York. Designed by James Renwick, begun in 1859, and consecrated in 1879, St. Patrick's wasn't completed until 1906. Irish Catholics picked one of the city's WASPiest neighborhoods for St. Patrick's. After the death of the John Cardinal O'Connor in early 2000, the Pope installed Bishop Edward Egan, whom he elevated to Cardinal in early 2001. If you don't want to come for Mass, you can pop in between services to get a look at the impressive interior. The St. Michael and St. Louis altar came from Tiffany and Co. (also on Fifth Ave.), while the St. Elizabeth altar—honoring Mother Elizabeth Seton, the first American-born saint—was designed by Paolo Medici of Rome.

Fifth Ave. (btwn 50th and 51st sts.). ⓒ **212/753-2261**. www.ny-archdiocese.org/pastoral/cathedral_about.html. Free admission. Sun–Fri 7am–8:30pm; Sat 8am–8:30pm. Mass Mon–Fri 7, 7:30, 8, and 8:30am, noon, and 12:30, 1, and 5:30pm; Sat 8 and 8:30am, noon, and 12:30 and 5:30pm; Sun 7, 8, 9, and 10:15am (Cardinal's Mass), noon, and 1, 4, and 5:30pm; holy days 7, 7:30, 8, 8:30, 9, 11, and 11:30am, noon, and 12:30, 1, and 5:30 and 6:30pm. Subway: B, D, F, V to 47–50th sts./Rockefeller Center.

Temple Emanu-El Many of New York's most prominent families are members of this Reform congregation—the first established in New York City. The largest house of Jewish worship in the world is a blend of Moorish and Romanesque styles, symbolizing the mingling of Eastern and Western cultures. The temple houses a remarkable collection of Judaica in the Herbert & Eileen Bernard Museum, including a collection of Hanukkah lamps ranging from the 14th to the 20th centuries. Three galleries also tell the story of the congregation from 1845 to the present. Free **tours** are given after services Saturday at noon. Inquire for a schedule of lectures, films, music, and symposiums.

1 E. 65th St. (at Fifth Ave.). ⓒ **212/744-1400**. www.emanuelnyc.org. Free admission. Daily 10am–5pm. Services Sun–Thurs 5:30pm; Fri 5:15pm; Sat 10:30am. Subway: N, R to Fifth Ave.; 6 to 68th St.

Trinity Church Serving God and Mammon, this Wall Street house of worship—with neo-Gothic flying buttresses, stained-glass windows, and vaulted ceilings—was designed by Richard Upjohn and consecrated in 1846. At that time, its 280-foot (84m) spire dominated the skyline. Its main doors, embellished with biblical scenes, were inspired in part by Ghiberti's famed doors on Florence's Baptistery. The historic church stood strong while office towers crumbled around it on September 11, 2001. The gates to the historic church serve as an impromptu memorial to the victims of 9/11, with countless tokens of remembrance left by both locals and visitors alike.

The church runs a brief free **tour** daily at 2pm (a second Sun tour follows the 11:15am Eucharist); groups of five or more should call © **212/602-0872** to reserve. There's a small museum at the end of the left aisle displaying documents (including the 1697 church charter from William III), photographs, replicas of the Hamilton-Burr duel pistols, and other items. Surrounding the church is a churchyard whose monuments read like a history book: a tribute to martyrs of the American Revolution, Alexander Hamilton, Robert Fulton, and many more. Lined with benches, this makes a wonderful picnic spot on warm days.

Also part of Trinity Church is **St. Paul's Chapel**, at Broadway and Fulton Street, New York's only surviving pre-Revolutionary church, and a transition shelter for homeless men until it was transformed into a relief center after September 11; it returned to its former duties in mid-2002. Built by Thomas McBean, with a templelike portico and Ionic columns supporting a massive pediment, the chapel resembles London's St. Martin-in-the-Fields. In the small graveyard, 18th- and early-19th-century notables rest in peace and modern businesspeople sit for lunch.

Trinity holds its **Noonday Concert series** of chamber music and orchestral concerts Monday and Thursday at 1pm; call © **212/602-0747** or visit the website for a schedule, and to see if programming had resumed at St. Paul's.

At Broadway and Wall St. © 212/602-0800, 212/602-0872, or 212/602-0747 (concert information). www.trinitywallstreet.org. Free admission and tours; $2 suggested donation for noonday concerts. Museum Mon–Fri 9–11:45am and 1–3:45pm; Sat 10am–3:45pm; Sun 1–3:45pm. Services Mon–Fri 8:15am, 12:05, and 5:15pm (additional Healing Service Thurs at 12:30pm); Sat 8:45am; Sun 9 and 11:15am (also 8am Eucharist service at St. Paul's Chapel, between Vesey and Fulton sts.). Subway: 4, 5 to Wall St.

7 Central Park ★★★ & Other Places to Play
CENTRAL PARK

Without the miracle of civic planning that is Central Park, Manhattan would be an unbroken block of buildings. Instead, in the middle of Gotham, an 843-acre retreat provides an escape valve and tranquilizer for millions of New Yorkers.

While you're here, take advantage of the park's many charms—not the least of which is its layout. Frederick Law Olmsted and Calvert Vaux won a competition with a plan that marries flowing paths with sinewy bridges, integrating them into the natural landscape with its rocky outcroppings, man-made lakes, and wooded pockets. The park's construction, between 1859 and 1870, provided employment during a depression and drew the city's population into the upper reaches of the island, which at that time were still quite rural. Nevertheless, designers predicted the hustle and bustle to come, and hid traffic from the eyes and ears of park-goers by building roads that are largely hidden from the bucolic view.

On just about any day, Central Park is crowded with New Yorkers and visitors. On nice days, especially weekend days, it's the city's party-central. Families come to play; in-line skaters fly through the crisp air and twirl in front of the band shell; couples stroll or paddle the lake; dog owners hike and throw Frisbees; and just about everybody comes to sunbathe at the first sign of summer. On beautiful

Central Park

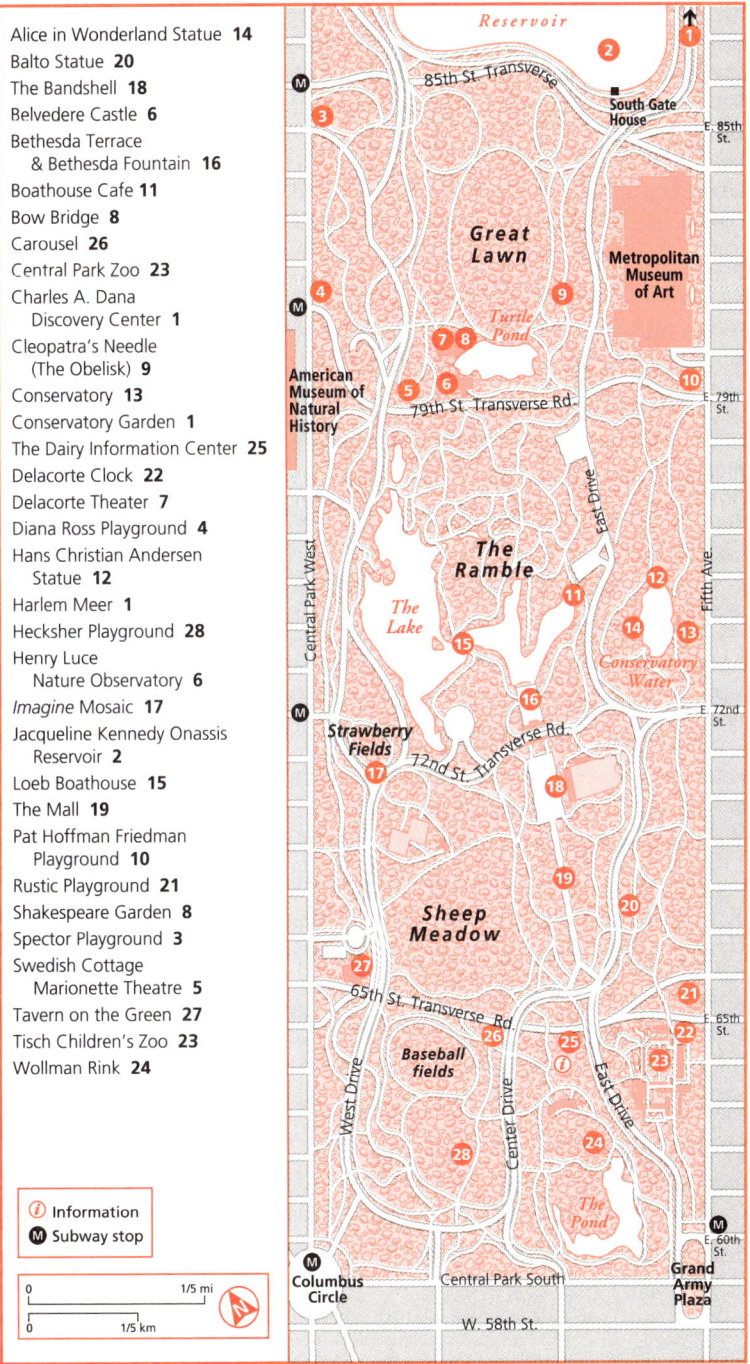

Alice in Wonderland Statue **14**
Balto Statue **20**
The Bandshell **18**
Belvedere Castle **6**
Bethesda Terrace
  & Bethesda Fountain **16**
Boathouse Cafe **11**
Bow Bridge **8**
Carousel **26**
Central Park Zoo **23**
Charles A. Dana
  Discovery Center **1**
Cleopatra's Needle
  (The Obelisk) **9**
Conservatory **13**
Conservatory Garden **1**
The Dairy Information Center **25**
Delacorte Clock **22**
Delacorte Theater **7**
Diana Ross Playground **4**
Hans Christian Andersen
  Statue **12**
Harlem Meer **1**
Hecksher Playground **28**
Henry Luce
  Nature Observatory **6**
Imagine Mosaic **17**
Jacqueline Kennedy Onassis
  Reservoir **2**
Loeb Boathouse **15**
The Mall **19**
Pat Hoffman Friedman
  Playground **10**
Rustic Playground **21**
Shakespeare Garden **8**
Spector Playground **3**
Swedish Cottage
  Marionette Theatre **5**
Tavern on the Green **27**
Tisch Children's Zoo **23**
Wollman Rink **24**

ⓘ Information
Ⓜ Subway stop

243

days, the crowds are part of the appeal—everybody comes to peel off their urban armor and relax. On these days, the people-watching is more compelling than anywhere else in the city. But even on the most crowded days, there's always somewhere to get away from it all.

ORIENTATION & GETTING THERE Look at your map—that great green swath in the center of Manhattan is Central Park. It runs from 59th Street (also known as Central Park S.) at the south end to 110th Street at the north end, and from Fifth Avenue on the east side to Central Park West (the equivalent of Eighth Ave.) on the west side. A 6-mile (9.5km) rolling road, **Central Park Drive,** circles the park, and has a lane set aside for bikers, joggers, and inline skaters. A number of **transverse (crosstown) roads** cross the park at major points—at 65th, 79th, 86th, and 97th streets—but they're built down a level, largely out of view, to minimize intrusion on the bucolic nature of the park.

A number of subway stops and lines serve the park. To reach the southernmost entrance on the west side, take an A, B, C, D, 1, or 9 to 59th Street/Columbus Circle. To reach the southeast corner, take the N, R to Fifth Avenue; from this stop, it's an easy walk to the Information Center in the **Dairy** (© **212/794-6564;** open daily 11am–5pm, to 4pm in winter), midpark at about 65th Street. Here you can ask questions, pick up information, and purchase a good park map.

If your time for exploring is limited, I suggest entering the park at 72nd or 79th streets (subway: B, C to 72nd St. or 81st St./Museum of Natural History). From here, you can pick up information at the visitor center at **Belvedere Castle** (© **212/772-0210;** open Tues–Sun 10am–5pm, to 4pm in winter), midpark at 79th Street. There's also a visitor center at the **Charles A. Dana Discovery Center** (© **212/860-1370;** open daily 11am–5pm, to 4pm in winter), at the northeast corner of the park at Harlem Meer, at 110th Street between Fifth and Lenox avenues (subway: 2, 3 to 110th St.). The Dana Center is an environmental center hosting workshops, exhibits, music programs, and park tours, and lends fishing poles for fishing in Harlem Meer (park policy is catch-and-release).

Food carts and vendors are at all of the park's main gathering points, so finding a bite is never a problem. You'll also find food counters at the **Conservatory,** on the east side of the park, north of the 72nd Street entrance; and at **The Boat House,** on the lake near 72nd Street and Park Drive North, which also offers a full-service menu (© **212/517-2233**).

GUIDED WALKS The **Central Park Conservancy** offers a slate of free walking tours; call © **212/360-2726** or check **www.centralparknyc.org** for the current schedule (click on the "Walking Tours" button on the left). The Dana Center hosts ranger-guided tours on occasion (call © **800/201-PARK** or 212/860-1370 for the schedule).

FOR FURTHER INFORMATION Call the main number at © **212/360-3444** for recorded information, or 212/310-6600 or 212/628-1036 to speak to a live person. Call © **888/NY-PARKS** for events information. The park also has two websites: The city parks department's site at **www.centralpark.org**, and the Central Park Conservancy's site at **www.centralparknyc.org**, each of which features maps and a rundown of attractions and activities. For a park **emergency,** dial © **800/201-PARK,** which will link you to the park rangers.

SAFETY TIP Even though the park has the lowest crime rate of any of the city's precincts, keep your wits about you, especially in the more remote northern end. It's a good idea to avoid the park entirely after dark, unless you're heading to one of the restaurants for dinner or to a SummerStage or Shakespeare in the Park event (see chapter 9), when you should stick with the crowds.

EXPLORING THE PARK

The best way to see Central Park is to wander along the park's 58 miles (93km) of winding pedestrian paths, keeping in mind the following highlights.

Before starting your stroll, stop by the **Information Center** in the Dairy (© **212/794-6464;** open daily 11am–5pm, to 4pm in winter), midpark in a 19th-century-style building overlooking Wollman Rink at about 65th Street, to get a good park map and other information on sights and events.

The southern part of Central Park is more formally designed and heavily visited than the relatively rugged and remote northern end. Not far from the Dairy is the **carousel** with 58 hand-carved horses (© **212/879-0244;** open daily 10:30am–6pm, to 5pm in winter; rides are 90¢); the zoo (see listing for "Central Park Zoo"); and the Wollman Rink for roller- or ice-skating (see "Activities," below).

The **Mall,** a long formal walkway lined with elms shading benches and sculptures of sometimes forgotten writers, leads to the focal point of Central Park, **Bethesda Fountain** ⭐ (along the 72nd St. transverse road). **Bethesda Terrace** and its sculpted entryway border a large **lake** where dogs fetch sticks, boaters glide by, and anglers try their luck at catching carp, perch, catfish, and bass. You can rent a rowboat at or take a gondola ride from **Loeb Boathouse,** on the eastern end of the lake (see "Activities," below). Boats of another kind are at **Conservatory Water** (on the east side at 73rd St.), a stone-walled pond flanked by statues of both **Hans Christian Andersen** and **Alice in Wonderland.** On Saturday at 10am, die-hard yachtsmen race remote-controlled sailboats in fierce competitions following Olympic regulations. (Sorry, model boats aren't for rent.)

Sheep Meadow on the southwestern side of the park is a designated quiet zone, where Frisbee throwing and kite flying are as energetic as things get. Another respite is **Strawberry Fields** ⭐, at 72nd Street on the West Side. This memorial to John Lennon, who was murdered across the street at the Dakota apartment building, is a gorgeous garden centered around an Italian mosaic bearing the title of this Beatle's most famous solo song, and his lifelong message: IMAGINE. In keeping with its goal of promoting world peace, the garden has 161 varieties of plants, donated by each of the 161 nations in existence when it was designed in 1985. This is a wonderful place for peaceful contemplation.

Bow Bridge, a graceful lacework of cast iron designed by Calvert Vaux, crosses over the lake and leads to the most bucolic area of Central Park, the **Ramble.** This dense 38-acre woodland with spiraling paths, rocky outcroppings, and a stream is the best spot for bird-watching and feeling as if you've discovered an unimaginably leafy forest right in the middle of the city.

North of the Ramble, **Belvedere Castle** ⭐ is home to the **Henry Luce Nature Observatory** (© **212/772-0210**), worth a visit if you're with children. From the castle, set on Vista Rock (the park's highest point at 135 ft./41m), you can look down on the **Great Lawn,** and the **Delacorte Theater,** home to Shakespeare in the Park (p. 312). The small **Shakespeare Garden** south of the theater is scruffy, but it does have plants, herbs, and trees mentioned by the playwright. Behind the Belvedere Castle is the **Swedish Cottage Marionette Theatre** ⭐ (© **212/988-9093**), hosting marionette plays for children.

Continue north along the east side of the Great Lawn, parallel to East Drive. Near the glass-enclosed back of the **Metropolitan Museum of Art** ⭐⭐⭐ (p. 211) is **Cleopatra's Needle,** a 69-foot (21m) obelisk originally erected in

Heliopolis around 1475 B.C. It was given to the city by the khedive of Egypt in 1880. (The khedive bestowed a similar obelisk, which now sits on the Embankment of the Thames, to the city of London.)

North of the 86th Street Transverse Road is the **Jacqueline Kennedy Onassis Reservoir,** so named after the death of the First Lady, who lived nearby and often enjoyed a run along the 1½-mile (2.5km) jogging track around the reservoir.

At the northeast end of the park is the **Conservatory Garden** (at 105th St. and Fifth Ave.), Central Park's formal garden, with a magnificent display of flowers and trees reflected in pools of water. (The gates to the garden once fronted the Fifth Ave. mansion of Cornelius Vanderbilt II.) **Harlem Meer** and its boathouse were recently renovated and look beautiful. The boathouse now hosts the **Charles A. Dana Discovery Center,** near 110th Street between Fifth and Lenox avenues (© **212/860-1370**), where children learn about the environment and borrow fishing poles for catch-and-release at no charge.

GOING TO THE ZOO

Central Park Zoo *Kids* It has been a decade since the zoo in Central Park was renovated, making it both more human and more humane. Sea lions frolic in the central pool area. The gigantic, graceful polar bears (one of whom, by the way, made himself a true New Yorker when he began regular visits with a shrink) glide back and forth across a watery pool that has glass walls through which you can observe very large paws doing very smooth strokes. The monkeys seem to regard those on the other side of the fence with knowing disdain. In the hot and humid Tropic Zone, large colorful birds swoop around in freedom, sometimes landing next to nonplused visitors.

The indoor Tropic Zone is a real highlight, its steamy rain forest home to everything from black-and-white colobus monkeys to emerald tree boa constrictors to a leaf-cutter ant farm; look for the dart poison frog exhibit, which is very cool. So is the large penguin enclosure in the Polar Circle, which is better than the one at San Diego's Sea World. In the Temperate Territory, look for the Asian red pandas (cousins to the black-and-white ones), which look like beautiful raccoons. Despite their pool and piles of ice, the polar bears still look sad.

The entire zoo is good for short attention spans; you can cover the whole thing in 1½ to 3 hours, depending on the size of the crowds and how long you like to linger. It's also very kid-friendly, with lots of well-written and -illustrated placards that older kids can understand. For the littlest ones, there's the $6 million **Tisch Children's Zoo.** With sheep, llamas, potbellied pigs, and more, this petting zoo and playground is a real blast for the 5-and-under set.

830 Fifth Ave. (at 64th St., just inside Central Park). © **212/861-6030.** www.wcs.org/zoos. Admission $3.50 adults, $1.25 seniors, 50¢ children 3–12, free for children under 3. Apr–Oct Mon–Fri 10am–5pm; Sat–Sun 10am–5:30pm. Nov–Mar daily 10am–4:30pm. Subway: N, R to Fifth Ave.

ACTIVITIES

The 6-mile (9.5km) rolling road circling the park, **Central Park Drive,** has a lane for bikers, joggers, and in-line skaters. The best time to use it is when the park is closed to traffic: Monday to Friday from 10am to 3pm (except Thanksgiving to New Year's) and 7 to 10pm. It's also closed from 7pm Friday to 6am Monday, but when the weather is nice, the crowds can be hellish.

BIKING Off-road mountain biking isn't permitted; stay on Central Park Drive or your bike may be confiscated by park police.

You can rent 3- and 10-speed bikes as well as tandems in Central Park at the **Loeb Boathouse,** midpark near 72nd Street and Park Drive North, just in from

Fifth Avenue (© **212/517-2233** or 212/517-3623), for $9 to $20 an hour, with a complete selection of kids' bikes, cruisers, tandems, and the like ($200 deposit required); at **Metro Bicycles,** 1311 Lexington Ave., at 88th Street (© **212/ 427-4450**), for about $7 an hour, or $35 a day; and at **Toga Bike Shop,** 110 West End Ave., at 64th Street (© **212/799-9625;** www.togabikes.com), for $30 a day. No matter where you rent, be prepared to leave a credit-card deposit.

BOATING From March through November, gondola rides and rowboat rentals are available at the **Loeb Boathouse,** midpark near 74th Street and Park Drive North, just in from Fifth Avenue (© **212/517-2233** or 212/517-3623). Rowboats are $10 for the first hour, $2.50 every 15 minutes thereafter, and a $30 deposit is required; reservations are accepted.

HORSE-DRAWN CARRIAGE RIDES At the entrance to the park at 59th Street and Central Park South, you'll see a line of **horse-drawn carriages** waiting to take passengers through the park or along certain of the city's streets. Horses belong on city streets as much as chamber pots belong in our homes. You won't need me to tell you how forlorn most of these horses look—skip it.

ICE-SKATING **Wollman Rink** ✶, on the east side of the park between 62nd and 63rd streets (© **212/439-6900;** www.wollmanskatingrink.com), is the city's best outdoor skating spot, more spacious than the rink at Rockefeller Center. It's open for skating from mid-October to mid-April, depending on the weather. Rates are $7 for adults, $3.50 for seniors and kids under 12, and skate rental is $3.50; lockers are available (locks are $6.75).

IN-LINE SKATING Central Park is the city's most popular place for blading. See the beginning of this section for details on Central Park Drive, the main drag for skaters. On weekends, head to West Drive at 67th Street, behind Tavern on the Green, where you'll find trick skaters weaving through an NYRSA slalom course at full speed, or the Mall in front of the band shell (above Bethesda Fountain) for twirling to tunes. In summer, **Wollman Rink** converts to a hot-shot roller rink, with half-pipes and lessons available (see "Ice-Skating," above).

You can rent skates for $20 a day from **Blades Board and Skate,** 120 W. 72nd St., between Broadway and Columbus Avenue (© **212/787-3911;** www.blades.com). Wollman Rink (see above) also rents in-line skates for park use at similar rates.

PLAYGROUNDS Nineteen Adventure Playgrounds are scattered throughout the park, perfect for jumping, sliding, swinging, and digging. At Central Park West and 81st Street is the **Diana Ross Playground** ✶, voted the city's best by *New York* magazine. Also on the west side is the **Spector Playground,** at 85th Street and Central Park West, and, farther north, the **Wild West Playground** at 93rd Street. On the east side is the **Rustic Playground,** at 67th Street and Fifth Avenue, a delightfully landscaped space rife with islands, bridges, and slides; and the **Pat Hoffman Friedman Playground,** behind the Metropolitan Museum of Art at East 79th Street, is geared toward older toddlers.

RUNNING Marathoners and wannabes run in Central Park along the 6-mile (9.5km) **Central Park Drive,** which circles the park (run toward traffic to avoid being mowed down by wayward cyclists and in-line skaters). For a shorter loop, try the midpark 1.5-mile (2.5km) track around the **Jacqueline Kennedy Onassis Reservoir** (keep your eyes ready for spotting Madonna and other famous bodies). It's safest to jog only during daylight hours and where everybody else does. Avoid the small walks in the Ramble and at the north end of the park.

OTHER PARKS

For parks in Brooklyn and Queens, see "Highlights of the Outer Boroughs" (p. 258). For more information on these and other city parks, go online to **http://nycparks.completeinet.org**.

Battery Park ⭐⭐ As you traverse Manhattan's concrete canyons, it's easy to forget you're on an island. But at Manhattan's southernmost tip, you get the real sense that just past Liberty, Ellis, and Staten islands is the Atlantic Ocean.

The 21-acre park is named for the cannons built to defend residents after the American Revolution. **Castle Clinton National Monument** (the place to purchase tickets for the Statue of Liberty and Ellis Island ferry) was built as a fort before the War of 1812, though it was never used as such. The 22-ton **bronze sphere** by Fritz Koenig that was recovered from the rubble of the World Trade Center, where it stood between the Twin Towers as a symbol of global peace, now stands—severely damaged but still whole—in the park as a temporary memorial to the nearly 3,000 victims of the World Trade Center terrorist attack. This may be the finest place in the city to pay tribute to those who were lost.

You'll likely recognize Battery Park for the role it played in *Desperately Seeking Susan*. Besides the T-shirt vendors and hot-dog carts, you'll find several statues and memorials throughout the park. This is quite the civilized park, with lots of STAY OFF THE GRASS! signs and Wall Streeters eating sandwiches on the park benches. Pull up your own bench for a good view across the harbor.

From State St. to New York Harbor. Subway: N, R to Whitehall St.; 1, 9 to South Ferry; 4, 5 to Bowling Green.

Bowling Green Park This patch of green at the end of Broadway is most notable for its early history. This is most likely the spot where, in 1626, Peter Minuit gave beads and other trinkets worth about 60 guilders ($24) to a group of Indians, and then claimed he had bought Manhattan. The local Indians didn't think they owned this island because Manhattan was considered communal hunting ground, so it isn't clear what the Indians thought the trinkets meant. Either (a) they thought the exchange was a way of closing an agreement to extend the shared hunting use to this funny-looking group of pale people with yellow beards; or (b) they were selling land that they didn't own in the first place, thus performing the first shrewd real-estate deal of the Financial District.

When George III repealed the Stamp Act in 1770, New Yorkers raised a statue of him here, although today it's just another lunch spot for stockbrokers. The statue lasted 5 years, until the day the Declaration of Independence was read to the public in front of City Hall (now Federal Hall) and a crowd rushed down Broadway to topple the statue, chop it up, melt it down, and transform it into 42,000 bullets, which they later used to shoot the British.

On the fringe of the park is the stunning 1907 beaux-arts **U.S. Customs House,** currently housing the National Museum of the American Indian (p. 232).

From State St. to New York Harbor. Subway: 4, 5 to Bowling Green; N, R to Whitehall St.

Bryant Park ⭐ Another success story in urban redevelopment, Bryant Park is the latest incarnation of a 4-acre site that was, at various times a graveyard and a reservoir. Named for poet and *New York Evening Post* editor William Cullen Bryant (look for his statue on the east end), the park rests atop the New York Public Library's underground stacks. Another notable statue is a squat and evocative stone portrait of Gertrude Stein.

This simple green swath is welcome relief from Midtown's concrete, taxi-choked jungle, and good weather attracts brown-baggers from neighboring office buildings. Just behind the library is **Bryant Park Grill** (© 212/840-6500; www.bryantparkgrill.com), a gorgeous, airy bistro with spectacular views but merely decent food. The grill's two summer alfresco restaurants—**The Terrace,** on the Grill's roof, and the **Cafe** are extremely pleasant on a nice day.

Additionally, the park plays host to New York's **Seventh on Sixth** fashion shows, set up in billowy white tents (open to the trade only) in the spring and fall.

In the summer, HBO sponsors the **Bryant Park Summer Film Festival,** in which a classic film—*Dr. Zhivago, Viva Las Vegas,* and the like—is shown on a 20-by-50-foot screen under the stars every Monday evening at sunset. Admission is free; just bring a blanket and a picnic. Rain dates are Tuesdays. For the current schedule, call © **212/512-5700** or visit www.hbobryantparkfilm.com.

Behind the New York Public Library, at Sixth Ave. between 40th and 42nd sts. www.bryantpark.org. Subway: B, D, F, V to 42nd St.; 7 to Fifth Ave.

Union Square Park Reclaimed from drug dealers and abject ruin in the late '80s, Union Square Park is now one of the city's best assets. This patch of green is the focal point of the fashionable Flatiron and Gramercy Park neighborhoods. Don't miss the grand equestrian statue of George Washington at the south end or the bronze statue (by Bartholdi, the sculptor of the Statue of Liberty) of the marquis de Lafayette at the eastern end, gracefully glancing toward France.

This charming square is the site of New York's premier **Greenmarket.** Every Monday, Wednesday, Friday, and Saturday, vendors hawk fresh veggies and fruits, organic baked goods, cider, wine, and even fresh fish and lobsters in booths that flank the north and west sides of the square. Fresh-cut flowers and plants are also for sale, as are books and postcards. During summer and fall, you can graze the bazaar and assemble a cheap and healthy lunch to munch under the trees or at the picnic tables at the park's north end. Musical acts play the small pavilion at the north end of the park, and in-line skaters take over the market space in the after-work hours. A **cafe** is open at the north end of the park in warm weather.

From 14th to 17th sts., btwn Park Ave. S. and Broadway. Subway: 4, 5, 6, L, N, R, Q, W to 14th St./Union Sq.

Washington Square Park You'll be hard-pressed to find much "park" in this mostly concrete square—a burial ground in the late 18th century—but it's undeniably the focal point of Greenwich Village. Chess players, skateboarders, street musicians, New York University students, couples, the occasional film crew, and not a few homeless people compete for attention throughout the day and most of the night. (If anyone issues a challenge to play you in the ancient and complex Chinese game of Go, don't take them up on it—you'll lose money.)

The lively scene belies a macabre past. Once marshland traversed by Minetta Brook, it became in 1797 a potter's field, and the remains of some 10,000 bodies are buried here. In the early 1800s, the square, or the infamous Hanging Elm in the northwest corner where MacDougal Street meets the park, was used for public executions. It wasn't until the 1830s that the Greek Revival town houses on **Washington Square North** known as "The Row" (note especially nos. 21–26) attracted the elite. Stanford White designed Washington Arch (1891–92) to commemorate the centenary of George Washington's inauguration as president. While in the neighborhood, peek down MacDougal Alley and Washington Mews, both lined with delightful old carriage houses.

At the southern end of Fifth Ave. (where it intersects Waverly Place btwn MacDougal and Wooster sts.). Subway: A, C, E, F, V to West 4th St./Washington Sq.

8 Affordable Sightseeing Tours

Reservations are required on some of the tours listed below, but even if they're not, it's always best to call ahead to confirm prices, times, and meeting places.

HARBOR CRUISES

Circle Line Sightseeing Cruises Circle Line is the only tour company that circumnavigates the entire 35 miles (56km) around Manhattan, and I love this ride. The **Full Island** cruise takes 3 hours and passes by the Statue of Liberty, Ellis Island, the Brooklyn Bridge, the United Nations, Yankee Stadium, the George Washington Bridge, and more, including Manhattan's wild northern tip. The panorama is riveting, and the commentary isn't bad. The big boats are basic but fine, with lots of deck room for everybody to enjoy the view. Snacks, soft drinks, coffee, and beer are available onboard for purchase.

If 3 hours is more than you or the kids can handle, go for either the 1½-hour **Semi-Circle** or **Sunset/Harbor Lights** cruise, both of which show you the highlights of the skyline. There's also a 1-hour **Seaport Liberty** version that sticks close to the south end of the island. But of all the tours, the kids might like **The Beast** best, a thrill-a-minute speedboat ride offered in summer only.

In addition, a number of adults-only **Live Music and DJ Cruises** sail regularly from the seaport from May through September ($20–$40 per person). Depending on the night of the week, you can groove to the sounds of jazz, Latin, gospel, dance tunes, or blues as you sail along the skyline.

Departing from Pier 83, at W. 42nd St. and Twelfth Ave. Also departing from Pier 16 at South St. Seaport, 207 Front St. © 212/563-3200. www.circleline.com, www.ridethebeast.com, and www.seaportmusiccruises.com. Sightseeing cruises $13–$25 adults, $11–$20 seniors, $7–$12 children 12 and under. Subway to Pier 83: A, C, E to 42nd St. Subway to Pier 16: J, M, Z, 2, 3, 4, 5 to Fulton St.

SPECIALTY TOURS
MUSEUMS & CULTURAL ORGANIZATIONS

In addition to the choices below, those interested in touring the Financial District with a guide should also consider the **World of Finance Walking Tour** offered Fridays at 10am by the Museum of American Financial History; see p. 228.

The **Municipal Art Society** (© 212/439-1049 or 212/935-3960; www.mas.org) offers excellent historical and architectural walking tours aimed at intelligent, individualistic travelers. A highly qualified guide who gives insights into the significance of buildings, neighborhoods, and history leads each tour. Topics range from the urban history of Greenwich Village to "Mies and the Moderns," examining the architectural legacy of Mies van der Rohe, to an examination of the "new" Times Square. Weekday walking tours cost $12; weekend tours cost $15. Reservations may be required depending on the tour, so call ahead. A full schedule is available online or by calling © 212/439-1049.

The **92nd Street Y** (© 212/415-5500 or 212/415-5628; www.92ndsty.org) offers a variety of walking and bus tours, many featuring funky themes or behind-the-scenes visits. Subjects can range from "Diplomat for a Day at the U.N." to "Secrets of the Chelsea Hotel," from "Artists of the Meat-Packing District" to "Jewish Harlem." Prices range from $20 to $60 (sometimes more for bus tours), but many include ferry rides, afternoon tea, dinner, or whatever suits the program. Guides are experts on their subjects, ranging from historians to an East Village poet, mystic, and art critic (for "Allen Ginsberg's New York" and "East Village Night Spots"), and many routes travel into the outer boroughs; some day trips even reach beyond the city. Advance registration is required for all walking and bus tours. Schedules are planned a few months in advance, so check the website for tours that might interest you.

INDEPENDENT OPERATORS

One of the most highly praised sightseeing organizations in New York is **Big Onion Walking Tours** ✦ (© **212/439-1090;** www.bigonion.com). Enthusiastic Big Onion guides (all hold degrees in American history) peel back the layers of history to reveal the city's secrets. The 2-hour tours are offered mostly on weekends, and subjects include the "The Bowery," "Presidential New York," "Irish New York," "Central Park," "Greenwich Village in Twilight," "Historic Harlem," "Jewish Ellis Island," "Brooklyn Bridge & Brooklyn Heights at Twilight," and historic takes on Lower Manhattan. One of the most popular is the "Multiethnic Eating Tour" of the Lower East Side, where you munch on everything from dim sum and dill pickles to fresh mozzarella. Tour prices range from $12 to $18 for adults, $10 to $16 for students and seniors. No reservations are necessary, but Big Onion *recommends that you call to verify schedules.*

All tours from **Joyce Gold History Tours of New York** ✦ (© **212/242-5762;** www.nyctours.com) are offered by Joyce Gold herself, an instructor of Manhattan history at New York University and the New School, who has been conducting walks around New York since 1975. Her tours can cut to the core of this town; Joyce is full of fascinating stories about Manhattan and its people. Tours are arranged around themes like "The Colonial Settlers of Wall Street," "The Genius and Elegance of Gramercy Park," "Downtown Graveyards," "The Old Jewish Lower East Side," "Historic Harlem," and "TriBeCa: The Creative Explosion." Tours are offered most weekends March to December and last from 2 to 4 hours, and the price is $12 per person; no reservations are required. Private tours can be arranged year-round, either for individuals or groups.

Behind the scenes is the focus of **Adventure on a Shoestring** ★★ (© **212/265-2663**), which offers 90-minute public walking tours on weekends (and some weekdays and holidays) year-round for just $5. One of the earliest entrants in the now-burgeoning walking-tour market, Howard Goldberg has provided unique views of New York since 1963, exploring Manhattan's neighborhoods with a breezy, man-of-the-people style. Tours run the gamut from historical and architectural walks of artsy SoHo, elegant Sutton Place, or little-known Roosevelt Island to themed walks like "A Salute to Jacqueline Kennedy Onassis" and "Greenwich Village Ghosts Galore." Most tours focus on Manhattan, but Mr. Goldberg occasionally leads tours to Astoria, Queens, home to the largest Greek population outside of Greece; the fascinating Russian quarter of Little Odessa, Brooklyn; and other ethic enclaves. One of the best budget bargains in New York. Walks go on regardless of the weather. Call for reservations.

Alfred Pommer has conducted **New York City Cultural Walking Tours** (© **212/979-2388;** www.nycwalk.com) in nearly every Manhattan neighborhood for over 15 years. He focuses on history and architecture, making the past come alive via photographs and stories. A number of his tours focus on specific subjects, such as "Gargoyles in Manhattan." His 2½-hour tours take place most Sundays at 2pm. The charge is $10 per person, and no reservation is needed; just show up at the assigned spot. Mr. Pommer also offers weekday walking tours that cost $20 per person and require reservations; call © **212/334-2211,** ext. 101, or

Value Absolutely Free Walking Tours

A number of neighborhood organizations and Business Improvement Districts (BIDs) offer free guided walks of their neighborhoods. For travelers on a budget, these introductory freebies are well worth taking advantage of:

The **Municipal Art Society** (© 212/935-3960; www.mas.org) offers a free walking tour of Grand Central Terminal on Wednesday at 12:30pm, which meets at the information booth on the Grand Concourse. The **Grand Central Partnership** (© 212/697-1245) runs its own free tour every Friday at 12:30pm, meeting outside the station in front of the Whitney Museum at Philip Morris gallery, at 42nd Street and Park Avenue. It's a real joy now that Grand Central has been restored. Call to confirm the schedule and meeting spot before you set out to meet either tour.

The Alliance for Downtown New York, the Business Improvement District in charge of Lower Manhattan, offers a free 90-minute **Wall Street Walking Tour** every Thursday and Saturday at noon, rain or shine. This guided tour explores the history and architecture of the nation's first capital and the world center of finance. Stops include the New York Stock Exchange, Trinity Church, Federal Hall National Monument, and other sites of historic and cultural importance. Tours meet on the steps of the U.S. Customs House (p. 232), at 1 Bowling Green (subway: 4, 5 to Bowling Green). Reservations are not required (unless you're a group), but you can call © 212/606-4064 or visit **www.downtownny.com** to confirm the schedule.

The **Orchard Street Bargain District Tour** (© 888/825-8374 or 212/226-9010; www.lowereastsideny.com) explores the history and retail culture of this neighborhood. This is a good bet for bargain-hunters, who will learn about the old-world shops and newer outlet stores in this discount-shopping destination. The free tours are given Sunday at 11am from April to December, rain or shine, and no reservation is required. Meet up with the guide in front of Katz's Delicatessen, 205 E. Houston St., at Ludlow Street.

If you're looking to tour a specific neighborhood with an expert guide, call **Big Apple Greeter** (© 212/669-8159; www.bigapplegreeter.org). This nonprofit organization consists of specially trained New Yorkers who volunteer to take visitors around town for a free 2- to 4-hour tour of a particular neighborhood. Reservations must be made in advance, preferably at least 1 week ahead of your arrival. Big Apple Greeter is also well suited to accommodate travelers with disabilities; see "Tips for Travelers with Special Needs" in chapter 2 for details.

---

go to www.imar.com/nycwalk. Private tours are available at $30 per hour for individuals or groups.

Self-proclaimed "radical historian" Bruce Kayton leads unconventional **Radical Walking Tours** (© 718/492-0069; www.he.net/~radtours) to conventional tourist sights. A tour of Harlem covers the Black Panthers, the Communist

Party, and Malcolm X in addition to the Apollo Theatre and the Schomburg Center, and a visit to the Lower East Side focuses on radical Jews such as Abraham Cahan (founder of the *Jewish Daily Forward* in 1897) and the Rosenbergs. Two Greenwich Village tours are offered, of course. Most tours cost $10 and last 2½ to 4½ hours; no reservations are required.

Would you like to cruise by Monica and Chandler's apartment building? How about the courthouse where the prosecutors of *Law & Order* fight the good fight? **On Location Tours** (✆ 212/334-0492 or 212/935-0168; www.sceneontv.com) offers narrated minibus tours on their **Manhattan TV Tour**; tickets are $20 for adults, $10 for kids 6 to 9, free for 5 and under. Or, if you want to see Carrie Bradshaw's Big Apple, take the 2½-hour *Sex in the City* **Tour**; tickets cost $25. Most tours take place on Saturdays and depart from the Times Square Visitor Center, at noon and 2:30pm respectively. There's a 3-hour *Sopranos* **Tour** that will take you to New Jersey for $30. Reservations are a must.

Recommended by the Harlem Travel and Tourism Association, **A La Carte New York Tours** (✆ 212/828-7360; www.alacartecity.com) also offers a slate of walking, bus, architecture, jazz, Apollo Theatre, and gospel tours of the Upper Manhattan neighborhood. Prices run from $15 to $75, depending on the options you choose. All guides are licensed and extremely knowledgeable.

New York Like a Native ★ (✆ 718/393-7537; www.nylikeanative.com) offers the city's best guided introduction to Brooklyn. The tours focus mainly on the best of brownstone Brooklyn, and you can choose from a 2½-hour version ($13), or an extended 4½-hour version ($35); the longer tour includes lunch, but you must cover your own bus and subway fares. Tours are generally offered on Saturdays from April through December, and meet at the Brooklyn Library on Grand Army Plaza (subway: 2, 3 to Grand Army Plaza). *Prepaid reservations are required;* visit the website or call ✆ **212/239-1124** to order.

9 Talk of the Town: Free TV Tapings

The trick to getting tickets for TV tapings in this city is to be from out of town. Visitors have a much better chance than we New Yorkers; producers are gun-shy about filling their audiences with obnoxious locals and see everybody who's not from New York as being from the heartland—their target TV audience.

If your heart's set on getting tickets to a show, request them as early as possible—6 months ahead isn't too early. You're usually asked to send a postcard. Always include the number of tickets you want, your preferred dates of attendance (be as flexible as you can), and your address *and* phone number. Tickets are always free. The shows tend to be pretty good about trying to meet your specific date requests, but don't be surprised if Ricki or Montel are far more responsive than, say, Dave Letterman. And even if you send in your request early, don't be surprised if tickets arrive as late as 1 or 2 weeks before tape date.

If you come to town without any tickets, all hope is not lost. Because they know that not every ticket holder will make it, many studios give out standby tickets on the day of taping. If you can get up early and don't mind standing in line for a couple (or a few) hours, you may get one. Now, the bad news: Only one standby ticket per person is allowed, so everybody who wants to get in has to get up at the crack of dawn and stand in line. And even if you get your hands on a standby ticket, it doesn't guarantee admission; they usually only start seating standbys after the regular ticket holders are in. Still, chances are good.

For additional information on getting tickets, call the NYCVB at ✆ **212/484-1222**. And remember—you don't need a ticket to be on the *Today* show.

If you attend a taping, bring a sweater! As anybody who watches Letterman knows, it's an icebox in those studios. And bring ID, as proof of age may be required.

Change of Heart   The syndicated dating show has relocated to the Big Apple, for better or worse. To score audience tickets, call © **877/485-7144**, or fill out the online ticket request form at www.changeofheart.warnerbros.com.

Emeril Live   If you haven't seen enough of superstar chef Emeril Lagasse, you can try to catch a taping of his show. Scoring tickets is no easy recipe; they're only available through the Food Network through periodic ticket lotteries. The best way to get in is to sign up for the weekly newsletter at FoodTV.com (click on "Newsletter" on the left-hand scroll bar), which announces ticket lotteries.

The Daily Show with Jon Stewart   Comedy Central's irreverent, often hilarious mock newscast tapes every Monday through Thursday at 5:45pm, at 513 W. 54th St. Make your advance ticket requests by phone at © **212/586-2477**, or check with them for any cancellation tickets for the upcoming week; the line is open Monday through Thursday from 10:30am to 4pm for tickets.

Good Morning America   Fans of ABC's weekday morning show can join Diane Sawyer and Charlie Gibson in their street-facing studio at Broadway and 44th Street as part of the live audience. To witness the 7 to 9am broadcast, fill out the online request at www.abcnews.go.com/sections/GMA (click on "GMA Tickets"), or call © **212/580-5176** during business hours.

Last Call with Carson Daly   Tapings of the MTV heartthrob's NBC late-night gabfest is much like a grown-up TRL, without the countdown or screaming sweet 16s. Tapings are on select weeknights at 7 and/or 9pm. You can reserve up to four tickets by calling © **212/664-3056**. Standby tickets are distributed on the day of taping at 9am outside 30 Rockefeller Plaza, on the 49th Street side of the building, on a first-come, first-served basis (*read:* Come early if you actually want to get one). Note that a standby ticket does not guarantee admission.

Late Night with Conan O'Brien   Conan tix might not quite have the cachet of a Dave ticket, but they're a very hot commodity—so start planning now. Tapings are Tuesday through Friday at 5:30pm (arrive by 4:45pm), and you must be 16 or older to attend. You can reserve up to four tickets by calling © **212/664-3056**. Standby tickets are distributed on the day of taping at 9am outside 30 Rockefeller Plaza, on the 49th Street side of the building (under the NBC Studios awning), on a first-come, first-served basis.

The Late Show with David Letterman   Here's the most in-demand TV ticket in town. Tapings are Monday through Thursday at 5:30pm (arrive by 4:15pm), with a second taping Thursday at 8pm (arrive by 6:45pm). You must be 18 or older to attend. Send your postcard 6 to 9 months in advance (two tickets max; one request only, or all will be disregarded), to *Late Show* Tickets, Ed Sullivan Theater, 1697 Broadway, New York, NY 10019. You can also register at www.cbs.com/latenight/lateshow (click on "Get Tickets") to be notified of tickets that may become available for specific dates you select over the next 3 months. On tape days, there are no standby lines anymore; call © **212/247-6497** at 11am for up to two standby tickets; start dialing early, because the machine will kick in as soon as all standbys are gone. If you do get through, you may have to answer a trivia question about the show to score tickets.

Live! with Regis and Kelly   Tapings with Regis Philbin and Kelly Ripa are Monday through Friday at 9am at the ABC Studios at 7 Lincoln Sq. (Columbus

Ave. and W. 67th St.) on the Upper West Side. You must be 10 or older to attend (under 18s must be accompanied by a parent). Send your postcard (four tickets max) at least a *full year* in advance to *Live!* Tickets, Ansonia Station, P.O. Box 230777, New York, NY 10023-0777 (✆ **212/456-3054**). Standby tickets are sometimes available. Arrive at the studio no later than 7am and request a standby number; standby tickets are handed out on a first-come, first-served basis.

Montel Williams Show Order tickets by calling ✆ **212/989-8101**. Shows typically tape on Wednesday and Thursday at 11:30am, 1:30pm, and 3:30pm. You must be 18 or older to attend.

The Ricki Lake Show Tickets can be requested by calling ✆ **800/GO-RICKI**, or filling out the online form at www.ricki.com. You can also use this line, or register on the website, to volunteer yourself as a guest for shows such as "I'm a 30-Year-Old Virgin—Will You Be My First?" or "Stop Being Naked Around My Man!" You must be 18 or older to attend.

Saturday Night Live SNL tapings are Saturday at 11:30pm from fall to late spring (arrival time 10pm); there's also a dress rehearsal at 8pm (arrival time 7pm). You must be 16 or older to attend. Tickets are so in demand that the lottery system for advance tickets is usually suspended. However, you can try for standby tickets on the day of the taping, which are distributed at 7am outside 30 Rockefeller Plaza, on the 49th Street side of the building, on a first-come, first-served basis; only one ticket per person will be issued. If you want to try your luck with advanced tickets, call ✆ **212/664-3056** *as far in advance of your arrival in New York as possible* to determine the current ticket-request procedure.

The Today Show Anybody can be on TV with Katie, Matt, and weatherman Al Roker. All you have to do is show up outside *Today*'s glass-walled studio at Rockefeller Center, on the southwest corner of 49th Street and Rockefeller Plaza, with your very own HI, MOM! sign. Tapings are Monday through Friday from 7am to 10am, but come at the crack of dawn if your heart's set on being in front. Who knows? If it's a nice day, you may even get to chat with Katie, Matt, or Al in a segment. Come extra early to attend a Friday Summer Concert Series show.

Total Request Live The countdown show that made Carson Daly a household name is broadcast live from MTV's second-floor glass-walled studio at 1515 Broadway, at 44th Street in Times Square, weekdays at 3:30pm. Crowds start gathering below at all hours, depending on the drawing power of the day's guest. Audience tickets can sometimes be reserved by calling the **TRL Ticket Reservation Hot Line** at ✆ **212/398-8549;** you must be between the ages of 16 and 24 to attend. If you're not able to score reservations, arrive by 2pm (preferably earlier) if you want a prayer of making it into the in-studio audience; a producer usually roams the crowd asking music trivia questions like "What's Britney Spears's middle name?" and "Who's the lead singer of Linkin Park?" giving away standby tickets for correct answers. And don't forget to make your WE LOVE YOU, CARSON! signs large enough to be captured on camera. You may also be able to watch or participate in other tapings; stop into the MTV Store on the corner of 44th and Broadway, where flyers for tapings and events are sometimes stacked next to the register.

The View ABC's popular girl-power gabfest tapes live Monday through Friday at 11am (ticket holders must arrive by 9:30am). Requests, which should be made 12 to 16 weeks in advance, can be submitted online (www.abc.go.com/theview) or via postcard to Tickets, *The View*, 320 W. 66th St., New York, NY 10023. Because exact date requests are not usually accommodated, try standby: Arrive at the studio before 10am and put your name on the standby list; earlier is better, because tickets are handed out on a first-come, first-served basis. You must be 18 or older to attend.

10 Especially for Kids

Some of New York's sights and attractions are designed specifically with kids in mind. But many of those I've discussed in the rest of this chapter are terrific for kids as well as adults; I've also included cross-references to the best of them.

Probably the best place of all to entertain the kids is in **Central Park** ✯✯✯, which has kid-friendly diversions galore (p. 242). For general tips and additional resources, see "For Families" under "Tips for Travelers with Special Needs," in chapter 2.

MUSEUMS

In addition to the museums specifically for kids, also consider the following: The **American Museum of Natural History** ✯✯✯ (p. 206), whose dinosaur displays are guaranteed to wow both you and the kids; the *Intrepid* **Sea-Air-Space Museum** (p. 224), on a battleship with an amazing collection of vintage and high-tech airplanes; the **Forbes Magazine Galleries** (p. 222), whose collection includes a number of vintage toys and games; the **New York City Police Museum** (p. 233); the **New York City Fire Museum** ✯ (p. 233), housed in a real firehouse; the **American Museum of the Moving Image** ✯ (p. 263), where you and the kids can learn how movies are made; the **Lower East Side Tenement Museum** ✯ (p. 227), whose weekend living-history program really intrigues school-age kids; the **New York Transit Museum** (p. 261), where kids can explore vintage subway cars and other hands-on exhibits; and the **South Street Seaport & Museum** (p. 235), which little ones will love for its theme park–like atmosphere and old boats bobbing in the harbor.

Children's Museum of Manhattan ✯ Designed for ages 2 to 12, this museum is strictly hands-on. Interactive exhibits and activity centers encourage self-discovery—and a recent expansion means there's now even more to keep the kids learning. The Time Warner Media Center takes children through the world of animation and helps them produce their own videos. The Body Odyssey is a zany, scientific journey through the body. This isn't just a museum for the 5-and-up set—there are exhibits designed for babies and toddlers, too. The busy schedule also includes daily art classes and storytellers, and a full slate of entertainment on weekends. Look for *Art Inside Out,* an interactive exhibit dedicated to introducing families to art and museums and featuring a video-making installation from photographer and Weimaraner lover William Wegman, among others, to run from October 2002 through the end of 2003.

212 W. 83rd St. (btwn Broadway and Amsterdam Ave.). © **212/721-1234.** www.cmom.org. Admission $6 adults and children, $3 seniors. Wed–Sun and school holidays 10am–5pm. Subway: 1, 9 to 86th St.

Children's Museum of the Arts Interactive workshop programs for children ages 1 to 12 and their families are the attraction here. Kids dabble in puppet making and computer drawing or join in singalongs and live performances. Also look for rotating exhibitions of the museum's permanent collection, featuring WPA work; an exhibit by contemporary artist Melissa Stern in early 2003; and the Piccolo Spoleto Festival from May through July 2003. Call or check the website for the current exhibition and activities schedule.

182 Lafayette St. (btwn Broome and Grand sts.). © **212/941-9198** or 212/274-0986. www.cmany.org. Admission $5 for visitors 1–65; pay what you wish Thurs 4–6pm. Wed and Fri–Sun noon–5pm; Thurs noon–6pm. Subway: 6 to Spring St.

New York Hall of Science 🎠 Children will love this huge hands-on museum, which bills itself as "New York's Only Science Playground." This place is amazing for school-age kids. Exhibits let them be engulfed by a giant soap bubble, float on air in an antigravity mirror, compose music by dancing in front of light beams, and explore the world of microbes. There are even video machines that kids can use to retrieve astronomical images, including pictures taken by the *Galileo* in orbit around Jupiter. There's a Preschool Discovery Place for the really little ones. But best of all is the summertime **Outdoor Science Playground** 🎠 for kids 6 and older—ostensibly lessons in physics, but really just a great excuse to laugh, jump, and play on jungle gyms, slides, seesaws, spinners, and more.

The museum is located in **Flushing Meadows–Corona Park,** where kids can enjoy even more fun beyond the Hall of Science. Not only are there more than 1,200 acres of park and playgrounds, there's a zoo, a carousel, an indoor ice-skating rink, an outdoor pool, and bike and boat rentals. Kids and grown-ups will love getting an up-close look at the Unisphere steel globe, which was not really destroyed in *Men in Black.* The park is also home to the **Queens Museum of Art** (p. 265) as well as Shea Stadium and the U.S. Open Tennis Center.

4701 111th St., in Flushing Meadows–Corona Park, Queens. © **718/699-0005.** www.nyhallsci.org. Admission $7.50 adults, $5 seniors and children 4–17, free to all Thurs–Fri 2–5pm. Extra $2 for Science Playground. Mon–Wed 9:30am–2pm (Tues–Wed to 5pm in summer); Thurs–Sun 9:30am–5pm. Subway: 7 to 111th St.

Sony Wonder Technology Lab Not as much of an infomercial as you'd expect. Both kids and adults love this four-level high-tech science-and-technology center, which explores communications and technology. You can experiment with robotics, explore the body through medical imaging, edit a video, mix a song, design a video game, and save the day at an environmental command center. The lab also features the first high-definition interactive theater in the United States. Admission is free; this place is popular, however, so make reservations in advance. Reservations can be made up to 2 weeks in advance by calling © **212/833-5414** on Monday, Wednesday, or Friday between 11am and 4pm. Otherwise, you may not get in, or you may get tickets that require you to return at a different time.

Sony Plaza, 550 Madison Ave. (at 56th St.). © **212/833-8100,** or 212/833-5414 for reservations. www.sonywondertechlab.com. Free admission. Sun, Tues–Wed, and Fri–Sat 10am–6pm; Thurs 10am–8pm; last entrance 30 min. before closing. Subway: E, V or N, R to Fifth Ave.; 4, 5, 6 to 59th St.

OTHER KID-FRIENDLY DIVERSIONS

In addition to the choices below, don't forget New York's theme restaurants, which are playgrounds unto themselves for kids; see "Theme Restaurant Thrills!" in chapter 6. For kid-friendly theater, see "Kids Take the Stage" in chapter 9.

ZOOS & AQUARIUMS Bigger kids will love the **Bronx Zoo** 🎠🎠🎠 (see below), while the **Central Park Zoo** 🎠 with its Tisch Children's Zoo (p. 246) is suitable to younger kids. At the **New York Aquarium** at Coney Island (p. 261), kids can touch starfish and sea urchins and watch bottlenose dolphins and California sea lions stunt-swim in the outdoor aqua theater. Brooklyn's **Prospect Park** 🎠🎠 (p. 262) also boasts a wonderful little zoo.

SKY-HIGH VIEW Kids of all ages can't help but turn dizzy with delight at incredible views from atop the **Empire State Building** 🎠🎠🎠 (p. 209).

ARCADES **Lazer Park,** in Times Square at 1560 Broadway (entrance at 163 W. 46th St.; © **212/398-3060;** www.lazerpark.com), has amusements ranging from old-fashioned pinball to virtual-reality games and a laser-tag arena. Even better is the brand-new **Broadway City** 🎠, 241 W. 42nd St., between Seventh and Eighth avenues (© **212/997-9797;** www.broadwaycity.com), a neon-bright, multilevel interactive game center designed on a Big Apple theme where you could lose your kids (and a year's supply of quarters) for an entire day.

SPECIAL EVENTS Children's eyes grow wide at the march of **parades** (especially Macy's Thanksgiving Day Parade), **circuses** (Big Apple, Ringling Bros. and Barnum & Bailey), and **holiday shows** (the Rockettes' Christmas and Easter performances). See "Calendar of Events," in chapter 2, for details.

11 Highlights of the Outer Boroughs

IN THE BRONX

In addition to the choices below, literary buffs might also want to visit the **Edgar Allan Poe Cottage,** the final home for the brilliant but troubled author of *The Raven, The Tell-Tale Heart,* and other masterworks. See "In Search of Historic Homes" (p. 238).

Bronx Zoo Wildlife Conservation Park ✧✧✧ *Kids* Founded in 1899, the Bronx Zoo is the largest metropolitan animal park in the United States, with more than 4,000 animals on 265 acres. This is an extremely progressive zoo as zoos go—most of the cages have been replaced by more natural settings, ongoing improvements keep it feeling fresh and up-to-date, and it's far more bucolic than you might expect. I think it's one of the city's best attractions.

One of the most impressive exhibits is the **Wild Asia Complex.** This zoo-within-a-zoo comprises the **Wild Asia Plaza** education center; **Jungle World,** an indoor re-creation of Asian forests with birds, lizards, gibbons, and leopards; and the **Bengali Express Monorail** (open May–Oct), which takes you on a narrated ride high above free-roaming Siberian tigers, Asian elephants, Indian rhinoceroses, and other nonnative New Yorkers (keep your eyes peeled—the animals aren't as interested in seeing you). The **Himalayan Highlands** is home to some 17 extremely rare snow leopards, as well as red pandas and white-naped cranes. The 6½-acre **Congo Gorilla Forest** is home to Western lowland gorillas, okapi, red river hogs, and other African rain-forest animals.

The **Children's Zoo** (open Apr–Oct) allows young humans to learn about their wildlife counterparts. Kids can compare their leaps to those of a bullfrog, slide into a turtle shell, climb into a heron's nest, see with the eyes of an owl, and hear with the acute ears of a fox. There's also a petting zoo. Camel rides are another part of the summertime picture, as is the **Butterfly Zone** and the **Skyfari** aerial tram (each an extra $2 charge).

If the natural settings and breeding programs aren't enough to keep zoo residents entertained, they can choose to ogle the two million annual visitors. But there are ways to beat the crowds. Try to visit on a weekday or on a nice winter's day. In summer, come early, before the heat of the day sends the animals back into their enclosures. Expect to spend an entire day here—you'll need it.

Getting There: Liberty Lines' BxM11 express bus, which makes stops on Madison Avenue, will take you to the zoo; call © **718/652-8400.** By subway, take the 2 train to Pelham Parkway and walk west to the Bronxdale entrance.

Fordham Rd. and Bronx River Pkwy., the Bronx. © **718/367-1010.** www.wcs.org/zoos. Admission $9 adults, $5 seniors and children 2–12, discounted admission Nov–Mar, free Wed year-round. There may be nominal additional charges for some exhibits. Nov–Mar daily 10am–4:30pm (extended hours for Holiday Lights late Nov to early Jan); Apr–Oct Mon–Fri 10am–5pm, Sat–Sun 10am–5:30pm.

New York Botanical Garden ✧ A National Historic Landmark, the 250-acre New York Botanical Garden was founded in 1891 and today is one of

America's foremost public gardens. The setting is spectacular—a natural terrain of rock outcroppings, a river with cascading waterfall, hills, ponds, and wetlands.

Highlights of the Botanical Garden are the 27 **specialty gardens** (the Peggy Rockefeller formal rose garden, the Nancy Bryan Luce herb garden, and the rock garden are my favorites), an **orchid collection,** and 40 acres of **uncut forest** as close as New York gets to its virgin state. The **Enid A. Haupt Conservatory,** a stunning series of Victorian glass pavilions that recall London's Crystal Palace, shelters a collection of tropical, subtropical, and desert plants as well as seasonal flower shows. There's also a **Children's Adventure Garden.** Natural exhibits are augmented by year-round educational programs, musical events, bird-watching excursions, lectures, special family programs, and many more activities. Snuff Mill, once used to grind tobacco, has a charming cafe on the banks of the Bronx River. There are so many ways to see the garden—tram, golf cart, walking tours—that it's best to call or check the website for more information.

Getting There: Take Metro North (© **800/METRO-INFO** or 212/532-4900; www.mta.nyc.ny.us/mnr) from Grand Central Terminal to the New York Botanical Garden station; it's a 20-minute ride. By subway, take the D or 4 train to Bedford Park, then bus Bx26 or walk southeast on Bedford Park Boulevard for 8 blocks. The garden operates a shuttle to and from Manhattan April through October on Fridays and weekends, Saturdays only in November and December. Round-trip shuttle and garden tickets are $15 for adults, $12 for seniors and students, $9 for children 2 to 12; call © **718/817-8700** for reservations.

200th St. and Southern Blvd., the Bronx. © **718/817-8700.** www.nybg.org. Admission $3 adults, $2 seniors and students, $1 children 2–12. Extra charges for Everett Children's Adventure Garden, Enid A. Haupt Conservatory, T. H. Everett Rock Garden, Native Plant Garden, and narrated tram tour; entire Garden Passport package is $10 adults, $7.50 seniors and students, $4 children 2–12. Apr–Oct Tues–Sun and Mon holidays 10am–6pm; Nov–Mar Tues–Sun and Mon holidays 10am–4pm.

Wave Hill ★ *Finds* Formerly a private estate with panoramic views of the Hudson River and the Palisades, Wave Hill has, at various times, been home to a British U.N. ambassador as well as Mark Twain and Theodore Roosevelt. Set in a bucolic neighborhood that doesn't look anything like you'd expect from the Bronx, its 28 gorgeous acres were bequeathed to the city of New York for use as a public garden that is now one of the most beautiful spots in the city. It's a wonderful place to commune with nature along wooded paths and in herb and flower gardens, where horticulturists have labeled all of the plants. Benches are positioned for quiet contemplation and spectacular views. It's a great spot for taking in the Hudson River vibe without having to travel to Westchester to visit the Rockefeller estate. Programs range from horticulture and environmental education, landscape history and forestry to dance performances and concerts. A new Visitor and Horticultural Center designed by Robert A. M. Stern is currently under construction, and should make this hidden jewel shine even brighter.

Getting There: Take the 1 or 9 subway to 231st Street, then take the Bx7 or Bx10 bus to the 252nd Street stop; or take the A subway to 207th Street and pick up the Bx7 to 252nd Street. From the 252nd Street stop, walk west across the parkway bridge and turn left; at 249th Street, turn right. Metro North trains (© **212/532-4900**) travel from Grand Central to the Riverdale station; from there, it's a pleasant 5-block uphill walk to Wave Hill.

675 W. 252nd St. (at Independence Ave.), the Bronx. © **718/549-3200.** www.wavehill.org. Admission $4 adults, $2 seniors and students, free in winter and Sat mornings and Tues in summer. Tues–Sun 9am–4:30pm; extended hours in summer (check ahead).

IN BROOKLYN

For details on walking the **Brooklyn Bridge** ⭐⭐, see p. 208.

It's easy to link visits to the Brooklyn Botanic Garden, the Brooklyn Museum of Art, and Prospect Park, because they're an easy walk from one another, just off **Grand Army Plaza.** Designed by Frederick Law Olmsted and Calvert Vaux as a suitably grand entrance to their Prospect Park, it boasts a grand Civil War memorial arch designed by John H. Duncan (1892–1901) and the main **Brooklyn Public Library,** an Art Deco masterpiece completed in 1941 (the garden and museum are just on the other side of the library, down Eastern Pkwy.). The entire area is a half-hour subway ride from midtown Manhattan.

Brooklyn Botanic Garden ⭐   Down the street from the Brooklyn Museum of Art (see below) is the most popular botanic garden in the city. This 52-acre sanctuary is at its most spectacular in May, when the deep pink blossoms of cherry trees are abloom. Well worth seeing is the **Cranford Rose Garden,** one of the largest and finest in the country; the **Shakespeare Garden,** an English garden featuring plants mentioned in his writings; a **Children's Garden;** the **Osborne Garden,** a 3-acre formal garden; the **Fragrance Garden,** designed for the blind but appreciated by all noses; and the extraordinary **Japanese Hill-and-Pond Garden.** The renowned **C.V. Starr Bonsai Museum** is home to the world's oldest and largest collection of bonsai, while the impressive $2.5 million Steinhardt Conservatory holds the garden's extensive indoor-plant collection.

1000 Washington Ave. (at Eastern Pkwy.), Brooklyn. © **718/623-7200.** www.bbg.org. Admission $3 adults, $1.50 seniors and students, free for children under 16, free to all Tues and Sat 10am–noon year-round and Wed–Fri mid-Nov to mid-Mar. Apr–Sept Tues–Fri 8am–6pm, Sat–Sun 10am–6pm; Oct–Mar Tues–Fri 8am–4:30pm, Sat–Sun 10am–4:30pm. Subway: Q to Prospect Park; 2, 3 to Eastern Pkwy./Brooklyn Museum.

Brooklyn Museum of Art ⭐⭐   One of the nation's premier art institutions, the Brooklyn Museum of Art rocketed into the public consciousness in 1999 with the controversial "Sensation: Young British Artists from the Saatchi Collection," which drew international media attention and record crowds, who came to see just what an artist—and a few conservative politicians—could make out of a little elephant dung.

Indeed, the museum is best known for its remarkable temporary exhibitions—which ranged from "Jewish Life in Ancient Egypt" to "*Star Wars:* The Magic of Myth" in mid-2002 alone—as well as its excellent permanent collection. The museum's grand beaux-arts building, designed by McKim, Mead & White (1897), befits its outstanding holdings, most notably the Egyptian, Classical, and Ancient Middle Eastern collection of sculpture, wall reliefs, and mummies. The distinguished decorative-arts collection includes 28 American period rooms from 1675 to 1928 (the Moorish-style smoking room from John D. Rockefeller's 54th St. mansion is my favorite). Other highlights are the African and Asian arts galleries, works by Rodin, a good costumes and textiles collection, and a diverse collection of American and European painting and sculpture that includes works by Homer, O'Keeffe, Monet, Cézanne, and Degas.

200 Eastern Pkwy. (at Washington Ave.), Brooklyn. © **718/638-5000.** www.brooklynmuseum.org. Suggested admission $6 adults, $3 seniors and students, free for children under 12, free to all 1st Sat of the month 5–11pm. Wed–Fri 10am–5pm; 1st Sat of the month 11am–11pm, each Sat thereafter 11am–6pm; Sun 11am–6pm. Subway: 2, 3 to Eastern Pkwy./Brooklyn Museum.

Brooklyn Tabernacle ⭐   Under the direction of passionate orator Pastor Jim Cymbala and his choral-director wife Carol, this nondenominational Christian revival church has grown into one of the largest—a congregation of nearly

10,000—and most renowned churches in the nation. Folks come from all over the world to see the 275-voice, four-time Grammy Award–winning **Brooklyn Tabernacle Choir,** one of the nation's most celebrated gospel choirs.

Brooklyn Tabernacle relocated to Smith Street in the heart of downtown Brooklyn, in mid-2002. The gloriously renovated seats nearly 4,000 for each service. Still, come early for a prime seat, especially when the choir sings (at the noon and 4pm Sun services).

17 Smith St. (btwn Fulton and Livingston sts.) Brooklyn. © 718/783-0942. www.brooklyntabernacle.org. Services Sun 9am, noon, and 4pm; Tues 7pm. Subway: 1, 2 to Hoyt St.; 4, 5 to Borough Hall; A,C, F to Jay St./Borough Hall; M, N, R to Lawrence St/Metro Tech.

New York Aquarium *Kids* Because of the long subway ride (about an hour from midtown Manhattan) and its proximity to the Coney Island boardwalk, this one is really for summer. The aquarium is home to hundreds of sea creatures. Taking center stage are Atlantic bottlenose dolphins and California sea lions that perform daily during summer at the **Aquatheater.** Also in the spotlight are Pacific octopuses, sharks, and a brand-new sea horses exhibit. Black-footed penguins, sea otters, and a variety of seals live at the **Sea Cliffs exhibit,** a re-creation of a Pacific coastal habitat. My favorites are the beautiful beluga whales, which exude buckets of aquatic charm. Look for a new alien stingers exhibit in autumn 2002. Children love the hands-on exhibits at **Discovery Cove.** There's an indoor ocean-view cafeteria and an outdoor snack bar, plus picnic tables.

If you've made the trip out, check out the human exhibits on **Coney Island**'s 2¾-mile (4.5km) boardwalk. Not much is left from its heyday, and it can be a little eerie when the crowds aren't around. But you can still use the beach, drop some cash at an arcade, and ride the wooden **Cyclone** roller coaster (still a terrifying ride, if only because it seems so . . . rickety). Also treat yourself to a **Nathan's Famous** hot dog, just off the boardwalk at Surf and Stillwell avenues. This is the original—where the term "hot dog" was coined in 1906.

502 Surf Ave. (at W. 8th St.), Coney Island, Brooklyn. © 718/265-3400. www.nyaquarium.com. Admission $9.75 adults, $6 seniors and children 2–12. Memorial Day to Labor Day Mon–Fri 10am–5pm, Sat–Sun 10am–7pm; Apr to Memorial Day and Labor Day to Oct daily 10am–5pm; Nov–Mar daily 1am–4:30pm. Subway: D, F to W. 8th St., Brooklyn.

New York Transit Museum *Kids* Under renovation at press time, this underground museum is scheduled to reopen in 2003. It's housed in a decommissioned subway station, and is a wonderful place to spend an hour or so. The museum is small but well done, with multimedia exhibits exploring the history of the subway from its groundbreaking (Mar 24, 1900) to the present. Kids and

---

Value An Arts Party Grows in Brooklyn

First Saturday is the Brooklyn Museum of Art's popular program that takes place on (you guessed it) the first Saturday of each month. It runs from 5 to 11pm and includes free admission and a slate of live music, films, dancing, talks, and other entertainment that can get esoteric—think karaoke, poetry, silent film, experimental jazz, and disco. On a recent Saturday, events included an Irish dance performance, a panel discussion on black photographers, a screening of *Hair,* and a dance party featuring a funk-and-soul deejay. As only-in-New-York events go, First Saturday is a good one—you can always count on a full slate of cool.

parents will enjoy the interactive elements and the vintage subway cars, wooden turnstiles, and station mosaics of yesteryear. New at reopening will be "On the Streets: New York's Trolleys and Buses." It's a minor but remarkable tribute to an important development in the city's history.

Remaining open throughout renovation is the **Gallery Annex & Store at Grand Central Station,** which houses rotating exhibitions and a transit-themed gift shop (see "Museum Stores," in chapter 8). A second museum store, and a travel information kiosk, is at the **Times Square Visitors Center;** see chapter 4.

Boerum Place and Schermerhorn St., Brooklyn. © 718/694-5100. www.mta.info/museum. Admission $3 adults, $1.50 seniors and children 3–17, free for seniors Tues noon–4pm. Mon–Fri 10am–4pm; Sat–Sun noon–5pm. Subway: A, C, F to Jay St.; N, R to Court St.; 2, 3, 4, 5 to Borough Hall. **Gallery Annex:** In Grand Central Terminal (on the main level, in the shuttle passage next to the Station Masters' office), 42nd St. and Lexington Ave. © 212/878-0106. Subway: 4, 5, 6, 7, S to 42nd St./Grand Central.

Prospect Park Designed by Frederick Law Olmsted and Calvert Vaux after their success with Central Park, this 562 acres of woodland, meadows, bluffs, and ponds is considered their masterpiece by many.

The best approach is from Grand Army Plaza, presided over by the **Soldiers' and Sailors' Memorial Arch** (1892) honoring Union veterans. For the best view of the landscape, follow the path to Meadowport Arch, and proceed through to the Long Meadow, following the path that loops around it (about an hour's walk). Other highlights include the 1857 Italianate mansion **Litchfield Villa** on Prospect Park West; the **Friends' Cemetery** Quaker burial ground (where Montgomery Clift is eternally prone—sorry, it's fenced off to browsers); the wonderful 1906 beaux-arts **boathouse;** the 1912 **carousel,** with white wooden horses salvaged from a Coney Island merry-go-round (open Apr–Oct; rides 50¢); and **Lefferts Homestead Children's Historic House Museum** (© 718/965-6505), a 1783 Dutch farmhouse with a museum of period furniture and exhibits geared to kids (open Apr–Nov Fri–Sun 1–4pm). There's a map at the park entrance that you can use to get your bearings.

On the east side of the park is the **Prospect Park Wildlife Conservation Center** (© 718/399-7339). This is a thoroughly modern children's zoo where kids can walk among wallabies, explore a prairie-dog town, and much more.

At Grand Army Plaza, bounded by Prospect Park W., Parkside Ave., and Flatbush Ave., Brooklyn. © 718/965-8951, or 718/965-8999 for events information. www.prospectpark.org. Zoo admission $2.50 adults, $1.25 seniors, 50¢ children 3–12. Zoo Apr–Oct Mon–Fri 10am–5pm, Sat–Sun 10am–5:30pm; Nov–Mar daily 10am–4:30pm. Subway: 2, 3 to Grand Army Plaza (walk down Plaza St. W. 3 blocks to Prospect Park W. and the entrance) or Eastern Pkwy./Brooklyn Museum.

BROOKLYN HEIGHTS HISTORIC DISTRICT

Just across the Brooklyn Bridge is **Brooklyn Heights**, a peaceful neighborhood of tree-lined streets, more than 600 historic houses built before 1860, landmark churches, and restaurants. Even with its magnificent promenade providing sweeping views of Lower Manhattan's ragged skyline, it feels more like its own village than part of the larger urban expanse.

This is where Walt Whitman wrote *Leaves of Grass.* In the 19th century, abolitionist Henry Ward Beecher railed against slavery at **Plymouth Church of the Pilgrims** on Orange Street between Henry and Hicks streets. If you walk down **Willow Street** between Clark and Pierrepont, you'll see three houses (nos. 108–112) in the Queen Anne style that was fashionable in the late 19th century, as well as a trio of Federal-style houses (nos. 155–159) built before 1829. Also visit **Montague Street,** the main drag of Brooklyn Heights, full of cafes and shops. And don't forget about **Grimaldi's Pizzeria** (p. 194), near the water on historic Old Fulton Street, which serves the city's best pizza.

GETTING THERE   Bounded by the East River, Fulton Street, Court Street, and Atlantic Avenue, the Brooklyn Heights Historic District is one of the most easily accessible sights beyond Manhattan. The neighborhood is reachable via several subway trains: the A, C, F to Jay Street; the 2, 3, 4, 5 to Clark Street or Borough Hall; and the N, R to Court Street. *Note:* Status of the N, R, and C lines was unknown at press time, but all other above-mentioned service is normal.

It's easy to link a walk around Brooklyn Heights and along its promenade with a walk over the **Brooklyn Bridge** ★★ (p. 208), a tour that makes for a lovely afternoon. Take a 2 or 3 train to **Clark Street** (the first stop in Brooklyn). Turn right out of the station and walk toward the water, where you'll see the start of the **Brooklyn Promenade.** Stroll along the promenade for the now-heartbreaking views of Lower Manhattan and the multimillion-dollar brownstones, or park yourself on a bench to contemplate.

The promenade ends at Columbia Heights and Orange Street. To head to the bridge from here, turn left and walk toward the Watchtower Building. Before heading downslope, turn right immediately after the playground onto Middagh Street. After 4 or 5 blocks, you'll reach a busy thoroughfare, Cadman Plaza West. Cross the street and follow the walkway through **Cadman Plaza Park;** veer left at the fork. At Cadman Plaza East, turn left (downslope) toward the underpass, where you'll find the stairwell up to the Brooklyn Bridge footpath on your left.

IN QUEENS

In summer 2002, the **Museum of Modern Art** ★ closed its midtown Manhattan campus for a 3-year renovation, opening an exhibit space in Long Island City called **MoMA QNS** ★ (p. 211). This 45,000-square-foot exhibition space will showcase many of the finest works in the museum's collection, making the quick and easy subway ride out to Queens more than worthwhile.

When you head to MoMA QNS, consider making a day of it. **Queens Artlink** (www.moma.org/qal) is a free weekend arts shuttle, running Saturday and Sunday from 11:30am to 5:30pm and linking all of the institutions below (except the Queens Museum of Art). You can also catch a weekend ride on the **Long Island City Art Loop,** a free shuttle bus between the Noguchi Museum, the Socrates Sculpture Park, and P.S.1, Saturday and Sunday between noon and 6pm. Any participating institution can answer questions about the shuttles.

For details on the **New York Hall of Science** ★ and **Flushing Meadows–Corona Park** (home to the Queens Museum of Art), see p. 257.

American Museum of the Moving Image ★ *Kids*   Head here if you truly love movies. Unlike Manhattan's Museum of Television & Radio (p. 229), which is more of a library, this is a thought-provoking museum examining how moving images—film, video, and digital—are made, marketed, and shown. It's housed in part of the Kaufman Astoria Studios, which once were host to W. C. Fields and the Marx Brothers, and more recently have been used by Martin Scorsese (*The Age of Innocence*), Bill Cosby (his *Cosby* TV series), and *Sesame Street.*

The museum's core exhibit, **"Behind the Screen,"** is an engaging two-floor installation that takes you step-by-step through the process of making, marketing, and exhibiting moving images. There are more than 1,000 artifacts, from technological gadgetry to costumes, and interactive exhibits where you can try your hand at sound-effects editing or create animated shorts, among other simulations. Special-effects benchmarks from the mechanical mouth of *Jaws* to the blending of past and present in *Forrest Gump* are explored and explained. And in a nod to nostalgia, memorabilia that wasn't swept up by the Planet Hollywood chain is displayed, including a Hopalong Cassidy lunchbox, an E.T. doll, celebrity coloring books, and Dean Martin and Jerry Lewis puppets. Also on display are sets from *Seinfeld*. Even better are the daily hands-on demonstrations, where you can watch film editors, animators, and the like at work.

"**Insiders' Hour**" **tours** are offered every day at 2pm. The museum also hosts **free film and video screenings,** often accompanied by artist appearances, lectures, or discussions. Seminars often feature film and TV pros discussing their craft; past guests have included Spike Lee, Terry Gilliam, Chuck Jones, and Atom Egoyan, so it's worth seeing if someone's on while you're in town. There's a terrific gift shop chock-full of affordable movie- and TV-themed gifts, too.

35th Ave. at 36th St., Astoria, Queens. © 718/784-0077 or 718/784-4777. www.ammi.org. Admission $8.50 adults, $5.50 seniors and college students, $4.50 children 5–18. Tues–Fri noon–5pm; Sat–Sun 11am–6pm (evening screenings Sat–Sun at 6:30pm). Subway: R to Steinway St.; N to Broadway.

Isamu Noguchi Garden Museum *Finds* No place in the city is more Zen than this indoor/outdoor garden museum showcasing the work of Japanese American sculptor Isamu Noguchi (1904–88). The original building in Long Island City, built in 1927 and purchased by Noguchi in 1975, will be closed for renovation until spring 2003. The museum has temporary exhibition space in nearby Sunnyside. While this temporary space is limited to indoor exhibitions, it's still worth visiting to see a beautiful collection of the artist's masterworks in stone, metal, wood, and clay; you'll even see theater sets, furniture, and models for public gardens and playgrounds. A free guided tour is offered at 2pm. The museum shop will continue to sell Noguchi's Akari lamps as well as books, cards, posters, and the like.

The museum is set to return home in spring 2003; summer visitors, however, should confirm the return before heading out.

Temporary site: 36-01 43rd Ave. (at 36th St.), Sunnyside, Queens. Subway: 7 to 33rd St. Walk north to 36th St., turn left and go 1 block to 43rd Ave. Original location, returning spring 2003: 32-37 Vernon Blvd. (at 33rd Rd.), Long Island City, Queens. © 718/204-7088. www.noguchi.org. Suggested admission $4 adults, $2 seniors and students. Wed–Fri 10am–5pm; Sat–Sun 11am–6pm. Subway: N to Broadway. Walk west on Broadway toward Manhattan until Broadway ends at Vernon Blvd.; turn left on Vernon and go 2 blocks.

Museum for African Art *Finds* This captivating museum is a leading organizer of temporary—and usually excellent—exhibits dedicated to historic and contemporary African art and culture. In September 2002, the museum moved out of SoHo into a long-term temporary home in Long Island City (the same building where the Isamu Noguchi Museum is temporarily housed), which it will occupy until its new Museum Mile home is ready on Fifth Avenue between 109th and 110th streets. Look for "Facing the Mask," a traditional installation of over 70 of the finest examples of masks from across the African continent, to run through February 2003. Weekend and evening programs include music and dance performances, art-making workshops, family events, and more.

36-01 43rd Ave. (at 36th St.), Long Island City, Queens. © 212/966-1313. www.africanart.org. Admission $5 adults; $2.50 seniors, students, and children. Tues–Fri 10:30am–5:30pm (to 8:30pm 3rd Thurs of each month); Sat–Sun noon–6pm. Subway: 7 to 33rd St. Walk north to 36th St., turn left and go 1 block to 43rd Ave.

P.S. 1 Contemporary Art Center If you're interested in contemporary art that's too cutting-edge for most museums, don't miss this MoMA affiliate museum. Reinaugurated in 1997 after a 3-year $8.5 million renovation of the Renaissance Revival building that was originally a public school (hence the name), this is the world's largest institution exhibiting contemporary art from America and abroad. You can expect to see a kaleidoscopic array of works from artists ranging from Jack Smith to Julian Schnabel; the museum is particularly well known for large-scale exhibitions by artists such as James Turrell.

22-25 Jackson Ave. (at 46th Ave.), Long Island City, Queens. © 718/784-2084. www.ps1.org. Suggested admission $5 adults, $2 seniors and students. Wed–Sun noon–6pm. Subway: E, V to 23rd St./Ely Ave. (walk 2 blocks south on Jackson Ave. to 46th Ave.); 7 to 45th Rd./Court House Sq. (walk 1 block south on Jackson Ave.).

Queens Museum of Art   One way to see New York in the shortest time (albeit without the street life) is to visit the Panorama, created for the 1939 World's Fair, a building-for-building architectural model of New York City complete with an airplane that takes off from LaGuardia Airport. The 9,335-square-foot (840 sq. m) Gotham City is the largest model of its kind, with 895,000 structures built on a scale of 1 inch = 100 feet. A red-white-and-blue ribbon is draped over the Twin Towers, which still stand in this Big Apple.

Also on display is a collection of Tiffany glass made at Tiffany Studios in Queens between 1893 and 1938. The Contemporary Currents series features exhibits focusing on the works of a single artist, often with an international theme (suitable to New York's most diverse borough). History buffs should take note of the museum's NYC Building, which housed the United Nation's General Assembly from 1946 to 1952. Art exhibitions, tours, lectures, films, and performances are part of the program, making this a strong museum on all fronts.

Next to the Unisphere in Flushing Meadows–Corona Park, Queens. © 718/592-9700. www.queensmuse. org. Suggested admission $5 adults, $2.50 seniors and students, free for children under 5. Tues–Fri 10am–5pm; Sat–Sun noon–5pm. Subway: 7 to Willets Point/Shea Stadium (follow the yellow signs for the 10-min. walk through the park to the museum, which sits next to the Unisphere).

Socrates Sculpture Park   This former riverside landfill is now the best exhibition space for large-scale outdoor sculpture in the city. No velvet ropes and motion sensors here—interaction with the artwork is encouraged. Well worth a look, especially on a lovely day. Check the website for the current exhibition schedule—or just let yourself be happily surprised.

Broadway at Vernon Blvd., Long Island City, Queens. © 718/956-1819. www.socratesscupturepark.org. Free admission. Daily 10am–sunset. Subway: N or W to Broadway; walk 8 blocks along Broadway toward the East River.

12 Spectator Sports

For details on the **New York City Marathon** and the **U.S. Open Tennis Championships,** see the "Calendar of Events" in chapter 2.

BASEBALL   With two baseball teams in town, you can catch a game almost any day from April to October. (Don't bother trying to get Subway Series tix—they're the hottest seats in town. Ditto for opening day or any playoff game.)

Star catcher Mike Piazza and the Amazin' **Mets** play at **Shea Stadium** in Queens (subway: 7 to Willets Point/Shea Stadium). For tickets (which ran $12–$43 for regular-season games in the 2002 season) and information, call the **Mets Ticket Office** at © **718/507-TIXX,** or visit **www.mets.com.** Also keep in mind that you can buy game tickets (as well as logo wear and souvenirs, if you want to dress appropriately for the big game) at the **Mets Clubhouse Shop;** see p. 290.

Never mind that the **Yankees** lost to the upstart Diamondbacks in 2001—let's see them build a franchise like this one. The Yanks, who won their 26th World Championship in 2000, play at the House That Ruth Built, otherwise known as Yankee Stadium (subway: C, D, 4 to 161st St./Yankee Stadium). For tickets ($8–$65 in 2002), call **Ticketmaster** (📞 212/307-1212 or 212/307-7171; www.ticketmaster.com) or **Yankee Stadium** (📞 718/293-6000; www.yankees.com). Serious baseball fans might check the schedule well in advance for **Old Timers' Day,** usually held in July, when pinstriped stars of years past return to the stadium to take a bow.

At Yankee Stadium, upper-tier box seats (which run about $33), especially those behind home plate, give you a great view. Upper-tier reserve seats are behind the box seats and much cheaper ($17). Bleacher seats are even cheaper, and the rowdy commentary from that section's bleacher creatures is free. Most of the expensive seats (field boxes) are sold out in advance. You can often purchase these same seats from scalpers, but you'll pay a premium. Tickets can be purchased at the teams' **clubhouse shops** in Manhattan; see p. 291. If you're interested in taking a tour of the House that Ruth Built, call 📞 **718/579-4531** or check **www.yankees.com** for details (click on "Yankee Stadium").

Minor-league baseball made a Big Apple splash in summer 2001 when the **Brooklyn Cyclones,** the New York Mets' farm team, and the **Staten Island Yankees** came to town. Boasting their own waterfront stadium, the Cyclones have been a major factor in the revitalization of Coney Island; spanking-new KeySpan Park sits right off the boardwalk (subway: F, N, Q, W to Stillwell Ave./Coney Island). The SI Yanks also have their own new field, the Richmond County Bank Ballpark, a 5-minute walk from the Staten Island Ferry terminal (subway: N, R to Whitehall St.; 4, 5 to Bowling Green; 1, 9 to South Ferry). With bargain-basement ticket prices (which topped out at $8 for the Cyclones, $10 for the Yanks in the 2002 season), this is a great way to experience baseball for a fraction of the major-league hassle and cost. Both teams have already developed a rabidly loyal fan base, so it's a good idea to buy your tickets for the 2003 summer season—which will run from June through September—in advance. For the Cyclones, call 📞 **718/449-8497** or visit www.brooklyncyclones.com; to reach the SI Yanks, call 📞 **718/720-9200** or go online to www.siyanks.com.

BASKETBALL Two pro teams call **Madison Square Garden,** Seventh Avenue between 31st and 33rd streets (📞 **212/465-6741** or www.thegarden.com; 212/307-7171 or www.ticketmaster.com for tickets; subway: A, C, E, 1, 2, 3, 9 to 34th St.), home court: Latrell Sprewell, Allen Houston, and the rest of the **New York Knicks** (📞 **877/NYK-DUNK** or 212/465-JUMP; www.nyknicks.com); and the **New York Liberty** (📞 **212/564-WNBA;** www.wnba.com/liberty), who electrify fans with their tough-playing defense led by All-Stars Teresa Weatherspoon and Tari Phillips. The cheapest tickets are $8, and the majority of decent upper-tier seats are $13—a bargain compared to the Knicks, whose cheap seats are a whopping $26.50 (there are a few $10 seats, but I defy you to score one). Knicks tickets are hard to come by, so plan ahead if you want a front-row seat near First Fan Spike Lee.

ICE HOCKEY The **New York Rangers** play at Madison Square Garden, Seventh Avenue between 31st and 33rd streets (📞 **212/465-6741;** www.newyorkrangers.com or www.thegarden.com; subway: A, C, E, 1, 2, 3, 9 to 34th St.). The 1994 Stanley Cup champions have reeled in recent years, but tickets are hard to get nevertheless, so plan well ahead; call 📞 **212/307-7171,** or visit www.ticketmaster.com for online orders.

Shopping for Big Apple Bargains

New York draws bargain hunters from around the globe with its wealth of values, range of merchandise, and unparalleled sales. As with anything, you just have to know where to look.

City **sales tax** is 8.25%, but there is **no tax on clothing and footwear items under $110.** If you're visiting from out of state, consider having your purchases shipped directly home to avoid paying sales tax.

1 The Top Shopping Streets & Neighborhoods

Here's a rundown of New York's most interesting shopping areas, with some highlights of each to give you a feel for the neighborhood. **If addresses and phone numbers are *not* given here,** refer to the store's expanded listing by category in "Shopping A to Z," later in this chapter.

DOWNTOWN
LOWER MANHATTAN & THE FINANCIAL DISTRICT

The Financial District's shopping scene was devastated by the demise of the World Trade Center, whose underground shopping mall had evolved into the city's best by 2001. **South Street Seaport** (© 212/732-7678; subway: 2, 3, 4, 5 to Fulton St.) carries the neighborhood's torch. Familiar names like Bath & Body Works and the Sunglass Hut line Fulton Street, the Seaport's main cobbled drag, and fill the levels at Pier 17, a barge-turned-shopping-mall. There's nothing here you can't get anywhere else; come for the historic ambience, the wonderful harbor views, and to spend a few dollars in Lower Manhattan, which needs all the support it can get. For a complete store list, visit www.southstreetseaport.com.

Lower Manhattan continues to shine in the discount department. New Yorkers were thrilled in March 2002 when the king of discount department stores, **Century 21,** reopened its doors (the store is across the street from the World Trade Center site). Electronics megamart **J&R** is still going strong, now occupying a full city block with its great prices on everything that you can turn on, plug in, or use to tune out, from cameras and computers to CDs and software.

CHINATOWN

Don't expect to find the purchase of a lifetime, but there's some quality browsing. The fish markets along Canal, Mott, Mulberry, and Elizabeth streets are fun for their bustle and exotica. Dispersed among them (especially along **Canal St.**), you'll find a mind-boggling collection of knock-off sunglasses and watches, backpacks, leather goods, and souvenirs. It's a fun browse, but don't expect quality, and be sure to bargain before you buy. **Mott Street,** between Pell Street and Chatham Square, boasts the most interesting off-Canal shopping, with an antiques shop or two among the storefronts selling blue-and-white Chinese dinnerware. The highlight is the **Pearl River** Chinese emporium (see "Gifts & Paper Goods" in "Shopping A to Z," later in this chapter).

THE LOWER EAST SIDE

The bargains aren't what they used to be in the **Historic Orchard Street Shopping District**—which runs from Houston to Canal along Allen, Orchard, and Ludlow streets, spreading outward along both sides of Delancey Street—but prices on leather bags, shoes, luggage, and fabrics on the bolt are still good. Be aware, though, that the hard sell on Orchard Street can be hard to take. Still, the district is a nice place to discover a part of New York that's disappearing. Come during the week, because most stores are Jewish-owned and therefore close Friday afternoon and all day Saturday. Sunday tends to be a madhouse.

The artists and other trendsetters who have been turning this neighborhood into a bastion of hip have added a cutting edge to its shopping scene. You'll find a growing crop of alterna-shops south of Houston and north of Grand Street, between Allen and Clinton streets to the east and west, specializing in up-to-the-minute fashions and club clothes for cutting-edge 20-somethings, plus funky retro furnishings, Japanese toys, and offbeat items. Before you browse, stop into the **Lower East Side Visitor Center,** 261 Broome St., between Orchard and Allen streets (© **888/825-8374** or 212/226-9010; subway: F to Delancey St.), for a guide that includes vendors both old-world and new. Or you can see the list online at www.lowereastsideny.com. *Money-saving tip:* Check the website or call the center for details about the **Go East card,** which will score cardholders discounts at neighborhood merchants.

SOHO

People love to complain about superfashionable SoHo—it's become too trendy, too tony, too Mall of America. True, **J. Crew,** 100 Prince St., between Mercer and Greene (© **212/966-2739**), is one of many big names to have supplanted the artists and galleries that used to inhabit the cast-iron buildings. But SoHo is still one of the best shopping neighborhoods in the city, and fun to browse. You'll find few bargains, as merchants have to cover those high rents. This is the epicenter of cutting-edge couture, with designers like Anna Sui and British legend Vivienne Westwood in residence. Most of these designer shops are likely to be *way* out of your price range, but the streets are full of unique boutiques, some hawking more affordable wares, and the eye candy is tops. End-of-season sales, when racks are cleared for incoming merchandise, are the best bet if you want to buy.

SoHo's prime shopping grid is from Broadway east to Sullivan Street and from Houston down to Grand Street.

NOLITA

Just a few years ago, **Elizabeth Street** was a nondescript adjunct to Little Italy. Today it's the grooviest shopping strip in town, star of the neighborhood known as Nolita. Elizabeth and **Mott and Mulberry streets** are dotted with an increasing number of shops between Houston and Spring streets, with a few pushing south to Kenmare. But don't expect cheap; Nolita is the stepchild of SoHo. Its boutiques are the province of shopkeepers specializing in high-quality, fashion-forward products and design, but a few yield quirkier, more affordable gifts—and the browsing is excellent. It's an easy walk from the Broadway/Lafayette stop on the F, V line here, since it starts just east of Lafayette Street; you can also take the 6 to Spring Street, or the N, R to Prince Street and walk east. **Prince Street** is probably the best stretch for affordable treasures.

THE EAST VILLAGE
The East Village remains the standard of bohemian hip, and is one of the city's best neighborhoods for wallet-friendly shopping. The easiest subway access is the 6 train to Astor Place, which lets you out by **Kmart** and **Astor Wines & Spirits;** from here, it's just a couple blocks east to the prime hunting grounds.

East 9th Street between Second Avenue and Avenue A has become one of my favorite shopping strips in the city. Lined with an increasingly smart collection of boutiques, it proves that the East Village isn't just for kids anymore. I'm happy to report that—so far, at least—prices have stayed within reach. Up-and-coming designers sell excellent, affordably priced fashions for women here, including **Jill Anderson, a. cheng,** and others, and a small branch of **Eileen Fisher** caters to bargain hunters by serving as the chain's outlet store. This is also an excellent stretch for gifts and little luxuries; see "Gifts & Paper Goods" in "Shopping A to Z," later in this chapter. Most of these shops don't open until around 1pm, and most are closed Mondays. If you're enjoying this 'hood, check out the offerings on surrounding blocks; they aren't as mature, but it won't take long.

If it's strange, illegal, or funky, it's probably available on **St. Marks Place,** 8th Street, running east from Third Avenue to Avenue A. It's like a permanent street market, with countless T-shirt and jewelry stands.

LAFAYETTE STREET FROM SOHO TO NOHO
Lafayette Street has a retail character of its own, distinct from the rest of SoHo. It has grown into a full-fledged Antiques Row, strong in midcentury furniture. The quality is high, but prices are higher. Lafayette is great to browse if you have an interest in design trends—stroll between Astor Place and Spring Street—but bargain hunters are better off elsewhere. Browsers should take the 6 train to Astor Place and work their way south, or get off at Spring Street and walk north. Dispersed among the stores are a number of cutting-edge clothiers; this is where skateboard fashion moved from the street to the catwalks.

GREENWICH VILLAGE
The West Village is great for browsing and gift shopping. Specialty book- and record stores, antiques and crafts shops, and gourmet food markets dominate. Except for NYU territory—**8th Street** between Broadway and Sixth Avenue for trendy footwear and affordable fashions and Broadway from 8th Street south to Houston, anchored by **Urban Outfitters** and dotted with skate and sneaker shops—the Village isn't much of a destination for fashion hunters.

The prime drag for strolling is **Bleecker Street,** where you'll find lots of leather shops and record stores interspersed with interesting, artsy boutiques. **Christopher Street,** just east of Seventh Avenue, is fun and loaded with Village character. Serious browsers should also wander west of **Seventh Avenue,** where boutiques are tucked among the brownstones, and along **Hudson Street.**

MIDTOWN
THE FLATIRON DISTRICT & UNION SQUARE
The epitome of uptown fashion a hundred years ago, **Sixth Avenue** from 14th to 23rd streets has grown into the city's discount shopping center. Superstores

and off-pricers fill the cast-iron buildings: **Filene's Basement, TJ Maxx,** and **Bed Bath & Beyond,** are all at 620 Sixth Ave., and **Old Navy** is next door; **Barnes & Noble** is just a couple of blocks away at Sixth Avenue near 22nd Street.

HERALD SQUARE & THE GARMENT DISTRICT

Herald Square—where 34th Street, Sixth Avenue, and Broadway converge—is dominated by **Macy's,** the self-proclaimed world's biggest department store, and other famous-name shopping. At Sixth Avenue and 33rd Street is the **Manhattan Mall** (© 212/465-0500; www.manhattanmallny.com), home to mall standards such as Foot Locker, LensCrafters, and Radio Shack.

A long block over on Seventh Avenue, not much goes on in the Garment District. This is, however, where you'll find that quintessential New York experience, the sample sale; see "Scouring the Sample Sales" on p. 282.

TIMES SQUARE & THE THEATER DISTRICT

This neighborhood has become increasingly family-oriented: with the rollicking **Virgin Megastore; Gap** at 42nd and Broadway; the new **Toys"R"Us** flagship on Broadway and 44th Street, with its own Ferris wheel; and the **E-Walk** retail and entertainment complex on 42nd Street between Seventh and Eighth avenues, overflowing with mall-familiar shops like the **Museum Company.**

West 47th Street between Fifth and Sixth avenues is the city's **Diamond District.** More than 90% of the diamonds sold the United States come through this neighborhood first, so there are some great deals if you're in the market for a nice rock or a piece of fine jewelry. The street is lined with showrooms; be ready to wheel and deal with the largely Hasidic dealers, who offer quite a juxtaposition to the crowds. For an introduction to the district, visit **www.47th-street.com**. If you're in the market for wedding rings, there's only one place to go: Herman Rotenberg's **1,873 Unusual Wedding Rings,** 4 W. 47th St., booth 86 (© 800/ 877-3874 or 212/944-1713; www.unusualweddingrings.com). For semi-precious stones, head to the **New York Jewelry Mart,** 26 W. 46th St. (© 212/ 575-9701). Virtually all dealers are open Monday through Friday only.

Shopper's alert: You'll notice a wealth of electronics stores throughout the neighborhood, many trumpeting GOING OUT OF BUSINESS sales. These guys have been going out of business since the Stone Age. That's the bait and switch; pretty soon you've spent too much money for not enough MP3 player. If you want to check out what they have to offer, go in knowing what the going price is on what you want. You can make a good deal if you know exactly what the market is, but these guys will be happy to suck you dry given half a chance.

FIFTH AVENUE & 57TH STREET

The heart of Manhattan retail is the corner of Fifth and 57th. Home to high-ticket names like Gucci, Chanel, Cartier, and Van Cleef & Arpels, this tony neighborhood has long been the province of the über-rich. In recent years, however, both Fifth Avenue and 57th Street have become more accessible as wallet-friendlier retailers such as the **Niketown** and the **NBA Store** have joined the fold. You'll also find kid wonderland **FAO Schwarz** as well as a number of national names such as **Banana Republic** and **Liz Claiborne,** which have further democratized Fifth by setting up their flagships along the avenue.

High traffic flow and real-estate costs keep prices up, and the flagships tend to send their sale merchandise to lower-profile shops. Still, the window-shopping is classic. And if you, like Holly Golightly, always dreamed of shopping at **Tiffany & Co.,** 727 Fifth Ave., at 57th Street (⌀ **212/755-8000;** www.tiffany.com), the world's most famous jewelry store is worth a stop. The multilevel showroom is so full of tourists that it's easy to browse. If you want to indulge, head upstairs to the gift level, where you'll find a number of items to suit a $75 budget. Everything comes packaged in the classic little blue box with an impeccable white ribbon.

UPTOWN
MADISON AVENUE
Welcome to Rich Man's Land. Madison Avenue from 57th to 79th streets has usurped Fifth Avenue as the toniest shopping stretch in the city. It's home to the most luxurious designer boutiques: Calvin, Prada, Versace, Valentino . . . the list goes on. Even the sales are ridiculous. ("This $1,200 sweater is on sale for $575? I'll take it!" Yeah, right.) Still, the window-shopping is unparalleled—even if you're not into fashion, the displays are entertainment in their own right. What's more, a stroll along the superchic avenue on a nice day often results in a star sighting. By all means, make a point of browsing even if you don't intend to buy.

For those of us with limited budgets, stores such as **Crate & Barrel** and the **Ann Taylor** flagship, 645 Madison Ave., at 60th Street (⌀ **212/832-2010;** www.anntaylor.com), make Madison Avenue seem a little more approachable.

THE UPPER WEST SIDE
The Upper West Side's best shopping street is **Columbus Avenue.** Small shops catering to the neighborhood's mix of young hipsters and families line both sides of the pleasant avenue from 66th Street to about 86th Street. For comfort over style (these city streets can be murder on the feet!), try **Aerosoles,** 310 Columbus Ave. (⌀ **212/579-8659**), or **Sacco** for women's shoes that offer a bit of both, and **Harry's** and **Tip Top Shoes** for men, women, and children. **Maxilla & Mandible** offers groovy natural science–based gifts (see "Museum Stores" in "Shopping A to Z," later in this chapter).

Boutiques dot Amsterdam Avenue, but main drag Broadway is more notable for its terrific gourmet edibles at **Zabar's** and **Fairway** markets, both legends in their own right (see "Edibles" in "Shopping A to Z," later in this chapter).

2 The Best Department Stores for Bargain Hunters

Bloomingdale's Bloomie's is more accessible than Barneys or Bergdorf's and more affordable than Saks, but still has the pizzazz that Macy's and Lord & Taylor now largely lack. Taking up a city block, it has just about anything you could want, from clothing (both designer and everyday basics) and fragrances to a full range of housewares. The frequent sales can yield unbeatable bargains; look for full-page advertisements in the *New York Times*. The main entrance is on Third Avenue, but pop up to street level from the 59th Street station and you'll be right at the Lexington Avenue entrance. 1000 Third Ave. (Lexington Ave. at 59th St.). ⌀ **212/705-2000.** www.bloomingdales.com. Subway: 4, 5, 6 to 59th St.

Century 21 *Value* Despite suffering severe damage in the terrorist attacks on the World Trade Center, Century 21 reopened its doors on March 1, 2002. The designer discount store is back, and it's better than ever.

Prices on designer goods are 40% to 70% off what you would pay at a department store or designer boutique. Don't think that $250 Armani blazer is a bargain? Look again at the tag—the retail price on it is upward of $800. This is the place to find those $5 Liz Claiborne tees, $20 Todd Oldham pants, or the $50 Bally loafers—not to mention underwear, hosiery, and ties so cheap that they're almost free. Kids' clothes, linens, and housewares are also part of the stock. The price you used to pay to get these deals was wrestling with the aggressive, ever-present throngs, but it's hard to say what the ambience will be now. Avoid the weekday lunch hour and Saturdays, if you can. 22 Cortlandt St. (btwn Broadway and Church St.). ⓒ 212/227-9092. www.c21stores.com. Subway: 1, 2, 3, 4, 5, M to Fulton St.; A, C to Broadway/Nassau St.; E to Chambers St.

Kmart Kmart is so out of place in the East Village that it has turned the mundane into marvelous camp: Japanese kids stare at gargantuan boxes of detergent as if they were Warhol designed, and multipierced locals navigate the name-brand maze alongside stroller-pushing housewives. Kitsch value aside, this multilevel store is a great bet for discount prices on practical items, from socks to shampoo. You'll also find a pharmacy, a food department where you can stock up on Cocoa Puffs and other kitchen supplies (sale prices on snack foods are rock-bottom), and even a photo studio. 770 Broadway (btwn 8th and 9th sts.). ⓒ 212/673-1540. Subway: 6 to Astor Place.

Lord & Taylor Okay, so maybe Lord & Taylor isn't the first place you'd go for a vinyl miniskirt, but I like its understated, elegant mien. Long known as an excellent source of women's dresses and coats, L&T stocks all the major labels for men and women, with a special emphasis on American designers. Their house-brand clothes (khakis, blazers, turtlenecks, and summer sportswear) are well made and a great bargain. Sales, especially around holidays, can be stellar. The store is big enough to have a good selection but doesn't overwhelm. The Christmas window displays are an annual delight. 424 Fifth Ave. (at 39th St.). ⓒ 212/391-3344. www.lordandtaylor.com. Subway: F, V to 42nd St.

Macy's A four-story sign on the side of the building trumpets "MACY'S, THE WORLD'S LARGEST STORE."—hard to dispute, since the 10-story behemoth covers an entire block. Macy's is a hard place to shop: The size is unmanageable, the service is dreadful, the din from the crowds on the ground floor alone will kick your migraine into action. The store's one-of-a-kind flair that I remember from my childhood is just a memory. But they do sell *everything*. What's more, sales run constantly, so bargains are guaranteed. And the store provides personal guides/shoppers at no charge. At Christmastime, come as late as you can manage (the store is usually open until midnight in the final shopping days).

Tips for sale seekers: One-day sales usually occur on Wednesdays and sometimes on Saturdays. Call the store when you arrive to find out whether your visit overlaps with one. Or check the *New York Times* any day of the week for full-page advertisements, which sometimes include clip-out coupons for additional 10% to 15% discounts. At Herald Sq., W. 34th St. and Broadway. ⓒ 212/695-4400. www.macys.com. Subway: B, D, F, N, Q, R, 1, 2, 3, 9 to 34th St.

3 Shopping A to Z
ANTIQUES & COLLECTIBLES

New York has a wealth of antiques shops, covering everything from ancient to Americana to Art Deco to midcentury modern. Prices are astronomical—much higher than virtually everywhere else in the country. Still, traditionalists will love the blocks off **Broadway near 10th and 11th streets,** where the bounty includes Kentshire Galleries (37 E. 12th St., © **212/673-6644**); and **East 59th, 60th, and 61st streets** around Second Avenue, not far from the Manhattan Art & Antiques Center (1050 2nd Ave., between 55th and 56th sts.; © **212/335-4400**), where about 2 dozen high-end dealers line the street and spill over onto surrounding blocks. Fans of midcentury furniture and Americana with a twist should browse **Lafayette Street** in SoHo/NoHo. Just about any dealer will have the current issue of the free *Greyrock Antiques Guide* and/or *Antiques New York,* which will lead you to specialty dealers around the city.

Chelsea Antiques Building *Value* Right around the corner from New York's best flea market (see the box below), more than 100 dealers occupy this 12-floor building, which is open daily. The permanent stalls run the gamut from 18th-century antiques to rare books to early-20th-century radios, jewelry, and toys. Prices are so good that it's known as a dealer's source, and shoppers are the type who love to prowl, touch everything, and sniff out a bargain. 110 W. 25th St. (btwn Sixth and Seventh aves.). © 212/929-0909. Subway: F to 23rd St.

J. Fields Studio & Gallery This gallery is the place for vintage and contemporary foreign and domestic film posters. A limited supply of music posters is on hand, too (including a selection of psychedelic posters from the '60s). J. Fields is considered the best vintage-poster restorer in the city, so quality is first-rate. Prices are high, but vintage lobby cards start at $15. 55 W. 17th St. (just east of Sixth Ave.), 6th floor. © 212/989-4520. www.avidcollectorposters.com. Subway: F to 14th St.

La Belle Epoque This shop specializes in original Art Deco and Art Nouveau posters—mostly European advertisements—from the 1890s through the 1950s, as well as conservation framing. If you're a buff with a limited budget, smaller framed pieces in the $100 range means that you can buy rather than just browse. 280 Columbus Ave. (at 73rd St.). © 212/362-1770. www.la-belle-epoque.com. Subway: B, C to 72nd St.

BEAUTY

Kiehl's Kiehl's is more than a store: It's a virtual cult. Models, stockbrokers, visitors, and just about everyone else stops by this old-time apothecary for its simply packaged, wonderfully formulated products for women and men. Lip Balm no. 1 is the perfect antidote for the winter winds. Kiehl's now has a counter at Saks, too but stop into the original if you can. 109 Third Ave. (btwn 13th and 14th sts.). © 212/677-3171. Subway: L, N, R, 4, 5, 6 to 14th St./Union Sq.

Ricky's Urban Groove This wild emporium of personal-care products is a blast to browse. Goodies run the gamut from chartreuse-hued wigs to temporary tattoos to nail colors you've never dreamed of. But Ricky's also makes a good stop for travel sizes, brushes, hair clips, and anything else you might've forgotten, all at low, low prices. The SoHo location is best. 590 Broadway (btwn Houston and Prince sts.). © 212/226-5552. www.rickys-nyc.com. Subway: L, N, R, 4, 5, 6 to 14th St./Union Sq. Also at 718 Broadway (near Astor Place); © 212/979-5232; subway: N, R to 8th St.); 466 Sixth Ave. (btwn 11th and 12th sts.); © 212/924-3401; subway: F to 14th St.); 44 E. 8th St. (at Greene St.; © 212/254-5247; subway: 6 to Astor Place); 988 Eighth Ave. (at 58th St.; © 212/957-8343; subway: A, B, C, D, 1, 9 to 59th St./Columbus Circle).

Sephora The Rock Center branch of the French beauty superstore is a three-floor bonanza of beauty. You'll find everything you could want, from scents to nail color to skin cleansers to bath salts to makeup brushes to hair accessories—

in a phenomenal number of lines that run the gamut from upscale lines Babor, Philip Thomas Roth, and Murad to funky bunches like Philosophy, Urban Decay, and Hard Candy. An incredible store, with an encyclopedic staff and testers galore. At Rockefeller Center, 636 Fifth Ave. (at 51st St.). ✆ **212/245-1633.** www.sephora.com. Subway: E, F to 51st St. Also at 1500 Broadway (btwn 43rd and 44th sts.; ✆ **212/944-6789**; subway: N, R, S, 1, 2, 3, 7, 9 to 42nd St/Times Sq.); 130 W. 34th St. (btwn Broadway and Seventh Ave.; ✆ **212/629-9315**; subway: B, D, F, Q to 34th St./Herald Sq.); 119 Fifth Ave. (at 17th St.; ✆ **212/674-3570**; subway: N, R to 23rd St.); 555 Broadway (btwn Prince and Spring sts.; ✆ **212/625-1309**; subway: N, R to Prince St.); 1129 Third Ave. (at 67th St.; ✆ **212/452-3336**; subway: 6 to 68th St.); 2103 Broadway (btwn 73rd and 74th sts.; ✆ **212/362-1500**; subway: 1, 2, 3, 9 to 72nd St.).

BOOKS
THE BIG CHAINS

Barnes & Noble B&N dominates the urban landscape with more locations than any other chain. The Union Square location is my favorite: The selection is huge and well organized, the store is comfortable and never feels overcrowded, and you're welcome to browse—or nab a chair and read—as long as you like. There's a cafe and an extensive magazine stand. Many locations host an active calendar of readings, often starring such luminaries as Martin Amis and Elmore Leonard. On Union Sq., 33 E. 17th St. ✆ **212/253-0810.** www.bn.com. Subway: L, N, R, 4, 5, 6 to 14th St./Union Sq. Also at 1972 Broadway (at 66th St.) ✆ **212/595-6859**; subway: 1, 9 to 66th St.); 4 Astor Place (btwn Broadway and Lafayette St.; ✆ **212/420-1322**; subway: 6 to Astor Place); 675 Sixth Ave. (near 22nd St.; ✆ **212/727-1227**; subway: F to 23rd St.); 160 E. 54th St. (at Third Ave.; ✆ **212/750-8033**; subway: 6 to 51st St.); 600 Fifth Ave. (at 48th St.; ✆ **212/765-0590**; subway: E, F to Fifth Ave.); Citicorp Center, 160 E. 54th St. (btwn Lexington and Third aves.; ✆ **212/750-8033**; subway: 6 to 51st St.); 2289 Broadway (at 82nd St.; ✆ **212/362-8835**; subway: 1, 9 to 79th St.); 105 Fifth Ave. (at 18th St.; ✆ **212/807-0099**; subway: F to 14th St.); 240 E. 86th St. (btwn Second and Third aves.; ✆ **212/794-1962**; subway: 4, 5, 6 to 86th St.).

Borders The selection of books and music at Borders is extensive, service is great, and the stores host a wealth of events, including appearances from authors to musician Lou Reed to ethereal pup Mr. Winkle. 461 Park Ave. (at 57th St.). ✆ **212/980-6785.** www.borderstores.com. Subway: 4, 5, 6 to 59th St. Also at 550 Second Ave. (at 32nd St.; ✆ **212/685-3938**; subway: 6 to 33rd St.).

SPECIALTY BOOKSTORES

New York has more terrific specialty bookstores than I can possibly recount here; these are just some of the best.

Argosy Books Antiquarian-book hounds should check out this 75-year-old store, with high ceilings, packed shelves, an intellectual air, an outstanding collection of rarities—including 18th- and 19th-century prints, maps, and autographs—and a solid sale table. 116 E. 59th St. (btwn Park and Lexington aves.). ✆ **212/753-4455.** www.argosybooks.com. Subway: 4, 5, 6 to 59th St.

Bluestockings Women's Bookstore & Cafe This feminist-focused bookstore/gallery/cafe/performing-arts space caters to the literary needs and wants of women, straight and gay, with fiction, nonfiction, memoirs, poetry, self-help, missives on racism, classism, sexism, empowerment, and more. Books are displayed for easy browsing, and the staff is happy to make suggestions. There's a pleasant cafe, as well as a small but well-chosen section of socially aware children's books. A full calendar of readings, meetings, and workshops is always on. 172 Allen St. (south of Houston St.). ☏ 212/777-6028. www.bluestockings.com. Subway: F to Second Ave. (use First Ave. exit).

Bookleaves *Value* This unassuming West Village used-book nook is wonderful for general-interest browsing at hand-me-down prices. Art-book enthusiasts, in particular, should seek this place out. 304 W. 4th St. (near Bank St.). ☏ 212/924-5638. Subway: A, C, E to 14th St.

Books of Wonder You don't have to be a kid to fall in love with this bookstore. Kids will love BOW's story readings; call or check the site for the latest schedule. 16 W. 18th St. (btwn Fifth and Sixth aves.). ☏ 212/989-3270. www.booksofwonder.com. Subway: L, N, R, Q, W, 4, 5, 6 to 14th St./Union Sq.

Complete Traveller Whether your destination is Texas or Tibet, you'll find what you need in this, possibly the world's best travel bookstore. There are maps and accessories, plus a collection of antiquarian travel books whose facts may be outdated but whose writers' perceptions continue to shine. The staff is attentive. 199 Madison Ave. (at 35th St.). ☏ 212/685-9007. Subway: 6 to 33rd St.

Forbidden Planet Here's the city's largest collection of sci-fi, comics, and graphic-illustration books. The range of products can't be beat, and the proudly geeky staff really knows what's what. Great sci-fi-themed toys, too. 840 Broadway (at 13th St.). ☏ 212/473-1576. www.forbiddenplanetnyc.com. Subway: L, N, R, Q, W, 4, 5, 6 to 14th St./Union Sq.

Gotham Book Mart Paris may have had Sylvia Beach, but New York was lucky enough to have Frances Steloff, who opened Gotham Book Mart in 1920. She championed such once-banned works as Henry Miller's *Tropic of Cancer*, and numbered among her admirers Ezra Pound, Saul Bellow, and Jackie Onassis. Frances has passed on, but her aura lives. The emphasis here is on poetry, literature, and the arts. Look for the sign that says WISE MEN FISH HERE. *Note:* The store is scheduled to move, but the location and date were unknown at press time; call before you go. 41 W. 47th St. (btwn Fifth and Sixth aves.). ☏ 212/719-4448. Subway: B, D, F, V to 47th–50th sts./Rockefeller Center.

Gryphon Bookshop *Value* Here's the Upper West Side's best used-book store. It's a browser's delight, stacked with used and rare fiction, nonfiction, and art books, plus the occasional reviewer's copy at discounted prices. 2246 Broadway (btwn 80th and 81st sts.). ☏ 212/362-0706. Subway: 1, 9 to 79th St.

Hagstrom Map & Travel Center This bookstore sells travel guides and an incredible selection of cartography to meet about any map need, including some of the best maps around of the Big Apple. 57 W. 43rd St. (btwn Fifth and Sixth aves.). ☏ 212/398-1222. Subway: B, D, F, V to 42nd St. Also at 125 Maiden Lane (at Water St.; ☏ 212/785-5343; subway: A, C, 2, 3, 4, 5 to Fulton St.).

Housing Works Used Books Cafe *Finds* Find your reading material at this spacious yet cozy used-book shop, sporting 45,000 books and records to browse. It's part of Housing Works, a not-for-profit organization that provides housing, services, and advocacy for homeless people living with HIV and AIDS. The collection is terrific and well organized, with lots of well-priced paperbacks, hardbacks and coffee-table books. There's a cafe that serves coffee and tea, sandwiches, sweets, and light bites, plus beer and wine, and you're welcome to read as you snack. The store often hosts readings as well as occasional music performances; call or check the website for the current calendar. 126 Crosby St. (south of Houston St.). ☎ 212/334-3324. www.housingworksubc.com. Subway: F, V to Broadway/Lafayette St.; 6 to Spring St.

Kitchen Arts & Letters Here's the ultimate cook's and food-lover's bookstore. You'll be wowed by the selection, which includes rare, out-of-print, and foreign-language titles focusing on food and wine. The staff will conduct searches for hard-to-find titles. The shop is an overstuffed jumble, but if this is your bag, you'll be browsing for hours. 1435 Lexington Ave. (btwn 93rd and 94th sts.). ☎ 212/876-5550. www.kitchenartsandletters.com. Subway: 6 to 96th St.

Madison Avenue Bookshop With the sad demise of Coliseum Books, this lovely shop is now my favorite general-interest bookstore if I want knowledgeable staff to point me to a great read. Author signings are a regular part of the calendar. 883 Madison Ave. (btwn 69th and 70th sts.). ☎ 212/535-6130. www.madisonavenuebookshop.com. Subway: 6 to 68th St.

Murder Ink Murder, she wrote, he wrote, they wrote. Murder Ink claims to be the world's oldest mystery-book store. They purport to sell every mystery in print, and also have a huge selection of out-of-print paperbacks, hard-to-find imports, and signed first editions. 2486 Broadway (btwn 92nd and 93rd sts.). ☎ 800/488-8123 or 212/362-8905. www.murderink.com. Subway: 1, 9 to 96th St.

Oscar Wilde Bookshop The world's oldest gay and lesbian bookstore is still going strong. The nice staff makes browsing this landmark a pleasure. 15 Christopher St. (btwn Sixth and Seventh aves.). ☎ 212/255-8097. www.oscarwildebooks.com. Subway: 1, 9 to Christopher St.

Partners & Crime This Village shop is as much fun as a good thriller. The new and used collections include signed first editions. Readings by well-known scribes are a regular event, and live actors perform a 1940s mystery radio show, complete with organist and sound effects, on the first Saturday of the month at 6 and 8pm ($5). 44 Greenwich Ave. (at Charles St.). ☎ 212/243-0440. www.crimepays.com. Subway: A, C, E, F, V, S to W. 4th St. (use 8th St. exit).

Rand McNally Travel Store Sheet maps, globes, city maps, international maps, laminated maps—so many maps that you might never get lost again. A wide range of travel guides, atlases, and such travelers' aids as voltage converters and inflatable pillows, too. 150 E. 52nd St. (btwn Lexington and Third aves.). ☎ 212/758-7488. www.randmcnally.com. Subway: E, F to Lexington Ave.; 6 to 51st St. Also at 555 Seventh Ave. (btwn 39th and 40th sts.); ☎ 212/944-4477; subway: 1, 2, 3, 7, 9, N, R, S to 42nd St./Times Sq.).

Revolution Books If you're looking for an alternative viewpoint, you'll find one at Revolution. Books on Marxism, feminism, and just about any other "ism" make up the bulk of this store. But it's not just political lit; fiction, poetry, magazines, and newspapers are on hand. 9 W. 19th St. (btwn Fifth and Sixth aves.). ☎ 212/691-3345. Subway: 4, 5, 6, L, N, R to 14th St./Union Sq.

Rizzoli This clubby Italian bookstore is the classiest—and most relaxing—spot in town to browse for visual-art and design books, plus quality fiction, gourmet cookbooks, and other upscale reading. There's a decent selection of foreign-language, music, and dance titles as well. 31 W. 57th St. (btwn Fifth and Sixth aves.). ☎ 212/759-2424. Subway: N, R to Fifth Ave.

St. Mark's Bookshop Established in 1977, this East Village bookshop is a great place to browse. You'll find lots of terrific alternative and small-press fiction and poetry, plus criticism, Eastern philosophy, and mainstream literature with an edge. You'll also find art, photography, and design books as well as an alternative 'zine rack. Lots of spoken-work CDs and cassettes, too. 31 Third Ave. (at 9th St.). © 212/260-7853. www.stmarksbookshop.com. Subway: 6 to Astor Place.

The Scholastic Store *Kids* This mammoth store is at the ground level of the headquarters for children's publisher Scholastic. The 6,200-foot retail space is a veritable interactive playground for kids. Books, toys, and software feature Scholastic's top-selling brands, from Clifford the Big Red Dog to Captain Underpants. Harry Potter and friends are also well represented. A full slate of in-store events, from author signings to craft workshops, keep kids busy; check the website or call for the schedule. 557 Broadway (btwn Prince and Spring sts.). © 212/343-6166. www.scholastic.com/sohostore. Subway: N, R to Prince St.

Shakespeare & Co. This boutiquelike bookstore stocks the latest bestsellers, and has a well-rounded inventory. The displays are enticing if you're looking for something new. 716 Broadway (at Washington Place). © 212/529-1330. www.shakeandco.com. Subway: N, R to 8th St. Also at 939 Lexington Ave. (at 69th St. © 212/570-0201; subway: 6 to 68th St.); 135 E. 23rd St. (at Lexington Ave.; © 212/505-2021; subway: 6 to 23rd St.); 1 Whitehall St. (at Broadway, next to U.S. Customs House, 1 block from Staten Island Ferry; © 212/742-7025; subway: 4, 5 to Bowling Green; N, R to Whitehall St.).

The Strand *Value* Something of a New York legend, The Strand is worth a visit for its "8 miles of books" as well as its extensive inventory of review copies and bargain titles at up to 85% off list price. It's the city's best book deal—there's almost nothing marked at list—and the selection is phenomenal (there's even a rare-book department). Still, you'll work for it: The narrow aisles mean you're always getting bumped; the books are only roughly alphabetized; and there's no air-conditioning in summer. The Lower Manhattan location is significantly smaller. 828 Broadway (at 12th St.). © 212/473-1452. www.strandbooks.com. Subway: L, N, R, 4, 5, 6 to 14th St./Union Sq. Strand Annex at 95 Fulton St. (btwn William and Gold sts.; © 212/732-6070; subway: 4, 5, 6 to Fulton St.).

Traveler's Choice This small, friendly travel-book store can meet all of your travel guide needs, from Antarctica to Zimbabwe. 2 Wooster St. (between Grand and Canal sts.). © 212/941-1535. Subway: A, C, E to Canal St.

Urban Center Books Housed in an architectural landmark (McKim, Mead & White's 1882 Villard Houses), the Municipal Art Society's bookstore boasts a terrific selection of new books on architecture, urban planning, and landscape design. In the Villard Houses, 457 Madison Ave. (at 51st St.). © 800/352-1880 or 212/935-3592. www.urbancenterbooks.com. Subway: 6 to 51st St.

CLOTHING
RETAIL FASHIONS
Fashion hounds should check out "The Top Shopping Streets & Neighborhoods," earlier in this chapter, for advice on prime hunting grounds for original designs. Also check out the listing for **Century 21** (p. 271), the biggest and best discount department store.

Fashion Flagships
Some New York flagship stores are an experience you won't find in your local mall. These stores are display cases for the complete line of fashions, so you'll often find much more to choose from than in your at-home branch.

Check out **Ann Taylor**, 645 Madison Ave., at 60th Street (☎ 212/832-2010; www.anntaylor.com); the **Banana Republic** flagship at Rockefeller Center, 626 Fifth Ave., at 50th Street (☎ 212/974-2350; www.bananarepublic.com); **Eddie Bauer**, 1960 Broadway, at 67th Street (☎ 212/877-7629; www.eddiebauer.com), which also carries the AKA Eddie Bauer line and sports and mountaineering line; **Liz Claiborne**, 650 Fifth Ave., at 52nd Street (☎ 212/956-6505; www.lizclaiborne.com), carrying all of Liz's lines; and the **Original Levi's Store** at 3 E. 57th St., between Fifth and Madison (☎ 212/838-2125). **Old Navy** has a flagship featuring its basics and signature sense of humor at 610 Sixth Ave., at 18th Street (☎ 212/645-0663; www.oldnavy.com).

For Men & Women

Afterlife   This shop sells cutting-edge sportswear and club-wear accessories to downtowners who aspire to Patricia Field's couture club wear but can't afford it. Expect lots of tiny Ts, clingy fabrics, and hip-hugging pants, plus accessories to heighten the hipper-than-thou look. 450 Broadway (btwn Grand and Canal sts.). ☎ **212/625-3167** or 212/625-0787. Subway: N, R, Q, W, 6 to Canal St.

Burlington Coat Factory *Value*   Burlington has a stash of off-price and slightly irregular designer togs for men, women, and kids, but come for the coats. You'll find an exhaustive selection at excellent prices, as well as a fine selection of discounted leather bags and shoes. 707 Sixth Ave. (btwn 22nd and 23rd sts.). ☎ **212/229-1300**. Subway: F to 23rd St.

Canal Jean Co. *Value*   This big, bright store almost single-handedly started the SoHo shopping revolution nearly 2 decades ago. You'll find scads of well-priced jeans, midriff-baring T-shirts, and flannels, with the requisite hip accessories thrown in. Go downstairs for vintage wear, but know that the stuff they have is geared to the skateboard set and tends to be a tad shopworn. Check for seasonal sales: the Winter Blowout in February (up to 75% off everything in the store), the Summer Hot Sale in July, September's Back to School sale bonanza, and the Holiday Super Sale in December. *Note:* At press time, it was announced that Canal Jean Co. may be relocating. Call or check website for the latest. 504 Broadway (btwn Spring and Broome sts.). ☎ **212/226-1130**. www.canaljean.com. Subway: N, R to Prince St.; 6 to Spring St.

Daffy's *Value*   Long before any of these Johnny-come-lately discounters arrived, Daffy's offered rock-bottom prices. They don't get the big brand names of Century 21, but you'll come across classic European sportswear (cashmere sweaters and the like) and staples, especially for men. The kids' collection—much of it trendy designer—is a well-kept secret among city moms. 111 Fifth Ave. (at 18th St.). ☎ **212/529-4477**. www.daffys.com. Subway: 4, 5, 6, L, N, R, Q, W to 14th St./Union Sq. Also at 462 Broadway (at Grand St.; ☎ **212/334-7444**; subway: N, R to Canal St.); 335 Madison Ave. (at 44th St.; ☎ **212/557-4422**; subway: 4, 5, 6, 7, S to 42nd St./Grand Central); 1311 Broadway (at 34th St.; ☎ **212/736-4477**; subway: 1, 2, 3, 9 to 34th St.); 125 E. 57th St. (btwn Park and Lexington aves.; ☎ **212/376-4477**; subway: 4, 5, 6 to 59th St.).

Filene's Basement *Value*   This Boston-based institution's Manhattan satellites pale when compared to the mother store. The stock can be hit-or-miss, but you will find discounts on men's and women's clothing, handbags, accessories, shoes, and a few brands of perfume. Every now and then a big-time European label pops up, but don't count on finding the current season's goods, especially in the downstairs men's store. Inventory turns over lightning-quick here, though, so you never know what a trip through can yield. 620 Sixth Ave. (btwn 18th and 19th sts.).

© 212/620-3100. www.filenesbasement.com. Subway: F to 14th St. Also at 2222 Broadway (at 79th St.); © 212/873-8000; subway: 1, 9 to 79th St.).

H&M *Value* The Swedish discounter Hennes & Mauritz took New York by storm in 2000 with its high-style fashions at budget-minded prices. The colorful, loud, bustling stores are mammoth, the departments better organized than most full-retail department stores, the men's and women's wearables ultrachic, and the prices low, low, low. It's a fave with teens, in particular. The main Herald Square store carries all lines, including babies, children's, and maternity wear. 1328 Broadway (at 34th St.). © 646/473-1165. www.hm.com. Subway: B, D, F, N, R, V to 34th St./Herald Sq. Also at 640 Fifth Ave. (at 51st St.); © 212/489-0390; subway: E, V to Fifth Ave.). Smaller location at 558 Broadway (btwn Prince and Spring sts.); © 212/343-2722; subway: N, R to Prince St.).

Loehmann's *Value* This enormous discount outlet occupies a chunk of the original Barneys, and it has latched on to the stylish vibe. But not the prices, though; here, you'll pay 30% to 65% off department store prices. Two floors of casual wear by makers such as Liz Claiborne and Laundry lead to one of the city's best finds: The "Back Room," where styles by big names—Versace, D&G, Donna Karan, Max Mara—are offered at a fraction of retail. There's also a floor of men's fashions, the best you'll find in the discount realm. Excellent shoes, too, with great prices on top-quality styles. 101 Seventh Ave. (btwn 16th and 17th sts.). © 212/352-0856. www.loehmanns.com. Subway: 1, 9 to 18th St.

Roots *Finds* This Canadian sportswear company got worldwide attention for outfitting the best-dressed teams at the 2002 Winter Olympics: Canada and the USA. This is one of their few American shops, and it's worth checking out. Roots sells their top-quality fleece, Ts, sweats, and casual wear—not to mention those Olympic berets—at Gap-comparable prices. 270 Lafayette St. (at Prince St.). © 212/324-3333. www.roots.com. Subway: 6 to Spring St., N, R to Prince St.

Syms *Value* Syms is the discount store for men and women who need career wear. Designer and brand name clothes are slashed 40% to 60% off their original retail value. Good buys on kids' clothes, too. *Money-saving tip:* Register at the website for an additional 10% savings. 42 Trinity Place (btwn Rector St. and Battery Park). © 212/797-1199. www.syms.com. Subway: 1, 9, N, R to Rector St. Also at 400 Park Ave. (at 54th St.; © 212/317-8200; subway: 6 to 51st St.).

Tristan & America This Canadian retailer sells affordable, nicely tailored clothing in muted palettes to men and women who love Banana Republic's clothes but need a break from the high prices there. Look for great men's sweaters, affordable women's suits, and nicely cut trousers and A-line skirts. Excellent sales. 1230 Sixth Ave. (at 49th St.). © 212/246-2354. www.tristan-america.com. Subway: B, D, F, V to 47th–50th sts./Rockefeller Center.

Urban Outfitters The store for basics is sort of a Gap for alternative guys and gals: Jeans, oversize and tiny T-shirts, and bright velours and stretchy polyesters. There's a good selection of funky jewelry, as well as a wonderfully offbeat, affordable housewares section with batik bedspreads, candles, glassware, and mod bathroom accessories. You'll also find lots of silly gifts, from *Mad Libs* books to boxes of genuine *South Park* Cheesy Poofs. 628 Broadway (at Bleecker St.). © 212/475-0009. www.urbn.com. Subway: 6 to Bleecker St. Also at 374 Sixth Ave. (at Waverly Place; © 212/677-9350; subway: A, C, E, F, V to W. 4th St.); 162 Second Ave. (at 11th St.; © 212/375-1277; subway: L to Third Ave.); 526 Sixth Ave. (at 14th St.; © 646/638-1646; subway: F to 14th St); 2081 Broadway (at 72nd St.; © 212/579-3912; subway: 1, 2, 3, 9 to 72nd St.).

X-Large Your teen will love you for taking him or her to this hot spot (co-owned by Beastie Boy Mike D) for skate and urban street wear. The emphasis is on supercasual, with cutting-edge takes on staples like tees and sweatshirts; it's also big with 20-somethings and hip Japanese. 267 Lafayette St. (btwn Prince and Spring sts.). © 212/334-4480. www.xlarge.com. Subway: 6 to Spring St.

Just Women

a. cheng Alice Cheng's retro-modern styles for women are fresh, pretty, and, best of all, affordable. The petite shop is a breezy delight. 443 E. 9th St. (btwn First Ave. and Ave. A). © 212/979-7324. Subway: Subway: 6 to Astor Place.

Anthropologie Funky-chic and affordable wearables and accessories mix with gifts and furniture. Geared to young women who've outgrown Urban Outfitters. 375 W. Broadway (btwn Spring and Broome sts.). © 212/343-7070. www.anthropologie.com. Subway: C, E to Spring St. Also 85 Fifth Ave. (at 15th St.; © 212/627-5885; subway: L, N, R, 4, 5, 6 to Union Sq.).

Eileen Fisher Making their way around the nation in her shops and through outlets such as Saks and the Garnet Hill catalog, Eileen Fisher's separates are a dream come true for stylish women looking for easy-to-wear classic pieces. She designs fluid clothes in a neutral palette with natural fibers that don't sacrifice comfort for chic. Prices are on the high side, but the quality, fabrics, and style make them worth it. The SoHo shop, at 395 W. Broadway, is Fisher's prime showcase, but bargain hunters should head for the East 9th location, which functions as an outlet store, with sale merchandise and seconds. 314 E. 9th St. (btwn First and Second aves.). © 212/529-5715. www.eileenfisher.com. Subway: 6 to Astor Place. Also at 395 W. Broadway (btwn Spring and Broome sts.; © 212/431-4567; subway: C, E to Spring St.); 166 Fifth Ave. (btwn 21st and 22nd sts.; © 212/924-4777; subway: N, R to 23rd St.); 521 Madison Ave. (at 53rd St.; © 212/759-9888; subway: 6 to 51st St.); 341 Columbus Ave. (near 77th St.; © 212/362-3000; subway: B, C to 81st St.); 1039 Madison Ave. (btwn 79th and 80th sts.; © 212/879-7799; subway: 6 to 77th St.).

Find *Value* It's one-stop sample-sale shopping all the time at this terrific outlet store, which sells the same designer threads on the racks at places like Barneys at prices that are a mind-blowing 50% to 90% what uptown girls are paying. A wallet-watching fashionista's dream come true! 361 W. 17th St. (btwn Eighth and Ninth aves.). © 212/243-3177. Subway: A, C, E to 14th St.

Foley & Corinna *Finds* The Lower East Side's best boutique specializes in affordable original designs with a '70s flair that's retro in a nonkitschy way. You'll find a few reconstructed vintage pieces mixed in (such as vintage Ts with added lace for a sexier look), plus an excellent handbag collection. 108 Stanton St. (btwn Essex and Ludlow sts.). © 212/529-2338. Subway: F to Delancey St.

Intermix The place to dress and accessorize like your favorite *Sex and the City* gals, at not-too-expensive prices. The Flatiron location is the original, and remains the best. 125 Fifth Ave. (btwn 19th and 20th sts.). © 212/533-9720. Subway: N, R to 23rd St. Also at 210 Columbus Ave. (btwn 69th and 70th sts.; © 212/769 9116; subway: B, C to 72nd St.).

Jill Anderson *Finds* Finally, a New York designer who creates affordable clothes for real women for real life—not just for 22-year-old size-2s. This narrow, peaceful shop and studio is lined with Jill's simple, clean designs, which drape beautifully and accentuate a woman's form without clinging. They're wearable for all ages and many figure types (her small sizes are small enough to fit petites, and her larges generally fit a full-figured size 14). Her clothes are feminine without being frilly, retro-reminiscent but modern, understated but stylish. If this sounds appealing, don't miss her shop. 331 E. 9th St. (btwn First and Second aves.). © 212/253-1747. www.jillanderson.com. Subway: 6 to Astor Place.

Jungle Planet   This Village boutique specializes in trendy, affordable young women's casual wear in cotton, synthetics, and knits—print skirts, cute Ts, and the like. Sale prices start at $10. 175 W. 4th St. (btwn Sixth and Seventh aves.). © 212/989-5447. Subway: A, C, E, F, V, S to W. 4th St.; 1, 9 to Christopher St.

Liberty House   This Columbia University–area boutique is a find. It specializes in women's wear in easygoing styles that transcend age lines and figure types. Great casual sweaters, Ts, cotton pants and skirts, linen separates, and more, all at affordable prices. You'll also find ethnic gifts at the front of the store, jewelry and accessories under the glass-topped counter, and a kids' shop specializing in unique styles that don't cost a fortune. 2878A Broadway (at 112th St.). © 212/932-1950. Subway: 1, 9 to Cathedral Pkwy./110th St.

Nicolina   This charming and sophisticated shop is a Theater District anomaly. Come for fashionable basics in high-quality materials: wide-legged linen pants, flowing A-line and princess-cut dresses in silk and cotton, sweaters from labels like Beyond Threads and Sarah Arizona in fine wools, cotton, and silk. Great accessories, too, plus a small selection of contemporary and vintage gifts. 247 W. 46th St. (btwn Broadway and Eighth Ave.). © 212/302-NICO. Subway: N, R, S, 1, 2, 3, 9 to 42nd St./Times Sq.

VINTAGE & CONSIGNMENT CLOTHING

Alice Underground   This lovely SoHo shop specializes is cheap-chic vintage wear, from Victoriana to *Mod Squad* era. The goods are displayed in an orderly fashion, and there's a good selection of vintage linens. 481 Broadway (btwn Broome and Grand sts.). © 212/431-9067. Subway: N, Q, R, W, 6 to Canal St.

Allan & Suzi (Finds)   Make it past the freaky windows and you'll find one of the best consignment shops in the city. Allan and Suzi have specialized in 20th-century designer wear for over a decade, and the selection is marvelous. Their vintage and contemporary couture collection—which ranges from Chanel to Halston and Versace—is so well priced that it's within reach of the average shopper. The wild one-of-a-kind pieces are worth a look unto themselves. 416 Amsterdam Ave. (at 80th St.). © 212/724-7445. Subway: 1, 9 to 79th St.

Andy's Chee-Pees   This vintage-clothing store sports two jam-packed levels of retro-chic wearables, including leather, denim, '50s Hawaiian prints, blazers, and much more. Prices aren't exactly "cheep," but the quality is high. 691 Broadway (btwn 3rd and 4th sts.). © 212/254-3610. Subway: 6 to Bleecker St.

Argosy   This narrow shop offers a small but pristine collection of '60s and '70s fashions, including an excellent collection of stylish leather jackets. Prices are reasonable considering the quality. 428 E. 9th St. (btwn First Ave. and Ave. A). © 212/982-7918. Subway: 6 to Astor Place.

Encore (Value)   This is one of the city's best resale shops, with two floors of quality women's wear, plus a small men's department and accessories, all sold at a fraction of the original cost. Periodic sales sweeten the deal: The Chanel suit I saw for $650 was the buy of the century, but you don't have to bring that much cash to go home with a bargain. 1132 Madison Ave. (btwn 84th and 85th sts.), 2nd floor. © 212/879-2850. www.encoreresale.com. Subway: 6 to 86th St.

> ### *Value* Scouring the Sample Sales
>
> Welcome to the ultimate New York bargain: the sample sale, where top-notch fashion designers recoup some losses by selling off the sample outfits they make to show to store buyers. Often, they throw in canceled orders, overstock, and discontinued styles. Prices are rock bottom. What's the drawback? Such sales aren't advertised because designers don't want to alienate the big retailers by stealing their customers.
>
> So how do you get the scoop? The **weekly columns** "Sales & Bargains" in *New York* magazine and "Check Out" in *Time Out New York* list current and future sales; you can find *New York* magazine's sale picks online at www.nymetro.com. The free site NYSale (www.nysale.com) is probably your best source; it'll let you in on otherwise-unadvertised sales. If you're in the Garment District (especially along Broadway and Seventh Ave.) in the morning, you'll probably be handed **flyers** advertising sales that day.
>
> A few tips as you venture into bargain land:
>
> - Don't go at lunch; you'll be elbow-to-elbow with rushed office workers.
> - Bring cash. Some designers do accept credit cards, but don't chance it.
> - Few, if any, of these spaces have dressing rooms, so be prepared to try things on over your clothes (or hope it fits). Furthermore, because these garments are samples, they don't always come in a wide array of sizes.
> - All items are sold "as is," and every sale is final, so inspect merchandise carefully before you buy.

Housing Works Thrift Shop *Finds* With consistently low prices (most pieces $25 or less), lots of designer names (Todd Oldham, Calvin Klein, Donna Karan), and clothes in excellent condition, why go anywhere else? Styles range from classic to funky. There's also a good used-jeans area and a miniboutique selling couture-ish items at slightly higher prices. There's furniture, too, but good pieces go very fast. A great place to shop—not only will you get a bargain, but sales benefit homeless people living with HIV and AIDS. 143 W. 17th St. (btwn Sixth and Seventh aves.). ⓒ 212/366-0820. www.housingworks.org/thrift. Subway: 1, 9 to 18th St. Also 202 E. 77th St. (btwn Second and Third aves.; ⓒ **212/772-8461;** subway: 6 to 77th St.); 306 Columbus Ave. (btwn 74th and 75th sts.; ⓒ **212/579-7566;** subway: B, C to 72nd St.); 157 E. 23rd St. (btwn Third and Lexington aves.; ⓒ **212/529-5955;** subway: 6 to 23rd St.)

Ina *Finds* This designer consignment boutique specializes in used wearables, vintage and current, for men and women from the world's top couture houses. Labels run the gamut from Halston to Calvin to Prada to Daryl K. A beautiful selection of shoes and accessories is on hand. The locations are so close that you can scour both in one trip. 21 Prince St. (btwn Mott and Elizabeth sts.). ⓒ **212/334-9048.** Subway: N, R to Prince St., 6 to Spring St. Also at 101 Thompson St. (btwn Prince and Spring sts. ⓒ 212/941-4757; subway: N, R to Prince St.

Kimono House   This SoHo shop is an excellent stop for low prices on vintage kimono and *yukata* (cotton kimono, which make great bathrobes). The fabrics alone are worth the price for folks looking to dress up their wardrobes and homes with brilliant jewel tones and Asian patterns. 131 Thompson St. (btwn Houston and Prince sts.). © 212/505-0232. Subway: C, E to Spring St.

Love Saves the Day   This is the store made famous in *Desperately Seeking Susan* (Madonna bought those groovy boots here). LSD hasn't changed much since, except the prices keep going up. In addition to the entertaining collection of tacky vintage clothes, there's another good reason to come: the impressive assortment of Donny and Marie memorabilia and other collectible kitsch. 119 Second Ave. (at 7th St.). © 212/228-3802. Subway: 6 to Astor Place.

Metropolis   Some of the biggest names in fashion scout this clean, orderly vintage shop for fashion ideas. With good reason: Some of the coolest old clothes in the world turn up here, from skater pants and micro-cords to gingham-checked Western shirts perfect for your very own hoedown or hullabaloo. 43 Third Ave. (btwn 9th and 10th sts.). © 212/358-0795. Subway: 6 to Astor Place.

Michael's *Value*   This consignment boutique boasts designer wear for women—including such names as Chanel, YSL, Prada, Gucci, and Escada—at a fraction of the original cost. The bridal salon is an unbeatable find for top-quality dress at an off-the-rack price. 1041 Madison Ave. (btwn 79th and 80th sts.), 2nd floor. © 212/737-7273. www.michaelsconsignment.com. Subway: 6 to 77th St.

New & Almost New *Finds*   This closet brims with well-chosen contemporary and retro designer wear, all like-new and at great prices. 65 Mercer St. (just north of Broome St.). © 212/22666-6677. Subway: J, M, N, R, Q, W to Canal St.

Screaming Mimi's *Value*   Screaming Mimi's is as neat and well organized as any high-priced boutique—yet prices are reasonable, especially given the pricey vintage shops that have popped up in recent years. The clothes and accessories are well chosen, and the display is top notch. The housewares department is a cornucopia of kitsch, and includes a selection of New York memorabilia; prices start under $10, so this is a great place to find a special souvenir. 382 Lafayette St. (btwn 4th and Great Jones sts.). © 212/677-6464. Subway: 6 to Astor Place.

Tokio 7 *Value*   This designer consignment shop features gently used couture from labels like Helmut Lang, Yohji Yamamoto, Vivienne Westwood, and others, at way-below-retail prices. 64 East 7th St. (btwn First and Second aves.). © 212/353-8443. www.tokio7.com. Subway: 6 to Astor Place, L to First Ave.

Tokyo Joe *Value*   This cramped boutique is the designer consignment shop for left-of-mainstream hipsters. Browsing can be hellish, but prices are great. The shoe collection is stellar, often boasting barely (or never) worn Manolos and Jimmy Choos, priced at a fraction of what the *Sex and the City* gals pay at the uptown boutiques. 334 E. 11th St. (btwn First and Second aves.). © 212/473-0724. Subway: L to First Ave. Also at 240 E. 28th St. (btwn Second and Third aves.; © 212/532-3605; subway: 6 to 28th St.).

EDIBLES

Balducci's   This gourmet grocery is a foodie's dream come true. It's relatively small and packed, but it overflows with imported foodstuffs; the best meats, fish, and breads; picture-perfect fruits and veggies, including exotica like star fruit and enoki mushrooms; and deli, cheese, and dessert counters to die for. The staff manages to keep its cool even at the height of the holiday bustle. You can put together a takeout meal at the prepared-foods counter. 424 Sixth Ave. (at 9th St.). © 212/673-2600. Subway: A, C, E, F, V, S to W. 4th St. (use 8th St. exit).

Chelsea Market Located in an old Nabisco factory, this big, dazzling food mall is the city's largest. Come for raw and ready-to-eat foods, including divinely inspired baked goods and cappuccino from **Amy's Bread; Hale and Hearty** for yummy soups; Manhattan's best brownie at **Fat Witch Bakery;** and much more, including the wonderful **Chelsea Wine Vault. Chelsea Market Baskets** is a great place to pick up gifts for home. 75 Ninth Ave. (btwn 15th and 16th sts.). © 212/243-5678. www.chelseamarket.com. Subway: A, C, E, L to 14th St.

Dean & Deluca The quality here is superb: In addition to the excellent butcher, fish, cheese, and dessert counters (check out the cakes and the great character cookies) and beautiful fruits and veggies, you'll find a dried-fruit-and-nut bar, a huge coffee-bean selection, a gorgeous cut-flower selection, lots of imported waters and beers, and a limited but quality selection of kitchenware. A small cafe makes a great stop for a cappuccino break. 560 Broadway (at Prince St.). © 212/431-1691. www.dean-deluca.com. Subway: N, R to Prince St.

Fairway Market *Value* This unpretentious gourmet-food megamarket is an excellent place to put together a sophisticated picnic for nearby Central Park or an eat-in meal. The fruits and vegetables are glorious, and prices are better than you'll find at similar-quality markets. An excellent section of prepared and prepackaged foods, too—perfect for preparing in your in-room kitchenette. 2127 Broadway (at 74th St.). © 212/595-1888. Subway: 1, 2, 3, 9 to 72nd St.

Gourmet Garage *Value* This SoHo store features a neighborhood-appropriate loftlike setting and some of the tastiest gourmet products in town. The Garage supplies many of the city's best restaurants, and sells to the public at wholesale, about 40% off the retail of fancier stores. This location also boasts a good selection of premade sandwiches and prepared foods. The Upper West Side store features an extensive department of kosher foods. 453 Broome St. (at Mercer St.). © 212/941-5850. Subway: N, R, Q, W, 6 to Canal St. Also at 2567 Broadway (btwn 96th and 97th sts.; © 212/663-0656; subway: 1, 2, 3, 9 to 96th St.).

Grand Central Market Gloriously restored Grand Central Terminal now has its own small but terrific gourmet food hall at street level, accessible from 42nd Street, with such vendors as **Adriana's Caravan** for spices; **Ninth Avenue Cheese** for a gourmet selection; **Corrado Bread & Pastry** carrying loaves and pastries from Bouley Bakery; and more. 42nd St. at Park Ave. www.grandcentralterminal.com. Subway: S, 4, 5, 6, 7 to 42nd St./Grand Central.

Zabar's Zabar's is an institution. This giant deli sells prepared foods, packaged goods from around the world, coffee beans, breads, and much more (no fresh veggies, though). This is the place for lox, and the rice pudding is the best I've tasted. You'll also find an excellent—and well-priced—collection of housewares and restaurant-quality cookware, plus a never-ending flow of Woody Allen stock characters who shop here daily. Prepare yourself for crowds. The attached cafe serves terrific sandwiches and takeout—ideal for a Central Park picnic. 2245 Broadway (at 80th St.). © 212/787-2000. Subway: 1, 9 to 79th St.

SWEETS

Black Hound This charming shop specializes in truffles, cookies, and cakes. This is a terrific choice for those who like their chocolates not too frilly or sweet. Just about everything comes packaged in a blond-wood box tied with a velveteen ribbon, making them simple but elegant gifts. 170 Second Ave. (btwn 10th and 11th sts.). © **212/979-9505**. Subway: 6 to Astor Place; L to Third Ave.

Dylan's Candy Bar *Finds* The brainchild of Dylan Lauren (Ralph's little girl) and Jeff Schwartz, this beautifully designed 5,500-square-foot (495-sq.-m) shop is nirvana for sweet tooths. Two levels boast an endless selection of goodies (they claim to carry more than 5,000 sweets from around the world), running the gamut from your favorite dime-store brands to private-label artistic confectionary gifts. This place is a blast—like *Willy Wonka and the Chocolate Factory* come to life. 1011 Third Ave. (at 60th St.). © **646/735-0078**. www.dylanscandybar.com. Subway: 4, 5, 6 to 59th St.; E, V to Lexington Ave.

Li-Lac Chocolates Li-Lac is one of the few chocolatiers still making sweets by hand. In business since 1923, this Village shop whips up its chocolate and maple-walnut fudge fresh every day. They also make pralines, caramels, and hand-dipped chocolates, including sweets for the holidays (bunnies and chocolate eggs for Easter, chocolate Santas for Christmas, and so on). 120 Christopher St. (btwn Bleecker and Hudson sts.). © **800/624-4784** or 212/242-7374. Subway: 1, 9 to Christopher St. Also at Grand Central Market (Grand Central Terminal; © **212/370-4866**; subway: 4, 5, 6, 7 to 42nd St./Grand Central).

ELECTRONICS

J&R Music World/Computer World This block-long Financial District emporium is the city's top discount computer, electronics, and office equipment retailer. The sales staff is knowledgeable but can get pushy if you don't know exactly what you want. Don't succumb—take your time and find what you need. Or better yet, peruse the store's catalog or website. Park Row (at Ann St., opposite City Hall Park). © **800/221-8180** or 212/238-9100. www.jandr.com. Subway: 2, 3 to Park Place; 4, 5, 6 to Brooklyn Bridge/City Hall.

GIFTS & PAPER GOODS

If you're looking for a special gift for a creative spirit, check out the shops that line **East 9th Street** in the East Village; the side streets of **SoHo,** where a good number of unusual boutiques still survive; **Nolita;** and Greenwich Village, especially in the wonderful cadre of one-of-a-kind shops in the **West Village.** See "The Top Shopping Streets & Neighborhoods," earlier in this chapter.

Alphabets This playful shop has two halves: one for cards, toys, and Ts, the other to creative housewares, from dishware to freeform vases. It's all fun and affordable. 2284 Broadway (btwn 82nd and 83rd sts.). © **212/579-5702**. Subway: 1, 9 to 86th St. Also at 115 Ave. A (at St. Marks Place; © **212/475-7250**; subway: 6 to Astor Place, L to First Ave.); 47 Greenwich Ave. (btwn Perry and Charles sts.; © **212/229-2966**; subway: 1, 9 to Christopher St.).

Card-O-Mat This big, bright shop stocks the city's most diverse collection of creative cards, notepads, address and date books, photo albums, stationery, and other paper goodies. You'll find styles here you won't see anywhere else thanks to a wide range of European imports. 2884 Broadway (btwn 112th and 113th sts.). © **212/663-2085**. Subway: 1, 9 to 110th St./Cathedral Pkwy.

Daily 235 This quirky card and candy store for artsy grown-ups is a great place to pick up creative under-$10 gifts, from small-print books to Buddha-shaped candles. 235 Elizabeth St. (btwn Prince and Houston sts.). © 212/334-9728. Subway: N, R to Prince St.; 6 to Spring St.

Extraordinary* *Finds* This warm, friendly gallery–cum–gift shop is worth going out of your way to discover. Owner J. R. Sanders, an interior designer who has created exhibits at many museums, has assembled a collection of gifts from around the world. Lacquered crackle-eggshell trays from Vietnam, carved mango bowls from the Philippines, rosewood utensils camouflaged as tree branches from Africa, and much more—all eye candy for those who thrive on whimsy and good design. Best of all, prices are reasonable—you'd pay twice as much at any other gallery or boutique—and late hours (usually daily to 10:30pm) make it easy to visit. Truly extraordinary! 251 E. 57th St. (just west of Second Ave.). © 212/223-9151. Subway: 4, 5, 6 to 59th St.

H This tranquil shop is one of my favorites for unusual housewares and gifts. The wonderful collection runs the gamut from Slinky vases to Japanese rice-paper coasters to old French electronics illustrations, suitable for framing. 335 E. 9th St. (btwn First and Second aves.). © 212/477-2631. Subway: 6 to Spring St.

House of Cards and Curiosities *Finds* This jam-packed shop, the West Village's own funky take on an old-fashioned nickel-and-dime, is a joy to browse for kooky trinkets and cards. 23 Eighth Ave. (btwn 12th and Jane sts.). © 212/675-6178. Subway: A, C, E, L to 14th St.

JAM Paper *Value* For stylish stationery at low prices, JAM is the place to go. Most papers are color-block solids, but the spectrum covers the rainbow. You'll also find a large, creative selection of well-priced supplies for your home and office. 111 Third Ave. (btwn 13th and 14th sts.). © 212/473-6666. www.jampaper.com. Subway: L to Third Ave. Also at 611 Sixth Ave. (btwn 17th and 18th sts.; © 212/255-4593; subway: F to 14th St.).

Kate's Paperie I could browse for hours in this delightful shop's handmade stationery and wrap, innovative invitations and thank yous, notebooks, writing tools, and other paper products, including lampshades. Lovely art cards, too—perfect for writing the folks back home. A joy! The SoHo location is best. 561 Broadway (btwn Prince and Spring sts.). © 888/941-9169 or 212/941-9816. www.katespaperie.com. Subway: N, R to Prince St. Also at 8 W. 13th St. (btwn Fifth and Sixth aves.; © 212/633-0570; subway: F to 14th St.); 1282 Third Ave. (btwn 73rd and 74th sts.; © 212/396-3670; subway: 6 to 77th St.).

Leekan Designs This high-ceilinged shop is packed with Asian, Oceanic, and Moroccan exotica, from beaded jewelry to folk art to tableware to textiles to floor mats. The collection is eye-popping, and prices are quite affordable. 93 Mercer St. (near Spring St.). © 212/226-7226. Subway: N, R to Prince St.

Mascot Studio *Finds* Stop into this rough-hewn custom frame shop for one-of-a-kind picture frames, most extremely affordably priced. The small shop also curates art and photography shows, so you might even find a worthwhile exhibit when you arrive. 328 E. 9th St. (btwn First and Second aves.). © 212/228-9090. Subway: 6 to Astor Place.

Mxyplyzyk *Value* Come to this unpronounceable Village shop for one of the city's most fun and creative collections of one-of-a-kind housewares, office ware, and gifts. Most everything is reasonably priced. 125 Greenwich Ave. (at 13th St., near Eighth Ave.). © 212/989-4300. Subway: A, C, E, to 14th St.

New York Firefighter's Friend *Finds* Purchase FDNY logo wear, including T-shirts, sweatshirts, hats, and more. The goods are all top-quality, and a portion of profits go in support of the widows and children of the 343 firefighters lost in the World Trade Center terrorist attacks. 263 Lafayette St. (btwn Prince and Spring sts.). © 212/226-3142. www.nyfirestore.com. Subway: 6 to Spring St.

New York 911 *Finds* Next to Firefighter's Friend (see above) you can shop for NYPD logo wear, and EMT, FBI, and NYC coroner gear. The goods include shirts, caps, patches, logo toys, and more. (Not all of the products are licensed by the city; I suggest trying to stick with those that are.) A portion of the proceeds goes to NYPD-related charities. 263 Lafayette St. (btwn Prince and Spring sts.). © 888/723-3907 or 212/219-3907. www.ny911.com. Subway: 6 to Spring St.

Old Japan Come to this small Village shop for vintage silk kimonos, Japanese dolls, Noguchi lamps, Mingei folk items, and other gifts from the Land of the Rising Sun, including scarves and handbags fashioned out of kimonos and buckwheat pillows covered in kimono cotton. Vintage kimonos run $300 to $1,500, but there's always a year-round sale rack with prices under $100, and small pieces are always affordable. 382 Bleecker St. (btwn Perry and Charles sts.). © 212/633-0922. www.oldjapaninc.com. Subway: 1, 9 to Christopher St.

Pearl River *Value* This three-floor Chinatown emporium overflows with affordable Asian exotica. Goods run from paper lanterns to Chinese snack foods to Mandarin-collared silk pajamas to mah-jongg sets. This place can keep you occupied for hours, and it's a great source for cheap, creative souvenirs. The smaller Grand Street branch is as enchanting. *Note:* Look for the main store to move 1 block north on Broadway, on the west side of the street, by the time you arrive. 277 Canal St. (at Broadway). © 212/431-4770. www.pearlriver.com. Subway: N, R to Canal St. Also at 200 Grand St. (btwn Mott and Mulberry sts.); © 212/966-1010; subway: S to Grand St.).

Royale The cutest card shop in the Village, and a good choice for oddball postcards to send back home. 177 W. 4th St. (btwn Sixth and Seventh aves.). © 212/929-1029. Subway: A, C, E, F, V, S to W. 4th St.; 1, 9 to Christopher St.

HOME FASHIONS & HOUSEWARES

ABC Carpet & Home This 10-floor emporium is the ultimate home-fashions and -furnishings store. The goods run the gamut from Moroccan mosaic-tile end tables to Tuscan pottery to Tiffanyish lamps to distressed bed frames made up with Frette linens to much more, all carefully chosen and exquisitely displayed. Prices aren't bad, but these are high-end goods. Some of the smaller items are affordable, and the sales yield substantial discounts. Across the street is the multifloor carpet store, which boasts a remarkable collection of area rugs. 881 and 888 Broadway (at 19th St.). © 212/473-3000. www.abccarpet.com. Subway: 4, 5, 6, L, N, R, Q, W to 14th St./Union Sq.

Amalgamated Home Looking for brushed metal switch plates for your groovy new stainless-steel kitchen? How about a purple velvet love seat straight out of a Looney Tunes cartoon? Or the hippest rice bowls in town? You'll find it all and more at this pair of home shops, which stocks eye-catching household goods you won't see anywhere else. 19 Christopher St. (btwn Sixth and Seventh aves.). © 212/255-4160 (furniture and lighting) or 212/691-8695 (hardware and household sundries). Subway: 1, 9 to Christopher St.

Broadway Panhandler If you're looking for restaurant-quality cookware and kitchen tools, this is the place. It has the best combination of selection, prices, and service in town. Don't just take it from me—*New York* magazine gave Broadway Panhandler the "Best Pots and Pans" nod in 2000. 477 Broome St. (btwn Greene and Wooster sts.). © 212/966-3434. Subway: C, E to Spring St.

Details These fun-and-funky home stores are the place to outfit the coolest pad in town with Day-Glo bath accessories, cool-print shower curtains, glassware, and the like. Everything's cute and affordable! 347 Bleecker St. (at W. 10th St.). © 212/414-0039. Subway: 1, 9 to Christopher St./Sheridan Sq. Also at 142 Eighth Ave. (at 17th St.; © 212/366-9498; subway: A, C, E to 14th St.); 188 Columbus Ave. (at 68th St.; © 212/362-7344; subway: 1, 9 to 66th St.).

Fishs Eddy *Value* What a great idea—selling remainders of kitschy, custom-designed china. Ever wanted a dish that *really* says "Blue Plate Special"? Or how about a coffee mug with the terse logo "Cup o' Joe to Go"? The store is Browse Heaven, and prices are low enough. Other items include vintage and retro-inspired flatware, bowls, and restaurant-supply glassware that can be hard to find, like soda-fountain and pint glasses. 889 Broadway (at 19th St.). © 212/420-9020. www.fishseddy.com. Subway: 4, 5, 6, L, N, R, Q, W to 14th St./Union Sq. Also at 2176 Broadway (at 77th St.; © 212/873-8819; subway: 1, 9 to 79th St.).

kar'ikter *Finds* New York's biggest collection of sleek and playful Alessi housewares from Italy (including Michael Graves's iconic teakettle with bird whistle), as well as European animation cells and toys starring Tintin, Babar, and Asterix. 19 Prince St. (btwn Elizabeth and Mott sts.). © 212/274-1966. www.karikter.com. Subway: 6 to Spring St.

Leader Restaurant Equipment & Supplies *Value* The Bowery is the place to find restaurant-supply-quality kitchenware, and Leader is the best dealer on the block. This big, bustling shop is a good source for Chinese and Japanese wares—chopsticks, rice and noodle bowls, sushi plates, sake cups, and the like. You'll see a lot of the same styles you'd find at the high-end stores in SoHo or the Village, but at a fraction of the prices. 191 Bowery (btwn Spring and Delancey sts.). © 800/666-6888 or 212/677-1982. Subway: 6 to Spring St.

Lighting by Gregory *Value* The stretch of the Bowery (Third Ave.) from Houston to Canal streets is considered the "light-fixture district" for its huge selections and great bargains on light fixtures, lamps, and ceiling fans. Gregory's multishowroom shop is by far the best of the bunch, with a first-rate selection of all the name brands (including ultraquiet Casablanca ceiling fans) and terrific prices. 158 Bowery (btwn Delancey and Broome sts.). © 888/811-FANS or 212/226-1276. www.lightingbygregory.com. Subway: J, M to Bowery.

LEATHER, HANDBAGS & LUGGAGE

Fine & Klein *Value* The Lower East Side's bargain district is a great source for discount handbags and luggage. The best of the bunch is this shop, offering good discounts (usually 20%) on name-brand handbags. 119 Orchard St. (near Delancey St.). © 212/674-6720. Subway: F to Delancey St.

Grace Bags *Value* So you've always wanted a Prada, Gucci, kate spade, or Tod's bag, but your budget's just not up to shelling out the big bucks? Then come to this bargain hunter's delight of a discount shop, where good-quality *faux* versions of the designer styles sell for just $10 to $45. 190 Orchard St. (btwn Houston and Stanton sts.). © 212/228-6118. Subway: F to Second Ave.

Greenwood This Village shop sells top-quality leather handbags, backpacks, luggage, wallets, from famous names like Frye and Latico at reasonable prices. The selection is excellent, and service is professional. 263 Bleecker St. (btwn Sixth and Seventh aves.). © 212/366-0825. Subway: 1, 9 to Houston St.

Jobson's *Value* In business since 1949, Jobson's is a great discount source for name-brand luggage and leather goods. Rather than simply offer a cut off the retail price, management marks most items at 10% above cost, which usually amounts to a whopping 40% to 60% break for the buyer. The shop also does a huge airline and professional flyers business, and they'll be happy to tell you what the pros buy. Negotiators sometimes prevail. 666 Lexington Ave. (btwn 55th and 56th sts.). © 212/355-6846. Subway: 6 to 51st St.

Jutta Neumann *Finds* If you stop into this shop, you're likely to find the artist herself behind the counter, cutting and stitching her bold-hued leather goods—bags, wallets, boots, and more. Her new mules and strappy sandals have made a big splash. 158 Allen St. (btwn Stanton and Rivington sts.). © 212/982-7048. www.juttaneumann-newyork.com. Subway: F to Delancey/Essex sts.

Manhattan Portage Ltd. Store Come here for the hippest nylon and canvas carryalls in town. Manhattan Portage manufactures its bags in the city, and they're made from hard-wearing materials that can stand up to an urban lifestyle. Popular styles include messenger bags, deejay bags, and backpacks (in standard and one-shoulder styles) in a range of colors from bright yellow to camouflage. Manhattan Portage bags are also sold through other outlets, but you'll find the most complete selection here. 333 E. 9th St. (btwn First and Second aves.). © 212/995-5490. www.manhattanportageltd.com. Subway: 6 to Astor Place.

Original Leather If you're in the market for a leather jacket, pants, or skirt, this is the best of the Village's discount leather shops in terms of quality and price. You'll get good value for your dollar here, and the sales people aren't *too* hard-sell (comparatively speaking, that is). 173 W. 4th St. (btwn Sixth and Seventh aves.). © 212/675-2303. Subway: A, C, E, F, V, S to W. 4th St. Also at 176 Spring St. (btwn Thompson and W. Broadway; © 212/219-8210; subway: C, E to Spring St.); 552 LaGuardia Place (btwn Bleecker and 3rd St.; © 212/777-4362; subway: A, C, E, F, V, S to W. 4th St.); 84 Seventh Ave. (btwn 15th and 16th sts.; © 212/989-1120; subway: 1, 2, 3, 9 to 14th St.); 256 Columbus Ave. (at 72nd St.; © 212/595-7051; subway: B, C to 72nd St.); 1100 Madison Ave. (btwn 82nd and 83rd sts.; © 212/585-4200; subway: 4, 5, 6 to 86th St.).

Tip: Compare prices and styles to **Janet Woo**, down the block from the West Village location at 189 W. 4th St. (© **646/638-3035**), another reasonable outlet.

Village Tannery The cream of the Greenwich Village leather crop, with gorgeous and well-priced handbags, backpacks, wallets, and organizers. 173 Bleecker St. (btwn MacDougal and Sullivan sts.). © 212/673-5444. Subway: 1, 9 to Houston St. Also at 742 Broadway (btwn Astor Place and Waverly St.; © 212/979-0013; subway: 6 to Astor Place).

LOGO STORES

Mets Clubhouse Shop New York's other favorite baseball team has its own logo store in Midtown. Stop in for goods galore—baseball caps, T-shirts, posters, Piazza jerseys, '69 Miracle Mets memorabilia, and much more. You can buy regular-season game tix here, too. 143 E. 54th St. (btwn Lexington and Third aves.). © 212/888-7508. www.mets.com. Subway: E, V to Lexington Ave.

The MTV Store This petite boutique sits street-side, just below the MTV studio. There's not much here—but your kids will surely find something they want, whether it's a *Jackass* bumper sticker, an *Osbournes* T-shirt, or one of any number of *TRL* souvenirs. Flyers are sometimes on hand at the register, advertising for audience members for MTV shows. 1515 Broadway (at 44th St.). © 212/258-8000. Subway: 1, 2, 3, 7, 9, N, R, S, Q, W to 42nd St./Times Sq.

NBA Store   For all things NBA and WNBA, go to this three-level store, a multimedia celebration of pro hoops, complete with bleachers for player appearances and signings. 666 Fifth Ave. (at 52nd St.). © 212/515-NBA1. www.nbastore.com. Subway: B, D, F, V to 47th–50th sts./Rockefeller Center.

NBC Experience   This mammoth, neon-lit store sits across from the *Today* show studio and sells all manner of NBC-themed merchandise. Your kids will enjoy the interactive features, like the virtual reality "Conan O'Brien's Wild Desk Ride" or "Al Roker's Weather Challenge," which lets you do the forecast alongside the meteorologist, as well as the candy shop. 30 Rockefeller Plaza (at 49th St.). © 212/664-3700. www.nbcsuperstore.com. Subway: B, D, F, V to 47th–50th sts./Rockefeller Center.

The Pop Shop *Finds*   For affordable and wearable art that makes supercool souvenirs, come here. This groovy store is full of items based on designs by artist Keith Haring, who died in 1990. T-shirts, posters, calendars, stationery, toys, notebooks, transparent backpacks—all sport the vivid colors and loopy stick-figure drawings Haring made famous. Best of all, the Pop Shop is a nonprofit, offering continued support to the AIDS-related and children's charities that the young artist championed in life. 292 Lafayette St. (btwn Houston and Prince sts.). © 212/219-2784. www.haring.com. Subway: F, V to Broadway/Lafayette St.

Yankees Clubhouse Shop   For all your Bronx Bombers needs—hats, jerseys, jackets, and so on. Tickets for regular-season home games are also for sale, and there's a limited selection of other New York team jerseys. 245 W. 42nd St. (btwn Seventh and Eighth aves.). © 212/768-9555. www.yankees.com. Subway: A, C, E to 42nd St. Also at 393 Fifth Ave. (btwn 36th and 37th sts.; © 212/685-4693; subway: 6 to 33rd St.); 110 E. 59th St. (btwn Park and Lexington aves.; © 212/758-7844; subway: 4, 5, 6 to 59th St.); 8 Fulton St., in the South Street Seaport (© 212/514-7182; subway: 2, 3, 4, 5 to Fulton St.).

MUSEUM STORES

In addition to these, check out the excellent shops at the **American Craft Museum**, the **New York Public Library**, the **Museum for African Art**, the **Jewish Museum**, the **American Folk Art Museum**, the **American Museum of the Moving Image**, and the **Isamu Noguchi Museum**; see chapter 7.

Maxilla & Mandible *Finds*   This shop is not affiliated with the American Museum of Natural History, but a visit here makes a good adjunct to your trip to the museum (which is right around the corner). It's a fascinating natural-history emporium. Inside, you'll find rocks and shells from around the world, luminescent butterflies in display boxes, even real fossils containing prehistoric fish and insects that come with details on their history. There's also a variety of natural history–themed toys for kids. 451 Columbus Ave. (btwn 81st and 82nd sts.). © 212/724-6173. www.maxillaandmandible.com. Subway: B, C to 81st St.

Metropolitan Museum of Art Store   Given the scope of the museum, it's no wonder the gift shop is outstanding. Many treasures from the museum's collection have been reproduced as jewelry, china, and other objets d'art. The range of books is dizzying, and there's a comprehensive selection of posters and children's toys. 1000 Fifth Ave. (at 82nd St.). © 212/570-3894. www.metmuseum.org. Subway: 4, 5, 6 to 86th St. Also at Rockefeller Center, 15 W. 49th St. (© 212/332-1360; subway: B, D, F, Q to 47th–50th sts./Rockefeller Center); 113 Prince St. (at Greene St.; © 212/614-3000;

subway: N, R to Prince St.); on mezzanine level at Macy's, 34th St. and Sixth Ave. (© **212/ 268-7266;** subway: B, D, F, N, R, Q, V, W to 34th St./Herald Sq.).

MoMA Design Store Across the street from the Museum of Modern Art in Midtown is this shop, whose stock ranges from posters and clever toys to reproductions of many of the classics of modern design, including free-form Alvar Aalto vases and Frank Lloyd Wright chairs. If these high-design items are out of your reach, don't worry: There are plenty of affordable outré home accessories from which to choose. The new SoHo store is equally fabulous. *Note:* The design store will remain open while the museum is closed for renovation. 44 W. 53rd St. (btwn Fifth and Sixth aves.). © **212/767-1050.** www.moma.org. Subway: E, F to Fifth Ave.; B, D, F, V to 47th–50th sts./Rockefeller Center. Also at 81 Spring St. (at Crosby St.); © **646/613-1367;** subway: 6 to Spring St.).

New York Transit Museum Store Lots of transportation-themed gifts; the cufflinks made out of subway tokens are great! Grand Central Terminal (on the main level, in the passage next to Station Masters' office), 42nd St. and Lexington Ave. © **212/ 878-0106.** Subway: 4, 5, 6, 7, S to 42nd St./Grand Central.

MUSIC & VIDEO

Music buffs will find a wealth of new-and-used shops in the West Village. Standouts include **Rebel Rebel,** 319 Bleecker St. (© 212/989-0770), for imports and New Wave and glam classics; **Rockit Scientist,** off Bleecker at 43 Carmine St. (© 212/242-0066), a tiny place with a huge folk and psych collection; and **Sonic Groove,** 41 Carmine St. (© 212/675-5284; www.sonicgroove.com), which supplies the sounds for many city deejays. **Bleecker Bob's Golden Oldies,** 118 W. 3rd St. (© 212/475-9677), has outlived its legend; it's just a little hole-in-the-wall with worn, badly organized vinyl.

Grungy **St. Marks Place** between Third and Second avenues in the East Village is another great bet, especially for used music at low prices. **Joe's CDs,** at 11 St. Marks (© 212/673-4606), is a standout, as is **Sounds,** at no. 20 (© 212/ 677-3444), the dirt-cheap granddaddy of the St. Marks shops, and **Norman's Sound & Vision,** around the corner at 67 Cooper Square (© 212/473-6610).

In the Financial District, **J&R Music World** has a big selection of new music, and brand-new releases are almost always on sale; see "Electronics," earlier in this chapter.

Academy Records & CDs This Flatiron District shop is always filled with classical, opera, and jazz junkies perusing the extensive, well-priced collection of used CDs and vinyl. There's also a variety of other music, from rare '60s pop songsters to spoken word. 12 W. 18th St. (btwn Fifth and Sixth aves.). © **212/242-3000.** www.academy-records.com. Subway: 4, 5, 6, L, N, R, Q, W to 14th St./Union Sq.

Bleecker St. Records This sizable, well-lit space is great for one-stop shopping. The clean, well-organized CD and LP collections run the gamut from rock, oldies, jazz, folk, and blues to Oi! punk. You'll find lots of imports, collectibles, and out-of-print records (including singles), a terrific collection of used CDs, and a mix of casual listeners and serious collectors cruising the bins. 239 Bleecker St. (near Carmine St., just west of Sixth Ave.). © **212/255-7899.** Subway: A, C, E, F, V to W. 4th St.

Footlight *Finds* A dreamy collection of vintage vinyl—strong in jazz and pop vocalists, soundtracks, and show tunes—for the serious collector. 113 E. 12th St. (btwn Third and Fourth aves.). © **212/533-1572.** www.footlight.com. Subway: 4, 5, 6, L, N, R, Q, W to 14th St./Union Sq.

Generation Records *(Value)* This store sells mostly CDs and is an excellent source for "import" live recordings. Originally specializing in hard-core, punk, and metal, the collection upstairs still has a heavy edge but has diversified. Downstairs is a well-organized, well-priced used-CD selection that's not as picked-over as most; there's also a good selection of LPs. Despite the help's tough look, they're quite friendly and helpful. 210 Thompson St. (btwn Bleecker and 3rd sts.). © 212/254-1100. Subway: A, C, E, F, V to W. 4th St.

Jazz Record Center *The* place to find rare and out-of-print jazz records. In addition to the extensive selection of CDs and vinyl (including 78s), videos, books, posters, magazines, photos, and other memorabilia are available. Prices start at $5 for vinyl, $10 for CDs, and soar from there, befitting the rarity of the stock. Owner Frederick Cohen is extremely knowledgeable, so come here if you're trying to track down something obscure. 236 W. 26th St. (btwn Seventh and Eighth aves.), 8th floor. © 212/675-4480. www.jazzrecordcenter.com. Subway: 1, 9 to 28th St.

Kim's Video & Audio This funky minichain is New York's underground alternative to Blockbuster Video, but they also stock a decent selection of indie vinyl and CDs as well as books and 'zines at Mondo Kim's, Kim's West, and Kim's Mediapolis. Kim's Video at 144 Bleecker St. (btwn Thompson St. and LaGuardia Place). © 212/260-1010. www.kimsvideo.com. Subway: A, C, E, F, V, S to W. 4th St. Also Kim's West at 350 Bleecker St. (at W. 10th St.; © 212/675-8996; subway: 1, 9 to Christopher St.). Mondo Kim's at 6 St. Marks Place (btwn Second and Third aves.; © 212/598-9985; subway: 6 to Astor Place). Kim's Mediapolis at 2906 Broadway (at 113th St.; © 212/864-5321; subway: 1, 9 to 110th St.).

NYCD *(Value)* This neat, narrow little store is home to one of the city's best collections of used rock CDs thanks to its off-the-beaten-track Upper West Side location. Downtown trollers simply don't make it this far uptown to prune the selection, so it's easy to find lots of top titles among the pickings. 426 Amsterdam Ave. (btwn 80th and 81st sts.). © 212/724-4466. Subway: 1, 9 to 79th St.

Other Music *(Finds)* Head to Other Music for the wildest sounds in town. You won't find a major label here. They focus on small international labels. The bizarro runs the gamut from Japanese spin doctors to Irish folk; needless to say, the world-music selection is terrific. Fascinating and bound to be filled with music you've never heard. The staff knows their stuff, so ask away. 15 E. 4th St. (btwn Broadway and Lafayette St.). © 212/477-8150. www.othermusic.com. Subway: F, V to Broadway/Lafayette St.; 6 to Astor Place.

Throb A popular stop for dance-club deejays, this CD/vinyl shop specializes in electronic genres: house, ambient, jungle, drum-and-bass, loungecore, trance, trip hop. Imports are big business here. You'll also find record bags and T-shirts. 211 E. 14th (btwn Second and Third aves.). © 212/533-2328. www.throb.com. Subway: L to Third Ave.

Tower Records A mighty chain it may be, but it's hard to complain about Tower. Both locations are superstores brimming with a huge collection of music—classical, jazz, rock, world, you name it. The Village location has a good selection of indie and alternative labels. Just behind it at West 4th and Lafayette is **Tower Books and Video** (© 212/228-5100), where you'll find videos, books, and magazines (although the video selection isn't as good as you might expect). Look for in-stores by big names. 692 Broadway (at W. 4th St.). © 212/505-1500. www.towerrecords.com. Subway: N, R to 8th St.; 6 to Astor Place. Also at 1961 Broadway (at 66th St.; © 212/799-2500; subway: 1, 9 to 66th St.).

Virgin Megastore In the heart of Times Square, this superstore bustles day and night. For the size of it, the selection isn't as wide as you'd think; still, you're likely to find what you're looking for among the two levels of domestic and imported CDs and cassettes. Other plusses are an extensive singles department, a phenomenal number of listening posts, plus a huge video department. There's also a bookstore, a cafe, and a movie theater, and you can even arrange airfare on Virgin Atlantic. Look for a busy schedule of in-stores at both locations. 1540 Broadway (at 45th St.). © **212/921-1020**. www.virginmega.com. Subway: N, R, 1, 2, 3, 7, 9 to Times Sq./42nd St. Also at 52 E. 14th St. (at Broadway; © **212/598-4666**; subway: 4, 5, 6, N, R, L, Q, W to 14th St./Union Sq.).

SHOES

Designer shoe shops are on **East 57th Street** and up **Madison Avenue,** becoming pricier as you move uptown. **SoHo** is an excellent place to search; the streets are overrun with shoe stores, with **Broadway** below Houston between Spring and Canal street the place to look for discount prices. Cheaper copies of the trendiest styles are sold in the shops along **8th Street** between Broadway and Sixth Avenue in the Village, which some people call Shoe Row. Most department stores have two sizable shoe departments—one for designer stuff and one for daily wearables—and sales can be terrific. The women's shoe department at **Loehmann's** (p. 279) is well stocked and unbelievably priced.

Harry's Shoes This large, always-bustling store focuses on selling first-class brands for men, women, and children—from Aerosoles to Timberland—at the lowest retail prices. Expect such brands as Clarks, Sebago, Ecco, Havana Joe, Rockport, and many, many more. You might do well to price-compare with Tip Top (see below), which sells many of the same brands. 2299 Broadway (at 83rd St.). © **866/4-HARRYS**. www.harrys-shoes.com. Subway: 1, 2, 3, 9 to 86th St.

Profiles Here are casual and trendy discount shoes for men, women, and kids. 294 Columbus Ave. (at 74th St.). © **212/799-1994**. Subway: B, C to 72nd St.

Sacco Mostly Italian-made women's shoes that cross style with supreme comfort. I especially love the fall and winter boots, which are comfortable enough to carry me around the city on even the most arduous of research days. Lots of terrific basic blacks and browns. Good prices and sales, too. 94 Seventh Ave. (btwn 15th and 16th sts.). © **212/675-5180**. Subway: 1, 9 to 18th St. Also at 14 E. 17th St. (btwn Fifth Ave. and Broadway; © **212/243-2070**; subway: 4, 5, 6, N, R, L, S, Q, W to 14th St./Union Sq.); 111 Thompson St. (btwn Prince and Spring sts.; © **212/925-8010**; subway: C, E to Spring St.); 324 Columbus Ave. (btwn 75th and 76th sts.; © **212/799-5229**; subway: B, C to 81st St.); 2355 Broadway (at 86th St.; © **212/874-8362**; subway: 1, 9 to 86th St.).

Shoe Mania *Value* Another terrific discount shoe store for men and women; here, the emphasis is on style and comfort, with brands like Kenneth Cole, Dr. Marten's, and Steve Madden dispersed among the Birkenstocks, Mephistos, ad Joseph Siebels (great European comfort shoes). 853 Broadway (at 14th St.). © **212/253-8744**. www.shoemania.com. Subway: 4, 5, 6, N, R, L, S, Q, W to 14th St./Union Sq. Also at 331 Madison Ave. (btwn 42nd and 43rd sts.; © **212/557-6627**; subway: 4, 5, 6, 7, S to 42nd St./Grand Central).

Stapleton Shoe Company *Value* If Imelda Marcos had been a man, her first stop would have been this shoe store, next to the American Stock Exchange. Stapleton sells men's brands like Bally, Timberland, and Johnston & Murphy, all at discounts so deep it'll feel like insider trading. 68 Trinity Place (at Rector St.). © **212/964-6329**. Subway: N, R to Rector St.

Tip Top Shoes If you find yourself discovering that the shoes you thought were so comfortable just aren't cutting it—trust me, it happens a lot—head over

> ### Value $50 Fabulous: Chinatown's Secret Treasure Trove
>
> You've come to the Big Apple ready to shop. But there's one thing holding you back: sticker shock. Unfortunately, that old adage—if you have to ask, you can't afford it—holds true in many of Manhattan prime shopping 'hoods.
>
> But no self-respecting fashionista would let a detail like a shoestring budget get in her way. You *can* come home with fabulous fashions, funky housewares, and boasting about that full-body massage—all for less than $50. Head for Chinatown, the mecca for intrepid bargain shoppers.
>
> **There's the Rub** Sure, SoHo's Bliss Spa is nice, but Chinatown can't be beat for the best deals on massages.
>
> At **Wu Lim Qi Gong,** 35 Howard St. (between Broadway and Lafayette sts. © **646/613-0208,** subway: N, R, W to Canal St.), prices range from $7 for 10 minutes to $42 for a full-hour massage. (Actually, 61 min.; increments are, inexplicably, 10, 16, 31, 46, and 61 min.) Reflexology treatments will set you back $28 for 40 minutes. Don't be frightened off by the basement entrance. Massages are given in a large, lovely room painted a calming green and lined with glass treatment compartments, each with two massage tables. You won't find robes and slippers, a steam bath, showers or munchies, but you will get immediate attention and a rigorous rub while covered in soft, thick towels. You get exactly what you pay for: Treatments are timed to the second. You can also try **New Land Chinese Reflexology Center,** 234-238 Canal St. (between Centre and Baxter sts. © **212/966-0306,** subway: J, M, Z to Canal St.), where prices are about the same.
>
> These spots are open day and night, so you almost never have a wait!
>
> **Knock It Off** On the streets of New York, you'll see tables of the newest and finest designer bags that are, ahem, somewhat less than genuine. Most are convincing imitations, and they function much like the real thing.

to Tip Top, New York's premier walking-shoe shop (since 1940). You'll find all of the top brands here for men and women, including Rockport, Mephisto, Dansko, Ecco, and hip Campers, plus tennies from New Balance and Puma. 155 W. 72nd St. (btwn Broadway and Columbus Ave.). © **800/WALKING** or 212/787-4960. www.tiptopshoes.com. Subway: 1, 2, 3, 9 to 72nd St.

TOYS

The Enchanted Forest *Finds* Here's a shop for kids and grown-ups alike. It overflows with stuffed animals and puppets, plus the kinds of simple but absorbing games that parents remember from the days before PlayStation, like PickUp Sticks and Chinese Checkers. There's also a book nook specializing in reissued classics like *The Phantom Toll Booth* and small-print children's and adult gift books. It's truly a special place. 85 Mercer St. (btwn Spring and Broome sts.). © **212/925-6677.** www.sohotoys.com. Subway: N, R to Prince St.

Lots of wallet-friendly knockoffs can be found in Chinatown, particularly along Canal Street between Lafayette and Mott streets (subway: J, M, Z to Canal St.) where small shops—usually no more than glorified stalls—offer a dazzling array of Vuitton-like, Prada-ish and almost-Channel bags, wallets, shoes, shirts, scarves, watches, perfume—all from the world's great design houses (or not). Why not pick up a not-exactly-Burberry hat for a 10-spot, and tote the savings in the not-quite kate spade purse you got for $15?

Cooking with Fusion   Nothing says fabulous like a cupboard full of exotic foodstuffs. Tucked in between the seafood and meat sellers, Asia **Market Corporation,** 71½ Mulberry St. (just below Canal St.; © **212/962-2028,** subway: J, M, Z to Canal St.), is no more promising from the outside than an old deli—but appearances can be deceiving. This grocery boasts a dizzying selection of goodies—many of the same brands found in the city's pricey food emporiums. Get everything from Café du Monde Chicory and Coffee (14 oz. for $3.75) to Calvé "Frites Saus," a mayonnaisey-type french-fry sauce from Holland ($3.25). Most of the stock is dedicated to Asian cooking—but these are some of the best prices on wasabi, nori, and exotic spices and rices that you will see.

Got Zen?   The corner of Baxter and Walker streets, just below Canal Street, is home to a variety of sellers hawking housewares, jade, and plants. Stop in **Peony Flowery Bonsai Fountain** at 106 Walker St. (between Lafayette and Centre sts.; © **212/334-1807,** subway: N, Q, R, W to Canal St.), where lovely bonsai trees start at $16. Then relax at **Dragon Land Bakery,** 125 Walker St. (just below Canal St.; © **212/219-2012,** subway: N, Q, R W to Canal St.), Chinatown's answer to Fauchon, where sweets, pastel puddings flavored with mango or green tea, and crisp cookies are available for between 75¢ and $1.75.

—*Maureen Johnson*

FAO Schwarz   The best-loved toy store in America was designed with an eye for fun: The elevator is shaped like a huge toy soldier, and there are plenty of hands-on displays to keep the little ones occupied. Entire areas are devoted to specific toy makers (Lego, Fisher Price, *Star Wars* action figures, Barbie). You and the kids will find plenty of affordable gifts to take home. 767 Fifth Ave. (at 58th St.). © 212/644-9400. www.fao.com. Subway: N, R to Fifth Ave.

Toys"R"Us   Geoffrey the Giraffe must be mighty pleased with this new home. It occupies almost an entire city block in Times Square, and boasts its own Ferris wheel kids can ride for free. The huge collection is well organized and the store's "ambassadors" are abundant and helpful; they'll even point you to restaurants and kid-friendly attractions in the neighborhood. Don't miss it if you're traveling with kids. 1514 Broadway (at 44th St.). © 800/869-7787. Subway: 1, 2, 3, 7, 9 to 42nd St. Also at 24–30 Union Sq. (© 212/674-8697; subway: 4, 5, 6, N, R, L, S, Q, W to 14th St./Union Sq.).

9

New York City After Dark

There's so much to see and do in New York at night that your biggest problem is going to be choosing among the many temptations.

There's no way that I can tell you what's going to be on while you're in town. So for the latest, most comprehensive listings, from theater and performing arts to live rock, jazz, and dance club coverage, *Time Out New York* (**www.timeoutny.com**) is my favorite source; a new issue hits newsstands every Thursday. The free weekly *Village Voice* (**www.villagevoice.com**) is available late Tuesday downtown and early Wednesday in the rest of the city. The arts and entertainment coverage is extensive. The *New York Times* (**www.nytoday.com**) features terrific entertainment coverage, particularly in the Friday "Weekend" section; the cabaret, classical-music, and theater guides are particularly useful. Other weekly sources are "Goings on About Town" in the *New Yorker* (**www.newyorker.com**); and *New York* magazine (**www.newyorkmag.com**), whose "Cue" features the latest happenings. *New York*'s **www.nymetro.com** site is an excellent Web source.

Bar-hoppers shouldn't pass up the comprehensive annual **Shecky's New York Bar, Club & Lounge Guide.** Its website (**newyork.sheckys.com**) is even more current, and all the information is free. **Shecky's Bar Phone** at © **212/777-BARS** offers up-to-the minute nightlife news for the cost of a phone call.

NYC/Onstage (© **212/768-1818;** www.tdf.org) is a recorded service providing schedules, descriptions, and details on theater and the performing arts. The bias is toward plays, but NYC/Onstage is a good source for music (including performances at Lincoln Center), dance, opera, cabaret, and family entertainment.

CultureFinder (**www.culturefinder.com**) is an excellent site for Big Apple arts and entertainment, with an emphasis on museums, theater, and classical music.

1 The Theater Scene

Nobody does theater better than New York. No other city—not even London—has a scene with so much breadth and depth, with so many alternatives. Broadway gets the most ink and airplay: This is where you'll find the big stage productions, from crowd-pleasers like *Phantom of the Opera* and *42nd Street* to newer phenomena like *The Lion King* and *The Producers*. But today's scene thrives beyond the bounds of Broadway. With bankable stars on stage, crowds lining up for tickets, and hits popular enough to generate major-label cast albums, Off-Broadway isn't just for culture vultures anymore.

Despite this vitality, plays and musicals close all the time, often with little warning. Before you arrive, or even once you get here, check the **publications** and **websites** at the beginning of this chapter to get an idea of what you might like to see. One useful source is the **Broadway Line** (© **888/BROADWAY** or

212/302-4111; www.broadway.org), where you can obtain details and descriptions on current Broadway shows, hear about special offers and discounts, and can ultimately be transferred to TeleCharge or Ticketmaster to buy tickets. There's also **NYC/Onstage** (© **212/768-1818;** www.tdf.org), providing the same kind of service for Broadway and Off-Broadway productions. (Don't buy tickets, though, until you read "Top Ticket-Buying Tips," below.)

Many top stars are heading for the New York stage these days: In the last couple seasons you could have seen Kevin Spacey, Patrick Stewart, Natasha Richardson, Kevin Bacon, and Liam Neeson onstage. But keep in mind that stars' runs are often short, and tickets sell out fast. If you hear that there's an actor you like on the New York stage, check with the box office to find out how long they'll be in the part, or if there are certain performances they don't do (like matinees), before you nail down your travel plans.

THE BASICS

LOCATIONS **Broadway, Off-Broadway,** and **Off-Off-Broadway** refer to theater size, pay, and other arcane details, not location—or, these days, even star wattage. Most of the Broadway theaters are in Times Square, around the thoroughfare for which the scene is named, but not on it: You'll find them on the side streets mostly in the mid-40s between Sixth and Eighth avenues, running north as far as 53rd Street. There's even a Broadway theater outside Times Square: the Vivian Beaumont in Lincoln Center, at Broadway and 65th Street.

Off-Broadway, on the other hand, is not that exacting. With the popularization of off-the-beaten-track productions, the distinction between Off- and Off-Off-Broadway has become fuzzier. Off-Off-Broadway shows tend to be more avant-garde and experimental. Off- and Off-Off-Broadway shows tend to be based downtown, but are sometimes found in Midtown and on the Upper West Side.

TIMETABLES Broadway shows tend to keep regular schedules. There are usually eight performances a week: evening shows Tuesday through Saturday, plus matinees on Wednesday, Saturday, and Sunday. Evening shows are usually at 8pm, while matinees are usually at 2pm Wednesday and Saturday, 3pm Sunday. But schedules can vary. Shows usually start on the dot; if you arrive late, you may have to wait until intermission to take your seat.

TICKET PRICES Ticket prices for Broadway shows vary dramatically. The high end for any given show is likely to be between $60 and $100, or higher. The cheapest end of the price range can be as low as $20 or as high as $50, depending on the theater. If you're buying tickets at the low end of a wide range, be aware that you may be buying obstructed-view seats. If all tickets are the same price or the range is small, you can pretty much count on all of the seats being pretty good. Otherwise, price is your barometer. Legroom can be tight in these old theaters, and you'll usually get more in the orchestra seats.

Off-Broadway and Off-Off-Broadway shows tend to be cheaper, with tickets often as low as $10 or $15. In fact, experimental theaters like the Off-Off-Broadway, Obie Award–winning **Dixon Place,** 309 E. 26th St. (© **212/ 532-1546;** www.dixonplace.org), offers drama at prices that range from free to $12. However, seats for the most established shows and those with star power can command prices as high as $50 or $60.

Don't let price be a deterrent to enjoying the theater. There are ways to pay less if you're willing to make the effort and be flexible, with a few choices at hand as to what you'd like to see. Read on.

Kids Take the Stage: Family-Friendly Theater

The family-friendly theater scene is flourishing. There's so much going on that it's best to check *New York* magazine, *Time Out New York,* or the Friday *New York Times* for current listings. Besides Broadway shows, the following are some dependable—and cheaper—entertainment options.

The **New Victory Theater,** 209 W. 42nd St., between Seventh and Eighth avenues (✆ 212/382-4020; www.newvictory.org), reopened as the city's first full-time family-oriented performing-arts center and has hosted companies ranging from the Trinity Irish Dance Company to the Flaming Idiots, who juggle everything from fire and swords to bean-bag chairs.

The **Paper Bag Players** (✆ 212/362-0431; www.paperbagplayers.org), called "the best children's theater in the country" by *Newsweek,* perform funny tales for children 4 to 9 in a set made from bags and boxes, in winter only, at Hunter College's Sylvia and Danny Kaye Playhouse, 68th Street between Park and Lexington avenues (✆ 212/772-4448). You can also call to inquire whether they'll be staging other performances about town.

TADA! Youth Theater, 120 W. 28th St., between Sixth and Seventh avenues (✆ 212/627-1732; www.tadatheater.com), is a youth ensemble that performs musicals and plays for kids, teens, and their families.

The **Swedish Cottage Marionette Theatre** (✆ 212/988-9093; www.centralpark.org) puts on marionette shows for kids at its 19th-century Central Park theater throughout the year. Reservations are a must.

The World Voices Club at the **New Perspectives Theatre,** 750 Eighth Ave., between 46th and 47th streets (✆ 212/730-2030; www.newperspectivestheatre.org), presents a new puppet show based on fables from various world cultures each month.

While David Mamet hardly seems like a playwright for the kiddies, the "Atlantic for Kids" series is at the **Atlantic Theater Company,** 453 16th St., between Ninth and Tenth avenues (✆ 212/691-5919; www.atlantictheater.org), which Mamet founded with actor William H.

TOP TICKET-BUYING TIPS

BEFORE YOU LEAVE HOME If you want to guarantee yourself a seat at a particular show by buying tickets in advance, it's almost impossible to get around paying full price. (The only exception is to register for one or more of the online theater clubs, which offer advance-purchase discounts to members; see "How to Save on Theater Tickets," below.) Phone ahead or go online for tickets to the most successful or popular shows as far in advance as you can; with shows such as *The Lion King* or *The Producers,* it's never too early.

Buying tickets can be simple, if the show you want isn't sold out. Call such general numbers as **TeleCharge** (✆ 212/239-6200; www.telecharge.com), which handles most Broadway and Off-Broadway shows and some concerts; or **Ticketmaster** (✆ 212/307-4100; www.ticketmaster.com), which also handles Broadway and Off-Broadway shows and concerts. If you're an American Express

Macy. Two of their hilariously offbeat productions made *Time Out New York*'s Best of 2000 list, and Mamet's version of *The Frog Prince* entertained crowds in winter 2002, so it's worth seeing what's on while you're in town.

Another excellent troupe that excels at children's theater is the **Vital Theatre Company,** 432 W. 42nd St., between Ninth and Tenth avenues (© **212/592-4508;** www.vitaltheatre.org); it's well worth seeing what's on.

If you want to introduce your kids to live opera, check out the "Opera in Brief" program, which runs most Saturdays at 11:30am, at **Amato Opera** (p. 303). For kid-friendly classical music, see what's on at **Bargemusic** (p. 30), which presents chamber-music concerts for kids throughout their season. Look for Young People's Concerts and Kidzone Live!, in which kids get to interact with orchestra members prior to curtain time, at the **New York Philharmonic** (p. 306). Also check to see what's on at **Carnegie Hall** (p. 309), which offers family concerts for a bargain-basement ticket price of just $5, plus the CarnegieKids program, which introduces kids ages 3 to 6 to basic musical concepts through a 45-minute music-and-storytelling performance. Finally, don't forget "Jazz for Young People," Wynton Marsalis's stellar family concert series at **Jazz at Lincoln Center** (p. 310).

Money-saving tip: **High 5 Tickets to the Arts** (© **212/HI5-TKTS;** www.high5tix.org) makes theater more accessible for kids 13 to 18. Teens can buy donated tickets for select theatrical performances for $5 each at weekend performances, or $5 for two (for the teen and a guest of any age) for Monday through Thursday shows. High 5 also offers discount museum passes at the wallet-friendly price of two for $5 (for the teen and a guest of any age). Check out the website for details on theater or museum tickets, which can usually be purchased with proof of age at any New York City Ticketmaster outlet or online. Also check the High 5 website for listings of free and nearly free events going on while you and your teen are in town.

cardholder, check to see if tickets are being sold through **American Express Gold Card Events** (© **800/448-TIKS;** www.americanexpress.com/gce). You'll pay full price, but Amex has access to blocks of preferred seating set aside for cardholders, so you may be able to get tickets to a show that's otherwise sold out, or better seats than you would otherwise be able to buy.

Theatre Direct International (TDI) is a ticket broker that sells tickets to select Broadway and Off-Broadway shows—including some of the most popular, like *Oklahoma!* and *Cabaret*—to individuals and travel agents. Check to see if they have seats to the shows in which you're interested by calling © **800/ BROADWAY** or 212/541-8457; you can also order tickets through TDI via their website, **www.broadway.com**. Because there's a service charge of $15 per ticket, try Ticketmaster or TeleCharge first; but because they act as a consolidator, TDI may have tickets for a specific show if the major outlets don't.

Value How to Save on Theater Tickets

If you employ a little patience, flexibility, and know-how, there are ways to pay less than full price for your theater tickets—sometimes a lot less.

For Advance Planners Your best bet is to try before you go. You might be able to purchase **reduced-price theater tickets** over the phone (or in person at the box office) by joining one or more of the online theater clubs. Membership is free and can garner you discounts of up to 50% on select Broadway and Off-Broadway shows. The deals are available to registered club members at **Broadway.com (www.broadway.com), Playbill Online** (www.playbill.com or www.playbillclub.com), and **TheaterMania** (www.theatermania.com). You can sign up to be notified by e-mail as offers change. I like the **Playbill Club** best; its discounts tend to be the most wide-ranging, often including the best Broadway and Off-Broadway shows. TheaterMania's **TM Insider** is the runner-up; the Broadway.com site wants a bit too much personal information for my taste. Nothing prevents you from signing up with all of them and taking advantage of the best deals.

You can sign up with the **Hit Show Club** (© 212/581-4211; www.hitshowclub.com), a free subscription club that offers its members discounts to Broadway and Off-Broadway shows. Once you sign up, you can find offers online or stop by their offices at 630 Ninth Ave. (between 44th and 45th sts., 8th floor; open Mon–Fri 9am–4pm), and pick up discount coupons for theater, dining, and attractions. I recommend calling the info line or checking the website before you leave. One advantage of the website is that it will let you "bid" on tickets for the Broadway and Off-Broadway shows in which you're interested. Maybe you can tell the folks back home how you scored *Phantom* tickets for just 20 bucks!

The Theatre Development Fund, which operates the TKTS same-day discount-ticket booth (see below), also runs the **TDF Voucher** program, which gives participants dirt-cheap access to a world of cutting-edge theater and performing arts that even most New Yorkers don't know about. Sign up for $28, and you'll get four vouchers that you can use at any number of events that will be on while you're in town: theater, ballet, light opera, dance, and more. That's $7 a ticket—cheaper than a bad movie. You can order your vouchers online at the TDF website (**www.tdf.org**; click on "TDF Programs," then "TDF Vouchers"), where you'll be able to review a list of current ongoing events that accept vouchers before you buy.

For In-Towners The best deal on same-day tickets for Broadway and Off-Broadway shows is the **Times Square Theatre Centre,** better known as the **TKTS** booth run by the nonprofit Theatre Development Fund at Duffy Square, 47th Street and Broadway (open 3–8pm for evening performances, 10am–2pm for Wed and Sat matinees, from 11am on Sun for all performances). Tickets for that day's performances are usually offered at half-price, with a few reduced 25%, plus a $2.50 per ticket service charge. Boards outside the ticket windows list available shows; you're unlikely to find the biggest hits, but most other shows turn up. Only cash and traveler's checks are accepted (no credit cards). There's often a line, so show up early for the best availability and be prepared to wait—but the crowd is part of the fun. If you don't have a specific show in mind, you can walk up to the window later in the day and something is always available.

Run by the same group and offering the same discounts is the **TKTS Downtown Theatre Centre,** at South Street Seaport (open Mon–Fri 11am–5:30pm, Sat 11am–3:30pm; subway: 2, 3, 4, 5, E, J, Z, M to Fulton St.; A, C to Broadway-Nassau). The advantages to coming down here are that the lines are generally shorter, and matinee tickets are available the day before, so you can plan ahead.

Visit www.tdf.org or call **NYC/Onstage** at © 212/768-1818 and press "8" for the latest TKTS information.

Many shows, particularly long-running ones such as *Cabaret* and *Phantom of the Opera,* offer **twofers,** which allow you to purchase two tickets for the price of one for certain performances. You can find these coupons at many places in the city: hotel lobbies, in banks, in shops, even at restaurant cash registers. They'll definitely be found at the **Times Square Visitors Center,** 1560 Broadway, between 46th and 47th streets (© 212/768-1560). They're also available at the **NYCVB Visitor Information Center** at 810 Seventh Ave., between 52nd and 53rd streets (© 212/484-1222); and at the information window on the main concourse of **Grand Central Terminal,** East 42nd Street at Vanderbilt Avenue, near the ticket-purchase windows directly across from the information kiosk.

For Theater Fans Willing to Go the Extra Mile Broadway shows—even blockbusters—sometimes have a limited number of tickets set aside for **students and seniors,** and they might be available at the last minute; many Off-Broadway houses make "rush" seats available to students 30 minutes to an hour before curtain. On Broadway, *Rent* has offered all kinds of bargains to keep younger theatergoers coming. Call the box office of the show in which you're interested to inquire about their discount policies.

If you don't mind staying on your feet, you can save big bucks—and often gain access to sold-out shows—with **standing-room** tickets, offered by many (but not all) Broadway shows. A limited number are usually sold on the day of show, and cost between $10 and $20. Call the box office in advance and they can fill you in on their standing-room policy.

Some Off- and Off-Off Broadway shows, including such fetching performances as the Blue Man Group, will let you see the show for free if you're willing to be an **usher.** This requires some advance legwork and willingness to put in extra hours, but it can pay off for theater fans on shoestring budgets. Again, inquire with the theater directly.

There are so many options for getting cut-rate tickets that any visitor can fill up a week with cheap shows. But there's never any guarantee that last-minute tickets or discounts will be available to a specific show. If there's one you absolutely must see, splurge on full-price advance-purchase tickets.

Other reputable brokers include **Keith Prowse & Co.** (© **800/669-8687** or 212/398-4175; www.keithprowse.com) and **Global Tickets Edwards & Edwards** (© **800/223-6108;** www.globaltickets.com). For a list of other licensed brokers, get a copy of the Official NYC Visitor Kit (see "Visitor Information" in chapter 2 for details). All kinds of ticket brokers list ads in the Sunday *New York Times* and other publications, but don't take the risk. Stick with a licensed broker recommended by the NYCVB.

If you don't want to pay a service charge, call the **box office.** Broadway theaters don't sell tickets over the phone—the major exception is the **Roundabout Theatre** (© **212/719-1300;** www.roundabouttheatre.org), which charges a $5-per-ticket "convenience" fee—but a good number of Off-Broadway theaters do sell tickets over the phone.

WHEN YOU ARRIVE Once you arrive, getting your hands on good tickets can take some smarts—and failing those, cash. Even if it seems unlikely that seats are available, always **call the box office** first. Single seats are often easiest to obtain, so people willing to sit apart may find themselves in luck.

You should also try the **Broadway Ticket Center,** run by the League of American Theaters and Producers at the Times Square Visitors Center, 1560 Broadway, between 46th and 47th streets (open Mon–Sat 9am–7pm, Sun 10am–6pm). They often have tickets available for otherwise sold-out shows, both for advance and same-day purchase, and charge about $5 extra per ticket.

If you want to deal with a broker, **Keith Prowse & Co.** has an office that accommodates drop-ins at 234 W. 44th St., between Seventh and Eighth avenues, Suite 1000 (© **800/223-6108;** open Mon–Sat 9am–6pm).

If you buy from one of the **scalpers** selling tickets in front of the theater, you're taking a risk. They may be legit—a couple from the 'burbs whose companions couldn't make it for the evening, say—but they could be swindlers passing off fakes for big money. It's a risk that's not worth taking.

One preferred **insiders' trick** is to make the rounds of Broadway theaters at about 5 or 6pm, when unclaimed house seats are made available to the public. These tickets—reserved for VIPs, friends of the cast, the press, etc.—offer great seats and are sold at face value without service charge.

Also, note that **Monday** is often a good day to cop big-name tickets. Though most theaters are dark that day, some of the most sought-after choices aren't. Locals are at home first night of the workweek, so all the odds are in your favor. Your chances will always be better on weeknights, or for Wednesday matinees.

2 Opera, Classical Music & Dance

In addition to the listings below, see what's on at **Carnegie Hall** and the **Brooklyn Academy of Music,** two of the most respected—and enjoyable—performing-arts venues in the city. The **92nd Street Y** also hosts lots of arts events, usually at low prices. I've listed the operatic and symphonic companies at **Lincoln Center;** also check the center's calendar for all offerings. See "Major Concert Halls & Landmark Venues," later in this chapter.

OPERA

In addition to the choices below, you might want to see what's on from the **New York Grand Opera** (© **212/245-8837;** www.newyorkgrandopera.org), which puts on free Verdi productions at Central Park's SummerStage (see the box on p. 309) as well as workshop programs throughout the year.

Fans with an ear for experimentalism might check out **American Opera Projects** (© **718/398-4024;** www.aopinc.org), which develops new American operas and other projects and showcases them at venues around town. Tickets generally run $10 to $30, and discounts may be available for students and seniors.

Amato Opera Theatre *Value*   This cozy, off-the-beaten-track venue functions as a showcase for talented young American singers. The 100-plus-seat house celebrated its 50th season in 2001 amid a rising reputation. The staple is full productions of Italian classics—Verdi's *La Traviata,* Puccini's *Madame Butterfly,* Bizet's *Carmen,* with an occasional Mozart tossed in—at great prices ($28, $23 for seniors and kids). Performances, usually held on Saturday and Sunday, now regularly sell out, so it's a good idea to reserve 3 weeks in advance.

Attention, moms and dads: On one Saturday a month, "Opera in Brief" offers fully costumed, kid-length versions of the classics with narration so Mom and Dad have a forum in which to introduce the little ones to opera. At $15 or so per ticket, these matinees are wallet-friendly, too. 319 Bowery (at 2nd St.). © **212/ 228-8200.** www.amato.org. Subway: F to Second Ave.; 6 to Bleecker St.

Metropolitan Opera   Tickets can cost a fortune—anywhere from $25 to $275. But for its full productions of the classic repertory and schedule packed with world-class singers, the Met ranks first in the world. Millions are spent on fabulous stagings of new works and repertory favorites, and the venue itself is a wonder of acoustics. To guarantee that its audience understands the words, the Met has outfitted the back of each row of seats with screens for subtitles—translation help

---

Value **Bargain Alert: The Classical Learning Curve**

The **Juilliard School,** 60 Lincoln Center Plaza (Broadway at 65th St.; © 212/769-7406 or 212/721-6500; www.juilliard.edu), the nation's premier music education institution, sponsors about 550 performances of high quality—at low prices—throughout the school year. With most concerts free and $20 as a maximum, Juilliard is one of New York's great cultural bargains. Though most would assume that the school presents only classical music, Juilliard offers other music as well as drama, dance, opera, and interdisciplinary works. The best way to find out about the wide array of productions is to call, visit the website (click on "Calendar of Events"), or consult the bulletin board in the building's lobby. Watch for master classes and discussions open to the public featuring celebrity guest teachers.

The **Manhattan School of Music,** at Broadway and 122nd Street (© 212/749-2802, ext. 4428; www.msmnyc.edu) hosts student concerts as well as daily recitals during the academic year. Most performances are free, and the top ticket price is usually $15. In addition to orchestral and chamber music, the school is highly regarded for its contemporary music and jazz as well as musical theater programs, so performances run the gamut. Look for free master classes, too. Call the box office weekdays between 9am and 5pm for the latest schedule, or check the website (click on "Concert Calendar"); tickets are usually required even for free events, so plan ahead.

> **Value** **Lincoln Center Alert: Last-Minute & Discount Ticket-Buying Tips**
>
> Most seats at **New York Philharmonic** performances are sold to subscribers, but there are ways to get tickets.
>
> When subscribers can't attend, they may return their tickets to the theaters, which resell them at the last moment. These can be in the most coveted rows of the orchestra. Ticket holders can return tickets until curtain time, so tickets that are not available in the morning may be available (at full price) later in the day. The hopefuls form "cancellation lines" 2 hours or more before curtain time for a crack at returned tickets.
>
> Periodically, some **same-day orchestra tickets** are set aside at the philharmonic, and sold in the morning for $25 (maximum two). They usually go on sale at 10am weekdays, 1pm Saturday (noon if there's a matinee).
>
> **Senior/student/disabled rush tickets** may be available for $10 (maximum two) on concert day, but never at Friday matinees or Saturday evening performances. To check availability for any of these programs at all performances, call **Audience Services** at © 212/875-5656.
>
> You're also invited to watch the Philharmonic at work by attending an **Open Rehearsal** for just $14. Not only is this a bargain-basement way to see a great orchestra, it's fascinating to watch how the conductor and musicians shape a piece. There are usually 30 or so of these throughout the season; call Audience Services or check the website for the schedule.
>
> Families with teenagers can participate in **Phil Teens,** which allows you and your teen between the ages of 12 and 17 to attend a New York Philharmonic Rush Hour Concert for just $10 each. Rush Hour concerts start at 6:45pm and last an hour. Your Phil Teen ticket also allows you to arrive as early at 5:30pm to meet guest artists, soloists, and special guests.
>
> Lincoln Center's **Alice Tully Hall** (where the Chamber Music Society performs and other concerts are held), **Jazz at Lincoln Center,** the

for those who want it, minimum intrusion for those who don't. James Levine is the brilliant and popular conductor of the orchestra.

The Met has a number of programs that allow access to cut-rate tickets; for details, see "Lincoln Center Alert: Last-Minute & Discount Ticket-Buying Tips," above. At the Metropolitan Opera House, Lincoln Center, Broadway and 64th St. © 212/362-6000. www.metopera.org. Subway: 1, 9 to 66th St.

New York City Opera This superb company attempts to reach a wider audience than the Metropolitan with its more "human" scale and significantly lower prices ($25–$98). It's also committed to adventurous premieres, newly composed operas, the occasional avant-garde work, American musicals presented as operettas (Stephen Sondheim's *Sweeney Todd,* and *Porgy and Bess*), and even obscure works by mainstream or lesser-known composers. Its mix stretches from the "easy" works of Verdi and Gilbert & Sullivan to the more

Metropolitan Opera, and the New York City Opera, offer last-minute-purchase and discount programs, as do Carnegie Hall and the Brooklyn Academy of Music. Policies differ; for instance, the New York City Ballet offers Student Rush tickets only, at $10 a pop, while the New York City Opera allows students to buy tickets a week in advance at half-price ($13–$53), as well as offering same-day rush tickets (Rush Hot Line: © 212/870-5630). In addition to senior and student rush tickets, Carnegie Hall offers some limited-view tickets for $10 (on sale Sat at 11am for the week's upcoming performances), and presents some totally free events through its neighborhood concert series. Check with the venue directly for details on their specific programs. And call the box office first to check on same-day availability before heading to the theater—or, if you're willing to risk coming away empty-handed, be there at opening time (or before) for first crack.

The Met Opera offers standing-room tickets for $12 to $16, which can be a bargain for budget-minded fans. It's not a bad situation, because you get to lean against plush red bars. (Don't tell the ushers I told you, but if subscribers fail to show, I've seen standees with eagle eyes fill the empty seats at intermission.) Wheelchair-access standing-room places are also available. Tickets go on sale Saturday at 10am for the following week's performances (Sat–Fri). The line sometimes forms much earlier, so plan ahead. Keep in mind that special performances may not be available to potential standees. Call © 212/362-6000 for details. It never hurts to inquire about standing-room availability at other venues as well.

Summer visitors should also keep in mind that both the Philharmonic and the Met Opera offer free concerts in the parks throughout the five boroughs, including Central Park, in July and August. For the current schedule, call © 212/875-5656 or 212/362-6000. The Philharmonic maintains a list of their upcoming park gigs throughout the five boroughs at www.newyorkphilharmonic.org; look under "Events and Performances."

challenging oeuvres of the likes of Arnold Schönberg and Philip Glass. For 2002 to 2003, look for the debut of *Dead Man Walking*, based on Sister Helen Prejean's book; and a double whammy from Puccini: *Madame Butterfly* and *La Bohème*. At the New York State Theater, Lincoln Center, Broadway and 64th St. © 212/870-5630 (information or box office), or 212/307-4100 for Ticketmaster. www.nycopera.com or www.ticketmaster.com. Subway: 1, 9 to 66th St.

New York Gilbert and Sullivan Players If you're in the mood for light-hearted operetta, try this lively company, which specializes in Gilbert and Sullivan's 19th-century English comic works. Tickets are affordable, usually in the $30-to-$50 range. The annual calendar generally runs from October through April and includes four shows a year, plus winter performances at City Center (p. 307). At Symphony Space, Broadway and 95th St. © 212/864-5400 or 212/769-1000. www.nygasp.org. Subway: 1, 2, 3, 9 to 96th St.

CLASSICAL MUSIC

Bargemusic *Value*   Many thought Olga Bloom peculiar when she transformed a 40-year-old barge into a chamber-music concert hall. More than 20 years later, Bargemusic is an internationally renowned recital room boasting more than 100 chamber-music performances a year. There are three shows per week, on Thursday and Friday evenings at 7:30pm and Sunday afternoon at 4pm. The musicians perform on a small stage in a cherry-paneled, fireplace-lit room accommodating 130. The barge may creak a bit and an occasional boat may speed by, but the music rivals what you'll find in almost any other New York venue—and the panoramic view through the glass wall behind the stage can't be beat. Neither can the price: Tickets cost $35 ($20 students), or $40 for performances by larger ensembles. Reserve well in advance. At Fulton Ferry Landing (just south of the Brooklyn Bridge), Brooklyn. © 718/624-2083 or 718/624-4061. www.bargemusic.org. Subway: 2, 3 to Clark St; A, C to High St.

New York Philharmonic   Symphony-wise, you'd be hard-pressed to do better than the New York Philharmonic. Now that legendary music director Kurt Masur has retired, the country's oldest orchestra is under the guidance of Lorin Maazel. Don't expect quality to falter one bit. Highlights of the 2002–03 season include a New Year's Eve Gershwin gala, a wealth of crowd pleasers from Beethoven's *Ninth* to Yo Yo Ma, and a season finale of Mahler's *Resurrection* symphony. There's a summer season in July, when themed classics brighten the hall, as well as summer concerts in Central Park.

Tickets run $21 to $88; opt for a rush-hour concert or a matinee for the lowest across-the-board prices. The acoustics of the hall are such that, at the midrange price points, I prefer the second tier (especially the boxes) over the more expensive rear orchestra seats. Go cheap if you have to; you're sure to enjoy the program from any vantage point. At Avery Fisher Hall, Lincoln Center, Broadway at 65th St. © 212/875-5656 for audience services, 212/875-5030 for box office information or Center Charge at 212/721-6500 for tickets. www.newyorkphilharmonic.org. Subway: 1, 9 to 66th St.

DANCE

In addition to the troupes below, some other venues to keep in mind are the **Brooklyn Academy of Music,** the **92nd Street Y, Radio City Music Hall,** and **Town Hall** (see "Major Concert Halls & Landmark Venues," below).

For innovative works, see what's on at the **Dance Theater Workshop,** in the Bessie Schönberg Theater, 219 W. 19th St., between Seventh and Eighth avenues (© **212/691-6500** or 212/924-0077; www.dtw.org), a first-rate launching pad for nearly a quarter-century; and **Danspace Project,** at St. Mark's Church, 131 E. 10th St. (© **212/674-8112** or 212/674-8194; www.danspaceproject.org), whose performances lean toward the avant-garde, with ticket prices usually falling between free and $15, depending on the performance. Also check for modern dance at **Dixon Place,** 309 E. 26th St. (© **212/532-1546;** www.dixonplace.org), where tickets range from free to $12.

In addition to regular appearances at City Center (see below), the **American Ballet Theatre** (www.abt.org) is in residence at Lincoln Center's Metropolitan Opera House (© **212/362-6000**) for 8 weeks each spring. The same venue also hosts such visiting companies as the Kirov, Royal, and Paris Opéra ballets.

The weekly *Time Out New York,* available on newsstands, maintains a section dedicated to dance events around town that's an invaluable resource to fans.

City Center Modern dance usually takes center stage in this Moorish dome-topped performing-arts palace. The companies of Merce Cunningham, Martha Graham, Paul Taylor, Alvin Ailey, Twyla Tharp, the Dance Theatre of Harlem (in residence in Sept, and celebrating its 30th year this season), and the American Ballet Theatre are often on the calendar. Don't expect cutting edge—but do expect excellence. Tickets generally run $25 to $80, depending on the performance; sightlines are terrific from all corners, and a new acoustical shell means the sound is pitch-perfect, so you won't lose out with cheaper tickets. City Center also presents a limited program schedule at the Cathedral of St. John the Divine (p. 240) at lower-than-average ticket prices ($15–$50). 131 W. 55th St. (btwn Sixth and Seventh aves.). ✆ **877/581-1212** or 212/581-1212. www.citycenter.org. Subway: F, N, R, Q, W to 57th St.; B, D, E to Seventh Ave.

Joyce Theater Housed in an old Art Deco movie house, the Joyce has grown into a modern dance institution. You can see everything from Native American dance to the works of Pilobolus to the Martha Graham Dance Company. In residence annually is Eliot Feld's company, Ballet Tech, which WQXR radio's Francis Mason called "better than a whole month of namby-pamby classical ballets." The Joyce has a second space, the **Joyce SoHo,** where you can see rising young dancers and experimental works in a 70-seat performance space. Tickets are usually $38 at the main theater, as little as $10 at the SoHo space. 175 Eighth Ave. (at 19th St.). ✆ **212/242-0800.** www.joyce.org. Subway: C, E to 23rd St.; 1, 9 to 18th St. Joyce SoHo at 155 Mercer St. (btwn Houston and Prince sts.; ✆ **212/431-9533**; subway: N, R to Prince St.).

New York City Ballet Highly regarded for its unsurpassed technique, the New York City Ballet is the world's best. The company renders with happy regularity the works of two of America's most important choreographers: George Balanchine, its founder, and Jerome Robbins. Under the direction of Ballet Master in Chief Peter Martins, the troupe continues to expand its repertoire and performs to a wide variety of classical and modern music. The cornerstone of the annual season is the Christmastime production of *The Nutcracker,* for which tickets usually become available in early October. Ticket prices for most events run $28 to $66. At the New York State Theater at Lincoln Center, Broadway and 64th St. ✆ **212/870-5570.** www.nycballet.com. Subway: 1, 9 to 66th St.

3 Major Concert Halls & Landmark Venues

Apollo Theatre Built in 1914, this legendary Harlem theater launched or nurtured the careers of countless musical icons—including Bessie Smith, Billie Holiday, Dinah Washington, Duke Ellington, Ella Fitzgerald, Sarah Vaughan, Count Basie, Aretha Franklin, and the Jackson Five—and is in large part responsible for the development and popularization of black music in America. By the 1970s, it had fallen on hard times, but a 1986 restoration breathed new life into the landmark. Today the Apollo is renowned for its African-American acts of all musical genres, from hip-hop to Wynton Marsalis's "Jazz for Young People" events. Wednesday's "Amateur Night at the Apollo" is a fun-filled night that draws in young talents with high hopes of making it big (a young Lauryn Hill started here—and didn't win!). Tickets are usually $15 to $27, slightly higher for finalist shows. 253 W. 125th St. (btwn Adam Clayton Powell and Frederick Douglass boulevards). ✆ **212/749-5838.** Subway: 1, 9 to 125th St.

Money-saving tip: For free tickets to *It's Showtime at the Apollo* (www.apolloshowtime.com), call ✆ **212/889-3532** or send a self-addressed, stamped

Park It! Shakespeare, Music & Other Free Fun

As the weather warms, New York culture comes outdoors to play.

Shakespeare in the Park, held at Central Park's Delacorte Theater, is the city's most famous alfresco arts event. Organized by the late Joseph Papp's Public Theater, the schedule consists of one or two summer productions, usually of the Bard's plays. Productions often feature big names and range from traditional (Andre Braugher as an armor-clad *Henry V*) to avant-garde (Morgan Freeman and Tracy Ullman in *Taming of the Shrew* as a Wild West showdown). The theater itself, next to Belvedere Castle near 79th Street and West Drive, is a dream—on a starry night, there's no better stage in town. Tickets are given out free on a first-come, first-served basis (two per person), at 1pm on the day of the performance at the theater. The Delacorte might have 1,881 seats, but each is a hot commodity, so people line up next to the theater 2 to 3 hours in advance (even earlier if a big name is involved). You can also pick up same-day tickets between 1 and 3pm at the Public Theater, at 425 Lafayette St., where the Shakespeare Festival continues throughout the year. For more information, call the Public Theater at © **212/539-8750** or the Delacorte at © **212/861-7277,** or go online at www.publictheater.org.

With summer also comes the sound of music. The **New York Philharmonic** and the **Metropolitan Opera** hold free concerts beneath the stars in Central Park, and in parks throughout the five boroughs. For the schedule, call © **212/875-5656** or 212/362-6000. The Philharmonic maintains a list of their upcoming gigs at www.newyorkphilharmonic.org; look under "Events and Performances."

The most active music stage in Central Park is **SummerStage,** at Rumsey Playfield, midpark around 72nd Street, which has featured everyone from James Brown to Patti Smith. Recent offerings have included concerts by Hugh Masekela, the Jon Spencer Blues Explosion,

---

envelope and the dates you'll be in the Big Apple to It's Showtime at the Apollo, 3 Park Ave., 40th Floor, New York, NY 10016.

Brooklyn Academy of Music *Finds* BAM is the city's most renowned contemporary arts institution, presenting cutting-edge theater, opera, dance, and music. Offerings have included presentations of baroque opera by William Christie and Les Arts Florissants; pop opera from Lou Reed; Marianne Faithfull singing Kurt Weill; dance by Mark Morris and Mikhail Baryshnikov; the Philip Glass ensemble accompanying screenings of *Koyannisqatsi* and Lugosi's original *Dracula;* the Royal Dramatic Theater of Sweden directed by Ingmar Bergman; and much more, including visiting companies from all over the world. Tickets run anywhere from $5 to $95, depending on the performance and the seats you choose; most performances offer a $25-to-$75 range.

Of particular note is the **Next Wave Festival,** from September through December, this country's foremost showcase for new experimental works. The **BAM Rose Cinemas** show first-run independent films, and there's free live music every Thursday, Friday, and Saturday night at **BAMcafé,** which can range

and Marianne Faithfull; "Viva, Verdi!" festival performances by the New York Grand Opera; cabaret nights; and more. The season usually lasts from mid-June to August. While some big-name shows charge admission, tickets aren't usually required; donations are accepted, however. Call the hot line at ⓒ 212/360-2777 or visit www.summerstage.org.

The calendar of free events heats up throughout the city's parks in summertime. You can find out what's happening by calling the **Parks and Recreation Special Events Hot Line** at ⓒ **888/NY-PARKS** or 212/360-3456, or pointing your browser to **nycparks.completeinet.net**.

HBO sponsors the **Bryant Park Summer Film Festival,** in which a classic film—think *Dr. Zhivago* or *Viva Las Vegas*—is shown on a large screen under the stars every Monday evening at sunset. Admission is free; just bring a blanket and a picnic. Rain dates are Tuesdays. For the schedule, call ⓒ **212/512-5700** or visit www.hbobryantparkfilm.com.

In Lower Manhattan, Trinity Church, at Broadway and Wall Street, hosts a chamber-music and orchestral **Noonday Concert** series year-round each Monday and Thursday at 1pm. This program isn't quite free, but almost: A $2 contribution is requested. Call the concert hot line at ⓒ **212/602-0747** or visit www.trinitywallstreet.org; see chapter 7 for further details.

Most of the city's museums offer free music and other programs on select nights. The **Metropolitan Museum of Art** has an extensive slate of offerings, including live classical music and cocktails on Friday and Saturday evenings. There's lots of fun to be had at others as well, including the **Guggenheim,** whose weekend Worldbeat Jazz series is a big hit; the **American Museum of Natural History,** which features live jazz in the Hall of the Universe in the Rose Center for Earth and Space; and the **Brooklyn Museum of Art,** which hosts the remarkably eclectic **First Saturday** program monthly. For details, see the museum listings in chapter 7.

from atmospheric electronica from coronetist Graham Haynes to radical jazz from the Harold Rubin Trio to tango band Tanguardia! ($10 food minimum). 30 Lafayette Ave. (off Flatbush Ave.), Brooklyn. ⓒ 718/636-4100. www.bam.org. Subway: 2, 3, 4, 5, M, N, Q, R, W to Pacific St./Atlantic Ave.

Carnegie Hall   One of the most famous venues in the world, Carnegie Hall offers everything from classics to the music of Ravi Shankar. The **Isaac Stern Auditorium,** the 2,804-seat main hall, welcomes visiting orchestras from across the country and the world. The legendary hall is both visually and acoustically brilliant. There's also the intimate 284-seat **Weill Recital Hall,** used to showcase chamber music and vocal and instrumental recitals. Carnegie Hall has also reclaimed the underground Zankel Concert Hall, occupied by a movie theater for 38 years; it should reopen as a 650-seat third stage in 2003. For last-minute and discount ticket-buying tips, see the feature on p. 304. 881 Seventh Ave. (at 57th St.). ⓒ 212/247-7800. www.carnegiehall.org. Subway: B, N, Q, R to 57th St.

Lincoln Center for the Performing Arts   New York is the world's premier performing-arts city, and Lincoln Center is its premier institution. Whenever you're planning an evening's entertainment, check the offerings here—which can include opera, dance, symphonies, jazz, theater, film, and more. Lincoln Center's many buildings serve as permanent homes to their own companies as well as major stops for world-class performance troupes from around the globe.

The **Chamber Music Society of Lincoln Center** (C 212/875-5788; www.chamberlinc.org) performs at Alice Tully Hall or the Daniel and Joanna S. Rose Rehearsal Studio, often with such high-caliber guests as Anne Sofie Von Otter and Midori. The **Film Society of Lincoln Center** (C 212/875-5600; www.filmlinc.com) screens a daily schedule of movies at the Walter Reade Theater, and hosts a number of film and video festivals as well as the Reel to Real program for kids, pairing silent-screen classics with live performance. **Jazz at Lincoln Center** (C 212/258-9800; www.jazzatlincolncenter.org) is led by the incomparable Wynton Marsalis, with the orchestra usually performing at Alice Tully Hall; the "Jazz at the Penthouse" program, where great jazz pianists like Ellis Marsalis and Tommy Flanagan play in a spectacular candlelit setting overlooking the Hudson River, is the hottest ticket in town.

Lincoln Center Theater (C 212/362-7600; www.lct.org) consists of the Vivian Beaumont Theater, a modern, comfortable venue with great sightlines that has been home to much Broadway drama, and the Mitzi E. Newhouse Theater, a well-respected Off-Broadway house that has also hosted theatrical triumphs.

For details on the **Metropolitan Opera,** the **New York City Opera,** the **New York City Ballet,** the **Juilliard School,** the phenomenal **New York Philharmonic,** and the **American Ballet Theatre,** which takes up residence here every spring, see "Opera, Classical Music & Dance," earlier in this chapter.

Most of the companies' **major seasons** run from about September or October to April, May, or June. **Special series** like Great Performers help round out the calendar. Indoor and outdoor events are held in warmer months: Summer kicks off with the **JVC Jazz Festival** in June; July sees **Midsummer Night's Swing** with partner dancing, lessons, and music on the plaza; August's **Mostly Mozart** attracts talents like Alicia de Larrocha and André Watts; the 3-year-old **Lincoln Center Festival** celebrates the best of the performing arts; **Lincoln Center Out-of-Doors** is a series of free alfresco music and dance performances also in August; there's also the **New York Film Festival,** and more. Check Lincoln Center's website to see what special events will be on while you're in town.

Tickets for all performances at Avery Fisher and Alice Tully halls can be purchased through **CenterCharge** (C 212/721-6500) or at www.lincolncenter.org (click on "Box Office & Schedule"). Tickets for all Lincoln Center Theater performances can be purchased through **TeleCharge** (C 212/239-6200; www.telecharge.com). Tickets for New York State Theater productions (New York City Opera and Ballet companies) are available through **Ticketmaster** (C 212/307-4100; www.ticketmaster.com), while tickets for films showing at the Walter Reade Theater can be bought up to 7 days in advance by calling C 212/496-3809. For last-minute full-price and discount ticket-buying tips, see p. 304. 70 Lincoln Center Plaza (at Broadway and 64th St.). C **212/546-2656** or 212/875-5456. www.lincolncenter.org. Subway: 1, 9 to 66th St.

Madison Square Garden Monsters of rock and pop fill this 20,000-seat arena, which is also home to the Knicks, the Rangers, and the WNBA's Liberty. The cavernous hulk is better suited to sports than to concerts, or in-the-round events such as Ringling Bros. Barnum & Bailey Circus. End up in the back for U2, and you'd better bring binoculars. You'll find better sightlines at the **Theater at Madison Square Garden,** an amphitheater-style auditorium with

5,600 seats that has played host to some major stars, from Barbra Streisand to Roxy Music. Watch for annual stagings of *The Wizard of Oz, A Christmas Carol,* and such family shows as *Sesame Street Live.* Newest at MSG is the **Comedy Garden** (www.comedygarden.com), the Garden's comedy club at the Theater, where talent runs the gamut from well-known local comics to Robin Williams.

The box office is located at Seventh Avenue and 32nd Street. Or you can purchase tickets through **Ticketmaster** (𝄪 **212/307-7171;** www.ticketmaster.com). On Seventh Ave. from 31st to 33rd sts. 𝄪 **212/465-MSG1.** www.thegarden.com. Subway: A, C, E, 1, 2, 3, 9 to 34th St.

92nd Street Y Tisch Center for the Arts *Value*   This generously endowed community center offers a phenomenal slate of cultural happenings, from classical to folk to jazz to world music to cabaret to lyric theater and literary readings. Great classical performers—Janos Starker, Nadja Salerno-Sonnenberg—give recitals here. The concert calendar often includes luminaries such as Max Roach, John Williams, and Judy Collins; Jazz at the Y from Dick Hyman and guests; the longstanding Chamber Music at the Y series; the classical Music from the Jewish Spirit series; and regular cabaret programs. The lectures and literary-readings calendar is unparalleled, with featured speakers ranging from Lorne Michaels to David Halberstam to Jeff Bezos (CEO of Amazon) to Katie Couric to Elie Wiesel. There's a regular schedule of modern dance, too, through the Harkness Dance Project. Best of all, readings and lectures are usually priced between $20 and $30 for nonmembers, dance is usually $20, and concert tickets generally go for $15 to $50—half or a third of what you'd pay at comparable venues. 1395 Lexington Ave. (at 92nd St.). 𝄪 **212/996-1100.** www.92ndsty.org. Subway: 4, 5, 6 to 86th St.; 6 to 96th St.

Radio City Music Hall   After an extensive renovation in 1999, this stunning Art Deco 6,200-seater continues to be a choice venue; the setting alone adds a dash of panache to any performance. Star of the Christmas season is the **Radio City Music Hall Christmas Spectacular,** starring the legendary Rockettes (tickets $36–$119). Visiting pop chart–toppers, from Patti LaBelle to Radiohead, also perform here. Thanks to perfect acoustics and uninterrupted sight lines, there's hardly a bad seat in the house. The theater also hosts dance performances, family entertainment, and a number of annual awards shows—including anything MTV is holding in town—so this is a good place to celeb-spot on show nights. 1260 Sixth Ave. (at 50th St.). 𝄪 **212/247-4777,** or 212/307-7171 for Ticketmaster. www.radiocity.com or www.ticketmaster.com. Subway: B, D, F, V to 49th–50th sts./Rockefeller Center.

Town Hall   This intimate landmark theater—a National Historic Site designed by McKim, Mead & White—is blessed with outstanding acoustics, making it an ideal place to enjoy many kinds of performances, including theater, dance, lectures, drama, comedy, film, and music. The grade is extremely steep, so unless Lurch sits in front of you, fellow audience members shouldn't block your view. Ticket prices vary depending on the show but are usually less than $40. 123 W. 43rd St. (btwn Sixth and Seventh aves.). 𝄪 **212/840-2824,** or 212/307-4100 for Ticketmaster. www.the-townhall-nyc.org or www.ticketmaster.com. Subway: N, R, S, 1, 2, 3, 7, 9, Q, W to 42nd St./Times Sq.; B, D, F, V to 42nd St.

4 Live Rock, Jazz, Blues & More

I discuss the top venues, both large and small, below. But there are many more, and new ones pop up all the time. For the latest, check the publications discussed earlier this chapter.

LARGER VENUES

For coverage of **Madison Square Garden**, the **Theater at MSG**, and **Town Hall**, see "Major Concert Halls & Landmark Venues," above.

Beacon Theatre This pleasing venue—a 1928 Art Deco movie palace with an impressive lobby, stairway, and auditorium seating about 2,700—hosts mainly pop music, usually for the over-30 crowd. Featured acts have ranged from Bryan Ferry to perennial faves the Allman Brothers. You'll also find such events as the bodybuilding "Night of Champions" on the calendar. 2124 Broadway (at 74th St.). © 212/496-7070. www.livetonight.com. Subway: 1, 2, 3, 9 to 72nd St.

Hammerstein Ballroom This midsize general-admission venue is one of the city's most popular rock stages, hosting everyone from Moby and Bush to Belle & Sebastian to prefab boy-band O-Town. The sound system is good, and the stage high enough that sightlines are decent from the main floor. The side balconies are for VIPs, but the main balcony level, graded for good views and boasting comfortable theater-style seating, is usually open to regular folk. You have to have a mezzanine-level ticket to gain access, so request one when you're buying if you want one (there's usually no cost difference). Otherwise, you'll end up on the standing-room-only floor, which some (not me!) prefer. At the Manhattan Center, 311 W. 34th St. (btwn Eighth and Ninth aves.). © 212/485-1534. www.concerthotline.com. Subway: A, C, E to 34th St./Penn Station.

Roseland This old warhorse, a 1919 ballroom, has been under threat of the wrecking ball for years. Everybody has played at this too-huge-for-its-own-good 2,500-capacity general-admission hall, from Marc Anthony to Hole to Busta Rhymes. Bands who inspire mosh pits like to book here (Nine Inch Nails, No Doubt), because there's plenty of space for slamming and surfing. Thankfully, there's also room to steer clear and enjoy the show. *Money-saving tip:* Purchase advance tickets at Irving Plaza (p. 313) sans the Ticketmaster service fee. 239 W. 52nd St. (btwn Broadway and Eighth Ave.). © 212/777-6800, 212/247-0200, or 212/307-7171 for Ticketmaster. www.roselandballroom.com or www.livetonight.com. Subway: C, E, 1, 9 to 50th St.

MIDSIZE & MULTIGENRE VENUES

For the most part, expect to pay a little more for shows at these venues than you would at smaller clubs—anywhere from $10 to $25, depending on the act.

B.B. King Blues Club & Grill This 550-seat venue is one of the prime anchors of Times Square's "new" 42nd Street. Despite its name, B.B. King's seldom sticks to the blues; instead you're likely to find pop, funk, and rock names, mainly from the past. The big-ticket talent runs the gamut from Nile Rodgers and Chic (cool!) to Big Bad Voodoo Daddy to the Turtles (yes, with Flo and Eddie) to Ice-T. A few more (relatively) esoteric acts take the stage on occasion, such as Luther "Guitar Junior" Johnson and Shemikia Copeland. Tourist-targeted pricing—$25 to $35, plus minimums—makes for an expensive night, and seating policies can be terribly convoluted, but there's no arguing with the quality of the talent. The Sunday gospel lunch is a genuine slice of joy. 42nd St. btwn Seventh and Eighth aves. © 212/997-4144, or 212/307-7171 for Ticketmaster. www.bbkingblues.com. Subway: A, C, E, Q, W, 1, 2, 3, 7, 9 to 42nd St.

The Bottom Line The Bottom Line built its reputation by serving as a showcase for the likes of Bruce Springsteen, and it remains one of the city's most well-respected venues. With table seating, waiter service, decent burgers and fries, and a no-smoking policy, it's one of the city's most comfortable. The Bottom Line is renowned for its sound and bookings of the best rock and singer/songwriters in the business. Shawn Colvin, Marshall Crenshaw, Lucinda Williams, Suzanne Vega, Steve Forbert, Emmylou Harris, Tower of Power, and David Johansen (and alter-ego Buster Poindexter) are among the artists who make this their favored venue for area appearances. There are usually two shows nightly. Tickets usually run $15 to $30, with most $20 or less. 15 W. 4th St. (at Mercer St.). © 212/502-3471 or 212/228-6300. www.bottomlinecabaret.com. Subway: N, R to Astor Place; A, C, E, F, V to W. 4th St.

Bowery Ballroom This marvelous space is run by the same people behind the Mercury Lounge (see below). The Bowery space is bigger, accommodating a crowd of 500 or so. The stage is big and raised to allow good sightlines from every corner. The sound couldn't be better, and Art Deco details give the place a sophistication that doesn't come easy to general-admission halls. My favorite spot is the balcony, which has its own bar and seating alcoves. This place is a favorite with alt-rockers like Melissa Ferrick, Shudder to Think, and Toshi Reagon, as well as acts like Warren Zevon, Neil Finn, and Patti Smith who thrive in an intimate setting. Tickets run $10 to $30, with most under $20. *Money-saving tip:* Buy advance tickets at Mercury's box office; you'll save the service charge, and up to $2 to $5 on the day-of-show price. 6 Delancey St. (at Bowery). © 212/533-2111. www.boweryballroom.com. Subway: F, J, M, Z to Delancey St.

Irving Plaza This high-profile midsize music hall is the prime stop for national-name rock bands that aren't quite big enough yet (or anymore) to sell out Hammerstein, Roseland, or the Beacon. Think Five for Fighting, Jars of Clay, Super Furry Animals, the Reverend Horton Heat, and Cheap Trick. From time to time, big-name artists also perform—Prince, Bob Dylan, and Trent Reznor have all played "secret" shows here. This is a nice place to see a show, with a well-elevated stage and lots of open space even on sold-out nights. There's an upstairs balcony that offers unparalleled views, but come early for a spot. Tickets range from $14 to $30, with most between $20 and $25. *Money-saving tip:* Buy tickets prior to the day of show to save $2 to $5. 17 Irving Place (1 block

---

> **Tips Ticket-Buying Tips**
>
> Tickets for events at all larger theaters and Hammerstein Ballroom, Roseland, Irving Plaza, B.B. King's, and S.O.B.'s can be purchased through **Ticketmaster** (© **212/307-7171**; www.ticketmaster.com).
>
> Advance tickets for an increasing number of shows at smaller venues—including CBGB, Bowery Ballroom, Mercury Lounge, Village Underground, Tribeca Blues, and Fez Under Time Cafe, plus Brooklyn's Warsaw and Northsix—can be purchased through **Ticketweb** (© **212/269-4TIX**; www.ticketweb.com). Do note that Ticketweb can sell out its allotted number of tickets without the show being completely sold out. If Ticketweb is sold out, check with the venue directly.
>
> Even if a show is sold out, that doesn't mean you're out of luck. There are usually people hanging around at showtime trying to get rid of extra tickets for friends who didn't show, and they're usually happy to pass them off for face value. You'll also see scalpers, who often peddle forgeries and are best avoided—it doesn't take a rocket scientist to tell the difference. Be aware, of course, that in New York City, it's illegal to sell a ticket for more than $5 above its face value.

west of Third Ave. at 15th St.). © **212/777-1224** or 212/777-6800. www.irvingplaza.com. Subway: 4, 5, 6, L, N, R, Q, W to 14th St./Union Sq.

The Knitting Factory New York's premier avant-garde music venue has four spaces, each showcasing performances ranging from experimental jazz and folk to spoken-word and poetry to multimedia. Regulars who use the Knitting Factory as their lab of choice include former Lounge Lizard John Lurie; around-the-bend experimentalist John Zorn; guitar gods Vernon Reid, Eliot Sharp, and David Torn; and Television's Richard Lloyd. (If these names mean nothing to you, chances are good that the Knitting Factory is not for you.) The schedule is peppered with edgy star turns from the likes of Cibo Matto, Gil Scott Heron, Taj Mahal, Faith No More's Mike Patton, and Lou Reed. There are often two shows a night in the pleasing main performance space, so it's easy to work a show around other activities. Prices usually run $7 to $20, with most falling between $10 and $15. The Old Office Lounge offers an extensive list of microbrews and free live entertainment. 74 Leonard St. (btwn Broadway and Church St.). © **212/219-3006.** www.knittingfactory.com. Subway: 1, 9 to Franklin St.

ROCK & MIXED-MUSIC CLUBS

Arlene Grocery This casual Lower East Side club boasts a friendly bar and a good sound system; unfortunately, music isn't always free, but the quality of the artists is usually pretty high, and the cover is around $5. Arlene Grocery serves as a showcase for hot bands looking for a deal or promoting their self-pressed record. The crowd is a mix of club-hoppers, rock fans looking for a new fix, and industry scouts looking for new blood. 95 Stanton St. (btwn Ludlow and Orchard sts.). © 212/358-1633. www.arlene-grocery.com. Subway: F to Second Ave.

The Baggot Inn *Value* This easygoing pub has become one of the best showcases in the city for unknown acts, especially if you like quality acoustic and folk-rock music. Blues, Irish music, poetry, and acoustic jams and open-mike nights also regularly pop up on the calendar. The cover is always bargain-priced—from free to $5—and happy hour until 7pm and nightly drink specials round out the entertainment value. 82 W. 3rd St. (btwn Thompson and Sullivan sts., below the Boston Comedy Club). © 212/477-0622. www.thebaggotinn.com. Subway: A, C, E, F, V to W. 4th St.

Bitter End Folk rock's legendary Bitter End has been going strong in the heart of the Village for 40-plus years, and it's still a relevant showcase for acoustic and electric rock and experimental sounds. Admission costs $5, with a few shows reaching $7. 147 Bleecker St. (btwn Thompson and LaGuardia sts.). © 212/673-7030. www.bitterend.com. Subway: A, C, E, F, V to W. 4th St.

Brownie's This bare-bones East Village showcase gets points for quantity with its nightly jam-packed lineup, and often features alterna-stars like J. Mascis (Dinosaur Jr.) and Craig Wedren (Shudder to Think), for $8 to $10. Advance tickets for many shows can be purchased without service charge at Other Music (p. 292). 169 Ave. A (btwn 10th and 11th sts.). © 212/420-8392. www.browniesnyc.com. Subway: L to First Ave.

CBGB The original downtown club has seen better days, but no other spot is so rich with rock history. This was the launching pad for New York punk and New Wave: the Ramones, Blondie, the Talking Heads, Television, Patti Smith, Stiv Bators and the Dead Boys—everybody got started here. These days, you've probably never heard of most acts here. Never mind—CB's still rocks. Come early if you have hopes of actually seeing the stage. Cover usually runs $6 to $10.

More today than yesterday is **CB's 313 Gallery,** a welcome spin-off that showcases alternative art on the walls and mostly acoustic singer/songwriters on stage; cover is usually $5, never higher than $8. Same goes for CB's **lounge,** which has a more cerebral alt edge to its sounds, plus regular poetry slams (cover free to $8). Within striking distance of the history, but more pleasant all the way around. 315 Bowery (at Bleecker St.). ✆ 212/982-4052, or 212/677-0455 for CB's 313 Gallery. www.cbgb.com. Subway: F to Second Ave.; 6 to Bleecker St.

The C-Note This Alphabet City boîte used to focus on contemporary jazz performers but has branched out to embrace singer-songwriter pop, rock, blues, country and roots, Latin music, and other genres. The quality tunes are almost always worth the price of admission, which ranges from free to $7. 157 Ave. C (at 10th St.). ✆ 212/677-8142. www.thecnote.com. Subway: L to First Ave.

Continental The cover ranges from free to $5 at this proudly skanky punk rock joint, where artists such as Spacehog occasionally surface among the unknowns. 25 Third Ave., at St. Marks Place. ✆ 212/529-6924. www.nytrash.com/continental. Subway: 6 to Astor Place.

The Cutting Room This Flatiron District music club and restaurant is co-owned by actor Chris Noth (*Sex and the City, Law & Order*), so don't be surprised if you spot a famous face or two. That said, the environment is usually easygoing, and the mix of entertainment runs the gamut from experimental synth ensemble Mother Mallard's Portable Masterpiece Co. to the terrific, Oingo Boingo-ish Niagras. A huge draw is Saturday night's Le Scandal (formerly Blue Angel Cabaret), sort of a feminist take on burlesque, with a dash of Jim Rose Circus Side Show thrown in. The cover is $10 to $12, but can rise to $15 when names like Midge Ure are there. 19 W. 24th St. (btwn Broadway and Sixth Ave.). ✆ 212/691-1900. www.thecuttingroomnyc.com. Subway: N, R to 23rd St.

Fez Under Time Cafe You have to reserve a seat a few days ahead for the popular Thursday night Mingus Big Band ($18), when the low-ceilinged basement performance space is filled with the cool sounds of jazz. The rest of the week brings an eclectic live-music-and-performance-art mix, which can range from Patti Rothberg to drag grande-dame Hedda Lettuce to tributes to acts like Queen and ABBA from Loser's Lounge. You never know who's gonna pop up; Joan Rivers did a few shows here in mid-2002. The stage is fronted by tightly packed picnic-style tables and a few booths. Time Cafe's pleasing, well-priced menu is served during performances (see chapter 6). I would love this space if it were better ventilated; if you need to escape the cigarette smoke, head upstairs to the lounge and bar, which has an *Arabian Nights* ambience. The cover ranges from $10 to $15, and a two-drink minimum might be required. *Money-saving tip:* Students holding a valid photo ID can usually attend the Mingus Big Band late show for just $10. 380 Lafayette St. (at Great Jones St.). ✆ 212/533-2680. www.feznyc.com. Subway: 6 to Bleecker St.

Mercury Lounge The Merc is everything a top-notch live-music venue should be: unpretentious, civilized, and with a killer sound system. The rooms are nothing special: a front bar and an intimate back-room performance space with a low stage and a few tables lining the brick walls. The calendar is filled with a mix of accomplished local rockers and national acts like Frank Black, Art Alexakis, and the Mekons. The crowd is grown-up and easygoing. The only downside is that it's consistently packed thanks to the high quality of the entertainment and all-around pleasing nature of the experience. The cover is likely to

> ### Value Free Music in the Clubs
>
> **Rodeo Bar** (see below) is the city's top no-cover club, but it's not the only free show in town.
>
> Others worth checking out include the **Living Room,** 84 Stanton St., at Allen Street (© 212/533-7235), an unpretentious bar/restaurant that's good for acoustic acts (the sound system isn't great for electric). The pass-the-bucket policy allows you to contribute to the performers' earnings (the venue suggests a $5 tip); there is a one-drink minimum. Also on the Lower East Side is **Luna Lounge**, 171 Ludlow St., between Houston and Stanton streets (© 212/260-2323; www.lunalounge.com), which usually hosts two bands a night. Monday's comedy night, Eating It, has become so popular that there's $7 cover (one drink included).
>
> East Village stalwart **Sidewalk,** 94 Ave. A, at 6th Street (© 212/473-7373), hosts live bands in the back room most nights for the price of two (cheap) drinks. Pretty good cheap eats serve as additional attractions. And—like sibling club **Manitoba's,** 99 Ave. B., between 6th and 7th streets (© 212/982-2511), the fun rock-and-roll bar from Dictators frontman Dick Manitoba—**Lakeside Lounge,** 162 Ave. B, between 10th and 11th streets (© 212/529-8463; www.lakesidelounge.com), also regularly hosts excellent-quality live music with no cover charge.
>
> Jazz fans can try **Arthur's Tavern,** in the Village at 57 Grove St., at Seventh Avenue South (© 212/675-6879), a comfortable club and piano bar attracting a mixed gay-and-straight crowd. Beware of the drinks, which can be pricey. In the East Village, "Live Jazz or Die" is the mantra at **Detour**, 349 E. 13th St., at First Avenue (© 212/533-6212; www.jazzatdetour.com), a high-quality club offering no-cover music

be between $8 and $10, maybe more for national acts. 217 E. Houston St. (at Essex St./Ave. A). © 212/260-4700. www.mercuryloungenyc.com. Subway: F to Second Ave.

Rodeo Bar *Value* Here's New York's oldest—and finest—honky-tonk. Hike up your Wranglers and head inside, where you'll find longhorns on the walls, peanut shells underfoot, and Tex-Mex on the menu. But this place is really about the music: urban-tinged country, bluegrass, swinging rockabilly, and Southern-flavored rock. Bigger names like Brian Setzer and up-and-comers on the tour circuit like Hank Williams III occasionally grace the stage, but regular acts like Dixieland swingers the Flying Neutrinos, cowpunk goddess Rosie Flores, and BBQ Bob and the Spareribs usually supply free music, keeping the urban cowboys plenty happy. A 10-gallon hat full o' fun. It's happy hour until 7pm; the music starts around 9:30pm nightly, and goes until at least 3am. 375 Third Ave. (at 27th St.). © 212/683-6500. www.rodeobar.com. Subway: 6 to 28th St.

Tonic *Finds* This quirky Lower East Sider has become the avant-garde jazz/experimental rock spot in the Knitting Factory vein, sometimes with big names like John Zorn's Masada, Cibo Matto, and Marc Ribot in the house. Tickets range from $8 to $12. A deejay spins mood music downstairs. Sunday's

nightly (two-drink minimum); $3 happy hour from 4 to 7pm maximizes the fun.

Harlem's **Showmans Cafe,** 375 W. 125th St., between St. Nicholas and Morningside avenues (© **212/864-8941**), hosts free music Monday through Saturday ranging from jazz to funky bebop that attracts music lovers and players from all walks of life, and the service is just as friendly whether you come from the neighborhood, downtown, or out of town.

Another excellent choice is **Smoke**, 2571 Broadway, between 105th and 106th streets (© **212/864-6662**; www.smokejazz.com), which offers first-class jazz, and there's almost never a cover. The first sets of the night on Friday and Saturday are smoke-free; happy-hour Cosmos, sidecars, and mojitos for just $3 (daily 5–8pm) round out the budget-minded fun.

Also keep in mind that a number of clubs listed in these pages offer free music 1 or more nights a week, such as **Cafe Wha?,** the **Continental,** the **Baggot Inn, Arlene Grocery, Chicago B.L.U.E.S.,** the **C-Note,** the lounge at **CBGB, 55 Bar, Tonic,** and the **Internet Cafe;** the **Knitting Factory** offers free music in its Old Office Lounge. There's also free live music every Sunday at SoHo's **24/8 Lounge** (see "Bars & Cocktail Lounges" later in this chapter). **Jazz at the Cajun** lets you listen to the finest old-school jazz in town for the price of a meal—and you have to eat anyway, don't you? The easiest way to check for free events while you're in town is to peruse the weekly *Time Out New York,* which announces no-cover shows with an easy-to-spot FREE! Sunday and Monday are big nights for freebies.

Remember that schedules and no-cover policies can change at any time, so always confirm in advance.

Klezmer brunch is definitely worth seeking out. *Money-saving tip:* You can usually save a few bucks by buying advance (rather than day-of-show) tickets, either at the Tonic box office, open daily from 8 to 11pm, or at Other Music (p. 292). 107 Norfolk St. (btwn Delancey and Rivington sts.). © **212/358-7503.** www.tonicnyc.com. Subway: F, J, M, Z to Delancey/Essex sts.

Village Underground *(Finds* The folks behind dear departed Tramps have opened this intimate, even romantic subterranean venue (which has a "no smoking" policy in the performance space). Some big-name talent turns up, including Buckwheat Zydeco, Michelle Shocked, Junior Brown, and R&B legend Solomon Burke (on the heels of his Rock and Roll Hall of Fame induction). Even if you don't recognize the names, you can count on quality music. Tickets run from $7 to $25; advance tickets can be purchased at www.ticketweb.com or at © **866/468-7619.** 130 W. 3rd St. (btwn Sixth Avenue and MacDougal St.). © 212/777-7745. www.thevillageunderground.com. Subway: A, C, E, F, V to W. 4th St. (use W. 3rd St. exit).

JAZZ, BLUES & MORE

A night at a top-flight jazz club can be expensive. Cover charges can vary dramatically—from as little as $10 to as high as $65, depending on who's taking the stage—and there's likely to be an additional two-drink minimum (or a dinner requirement, if you choose an early show). Call ahead so you know what you're getting into; reservations are also an excellent idea at top spots.

For those of you who like your jazz with an edge, see what's on at the **Knitting Factory** (p. 314), **Tonic** (p. 316), and the **C-Note** (p. 315). Trad fans should also consider the Thursday Mingus Big Band Workshop at **Fez Under Time Cafe** (p. 315), while swingsters should consider **Swing 46** (p. 331). **Smoke** (p. 317) is probably your best bet for quality jazz without a cover. Lovers of Latin and world music can't do better than terrific **S.O.B.'s** (p. 331).

There's also world-beat jazz every Friday and Saturday from 5 to 8pm in the rotunda at the **Guggenheim Museum;** see chapter 7. And don't forget **Jazz at Lincoln Center** (p. 310), the nation's premier forum for the traditional and developing jazz canon.

Birdland   While the legends of Parker, Monk, Gillespie, and other bebop pioneers still hold sway, Birdland isn't a crowded, smoky joint of yesteryear. The big room is spacious, comfy, and classy, with excellent sound and top-notch talent. Expect lots of accomplished big bands and jazz trios, plus occasional appearances by stars like Dave Brubeck. You can't go wrong with the Sunday night show, starring Chico O'Farrell's smokin' Afro-Cuban Jazz Big Band. The Southern-style food is pretty good. At press time, Tuesdays were the domain of the Duke Ellington Orchestra, lead by Duke's grandson Paul Ellington every other week. The cover runs a hefty $20 to $35, with a $10 food-and-drink minimum. *Money-saving tip:* You can avoid the minimum by sitting at the bar rather than a table, and you'll also score a complimentary beverage (at press time, anyway; check current policy). 315 W. 44th St. (btwn Eighth and Ninth aves.). © 212/581-3080. www.birdlandjazz.com. Subway: A, C, E to 42nd St.

Blue Note   Celebrating its 20th birthday in 2001, the Blue Note attracts the biggest names in jazz to its intimate setting. Just about everyone of note has played here. The sound system is excellent, and every seat in the house has a sightline to the stage. A night here can get expensive—the cover is usually $30 to $35 per person—but how often do you get to enjoy jazz of this caliber? There are two shows per night, and dinner is served. 131 W. 3rd St. (at Sixth Ave.). © 212/475-8592. www.bluenote.net. Subway: A, C, E, F, V to W. 4th St.

55 Bar *Value*   This prohibition-era Village dive hosts high-quality jazz and blues nightly, with guitarists a specialty (think Wayne Krantz, Hiram Bullock). The house guitar trio is definitely worth a listen, and if saxist Ed Palermo is on the bill, go. The cover ranges from free (two-drink minimum) to $15; it's usually in the $3-to-$5 range. 55 Christopher St. (just east of Seventh Ave.). © **212/929-9883.** www.55bar.com. Subway: 1, 9 to Christopher St.

Internet Cafe *Value*   Those looking for an affordable jazz fix should visit this casual online cafe, which features well-regarded jazz from up-and-coming acts nightly, plus a full bar. The cover charge is never more than $8, usually less; at press time, legendary bluesman Bobby Radcliffe had a standing gig on Friday nights with no cover. 82 E. 3rd St. (btwn First and Second aves.). © **212/614-0747.** www.bigmagic.com. Subway: F to Second Ave.

Iridium   This snazzy jazz club has relocated from its longtime perch across from Lincoln Center to a heart-of-the-Theater District location. Everything else remains the same, including the talent and big-name acts. Like the Energizer bunny, Les Paul keeps on going, playing every Monday night (tickets $27.50, plus $15 minimum). Other top-notch performers include Nicholas Payton, Mose Allison, McCoy Tyner and Bobby Hutcherson, and the Jazz Messengers. A full, rather sophisticated dinner menu is served. 1650 Broadway (at 51st St.). © 212/582-2121. www.iridiumjazzclub.com. Subway: 1, 9 to 50th St.

Jazz at the Cajun *Finds* This cozy, casual New Orleans–themed supper club is the best venue in town for prewar big-band and Dixieland jazz—think Jelly Roll Morton, Scott Joplin, early Duke. The crowd comes from all walks of life, united in their love of the old school. Cajun is home base for Vince Giordano's Nighthawks, who are masters of yesteryear—a joy to watch!—but the place jumps no matter what crew takes the stage. There's no cover charge, and food is affordable and just fine, with entrees in the low and mid-teens; reserve in advance. 129 Eighth Ave. (btwn 16th and 17th sts.). © **212/691-6174.** www.jazzatthecajun.com. Subway: A, C, E to 14th St. L to 8th Ave.

Jazz Standard *Finds* Boasting a retro-speakeasy vibe, the Jazz Standard is one of the city's largest jazz clubs, with well-spaced tables seating 150 and a $15 cover ($20 on weekends). The rule is straightforward, mainstream jazz by new and established musicians, including such stars as Branford Marsalis. Now that the restaurant is **Blue Smoke** from Danny Meyer (Union Square Cafe, Gramercy Tavern), serving mouthwatering gourmet Southern barbecue at affordable prices, you really can't go wrong. This makes for one fantastic night on the town. 116 E. 27th St. (btwn Park Ave. S. and Lexington Ave.). © **212/576-2232.** www. jazzstandard.net. Subway: 6 to 28th St.

Lenox Lounge *Finds* Harlem's best jazz club is this beautifully renovated classic. Said to be a favorite of Billie Holliday's, the intimate, Art Deco–cool back room—complete with zebra stripes on the walls and banquettes—hosts top-flight jazz vocalists, trios, and quartets for a crowd that comes to listen and be wowed. The cover never goes higher than $15 (one-drink minimum). Good soul food is served—or pair your visit with dinner at nouveau Creole Bayou or soul-food landmark Sylvia's (see chapter 6). Well worth the trip uptown for those who want a genuine Harlem jazz experience. 288 Malcolm X Blvd. (Lenox Ave.; btwn 124th and 125th sts.). © **212/427-0253.** Subway: 2, 3 to 125th St.

Small's *Value* Here's a great destination for committed jazzophiles: If you just don't want to stop grooving after the other clubs close, head to this basement hideaway, which stays open all night. Scheduled performers, who often include cutting-edge acts or overlooked talents, play from around 10pm to 2am, followed by a nightly jam session until dawn (and often beyond). No alcohol is served, but that doesn't keep the crowds away—they're happy to come just for the music. Drinks are free with the $10 cover (you're also welcome to BYO), and all ages are welcome. 183 W. 10th St. (just off Seventh Ave.). © **212/929-7565.** www. smallsjazz.com. Subway: 1, 9 to Christopher St.

Terra Blues This artsy blues club hosts an active calendar of local and national acts, with a $5 to $10 cover, even on weekends; plan on a two-drink minimum. 149 Bleecker St. (btwn Thompson St. and LaGuardia Place). © **212/777-7776.** www.terrablues.com. Subway: A, C, E, F, V to W. 4th St.

Tribeca Blues This club has taken over where the legendary Wetlands left off, catering to funked-up jazz fans and Deadheads. It hosts a calendar of local and national blues acts, with an occasional star turn from folks like Commander Cody and Trey Anastasio. The cover is usually between $5 and $12, but can go as high as $15 if a famous name is on. 16 Warren St. (btwn Broadway and Church St.). © 212/766-1070. www.amdmusic.com. Subway: A, C, E to Chambers St.

The Village Vanguard What CBGB is to rock, the Village Vanguard is to jazz. One look at the photos on the walls will show you who's been through since 1935, from Coltrane, Miles, and Monk to Branford Marsalis and Joshua Redman. Expect a mix of established names and high-quality local talent, including the Vanguard's own jazz orchestra on Monday nights. The sound is great, but sightlines are terrible, so come early for a front table. The crowd can seem either overly serious or overly touristy, but don't let that stop you—you'll always find great music. Covers range from $15 to $30; Sunday through Thursday nights are cheapest. 178 Seventh Ave. S. (just below 11th St.). © 212/255-4037. www.villagevanguard.net. Subway: 1, 2, 3, 9 to 14th St.

5 Stand-Up & Sketch Comedy

Comedy Cellar *Finds* This intimate subterranean spot is the club of choice for stand-up fans in the know, thanks to the most consistently impressive lineups in the business. I'll always love the Comedy Cellar for introducing an uproariously funny unknown comic named Ray Romano to me a few years back. $10 weekdays, $12 weekends, two-drink minimum. *Money-saving tip:* Check website to order free tickets and free drinks for select nights. 117 MacDougal St. (btwn Bleecker and W. 3rd sts.). © 212/254-3480. www.comedycellar.com. Subway: A, C, E, F, V to W. 4th St. (use 3rd St. exit).

Gershwin Hotel *Value* One of New York's best budget hotels (see chapter 5) hosts some of the city's best comedy lineups in the Living Room lounge, for a $5 cover charge. Comedians usually take the stage 4 nights a week; best of the bunch is Thursday's terrific Great $5 Comedy Show, which regularly hosts the best funny-men and -women in the biz. 7 E. 27th St. (btwn Fifth and Madison aves.). © 212/545-8000. www.gershwinhotel.com. Subway: N, R, 6 to 28th St.

New York Comedy Club *Value* With a $7 cover charge on weekdays ($10 Fri–Sat) plus two-beverage minimum, this small club offers the best value for your money. Despite what the owners call their "Wal-Mart approach" to comedy, the club has presented Damon Wayans, Chris Rock, and Brett Butler, among others, in its two showrooms. Monday's Open Mike Night (5pm) is $3 with unlimited soft drinks, and you're welcome to get on stage for your 5 minutes of fame. Weekends set aside time for African-American and Latino comics. Come early for a good seat. 241 E. 24th St. (btwn Second and Third aves.). © 212/696-5233. www.newyorkcomedyclub.com. Subway: 6 to 23rd St.

Stand-Up New York The Upper West Side's premier stand-up comedy club hosts some of the brightest comics in the business, plus drop-ins like Dennis Leary, Caroline Rhea, Robin Williams, and Mr. Upper West Side himself, Jerry Seinfeld. Cover is $10 to $15, with a two-item food or drink minimum. *Money-saving tip:* Order your tickets for PrimeTime shows (Thurs–Sat) online at the website and you'll save $5 per ticket. 236 W. 78th St. (at Broadway). © 212/595-0850. www.standupny.com. Subway: 1, 9 to 79th St.

Upright Citizens Brigade Theater *Value* You've seen their twisted, highly original sketch comedy on Comedy Central—now you can see the Upright Citizens Brigade, New York's premier alternative comedy troupe, live. The best of the nonstop hilarity is *A.S.S.S.C.A.T.*, the troupe's extremely popular long-form improv show, which often sells out in advance. You won't pay more than

$5 for any show; reservations are a must. 161 W. 22nd St. (btwn Sixth and Seventh aves.) © **212/366-9176**. www.ucbtheater.com. Subway: 1, 9 to 23rd St.

6 Cabaret Rooms & Piano Bars

The city's top supper clubs and cabarets are not for the budget-minded. At places like **Cafe Carlyle,** in the Carlyle Hotel, 781 Madison Ave. (© **212/570-7189**), home to the legendary Bobby Short (and Woody Allen in the Eddy Davis New Orleans Jazz Band most Mondays), and the Algonquin's **Oak Room,** 59 W. 44th St. (© **212/840-6800**), covers usually run in the neighborhood of $75, plus two-drink or dinner-check minimums; count on a $300 night on the town.

But never fear: One of these more casual, less-expensive options will result in a wallet-friendly night. Reservations are suggested for cabaret shows, and are not usually necessary for piano bars (although it never hurts to check).

Brandy's Piano Bar A mixed crowd—Upper East Side locals, waiters off work, gays, straights, all ages—comes to this intimate, old-school piano bar for the atmosphere and nightly entertainment. The talented wait staff does most of the singing while waiting for their big break, but enthusiastic patrons regularly join in. The sounds tend to familiar adult-contemporary radio hits and cabaret tunes. This place is so unhip that it's downright cool; it makes for a fun and affordable night on the town. No cover charge; two-drink minimum. 235 E. 84th St. (btwn Second and Third aves.). © **212/650-1944**. Subway: 4, 5, 6 to 86th St.

Danny's Skylight Room You'll find this Theater District showroom tucked away in, of all places, the rear of a Thai restaurant. It offers surprisingly strong lineups, including the fabulous Blossom Dearie and her world-class trio, with a cover that ranges from $12 to $25 (usually $15 or less), plus a $10 minimum; ask about dinner/show packages. There's no cover in the piano bar, where you'll hear first-class tunes from the American songbook. Happy hour (weekdays 4:30–7pm) means two-for-one beer and wine. At Danny's Grand Sea Palace, 346–348 W. 46th St. (btwn Eighth and Ninth aves.). © **212/265-8133** or 212/265-8130. www.dannysgrandseapalace.com. Subway: A, C, E to 42nd St.

Don't Tell Mama You'll find an evening of torch songs, comedy, and much more in a friendly, and affordable, atmosphere at this wonderful two-room Theater District cabaret. The cover charge ranges from free to $20, depending on the show, plus a two-drink minimum. Drinks only, no dinner. The piano bar is particularly lively, and always free (two-drink minimum). 343 W. 46th St. (btwn Eighth and Ninth aves.). © **212/757-0788**. Subway: A, C, E to 42nd St.

Duplex Cabaret Expect a high camp factor and lots of good-natured fun in this multilevel space, New York's oldest cabaret. A mixed gay/straight crowd of locals and out-of-towners sit at outdoor tables, gather around the downstairs piano (singalongs from around 9pm), or head upstairs to the cabaret for shows that run from minimusicals to drag revues to stand-up comedy. No cover at the piano bar (two-drink minimum), $5 to $15 in the showroom. 61 Christopher St. (at Seventh Ave.). © **212/255-5438**. www.theduplex.com. Subway: 1, 9 to Christopher St.

Judy's Chelsea This lovely cabaret room is the newest on the scene (since 1999), but has already settled in as one of the top cabaret rooms in town, with a smart modern look and an easygoing vibe. Talent runs the gamut from rising stars to well-known vets of the cabaret stage. Covers vary depending upon who's on stage, but usually sticks between $10 and $15 (no cover for the piano bar);

there's also a $10 food-and-drink minimum. 169 Eighth Ave. (btwn 18th and 19th sts.). © 212/929-5410. www.judyschelsea.com. Subway: A, C, E, L to 14th St.

7 Bars & Cocktail Lounges

TRIBECA
In addition to the choices below, consider **Walker's**, 16 N. Moore St., at Varick St. (© 212/941-0142), a holdout from pre-fabulous TriBeCa; see chapter 6.

Grace *Finds* This spacious and unpretentious lounge has made itself right at home with a sophisticated yet down-to-earth vibe; a good selection of cocktails, single-malts, and on-tap beers from the sweeping, welcoming mahogany bar; and an affordable menu of elegant yet unpretentious Pan-Asian–influenced New American dishes ($8–$14) that make great late-night cocktail nibbles. There's an airy dining room in back, too, if you'd like to reserve a nook for yourself. 114 Franklin St. (btwn W. Broadway and Church St.). © 212/343-4200. www.gracebarandrestaurant.com. Subway: 1, 9 to Franklin St.

Liquor Store Bar Housed in, yes, a former liquor store, this wonderful little oak-and-brass tavern is the best place for an affordable drink with a dash of style in TriBeCa. Come midweek to beat the Friday and Saturday crowds. 235 W. Broadway (at White St.). © 212/226-7121. Subway: A, C, E to Canal St.

The Sporting Club The city's best sports bar (rated No. 1 in the *Daily News*) is a guy's joint if there ever was one. The space is big, with giant TV screens at every turn tuned to just about every game on the planet. (Wall Streeters bring their international cohorts here to catch everything from English football to Japanese sumo.) The menu is what you'd expect: wings, burgers, club sandwiches, and *lots* of beer. Reservations accepted (a good idea when the big game's on). When the big games are over, this turns into a surprisingly popular singles place. 99 Hudson St. (btwn Franklin and Leonard sts.). © 212/219-0900. www.thesportingclub.net. Subway: 1, 9 to Franklin St.

CHINATOWN & LITTLE ITALY
Double Happiness *Finds* The only indicator to the subterranean entrance is a WATCH YOUR STEP sign. Once through the door, you'll find a beautifully designed speakeasy-ish lounge with artistic nods to the neighborhood, plus a low-key vibe. The space is large, but a low ceiling and intimate nooks add a hint of romance (although the loud music mix may deter true wooing). The fabulous food is from the upstairs restaurant, Wyanoka, so this is a great place to satisfy the munchies, too. Don't miss the green-tea martini, an inspired house creation. 173 Mott St. (btwn Grand and Broome sts.). © 212/941-1282. Subway: 6 to Spring St.

Mare Chiaro This authentic corner of Little Italy now hosts a bizarro mix of slumming Nolita hipsters, uptown singles, and neighborhood holdovers from an age when this was just a drinking man's bar. But Mare Chiaro still works its crusty magic, transporting you back to another era with its gentrification-resistant vibe. A great place for a cheap beer at a crossroads of city life. 176½ Mulberry St. (at Broome St.). © 212/226-9345. Subway: 6 to Spring St.

THE LOWER EAST SIDE
Also consider **Le Pere Pinard** (p. 144), 175 Ludlow St., south of Houston (© 212/777-4917), an affordable, terrific, and *très français* wine bar. There's also **Mercury Lounge**, 217 E. Houston St. (© 212/260-4700), which has a casual, comfortable bar up front; see p. 315.

Barramundi This nice lounge is notable for its fairy-tale outdoor garden, friendly staff, and settled-in feel in a neighborhood overrun by hipster copycats. Come on a weeknight to snare a table in the little corner of heaven out back. A fireplace makes Barramundi almost as appealing on cool nights. 147 Ludlow St. (btwn Stanton and Rivington sts.). © 212/569-6900. Subway: F to Second Ave.

Good World Bar & Grill *Finds* Don't worry about running into your fellow tourists here; this former Chinese barbershop is completely off the beaten track. Despite the location and utter lack of decor, it draws a young alterna-hip crowd with its refreshing lack of pretensions, low prices on good on-tap beers, and surprisingly good—and affordable—Scandinavian eats. 3 Orchard St. (btwn Division and Canal sts.). © 212/925-9975. Subway: F to East Broadway.

Idlewild *Finds* It may look unapproachable from the street, with nothing but an unmarked stainless-steel facade, but inside you'll find a fun, easygoing bar that's perfect for lovers of retro-kitsch. The interior is a larger-scale repro of a jet airplane, complete with reclining seats, tray tables, and too-small bathrooms. There are booths in back for larger crowds, and an *Austin Powers*–style bar to gather around at center stage. The crowd is a mix of downtown locals and hip tourists, and the deejay spins a listener-friendly mix of light techno, disco in the funkadelic vein, and '80s tunes from the likes of the Smiths and the Cure. Drinks are affordable. 145 E. Houston St. (btwn First and Second aves., on the south side of Houston). © 212/477-5005. Subway: F to Second Ave.

Rivertown Lounge *Value* This spacious, low-key neighborhood boîte is an excellent place to hang with the locals and nurse a beer. Happy hour lasts all day: Enjoy $3 wine and drafts Monday through Friday from 1 to 8pm. There's a dartboard and a pool table. Deejays speed up the vibe most nights. 187 Orchard St. (south of Houston St.). © 212/388-1288. Subway: F to Second Ave.

Whiskey Ward *Finds* Here's the second-best bar in town for serious whiskey fans (only behind the East Village's dba): First-class single malts and bourbons from which to choose, and no pretensions. Decor is kept to a minimum in traditional saloon style, but the jukebox rocks and a pool table provides additional entertainment. Nice on-tap and bottled beer selection, too. 121 Essex St. (btwn Rivington and Delancey sts.). © 212/477-2998. Subway: F to Delancey St.

SOHO

Also consider old-world **Fanelli's Cafe** (p. 146), 94 Prince St., at Mercer Street (© **212/226-9412**), for a brew and a burger—but come early to avoid the crowds. Another terrific choice for a pint-and-plate combo is **Puck Fair** (p. 148), 298 Lafayette St., just south of Houston (© **212/431-2100**).

Ear Inn This far-west SoHo pub has been a local fave since before the Civil War, thanks to its casual ambience, huge selection of beers, and bartenders who aren't looking for their big break. This is the kind of place where bikers can pony up to the bar next to bankers, and everybody gets along. 326 Spring St. (btwn Greenwich and Washington sts.). © 212/226-9060. Subway: C, E to Spring St.

Value Money-Saving Tip for Cabaret Fans

At **Cafe Carlyle,** value-minded cabaret fans can save by reserving standing room (which usually results in a spot at the bar) for just $35.

Merc Bar Notable for its long tenure in the fickle world of beautiful-people bars, upscale Merc Bar has mellowed nicely. You'll still find a good-looking crowd in the superbly appointed lounge, but now it's a confident rather than trend-happy one. The decor bespeaks civilized rusticity with warm woods, a canoe over the bar, copper-top tables, and butter-leather banquettes. A great place to nestle into a comfortable couch with your honey, splurge on a classy cocktail, and enjoy the scene. The European martini (Stoli raspberry and Chambord) is divine. Look carefully, because there's no sign. 151 Mercer St. (btwn Prince and Houston sts.). © 212/966-2727. www.mercbar.com. Subway: N, R to Prince St.

24/8 Lounge The upstairs Aussie restaurant **Eight Mile Creek** is a bit pricey, but the downstairs Down Under–themed boîte is always accessible. The mood is easygoing, the drinks are well poured, and affordable versions of the upscale upstairs menu are available ($7–$14). Thursdays are deejay nights, while Sundays are set aside for groovy live music. 240 Mulberry St. (btwn Prince and Spring sts.). © 212/431-4635. www.eightmilecreek.com. Subway: 6 to Spring St.

THE EAST VILLAGE & NOHO

In addition to the choices below, also consider **Fez**, 380 Lafayette St., at Great Jones St. (© 212/533-2680; www.feznyc.com), a dimly lit Moroccan-themed bar and lounge that I prefer to the downstairs performance space; see p. 315.

Burp Castle *Finds* This theme bar is a must for serious beer lovers. It's styled as a "Temple of Beer Worship," complete with medieval-inspired decor, choral music on the sound system, and soft-spoken waiters in monkish garb. Before you have time to let the weirdness sink in, you'll be distracted by the incomparable beer list. There are more than 500 bottled and on-tap beers from which to choose—including a phenomenal collection of Trappist ales, of course. The staff is courteous but a bit too studiedly monkish in its behavior; I couldn't wrest an actual recommendation out of them. 41 E. 7th St. (btwn Second and Third aves.). © 212/982-4576. Subway: 6 to Astor Place.

dba *Finds* dba has completely bucked the loungey trend that has taken over the city, instead remaining firmly and resolutely an unpretentious neighborhood bar. Everyone is welcome in this beer- and scotch-lover's paradise, which posts a massive drink menu on chalkboards. Owner Ray Deter specializes in British-style cask-conditioned ales (the kind that you pump by hand) and stocks a phenomenal collection of single-malt scotches. The crowd is a pleasing mix of connoisseurs and casual drinkers who like the choices and egalitarian vibe. Ray has enclosed the back garden, transforming it into an East Village beer garden. Excellent jukebox, too. 41 First Ave. (btwn 2nd and 3rd sts.). © 212/475-5097. www.drinkgoodstuff.com. Subway: F to Second Ave.

Dempsey's Pub This is the place for a well-priced pint, happy-hour specials, and homey atmosphere, plus traditional Irish music on Tuesdays. 61 Second Ave. (btwn 2nd and 3rd sts.). © 212/388-0662. Subway: F to Second Ave.

Drinkland This Alphabet City boîte boasts a retro-futuristic pop-art interior by the designer for *Austin Powers* and deejays from around the world, who spin techno, house, jungle, trance, and other electronic sounds Tuesday through Sunday nights for a crowd that really comes to listen. There's almost never a cover (usually $5 on Sat only), but call to confirm. 339 E. 10th St. (btwn aves. A and B). © 212/228-2435. www.drinkland.com. Subway: L to First Ave.

KGB Bar This former Ukrainian social club still boasts its Soviet-themed decor, but it now draws creative types who like the low-key boho vibe. Sunday nights are the biggest draw, thanks to the success of KGB's excellent reading series, where an increasingly talented pack of up-and-coming and published writers read their prose to a receptive crowd starting at 7pm. Past readers have included Rick Moody (*The Ice Storm*) and Kathryn Harrison (*The Kiss*). 85 E. 4th St. (btwn Second and Third Aves.). © 212/505-3360. Subway: 6 to Astor Place.

McSorley's Old Ale House   In business for more than 140 years, McSorley's window proudly claims WE WERE HERE BEFORE YOU WERE BORN. Only McSorley's Ale is served, light or dark, and two at a time. Come to bask in the old-time New York vibe, not to nurse a Diet Coke. This is an ale-sodden frat-boy madhouse most nights and an Irish Armageddon on St. Patrick's Day, but everybody seems to love it. Although it's also a McSorley's tradition to urinate on the wall outside, they prefer you honor that one in the breach, not in the commission. 15 E. 7th St. (btwn Second and Third aves.). © 212/473-9148. Subway: 6 to Astor Place.

Tom & Jerry's (288 Bar) *Finds*   Here's a pleasing neighborhood bar minus the grunge factor that usually plagues such joints. The place has an authentic local vibe, and the youngish, artsy crowd is unpretentious and chatty. The beer selection is very good and the mixed drinks are better than average. Flea-market hounds will enjoy the vintage collection of "Tom & Jerry" punchbowl sets behind the bar, and creative types will enjoy the rotating collection of works from local artists, which changes monthly. There's no sign, but you'll spy the action through the plate-glass window on the east side of Elizabeth Street just north of Houston. 288 Elizabeth St. © 212/260-5045. Subway: 6 to Bleecker St.

GREENWICH VILLAGE & THE MEAT-PACKING DISTRICT

Chumley's   Many bars in New York date to Prohibition, but Chumley's still has the vibe. The college-age crowd doesn't date back as far, however. Come to warm yourself by the fire and indulge in a once-forbidden pleasure: beer. The door is unmarked, with a metal grille on the small window; another entrance is at 58 Barrow St., which takes you in through a back courtyard. 86 Bedford St. (at Barrow St.). © 212/675-4449. Subway: 1, 9 to Christopher St.

Hogs & Heifers   This roadhouse-style bar is it: the *Coyote Ugly* bar, complete with "bra tree," bar-top hip-shaking, and free-flowing shots. It's pretty much devoid of its original rough-and-tumble local appeal, but still offers fun for those who don't mind the tourist trappings. The bridge-and-tunnel, frat-boyish crowd gets wild as the night wears on, especially on weekends. 859 Washington St. (at 13th St.). © 212/929-0655. Subway: A, C, E, L to 14th St. Also at 1843 First Ave., btwn 95th and 96th sts. (© 212/722-8635; subway: 6 to 96th St.).

White Horse Tavern   Poets and literary buffs pop into this 1880 pub to pay their respects to Dylan Thomas, who tipped his last jar here. Best enjoyed in the warm weather when there's outdoor drinking, or at happy hour for the cheap drafts that draw in a big frat-boy and post-frat yuppie crowd. 567 Hudson St. (at 11th St.). © 212/243-9260. Subway: 1, 9 to Christopher St.

CHELSEA

Chelsea Brewing Company *Moments*   Affordable American pub grub, good house-label brews, and great Hudson River views from a waterfront terrace make this an excellent choice for a few beers and some easygoing socializing. Even if it's too cold (or crowded) for alfresco enjoyment, you'll find an attractive, high-ceilinged wood-and-brass brewpub inside—nothing unique, but comfortable and view-endowed. At Pier 61, Chelsea Piers, Eleventh Ave. and 18th St. © 212/336-6440. www.chelseabrewingco.com. Subway: C, E to 23rd St.

Gaslight The ideal cross between a cozy English pub and an elegant Victorian lounge. No taps, though—but a dependably good hangout nonetheless. 400 W. 14th St. (at Ninth Ave.). © 212/807-8444. Subway: A, C, E to 14th St.

Serena *Finds* This plush and popular basement boîte has managed to stay fresh by reinventing itself. Done in deep, sexy reds, Serena is again as hip as can be—I've even spotted Moby here. It's relatively unpretentious considering its hot-spot status; still, dress the part if you want to make it past the doorman. The crowd is young and pretty, and the music mix is a blast—think Fatboy Slim meets ABBA meets Foghat and you'll get the picture. In the basement level of the Hotel Chelsea, 222 W. 23rd St. (btwn Seventh and Eighth aves.). © 212/255-4646. Subway: C, E, 1, 9 to 23rd St.

THE FLATIRON DISTRICT, UNION SQUARE & GRAMERCY PARK

Also consider the **Old Town Bar & Restaurant** (p. 165), 45 E. 18th St., between Broadway and Park Avenue South (© 212/529-6732), a genuine tin-ceilinged 19th-century bar that's a terrific place to soak up some old New York atmosphere. Sleek noodle house **Republic** (p. 166), 37 Union Sq. W. (© 212/627-7172), boasts an up-front bar that's popular with a wallet-watching cocktail crowd who come to enjoy such creative libations as the Sake Dragon martini (sake and Chambord) and a Fuji apple Cosmopolitan.

Dusk *Finds* This casual, artsy lounge is a great choice for a cocktail. There's a fab mirrored mosaic wall, banquettes opposite, a friendly bar serving affordable drinks, a pool table, and mostly U.K. tunes—from drum-and-bass to Super Furry Animals to Blur to Enya—on the sound system. Expect an easygoing, youngish crowd that stays relaxed and unpretentious into the evening. No sign, but look for the three blue lights attached to a dark storefront. 147 W. 24th St. (btwn Sixth and Seventh aves.). © 212/924-4490. Subway: F to 23rd St.

Heartland Brewery The food leaves a bit to be desired, but the house-brewed beers are first-rate. Great American Beer Festival three-time award-winner Farmer Jon's Oatmeal Stout is always on hand, as are three or four handcrafted ales and a lager or two. A good selection of single malts and tequilas, too. The two-level bar is big and appealing, but expect a loud, boisterous after-work crowd, plus a good number of Germans and Brits (testament to the quality of the brew). 35 Union Sq. W. (at 16th St.). © 212/645-3400. www.heartlandbrewery.com. Subway: 4, 5, 6, L, N, R, Q, W to 14th St./Union Sq. Also at 1285 Sixth Ave. (at 50th St., across from Radio City Music Hall; © 212/582-8244; subway: B, D, F, V to 47th–50th sts./Rockefeller Center).

Park Avenue Country Club More polished than your average sports bar, this is a comfortable place to hunker down over a club sandwich and a beer to watch the game. There are TVs at every turn, and a mahogany central bar serves up an extensive list of bottled and on-tap brews. Pool tables are on hand for halftime and seventh-inning stretches. 381 Park Ave. S. (at 27th St.). © 212/685-3636. www.parkavenuecountryclub.com. Subway: 6 to 28th St.

Pete's Tavern The oldest continually operating establishment in the city, Pete's opened while Lincoln was president. It reeks of history—and more importantly, there's Guinness on tap and a terrific happy hour. The crowd is a mix of locals from Gramercy Park and more down-to-earth types. 129 E. 18th St. (at Irving Place). © 212/473-7676. www.petestavern.com. Subway: 4, 5, 6, L, N, R, Q, W to 14th St./Union Sq.

Slate The former Chelsea Billiards has been upscaled into Slate, the sleekest, chicest pool hall in town; *Sex and the City* has filmed here. The room is dressed in fiery reds and cool grays; a deejay spins hip-hop, top 40, and techno tunes as you rack 'em up. Still, this is a serious billiard palace, with 34 top-flight Steel and Brunswick tables. Expect to pay $12 to $16 per hour for two, plus $3 extra for a third person; rates are cheapest midday, midweek. There's an excellent selection of international beers as well as cocktailesque libations. 54 W. 21st St. (btwn Fifth and Sixth aves.). © 212/989-0096. www.chelseabilliard.citysearch.com. Subway: N, R to 23rd St.

TIMES SQUARE & MIDTOWN WEST

Joe Allen (p. 172), the legendary Broadway pub on Restaurant Row, 326 W. 46th St., between Eighth and Ninth avenues (© **212/581-6464**), is great for an after-theater cocktail even if you don't dine here. A second branch of **Heartland Brewery** (p. 326) is across from Radio City at 1285 Sixth Ave., at 51st Street (© **212/582-8244**). There's also **ESPN Zone** (p. 174), 1472 Broadway, at 42nd Street (© **212/921-3776**), the ultimate sports bar.

Algonquin Bar The oak-paneled lobby of this venerable literati-favored Arts and Crafts hotel is the comfiest and most welcoming in the city, made to linger over pre- or post-theater cocktails. You'll feel the spirit of Dorothy Parker and the Algonquin Round Table that pervades the room. Try the Matilda, a light blend of orange juice, Absolut Mandarin, triple sec, and champagne, named after the Algonquin's feline in residence. Adjacent is the clubby **Blue Bar,** home to a rotating collection of Hirschfeld drawings. Well worth a few spare bucks if you want to soak in old New York atmosphere at its finest. 59 W. 44th St. (btwn Fifth and Sixth aves.). © 212/840-6800. Subway: B, D, F, V to 42nd St.

M Bar *Finds* This library-style lounge transcends its hotel-bar status with a circular bar, a first-rate cocktail menu, comfortable seating, a dark and romantic Art Deco mood, and a warmth that will make pretension-phobes feel right at home. Prices are reasonable too, considering the neighborhood. The weekly Wednesday jazz night has turned into a big hit with locals—so much so that the calendar has expanded to include cabaret nights and wine tastings. A real gem! Adjacent to the Mansfield hotel, 12 W. 44th St. (btwn Fifth and Sixth aves.). © 212/944-6050. Subway: B, D, F, V to 42nd St.

Mickey Mantle's Of course, it's terribly sad that the Mick, who gave his life to the bottle, should have his name on a bar. But if you're a fan, it's worth a visit to his mahogany-and-brass sports bar and restaurant, which chronicles his life and career in photos. The crowd is a laid-back mix of white-collar workers and tourists. Moderately priced burger fare is available, plus the requisite souvenirs. A great place to watch the game. 42 Central Park S. (btwn Fifth and Sixth aves.). © 212/688-7177. www.mickeymantles.com. Subway: F to 57th St.

Russian Vodka Room *Finds* This old-school lounge is a Theater District find. It's not going to win any style awards, but it's comfortable and knows what's what when it comes to vodkas. More than 50 are on hand, plus the RVR's own infusions; you can order an iced rack of six if you can't decide between such yummy flavors as cranberry, apple cinnamon, ginger, horseradish, and more (the raspberry makes a perfect Cosmo). The 30-something-and-up crowd is peopled with post-Soviet imports as well as New Yorkers in the know. A martini or Cosmo is about $10, but you could do the backstroke in it. Come early if you want to snag a bar table. 265 W. 52nd St. (btwn Broadway and Eighth Ave.). © 212/307-5835. Subway: C, E, 1, 9 to 50th St.

Tír Na Nóg This festive place is a standout among the Irish pubs that line Eighth Avenue near Penn Station. The decor lends the place a genuine Celtic vibe, as does the Murphy's on tap and the lilt of the bartender. The bar has established itself among both locals and bridge-and-tunnel types for its unpretentious, lively air. There's good upscale pub grub, a dance floor, and live foot-stompin' Irish music Friday and Saturday nights. The ideal place to celebrate St. Patrick's Day. 5 Penn Plaza (Eighth Ave. between 33rd and 34th sts.). © 212/630-0249. www.tirnanognyc.com. Subway: A, C, E to 34th St./Penn Station.

MIDTOWN EAST & MURRAY HILL

Bull & Bear The name speaks to its business-minded clientele; there's even a stock ticker in constant service for those three-martini lunches. The Bull & Bear is like a gentlemen's pub, with leather chairs, a waistcoated staff, and a troika-shaped mahogany bar polished to a high sheen at the center of the room. Still, it's plenty comfy for casual drinkers. Ask Oscar, who's been here for more than 30 years, or one of the other accomplished bartenders to blend you a classic cocktail. Or just order a beer—either way, you'll be right at home here. An ideal place to kick back after a hard day of sightseeing. At the Waldorf-Astoria. 301 Park Ave. (btwn 49th and 50th sts.). © 212/872-4900. Subway: 6 to 51st St.

The Ginger Man The bait at this appealing and cigar-friendly upscale bar is the 66 gleaming tap handles lining the wood-and-brass bar, dispensing everything from Sierra Nevada and Hoegaarden to cask-conditioned ales. The cavernous space has a clubby feel, as Cohiba-toking Wall Streeters and the young men and women they flirt with lounge on sofas and chairs. The limited menu is well prepared, and prices are better than you'd expect from a place like this. 11 E. 36th St. (btwn Fifth and Madison aves.). © 212/532-3740. Subway: 6 to 33rd St.

King Cole Room The birthplace of the Bloody Mary, this spot may just be New York's best classic hotel bar. The Maxfield Parrish mural is worth the price of a classic cocktail (ask the bartender to tell you about the "hidden" meaning of the painting). The sophisticated setting demands proper attire, so dress for the occasion. The *New York Times* calls the bar nuts "the best in town," but there's an elegant bar-food menu if you'd like something more substantial. Avoid the after-work hours at holiday time, when the crowd can ruin the mood. At the St. Regis hotel, 2 E. 55th St. (at Fifth Ave.). © 212/339-6721. Subway: E, F to 53rd St.

THE UPPER WEST SIDE

The subterranean **All State Cafe** (p. 184), 250 W. 72nd St., between Broadway and West End Avenue (© 212/874-1883), is one of the best workaday pubs in town, with a loyal and easygoing grown-up crowd, great burgers, a terrific jukebox, and a cozy fireplace.

Also consider **Fez** at **Time Cafe**, 2330 Broadway, at 85th St. (© 212/579-5100), a second Moroccan-themed cafe from the people behind the ultra-groovy original Fez at Time Cafe in NoHo (p. 315). Closer to Columbia, there's also a terrific bar that rollicks well into the wee hours at **Nacho Mama's**, 2893 Broadway, between 112th and 113th streets (© 212/665-2800).

Amsterdam Billiard Club A straight-ahead, top-flight billiard bar with a completely unpretentious ambience, good beers on tap, and a lively local crowd make this one of the best pool bars in NYC. 344 Amsterdam Ave. (btwn 76th and 77th sts.). © 212/496-8180. Subway: 1, 9 to 79th St. Also at 210 E. 86th St. (btwn Second and Third aves.; © 212/570-4545; subway: 6 to 86th St.).

The Heights Bar & Grill *Value* This Columbia U. hangout is a great bet for bargain hunters. It boasts an attractive, tree-lined view of Broadway (with open-air appeal in warm weather) and bargain drinks, from $7 10-oz. martinis and margaritas to blended drinks in pint glasses ($6) to a wide world of beers. Ah, the joys of college life! The Heights doubles as a restaurant, so come late for the bar scene. 2867 Broadway (btwn 111th and 112th sts.), 2nd floor. ℂ 212/866-7035. www.theheightsbarandgrill.com. Subway: 110th St./Cathedral Pkwy.

Hi-Life Bar & Grill Amsterdam Avenue from 72nd to 86th streets has evolved into a major barhopping strip, dotted with yuppified bars and an ever-growing list of trendy lounges—but this longstanding neighborhood joint still holds its own. The stainless-steel-and-mahogany Hi-Life feels like a page out of the days when men wore gray flannel suits and everybody had a doozy of a before-dinner cocktail. It has a pleasant alfresco patio, an easygoing atmosphere, and bartenders who blend the best martinis in town for the money. 477 Amsterdam Ave. (at 83rd St.) ℂ 212/787-7199. Subway: 1, 9 to 86th St. Also at 1340 First Ave. (at 72nd St.; ℂ 212/249-3600. Subway: 6 to 68th St.).

Shark Bar This popular upscale spot is well known for its good soul food and even better singles' scene. It's also a favorite hangout for sports celebs, so don't be surprised if you spot a New York Knick or two. 307 Amsterdam Ave. (btwn 74th and 75th sts.). ℂ 212/874-8500. Subway: 1, 2, 3, 9 to 72nd St.

THE UPPER EAST SIDE

There's an outpost of the Meat-Packing District roadhouse **Hogs & Heifers** (p. 325) at 1843 First Ave., between 95th and 96th streets (ℂ 212/722-8635; subway: 6 to 96th St.). Despite its offshoot status, this one's slightly more laid-back and boasts more genuine saloon style. If you have a game of pool in mind, head to the east-side branch of the **Amsterdam Billiard Club** (p. 328), 210 E. 86th St., between Second and Third avenues (ℂ 212/570-4545; subway: 6 to 86th St.). Also look for another retro-cool branch of the **Hi-Life** (above), at 1340 First Ave., at 72nd Street (ℂ 212/249-3600; subway: 6 to 68th St.).

Great Hall Balcony Bar *Moments* One of Manhattan's best cocktail bars is only open on Friday and Saturday—and only from 4 to 8:30pm, to boot. The Metropolitan Museum of Art transforms the lobby's mezzanine level into a cocktail-and-classical music lounge twice weekly, offering an only-in-New-York experience. The music is usually provided by a grand piano and string quartet. The setting couldn't be grander, especially when the hall is transformed into a Christmas paradise at holiday season. You'll have to pay the $10 admission, but the galleries are open until 9pm. At the Metropolitan Museum of Art, Fifth Ave. at 82nd St. ℂ 212/535-7710. www.metmuseum.org. Subway: 4, 5, 6 to 86th St.

Subway Inn Now, here's a dive bar if there ever was one—and that's the Subway Inn's charm. Every time I go to Bloomingdale's, I get a perverse joy at seeing this hole-in-the-wall in the shadow of the department store, as the high-rent neighborhood around it grows more upscale and out-of-reach to the average Joes inside. A great spot for a spouse to nurse a cheap beer while the shopper of the couple exercises the plastic at Bloomies. Note to film buffs: This was Montgomery Clift's local bar; he lived just down the street for years. 143 E. 60th St. (just east of Lexington Ave.). ℂ 212/223-8929. Subway: 4, 5, 6 to 59th St.

HARLEM

Lenox Lounge More famous for its status as Harlem's best jazz club (p. 319), Lenox Lounge also boasts Harlem's best bar scene. This old-world throwback (scotch comes Johnnie Walker, not single-malt) is warm, cozy, and immensely popular with grown-ups from all walks of life. 288 Malcolm X Blvd. (Lenox Ave., btwn 124th and 125th sts.). ℂ 212/427-0253. Subway: 2, 3, to 125th St.

8 Dance Clubs & Party Scenes

No slice of New York nightlife is as mutable as the club scene. In this world, hot spots don't even get 15 minutes of fame—their time in the limelight is usually more like a commercial break.

First things first: Finding and going to the latest hot spot is not worth agonizing over. Clubbers spend their lives obsessing over the scene. My rule of thumb is that if I know about a place, it must not be hip anymore. Just find someplace that amuses you, and enjoy the crowd.

"Clubs" as actual, physical spaces don't mean much anymore. The hungry-for-nightlife crowd follows events of certain party "producers" who switch venues and times each week. A number of bars and lounges listed in the previous section—like **Idlewild** and **Drinkland,** to name just two—host deejay parties and "club" scenes on various nights of the week.

I've concentrated on a wide variety of scenes below, from performance-artsy to perennially popular discos, most of which are generally easy to make your way into. You can find listings for the most current hot spots and movable parties in the **sources** listed in the introduction to this chapter.

New York nightlife starts late. With the exception of places that have scheduled live performances, it's almost useless to show up anywhere before 11pm. Don't depend on plastic; bring cash, and plan on dropping a wad. Cover charges start out anywhere from $5 to $30 and often get more expensive as the night wears on. *Time Out New York* is a great source to check, as it lists cover charges for the week's big events and clearly indicates which are free.

Money-saving tips: Additional online sources that might score you discount admissions to select clubs include **www.promony.com**. No matter what, **always call ahead,** because schedules change constantly and can do so at the last minute. Even better: You also may be able to put your name on a guest list that will save you a few bucks at the door. You can also check **newyork.sheckys.com** for VIP guest list access. And always check the clubs' websites directly for special deals.

Baktun This club has been hot since the word go. Sleek Baktun was conceived in 2000 as a multimedia lounge, and incorporates video projections (shown on a clever double-sided video screen) into its dance parties as well as live cybercasts. The music tends toward electronica, with some live acts. At press time, Saturday's Direct Drive was still the key drum 'n' bass party in town. The cover runs $3 to $10. 418 W. 14th St. (btwn Ninth Ave. and Washington St.). © 212/206-1590. www.baktun.com. Subway: A, C, E, L to 14th St.

Cafe Wha? You'll find a carefree crowd dancing in this casual basement club any night of the week. From Wednesday through Sunday, the stage features the house's own Wha Band, which does an excellent job of cranking out crowd-pleasing covers of familiar rock-and-roll hits from the '70s, '80s, and '90s. Monday night is the hugely popular Brazilian Dance Party, while Tuesday night is Classic Funk Night. Expect to be surrounded by lots of Jersey kids and out-of-towners on the weekends, but so what? You'll be having as much fun as they are. Reservations are a good idea. The cover runs from free to $10, making Wha a good value to boot. 115 MacDougal St. (btwn Bleecker and 3rd sts.). © 212/254-3706. www.cafewha.com. Subway: A, B, C, D, E, F, V to W. 4th St.

Centro-Fly This swank Op Art club is so fab that Mary J. Blige used it as a video set. The sunken bar must be the coolest in town. Despite its fabulousness, Centro-Fly is quite welcoming. Two mondo sound systems and a four-turntable booth lure in top-notch deejay talent ranging from Junior Sanchez to Dimitri from Paris to Paul Oakenfold. Depending on the night, look for deep house, hip-hop, or another edgy music mix. The Friday-night funky-soulful British house party GBH (www.gbh.tv), New York's longest-running house party, may be the best reason to come. *Money-saving tip:* Sign up for Centro-Fly's weekly e-mailer for access to reduced $10 admission. 45 W. 21st St. (btwn Fifth and Sixth aves.). © 212/627-7710. www.centro-fly.com. Subway: F to 23rd St.; N, R to 23rd St.

Club Shelter The popular Saturday-night club Shelter now has its own Midtown home. Maestro deejay Timmy Regisford spins top-flight techno, soulful house, garage, and New Wave in an inspired mix, and the crowd is diverse, music-loving, and welcoming. Admission is $12 before 1am, $17 thereafter. Call or check the website for the list of other parties, such as Subliminal Sessions, the favorite U.K.-inspired house party that should take root on Thursdays. Shelter also hosts the occasional live performance. 20 W. 39th St. (btwn Fifth and Sixth aves.). © 212/719-4479. www.clubshelter.com. Subway: A, C, E to 42nd St.

Don Hill's This long-lived, eccentric, divey club draws a heavily integrated gay-lesbian/straight crowd that comes for rock, glam, and punk some nights, campy parties on others. Röck Cändy is a fun neo-glam resurrection, featuring live hair-metal bands (yes, there are still some out there). Ultimate groupie Bebe Buell (Liv Tyler's mom) shows up on the bill occasionally. The cover always falls between $5 and $10, and drinks are affordable. 511 Greenwich St. (at Spring St.). © 212/219-2850. Subway: 1, 9 to Canal St.

Nell's *Finds* Nell's calls itself "The Classic New York Nightclub," and it has earned the moniker. It was the first to establish a loungelike atmosphere years ago. It has been endlessly copied. Nell's attracts a grown-up crowd that ranges from homeboys to Wall Streeters, and it's as marvelous as ever. Although the entertainment can run the gamut from comedy and spoken word to Cuban sounds, most of the parties have a soulful edge. The gem of the New York nightlife scene! The cover is a well-worth-it $7 to $15, depending on the night. Dress nicely—Nell's deserves respect. 246 W. 14th St. (btwn Seventh and Eighth aves.). © 212/675-1567. www.nells.com. Subway: A, C, E, 1, 2, 3, 9 to 14th St.

S.O.B.'s *Finds* If you like your music hot, hot, hot, S.O.B.'s is the place. This is the city's top world-music venue, specializing in Brazilian, Caribbean, and Latin sounds. The packed house dances and sings along nightly to calypso, samba, mambo, African drums, reggae, or other global grooves, united in the feel-good vibe. Bookings include top-flight performers from around the globe; Astrud Gilberto, Ruben Blades, King Sunny Ade, Eddie Palmieri, Beausoleil, and Celia Cruz are only a few of the names who have graced this lively stage. The room's Tropicana Club style has island pizzazz that carries through to the Caribbean-influenced cooking and extensive tropical drinks menu. This place is so popular that it's an excellent idea to book in advance, especially if you'd like table seating. Monday is dedicated to Latin sounds, Tuesday to reggae, Friday features a late-night French Caribbean dance party, while Saturday is reserved for samba. The cover runs $10 to $25, but frequently stays at or below the $15 mark. *Money-saving tip:* Check the website for a $5 off coupon. 204 Varick St. (at Houston St.). © 212/243-4940. www.sobs.com. Subway: 1, 9 to Houston St.

Swing 46 Swing is still a nightly affair at this jazz and supper club (supper not required). Music is live nightly, and runs the gamut from big band to boogie-woogie to jump blues. Don't miss Vince Giordano and His Nighthawks if they're on the bill, especially if sharp-dressed Casey McGill is singing and strumming his ukulele too. The Harlem Renaissance Orchestra is another great choice. Even first-timers can join in the fun, as free swing lessons are offered nightly at 9:15pm. The cover is $7 Sunday through Wednesday, $12 Thursday through Saturday. No jeans or sneakers. 349 W. 46th St. (btwn Eighth and Ninth aves.). © 212/262-9554. www.swing46.com. Subway: C, E to 50th St.

13 *Value* This little lounge is a great place to dance the night away. It's stylish but unpretentious, with a steady roster of fun weekly parties. Sunday night's no-cover Britpop fest Shout! lives on, as popular as ever—and with no cover, to boot. The rest of the week runs the gamut from '70s and '80s New Wave and glam night to progressive house and trance to poetry slams and performance art. If there's a cover, it's usually $5, occasionally $7 or $10. Happy hour offers two-for-one drinks (and no cover) from 4 to 8pm. 35 E. 13th St. (btwn Broadway and University Place), 2nd floor. © 212/979-6677. www.bar13.com or www.shoutnewyork.com. Subway: 4, 5, 6, N, R, L, Q, W to 14th St./Union Sq.

Vinyl *Finds* No alcohol is served at Vinyl—but that doesn't keep the rapturous masses at bay. This TriBeCa club welcomes a big, mixed black/white, gay/straight crowd to the best roster of weekly parties on the planet—mainly hip-hop- and house-flavored party nights ruled by a first-rate crop of deejays. The now-legendary Body and Soul (www.bodyandsoul-nyc.com) is a Sunday-afternoon party extraordinaire. Even better is Friday's Be Yourself, superstar deejay Danny Tenaglia's weekly rave, which doesn't relent until the Saturday-morning cartoon hours. 6 Hubert St. (btwn Hudson and Greenwich sts.). © 212/343-1379. Subway: A, C, E to Canal St.; 1, 9 to Franklin St.

9 The Gay & Lesbian Scene

To get a thorough, up-to-date take on what's happening in gay and lesbian nightlife, pick up copies of *HX* (www.hx.com), *New York Blade* (www.nyblade.com), *Next* (www.nextnyc.com), and *Gay City News* (www.gaycitynews.com), available for free in bars and clubs all around town, at news boxes throughout the city, or at the **Lesbian, Gay, Bisexual & Transgender Community Center,** at 208 W. 13th St., between Seventh and Eighth avenues (© **212/620-7310;** www.gaycenter.org). The weekly *Time Out New York* boasts a terrific gay and lesbian section; another great source is the legendary free weekly *Village Voice.* Always remember that asking people in one bar can lead you to discover another that fits your tastes.

In addition to the choices below, be sure to see what's happening at such clubs as **Vinyl** and **Don Hill's,** which cater to gay and/or gay/straight mixed crowds; see "Dance Clubs & Party Scenes," above. You might also wish to consider **Duplex** and **Don't Tell Mama** if cabaret's more your style (p. 321). Women might wish to see what's on at **Bluestockings** bookstore and cafe (p. 274).

Barracuda Chelsea is central to gay life—and gay bars. This trendy, loungey place is a continuing favorite, voted "Best Bar" by *HX* and *New York Press* for 2 years running, while *Paper* singles out the hunky bartenders. There's a sexy bar for cruising out front and a comfy lounge in back. Look for the regular drag shows. 275 W. 22nd St. (btwn Seventh and Eighth aves.). © 212/645-8613. Subway: C, E, 1, 9 to 23rd St.

Big Cup Big Cup isn't a bar but a coffeehouse. Still, you'd be hard-pressed to find a cooler, comfier pickup joint, or a more preening crowd. This is where all the Chelsea boys hang; just think of it as a living room–style lounge without the alcohol. By the way, it also happens to be a fab coffeehouse. 228 Eighth Ave. (btwn 21st and 22nd sts.). ✆ **212/206-0059.** Subway: C, E to 23rd St.

Boiler Room This East Village bar is everybody's favorite gay dive. Despite the mixed guy-girl crowd, it's a cruising scene for well-sculpted beautiful boys who love to pose, and a fine hangout for those who'd rather play pool. 86 E. 4th St. (btwn First and Second aves.). ✆ **212/254-7536.** Subway: F to Second Ave.

Chase *Finds* This serene and stylish multiroom lounge on the northern fringe of Hell's Kitchen is symbolic of how far this neighborhood has come over the last half-dozen years. The pretty-boy staff is welcoming to locals and visitors alike. The relaxed weeknight ambience transforms into quite a party scene on weekends. 255 W. 55th St. (btwn Broadway and Eighth Ave.). ✆ **212/333-3400.** Subway: A, B, C, D, 1, 9 to 59th St./Columbus Circle.

The Cock *Finds* This gleefully seedy East Village joint is the most envelope-pushing gay club in town. A self-proclaimed "rock and sleaze fag bar" is dedicated to good-natured depravity. Head elsewhere if you're the retiring type. 188 Ave. A (at 12th St.). ✆ **212/777-6254.** Subway: L to First Ave.

Crazy Nanny's This lesbian bar and club is huge, friendly, and perpetually trendy. There are two floors, two bars, a groovy jukebox, dancing, a pool table, video games, and a variety of theme nights, including Dance Party on Thursday, and karaoke on Sunday and Wednesday (free cover). Out-of-towners are welcome. There's usually an $8 cover; drinks are half-price Monday through Friday from 4 to 7pm. 21 Seventh Ave. S. (at Leroy St.). ✆ **212/366-6312.** www.crazynannys.com. Subway: 1, 9 to Houston St.

The Eagle Everybody's favorite leather bar has been beautifully re-created in this far west Chelsea bilevel space. 554 W. 28th St. (btwn Tenth and Eleventh aves.). ✆ **646/473-1866.** Subway: C, E to 23rd St.

Hell This glamorous lounge is a sexy haven for a predominantly gay weekend crowd in the hipper-than-hell Meat-Packing District. The cocktails are well mixed, and plenty of comfy sofas are on hand for getting cozy. Ahead of its time in the 'hood, Hell is not quite as ultrahot as it used to be, but that just means there's more room for you. 59 Gansevoort St. (btwn Washington and Greenwich sts.). ✆ **212/727-1666.** Subway: A, C, E to 14th St.

Henrietta Hudson *Finds* This friendly, popular, and sometimes raucous women's bar/lounge is known for drawing in an attractive, upmarket lipstick lesbian crowd that comes for the jukebox and videos as well as the pleasingly low-key atmosphere. There's a $5 to $7 cover on weekends, when deejays spin tunes (Fri–Sat) and live bands are in the house (Sun). 438 Hudson St. (at Morton St.). ✆ **212/924-3347.** Subway: 1, 9 to Houston St.

Meow Mix Owner Brooke Webster has made this funky, divey East Village bar a great hangout since 1994. It draws in a young, attractive riot *grrrrl* crowd with nightly diversions like deejays and live bands, a pool table and authentic Ms. PacMan machine in the basement lounge, and is the place to watch New York Liberty away games on the big-screen TV. Two-for-one happy hour daily from 5 to 8pm. 269 E. Houston St. (at Suffolk St.) ✆ **212/254-0688.** www.meowmixchix.com. Subway: F to Second Ave.

Rubyfruit Bar & Grill This cozy bar and restaurant is a popular hangout, and less raucous than most of the other all-girl party scenes listed here. Choose a romantic dinner downstairs, or head upstairs for the playful, friendly pickup or hangout scene—whichever you prefer. 531 Hudson St. (btwn Charles and W. 10th sts.). ☎ 212/929-3343. Subway: 1, 9 to Christopher St.

Splash/SBNY After 10 years, this campy and fun dance club still manages to be one of the hottest scenes on the men's circuit. In fact, an end-of-2001 rebirth has breathed new life into the scene; *New York* magazine even chose it best gay dance club for 2002. Beautiful bartenders, video screens, New York's best drag queens—Splash has it all. Theme nights are a big deal. Best of the bunch is Musical Mondays, dedicated to Broadway video clips and music. Musical Mondays' famous singalongs are such a blast that they draw a crossover gay/straight mixed crowd as well as celebs like Nathan Lane and the cast of ABBA musical *Mamma Mia!*. 50 W. 17th St. (btwn Fifth and Sixth aves.). ☎ 212/691-0073. www.splashbar.com. Subway: F, V to 14th St.; 4, 5, 6, N, R, L, Q, W to 14th St./Union Sq.

Stonewall Bar The spot where it all started. A mixed gay and lesbian crowd—old and young—makes this an easy place to begin. At least pop in to relive a defining moment in queer history. 53 Christopher St. (east of Seventh Ave.). ☎ 212/463-0950. Subway: 1, 9 to Christopher St.

Townhouse Bar Here's a first-class watering hole for men who want to relax rather than cruise. Friendly and open to all. 236 E. 58th St. (btwn Second and Third aves.). ☎ 212/754-4649. Subway: 4, 5, 6 to 59th St.

Ty's Bar This friendly, unassuming gay bar has been a part of the Village men's scene for about a million years. The second Tuesday of each month is Firemen's Night, if you want to chat up some of New York's bravest. 114 Christopher St. (btwn Bleecker and Bedford sts.). ☎ 212/741-9641. www.tys.citysearch.com. Subway: 1, 9 to Christopher St.

View Bar *Finds* View Bar is more Will Truman than Jack McFarland, if you know what I mean. Up front is a very attractive and comfortable lounge, in back is a pool room with the name-worthy view; throughout you'll find friendly bartenders, affordable drinks, and Kenneth Cole–dressed boys who could pass on either side of bi. A welcome addition to the scene. 232 Eighth Ave. (btwn 21st and 22nd sts.). ☎ 212/929-2243. Subway: C, E to 23rd St.

Index

A AA (American Automobile Association), 61
Abyssinian Baptist Church, 8, 240
Accommodations, 1, 97–131
    best, 9–13
    family-friendly, 126–127
    money-saving tips, 20–26
    reservations services, 21–22
Addresses, finding, 68, 80
Airfares, 17–19, 59
Airports, 17, 44–52
AirTrain Newark, 1, 17, 20, 44, 48
Air travel, 44, 58–60
American Craft Museum, 218
American Folk Art Museum, 2, 218–219
American Jewish Historical Society, 220
American Museum of Natural History, 206–208
American Museum of the Moving Image (Queens), 263–264
American Sephardi Federation, 220
Ansonia, 236
Antiques and collectibles, 272–273
Apartment/home stays, 23–25
Apollo Theatre, 307–308
Aquarium, New York (Brooklyn), 261
Arcades, 257–258
Architecture, 7
Area codes, 94
Art galleries, 8–9, 230–231
Asia Society, 2, 220
Astor Row Houses, 237
ATMs, 56–58

B allet, 308–309
Bars, 324
Baseball, 265–266
Basketball, 266
Battery Park, 9, 219, 248
Beauty and bath products, 273–274
Bicycling, 34–35, 246–247
Bloomingdale's, 271
Boating, 247
Bookstores, 274–277
Botanical Garden, New York (the Bronx), 258–259
Botanic Garden, Brooklyn, 260
Bowling Green Park, 248
Bronx, the, 258–259
Bronx Zoo, 258
Brooklyn, 130, 194
    sights and attractions, 260–263
Brooklyn Academy of Music (BAM), 308–309
Brooklyn Botanic Garden, 260
Brooklyn Bridge, 7, 208
Brooklyn Cyclones, 266
Brooklyn Heights, 262–263
Brooklyn Museum of Art, 260
Brooklyn Public Library, 260
Brooklyn Tabernacle, 260–261
Bryant Park, 248–249
Bus travel, 19, 53, 60, 87–89
    to/from airports, 46–49

C abarets and piano bars, 321–322
Calendar of events, 33–38
Carnegie Hall, 311
Car rentals, 61
Car travel, 53, 58, 90–91
Castle Clinton National Monument, 248
Cathedral of St. John the Divine, 240–241
Center for Jewish History, 220
Central Park, 7, 35, 206, 242–247
Central Park Drive, 246
Central Park Zoo, 246

Century 21, 271
Chelsea, 75–76
    accommodations, 103–108
    art galleries, 231
    bars, 325–326
    restaurants, 160–163
Chelsea Market, 284
Chelsea Piers, 76
Children. *See* Families with children
Children's Museum of Manhattan, 256
Children's Museum of the Arts, 256
Children's Zoo (the Bronx), 258
Chinatown, 70, 72
    bars, 324
    restaurants, 141–143
    shopping, 267–268, 294
Chinese New Year, 33
Christmas, 8, 37–38
Chrysler Building, 236–237
City Hall, 70
CityPass, 27–28
Classical music, 8, 306
Cloisters, the, 211, 220–221
Comedy clubs, 320–321
Consolidators, 18
Cooper-Hewitt National Design Museum, 221
Credit cards, 57
Crime, 92–93
Currency, 56–57
Customs regulations, 55–56

D ahesh Museum of Art, 221
Dakota, 236
Dance clubs, 330–332
Dance companies, 306–307
Department stores, 271–272
Dia Center for the Arts, 221–222
Diamond District, 270
Disabled travelers, 40–42
Doctors, 94
Drinking laws, 61

E

Easter Parade, 34
East Village, 73–74
    accommodations, 100, 102
    bars, 326–327
    restaurants, 149–155
    shopping, 269
Edgar Allan Poe Cottage (the Bronx), 238, 258
Electricity, 61
Ellis Island, 6, 208–209, 215
El Museo del Barrio, 218, 222
E-mail, 76–77
Embassies and consulates, 62
Emergencies, 62, 94
Empire State Building, 33, 209–210
Entertainment book, 16
Entry requirements, 54–55
Eva and Morris Feld Gallery, 219

F

Families with children, 23, 40
    accommodations, 126–127
    deals for teens, 28
    sights and attractions, 256–258
    theater, 298–299
Fashions, 277–283
Federal Hall National Memorial, 222
Festivals, 33–38
Fifth Avenue, 81, 270
57th Street, 270
Film Festival, New York, 36
Financial District, 69, 137–138, 267
Flatiron Building, 237
Flatiron District. *See* Union Square, Flatiron District, and Gramercy Park
Fleet Week, 34
Flushing Meadows-Corona Park, 257
Food
    shopping for, 283–285
    festivals, 34, 36
Forbes Magazine Galleries, 222
Foreign visitors, 54–65
Fourth of July Fireworks Spectacular, 35
Fraunces Tavern Museum, 2, 222–223
Free and affordable events and activities, 6–9, 29–30, 224–225, 316–317
Frick Collection, 223

G

Garment District, 80–81, 270
Gasoline, 62
Gays and lesbians, 35, 42–43, 332–334
GE Building, 213
Gifts, 285–287
Gramercy Park. *See* Union Square, Flatiron District, and Gramercy Park
Grand Army Plaza (Brooklyn), 260
Grand Central Terminal, 7, 210, 252
Greenmarket, 249
Greenwich Village, 37, 74–75
    accommodations, 102–103
    bars, 325
    restaurants, 155–160
    shopping, 269
Ground Zero, 9, 219
Guggenheim Museum, 213

H

Halloween, 37
Hanukkah, 38
Harbor cruises, 250
Harlem, 8, 36, 82–83
    accommodations, 129–131
    jazz club, 329
    restaurants, 193–194
    sights and attractions, 237
Health concerns, 38–39
Hell's Kitchen, 79
Herald Square, 270
Holidays, 8, 62
Horse-drawn carriage rides, 247
Hospitals, 94
Hostels, 23–26
Hot lines, 94–95

I

Ice hockey, 266
Ice-skating, 37, 247
Immigration and customs clearance, 59–60
In-line skating, 247
Insurance, 39, 56
International Building, 213
International Center of Photography, 223
International visitors, 54–65
Internet access, 76
Intrepid Sea-Air-Space Museum, 224–226
Inwood, 83
Isamu Noguchi Garden Museum (Queens), 2, 264

J

Japan Society, 226
Jazz clubs, 317–320
Jewish Museum, 226–227
John F. Kennedy International Airport (JFK), 44–47, 49–52
Joyce Theater, 307
Juilliard School, 303
Jumel Terrace Historic District, 237

K

Knitting Factory, 314

L

Lafayette Street, 269
LaGuardia Airport, 44–46, 48–52
Layout of New York City, 67–68
Leather goods, 288–289
Legal aid, 63
Leo Baeck Institute, 220
Lever House, 236
Liberty Island, 6, 214
Libraries, 95
Lincoln Center for the Performing Arts, 35, 304–305, 309–310
Liquor laws, 95
Little Italy, 72
    bars and cocktail lounges, 322
    restaurants, 141–143
Live-music clubs, 311–320
Logo stores, 289–290
Lord & Taylor, 272
Lower East Side, 72–73
    accommodations, 99
    bars, 322–323
    restaurants, 143–146
    shopping, 268
Lower East Side Tenement Museum, 227
Lower Manhattan, 69

M

MacArthur Airport, 50
Macy's, 272
Macy's Thanksgiving Day Parade, 37
Madame Tussaud's New York, 227–228
Madison Avenue, 81, 271
Madison Square, 78
Madison Square Garden, 310–311
Mail, 63
Manhattan School of Music, 303
Marathon, 37
McGraw-Hill Building, 213

INDEX

Meat-Packing District, 76–77, 155–160, 325
Merchant's House Museum, 238
MetroCard, 20, 84–85
Metropolitan Museum of Art, 211, 218, 290
Metropolitan Opera, 303, 305, 308
Mets, 265
Midtown, shopping, 269–271
Midtown East and Murray Hill, 81
    accommodations, 120–123
    bars and cocktail lounges, 328
    restaurants, 179–181
Midtown West, 78–79
    accommodations, 111–120
    bars and cocktail lounges, 327–328
    restaurants, 168–179
MoMA QNS (Queens), 2, 211–212, 263
Money, 30–32, 56–58
Money-saving tips, 4–6, 16–30
Morgan Library, 228
Morris-Jumel Mansion, 238
Mother A.M.E. Zion Church, 8, 241
Mount Vernon Hotel Museum & Garden, 228
Municipal Art Society, 210, 250, 252, 277
Murray Hill. *See* Midtown East and Murray Hill
Museum for African Art (Queens), 264
Museum Mile, 34, 218
Museum of American Financial History, 228–229
Museum of Jewish Heritage, 2, 229
Museum of Modern Art/ MoMA QNS, 2, 211–212, 263, 291
Museum of Television & Radio, 229
Museum of the City of New York, 9, 229–232
Museums, 6–7
    tours, 250–251
Museum stores, 290–291
Music and video stores, 291–293

NASDAQ billboard, 216
National Academy of Design, 232

National Museum of the American Indian, 232
Natural History, American Museum of, 206–208
NBC studios, 213
Neighborhoods, 7, 69–83
    downtown, 69–75
Neue Galerie New York, 2, 232
Newark International Airport, 1, 44–46, 48–52, 58, 65, 90
New Museum of Contemporary Art, 232–233
Newspapers and magazines, 63, 95
New Year's, 8, 38
New York Aquarium, 261
New York Botanical Garden (the Bronx), 258–259
New York City Ballet, 307
New York City Fire Museum, 9, 233
New York City Police Museum, 2, 233
New York for Less guidebook, 16
New York Hall of Science, 257
New-York Historical Society, 9, 233–234
New York Knicks, 266
New York Liberty, 266
New York Philharmonic, 304, 306, 308
New York Public Library, 238–239
New York Rangers, 266
New York Stock Exchange (NYSE), 217
New York Times, 66
New York Transit Museum (Brooklyn), 210, 261–262, 291
Nightlife and entertainment, 296–336
    money-saving tips, 29–30
92nd Street Y, 250, 302, 306, 311
Noguchi, Isamu, Garden Museum (Queens), 2, 264
NoHo, 74, 149–155, 324–325
Nolita, 73, 146–149, 268–269
NYC & Company, 2, 16

Opera, 302–305
Orchard Street, 72, 73, 252, 268

Package deals, 16, 46–47
Paper goods, 285–287
Parking, 91
Petrol, 62
Pharmacies, 95
Pizza restaurants, 136, 147, 152, 158, 166, 172, 189, 192, 194
Playgrounds, 247, 257
Poe, Edgar Allan, Cottage (the Bronx), 238, 258
Port Authority Terminal, 53, 92
Prospect Park (Brooklyn), 262
P.S. 1 Contemporary Art Center (Queens), 264–265

Queens, sights and attractions, 263–265
Queens Artlink shuttle, 2, 212, 263
Queens Museum of Art, 257, 265

Radio City Music Hall, 37, 213, 311
Religious institutions, 240–242
Restaurants, 1–2, 8, 33, 35, 132–194
    best, 13–15
    by cuisine, 133–137
    family-friendly, 188
    money-saving tips, 26–27
    pizza, 136, 147, 152, 158, 166, 172, 189, 192, 194
    theme, 174–175
Restrooms, 65, 95
Rink at Rockefeller Plaza, 213
Rockefeller Center, 79–80, 212–213
Roosevelt, Theodore, Birthplace, 236
Rose Center for Earth and Space, 206–207
Running, 247

Safety, 58, 92–93
St. John the Divine, Cathedral of, 240–241
St. Patrick's Cathedral, 241
St. Patrick's Day Parade, 34
St. Paul's Chapel, 242
San Gennaro, Feast of, 36
Scandinavia House: The Nordic Center in America, 234

INDEX

Schomburg Center for Research in Black Culture, 234
Seagram Building, 236
Seasons, 32–33
Security, air travel, 45
Senior travelers, 42
Shakespeare in the Park, 35, 308
Shoe stores, 293–294
Shopping, 28–29, 267–295
Sights and attractions, 2
    for kids, 256–258
    money-saving tips, 27–28
    by neighborhood, 195–205
    suggested itineraries, 205–206
    tours, 250–253
Skyscraper Museum, 234–235
Skyscrapers, 236–240
Socrates Sculpture Park (Queens), 265
SoHo, 73
    art galleries, 231
    bars and cocktail lounges, 323–324
    restaurants, 146–149
    shopping, 268
Solomon R. Guggenheim Museum, 213–214
Sony Building, 236
Sony Wonder Technology Lab, 257
South Street Seaport, 69
South Street Seaport & Museum, 235
Spanish Harlem (El Barrio), 83
Special events and festivals, 33–38
Spectator sports, 9, 265–266
Staten Island Ferry, 6, 214
Staten Island Yankees, 266
Statue of Liberty, 6, 214, 215–216
Stolen wallet or credit cards, 31–32
Strivers' Row, 237
Students, 43
Studio Museum in Harlem, 235
Subway, 20, 84–87
    to/from airports, 46–49
    safety tips, 93

    service interruption notes, 86
    transit information, 87
Sugar Hill, 237
SummerStage, 35, 308
Sylvan Terrace, 237

Taxes, 63, 95
Taxis, 51, 89–90
Telephones, 63–64
Television shows, tapings of, 7–8, 253–256
Temple Emanu-El, 241
Thanksgiving Day Parade, 37
Theater, 2–3, 8, 36, 296–302
Theater District, 79, 270
Time Out New York, 66–67
Times Square, 79
    accommodations, 111–120
    bars and cocktail lounges, 327–328
    restaurants, 168–179
    shopping, 270
    sights and attractions, 216
Time zones, 64
Tipping, 64–65
Tisch Children's Zoo, 246
Titanic Memorial Lighthouse, 235
TKTS booth, 29
Toilets, public, 65
Tours, package, 16
Town Hall, 311
Toys, 295
Train travel, 19–20, 52–53, 60
    AirTrain Newark, 1, 17, 20, 44, 48
Transit information, 96
Transportation, 83–92
    to/from airports, 44–52
    by bus, 87–89
    by car, 90–91
    money-saving tips, 20
    to the suburbs, 92
    by subway, 84–87
    by taxi, 89–90
Travelers Aid, 65
Traveler's checks, 57
TriBeCa, 70
    accommodations, 98
    bars, 322
    restaurants, 138–141
Trinity Church, 9, 219, 241–242

Union Square, Flatiron District, and Gramercy Park, 78
    accommodations, 108–111
    bars and cocktail lounges, 326–327
    restaurants, 164–167
    shopping, 269–270
Union Square Park, 249
United Nations, 239
Upper East Side, 82
    bars and cocktail lounges, 329
    restaurants, 191–192
Upper West Side, 81–82
    accommodations, 123–129
    bars and cocktail lounges, 328–329
    restaurants, 181–191
    shopping, 271

Village Voice, 67
Visas, 54
Visitor information, 30, 66–67

Walking tours, 250–253
Wall Street, 217, 252
Washington Heights, 83
Washington Square Park, 249–250
Wave Hill (the Bronx), 259
Weather, 32–33, 96
Websites, 12
West Chelsea, 76–77
Western Union, 31–32
Whitney Museum of American Art, 217
    at Philip Morris, 217, 236
Wollman Rink, 247
Woolworth Building, 239–240

Yankees, 265–266, 290
Yeshiva University Museum, 220
YIVO Institute for Jewish Research, 220

Zabar's, 284
Zoos, 246, 258

FROMMER'S® COMPLETE TRAVEL GUIDES

Alaska
Alaska Cruises & Ports of Call
Amsterdam
Argentina & Chile
Arizona
Atlanta
Australia
Austria
Bahamas
Barcelona, Madrid & Seville
Beijing
Belgium, Holland & Luxembourg
Bermuda
Boston
Brazil
British Columbia & the Canadian Rockies
Budapest & the Best of Hungary
California
Canada
Cancún, Cozumel & the Yucatán
Cape Cod, Nantucket & Martha's Vineyard
Caribbean
Caribbean Cruises & Ports of Call
Caribbean Ports of Call
Carolinas & Georgia
Chicago
China
Colorado
Costa Rica
Denmark
Denver, Boulder & Colorado Springs
England
Europe
European Cruises & Ports of Call
Florida
France
Germany
Great Britain
Greece
Greek Islands
Hawaii
Hong Kong
Honolulu, Waikiki & Oahu
Ireland
Israel
Italy
Jamaica
Japan
Las Vegas
London
Los Angeles
Maryland & Delaware
Maui
Mexico
Montana & Wyoming
Montréal & Québec City
Munich & the Bavarian Alps
Nashville & Memphis
Nepal
New England
New Mexico
New Orleans
New York City
New Zealand
Northern Italy
Nova Scotia, New Brunswick & Prince Edward Island
Oregon
Paris
Philadelphia & the Amish Country
Portugal
Prague & the Best of the Czech Republic
Provence & the Riviera
Puerto Rico
Rome
San Antonio & Austin
San Diego
San Francisco
Santa Fe, Taos & Albuquerque
Scandinavia
Scotland
Seattle & Portland
Shanghai
Singapore & Malaysia
South Africa
South America
South Florida
South Pacific
Southeast Asia
Spain
Sweden
Switzerland
Texas
Thailand
Tokyo
Toronto
Tuscany & Umbria
USA
Utah
Vancouver & Victoria
Vermont, New Hampshire & Maine
Vienna & the Danube Valley
Virgin Islands
Virginia
Walt Disney World® & Orlando
Washington, D.C.
Washington State

FROMMER'S® DOLLAR-A-DAY GUIDES

Australia from $50 a Day
California from $70 a Day
Caribbean from $70 a Day
England from $75 a Day
Europe from $70 a Day
Florida from $70 a Day
Hawaii from $80 a Day
Ireland from $60 a Day
Italy from $70 a Day
London from $85 a Day
New York from $90 a Day
Paris from $80 a Day
San Francisco from $70 a Day
Washington, D.C. from $80 a Day

FROMMER'S® PORTABLE GUIDES

Acapulco, Ixtapa & Zihuatanejo
Amsterdam
Aruba
Australia's Great Barrier Reef
Bahamas
Berlin
Big Island of Hawaii
Boston
California Wine Country
Cancún
Charleston & Savannah
Chicago
Disneyland®
Dublin
Florence
Frankfurt
Hong Kong
Houston
Las Vegas
London
Los Angeles
Los Cabos & Baja
Maine Coast
Maui
Miami
New Orleans
New York City
Paris
Phoenix & Scottsdale
Portland
Puerto Rico
Puerto Vallarta, Manzanillo & Guadalajara
Rio de Janeiro
San Diego
San Francisco
Seattle
Sydney
Tampa & St. Petersburg
Vancouver
Venice
Virgin Islands
Washington, D.C.

FROMMER'S® NATIONAL PARK GUIDES

Banff & Jasper
Family Vacations in the National Parks
Grand Canyon
National Parks of the American West
Rocky Mountain
Yellowstone & Grand Teton
Yosemite & Sequoia/Kings Canyon
Zion & Bryce Canyon

FROMMER'S® MEMORABLE WALKS

Chicago	New York	San Francisco
London	Paris	Washington, D.C.

FROMMER'S® GREAT OUTDOOR GUIDES

Arizona & New Mexico	Northern California	Vermont & New Hampshire
New England	Southern New England	

SUZY GERSHMAN'S BORN TO SHOP GUIDES

Born to Shop: France	Born to Shop: Italy	Born to Shop: New York
Born to Shop: Hong Kong, Shanghai & Beijing	Born to Shop: London	Born to Shop: Paris

FROMMER'S® IRREVERENT GUIDES

Amsterdam	Los Angeles	San Francisco
Boston	Manhattan	Seattle & Portland
Chicago	New Orleans	Vancouver
Las Vegas	Paris	Walt Disney World®
London	Rome	Washington, D.C.

FROMMER'S® BEST-LOVED DRIVING TOURS

Britain	Germany	Northern Italy
California	Ireland	Scotland
Florida	Italy	Spain
France	New England	Tuscany & Umbria

HANGING OUT™ GUIDES

Hanging Out in England	Hanging Out in France	Hanging Out in Italy
Hanging Out in Europe	Hanging Out in Ireland	Hanging Out in Spain

THE UNOFFICIAL GUIDES®

Bed & Breakfasts and Country Inns in:
 California
 Great Lakes States
 Mid-Atlantic
 New England
 Northwest
 Rockies
 Southeast
 Southwest
Best RV & Tent Campgrounds in:
 California & the West
 Florida & the Southeast
 Great Lakes States
 Mid-Atlantic
 Northeast
 Northwest & Central Plains
 Southwest & South Central Plains
 U.S.A.
Beyond Disney
Branson, Missouri
California with Kids
Chicago
Cruises
Disneyland®
Florida with Kids
Golf Vacations in the Eastern U.S.
Great Smoky & Blue Ridge Region
Inside Disney
Hawaii
Las Vegas
London
Mid-Atlantic with Kids
Mini Las Vegas
Mini-Mickey
New England and New York with Kids
New Orleans
New York City
Paris
San Francisco
Skiing in the West
Southeast with Kids
Walt Disney World®
Walt Disney World® for Grown-ups
Walt Disney World® with Kids
Washington, D.C.
World's Best Diving Vacations

SPECIAL-INTEREST TITLES

Frommer's Adventure Guide to Australia & New Zealand
Frommer's Adventure Guide to Central America
Frommer's Adventure Guide to India & Pakistan
Frommer's Adventure Guide to South America
Frommer's Adventure Guide to Southeast Asia
Frommer's Adventure Guide to Southern Africa
Frommer's Britain's Best Bed & Breakfasts and Country Inns
Frommer's Caribbean Hideaways
Frommer's Exploring America by RV
Frommer's Fly Safe, Fly Smart
Frommer's France's Best Bed & Breakfasts and Country Inns
Frommer's Gay & Lesbian Europe
Frommer's Italy's Best Bed & Breakfasts and Country Inns
Frommer's New York City with Kids
Frommer's Ottawa with Kids
Frommer's Road Atlas Britain
Frommer's Road Atlas Europe
Frommer's Road Atlas France
Frommer's Toronto with Kids
Frommer's Vancouver with Kids
Frommer's Washington, D.C., with Kids
Israel Past & Present
The New York Times' Guide to Unforgettable Weekends
Places Rated Almanac
Retirement Places Rated

America Online Keyword: Travel

Booked seat 6A, open return.

Rented red 4-wheel drive.

Reserved cabin, no running water.

Discovered space.

With over 700 airlines, 50,000 hotels, 50 rental car companies and 5,000 cruise and vacation packages, you can create the perfect getaway for you. Choose the car, the room, even the ground you walk on.

Travelocity.com
A Sabre Company
Go Virtually Anywhere.

Travelocity.® Travelocity.com® and the Travelocity skyline logo are trademarks and/or servicemarks of Travelocity.com L.P. and Sabre® is a trademark of an affiliate of Sabre Inc. © 2002 Travelocity.com L.P. All rights reserved.

America Online Keyword: Travel

You Need A Vacation.

700 Airlines, 50,000 Hotels, 50 Rental Car Companies, And A Million Ways To Save Money.

Travelocity.com
A Sabre Company
Go Virtually Anywhere.

Travelocity,® Travelocity.com® and the Travelocity skyline logo are trademarks and/or servicemarks of Travelocity.com L.P. and Sabre® is a trademark of an affiliate of Sabre Inc. © 2002 Travelocity.com L.P. All rights reserved.